CULTURES OF THE DEATH DRIVE

Post-contemporary

Interventions

Series Editors:

Stanley Fish and

Fredric Jameson

CULTURES OF THE DEATH DRIVE

Melanie Klein and Modernist Melancholia

ESTHER SÁNCHEZ-PARDO

DUKE UNIVERSITY PRESS   Durham and London 2003

© 2003 Duke University Press
All rights reserved
Printed in the United States of America on acid-free paper ∞
Typeset in Quadraat by Keystone Typesetting, Inc.
Library of Congress Cataloging-in-Publication Data
appear on the last printed page of this book.

For Juan

CONTENTS

ACKNOWLEDGMENTS

Cultures of the Death Drive was written with the support of a fellowship from the Spanish Ministry of Education and the Del Amo-Universidad Complutense Foundation, which covered my stay at the Rhetoric Department, University of California-Berkeley, in 1995–96. A preliminary version of chapter 4 first appeared as "Melancholia as constitutive of male homosexuality: A Kleinian approach" in Gender and Psychoanalysis 3 (1998).

I am greatly indebted to the counsel of colleagues and teachers at the University of California at Berkeley and Santa Cruz and at Cornell University at different times in my nomadic roaming around the United States. Among these people, I must mention Fredric Jameson, Hayden White, and Judith Butler, the latter of whom was responsible for making my stay at Berkeley both possible and fruitful. Reynolds Smith, Executive Editor at Duke University Press, engaged this project with enormous interest and respect from the beginning. I am very grateful for his insightful and efficient contribution to the final version of this volume.

My friends Marcia Baker, Jacques Lezra, and Osvaldo Sabino should also be credited for supporting me through difficult times in this long war of attrition.

I also extend my thanks to my graduate students in the English Department, Universidad Complutense, for their encouragement and interest in our common work.

Finally, I would also like to mark the great debt I owe to my parents, Piedad and Jesús, for their encouragement, love, and blind faith in me. And above any other reader of my work I would like to thank Juan Imperial, to whom this book is dedicated, for his constant friendship and invaluable intellectual partnership.

Works by Melanie Klein are identified in the text by means of the following abbreviations.

A & G   On the theory of anxiety and guilt, 1948.

Appendix   Appendix: The scope and limits of child analysis, 1932.

AW&RI   Our adult world and its roots in infancy, 1959.

CT   Criminal tendencies in normal children, 1927.

CTP   On the criteria for the termination of a psycho-analysis, 1950.

DC   The development of a child, 1921.

DMF   On the development of mental functioning, 1958.

E&G   Envy and gratitude, 1957.

EA   Early analysis, 1923.

EASB   The effects of early anxiety-situations on the sexual development of the boy, 1932.

EASDE   The significance of early anxiety-situations in the development of the ego, 1932.

EASG   The effects of early anxiety-situations on the sexual development of the girl, 1932.

ELI   Some theoretical conclusions regarding the emotional life of the infant, 1952.

EOC&S   Early stages of the Oedipus conflict and of super-ego formation, 1932.

IASWA   Infantile anxiety situations reflected in a work of art and in the creative impulse, 1929.

IS-F   The importance of symbol-formation in the development of the ego, 1930.

LGR   Love, guilt and reparation, 1937.

M-DS   A contribution to the psychogenesis of manic-depressive states, 1935.

MM-D   Mourning and its relation to manic-depressive states, 1940.

NChP   Narrative of a child psycho-analysis, 1961.

OCEA   The Oedipus complex in the light of early anxieties, 1945.

ON&ES   The relations between obsessional neurosis and the early stages of the super-ego, 1932.

OT   The origins of transference, 1952.

PCh   *The psycho-analysis of children*, 1932.

SL   On the sense of loneliness, 1963.

SM   Notes on some schizoid mechanisms, 1946.

And melancholy is the nurse of frenzy.
—William Shakespeare

What is now holding sway in the superego is, as
it were, a pure culture of the death instinct, and
in fact it often enough succeeds in driving the ego
into death, if the latter does not fend off its tyrant
in time by the change round into mania.
—Sigmund Freud

We keep enshrined in our minds our loved people.
—Melanie Klein

Introduction: Anxieties and Their Vicissitudes

Klein does theory otherwise.—Jacqueline Rose

The question is this: is it ever possible to assess the relative merits of orthodoxy as against heterodoxy in psychoanalysis?—Roy Schafer

This book seeks to interrogate the complex interrelations between two central modernist discourses, psychoanalysis and literary and artistic modernism. Modernism is understood as a discursive and historical field situated at the crossroads of other discourses and events that configured the cultural map of the first decades of the twentieth century. This project is thus a hybrid, partly psychoanalytical and partly literary and visual. It is an inquiry into the relations among sexuality, melancholia, and representation in literary and visual texts that can be read at the intersection of psychoanalysis and the arts in modernism.

As was the case with the beginnings of psychoanalysis, early modernist texts were experienced as shocking, unintelligible, and disruptive. I will try to explore the radical implications of a new rhetoric pervaded by revolutionary tropes flowing intertextually both ways, from literature and art to psychoanalysis and vice versa. The problem of the self, embedded, crossed and inflected by different discourses, comes to be read differently by means of recourse to the unconscious and, in my view, specifically to the Kleinian notion of unconscious phantasy.[1] Literary modernisms show a heightened degree of language skepticism, and this allies modernisms and psychoanalyses in their radical critique.

In this volume, I will argue that melancholia has a constitutive role in modernist sexualities. Modernism was also a time when gender visibility was very high. Drawing from the modernist—and later postmodernist—insight into gender as a continuous process of constructing ideas about male and female characteristics and differences, as the process through which this construction is regulated and disseminated, in its flaws, its instabilities, and the marginalized forms of submission to and rebellion against the norm, my aim is to explore to what extent what I call modernist cultures of the death drive mold and inflect modernist sexualities in the turn of the century emergence of alternatives to traditional femininities and masculinities. It is my contention that, on account of the magnitude of the generalized calling into question of the binary in the emergent modernist discourses of literature and the arts, and in the debates and crises of representation echoed in psychoanalysis, psychiatry, anthropology, and the law, we can indisputably trace the poststructuralist impulse to dismantle the dichotomous approach to gender to the modernist critique of normative notions of masculinity and femininity.

In the hierarchical structure of the binary, in the alleged universalization and homogenization that it presupposes, and in the violence of the exclusions that it performs, the modernist and postmodernist critiques share some ground for contestation, deconstruction, and new developments. The gender binary, in its privileging of anatomical difference, genitality, and reproduction, fails to accommodate all those subject positions that do not correspond to anatomy and the various degrees of biological variation within the anatomical realm. Kleinian theory introduces important changes in the psychosexual evolution of the boy and the girl. The Kleinian emphasis on the flexibility and malleability of positions, renders bodies capable of representations that exceed binary divisions and thereby redistribute symbolic authority and routes of desire.

During the 1920s, the important influx of Viennese analysts led to a difficult state of affairs in the British Psycho-analytical Society.[2] Melanie Klein had come to London from Berlin in 1926 encouraged by Ernest Jones, who firmly believed in the importance of her work in the analysis of children.[3] By the early 1930s Klein's influence was substantial. At that time, she was supported by Jones, by the early nucleus of the Kleinian group (Susan Isaacs, Paula Heimann, and Joan Riviere), and by her own psychoanalyst daughter, Melitta Schmideberg.

By 1935, opposition to Klein's views emerged. This opposition was led by Edward Glover and later joined by Schmideberg. Glover utterly opposed the assumption put forward by the Kleinians that only those trained in the analysis of children as well as those concerned with the analysis of psychosis should be regarded as first-class analysts. He also feared that Klein and her followers were increasingly taking over training in the Society and would thus ensure the dominance of their views. Consequently, Glover and a fairly large group of Viennese analysts came to derogate Klein's contributions as mere deviations from the Freudian norm. Although her "unorthodox" approach gained momentum, the strong opposition of her adversaries made the situation untenable. This led to the series of debates known as the Controversial Discussions (1941–45).[4] The theoretical issues, challenges, and questions dealt with during the discussions have also been central to the articulation of this project.

In my reading of Klein's oeuvre, I have found a remarkable antiessentialist and deconstructive potential that partakes of her contemporary concerns and many of our own with regard to gender and sexualities. Klein's texts contain deeply ingrained and richly suggestive postbinaristic notions, radicalizing, so to speak, many of Freud's later ideas and theories, such as the issue of the death drive. Klein's concept of unconscious phantasy and her ideas on melancholia and manic depression render the simplistic establishment of the (hetero)sexual relation an impossible and untheorizable horizon and complicate and destabilize the inadequate polar vocabularies of nature versus culture and psyche versus body.

Klein is perhaps the woman analyst who, on account of the strength of her opposition to the Freudian establishment, explores most deeply the role of the Oedipus conflict as what I call melancholic apparatus.[5] In "The Oedipus complex in the light of early anxieties" ([1945] 1975), Klein moves from her former postulates, which located the release of the first oedipal impulses in the oral frustration of weaning, and holds instead that the onset of the Oedipus complex coincides with the onset of the depressive position. Since the publication of "Mourning and its relation to manic-depressive states" ([1940] 1975) Klein states that the depressive position is a melancholia in statu nascendi.

This study, in its psychoanalytical aspects, is in many ways an interrogation of Klein's theories and the Kleinian school's contributions in their attempt to move beyond Freud in order to see to what extent their postulates and ideas work in the interests of a feminist and antihomophobic project.

From the first attempts to define *melancholia*, the concept has continued to shift, inhabiting a sort of middle ground or borderline state between psychosis and neurosis. In most cases, melancholia has been placed in the vicinity of paranoia, schizophrenia, and obsessional neurosis. In its extreme manifestations, melancholia brings us to the verge of madness. The close relationship between melancholia and all these symptoms, in its contemporaneous development with modernist literary, artistic, medical, anthropological, legal, and other discourses, led me to inquire into the intense melancholia that I perceived in the Kleinian oeuvre and the possibility of using it as a strategy of reading in this project.

In my view, Melanie Klein is the theorist of melancholia par excellence. In this volume, I explore the role that Abraham's and Freud's previous ideas on melancholia play in the development of Klein's own thinking. What is at the center of Kleinian psychoanalysis if not a melancholic story of the vicissitudes of the internal object on its difficult way to the external world? And what are the traces that these primary internal objects, in their condition of being always already lost, leave in our psyche?

Psychoanalysis partakes of the impulse of the modernist enterprise. Its emphasis on giving form or structure to the individual's psychic experience comes close to the modernist endeavor to organize human experience along the lines of a pattern, a design, a cluster of narratives expressing the tensions between containment and breaking loose. In this respect, Jean Laplanche has written: *"The object of psychoanalysis is not the human object in general.* It does not deal with 'man,' a concept which can be defined by many other sciences such as psychology, sociology, history, anthropology, but with the human object insofar as it formulates that object and insofar as it gives its own experience a form. It is of course essentially within clinical language that it formulates its experience but, at a deeper level, this is its very life-blood" ([1987] 1989, 10). He sees in the German *Erfahrung* what he understands by "experience" and defines as "a movement which brings us into contact with an object and into contact with the movement of that object" (16). The issue of the object, as an object of inquiry, an object of theorization, will take center stage in the Kleinian elaboration in both its epistemological and its clinical work.

Klein takes issue with the central tenets of Freudian metapsychology, such as the unconscious and the theory of the drives, and takes the death drive, anxiety and its vicissitudes, and the mechanisms of projection and introjection as her center of attention. From a consideration of anxiety in the Freudian sense as a transformation of prohibited desire, Klein moved to the idea that anxiety is the clearest manifestation of the death drive. I read Kleinian metapsychology as haunted by the dynamics of object loss and marked by the oscillation between the paranoid-schizoid and the depressive position. To some extent, Klein partakes of the gesture shared by so many women analysts during the 1920s and 1930s, which seeks to call into question the fact that the masculine parameter for sexuality and eroticism is allegedly universalized in the Freudian paradigm.

Another way to speak of these issues may be that of reading object loss and melancholia as illnesses of love. Love suffers from many illnesses, but not all kinds of love manifest the same symptoms. And not all the psychic wounds produced by love can be healed with the same *pharmakos*. This project is concerned with the kinds of love that "dare not speak [their] name[s]" in the chronological period of modernism and with the discursive, textual, and cultural production of melancholia in a variety of idiosyncratic personal styles.[6] My exploration of melancholia from a psychoanalytic perspective aims to open up a dialogue between the psychic and the social and the domains of phantasy and external reality, interrogating the extent to which their interaction at a specific point within a definite historical configuration produces a subject, regardless of whether it is a fully healthy or a defective one.

Why is melancholia a pathology that has for so long resisted definition, categorization, and classification? And why is it so often attributed to creative artists and women? Which factors are determinant in the aetiology of melancholia? This project aims to find ways to give at least partial answers to these questions. I want to suggest that melancholia, by virtue of its very implication in a domain where the psychic and the social are intimately interwoven—as is indeed the case in issues such as that of superego formation, mechanisms of introjection-projection, and the development of a disease with distinctive symptoms—participates in a complex dual economy. Its multiple manifestations in the language of symptoms, dreams, and art or in the material practices of those affected, and the enigma of its resolution (attempts to cure, cycles of repetition, and suicide) are avenues for my inquiry.

A recent feminist "return to Klein" has followed the increased interest in non-Kleinian object-relations theory and in the rereadings of Freud and Lacan and the exploration of the pre-oedipal that took place in the 1970s and 1980s, particularly in American academia.[7] One of the aims of this project to return to Klein may be rethought along the lines of Jean La-planche's well-known statement about his own return to Freud: "I would prefer to speak of *going back over* Freud, as it is impossible to return to Freud without working on him, without making him the object of work" ([1987] 1989, 16). This renewal through "going back" to Klein is also a crucial part of the scope of this study of melancholia and modernism.

From a Kleinian perspective, the central developmental task for every individual is to attempt to enter and remain within the depressive position. Although men and women will perform this task in different ways, as Klein shows, these differences are overshadowed in comparison with the task that every human being must face, that of integrating love and hate.[8] Some feminist theorists, dissatisfied with Freud's narrative of the male and fe-male paths to the Oedipus complex and its detrimental effects on women, have embraced the Kleinian perspective. In this respect, Juliet Mitchell has emphasized the idea of the "new" in Klein's contributions: "What she [Klein] did was new. She was an outstanding clinician and her ideas, despite problems with their presentation, represent an important new de-parture in the theory of mental processes" (1986, 9). The importance of the Kleinian breakthrough can be read along the lines of the crucial role that the sense of "newness" played in modernism.

In her previous work, Jacqueline Rose had remarked that feminism's affinity with psychoanalysis rests above all in the recognition that there is a resistance to identity at the very heart of psychic life (1986, 91). Central to Rose's work is the tension between identity and nonidentity and identity and negativity. Not only feminist but all progressive politics must take account of the need to maintain the tension of identity. In this respect, we must also acknowledge that some form of psychic integration must be seen as the precondition for any effectivity in the social. The capacity to maintain some sort of integration or coherence of the self is also the precondition for any commitment to an ethical or political position. Along this line of thought, melancholia, with its self-evading ruses, can hardly be offered as a revolutionary ideal. It can be read, though, as a form of active resistance to the dispossession that the social as a devouring agent perpetrates upon the subject.

To those critiques that charge Klein with granting excessive weight to a supposedly omnipotent and phallic mother and the overfeminization of psychoanalysis, the best corrective is, no doubt, to advocate a rereading of the whole Kleinian oeuvre with close attention paid to her rhetoric questioning of what this both reveals and conceals. There is an urgent need to go back to Klein's own language so as to discard previous oversimplifications, which are often unrigorous and sometimes simply dishonest, and critically assess the importance and the value of her insights for our current projects and concerns. In the Kleinian oeuvre, there is great potential for interrogation, contestation, and resignification. From the multiplicity of perspectives and approaches provided by gender studies (feminist and queer theory—in its most ample sense) and cultural studies, my return to Klein will take issue with recent and urgent questions about the contingent—unstable and precarious—status of sexualities in their relation to modernist discourses. My aim is to explore an endemic *mal du siècle* that under the guise of melancholia, depression, or manic-depressive illness came to the fore in the period between the two world wars.

The Kleinian version of the world of the infant, one in which good things are not simply unambivalently recognized as such but are sadistically and enviously attacked in phantasy, gives a disquieting view of primary mother-infant relations. Despite all this, Klein made no attempt to meet criticisms of the death drive. She was so firm in her position that destructive processes are obvious and empirically observed in infancy that no theoretical objection would make her change her mind. The Kleinian oeuvre raises many questions of how to read the death drive in her departure from Freud.[9]

There are no easy solutions, no falling into complacency, in Klein's thinking on the complex relationship between mother and child. There is no fusion but separation, no oceanic oneness but differentiation and early processes of individuation (introjection, projection, projective identification, and defense mechanisms). Klein's account of the mother-child dyad seems to be the one that is most in consonance with contemporary developments in biological research on intrauterine life and early attachment of the fetus to the mother.

There is no doubt at present that an embryo is separated from the mother from the start.[10] Gayatri Chakravorty Spivak has underscored the importance of Klein as a theorist of mother-child relations who advocates differentiation, separation, and opposition in an attempt to counter recent readings that tend to oversimplify her contributions. She writes: "That part of psychoanalysis that, even in its ruins, still has the intention of taking seriously the sub-individual zone of sense-making, playing by the rules of sub-jecting to restore social agency, and that part of deconstruction, which must work at the bond between intentional subjectivity and responsibility, find a haven here. This is Melanie Klein, another major player in my field of alternatives, read against the grain, particularly (though not only) against the grain of her readers, who fetishize the object rather than the relationship, fetishize the mother rather than the human child as assigned and sign-making" (1994, 186). Along the same lines, Ann Scott has written that the "move from a 'Lacanian feminism' to a 'concern with Klein' . . . represents a shifting locus of perspective: not just from Oedipal to pre-Oedipal, as it is so often termed, but from the constitution of the subject to the subject's constitution of its 'world' " (1990, 128). What are we to make of biased, reifying, and even fetishizing versions in the contemporary reading and reception of Klein's work? In a very important way, this is also at stake in the writing of this book.

In current critical discourse, Naomi Schor had recently announced that "In the marketplace of ideas there is no room and no time for mourning and melancholia. Mourning is viewed as somehow shameful, not to say retrograde. Furthermore, in the age of postmodernist 'waning of affect,' those who wish to bring back affects such as depression are not viewed as very good company" (1995, 159). In the 1990s, critical vocabularies exhibited a destabilization of gender as a privileged category of difference and the decentering of narrative as a crucial mode of cultural expression. In what she ironically identifies as a common "postmodern predicament" for early feminist critics, and if feminist literary criticism can have a future at all, she advocates the permanence of these two categories reconfigured and refashioned through the interplay of different discourses.

In this project, then, I am interested in several things at once. The first is reading and tracing melancholia in modernist discourses across disciplines. The psychoanalytic dissemination of the concept by Freud led me to ask whether Freud was the ultimate theorist of melancholia or whether there were others for whom melancholia was more central and supportive of their analytic edifice. Hence my return to Klein, to an exploration of the genealogy of the concept, and to an investigation of its ramifications and connections to crucial analytical concepts such as anxiety, identification, narcissism, introjection, and projection. I will try to address these and related questions in the course of this study through a reading of Kleinian texts and a selection of modernist literary and visual texts that exhibit a rhetoric of melancholia through a variety of discourses. I am also exploiting what I see as a fruitful tension between using melancholia as a way of presenting Klein's thought and introducing Klein's thought with the aim of demonstrating the prominent place melancholia occupies in her theorization.

Part I is concerned with an extensive and close reading of Klein's works in an attempt to read her otherwise. Not ignoring her links to Freud, I move on to consider her elaboration as autonomous, as an innovative construction of the foundations of a psychoanalytical school that, after the schism brought about by the Controversial Discussions, thrives even more. Klein and her associates Susan Isaacs, Joan Riviere, and Paula Heimann, the main initiators, are followed by Herbert Rosenfeld, Wilfred Bion, Donald Meltzer, and Hanna Segal, among others.

One of the central sections of this book contains a close reading of Melanie Klein's work. In The psycho-analysis of children ([1932] 1975e) and owing to the quality of the Kleinian text, it seems indisputable that we should read her in a dialogue with Freud. I read the Kleinian superego as a melancholic agency built upon identifications with lost objects on the basis of the lost mother and father. I examine all of the theoretical essays included in The psycho-analysis of children in an attempt to trace the origins of Kleinian thought and all the concepts that have to do with her further theorization of melancholia.

I also trace the connections between melancholia, paranoia, and female and male homosexuality, and I argue that the more or less extensive exclusion of reality in melancholia, homosexuality, and paranoid states is in direct proportion to the major or minor degree of the practices of exclusion that reality imposes on the individual. After a detailed analysis of the close link between the Kleinian superego and the death drive, I argue that the melancholic response is at the core of the differences between Klein and Freud. Kleinian melancholia is a specific mode of object relations, far from the narcissistic movement of turning back upon the ego of Freudian melancholia.

The concept of unconscious phantasy is also crucial in Kleinian metapsychology. Phantasy is a concept that problematizes the relationships between linguistic and visual representation, the issue of origin and ground. It is a rich psychoanalytic concept that resists essentialization, reification, and closure. In this book, I have decided to write phantasy with a ph in reference to the Kleinian unconscious phantasy. Since many times it is difficult to discriminate among types of phantasy, my attempt has been one of defamiliarization of our current way of reading the term fantasy in its most common usage. This "graphic" maneuver seeks, then, to problematize and destabilize our perception and apprehension of the term. The ph spelling marks the eruption of the unconscious in the subject's life and consequently the eruption of the unconscious in the text.

In "The nature and function of phantasy" ([1952] 1983)—the Kleinians' definitive statement on this issue—Susan Isaacs rigorously defines and describes the structuring function of phantasy in psychic life. I explore the connections that Isaacs traces between phantasy and the body and move on to consider the relationship between the origins of symbol formation and the containment of anxiety. The symbolic equation, as a more or less rigid operation, can be thought of in terms of projective identification, and whereas the symbol serves to overcome an accepted loss (the mourning process inherent in language) the symbolic equation disavows separation between subject and object and comes to attain melancholic proportions.[11] It lies at the root of the concrete thought characteristic of the psychoses.

Anxious Modernisms?

In the atmosphere of anxiety, insecurity, and transformation of the period between the wars, the ontological dilemma posed by different modernisms is the cost of losing metaphysical assurances. It results in an urgent battle between the public sphere and the private domain. The beginnings of the twentieth century make us increasingly aware of the social and political ramifications of this struggle. Lacking a foundation in universals, we are squarely placed within history, and the issues of power at stake in modernism reside in the cultural struggle between tradition and resistance to established norms. This state of affairs opens part II in this study.

In the field of cultural production, many modernist texts are riven with the horror of the war and haunted by the unprecedented specter of anxiety neurosis, the effects of shell shock, manic depression, and melancholia. Elements of anxiety, fear, and aggression pervade the dynamics of modernist texts.[12] Nonetheless, in the midst of this devastation, different modernisms counterattacked with a belief in movement, change, mutability, and transformation. Between the two world wars, various avant-garde projects erupt into the old space of representation, and they unsettle and defamiliarize both words and images and leave readers and audiences longing for a recognizable relationship that may bridge the gap between art and experience.

In this project, I am interested in examining in what ways melancholia opens up another space within modernist culture, a troubled interior space that poses a traumatic relationship with exteriority. To explore the space of melancholia also implies the exploration of the space of phantasy. Unconscious phantasy pervades all human activity, our bodies, our private and public architectures (appearance and all those things through which we make the world our own), and the way we internalize the world. The spaces we make to house this continual activity of interiorization and exteriorization are the site of the problem. The system of appearances of external coherence that we present to the world is, in Kleinian theory, part of a complex process of introjections and projections that also gives shape to our inside. Interiority and exteriority are constituted not as opposites but as intimately and problematically linked.[13] In these basic spatial forms, the struggle between the life and death drives repeats itself ad infinitum.

The problematization of the boundaries between inside and outside is a dilemma peculiar to all approaches to life and art that nonetheless gained a more acute impulse during modernism. Many modernist texts similarly stage a battle between mind and body, memory and desire, and the conflict between the need to remember and the longing to forget. In literary modernisms, the stream of consciousness technique becomes the privileged medium in which to express the unconscious, a dramatic way of expressing a divided self. Free indirect discourse has been read as a celebration of division. The tension of the double voice signifies the writer's particular understanding of modernism.

The modernists were also highly aware of the new possibilities that the modes of communication already available had for their diverse enterprises. Thus, imagism was implicitly predicated on the authority of the photographic image; *The waste land*, and at times *The cantos*, replicate cinematic effects, and much of modernist technique is informed by the methods of montage. Arguably, the very dislocation of genre and disruption of syntax in modernist texts acknowledge the breakup of the old hegemony of writing as a means of representation.

It has been argued that in the field of modernist architecture, instead of the narrative of function, which assigned great importance to the empty spaces of public appearance where the artificiality of institutional power was celebrated, flexible and nonsignificant spaces were proposed. Instead of the solid walls of fear and the roofs of shelter, architects proposed new planes of possibility.[14] The new world of film also redefined space. As Walter Benjamin put it, "The enlargement of a snapshot does not simply render more precise what in any case was visible, though unclear: it reveals entirely new structural formations of the subject" (1968b, 236). Benjamin goes on to equate the camera's operation in space with that of psychoanalysis in the psyche: "Evidently a different nature opens itself to the camera than opens to the naked eye—if only because an unconsciously penetrated space is substituted for a space consciously explored by man. . . . The camera introduces us to unconscious optics as does psychoanalysis to unconscious impulses" (236–37). Even though psychoanalysis tends to elevate word over image, many psychoanalytic constructs draw inspiration from or are expanded or limited by specific images.

In an attempt to create alternatives to narrative, modernist spatializing techniques juxtapose scenes in order to produce not a sense of continuity and synchronicity but fragments of experience or time in discontinuous chains. The reader has to make sense of these constructions and generate a narrative out of these heteroclite elements, out of these snapshots and discontinuous stills. Narratives, painting, and film attack our facile assumption of an identification between words and the essence of things. They disorient readers and beholders with a heightened sense of epistemic disequilibrium.

Space in Kleinian theory is not something that has to be conquered but something that must be experienced in all its complexity. It is also a space that is empty enough to allow the (lost) object to emerge. Through a reflection on the complex dynamics of the mechanisms of introjection and projection, I see the Kleinian model of the psyche as a corporeal one derived from bodily prototypes of oral incorporation and anal expulsion.

Juliet Mitchell has remarked that Klein's contribution is "to chart an area where present and past are one and time is spatial, not historical. This area has all the characteristics of a descriptive unconsciousness, an unconscious that has not been constructed by repression" (1986, 28).[15] In my study of Klein's metapsychology, I argue that her notion of positions spatializes the psyche. This is crucial to assessing the numerous signs of convergence between Kleinian psychoanalysis and different modernisms.

As such, modernisms pose a challenge not just to the social order but to the division of the sexes. It was Walter Benjamin who read woman as an allegory of the modern in the images of Baudelaire's poetry (prostitute, lesbian, androgyne). In this project, I want to argue that not only women but the blurring of the boundaries between the sexes in the debates over the "third sex" in medicine and psychiatry and the troubled political atmosphere of Europe in the period leading to and between the two world wars contributed to the rise of what I am calling modernist cultures of the death drive. I take these to be the material historical processes, trends, forces, and regulations that through involution and the deadening movement of repetition, inertia, and stasis force themselves upon individuals (or groups) and implement social and psychic exclusionary spaces encumbered and haunted by the physicality of their lost objects. These internal lost objects cannot be mourned and are instead clandestinely preserved inside the ego.

Through an extensive and close reading of Melanie Klein's work, it is my aim in this book to study and characterize the particular modality of melancholia that I am calling "modernist" at the crossroads where modernism as an artistic and cultural configuration intersects with modernity, a much larger enterprise whose limits, extension, and decline are still being debated in the West. In modernism, there is a new muffled sense of history in which the alienation and attenuation of experience (spleen, ennui, melancholia) characteristic of modernity unfold. I would argue that modernism ranks among those projects that both elaborate a critique of modernity from ideological and aesthetic postulates and show signs of a shattering, fragmentation, or splitting of consciousness that finds its correlate in the shattering of the world.

In this project, I am concerned with modernist melancholic discourses, with the variety of tropes through which melancholia and sexualities are figured in modernism, with the impairment and threat that melancholia poses to verbal and visual communication, and with the ways in which this is expressed or bypassed in a multiplicity of voices and styles that give rise to distinctive practices, strategies, and modes of overcoming anxiety. I am concerned with ways of representing melancholia and its symbolics of loss in modernist narratives, poems, and visual art. My emphasis is on the literal and the visual as specific sites where the struggle for individuality, sexuality, expressive freedom, and social visibility are played out.

I am interested in exploring in what ways the cultural production of modernist stereotypes of gender and idealized norms of conduct provide specific modes of inhabiting social relations and securing recognition for some subjects while others are excluded and deemed sick. Melancholia and manic depression, in the nascent discourses of psychiatry and psychoanalysis, are instruments of control in the hands of the medical profession and means through which the social executes its exclusionary practices. In the cultures of the 1920s and 1930s, gendered imagos are especially destabilized, and new forms opposed to traditional "femininities" and "masculinities" begin to proliferate and find their place in the cultural repertoire of images and narratives. The 1920s and 1930s also were critical decades for the emergence of controversies and debates about the nature of female sexuality. Coincident with the expansion of modernism, this period saw important elaborations of ideas for and against Freud's views on "normative" sexualities and perversion.

In this study, the readings that follow the lengthy genealogy of melancholia are critical interventions into several modernist texts that draw on different versions to theorizing melancholia. They traverse the range of Kleinian orientations to melancholia marked by the two crucial phases of Klein's career, the first, from 1921 to 1945, and the second from 1946 until the publication of her last papers. My selection of texts bears an interesting relation to an already established canon of modernist writing. My choice of writers and artists shows differences and intersections with canonical high modernism. Virginia Woolf, René Magritte, Lytton Strachey, Djuna Barnes, and Countee Cullen present a wide variety of alternatives in literary and artistic production during the first decades of the twentieth century. Two of them are associated with the Bloomsbury Group, one with the American expatriate fraction in Paris, and one with the Harlem Renaissance. René Magritte, whose paintings I read in a dialogue with Woolf, was among the leading members of the surrealist avant-garde. They worked in three of the meccas of modernism, Paris, London and New York, and they all had complex homosexual and heterosexual love relationships.[16] The intersections of gender, sexuality, race, class, and cultural and geographical location are crucial elements in the construction of different modernisms and will lead my inquiry into melancholia in its psychic dimension and social implications.

Virginia Woolf's writing was totally seized by sight. A large part of the singularity of her texts comes from the vividness of her vision. In chapter 9, I suggest the proximity of Woolf's and Magritte's projects in a reading across disciplines, from literature to art to psychoanalysis. They both orchestrate a radical modernist critique of form and by extension of genre. Whereas Woolf, by transgressing the boundaries between narrative and lyrical discourse, aims to explore the irreducible elegiac dimension of signification, Magritte dismantles any ascription to taxonomies of genre painting. My reading of Woolf's *To the lighthouse* (TLC) focuses on the melancholic nature of the fetish through a Kleinian lens. My readings of Magritte are interspersed with instances ranging from Lily Briscoe's canvas in TLH to Melanie Klein's discussions of her patient Richard's drawings and the paintings of one of Paula Heimann's analysands as reported in clinical papers. Woolf's and Magritte's projects interrogate art as representation, challenging its boundaries, power, and functions head on, a crucial issue at stake for all modernist intellectuals and artists.

In TLH, only the alleviating function of the fetish comes to rescue the subject from a universe in wrack and ruin. Woolf devises a grief practice that comes too close to the Kleinian theorization on mourning, melancholia, and manic-depressive states. In my reading, TLH as a melancholic text draws the repeated and repeatable transit between paranoid-schizoid and depressive modes of object relations. I read Woolf's attempts to substitute the lost object of love with the aesthetic object of Lily's canvas as a failure that has to do with the impossibility of ever restoring or retrieving the image of the good mother. By recourse to the intrinsic mobility and substitutability of the fetish, Lily Briscoe's canvas frames the fetish outside the domain of perspective and within the lyrical internal movement of Woolf's writing. Lily's melancholic happiness at the end of the novel may be read between the ecstatic experience of the modernist epiphany and the psychotic delirium of hallucination. One still unanswered, and perhaps unanswerable, question is: where does the labor of melancholia come to an end, and how, if at all, can we begin the work of mourning?

In chapter 10, I explore Lytton Strachey's biographical projects at the crossroads of history, biography, and personal narrative. In a reflection upon the writing of biography as a melancholic, projective exercise and on the permanent oscillation between history and fiction, Strachey assuages his concern with form. In my reading of *Elizabeth and Essex*—Strachey's most personal biography—Riviere's and Klein's arguments on masquerade are crucial to an understanding of the textual and psychic dynamics between Elizabeth, Essex, and Strachey as the main characters within this drama.

In *Elizabeth and Essex*, Strachey reflects upon love, aggression, and melancholia in the paranoid context of Elizabethan England at the height of melancholia during the Renaissance. And simultaneously this biography bears an uncanny resemblance to Strachey's own melancholia. Strachey had openly embraced the Wildean stereotype for himself, and in *Elizabeth and Essex*, he presents us with a new sexual subject produced by Elizabethan England, the effeminate man. In my reading, protected and preserved behind a mask, Strachey performs a subversive destabilization of normative masculinity, and by means of recourse to the melancholia implicit in the camp object he mitigates a series of losses in the real world through his rewriting.

In chapter 11, I read Djuna Barnes's *Ryder* as a modernist collage made up of a pastiche of voices, genres, and styles in which melancholia and paranoia flourish. The issue of the law in the domains of the familial and the social is placed at center stage in a narrative that shows women's sexualities in their most profound imbrication with the workings of the death drive. Barnes's inscription of women's—especially daughters'—and other outlaw desires displays an almost psychotic rhetoric in order to show the abyss that mediates between the body in pain and the wor(l)d. Part of the project of *Ryder* aims to render representable the unrepresentability of the sterile female body, the body of the invert, and the abject prostitute body as potential threats to the social heterosexual order through non-reproductivity. Following Barnes's sombre reflection on the patriarchal enforcement of maternity upon women, I argue that in one of the child-birth scenes in the novel we attend to a modernist version of the rebirth of melancholia. Barnes's apt rewriting of melancholia is also manifest in her (auto)biographical project through the inversion of the Freudian notion of the *Familienroman*. Her ventriloquizing of diverse voices and styles erupts in a sense of "paranoia as paraphrenia." Through a Kleinian reading that focuses on anxieties, projective identification, and defense mechanisms such as splitting, idealization, and manic denial, I reflect on the movement from the paranoid-schizoid to the depressive regime of object relations in this text.

The figure of the New Negro constitutes itself as the emblem of the Harlem Renaissance. Countee Cullen's well-known statement that to be "à la mode" was as important as being a Negro, since it implied being peculiar and apart, was discussed together with his poetry in the literary and artistic beginnings of the movement.

Harlem's celebratory insistence on its mission to preserve black heritage and culture and to foster new aesthetic black forms is inadvertently oblivious to the inscription of misogyny and homophobia as pure cultures of the death drive in its material practices. In chapter 12, I examine the anxieties over gender that were embedded in the atmosphere of the Harlem

Renaissance and Cullen's own conflictual position in his life and writings. Through a reflection on strategies such as linguistic mimicry and racial masquerade, and on the notion of the mask (especially the minstrel mask), I approach the complex dynamics of introjection-projection and aggression-retaliation inscribed in the Harlem Renaissance as part of the ideologies of modernism.

From Cullen's acknowledgment that he is bounded by his race and his figuring race as an unwanted container for different parts of the self, I aim to explore how the relationship between container and contained is articulated in his poetry. Through a reflection on poetic and narrative form—in his essays and his only novel, *One way to heaven* (1932)—I explore the idea of form as container of experience, its relationship with melancholia, and its problematization of form.

The melancholic dimension of Cullen's writings has been foregrounded in a genealogical sense that links his poems to the tradition of culturally white aesthetic and poetic forms. I read them through Klein's insights on splitting (of the object and the ego) and the oscillation between the paranoid-schizoid and the depressive position. It is my contention that Cullen does not simply adopt the conventional melancholy tone of the Romantics. Rather, he ascribes to the new modernist melancholia, which is manifest in his writings as they are traversed by modernist cultures of the death drive that have the issues of race, homosexuality, and a complex oedipal configuration as their targets. A Kleinian reading of the racist ego is in line with my former reflections on the phobic character of modernism and the emergence of phobic objects that polarize projections coming from outside. Finally, I attempt to explore the specific relationship between the subject's melancholia and the melancholia associated with race. Can we speak of a sense of collective melancholia in Cullen's writings?

Crucial for my reflection on modernist melancholia is a consideration of the kinds of agency and the possibilities available to these artists in their different social and cultural locations. I also endeavor to approach melancholia at the complex crossroads where individuality, community, and institution intersect.

Literary modernism problematized the means whereby the "self" could be expressed. Multiple factors are involved in this obsessive interest in representing the self, including a pervasive atmosphere of social alienation, the rise of psychoanalysis, the sense of shock brought about by World War I, and increasing experimentalism in all the movements in the domain of the arts. Modernism is urged to experiment, sometimes aggressively.

Modernist literary discourses are haunted by the specter of object loss: loss of a coherent and autonomous self, loss of a social order in which stability reigned, loss of metaphysical guarantees, and in some cases loss and fragmentation of an empire. In modernist narratives, the obsessive reverberation of the individual's lost objects of love comes to shatter his or her identity. With regard to the interimplications of narrative and psychoanalytic selves, the crises and disintegration of old notions of the self find expression in a desperate search for the subject as the lost object par excellence. Modernist literature celebrates not only the splitting of the self but the multiplicity and diversity of selves that provide a plethora of possibilities in terms of role playing, impersonation, passing, and phantasmatic identification. We may say that, to some extent, there is an effect of liberation of the ghost of unity and a movement toward plurality. Narrative control was undermined through syntactical disruption, ambiguity, repetition, and parody. Literary modernism attempted to rewrite the self in terms of contingent and self-reflexive formulations.

Modernist literary and visual texts strive on many levels to deny the contemporaneous sense of loss, to hide its sadness, to mark and disavow its absence, to vent and contain rage, and to doubt any project of reparation. In their attempt to replay the shattering moments of trauma, modernist texts ultimately comment on art, vision, and the very limits of representation. The traumatic marks precisely what has eluded human comprehension, the experience of an originary phantasy of violence experienced by the subject as victim.

How can we account for the fact that melancholia (depression in its present form) affects some individuals—especially women and various deviant subjects—and not others? We need to find answers to these questions in a space between the psychic and the social, in the space of cultural representation where the battles over meaning and the legitimacy of interpretations are waged.

I see in Kleinian theory the potential for reconceptualizing the complexities of identity and social relations through the concept of unconscious phantasy. Kleinian theory also helps us trace the aggression that fuels the literary and artistic text and fully apprehend its dynamics. Ultimately, this book aims to bear witness to the issues, arguments, and controversies that modernisms and psychoanalyses brought to the forefront during the first decades of the twentieth century by revolutionizing prior ideas about the self, gender, sexuality, and relations and by creating new modes of discourse to express this.

The social and political implications of Kleinian theory need to be rethought and developed. At present, a number of critics and analysts working within a Kleinian framework have put forward suggestions for integrating some of these ideas into the sphere of the social. The Kleinian elaboration of the depressive position incorporates much needed notions such as tolerance, openness, and integration.[17] Kleinian theory points toward a politics of inclusion. If we follow Klein's idea that the infant world is retained throughout adult life, then her representation of the infant's early experiences will have significant repercussions for our view of family and group relations, political identifications, and social organization.

In this study, I argue that love and melancholia can be read interchangeably as "illnesses" that storm the subject in its passage through object relations, specifically through sexuality and aggression. Looking into a number of aspects in which melancholia appears to be figured under different masks, my approach has sought to produce a cluster of narratives in order to refuse the dualistic gap that theory tries to open between art and life, process and product. This book attempts to blend many voices. Inherently interdisciplinary, it partakes of current concerns that seek to complicate hegemonic assumptions about the continuities among anatomical sex, social gender, gender identity, sexual identity, sexual object choice, and sexual practice. All too often, gender, identity, and race are cast in terms of fixity. From its enigmatic social nonplace, melancholia crucially problematizes the reification of these categories. It reads losses, discontinuities, and ruptures in the apparent narrative of the advance and progress of the modern(ist) subject.

PART ONE

1

Itineraries

Abraham and Freud: Epistolary Anxieties and the Origins of Melancholia

Karl Abraham was in truth *un preux chevalier* of Science, *sans peur et sans reproche.*—Ernest Jones

In his *The life and work of S. Freud* (1953–57), Ernest Jones likens the relationship Sigmund Freud had with Karl Abraham to the one he had with Sándor Ferenczi. As in the case of Fliess and Jung, with Ferenczi, Freud had been seduced by "the sight of this unchecked imagination" (158). Abraham, as much as Jones himself, was "certainly the most normal of the group" (159). In 1907, Abraham sent Freud his manuscript "On the significance of sexual trauma in childhood for the symptomatology of dementia praecox." Thus began their correspondence, a correspondence that was fraught with hesitation and submissiveness on the part of Abraham and with patronizing demands of discipleship on the part of Freud (Freud and Abraham, 1965).

Abraham felt almost pathologically indebted to Freud. He had asked him for advice when he decided to abandon his appointment at the Burghölzli Psychiatric Hospital in Zurich and settle in Berlin in private practice. At that time, Abraham asked Freud if he could refer patients to him and consult him on analytic matters. At this conjuncture, Freud was invested as patron and master and Abraham took up the role of faithful disciple and son.

Upon Freud's request, Abraham's mission would be to gain the sympathy of the German public (Letter, October 8, 1907; 1965, 9) and win it over to the analytic cause. As he writes in a letter addressed to Freud at the beginning of their correspondence, he is bound to represent psychoanalysis in partibus infidelium (Letter, June 11, 1908; 1965, 41). He never had the chance to be geographically close to the Freudian group in Vienna. From the orphanage of his intellectual exile, there was an undercurrent that intimately linked both men, their common Jewish origin. Freud phantasized a feeling of kinship that enabled their common "understanding" (Letter July 23, 1908; 1965, 46). Nevertheless, their relationship was not free of ambivalence. Whereas Jung's initial allegiance to Freud was overestimated on the basis of the bridging of the former's original resistance, Abraham's was simply taken for granted.[1]

The geographical space of Abraham's mission was also highly emblematic. Berlin was the city where Wilhelm Fliess had been living for many years. As is well known, after Fliess's unfortunate claims of originality in some of the ideas developed by Freud—the universal bisexual disposition being the most notorious—and their disputes, Freud decided to break off his relationship with his friend and confidant. The horizontal model of Fliess's mirroring function would be displaced onto a vertical genealogical paradigm. Freud is inscribed there as paterfamilias of a long line of legitimate and illegitimate sons, whose discipleship would prove to be either fruitful (uncritically continued) or barren (rebellious and consequently rejected).

In September 1911, Abraham gave a lecture at the Third Congress of Psychoanalysis, which was published in the Zentralblatt and entitled "Notes on the psycho-analytical investigation and treatment of manic-depressive insanity and allied conditions" ([1912] 1949). In 1915, Freud wrote "Mourning and melancholia" ([1915, 1917] 1953). On February 18, 1915, Freud told Abraham that he was about to receive a manuscript written by Ferenczi on melancholia and that he himself wished to send him a technical paper for his opinion.

On February 28, Abraham responds: "I must first of all thank you for the proofs. I found nothing to criticise from the first word to the last. To my great satisfaction everything in this paper corresponds with my own experiences. In saying this is your first paper that did not give me anything new, I only mean that—for once—I did not need to do any re-thinking. On the other hand my own observations were not yet so clearly formulated and I therefore learnt quite a lot from the way you structured your paper" (Letter, February 28, 1915; 1965, 212).

We do not know whether by the time Abraham received this letter Freud's manuscript "Mourning and Melancholia" had reached him yet. It is when Freud has just written his essay that an impasse seems to occur in their relationship. Abraham comes to realize that Freud's concepts, as they are outlined in this essay, signify nothing new to him; to some extent, they are similar to ideas of his own that remain in the shadows, untheorized. In this particular instance, he feels as if he were released from his debt of intellectual loyalty.

By March 27, Freud, not having heard from Abraham, writes a second letter in search of reassurance: "I . . . have found confirmation of the elucidation of melancholia in a case I studied for two months, though without visible therapeutic success, which, however, may follow" (Letter, March 27, 1915; 1965, 215). This time, Abraham's response is revealing.

> I have long postponed commenting on your "Outline of a Theory of Melancholia"—this was not only because I have no real leisure for work. Some years ago I myself made an attempt in this direction but was always aware of its imperfections, and was therefore afraid that my attitude to your new theory might easily be too subjective. I think I have now got over this difficulty and am able to accept all the essentials in your work. I do think, however, that an element from my earlier work should be more greatly stressed than it is in yours, and should like to put forward a suggestion which may solve the question left open by you. Important questions do of course remain unanswered, and I have no explanation for them at the present time. I should like to remind you—not to assert my priority but merely to understand the points of agreement in our findings—that I also started from a comparison between melancholic depression and mourning. I found support in your paper on Obsessional Neurosis (The Rat Man). (Letter, March 31, 1915; 1965, 215–16)

Freud's anxiety of authorship rendered untenable Abraham's position as a disciple. Abraham's ideas had been silently incorporated into the Freudian construction of "Mourning and Melancholia."[2] And Freud was not even willing to give him credit for that.

In Freud's response, dated May 4, he includes a critique of Abraham's understanding of melancholia based on two main points: lack of emphasis on the topographic aspect, the regression of the libido, and the abandonment of unconscious object cathexes; and the placing of anal sadism and eroticism in the foreground. Freud requires the consideration of dynamic, topographic, and economic factors in order to reach a "true explanation" of melancholia (Letter, May 4, 1915; 1965, 220). Indeed, the regression of the libido constitutes the core of Freud's hypothesis and has nothing to do with Abraham's. And it is Freud alone who foregrounds anal eroticism. Abraham's original contribution to the theory of melancholia lies precisely in the paramount role played in it by orality.

In his response, Abraham adds one more reservation. He is not persuaded yet that in melancholia the reproaches addressed to the other are turned back on the ego. He resists the idea of an independent, autonomous ego for which the other exists only as long as it is incorporated and transformed into a psychic instance. His reservations on the turning of reproaches against the other into self-reproaches comes from his skeptical view of placing narcissism center stage and, more broadly, of the solipsism of Freudian thought.

Finally, Abraham surrenders. He goes on to consider Freud's "Mourning and melancholia" as the "most fundamental and important of your papers for a long time" (Letter, April 1, 1916; 1965, 233). Upon receiving Freud's printed version of the original manuscript, Abraham's response is worth quoting at length.

> I am pleased to note that my "incorporation phantasy" could be fitted into the larger framework of your own theory. I haven't any important criticisms of this paper either, and can only admire your ability to complete a theoretical structure of this kind at such a time. One very minor criticism is the following. The so-called ideas of inferiority found in the melancholic only seem to be such. Sometimes they in fact represent delusions of grandeur, as for instance when the patient imagines that he has committed all the evil since the creation of the universe. Even though the self-reproaches may be aimed at the love-object, they signify at the same time a narcissistic over-estimation of the patient's own criminal capacities (similar to obsessional neurotics who think themselves capable of monstrous crimes). (Letter, April 16, 1918; 1965, 274)

Abraham's premonitory "incorporation phantasy" turns out to have been swallowed and incorporated by Freud into his own theory. As much as the object is internalized and disappears in Freudian melancholia, here the loyal disciple suffers the same fate. The *delusions of inferiority* of the melancholic are in fact *delusions of grandeur*, an obvious manifestation of his omnipotent feelings. This insistence upon the narcissistic character of melancholia runs parallel to Abraham's former reluctance to admit that the melancholic's self-reproaches are addressed to his object of love. He gives a further twist to the argument by talking about "criminal capacities," striving to find a way out of intrapsychic conflicts dominated by ambivalence and feelings of guilt, to envision the possibility of relating to an other that is real—as real as to be the target of our own destructive tendencies. By operating this shift from ambivalence to omnipotence of thought in the Freudian account of melancholia, the issue of the existence of a radical other comes to the forefront. How is Freud going to integrate this notion of the radical alterity of the lost object of love into the workings of mourning and melancholia?

Early on, in Abraham's essay "Notes on the psycho-analytical investigation and treatment of manic-depressive insanity and allied conditions" ([1912] 1949), his premises are far from those that Freud would later develop. He introduces four psychic categories interwoven in a complex system of relationships: anxiety, fear, depression, and mourning. He never uses the concept of melancholia, adopting depression instead. Whereas there is a significant number of studies on anxiety neuroses, psychoanalytic literature does not abound with studies of depression. Abraham is interested in drawing the distinction between both illnesses.

Reviewing psychoanalytical ideas on these matters, Freud first stated that neurotic anxiety originates in sexual repression. This sexual aetiology of anxiety is what allows us to differentiate it from fear. Following along these lines, and according to Abraham, we can distinguish between mourning and neurotic depression, with the latter caused by repression on the basis of unconscious desires. There exists an analogous relationship between anxiety and depression on one side and fear and mourning on the other. We fear the possibility of future unhappiness, whereas we mourn the unhappiness of a past satisfaction. Neurotics are prey to anguish over the impossibility of satisfying the demands of their drives by virtue of repression. Depression overwhelms the individual when he has neither successfully nor satisfactorily renounced his sexual aim. He feels incapable of being loved, and this is why he has mixed feelings about his life and his future. Abraham writes: "Anxiety and depression are related to each other in the same way as fear and grief. We fear a coming evil; we grieve over one that has occurred. A neurotic will be attacked with anxiety when his instinct strives for a gratification which repression prevents him from attaining; depression sets in when he has to give up his sexual aim without having obtained gratification. He feels himself unloved and incapable of loving, and therefore he despairs of his life and his future ([1912] 1949, 137–38).

In his 1912 essay, Abraham inquires into the nature of depression, an issue that has been frequently overlooked in psychoanalytic literature to date. His positing of a difference between anxiety and depression adds an unexplored and untheorized dimension to Freudian thought. When he states that the depressive has renounced his sexual aim "without having obtained gratification," he advances an irreconcilable idea within the domain of Freudian theory, disengaging himself from a notion of repression based on a conflict between desire and interdiction. In Abraham's view, depression is brought about by renunciation, not by repression. Depression, as well as mourning, follows the occurrence of a psychic event. Thus, Abraham introduces a concept of depression that is distinguishable and different from anxiety. Whereas anxiety originates in considering a satisfaction to come, depression stems from a renouncement that has already taken place. So depression rests on the idea of something that in the actual course of events has already happened and on the idea of the exteriority of the event. This exteriority does not mean that it has to represent any "real event" but rather underscores the impossibility in the relationship with the other.

In 1924, Abraham published "A short study of the development of the libido viewed in the light of mental disorders" ([1924] 1949). He introduced the first section of this essay with a reference to his 1912 paper: "More than ten years have passed since I first attempted to trace the aetiology of manic-depressive disorders on psycho-analytical lines. I was quite aware at the time of the shortcomings of that attempt and was at pains to make this clear in the title of my paper. But we should do well to remember how very little had been written as yet on any psycho-analytical subject. . . . Nevertheless, in spite of the shortcomings of that first attempt, its results have proved to be correct in certain not unimportant particulars. Freud's paper, 'Mourning and Melancholia,' confirmed my view that melancholia stood in the same relation to normal mourning for a loss as did morbid anxiety to ordinary fear" (418–19).

Abraham presents Freud's text as a confirmation of his paper. Whereas he establishes his anteriority in time, he foregos any claims to originality, putting aside his insight concerning the differences between anxiety and depression: "And we may now regard as definitely established the psychological affinity between melancholia and obsessional neuroses. Furthermore, these two illnesses show similarities in regard to the process of the disengagement of the libido from the external world. On the other hand, it had not hitherto been possible to discover anything concerning the point of divergence of melancholical and obsessional states; nor indeed had any light been shed as yet on the problem of the specific cause of the circular insanities" ([1924] 1949, 419).

Abraham raises questions that are crucial to Freudian theory. He suggests that Freud does not make clear the distinction between pathological mourning and melancholia. Abraham takes up the challenge and embarks on an arduous attempt to distinguish between melancholia and obsessional neurosis. This will lead him to develop his own theory of developmental stages, a theory that results in a thorough and detailed explanation and broadening of the one postulated by Freud. He believes it to be of utmost importance to introduce two substages within the anal sadistic stage: "This differentiation of the anal-sadistic stage into a primitive and a later phase seems to be of radical importance. For at the dividing line between those two phases there takes place a decisive change in the attitude of the individual to the external world. Indeed we may say that this dividing line is where 'object love' in the narrower sense, begins, for it is at this point that the tendency to preserve the object begins to predominate" ([1924] 1949, 432).

This subdivision of the anal sadistic stage, as much as regression in the melancholic—"the process of regression in melancholia does not stop at the earlier level of the anal-sadistic stage, but goes steadily back towards a still more primitive organization of the libido" ([1924] 1994, 432–33)— calls for subsequent subdivisions at every stage. Abraham adds one further innovation, namely, that these developmental stages of the libido go hand in hand with stages in the development of object love. He uses the schema I reproduce in table 1, by means of which he makes clear that upon completion of the final genital stage the subject attains postambivalent object love.

One of Abraham's most important contributions, and one that was crucial for the development of Melanie Klein's thinking, was the concept of "partial object love" as a stage in the development of object love. In

Table 1. Schema

Stages of Libidinal Organization	Stages of Object-love	
6 Final genital stage	Object love	Postambivalent
5 Earlier genital stage (phallic)	Object love with exclusion of genitals	
4 Later anal-sadistic stage	Partial love	
3 Earlier anal-sadistic stage	Partial love with incorporation	Ambivalent
2 Later oral stage (cannibalistic)	Narcissism (total incorporation of object)	
1 Earlier oral stage (sucking)	Autoerotism (without object)	Preambivalent

Abraham's view, partial object love was the beginning of a new attitude toward the object. He writes, "On that later level [of partial cannibalism] the individual shows the first signs of having some care for his object. We may also regard such a care, incomplete as it is, as the first beginnings of object-love in a stricter sense, since it implies that the individual has begun to conquer his narcissism" ([1924] 1994, 488). Prior to this stage, the infant paid no attention to the needs of its objects and was willing to destroy them at the height of his or her aggressivity. When the infant comes to care for the existence of the object even at the most primitive level—as a part (of the body) and not as a whole—he or she starts restricting these aggressive impulses. This constitutes the beginning of object love. The stage of partial love is thus an intermediary stage on the infant's way to total love. Abraham's ideas of a progression in the development of the capacity for concern for the object will be taken up by Melanie Klein and will play a central role in her theory of the paranoid-schizoid and the depressive position. In the Freudian elaboration, narcissism emerged as an intermediary stage between autoerotism and alloerotism ([1911] 1953, 60–61), although this may sound like an oversimplification when we consider the complexity of narcissism and object relations in the whole of Freud's works.[3]

In his paper, Abraham mostly focused his ideas on the central role of aggressivity toward the love object, specifically the connection between aggressivity and orality. In his view, the aggressive oral impulse to devour the love object underlies the narcissistic identification with the object. The melancholic feels guilty for having caused damage to his or her object and ultimately masochistic self-punishment is the only way to assuage the guilt.[4] Abraham showed that the ego can emerge from ambivalence only by acknowledging hostility toward the object. Sadism and an unconscious oral attachment to the object were evident signs in the depressive patient. And for Abraham the object is lost as a result of the individual's sadistic impulses.

According to Abraham, in melancholia the process of introjection takes two forms. In the first, the patient has introjected the original love-object on which his or her ego-ideal had been built; this object takes over the role of conscience, and it is from this introjected object that the pathological self-criticism of the melancholic emanates. In the second form, the content of those self-reproaches is ultimately a harsh criticism of the introjected object. Abraham graphically explains the fate of the object in melancholia: "We may truly say that during the course of an attack of melancholia the love-object goes through a process of psychological metabolism within the patient" (464). When Abraham uses the term *introjected object*, he is attempting to describe the psyche and its mental processes in terms of interactions among various objects. Departing from the Freudian structural model, he lays the foundation for Klein's future work in terms of both its points of agreement and its divergence from Freud.

It is also important to note that in the rhetoric of Abraham's papers there is an emphasis on spatiality, spatial metaphors, and spatial phantasies. His repeated allusions to "taking in," "being outside," "evacuating," and "expelling" are obvious tropes for figuring the oral and anal components in the infant's relation to the external world. This pervasive rhetoric of spatiality will later be prominent in Melanie Klein's writings, in which all interactions between psychic space and external reality are figured in terms of introjection and projection.

Abraham died in 1925. Jones describes how Fliess nursed him when he suddenly fell ill upon returning to Berlin from a conference in Holland. It seems that no doctor was able to give a consistent diagnosis of his illness. His phantasies of his "painful and swollen liver" (Jones 1953–1957, 3: 115) persuaded him of his need to undergo an operation. This by no means cured him of this mysterious illness. His sudden death was a shock to his friends and colleagues.

Today we know that Abraham died of a feverish bronchitis contracted after a pharingeal injury produced by the unfortunate ingestion of a fish-bone. Abraham was the most distinguished theorist of craving orality. His premature death sounds like a lethal joke, a fatal slip of the throat that carves out an absence in the evenness of Freud's faithful progeny. Uncannily and insatiably, his irretrievable lost voice haunts us today under the guise of a demand for knowledge, for a fresh inquiry into the blind spots and unsolvable problems he uncovered in the beginnings of psychoanalysis. As his disciple Melanie Klein teaches us, this epistemophilic urge originates also in a search for oral satisfaction, for the remnants of some melancholic incorporation, which is ultimately and most poignantly a demand of love.

Sándor Ferenczi: The Vicissitudes of Introjection

Sándor Ferenczi was an original theorist and a staunch supporter of his own views in the emerging field of psychoanalysis. He was mostly interested in studying the infant's earliest stages of attachment to the world, placing much emphasis on interpersonal relations, which he believed were of major importance for the child's future development.

The concept of introjection was first formulated and introduced by Ferenczi in one of his earliest papers "Introjection and Transference" ([1909] 1956). A few years later, he devoted his essay "On the Definition of Introjection" ([1912] 1955) to developing and explaining introjection in depth. He used the notion of introjection to refer to all processes whereby the ego forms a relationship with an object, which results in the inclusion of that object in the ego. In his words,

> I described introjection as an extension to the external world of the original autoerotic interests, by including its objects in the ego. I put the emphasis on this "including" and wanted to show thereby that I considered every sort of object love (or transference) both in normal and in neurotic people (and of course also in paranoiacs as far as they are capable of loving) as an extension of the ego, that is, as introjection. In principle, man can love only himself; if he loves an object he takes it into his ego. . . . I used the term "introjection" for all such growing onto, all such including of the loved object, in the ego. As already stated, I conceive the mechanism of all transference onto an object, that is to say all kinds of object love, as an extension of the ego. I described the excessive proneness to transference of neurotics as unconscious exaggeration of the same mechanism, that is, as addiction to introjection. (316–17)

Freud used introjection mostly to refer to the process of setting up the parents in the mind of the child as the superego ([1923] 1953) or to the process of internalization of the object in melancholia. Also, following Abraham ([1924] 1949), many analysts elaborated on the instinctual aspect of introjection, and it was frequently referred to as the psychic process analogous to the infant's oral incorporation at the breast (Fenichel [1925] 1953, Fuchs 1937). In Freud's writings, both incorporation and introjection are inextricably bound to the notion of identification; their overlapping and lack of specificity make it difficult to differentiate among the three of them.

Ferenczi's definition of *introjection* was very wide. It included all emotional relations, attachments, and interests in other people and in other objects in the most general sense. In his view, introjection was a basic process that enabled all kinds of attachments to objects in the external world. From here, he moved on to distinguish between two stages of development, the stage of introjection and the stage of projection. The former was related to an earlier stage of omnipotent thought and the latter to the development of reality-oriented thought.[5] According to him, the mechanism of introjection, when "unconsciously exaggerated," was the essential feature of neurosis, as opposed to projection, which characterized paranoia.

While Ferenczi was attempting to explain how the ego is established very much on the basis of introjection, Freud was at that time working on processes related to the cathexis of external objects and those related to the cathexis of the ego.[6] Freud's "On narcissism: An introduction" was published in 1914 and opened up the path that would lead to his formulation of the structural theory of the psyche. Ferenczi's arguments on introjection and projection as developmental stages were not fully compatible with the new Freudian postulates. Whereas Ferenczi believed that attachment to the object takes place at a very early stage (by means of introjection) and the mechanism of projection basically serves to differentiate between the inner world and external reality as a later development, Freud believed that the relationship with the object comes later in development and projection—a defense mechanism in paranoia—constitutes a regression to an earlier, narcissistic stage. With Freud's development of his ideas on narcissism ([1914] 1953) the concept of identification gained more importance. So far, identification had typically been conceived as an active process in the formation of symptoms or dreams, and from On narcissism: An introduction it came to be recognized as an important developmental process. In this sense, Freud, following Abraham's ideas, moved on to consider identification as it is related to the oral instinctual impulse of incorporation. Its mental counterpart came to be called introjection after Ferenczi's introduction of the term.

Later Freud did not mention Ferenczi's concept of introjection in his "Mourning and melancholia" ([1915, 1917], 1953) in spite of Ferenczi's suggestion to Freud (in a letter dated February 22, 1915, Freud and Ferenczi, 1993) that the term was appropriate to describe processes at work in melancholia. Freud did not share his view, for what he was proposing in his description of melancholia was that the trauma of object loss leads to an incorporation of the object within the ego. The narcissistic identification of the ego with the object in melancholia was a result of the loss of the object and the concomitant withdrawal of libido from it. Ferenczi's concept of introjection did not imply the abandonment of object-love and narcissistic regression. Rather, it emphasized the possibility of an ongoing attachment to the object. And it is quite clear from Ferenczi's text that introjection cannot have as its cause the loss of a love object. As we have just mentioned, Freud eventually adopted the term introjection, but he totally modified it in reference to his own views on the relationship between object loss and introjection ([1921] 1953). He also used introjection later to describe the process of superego formation related to the resolution of the Oedipus complex. Freud and Ferenczi also equated introjection with identification, using the terms synonymously. For both, identification constituted a regression from object-love.[7] In Ferenczi's view, object-love was an aspect of introjection and not a later developmental stage. In 1922, he claimed that identification was an attempt to bridge the gap between the self and the outer world ([1922] 1955, 374), and in his last paper he called the stage of identification that of "passive object-love, or tenderness" ([1933] 1955, 163).

Ferenczi, who for many years was Freud's closest collaborator, came to develop ideas different from some of Freud's major theses, and this abruptly ended their relationship. It seems that Freud disapproved of what he called Ferenczi's "departure from our 'classical technique'" (Jones 1955, 61) and of his emphasis on clinical practice, leaving aside central metapsychological issues.

Ferenczi spent a number of years conducting research on the influence of trauma on the development of the human personality. He was interested in the development of personality as a whole—not so much in specific instances as, for example, the role of trauma as the pathogenic agent in neurosis—and the effects of traumatizing relationships with objects (mainly parental figures) on this process. Along these lines, he developed the concept of "introjection of the aggressor," whereby children may "subordinate themselves to the will of the aggressor, to divine each of their desires and to gratify these" ([1933] 1955). He fully described how this process influenced the inner world of the child and allowed the child to deny the occurrence of the aggression in relation to external reality and continue "maintaining the previous situation of tenderness" (162). Later these important ideas came to deeply influence and inspire a good number of object relations analytical approaches, especially that of Melanie Klein.

What it is most interesting for our purposes is Ferenczi's positing of a physiological precursor of the superego. The severity of the feelings of guilt that arise in the genital stage are closely linked to pregenital trends and are associated by regression with early training in cleanliness. From their analysis of adults, Ferenczi and Klein agreed on the direct connection between that early training and the severity of the guilt experienced. This led Ferenczi to suggest in his "Psychoanalysis of sexual habits" ([1925] 1952) that there may be a kind of physiological precursor of the superego, which he called "sphincter morality" (267).

There is further disagreement between Freud and Ferenczi with regard to the question of the severity of the superego. In Civilization and its discontents ([1929, 1930] 1953), Freud subscribed to Melanie Klein's view, which attributed an internal origin to the severity of the superego. It seems that Ferenczi opposed this idea in a letter to Freud (November 11, 1930, Freud and Ferenczi, 1993). He claimed that it was the nature of the relationship with the parents that should be considered as the origin of the superego's severity. In Ferenczi's view, the superego was formed through introjection.

Ferenczi's most innovative contribution to psychoanalysis may have been precisely his notion of introjection. Like Abraham, rather than focusing as much as Freud did on intrapsychic processes, he emphasized the role of interpersonal relations and the influence of external factors in the development of the infant's inner world.

Ferenczi's Legacy: Abraham and Torok on the Vicissitudes of Introjection

Drawing on Ferenczi's notion of introjection, Nicholas Abraham and Maria Torok have worked on the question of pathological introjection—

which they call "endocryptic identification"—in the melancholic object relation. Abraham and Torok first edited and introduced a selection of Melanie Klein's papers in French in 1967. Since then, they have developed their ideas on mourning, melancholia, and mechanisms of introjection in a number of papers in which they mostly follow Ferenczi and differ from Klein.

The concluding passage of their introduction to the 1967 volume (entitled "Qui est Mélanie Klein?") is to a great extent symptomatic of how much the reception of Klein's work has been affected by some early readings that led to some limited and biased interpretations of her arguments and theories. They write: "And certainly, for a long time to come, the great figure of Melanie Klein shall project her 'shadow' and her 'sparkle' on the psychoanalytic movement. But those of us who live after her will not make her really ours until—having gone through the mourning of idolatry, both positive and negative—we have understood the real meaning of her confrontations and we have completely assimilated and incorporated her into the momentum of our own work" (reprinted in 1978, 198–99).

Echoing Freudian rhetoric, Abraham and Torok give us a melancholic full-length portrait of Klein using the pictorial chiaroscuro conventions of "Mourning and melancholia." The well-known Freudian phrase "the shadow of the object fell upon the ego" (1953, 14:249) turns into an object wearing a Kleinian mask that now projects its ominous shadow onto the analytical community. This objectification of Klein suggests an ambivalent love-hate relationship that, in strict Kleinian terms, should be placed in the stage of partial incorporation: Melanie Klein as part object. Deep-seated anxieties, fear, and the imposing threat from the lines of the adversaries mobilize a heavy artillery of defense mechanisms. Anything goes.

The overdetermination and near intoxication carried by the institution of Klein's very name mystifies the figure of the rebellious woman analyst as "a sort of Mother, loved and feared, flattered and hated, both encumbering in her scope and indispensable in her gifts" (Abraham and Torok 1978, 197). The cliché of the monstrous mother is used again to counterattack her unsettling ideas of dissent. Melanie Klein's body (of work) was turned into a fetish that keeps safe the pillars of psychoanalysis, a science loyal to the legacy of its father.

The mourning of idolatry resumed, we can fully appropriate Klein's thought and assimilate it into our projects. In Abraham and Torok's rhetoric, the body of Kleinian thought haunts psychoanalysis as the *cadavre exquis*, the "exquisite corpse," incorporated rather than assimilated by one of these vicissitudes of fate.[8] It would be interesting to submit Abraham and Torok's text to the scrutiny of their own cryptonymic analysis. Is it not the case that "completely assimilated" turns out to be symptomatic when it is examined under their analytic lens? First of all, what do they mean by *assimilation*? It was precisely Paula Heimann, one of Klein's closest collaborators, who introduced *assimilation* into the glossary of Kleinian thought. In her 1942 essay, "A Contribution to the problem of sublimation and its relation to processes of internalization," Heimann defines assimilation of internal objects in the context of her wider discussion of sublimation as that process "by which the subject acquires and absorbs those qualities of his internal parents which are suitable and adequate to him" (1942, 16).

Whereas this uncanny "completely assimilated" seems to point to the Kleinian theorization of the depressive position and its resolution in the attainment of the perception of whole objects and *total love*, it also evokes Abraham and Torok's entrapment in the very logic they seek to undo. In "Mourning or melancholia: introjection *versus* incorporation," they write: "The crucial move away from introjection (clearly rendered impossible) to incorporation is made when *words* fail to fill the subject's void and hence an imaginary thing is inserted into the mouth in their place" (1994, 128–29). Instead of this *mouth work*—speaking to the analytical community about the loss of Melanie Klein—another type of mouth work is utilized, in their own words, "one that is imaginary and equipped to deny the very existence of the entire problem" (129). Here again their rhetoric is reminiscent of Susan Isaacs's description of the mechanism of "compulsive confession" in her splendid essay on phantasy (1952), which "implies such unconscious argument as the following: 'If I say it, no one else will,' or 'I can triumph over them by saying it first, or win their love by at least appearing to be a good boy'" (106). What is the "object" of Abraham and Torok's harsh critique? Was it that Klein was not a good girl by closely following her master Ferenczi's original ideas? What is the point in their critique of what they call "Kleinian pan-fantasism" (1994, 125)? Abraham, in his work on Ferenczi, seems unproblematically ready to embrace what he calls Ferenczi's "pansymbolisme psychanalytique" in the latter's idea of "bioanalysis" (Abraham and Torok 1978, 24).[9]

Abraham and Torok's reelaboration of the notion of introjection bears a strong resemblance to Paula Heimann's notions of internalization and sublimation. Heimann considers "internal freedom and independence" (1942, 15) as necessary conditions for successful sublimation. She uses the metaphor of dramatic action to describe the dynamic scenario of the internal world, where memory traces of psychical experience interact with internal and external objects. She summarizes her argument as follows, stating that "the inner world is a never-ending drama of life and action. Life is bound up with the dynamic processes set up by aggression, guilt, anxiety and grief about the internal objects, and by the impulses of love and restoration; Love and Hate are urging the subject to strive for sublimation. The internal freedom to which I refer is a relative, not an absolute fact; it does not abolish conflicts, but it enables the subject to enlarge and unfold his ego in his sublimation" (17). In "The illness of mourning and the fantasy of the exquisite corpse," Maria Torok claims she wants to eliminate the misleading synonymy between introjection and incorporation (Abraham and Torok 1994, 113). Is it not the case that Heimann's enlargement and unfolding of the ego are paradoxically too closely related to Torok's rendering of introjection as follows: "By broadening and enriching the ego, introjection seeks to introduce into it the unconscious, nameless or repressed libido. Thus, it is not at all a matter of 'introjecting' the object, as it is all too commonly stated, but of introjecting the sum total of the drives, and their vicissitudes as occasioned and mediated by the object . . . introjection transforms instinctual promptings into desires and fantasies of desire, making them fit to receive a name and the right to exist and to unfold in the objectal sphere" (113).

The arguments of Abraham and Torok's critique of Klein are nothing new, for they do not seem to go beyond the debates on introjection and incorporation held during the Controversial Discussions in the 1940s. Their indebtedness to Klein shows in the development of their own ideas on endocryptic identification, symbol, psychic tomb, and cryptonymy, among others. In their reading, Klein is still in a state of partial incorporation, partial as result a great number of contemporary and even current appreciations of her work. It seems that it is about time to begin assessing Klein's outstanding contributions to psychoanalysis in a fair and unbiased way, at the very least on equal terms with those of her contemporaries. Only then can her work be read and received as a whole object. With the possibility of postambivalent love open and not foreclosed, the avenues for total disagreement will be closer to reality as well.

Sándor Radó: Melancholia Transfigured

I once described melancholia as a great despairing cry for love, and I believe
that our present context justifies us in so conceiving of it.—Sándor Radó

In "The problem of melancholia" (1928), Sándor Radó addressed the issue
of melancholia with significant variations from Freud's ideas. Radó introduced the concept of a double introjection in his account of the processes
at work in melancholia. His aim was to show to what extent analysis of the
ego and narcissism could provide new insights into the nature of melancholia, with special attention paid to the changes of mood characteristic of
manic depression, melancholia, and mania.

For Radó, the most striking feature displayed by the symptoms of
depressive conditions is the decline in self-esteem and self-satisfaction. In
melancholia, this finds clamorous expression in the melancholic's delusional self-accusations and his or her delusions of moral inferiority. Freud
identified a mental attitude of rebellion in melancholia which Radó places
prior to the acute phase of it—"a period of arrogant and embittered rebellion" (1928, 421).[10] Radó describes in detail the process that leads to this
rebellion. We can briefly summarize it in two steps. First, the ego of melancholics shows a strong craving for narcissistic gratification and considerable narcissistic intolerance, so that even to trivial offences and disappoint-
ments melancholics react with a drop in their self-esteem. Second, their
sadism fastens on their love objects, "as though it were their intention to
devour them altogether" (423). All of this precedes the subject's aggressive
tendencies directed against himself in melancholia. For Radó, the melancholic's "contrition" is a reaction to the failure of his or her rebellion. The
withdrawal in narcissistic fashion to the inner world is not an attempt to
gain the pardon and love of the object but rather those of the melancholic's
superego, which in Radó's own words constitutes a "regressive step, [by
which] the ego is removed from reality" (424).

Radó is interested in reconstructing the way in which the melancholic
produces his or her mechanism of self-punishment: the punishments of
the actual parents are unconsciously reproduced and he or she attempts to
win their love, but the intention underlying this is to win the reconciliation
to the superego. The ego in melancholia thus breaks off its relations with
reality. This is an important remark insofar as it clearly shows that in most
melancholic and manic-depressive disorders there is a flight from reality,
which places them in the proximity of psychosis.

For Radó, when the child begins to grasp the idea of guilt "it seems as though he were already prepared for this experience" (1928, 425), and he or she understands straight away its connection with punishment, expiation, and forgiveness. The differences with Melanie Klein are quite clear. Radó does not give an explanation of how or why this sense of guilt emerges, and he assumes an innate capacity to recognize and experience guilt. It is in the rage of the hungry infant that he situates the origin of all later forms of aggressive reaction to frustration, and it is on this aggressivity that the ego in the period of latency concentrates its whole sense of guilt. During the phallic phase, the superego is formed as a "primary function of self-observation" (426) and the ego becomes aware of the criticisms of this institution in the form of a dread of conscience, the sense of guilt.

For Radó, the torments of hunger are the mental precursors of later punishments. In fact, they come to be the primal mechanism of self-punishment. Thus, in Radó's view, "At the bottom of the melancholiac's profound dread of impoverishment there is really simply the dread of starvation (that is of impoverishment in physical possessions)" (1928, 427). According to this argument, the deepest fixation point in the melancholic disposition is to be found in the hunger situation of the infant. Radó had already identified a process he called "alimentary orgasm," which he had assumed to be the precursor of the later genital orgasm. He writes that we "cannot fail to recognize that the infant's dawning ego acquires in this narcissistic gratification that mental quality which it will later experience as self-satisfaction" (428).[11]

For Radó, the ego feels guilty because by its aggressive attitude it feels that it has itself to blame for the loss of the object. Nevertheless, there is yet another psychic process at work. The sadistic trend of the hostility of the ego toward the object translates into the idea that the object alone is to blame, that it provoked the rigor of the ego by means of its caprices and unreliability. When the ego fails to carry through the claims of its aggressive impulses toward the object and adopts an attitude of masochistic remorse toward the superego, Radó claims that "the aggressive tendency of the id goes over to the side of the superego and forces the ego itself, weakened by its expiatory attitude, into the position of the object" (1928, 430). In this sadomasochistic scenario, the ego, thrust into the place of the hated object, loses to a large extent its relationship with reality and becomes subjected to the tyranny of the sadistic superego and the id.

For Radó, it is imperative that the object undergo two different processes of incorporation, being absorbed not only by the superego but by the ego. In his view, it is of crucial importance that the child achieves what he calls the "synthetic function" and is able to realize that there is only one mother who gathers together "good" and "bad" aspects instead of two different figures, one idealized and another hated. The ego thus is able to confront the conflict of ambivalence. The superego is a creation of the ego, and it is "an attempt of the ego to realize its desire to transform the alternately 'good' and 'bad' parents into parents who are only 'good'" (1928, 433).

It is important to note that Radó refers to a certain quality of "femininity" in his description of patients with depressive dispositions. He writes, "My purpose was simply to define the type of individuals, feminine in their narcissism, to which persons of depressive disposition conform. With this type the mere 'danger of loss of love' is sufficient to compel formation of the superego" (1928, 434). From a different angle than that of Klein, it is striking to note how Radó reaches similar conclusions to the ones I drew in my discussion of melancholia and gender. Nevertheless, Radó does not pursue this idea further in his essay.

In Radó's view, in melancholia the "good object," whose love the ego desires, is introjected and incorporated in the superego, whereas the "bad object," which has been split off from the object as a whole, is incorporated in the ego and becomes the victim of the superego's sadistic tendencies. From Radó's viewpoint, it is quite clear that mania—not mourning—is the logical outcome of melancholia.

> Now if the "bad object" which resides within the ego is chastised and finally destroyed, all that remains is the object purged of its "bad" element, i.e. the "good object"; moreover, the hostility of the ego (of the id) is satisfied and has spent itself. Nothing now stands in the way of the purified ego's uniting itself with the object, which is also purged of offence, in reciprocal love! When the subject swings over to mania this, the goal of the melancholic process (in the region of the pathological) is fully attained. The "bad object" (as Abraham recognized) is expelled from the ego by an anal act and this is synonymous with its being killed. The ego, freed of its own aggressive tendencies and its hated enemy, heaves a sigh of relief and with every sign of blissful transport unites itself with the "good object", which has been raised to the position of the super-ego. (1928, 435)

Radó is obsessed with the operation of the purging of the "bad object" and the manic attempt to revive the ego's self-regard as a consequence of the loss of love. He even claims that the process of melancholia is "as it were a prophylactic measure against the ego's ever suffering such sever injury again. . . . From this purely psychic act, however, there ensues an important *real* result: the restoration of the subject's self-esteem—indeed, its leap into the exaltation of mania" (1928, 436). It is specifically mania that turns the ego back into the object world.[12] But melancholia is not fully exhausted in mania. In the remission of the manic phase, the subject's character is tinged with obsessive traits, which by means of extensive ideal formation allow the channeling of its aggressive impulses into the social and thus provide narcissistic identification in accordance with reality.

This channeling into the social of the manic's aggressivity under the guise of obsessional neurosis can be read as Radó's only possibility for a socially explained and acceptable melancholia that is founded upon its own erasure and invisibility. Melancholia metamorphosizes into mania, and this in turn becomes obsessional neurosis. There is a progressive taming of the psychotic and depressive features of melancholia into the most tractable rituals of obsessional neurosis. The melancholic dysfunctional subject is recovered and brought back to society, where his former rebellion—of a profoundly asocial character—will be, in Radó's view, narcissistically understood. There is no trace of the "bad object" whatsoever, only a superegoic good object that restores the subject's self-esteem if it acts in obedience to its demands. Social psychosis is avoided, but its avoidance has a significant cost, that of the repudiation and elimination of all bad objects, of all the subject's ancient objects of love.

Radó concludes his essay with a comparison between neurotic depression and melancholia. Neurotic depression is a kind or partial melancholia. The main difference between them lies in the fact that, whereas the ego of the melancholic is almost "consumed" (1928, 437) by depressive processes and loses its relationship with reality, in neurotic depression these processes are, in Radó's words, "merely superimposed upon an ego which is, indeed, neurotic but is more or less intact" (437). In neurotic depression, both the object and its relationship with reality are preserved, but the subject's hold on them is loosened and there is a narcissistic regression so as to take refuge in the "oral narcissistic reparation-mechanism" (437). Radó does not pursue his arguments further. It is quite clear that, in agreement with Abraham's findings, he places regression to the oral stage at the center of melancholia and neurotic depression. His explanation of the double introjective process at work in melancholia notwithstanding, he fails to address the issue of the origin of guilt and the negative, aggressive, and punitive aspects of the superego in later development. In an eclectic mixture of Abraham's and Freud's ideas on this issue, Radó gives a far-fetched solution to the problem of the dysfunctional subject of melancholia. Individual and social psychoses pass unrecognized, thus leaving aside one of the most intractable and painful questions at the beginning of psychoanalysis.

Freudian Melancholia: For They Know Not What They Have Lost

So by taking flight into the ego love escapes extinction.—Sigmund Freud

In the two opposed situations of being most intensely in love and of suicide the ego is overwhelmed by the object, though in totally different ways.—Sigmund Freud

In the context of the first period of Freud's metapsychological papers, "Mourning and melancholia" ([1915, 1917] 1953) is an enquiry into the similarities and differences between a normal and a pathological affect. In the Freudian conception of melancholia, everything takes place inside a psyche conceived of as self-contained and autonomous. When Freud introduces the idea of the triumph over the object in the passage from melancholia to mania, he is indebted to former ideas developed by Abraham. The latter had already suggested in his previous work ([1924] 1949) how behind the manifest self-debasement of the melancholic there lurks a narcissistic overestimation of the power of the ego. When the melancholic, in phantasy, kills the object, he or she is eliminating an object that is already dead. The blurring of the boundaries and subsequent appropriation of mourning by melancholia follows along these lines. The movement of the psyche turning back upon itself reveals a denial of alterity that is inscribed in the very rhetoric of "Mourning and melancholia." Freud's denial of alterity in the figures of his disciples and in the body of his doctrine, by virtue of successive melancholic incorporations, is a mise-en-abyme or specular replication of a theoretical construction that extends its implications far beyond what he himself was able to foresee.

The rhetoric of "Mourning and melancholia" echoes an impossibility, that of opening up a way to express mourning. An omnipresent melancholia pervades the Freudian text. All space is conceived as intrapsychic space where the other does not exist as a separate entity; it has been incorporated in the process of narcissistic regression of a split ego. Abraham had warned the Freudian melancholic of the omnipotent delusion that accuses him or her of having caused the death of the object of love. Melancholia poses a critical unsolvable problem, that of the misrecognition by the subject of the boundary between psychic and external reality.

The victory over the object inflicts an open wound on the ego. Tearing itself away from its external object to recoil in narcissistic autonomy, the ego tears itself away from a part of itself. Moreover, by virtue of the ego's misrecognition of the loss of the object, the object itself frequently returns under the guise of psychic pain. When mourning becomes impossible, a somatic transcription emerges inside the body of the subject as a residue devoid of symbolic meaning. This wound or psychic trace left by the death of the object effects an encystation, a demetaphorization of the body, which now comes to impersonate the object. This pregnant physicality of the body turns out to be inaccessible to meaning. Incorporation of the object emerges out of a failure of symbolization. In mourning, psychic pain can gain access to symbolization, whereas in melancholia there is a blockage, an inability to symbolize out of an excess of incorporation.

"Mourning and melancholia" opens with a Freudian reverie, one that melancholically harbors his readers into the enclosures of his founding theoretical phantasy, outlined in *Interpretation of dreams*, whereby he seeks to provide a ground for reflecting upon the distinction between a normal and a pathological affect. In this reverie, the centrality of narcissistic disorders as opposed to "normal [psychic] life" operates as the bedrock on which the Freudian metapsychological edifice rests.[13] Freud warns us of fluctuations in the definition of *melancholia* in psychiatry. Mourning and melancholia share the following traits: "a profoundly painful dejection, cessation of interest in the outside world, loss of the capacity to love, [and] inhibition of all activity" ([1915, 1917] 1953, 244), whereas melancholia distinguishes itself in "a lowering of the self-regarding feelings to a degree that finds utterance in self-reproaches and self-revilings, and culminates in a delusional expectation of punishment" (244). Freud points out that in some people the same circumstances produce melancholia instead of mourning and that this makes them "suspect of a pathological disposition" (243).

Early in his first analytical work in Draft G ([1895?] 1953) Freud states that the affect in melancholia is analogous to that of mourning, for both operate upon the regret that something was lost. Melancholia is at that time a loss at the level of the drives and specifically a work of mourning brought about by a loss of libido. Its aetiology comes from a "psychic impoverishment" ([1915, 1917] 1953, 246), which Freud figures under the shape of a hole in the psyche. This troping of the hole will be most frequently taken to represent depressive processes in a broad phenomenological sense, while for Freud at the time it was a hole through which libidinal energy drained away.[14]

As noted, there is a fundamental difference between mourning and melancholia, and that difference is the loss of self-esteem in melancholia. In "On narcissism: An introduction," Freud argues that the loss of the object reactivates the libidinal cathexis that can be protracted under the shape of a disavowal of reality and may lead to "hallucinatory wishful psychosis" ([1914] 1953, 244). Nevertheless, the reality principle will impose on the subject who has lost his or her object psychic work that demands a great expenditure of both libidinal energy and time. Throughout this work, the lost object is tracked down in the psyche before it can be relinquished by the libido on its way to regaining the capacity to cathect new objects as substitutes for the lost one. According to Freud, the mood of mourning is a "painful" one, and, whereas in mourning the lost object is always perceived as distinct and separate, in melancholia there is an essential misrecognition of what has been lost. The subject knows that he or she has lost something but ignores what it is, its contents being unknown and hidden deep in the unconscious. In the work of mourning, the loss, in bringing back to consciousness the contents represented by the object, has to some extent a function that works to reveal the object itself. In melancholia, the unknown character of the loss constitutes an enigma: "The object has not perhaps actually died, but has been lost as an object of love. . . . In yet other cases one feels justified in maintaining the belief that a loss of this kind has occurred, but one cannot see clearly what it is that has been lost, and it is all the more reasonable to suppose that the patient cannot consciously perceive what he has lost either. This indeed might be so even if the patient is aware of the loss which has given rise to his melancholia, but only in the sense that he knows *whom* he has lost but not *what* he has lost in him" (245).

In melancholia, it seems as if the loss only had to do with the ego and not the object itself, as if the spectral return of the object were in fact a (re)turning back upon the ego: Freud, immersed in his previous work on narcissism, argues that object choice operates narcissistically and in melancholia contrary to what happens in mourning; both the return of the libido and its displacement onto a different object is blocked. Immediately following the suppression of the narcissistic object cathexis, the libido turns back upon the ego: "Thus the shadow of the object fell upon the ego, and the latter could henceforth be judged by a special agency, as though it were an object, the forsaken object" ([1914] 1953, 249). In "On narcissism," Freud had already distinguished between "the formation of an ego-ideal" and sublimation. The ego-ideal, "heightens the demands of the ego and is the most powerful factor favoring repression; sublimation is a way out, a way by which those demands can be met without involving repression" (95). The ego-ideal thus comes to be a first repressive agency prior to the Freudian elaboration of the structural theory of the psyche.

When in "Mourning and melancholia" Freud refers to the abandoned object, he identifies the endopsychic path to object loss according to which it is not only the object that disappears (object-ive loss) but also the ego that splits (subject-ive loss). In melancholia, the preservation of the object rests upon the mode of narcissistic identification. The narcissistic enclosure is at its height insofar as the object was chosen in the narcissistic mode. Narcissistic identification is thus central to melancholia. Freud writes that "the object choice [in melancholia] has been effected on a narcissistic basis, so that the object-cathexis, when obstacles come in its way, can regress to narcissism. The narcissistic identification with the object then becomes a substitute for the erotic cathexis, the result of which is that in spite of the conflict with the loved person the love-relation need not be given up. This substitution of identification for object-love is an important mechanism in the narcissistic affections" ([1915, 1917] 1953, 249). For Freud, identification is a preliminary stage of object-choice that is expressed in ambivalent fashion and in which the ego wants to incorporate the object into itself by devouring it "in accordance with the oral or cannibalistic phase of libidinal development" (249). In Freud's view, melancholia borrows some of its features from mourning and the others "from the process of regression from narcissistic-object choice to narcissism" (249).[15]

Freud moves on to consider what the particular psychic instance that judges the ego may be. This instance comes out of a splitting in the ego between a critical agency—ego-ideal in "On narcissism" and later the superego in Group psychology and the analysis of the ego ([1921] 1953), The ego and *the id* ([1923] 1953), and subsequent works—and that part of the ego that is transformed on the basis of its identification with the object.[16] Ambivalence between love and hate is distributed between both of them.

> This conflict due to ambivalence, which sometimes arises from more real experiences, sometimes from more constitutional factors, must not be overlooked among the preconditions of melancholia. If the love for the object—a love which cannot be given up though the object itself is given up—takes refuge in narcissistic identification, then the hate comes into operation on this substitutive object, abusing it, debasing it, making it suffer and deriving sadistic satisfaction from its suffering. The self-tormenting melancholia, which is without doubt enjoyable, signifies, just like the corresponding phenomenon in obsessional neurosis, a satisfaction of trends of sadism and hate which relate to an object, and which have been turned around upon the subject's own self in the ways we have been discussing. ([1915, 1917] 1953, 251)

Freud will further pursue the definition and characterization of this splitting in *Group psychology and the analysis of the ego* and *The ego and the id*.[17]

In Freud's view, the self-criticisms of the melancholic seem to be addressed to his or her love object, the loss of which has triggered the psychic illness. He suggested that the melancholic identified with the love object and criticized it via him or herself. Freud described this operation as "a cleavage between the critical activity of the ego and the ego as altered by identification" ([1915, 1917] 1953, 249). The function of self-criticism may thus be conceived as an intrapsychic relationship between two parts of the ego, the one attacking the other.[18] Furthermore, in "Mourning and melancholia" Freud argued that melancholics blame themselves not only for their losses but for not having been loved from the beginning. As a result, they suffer from various degrees of self-alienation and are plagued with feelings of guilt, self-debasement, and self-hatred.

Freud's revision of his former views on superego formation together with his reflections on the role of aggression in *Civilization and its discontents* ([1929, 1930] 1953) bring his theory close to the notion of introjection in melancholia. In his attempt to find an explanation for the harshness of the superego, he claims that its aggression is nothing but the individual's own aggression directed inward. The severity of the superego could not be satisfactorily explained only in terms of the internalization of the parents' behavior. In line with Melanie Klein's new findings, Freud embraced the view of the redirection of aggression.

Freud himself acknowledged the influence of Klein's new ideas in a footnote to the text in *Civilization and its discontents*. Leo Bersani also writes of the importance of Klein's views on the severity of the superego. He notes, "Freud speaks of a kind of meta-aggressiveness, an aggressiveness developed in response to an external authority which refuses to satisfy our earliest wishes. The child will ingeniously identify with that authority, not in order to continue its punishments internally, but rather in order to safely possess it, on the inside, as the object or victim of its own aggressive impulses" (1986, 22). Bersani aptly sets up a melancholic Freudian scenario of anthropomorphized figures in which the conflict between a child and a father "becomes an internal confrontation between an internal superego having all the aggressiveness which the child would have liked to direct toward its father (as well as the punitive aggression expected from the father), and an inner father degraded to the status of a punished ego" (22).

Morality and Melancholia

The reactions expressed in their behaviour still proceed from a mental constellation of revolt, which has been, by a certain process, passed over into the crushed state of melancholia.—Sigmund Freud

Jean Gillibert has suggested that we can read Freud's "Mourning and melancholia" as if it were a treatise on morals. Its privileged place in Freudian metapsychology follows up the brilliant insight put forward in his *Project for a scientific psychology* ([1887–1902, 1950] 1953) that "The initial helplessness of human beings is the primal source of all moral motives" (318). Gillibert, echoing a Freudian "rhetoric in mourning," writes, "The shadow zones [in "Mourning and melancholia"] do not correspond to spaces where Freud was thinking obscurely; they are rather those spaces where truth is most difficult to think of" (1979, 160). Freud's remarks about "an exclusive devotion to mourning which leaves nothing over for other purposes or other interests" ([1915, 1917] 1953, 244), the patient's representation of his ego as "worthless, incapable of any achievement and morally despicable" (246), the melancholic's "delusion of (mainly moral) inferiority" (246), and the melancholic's "dissatisfaction with the ego on moral grounds" (247–48) remind us of the importance of "morality" in the issues at stake. To acknowledge that melancholia is a "narcissistic neurosis" or a "moral illness" is to propound narcissism as a nondestiny, since death is our final destiny and narcissism wants to be immortal. The cruel torture inflicted by the superego (orally sadistic and with highly regressive tendencies) on the ego risks being the last vicissitude of an immortal desire of this vital agency that is the ego, now bereft of what used to be its main support, its self-esteem. Freud writes that whereas the ego of the melancholic is a desert and it is the whole world that is a desert for the mourner, the melancholic "displays something else besides which is lacking in mourning—an extraordinary diminution in his self-regard, an impoverishment of his ego on a grand scale. In mourning it is the world itself which has become poor and empty; in melancholia it is the ego itself" (246).[19] Freud also points out that the melancholic is not much concerned with bodily accidents—infirmity, ugliness, weakness—or social inferiority, but with regard to the latter "it is only his fears and asseverations of becoming poor that occupy a prominent position" (248). He further relates the fear of becoming poor to anal erotism, "which has been torn out of its context and altered in a regressive sense" (252).[20]

This situation of ego impoverishment may lead the subject to commit suicide. Suicide partakes of a sacrificial logics. The melancholic *dies for* the superego (in the form of suicide, war, an ideal, and so on), and therefore no one can dispossess the melancholic of his or her own death.[21]

The lost object can be recovered in delirium, in the "hallucinatory wishful psychosis" (Freud [1915, 1917] 1953, 244). Indeed the thematics of object loss haunt the Freudian elaboration from castration to desire. We may as well argue that desire is always already in mourning (in pain by virtue of its proper unsatisfiability), but in order to arrive at such a conclusion we must first pass through narcissism and pleasure. Facing the verdict of reality—in itself the painful space where the individual passes from primary to secondary process—the performance of sexuality is represented as a "hallucinatory satisfaction of a wish" (Wunsch), where hallucination is not a perception without an object but rather the strongest external cathexis transferred to the individual's internal world. In this highly idealized fiction, Freud pushes his rhetoric to the edge by arguing that all desire is at its root psychotic and that desire implies first and foremost a kind of violence—in its tireless attempt to fuse inside and outside—traversed as it is by the death drive (Eros and Thanatos unified). In this scenario, maternal care and nurturance are inscribed as the longed for and deferred responses to hallucinatory pleasure. In the absence of maternal care, the system breaks down and the individual dies. Hallucinatory pleasure can no longer maintain life. It kills instead.

Since mourning—the time span during which mourning exists—denotes in a straightforward fashion object loss and separation, we may raise a question: what does it mean to lose in the Freudian account? When one reads "Mourning and melancholia" in detail, one is struck by the fact that it is to lose what turns out to be most important, much more than the actual object itself. The object is only significant as an empty holder of the individual's libidinal cathexis and as responsible for transforming this cathexis into a double polarity. The object is an empty carrier of life or death, of the ambivalence inherent to the drives, but we can no longer discern whether the dead are going to persecute the living—as is frequently seen in cases of pathological mourning—or whether guilt is nothing but the return of aggressivity and hate.

The main difference between mourning and melancholia in Freud is the loss of self-esteem in the latter. In his reconstruction of the melancholic process, Freud says that the ego of the melancholic has been offended and deceived by the loved object. But, according to Gillibert, it is important to retain the positive aspects of these modes of aggression and to note that an offense does not necessarily entail guilt. One is not guilty because one offends. There is no efficient causality between suffering and guilt. We can draw an analogy between the ill treatment inflicted by the superego upon the object-ego and that inflicted by the superego (i.e., fate) upon the ego in mourning. One of the strongest temptations of mourning is indeed the process of melancholization. The mourner's ego in its work of decathexis must constantly decide whether or not to share the fate of the lost object. The ego must make a choice between itself—narcissistic satisfaction—and the desire to go on living or between that part of itself—libidinally cathected—that is already lost and the desire to die.

Gillibert writes, "Were the world human, mourning will certainly become melancholia" (1979, 163). In other words, mourning does not become melancholia—pathological mourning—lest the world be lived *as if it were human*. He gives a good example to illustrate this idea. He dramatizes the parents' reaction to reckless infantile behavior that puts the life of the child at risk. One of the most primitive reactions is that of inflicting aggressive—verbal or physical—punishment. This aggressive act can be interpreted as a defense against an actual life-threatening situation lived as being possible at the moment. It is a reaction against the aggressive feelings of ambivalence toward the love object, and simultaneously it is self-punishment for the threat posed to one's own narcissism. Aggressivity effects here a reversal of roles. The father asks "do you wish to kill me?" of the child who was about to die. The circuit of liberation of aggressive tendencies and libido, suddenly repressed, needs the mediation of another desire, in this case that of the child, who one immediately imagines having the desire to die. This almost fatal mistake on the part of the child is not interpreted as contingent—later the father may remark, "You should have paid more attention to that"—but rather as an absolute for the father's narcissism. Narcissism cannot but think of events in an absolute or totalizing way.[22]

The original character of pain, of living pain as a holding structure—as in the psychosis of pain, so to speak—makes us aware of the intimate connection between the pleasure principle and its correlate, the reality principle, satisfaction, and anxiety-pain, Eros and Thanatos in all human activities, from the infant at the breast to adult sexuality.

The shameless pain of the melancholic is a most cherished pleasure. Yet absolute pleasure kills. Only orality fully provides the orgasm of the feast (Freud [1912–13] 1953) and mourning: "The self-tormenting melancholia, which is without doubt enjoyable, signifies, just like the corresponding phenomenon in obsessional neurosis, a satisfaction of trends of sadism and hate which relate to an object, and which have been turned around upon the subject's own self in the ways we have been discussing. . . . The melancholic's erotic cathexis in regard to his object has thus undergone a double vicissitude: part of it has regressed to identification, but the other part, under the influence of a conflict due to ambivalence, has been carried back to the stage of sadism which is nearer to that conflict" (Freud [1915, 1917] 1953, 251).[23] Melancholia is a purely libidinal illness between the species and the individual (the ego seen as its object). Feelings of shame in front of others are lacking in the melancholic, and Freud uncovers instead "an almost opposite trait of insistent communicativeness which finds satisfaction in self-exposure" (247). There is no longer shame, no longer any reference to the ego; the pure culture of the death drive resides in the superego.

The Freudian notion of melancholia is close to an open wound, a black hole, an abyss of dereliction.[24] There is no real object loss in melancholia, no mourning; rather there is a pseudomourning, which threatens the object. The lost object leaves its psychic trace inside—introjection and incorporation—and there is a disavowal of object loss. The subject mimics real mourning for the phantasmatic possession of the object and out of its own cannibalistic devoration. It seems as if there will be no real mourning lest the ego be lost through suicide, at which time the ego of the melancholic might then be mourned by its object. Melancholia is the most impossible, unlikely, and risky stage of love, the stage of loving cannibalistic ingestion.

For Gillibert, the melancholic can be the redeemer of a race through the sacrifice of ego and the exhibition of pain. The melancholic can also fulfill the narcissistic ideal of his or her ego by committing suicide, leaving to others the legacy of the abstract idea of his or her ego by forcing them to remember. Leo Bersani, in his discussion of Freud's *Civilization and its discontents*, has also pointed to the melancholy opposition between the individual and society, arguing that "the repression of the masochistic, nonnarrative, timelessly replicative grounds of the sexual is also consonant with the melancholy opposition between individual happiness and civilization in C&D, an opposition which should be understood as a return of the repressed, as the disguised reemergence of biological masochism in an anthropological fable about the oppositional, destructive nature of all confrontations between the claims of pleasure and the claims of history" (1986, 112–13). Human desire radically opposes civilization.[25]

Freud described mania melancholically. Mania is the mad triumph of the conflation between the ego and the ego-ideal, and along with it goes a total absence of shame.[26] In the back room of melancholia, Freud leaves the ego-ideal, the narcissistic ideal of autonomy, and the desire of recognition, the desire to be loved, which merged with shame is modified by the ego through the introjection of the object. The maniac in Freud fulfills the imperative of the ego-ideal, which is ideal morality.

The lost object introjected and incorporated inside the ego is a corpse in melancholia. It is a corpse that demands that the ego make a choice to get resuscitated; become a memory, a souvenir; or die. Melancholia refuses object loss, as is the case with projective identification and narcissistic identification. The melancholic has lost not just the object but the love the object feels for the ego. A severe narcissistic injury is effected, an open wound. There is neither mourning nor hallucination, only long and mute pain. In Freudian melancholia, pain takes the place of the object, masking the disavowal of loss.

The absence of the object in mourning and the empty presence of hallucination are not one and the same thing, but there is an analogical resemblance between them. In both cases there is nostalgia. Psychic reality and external reality have a passion for resemblances. Nevertheless, they are never identical except in the case of psychosis. Melancholia also resembles mourning in its temporality, insofar as in both of them the subject withdraws from the present and dwells on the past. But in melancholia it is impossible to leave the past behind. The melancholic appears to be stuck without a sense of direction for the future. Withdrawal and grief do not end, since they have become a way of retaining forever in phantasy what has long since been lost in reality.

The ego of the melancholic is impoverished but megalomaniac; it falls into the violence of a certain moral pain. The ego of the melancholic resembles its object, and this is the stance it takes toward the superego. The shameless exhibition of the ego of the melancholic out of its own delirium of guilt emerges from an intimate loss of the subject of representation in favor of a unique subjectivity that presents itself in an intolerable exhibition, the exhibition of the melancholic that leaves the analyst powerless.[27]

A Kleinian Epilogue

In Kleinian theory, we may say that to some extent it is out of pain that the internal object is born. The Freudian hallucination of the object is translated in Kleinian phantasy as a primitive form of projection that is reintrojected anew. In Kleinian theory, it is not so much the absence or loss of the external object but the risk that the internal object runs, that produces melancholia and psychic pain in the most general sense. For Klein, anxiety about object loss is primarily connected to aggressive phantasies of destruction of the object. In her view, fear of the disappearance of the object may be experienced in paranoid form—the predominant anxiety being that of being attacked by the object—or depressive form—the fear of losing the internalized good object. The pain in melancholia comes in Kleinian terms from a regression to the depressive position. Incorporation of the object, which is always a bad object (the absence of the object automatically makes it bad), and sadistic reinforcement of the superego, which relentlessly judges and devalues the ego assimilated to its lost object, bring about the melancholic condition.

For Klein, the ego and the object are perceived from birth and there is no theorization of a phase of primary narcissism. Nevertheless, what comes nearest to the notion of narcissism is her notion of projective identification, which allows simultaneously for object relations and a confusion of boundaries in the subject-object differentiation.

Klein enriched Freud's concept of mourning with the idea that this process provides the mourner with some sort of psychological compensation for his or her loss: an image of the loved one is summoned from memory and installed among the images that constitute the inner world. For Klein, mourning is fundamental for keeping our psychological integrity even as we separate from others and lose them. Loss is so profoundly inscribed in our psyches that it is always already there, even prior to perception of the object. There is certainly a phylogenetic, hereditary aspect to loss that in post-Kleinian thought can be linked to what Bion has identified as a "preconception of the absence of the breast" (1962b). This archaic inscription of loss is already an inscription of the death drive, a precocious somatic absorption of this originally physic energy that comes to be figured as the death drive. The actual loss of the object reactivates its trace.

2

Kleinian Metapsychology

Kleinian Metapsychology: The Psychoanalysis of Children

Melanie Klein's *The psycho-analysis of children* ([1932] 1975e) opens with a melancholic dedication pervaded with psychoanalytic undertones: "To the Memory of Karl Abraham. In Gratitude and Admiration." This can be naively read as Klein's personal tribute of fidelity and praise for the remarkable work of her former mentor and analyst. It also acknowledges a labor of love and an intellectual debt. More shrewdly, it anticipates and uncovers what her position will be in the contested field of Freud's new science. It is a primal scene of origins in which the analyst-daughter, haunted by the presence of the analyst-father, tells the story of her analytic family, one with no mother. Klein attempts to bring Abraham back to life in a restitutive moment. It seems as if the evolution of Klein's future thought were beautifully condensed in the elegiac epigram "In gratitude." The absence of a nurturing mother figure in her intellectual growth will later be overcompensated for with her theorization of an almost omnipotent mother, which will mark a turning point in the history of psychoanalysis. I want to suggest that evoking the name of Karl Abraham on the opening page of her major work acts as a screen memory that all too vividly both covers and uncovers the troubled conflict behind Klein's own life: the obstacles to her maturity and independence under the excessive control of an intrusive mother, the hindrances that a meaningless marriage and early motherhood posed for her, the impossibility of finding the phantasy of a good and solid transference-love. Klein's analysis came to an abrupt end with the death of Abraham. At a time when her personal life was falling to pieces, she had to mourn for her lost teacher and analyst.[1] One of my aims in this book is to show when in Klein's new approach to the old questions of psychoanalysis mourning becomes melancholia, the state in which bereavement cannot be resolved.

Much of the value of reading Klein's work today lies in the opening up of new ways of rethinking issues such as the role of aggressivity in our lives, the violence implicit in systems of representation, and the complex interplay between private and/or collective phantasies and social reality. Kleinian theory offers new ways of thinking about the political as a confrontational arena in which contending hegemonies struggle for power.

The theoretical conclusions Klein puts forward are almost always based on actual analyses of small children. In the appendix to her major work, The psycho-analysis of children ([1932] 1975e), she specifies the aims of child analysis that laid the foundations for all subsequent developments in the field within the Kleinian group. The benefits of child analysis are manifold. Her emphasis lies in the lessening of early anxiety situations, the resolution of the sadistic fixations of the child, and mitigation of the severity of the superego. The attainment of the standards proper to each age depends on "an adjustment between the super-ego and the id, and the consequent establishment of an adequately strong ego" (Appendix, 279).

The pressure of the superego must be relieved and its requirements reconciled with those of reality. In the regular course of events from pregenital stages to the genital stage, every advance made in the reduction of the severity of the superego means that the libidinal impulses have gained power in relation to the destructive ones and that the libido has fully attained the genital stage.

For Klein, the infant's first relationship is determined by the death drive, although it appears to go hand in hand with the instinct for self-preservation. It is therefore evident that one of the major aims of analysis should be to enable the patient to cope with the toll the death drive struggles to extract.[2] Psychoanalysis shows that factors producing psychoneuroses in the adult already existed in a latent form in his or her childhood and, "as a result of certain events, it entered upon an acute stage which made it an illness from a practical point of view" (Appendix, 280–81). For Klein, the basis of all psychoneurotic affections are the child's early anxiety situations. Since psychoanalysis profoundly affects the psychosexual development of the child, it "can do for children, whether normal or neurotic, all that it can do for adults and much more" (282). It can prove effective within a remarkable range of conditions such as psychoses and psychotic traits, malformations of character, asocial behavior, grave obsessional neuroses, and inhibitions of development. Without hesitation, Klein posits the possibility of therapeutic success while the individual is still young.

Nonetheless, her concern with the social function of psychoanalysis is clearly stated in her last paragraph: "If every child who shows disturbances that are at all severe were to be analysed in good time, a great number of those people who later end up in prisons or mental hospitals, or who go completely to pieces, would be saved from such a fate and be able to develop a normal life. If child analysis can accomplish a work of this kind— and there are many indications that it can—it would be the means not only of helping the individual but of doing incalculable service to society as a whole" (*Appendix*, 282). This will lead her to devote attention to asocial behavior and related problems, as she did in "Criminal tendencies in normal children" ([1927] 1975a) and other essays. In chapter 8 of *PCh*, "Early stages of the Oedipus conflict and of super-ego formation" ([1932] 1975b), Klein stated that very strong early anxiety situations and terror of the superego compels individuals to destroy their objects and forms the basis for the development of a criminal type of behavior (*EOC&S*, 143).[3]

A Precocious Superego

The idea of an infant of from six to twelve months trying to destroy its mother by every method at the disposal of its sadistic trends—with its teeth, nails and excreta and with the whole of its body, transformed in phantasy into all kinds of dangerous weapons— presents a horrifying, not to say an unbelievable, picture to our minds. And it is difficult, as I know from my own experience, to bring oneself to recognize that such an abhorrent idea answers to the truth. But the abundance, force and multiplicity of the cruel phantasies which accompany these cravings are displayed before our eyes in early analyses so clearly and forcibly that they leave no room for doubt.—Melanie Klein

In "Early stages of the Oedipus conflict and of super-ego formation," Klein begins to delineate her main differences (and later disagreements) with Freud and his disciples. She fully develops her ideas on the early superego and the Oedipus complex, the effect of early anxiety situations in the development of the ego, and the workings of the mechanisms of introjection and projection.[4] Her prompt adherence to Freud's notion of the death drive would result in a new and very ambitious form of elaboration of this controversial psychoanalytic concept.

Klein sets out to give an account of the origin and structure of the superego. Deeply influenced by Abraham, she places her emphasis on the early oral stage of development. The oral frustrations that children undergo release the oedipal impulses in them. The superego begins to form at the same time. These impulses extend from the middle of the first year to the third year of the child's life. In agreement with Abraham, Klein writes that the child's inability to obtain sufficient pleasure during its sucking period depends on the circumstances under which it is fed and that "Lack of satisfaction at the oral-sucking stage increases its need for gratification at the oral-biting stage" (EOC&S, 123). Inability to obtain oral gratification from sucking is the consequence of "internal frustration," which derives from an abnormally increased oral sadism. The interplay of life drives and death drives is present from these early stages. The death drive appears very early, and it is manifest in this emergent oral sadism "as a sign that its destructive instinctual components tip the balance" (124). Nevertheless, oral sadism is a necessary condition for the normal development of the child.

Freud's theorization of anxiety in *Inhibitions, symptoms, and anxiety* ([1925, 1926] 1953) is central to Klein's argument. For Freud, the emergence of anxiety is linked to a "danger-situation in which, as at birth . . . the ego finds itself helpless in the face of growing instinctual demands, i.e. that situation which is the first and original condition for the appearance of anxiety" (78). For Klein, the clearest instance of the conversion of the unsatisfied libido into anxiety is the reaction of the suckling to tensions caused by its physical needs (EOC&S, 125–26). These tensions strengthen the sadistic instincts of the infant. Sadism and destruction are indissolubly linked from the beginning. The destructive instinct is directed against the organism itself and must therefore be regarded by the ego as a danger. This danger is experienced by the individual as anxiety. Klein concludes: "Therefore anxiety would originate from aggression" (126).

For Freud, the narcissistic libido of the organism deflects the death drive outward in order to prevent it from destroying the organism itself. This process is at the bottom of the individual's relations with objects and underlies the mechanism of projection. The remaining part of the death drive that stays within the organism and is libidinally bound there is the origin of erotogenic masochism. For Klein, the ego has yet another means of mastering destructive impulses, through the splitting of the id. This is the first step in the formation of instinctual inhibitions and the superego.[5] In her view, a division of this sort is made possible by the fact that as soon as the process of incorporation has begun the incorporated object becomes the vehicle of defense against the destructive impulses within the organism. In a footnote, Klein advances her main thesis in this essay, namely, that the incorporated object at once assumes the functions of the superego (EOC&S, 127).

At these early stages, the child focuses his or her fears on external objects as potential sources of danger, against which his or her sadistic feelings are directed. These fears seem to have their basis in external reality, in the child's growing knowledge—a knowledge based on the development of the ego and its concomitant power of reality testing—of the mother as someone who either gives or withholds gratification. The external object is perceived as all powerful in relation to the satisfaction of the child's needs. The child's immature ego then seeks to protect itself by destroying his or her objects.

For Klein, the deflection of the death drive outward influences the child's relationship with his or her objects and leads to the full expansion of sadism. The phase of maximum oral sadism reaches its climax during and after weaning. Oral-sadistic phantasies of a quite definite character predominate, linking the oral-sucking and oral-biting stages. The child desires to suck and scoop out the contents of the mother's breast and by extension the interior of her body. Progressively, libidinal frustration increases sadism, and under the pressure of frustration the child develops an envy of his or her parents imagined in sexual intercourse. This *oral envy* is what makes children want to push their way back into their mother's body and is the motive force that arouses the epistemophilic instinct allied with that desire. Destructive impulses are soon directed toward the father, whose penis the child imagines inside the mother's body, incorporated after copulation. The child's fear of the father's penis is effected by metonymic displacement of pars pro toto, in Klein's own words, since it represents the father in person. Moreover, at this stage the penis inside the mother stands for a combination of the father and mother in one person and is regarded as being particularly terrifying and threatening.[6]

In Klein's account of these early stages of the Oedipus conflict, it is clear that heterosexual and homosexual tendencies arise side by side. The predominance of one position over another will be determined by a great number of internal and external elements: "genital desires for the parent of the opposite sex and jealousy and hatred of the parent of the same sex [begin to be felt] and to experience a conflict between its love and its hatred of the latter" (EOC&S, 133).[7]

Klein's views are radically different from Freud's at this point. According to Klein, genital impulses set in at the same time as the pregenital ones and influence and modify them. Moreover, she goes on to advance subversive ideas on the central role that masturbatory phantasies play in the oedipal situation and later in the sexual life or every individual. The sense of guilt the child experiences on account of its libidinal impulses is really a reaction to the destructive impulses that are knit up with them.

One of Freud's first essays on screen memories ([1899] 1953) is a pseudonymous paper dealing with memories that have to do with masturbation. Masturbation is an issue both crucial to and disruptive of psychoanalytical theory.[8] The nonnecessity or impossibility of having sexual relations with an other, is supplanted by an autoerotic search for satisfaction. Psychoanalysis, in its attempt to socialize every sexual impulse experienced by the subject, turns away from the potentially disruptive solipsism of masturbation. This is clearly manifested in Freud's "A child is being beaten" ([1919] 1953) and Anna Freud's "Beating fantasies and daydreams" ([1922] 1974) and "About losing and being lost" ([1953] 1978). Furthermore, we should remember that these are all autoanalytic texts. Throughout these essays, the repetition of a primordial loss is staged, which will inexorably lead us to rethink the compulsion to repeat as theorized by Freud in *Beyond the pleasure principle* ([1920a] 1953). And it raises many questions. What is at stake in autoanalytic and heteroanalytic writing in psychoanalysis? What does this tell us about institutional protocols? What do all these texts suggest when they attempt to turn an illegitimate pleasure into a legitimate one? And maybe, in a more covert manner, how do we turn masturbation into professional activity?[9]

In "Instincts and their vicissitudes" ([1915] 1953), Freud stated that the relationship between hate and objects is older than that of love. For him, hate is derived from the primal repudiation by the narcissistic ego of the external world. The ego strives to destroy all objects that are a source of painful feelings. Klein posits the existence of an early superego, contrary to the orthodox view that the formation of the superego begins in the phallic phase. In her view, the objects that have been introjected in the oral-sadistic phase—the first object cathexes and identifications—form the beginnings of the early superego and "the nucleus of the super-ego is to be found in the partial incorporation that takes place during the cannibalistic phase of development; and the child's early imagos take the imprint of those pregenital impulses" (EOC&S, 136–37).

For Klein, Freud's ideas mainly follow two lines of thought. According to one, the severity of the superego is derived from the severity of the real father, whose prohibitions and commands it repeats. According to the other, its severity is an outcome of the destructive impulses of the subject. This second line has been abandoned in favor of the idea that the superego is derived from parental authority, making this theory the basis of all further inquiry into the subject. Nevertheless, Klein states that Freud confirmed her view in *Civilization and its discontents* ([1929, 1930] 1953), by stressing the importance of the impulses of the individual as a factor in the origin of the superego and the fact that the superego is not identical with real objects.[10] Klein suggests calling the early identifications made by the child the *early stages of superego formation*. They differ in quality and mode of operation from later identifications. The superego as derived from the introjection of objects in the oral-sadistic phase is also the agency from which instinctual inhibitions proceed. Klein's superego is a melancholic agency, built upon identifications with lost objects—on the basis of the lost mother and father.[11] The early superego is also especially severe, and in no period of life is the opposition between ego and superego so strong as in early childhood.

Anxiety and sadism go hand in hand, so that the pressure of anxiety at this early stage will correspond in degree to the amount of sadism originally present. Later, in the anal-sadistic stage, the child ejects his object, which he perceives as hostile to him and which he equates with excrement. For Klein, this is a means of defense employed by the ego against the superego; it expels internalized objects and projects them into the outer world. The mechanisms of projection and expulsion are therefore closely bound up with the process of superego formation.

Klein agrees with Abraham's idea that "the tendency to spare the object and to preserve it has grown out of the more primitive destructive tendency by a process of repression" (quoted in EOC&S, 141). Therefore, when facing the possibility of the destruction of the object—initially a love object and by displacement a substitute for the mother—the subject, out of this primitive process of repression, opts for its preservation by introjecting it inside its body. This operation is an accurate description of the first move of the mechanism of melancholia.

The introduction of an early superego into the picture sheds new light on the child's development of object relations. The fact that by virtue of his or her own sadistic impulses the child creates a distorted picture of his or her objects and fears their introjection sets in motion the mechanisms of ejection and projection. The reciprocal action between introjection and projection is crucial in the formation of the superego, the development of object relations to persons, and subsequent adaptation to reality.

Crucial for my purpose is Klein's account of disturbances in the mechanism of projection that accompany a negation of intrapsychic reality, as happens in schizophrenia. Those affected deny, and to a certain extent eliminate, not only the source of their anxiety but its affects as well. As early as 1926, Laforgue suggested the term *scotomization* for this defensive mechanism. I want to suggest that in melancholia an analogous mechanism is in play.[12] Intrapsychic reality is not denied; rather, the opposite applies. There is a denial of external reality and a staging and reorganization of the individual's relations to the lost object of love inside the psyche, together with a parallel elimination of affect. Whereas introjection is in full force, the mechanism of projection remains blocked. The source of anxiety—the dangers and risks with which the external world threatens the object—is eliminated through introjection, which is followed by an eradication of affect. Therefore, we can claim that melancholia and psychotic states have in common a scotomization of affect.

In "The importance of symbol-formation in the development of the ego" ([1930] 1975), Klein is in agreement with Abraham's view that in the paranoiac the libido regresses to the earlier anal stage. According to Klein, the phase of maximal sadism is introduced by oral-sadistic impulses and comes to an end with the decline of the earlier anal stage. In her detailed description of this stage in EOC&S, she adds something new. In the period in which the child attacks by means of poisonous excreta, his or her mechanisms of projection are pushed to their furthest limits. This anxiety is diffused and distributed over many objects in the outer world, so that the child now expects to be attacked by a number of persecutors. Klein describes the paranoiac's characteristic features as follows: "The quality of secrecy and cunning which it attributes to those attacks leads it to observe the world about it with a watchful and suspicious eye and increases its relations to reality, though in a one-sided way; while its fear of the introjected object is a constant incentive to keep the mechanisms of projection in operation" (EOC&S, 146). The various techniques of sadism are employed in conjunction and to their fullest capacity, and the urethral-sadistic tendencies, as well as the oral-sadistic ones, are of fundamental importance. Klein places the fixation point for paranoia during the phase of maximal sadism. The child's attacks upon the mother's body and the phantasized incorporated penis are carried out by means of poisonous and dangerous excreta, and delusions of persecution spring from the anxiety situations attached to those attacks.

According to Klein, the child's fear of introjected objects urges him or her to displace that fear into the external world. By equating internal objects, organs, feces, and the contents of the whole body with his or her external objects and distributing fear over a great number of objects, the child employs a *phobic anxiety mechanism*. This is a further advance in the establishment of a relationship with objects and adaptation to reality. As Ferenczi observed, the child seeks to rediscover his or her organs and their functions in every outside thing by means of identification, which is the precursor of symbolization.[13]

The child's libidinal relations with his or her objects and the influence exerted by reality counteract the fear of internal and external enemies. Klein concludes by stating that superego formation, object relations, and adaptation to reality are thus "the result of an interaction between the projection of the individual's sadistic impulses and the introjection of his objects" (EOC&S, 148). The child's future development evolves out of cycles of introjection and projection whose psychic traces can be traced back to these early stages. The predominance of introjection and the blockage of projection are at work in the mechanism of melancholia. Analytical work on melancholia attempts to clear the way for projection and consequently to dislodge the afflicting object from the ego. Only then can a new work of mourning be completed.

In "The relations between obsessional neurosis and the early stages of the super-ego" ([1932] 1975f), Klein sets out to examine in what way the child's libido and his or her relationship with real objects bring about a modification of early anxiety situations. This is a crucial essay in which Klein investigates the proximity between neuroses and psychoses; introduces her ideas on phobias and phobic mechanisms; and theorizes on the compulsive character of the early superego, its role in obsessional neurosis, and the origins of guilt feelings. Melancholia, in its multiple manifestations, is viewed here as a set of disorders that share neurotic and psychotic traits.

In the early stage of development that Klein calls the phase of maximal sadism, the interaction between the life and death drives is a fundamental factor in the dynamic processes of the mind. Libido and destructive tendencies are indissolubly bound and "the vicious circle dominated by the death-instinct, in which aggression gives rise to anxiety and anxiety reinforces aggression can be broken by the libidinal forces when these have gained in strength" (ON&ES, 150). In these early stages, the need for the life instinct to overpower the death drive stimulates the growth of the sexual life of the individual. The child then maintains two kinds of relations, those with his or her real objects and those based on attachments to unreal imagos as both excessively good and excessively bad figures.

By the end of the oral-sadistic stage, when sadistic tendencies diminish, the threats made by the superego are reduced as well. The ego then tries to defend itself, first by scotomizing the superego and then by ejecting it. As the later anal stage sets in, the ego recognizes the necessity of obeying the commands of the superego, and its principal method to overcome anxiety is to try to satisfy both external and internalized objects. The ambivalence of the child toward his or her objects at this point is a very important mechanism for overcoming fear of the superego by directing it outward and distributing it over a number of objects. At the genital stage, the superego changes its mode of behavior—its threats become admonitions and reproaches—and the ego finds support through positive relationships with the child's objects by employing restitutive mechanisms with them.

It is at this stage that sublimation can set in. Restitutive tendencies are a fundamental motive force in all sublimations. According to Klein, "A precondition for the development of restitutive tendencies and of sublimations is that the pressure exerted by the super-ego should be mitigated and felt by the ego as a sense of guilt" (ON&ES, 154).[14] As the genital impulses gain in strength and more positive object relations develop, there is less friction, less violence, and therefore more satisfactory relations between ego and id and superego and ego.

Klein moves on to examine the fixation points for psychoses and neuroses. According to her, the boundary between the earlier and later anal stages forms the line of demarcation between psychosis and neurosis.

When anxiety situations reach a certain intensity, every child will at some time or other produce psychotic symptoms. For Klein, the abrupt changes in mood characteristic of melancholic disorders are also regularly found in children: "analytic observation has taught me that their sadness and depression, though not so acute as the melancholic depression of the adult, have the same causes and can be accompanied by thoughts of suicide" (ON&ES, 156). Melancholia is thus on the boundary between neuroses and psychoses.

Phobias: A Devouring Superego?

In the same essay, Klein puts forward her ideas on phobias and her differences with Freud on the subject. She suggests an answer to the dilemma Freud posed in *Inhibitions, symptoms, and anxiety* ([1925, 1926] 1953), namely, that the earliest phobias of children had provided no explanation whatsoever. For Freud, a phobia was "a matter of substituting one external danger for another" (77), the maximum fear being the threat of castration. For Klein, early phobias contain anxiety arising from the early stages of the formation of the superego and what lies at the root of a phobia is an internal danger. After reviewing Freud's approach to phobias in the cases of Little Hans and the Wolf Man, Klein states that animal phobias are already "a far-reaching modification of the fear of the super-ego" (ON&ES, 157). Phobias are not a mere distortion of the idea of being castrated by the father; underlying them there is an earlier fear of being devoured by the superego, so that a phobia would actually be a modification of early anxiety situations. Little Hans's neurosis showed no obsessional traits, whereas the Wolf Man quickly developed a regular obsessional neurosis due to stronger disturbances in his development.[15]

By stressing the importance of powerful anxiety situations that arise in the phase of maximum sadism, we can conclude with Klein that melancholia, paranoia, and female and male homosexuality share in common and in different degrees "a very extensive exclusion of reality and the production of severe obsessional and paranoid traits" (ON&ES, 161).[16] This is why it is of great importance to stress differences in degree among the whole range of melancholic disorders, paranoid states, and homosexualities. Klein's intent is far from pathologizing homosexuality. In fact, she tries to avoid the pitfalls into which most of her contemporaries' analytic theories and practices often fell. The link between male homosexuality and paranoia was first established by Freud in his analyses of Schreber and the Wolf Man. It was developed from a more openly social perspective in *Group psychology and the analysis of the ego*.[17] An original and unusual overly strong sadism that was not successfully modified and led to excessive anxiety at a very early stage of life is at the root of these disorders. From Klein's position, it is clear at this point that there is an exclusion of reality that produces neurotic and/or psychotic symptoms in melancholia, homosexuality, and paranoid states. But what is at stake here is no doubt how and why this mechanism of exclusion of reality operates. What is it that causes the individual to move away from reality to retreat into his or her symptoms? And why is early excessive anxiety so hard to overcome in melancholia, homosexuality, and paranoia? What happens when reality becomes unbearable and unlivable for the individual? I want to suggest that turning away from reality is a defense mechanism intended to protect the individual from powerful aggressions and hostilities that may end up putting his or her life—psychic and beyond—at risk. Thus, in melancholia suicide is a plausible denouement (ON&ES, 156). Acute obsessional neurosis may develop into paranoia—as in the case of the Wolf Man—and homosexuality, when repressed and unable to find expression in the open, may develop into a melancholic syndrome. The more or less extensive exclusion of reality, I am arguing, is in direct proportion to the major or minor degree of the practices of exclusion that reality imposes on the individual.[18]

Klein believes that the process of modification of a phobia is linked to the mechanisms upon which the obsessional neurosis is based. These mechanisms begin to be active in the later anal stage, and obsessional neurosis is "an attempt to cure the psychotic conditions of the earliest phases" (ON&ES, 162). Whereas discrete obsessional traits may emerge very early—in the later anal stage—they are not organized into what we regard as obsessional neurosis until the beginning of the latency period. In *Inhibitions, symptoms, and anxiety*, Freud maintained that obsessional neurosis did not set in until the phallic stage was attained ([1925, 1926] 1953, 53; see also Klein, ON&ES, 163–64).

Klein's views on regression are also crucial for some of the central arguments in this volume. She writes that "we regard as regression the fluctuation between the various libidinal positions—such fluctuation is, in my opinion, a characteristic of the early stages of development as regression in which the already cathected genital position is repeatedly abandoned for a time until it has been properly strengthened and established"

(ON&ES, 163). In other words, Klein maintains that there is no such thing as a linear psychosexual development. Development is rather a flexible process characterized by advancements and regressions. Genitality both attracts and repels and is continually being abandoned for previous positions. The success of genitality—that is, "compulsory heterosexuality"— seems to lie in being "properly strengthened and established." And the institution of the "proper" imposes a violent logic over the unproper/ improper, which sadistically strives to repress and subjugate.

The view that obsessional mechanisms arise very early in childhood— toward the end of the second year—fits into Klein's general theory of early superego formation. The superego is first felt by the ego as anxiety and then as a sense of guilt. This anxiety belonging to early danger situations is closely associated with the beginnings of obsessive traits and gives rise to an obsessive desire for knowledge. The uncertainties that assail obsessives about the inside of their bodies and their internal objects play a part in "stimulating exactness and order and the observance of certain rules and rituals, and the like" (ON&ES, 166).

In Klein's account, the extreme severity of the early superego increases the sadistic fixations of the child, forcing him or her to repeat destructive acts in a compulsive way. The superego, therefore, erects itself as privileged representative of the death drive. The conspicuous compulsive character of obsessional neurosis provides us with a vantage point from which to rethink the relationships between Klein's theories of early superego formation and the death drive.

When the children's destructive tendencies become less violent and more adaptable to the demands of the superego, they begin thinking that the restoration of their persons depends on the restoration of their objects. For Klein, the beginning of the Oedipus conflict is accompanied by masturbatory phantasies dominated by sadistic instincts directed against the parents in copulation. Crucial in Kleinian theory is the idea that the sense of guilt that arises at this stage is attached to the child's destructive instincts and not to its libidinal and incestuous instincts. When an excessive sense of guilt sets in motion obsessive actions as a defense, the child will employ those for the purpose of making restitution in a compulsive way based on a belief in the omnipotence of his or her thoughts. An exaggerated sense of omnipotence results in great obstacles to restitution.

The connection between epistemophilic and sadistic instincts is formed very early during the phase of maximum sadism. The first object of the child's epistemophilic instincts is the interior of the mother's body. The disappointment derived from the frustrated desire to know—on the basis of the mother's initial frustration of the child's oral desires—can be the source of severe disturbances in the development of the epistemophilic instinct. Knowledge at this point becomes a means of mastering anxiety. Finally, as the libidinal impulses grow stronger and the destructive ones weaker, the superego makes itself increasingly felt by the ego as an admonitory influence. Anxiety diminishes, restitutive mechanisms become less obsessive in character, and reactions belonging to the genital stage emerge. The attainment of a more balanced relationship between introjection and projection and between superego formation and object relations means that "the positive element has attained predominance" (ON&ES, 175).

Early Anxiety Situations and Ego Development

In "The significance of early anxiety-situations in the development of the ego" ([1932] 1975g), Klein stresses the importance of the pressure exerted by early anxiety situations in the development of the ego. She refers to Freud's analysis of the Fort-Da game in *Beyond the pleasure principle* and remarks that in play the child not only overcomes painful reality but also manages to master his or her fears and internal dangers by projecting them into the outer world. With the deflection of destructive instincts outward, external objects gradually become more important. Reality testing is crucial at this point so that the child can learn whether his or her counterattacks on external dangers have been successful. This also constitutes a strong incentive for the development of the epistemophilic instinct.

Klein equates the interaction between introjection and projection with the interaction between superego formation and object relations. As a consequence of these processes, the child finds a refutation of his or her fears in the outer world and allays anxiety by introjecting his or her real good objects. As the relationship with reality advances, the child uses his or her relations to objects and various activities and sublimations as points of support against fear of the superego and destructive impulses.

According to Klein, there is a deliberate effort on the part of the child to conflate his or her objects and the superego. The child "is continually endeavouring to make them interchangeable, partly so as to lessen its fear of its super-ego, partly so as to be better able to comply with the requirements of its real objects, which did not coincide with the phantastic commands of its introjected objects" (EASDE, 180). This failed metaphoric operation can thus be considered a strategy designed to liberate the ego from the contradictory burden of the demands made by its superego and its real objects. The superego, in Klein, is often mimetically dressed in the clothing of both internal and external objects. In 1932, when Klein was writing this essay, it is quite clear that they are considered to be separate entities. The early superego is allied with the presence of the death drive in the psyche from the very beginning of life. Internal objects can be theorized after the mechanisms of introjection and projection are operative. The complex dynamics that inform the interactions between superego and internal and external objects and among superego, ego, and id, and their consequences, are elaborated in depth for both sexes (this will be discussed later in this volume).[19] The ego of the child is thus "constantly wavering between its introjected objects and its real ones—between its world of phantasy and its world of reality" (EASDE, 180).

At the onset of the latency period, when the ego is strengthened, it joins with the superego in setting up a common standard that includes above all the subjection of the id and its adaptation to the demands of real objects and the external world. The onset of the latency period can thus be read as the point of capitulation of the ego—and domestication of the id—in its alliance with the superego to the demands of the latter and those of reality. External reality gains progressively more weight to the detriment of phantasy and internal reality.

The character of receptivity or exclusion of the external environment is decisive for the future adaptation or maladjustment of the individual and determines standards of health and illness. Melancholia arises as an acute response to the dangers and lethal traps with which external reality threatens our objects of love, admiration, and idealization. In a desperate attempt to safeguard the object at risk, its incorporation and preservation inside the psyche seems to be the most effective maneuver, but it has a very high cost. Along with the loss, the effacement of the object, a retreat of the subject from reality is also present in acute melancholic states—manic depression and involutional melancholia.[20] Melancholia is a measure of the intolerance and rejection that external reality imposes upon the individual. A weakened ego, assailed by the pressures of the id and unable to comply with the immoderate demands of the superego and reality, yields to an infinite distress. The afflictions and ailments of the melancholic can be approached from a Kleinian perspective by stressing the *décalage* that exists from very early on between superego formation and object relations. The melancholic response is at the core of Kleinian theory and at the core of the differences between Klein and Freud. In Freud's "Mourning and melancholia," the melancholic's movement of turning back upon his or her ego in a solipsistic moment of narcissistic dimensions translates into a Kleinian scenario in which the object is not simply absorbed, incorporated, and conflated with the ego. Object relations—and the early superego—are at play from the beginning and continue as long as psychic life exists. Kleinian melancholia is thus a specific mode of object relations. It is one in which an excessive introjection and a defective—or rather, blocked—projection, together with a new internal object that, after the attacks of external forces, needs our restitution, create a distortion in the regular, specific dynamics of object relations.

An excess of sadistic tendencies turns into masochism. From Klein, we know that women, feminine masochists, and female and male homosexuals are more prone to melancholia. It is not difficult to infer from this that the patterns of demand of these subjects from reality have something in common in the quality of their severity.

In the latency period, the child's ego-ideal is "the well-behaved 'good' child that satisfies its parents and teachers" (EASDE, 180). Ego and superego are now pursuing the common aim of achieving an adaptation to their environment and adopting ego-ideals that belong to that environment. At this stage, mastery of anxiety is achieved when the ego "obtains the sanction of those in authority over it" (185). Klein states: "In the latency period the normal girl will often master her anxiety in pre-eminently masculine ways, and the boy can still be described as normal even though he chooses more passive and feminine modes of behaviour for the same purpose" (186). The latency period therefore allows for great flexibility between masculine and feminine positions.

The major changes that occur in puberty allow the boy to abandon his fear of being castrated by his father and to see him as a good figure. The girl, in general more dependent than the boy on the approval of her objects, seeks to please parents and teachers with her "mental achievements" (EASDE, 190). Klein stresses that the activities, interests, and sublimations of the individual also serve to master anxiety and the sense of guilt, their motive force being not only to gratify aggressive impulses but to make restitution to the child's objects and to restore his or her own body and genitals.

Klein's contribution in this essay shows how the ego of the individual attempts to master its infantile anxiety situations. Success in the process is of fundamental importance for the development of the ego and is a decisive factor in securing mental health. Reassurance against anxiety is constantly needed. According to Klein, it "constantly flows from many sources . . . derive[d] from his activities and interests and from his social relations and erotic satisfactions—that enables him to leave his original anxiety-situations far behind and to distribute and weaken the full force of their impact upon him" (EASDE, 192). The "normal" individual usually achieves a high degree of removal from anxiety situations, but this does not amount to a relinquishment of them; under certain circumstances, their effects may reappear.[21]

3

Femininities: Melancholia, Masquerade, and the Paternal Superego

Freud wrote "The psychogenesis of a case of homosexuality in a woman" in 1920 ([1920b] 1953). In this peculiar case study of a patient with no apparent symptoms, Freud found out that the young female protagonist's adoration of "a society lady" concealed an identification with the woman's father.[1] In his view, this identification was based on disappointment at not having received a child from her father. As a result, "she changed into a man and took the mother in place of her father as the object of her love" (158). Freud inscribes his analysand's identifications in an oedipal scenario, with oedipal objects introjected regressively. He remarks that the identification with her father was "a kind of regression to narcissism" similar to melancholia (in its cannibalistic oral incorporation of the object). His patient resisted the analysis, and when Freud became aware that in countertransference he was becoming the butt of the young woman's hostility toward her father he suggested discontinuing treatment and advised her to consult a woman analyst.

Jean-Michel Quinodoz (1989) has traced the early history of psychoanalytic literature on female homosexuality. In 1920, Abraham stressed the importance of anality in the positive structure of femininity ([1920] 1922). He showed that the failure of the wish to have a child by the father is a substitute for the penis and that the failure of a daughter's identification with her mother may lead to homosexuality in women ([1920] 1922, 6). He believed that female homosexuality could be manifested in two forms: first, excessive penis envy, revealed in symbolic form (cathexis of a body part, "the look"); and, second, a wish to exact excessive revenge on men, with the phantasy of castrating them by first attracting and then despising them ([1920] 1922, 16).[2] Abraham's paper was very influential and stimulated further research on the specificities of female development. The issue was taken up and discussed by many analysts in ardent debates about female sexuality in the 1920s and early 1930s.

Ernest Jones's "The early development of female sexuality" (1927) is based on the analysis of five female homosexual patients. In his view, pregenital factors and oral aggressiveness are of the utmost importance in the genesis of female homosexuality. According to the level of regression, he differentiates between two forms. In the first, the woman goes on having relationships with men but competes aggressively with them, she still harbors the wish to be acknowledged as a man. In the second, the homosexual woman has withdrawn interest from men altogether. Jones believes that identification with the father is common to all forms of female homosexuality (1927, 468). He posits that little girls as well as little boys share a precocious awareness of the specific female organs and their functions, thus holding an opposite view from Freud's.

Jones's paper broadened the debate about sexual difference, which until then had only focused on the issue of the presence or absence of a penis. What characterizes a woman is therefore the presence of the female sexual organs, and although these are less conspicuous than those of their male counterparts they are by no means less well perceived in reality or phantasy. As is well known, Jones introduced here the term *aphanisis* to designate the fear of "total and permanent extinction of the capacity for sexual enjoyment" (1927, 461) in children of both sexes, as distinct from castration, which should be reserved for the male fear of losing the penis.[3] Jones suggests that all women experience the fear of losing their female organs and functions rather than the fear of losing a penis, which they do not possess.

In 1929, R. de Saussure's "Les fixations homosexuelles chez les femmes névrosés" was a pioneer study in its emphasis on the importance of early object relations and projection. In fact, he was the first analyst to mention the importance of the mechanism of projection in female homosexuality: "These women project outside themselves sometimes their masculinity and sometimes their femininity; they become attached to types of women opposite to themselves. As it happens, they are much more concerned to identify with their partners than to love them as object. The object for them is a mirror, which they invest with male or female narcissism depending on the type of woman in front of them" (70). He follows Abraham's insights on the partial nature of objects in phantasies and foregrounds the part played by bad weaning experiences in the origin of homosexual fixations.

Melanie Klein placed the regression and fixation points of female homosexuality at an earlier stage than Freud. In "The effects of early anxiety-situations on the sexual development of the girl" ([1932] 1975d), she provided a detailed account of the development of heterosexual and homosexual tendencies in relation to different anxieties. In this essay, Klein acknowledges that psychoanalysis "has thrown much less light on the psychology of women than on that of men" (194). Freud identified fear of castration as the underlying motive force in the formation of neurosis in men. In the case of women, castration was considered "an accomplished fact" ([1925, 1926] 1953, 63). For Klein, it is imperative to find out which kind of anxiety is in the aetiology of psychoneuroses in women.

Whether the ego is threatened by an excess of stimulation that it cannot master, according to Freud's view, or threatened with annihilation as a direct consequence of the death drive, as Klein holds—this conception being not far removed from Freud's—the ego defends itself by means of the production of anxiety and the building of defenses, with the aim of protection from both external and internal dangers.

In "Early stages of the Oedipus conflict" ([1928] 1975), Klein had advanced the view that the girl's deepest fear was that of having the inside of her body robbed and destroyed. As a result of the oral frustration she experiences with her mother, the female child turns away from her and takes her father's penis as her object of gratification. At that time, all that is desirable, including the father's penis, is contained inside the mother's body. The girl, increasingly frustrated, produces sadistic phantasies of attacking and destroying the mother's interior. Here lies the nucleus of children's early sexual theories, which derive from their phantasies of envy and hatred at being frustrated by both parents. The projection of children's sadistic desires onto their parents gives rise to a strong sense of guilt in their minds.

Klein refers to Jones's concept of aphanisis.[4] In her view, aphanisis implies the destruction of the girl's genital organs. The girl's sadistic impulses, addressed originally toward her mother, are now turned back upon herself. She fears having her genital organs destroyed or damaged in the course of the mother's attacks upon her body. In Klein's view, "the girl's Oedipus tendencies are ushered in by her oral desires for her father's penis. These desires are already accompanied by genital impulses" (EASG, 195).

With regard to the onset of the Oedipus complex, Klein agrees with Freud on two points: that the girl wants to have a penis and that she hates her mother for not giving her one. But altogether Klein puts forward some very different ideas. For her, the little girl does not want a penis of her own as an attribute of masculinity but in order to incorporate the father's penis as an object of oral gratification. This desire is not an outcome of her castration complex. In Klein's words, it is "the most fundamental expression of her Oedipus trends, and . . . consequently the female child is brought under the sway of her Oedipus impulses not indirectly, through her masculine tendencies and her penis-envy, but directly, as a result of her dominant feminine instinctual components" (EASG, 196). After the frustration suffered at her mother's breast, the little girl phantasizes her father's penis as an organ that "can provide her with a tremendous and never-ending oral gratification" (196). Klein agrees with Helene Deutsch[5] on this unconscious equation of the father's penis with the mother's breast and on the fact that the vagina takes on the passive role of the sucking mouth "in the process of displacement from above downwards" (quoted in EASG, 196). The female genitals have "oral, receptive qualities at an early age" (197) and this process of displacement "thus clears the way for the little girl's Oedipus tendencies—though these, it is true, do not unfold their full power until much later—and lays the foundation of her sexual development" (197). It is quite evident that both Deutsch and Klein, women analysts working in the framework of patriarchal psychoanalytic institutions, were confused as to their attribution of the qualities of activity and passivity in some conspicuous cases. If at this stage the equation "the penis works as a substitute for breast" holds true, and breast is the organ that is (passively) sucked, is it not the lips (or by extension the mouth) in this case that play the active role? Is it not the vagina, as an essentially oral organ in Klein's and Deutsch's views, the organ that would play the active role in sucking?

The shift to the father, with its essential ambivalence, is the beginning of the feminine phase in girls. The father's penis becomes the object of the girl's oral, urethral, anal, and genital impulses. Furthermore, her desires are intensified, since in her unconscious sexual theory her mother has incorporated her father's penis, and she consequently envies her. In view of all this, the girl has two alternatives: to retain a predominantly feminine position, which leads her "to assume a humble and submissive attitude towards the male sex" (EASG, 197); or to take up a masculine position with intense feelings of hatred as a consequence of having been denied access to her father's penis. The latter can give rise to all the signs and symptoms of penis envy in her.

The little girl may also fear the extremely dangerous "bad penis"—a composite of sadistic impulses drawn from her own phantasies—even when "her deepest and more powerful anxiety" is "her fear of her mother," and through displacement she passes it on to her father's penis (EASG, 198). This has severe consequences for her development, which may be manifested in a distorted attitude toward the male sex, a defective relationship to her objects, and the inability to completely overcome the stage of partial love.[6]

Part Objects and Superego Formation

At this stage of partial incorporation, the omnipotence of the girl's oral desire makes her believe that she has in fact incorporated the father's penis, which stands in for his whole person. From here, Klein moves on to talk of superego formation. At the level of representation, she states that "the child's earliest father-imagos—the nucleus of the paternal superego—are represented by his penis" (EASG, 198). The terrifying and cruel character of the superego in children of both sexes is due to the fact that they begin introjecting their objects at a period of development when sadism is at its maximum. However, the girl's impulse to introject the father's penis is stronger than that of the boy—on the basis, she claims, of her receptive genital disposition—so that "under normal circumstances the girl's Oedipus trends are to a far greater extent under the dominance of oral impulses than are those of the boy" (199). So for Klein in the psychosexual development of children it is crucial whether their dominant phantasies are those of a "good" or a "bad" penis. The girl has a more complicated path in her development. Klein summarizes the obstacles she encounters as follows: "the girl, being more subordinated to her introjected father is more at the mercy of his powers for good or evil than the boy is normally in relation to his super-ego. And her anxiety and sense of guilt in regard to her mother serve to complicate still further her divided feelings about her father's penis" (199). Strangely enough, in a footnote

Klein introduces the idea that "the girl's superego is . . . more potent than the boy's" (199), something she would take up later in the essay. Her choice of the adjective *potent* to qualify the girl's superego cannot possibly pass unnoticed. In the context of "penile reference," this *lapsus calami* is not gratuitous.[7] At the very least, it raises several questions that point to a number of blind spots in the text. For example, what is at stake in the Kleinian project when she (deliberately?) confuses activity with passivity, equates superego representation with the penis, and attributes more potency to the girl's superego rather than to the boy's? Raising the issue of the little girl's phantasies of fellatio in agreement with Helene Deutsch's findings—"in one phase of her development her unconscious equates her father's penis with her mother's breast as an organ for giving suck" (196)— and acknowledging that her Oedipus tendencies are "to a far greater extent under the dominance of oral incorporative impulses than are those of the boy" (199), Klein sets the premises for an explanation of women's melancholia as an outcome of the feminine phase of her Oedipus complex.[8]

In this section, Klein is constantly writing about "oral desires" and the fact that the incorporative oral desire is stronger and more acute in the case of girl than in that of the boy. It seems as if the cravings of desire have an insatiable oral nature. As in the Lacanian version, desire is by definition unsatisfiable.[9] And if the more receptive anatomical characteristics of the girl fuel her incorporative tendencies this will surely make her into a perfect candidate for melancholia. At this stage, all sexual activities for the little girl—Klein lists fellatio, coitus per anum, and normal coitus— constitute appropriate tools for gaining the knowledge to help her ascertain whether the fears she associates in her mind with copulation are well grounded. Sexuality thus becomes a lure for knowledge, and this links it to epistemophilia, the compulsion to repeat, and finally the death drive. This is clear in Klein's account of the girl's fears of sexual intercourse as expressed in her phantasies of her mother's utter destruction in coitus, and her explanation of genital sexuality, following Freud's model of the death drive in *Beyond the pleasure principle* ([1920a] 1953). The sexual act is described as both a situation of extreme danger and "the most powerful method of mastering anxiety" (EASG, 200). Klein writes that "the libidinal gratification that accompanies it [the sexual act] affords her the highest attainable pleasure and thus lessens her anxiety on its own score" (200).

When Klein gives her account of the girl's Oedipus complex and states her disagreement with Freud in chapter 11 of *The psychoanalysis* of children, she cannot forego her patriarchal background and give instead the feminist or feminized version of it. Right in the middle of the section "Early stages of the Oedipus conflict," when she is writing about the little girl's fears associated with copulation, she turns to a general explanation "on the motives which urge the individual to perform the sexual act" (EASG, 200). Her originally female individual is transformed into the more neutrally universal male. So we move abruptly from female to male sexuality with no smooth transition. Disconcertingly enough, there are all too many coincidences in the manifest content of the text, which make us wonder why is it that female sexuality—even at the core of the Kleinian project— is always already narrated by the offstage voice of a male.[10] By way of a telling illustration, let me quote the following: "on the one hand, his anxiety intensifies his libidinal needs, and on the other, the libidinal satisfaction of all erotogenic zones is used in the service of mastering anxiety. Libidinal satisfaction diminishes his aggressiveness and with it his anxiety" (201). The aporias of engaging in a project of rescuing and reinscribing the female voice in psychoanalysis in the 1930s show patently in this fragment.

It is important to remark that when Klein writes about the girl's future "love relationships" (EASG, 202) she is extremely careful to avoid any reference to the sexual identity of her partner. This is most revealing when we note that in the previous paragraph she has been alluding to a supposedly universal male subject. This passage is worth quoting at length: "If the girl, who tests her anxiety-situations by means of the sexual act which corresponds to a test by reality, is supported by feelings of a confident and hopeful kind, she will be led to take as her object a person who represents the 'good' penis. . . . But if the circumstances are unfavourable and her fear of the introjected 'bad' penis predominates, the necessary condition for her ability to love will be that she shall make this reality-test by means of a 'bad' penis—i.e., that her partner in love shall be a sadistic person" (201–2). Klein seems to suggest at this point that she is talking about a "phantasy penis," a phantasmatic object by definition, whose possession could be attributed to either sex. The little girl's pleasurable or unpleasurable perception is of paramount importance in terms of her future sexual and/or love relationships.[11]

From the vantage point of Klein's discussion of sadism and masochism, we gain access to her theory of melancholia, which is central to our purposes. Klein introduces an important observation with regard to the

Freudian notion of secondary or feminine masochism. In *Beyond the pleasure principle* ([1920a] 1953) and "The economic problem of masochism," ([1924] 1953), Freud writes about the interaction between sadistic and masochistic tendencies in psychic life. Klein summarizes Freud's ideas as follows. Sadism first becomes apparent in relation to an object, although it was originally a destructive instinct directed against the organism itself (primal sadism) and was only later diverted from the ego by the narcissistic libido. Erotogenic masochism is that portion of the destructive instinct that has not been turned outward and has remained within the organism and been libidinally bound there. Furthermore, Freud thinks that insofar as any part of the destructive instinct that has been directed outward is once more turned inward and drawn away from its objects it gives rise to secondary or feminine masochism.

Klein's contribution is linked to her theory of internal objects. For her, "when the destructive instinct has reverted in this way it still adheres to its objects; but now they are internalized ones, and in threatening to destroy them, it also threatens to destroy the ego in which they are situated" (*EASG*, 203). Klein believes that there are certain points in common between the self-tormenting behavior of the masochist and the self-reproaches of the melancholiac; both of them, in her view, are directed toward their introjected objects. Feminine masochism is thus directed toward the ego as well as the introjected objects.

The Kleinian account places melancholia side by side with feminine masochism. In melancholia, incorporation and preservation of the object also means its destruction. The feminine masochistic/melancholic machinery seems to be working this way: hostility and aggression coming from the external world result in the individual's sadistic attacks on it. Fear of the destruction of some external object drives the little girl masochistically to incorporate the object, and right away a feeling of ambivalence arises toward her new introjected object. This new encysted object influences her future object relations. In melancholia, as much as in feminine masochism, the individual struggles to destroy its ego, now prey to anxiety after losing its object (in melancholia, it is always already a love object). The more *potent* nature of the feminine superego makes implacable its sanctions and interdictions, and the love object, when deemed unacceptable or abject, must be relinquished. Disappearance or invisibility being the only alternatives, this love object may be incorporated, closeted, and housed in a phantasmatic psychic space. Women and feminine masochists (of either sex) are therefore more prone to melancholia, a malady that may accurately be called the illness of love.

Feminine Sexualities

In the section "The omnipotence of excreta," Klein asserts that, "the girl's sexual life and ego are more strongly and enduringly influenced in their development than are those of the boy by this sense of omnipotence of the function of the bladder and bowels" (EASG, 205). The girl's destructive impulses directed against her mother's body are also more powerful and enduring than the boy's. From this, Klein deduces that women attach their narcissism to their bodies as a whole due in part to connecting their sense of omnipotence to various bodily functions, whereas men focus it more upon their genitals. In the girl's early relations with her mother, the importance of the mother-imago as a helping figure and the strength of their attachment is crucial, since in her phantasies her mother possesses the nourishing breast, the father's penis, and children. Such a mother has the power to gratify all her needs.

In the section "The role of the vagina in infantile sexuality," Klein writes about the girl's unconscious knowledge of her vagina and the paramount role of the clitoris in her early sexual organization. Most of the phantasies associated with clitoral masturbation are of a pregenital kind, but as soon as the girl's desire to incorporate her father's penis grows stronger "they assume a genital and vaginal character . . . and thus, to begin with, take a feminine direction" (EASG, 211).

Her section "The castration complex" is central to my purposes, and I will dwell on it for some time. Klein begins by saying that the identification with the father, which the girl displays in the phallic phase and which bears signs of penis envy and the castration complex, is the outcome of a process comprised of many steps. Central to her argument is the fact that the identification with the father is affected by anxiety arising from the girl's feminine position (or phase) and that the adoption of a masculine position in each of her phases of development is "superimposed" upon a masculine position belonging to an earlier phase. At this point, Klein is giving us a version of the "masculinity complex" in women using an almost photographic rhetoric of the image. Spatial tropes of positions and superimpositions grant the feminine subject a specific quality by virtue of her former adherence to a constructed pattern, that of the very primitive or urposition, which leaves its trace in future and further editions of it. Klein mentions Karen Horney's "On the genesis of the castration complex in women" (1924) as the first essay that connected the castration complex of the woman to her early feminine position as a little girl. For Horney, the same factors that induce the girl to take up a homosexual attitude lead, though in a minor degree, to the production of the castration complex in her.[12]

Klein agrees with Jones's (1927) description of one of the types of female homosexuality whose features would later be characterized in depth by Joan Riviere in her well-known "Womanliness as a masquerade" (1929). This portrait of the masquerade of femininity has an obvious and often misread content of lesbianism. By way of summary, Klein writes that "the presence of very strong phantasies of fellatio in the female, allied to a powerful oral sadism, prepares the way for a belief that she has taken forcible possession of her father's penis and puts her into a special relation of identification with him. In her homosexual attitude, derived in this way, she will show a lack of interest in her own sex and a strong interest in men. Her endeavour will be to gain recognition and respect from men, and she will have strong feelings of rivalry, hatred and resentment against them. As regards character-formation, she will exhibit in general marked oral-sadistic traits; and her identification with her father will be employed to a great degree in the service of her castration wishes" (EASG, 214). For Riviere, the girl's sadistic position, reinforced by her anxiety, forms the basis of her masculinity complex. And precisely the intensity of her sadism and the extent of her capacity to tolerate anxiety will help to determine whether she will take up a heterosexual line or a homosexual one.

In Klein's view, the girl's homosexual position springs from her restitutive tendencies toward her mother after the attempt to destroy her by means of her father's dangerous penis and moved by identification with her sadistic father. Klein writes: "As soon as her reactive trends and her desires to make restitution set in force, she will feel urged to restore her mother by means of a penis with healing powers and thus her homosexual tendencies will become reinforced" (EASG, 216). She quotes Jones and refers to his thesis that female homosexuality may emerge in sublimated ways, especially in those cases in which the oral-sucking fixation is very strong. Klein seems to be mostly in agreement with Jones at this point. Excessive orality acts as an obstacle to genitality. In other words, a melancholic disposition works against the achievement of genital sexuality. Feminine melancholia is here understood as disruptive of the teleology of psychosexual evolution. Both feminine masochism (in its incorporative moves) and creativity may thus be understood as deviations from or sublimations of the death drive. In what Klein calls the "post-phallic phase," the girl makes her choice between retaining the feminine position or abandoning it.

In the section "Restitutive tendencies and sexuality," Klein introduces an important distinction between the consolidation of a homosexual versus a heterosexual position. She states that the consolidation of the girl's heterosexual position "depends upon that position being in conformity with the requirements of her super-ego" (EASG, 218). Whereas the achievement of the homosexual position seems to escape the sanction of the superego, the consolidation of a heterosexual position must meet the superego's requirements.[13] This raises questions as to the possibility of ever achieving a homosexual position since it evades the implacable demands of the superego and situates female homosexuality in a psychic space that is outside the law. The possibility of ever achieving a homosexual or heterosexual position depends on the girl's sadistic tendencies and the means she employs to master her anxiety.

In Klein's own words, "the final outcome of the infantile sexual development of the individual is the result of a long-drawn-out process of fluctuation between various positions and is built up upon a great number of interconnected compromises between his ego and his super-ego and between his ego and his id" (EASG, 220). By the end of the genital stage, together with a progressive decrease of anxiety and guilt, the girl lets her mother resume a feminine and maternal role. She takes on a similar role herself and sublimates her male components. It is thus quite clear that achieving the genital stage is synonymous with achieving heterosexuality. By the period of puberty, physiological changes accompanied by changes at the level of the drives bring about a crisis that makes untenable the feminine as well as the masculine position for the girl.

In her section "Ego-development" and the postscript to this long essay, Klein clearly states her differences with Freud on the issue of the girl's superego formation and sexual evolution. In "Some psychical consequences of the anatomical distinction between the sexes" ([1925b] 1953), Freud elaborates on the differences between the superego formation of girls and boys as associated with anatomical sexual differences. For Klein, anatomical differences—such as the absence of a penis or the receptive function of female genitals—stress the importance of oral impulses and introjective tendencies in the girl, resulting in "the introjection of her super-ego [being] more extensive than in the boy" (EASG, 232–33). In women, the superego is "more strongly operative" (233), and this causes them to be "more dependent upon their objects, more easily influenced by the outer world and more variable in their moral standards—that is, apparently less guided by the requirements of a super-ego" (233). The processes of introjection and projection are also stronger in women, and this is of vital importance for the development of their egos. The loosening of the surveillance exerted by the superego interestingly links women, feminine masochists, and the female homosexual position. In Klein's view, the girl's desire to incorporate her father's penis is the foundation and starting point of her sexual development and the formation of her superego.

Klein agrees with Freud's views in The ego and the id ([1923] 1953) insofar as we may extend our knowledge about the ego with regard to its multiple identifications. The girl finds it difficult to identify herself with her mother on the basis of an anatomical resemblance, owing to the fact that the female genitals are internal and that possessing or not possessing children—in the girl's phantasies, they are inside the mother's body—does not admit reality testing. Nevertheless, the girl manages to develop a very strong ego as a consequence of the much stronger introjection of her Oedipus object than the boy's, and "she leans on the powerful super-ego within partly in order to dominate or to outdo it" (EASG, 236).

What would it have meant for the institution of psychoanalysis at this point if the idea of a maternal superego as prior and determinant in psychic development had been accepted?[14] In The ego and the id ([1923] 1953) Freud had unconsciously forgotten and later reintroduced the mother into the formation of the superego. Klein was strongly asserting the importance of the mother in complex ways. It is no question of the pre-oedipal mother and the blissful attachment of mother and child in this symbiotic dyad. Klein is addressing the multiplicity of conflicting relationships that mother and daughter entertain in both the pre-oedipal and oedipal situations. In the context of cultural, social, and political dispossession of women's rights—and rights with regard to their children as a case in point—Klein narrates the ineluctable psychic dispossession of a maternal superego. The superego was and always had been a paternal instance.

Klein gives us a totally disruptive view of the development of female sexuality by the end of this essay. The achievement of genitality and by extension heterosexuality is a consequence of the girl's good mother-imagos. I think the force (and the ironies) of the display of Klein's rhetoric in this final section of her essay are so revealing and superb that it is worth quoting the following fragment at length.

> If she is in a position to entrust herself to the internal guidance of a paternal super-ego which she believes in and admires, it always means that she has good mother-imagos as well; for it is only where she has sufficient trust in a "good" internalized mother that she is able to surrender herself completely to her paternal super-ego. But in order to make a surrender of this kind she must also believe strongly enough in her possession of "good" things inside her body—of friendly internalized objects. Only if the child which, in her imagination, she has had, or expects to have, by her father is a "good" and "beautiful" child—only, that is, if the inside of her body represents a place where harmony and beauty reign (a phantasy which is also present in a man)—can she give herself without reserve, both sexually and mentally, to her paternal super-ego and to its representatives in the external world. (EASG, 237)[15]

Klein's hyperbolic patriarchal metaphors are no doubt intended to undermine any literal reading of this text. Tropes that allude to the patriarchal crippling of women—"entrust herself to the internal guidance of a paternal superego"—seduction, and (abuse) rape—"surrender herself completely"—reach their climax in this beatific scenario in which harmony and beauty reign and "she can give herself without reserve, both sexually and mentally, to her paternal superego and to its representatives in the external world." It is impossible to read these lines and not perceive Klein's own ironic surrendering. With great ability, she undoes this intrusive patriarchal logic by means of a mise en abyme and an erasure of the maternal superego and by providing strategies intended to undermine the silent acceptance of such a crippled feminine fate.

In the Kleinian narrative of the sexual development of the girl, the masculine position seems to be the best possible liberatory scenario for the future woman. The phantasy of the imaginary possession of a penis will produce radical changes in her attitude. Klein makes a crucial point: "As regards her activities and sublimations—which she regards in her unconscious as a reality-evidence of her possession of a penis or as substitutes for it—these are not only used to compete with her father's penis but invariably serve, in a secondary way, as a defence against her super-ego and in order to weaken it. In girls of this type, moreover, the ego takes a stronger lead and their pursuits are for the most part an expression of male potency" (EASG, 237).

If we follow the line of associations in the rhetoric of this essay, we will undoubtedly recognize the uncanniness of something all too familiar, namely, the connection between the woman's more "potent" superego—which barely appeared in a footnote—and the "weakened" superego of these types of girls (women who adopt a masculine position or lesbians), which results in pursuits that express male "potency." In other words, the harsher the superego, the more feminine attitude. The Oedipus complex appears clearly as a melancholic apparatus. This "secondary way" can be understood as a subversive strategic move undertaken to avoid an all too dangerous introjection and the melancholia attached to it.

In her postscript, Klein strongly disagrees with Freud's views in his recently published essay "Female sexuality" ([1931] 1953). In his discussion, Freud endeavors to isolate the period of the girl's attachment to her mother from the operation of her superego and her sense of guilt. According to Klein, it is precisely the anxiety and sense of guilt arising from the girl's aggressive impulses that intensify her primary libidinal attachment to her mother at a very early age. Whereas Freud believes that the girl's long attachment to her mother is an exclusive one and takes place before she has entered the Oedipus situation, Klein states: "my experience of analysis of small girls has convinced me that their long-drawn-out and powerful attachment to their mother is never exclusive and is bound up with Oedipus impulses" (EASG, 239).

Klein is the first analyst who writes extensively on the complex, troubled, and conflictual relationship of the infant girl with her mother. Far from suggesting simple solutions that translate into continuity, symbiosis, and mutual satisfaction in the mother-daughter relationship, she underscores what she believes is an essential misrecognition on the part of psychoanalysis. Anxiety, guilt, fear, and aggressivity also tinge their bond. The death drive is present from the very beginning of psychic life. Elements such as oral frustration with the breast and envy of parents' oral gratification in copulation, together with the equation of breast with penis, incline the girl to turn toward her father's penis. This attachment to her father, which for Klein takes place in the second half of the girl's first year, is fundamentally affected by her attachment to her mother: "If the small girl is too frightened of her mother she will not be able to attach herself strongly enough to her father and her Oedipus complex will not come to light" (EASG, 239). Klein ends her essay by alluding to Freud's basic agreement with some of her views. He also believed that the girl's attachment to her father is built on her early relationship with her mother and that many women repeat their relationships with their mothers in their relationships with men.

Envy and Gratitude

My work has taught me that the first object to be envied is the feeding breast, for the infant feels that it possesses everything he desires and that it has an unlimited flow of milk, and love which the breast keeps for its own gratification. This feeling adds to his sense of grievance and hate, and the result is a disturbed relation to the mother. If envy is excessive, this, in my view, indicates that paranoid and schizoid features are abnormally strong and that such an infant can be regarded as ill.—Melanie Klein

"Envy and gratitude" ([1957] 1975) is Klein's last major theoretical essay. This is a work of maturity in whose opening section she once again pays tribute to Abraham's memory, his teaching and the importance of his contributions to psychoanalysis. She writes: "As I am about to publish Envy and Gratitude, three decades after Abraham's death, it is a source of great satisfaction to me that my work has contributed to the growing recognition of the full significance of Abraham's discoveries" (E&G, 177). Nevertheless, Klein no longer hesitates, opening the second section of this piece by claiming full autonomy and responsibility for what her work has taught her after a long career in clinical practice. Klein was an indefatigable believer in the value of a work, whose validity was put to the test every day in encounters with her patients.

In "Envy and gratitude," Klein conceives envy as a primary affect that is clearly related to the death drive, it "is an oral-sadistic and anal-sadistic expression of destructive impulses, operative from the beginning of life and has a constitutional basis" (E&G, 176). Envy is closely allied to jealousy and greed but differs from them in seeking to spoil and rob the mother with the aim of destroying her creativeness. All of this is based on the phantasy that the breast is mean and grudging and would rather enjoy itself than satisfy the infant. The scenario of the infant's destructive attacks on the mother now has envy as its central part. Envy is mainly bound up with projection, and it can be identified as a destructive aspect of projective identification. Klein states her position and differences with Freud clearly. She writes: "The threat of annihilation by the death instinct within is, in my view—which differs from Freud on this point—the primordial anxiety, and it is the ego which, in the service of the life instinct—possibly even called into operation by the life instinct—deflects to some extent that threat outwards. This fundamental defence against the death instinct Freud attributed to the organism, whereas I regard this process as the prime activity of the ego" (E&G, 191). The experience of envy inevitably presupposes boundaries between infant and mother that Klein assumes exist from birth.

On the opposite side, gratitude is the feeling that springs from a good feed and a good breast. It leads to a sense of being full of good objects, to generosity, and is closely related to the process of restitution. It is the product of an alliance of the ego with the life drive. For Klein, it is enjoyment and the gratitude to which it gives rise that mitigate destructive impulses, envy, and greed.

Klein's contribution on the role of envy in premature genital excitement in infancy and childhood is also crucial. A rejecting mother is an important element in the result, even when the symptoms originate from a failure to work through the depressive position owing to an excess of envy. If the oral phase goes unresolved, the infant attempts to find substitute gratification in premature genital satisfactions, which then start to exhibit compulsive characteristics. The importance of the relationship among envy and gratitude; schizoid, depressive, and paranoid reaction patterns; idealized processes; and the growth of the ego is also amply elaborated in E&G.

Phantasies of Interpretation

In the chapter devoted to Klein included in *Wild desires and mistaken identities: Lesbianism and psychoanalysis* (1993) Noreen O'Connor and Joanna Ryan elaborate a critique of Klein by arguing that Kleinian-oriented feminist psychotherapists and psychologists "have failed to discuss Klein's specification of female homosexuality as oral-sadistic, destructive, fixated at the paranoid-schizoid position. There is no critique of the normativeness of Klein's metapsychology, notably her privileging of heterosexual dynamics" (74). They contend that for Klein female homosexuality "occurs because of unresolved difficulties at the paranoid schizoid position. . . . According to

Klein, female homosexuality can therefore be only a relationship of part objects" (77). Although I am most sympathetic toward a project that claims to uncover the biased and pathologized view that psychoanalytic theory has held on homosexualities, and most specifically on lesbianism, as I will try to show in what follows, O'Connor and Ryan base most of their critique on a partial and superficial reading of a limited part of Klein's work.

"The phantasy that anatomy is destiny" is the title of the section that O'Connor and Ryan devote to their discussion of Klein. This title seems to me not to go beyond a witty remark that in its very formulation proves to be a rather tendentious and encrypted subversion of Kleinian theory. Even if O'Connor and Ryan's purpose is to review and critique a good number of analysts and schools, the relative extension of the scope of their project—which I certainly see as significant and much needed—does not exempt them from the task of reading and examining in depth the complete works of the theorists with which they are dealing if they want to be consistent and effect a well-grounded and serious critique. They are careful to warn their readers that they must present "a general outline of her position on the Oedipus complex and the pre-oedipal psyche in order to set the context for understanding her position on homosexuality and lesbianism" (1993, 75) since they claim it is not possible "to extricate her position on solely the aetiology—the family background—of lesbianism" (75). Nevertheless, they never quite engage the larger picture of "homosexuality."

O'Connor and Ryan basically contend that Klein retains "stereotypical gender descriptions . . . present from earlier infancy," that she theorizes sexuality as "intrinsic to gender differences," and that she assumes "a natural causality connecting, sex, gender and desire, such that sexuality and desire are presented as the 'natural' expression of a given gender" (1993, 75). In this picture, female homosexuality is regarded as " 'oral-sadistic,' pregenital and immature" (Klein [1952] 1975c, 93). These sweeping statements suffer from overgeneralization, and they are certainly part of a somewhat long and unfortunate tradition of disqualifications and misreadings of the Kleinian canon. They launch very serious charges against Klein that, as I have tried to show, are not grounded in a careful close reading of and reflection on Klein's whole work.[16] At this point, and taking into account the ideas put forward in this book, I wish to critically engage the specific charges that O'Connor and Ryan develop in their essay.

First of all, O'Connor and Ryan never bother to clarify which notion of phantasy they are addressing or to consider what is at stake in the highly complex Kleinian notion of phantasy, how we can critique the Kleinian school's tenets and assumptions from their very roots (from the notion of "unconscious phantasy"). Nor do they suggest a plausible alternative location from which to start. The title of this essay and their discussion depict Klein very much as following the path traced by Freud, which seems, at the very least, unfair to and oblivious of the schism in the British Psychoanalytical Society and of what the period of the Controversial Discussions meant for the history of psychoanalysis. If we assume that Melanie Klein holds the phantasy that anatomy is destiny, we will miss the whole point at the center of Kleinian theory. First of all, and in the most basic and general sense, when Klein is talking about the breast or the penis she is obviously not referring to concrete anatomical organs. She is rather trying to establish the way in which the symbolic equation—in its linking of internal and external reality—works. She is by no means mapping "real" anatomies but what we may call "virtual" anatomies, granting them the flexibility that intrapsychic life and its intersubjective manifestations exhibit.

O'Connor and Ryan claim that Klein's paper "On the criteria for the termination of a psycho-analysis" ([1950] 1975), specifies " 'heterosexuality' as a major criterion for the termination of an analysis—that is to say, heterosexuality is a criterion for being psychically healthy, 'cured' of pathology (1993, 75). They quote the following passage from ELI: "The question arises how far the approach I am suggesting is related to some of the well-known criteria, such as an established potency and heterosexuality, capacity for love, object-relations and work, and certain characteristics of the ego which make for mental stability and are bound up with adequate defences" (75).

First, it is quite clear that in this passage Klein is formulating a question that she will attempt to address in the last pages of her paper. Klein takes great care in explaining the complexity of the development of the ego, emotions, the reduction of anxieties, and the work of mourning that the termination of analysis entails. Her emphasis is on working through persecutory and depressive anxieties to achieve a greater synthesis between the various aspects of the superego, diminishing splitting processes and reaching integration of the ego in depth.[17] Klein explicitly condenses in one short paragraph the prominent criterion for the termination of analysis. She writes: "I have made it clear throughout this paper that the criterion I suggest presupposes that the analysis has been carried back to the early stages of development and to the deep layers of the mind and has included the working through of persecutory and depressive anxieties" (CTP, 46). O'Connor and Ryan overlook the fact that Klein does not devote a single line in this paper to developing the issue of "potency and heterosexuality."[18] Most importantly, she stresses that this remains a question (or is at least questionable). Klein's silence is far more revealing than any explanation could be.

These writers claim that Klein retains Freud's alignment of gender and sexuality by attributing "appropriate" sexual desires to each gender. They quote one passage from "Early stages of the Oedipus conflict" ([1928] 1975) and another from "Our adult world and its roots in infancy" ([1959] 1975). The latter they take as indicative of Klein's unchanging views on this subject. In this last instance, the extension of their quote is tendentiously cut short before Klein is able to make her point and question and problematize the whole oedipal situation. This is a blatant instance of interested misapprehension that deserves to be quoted at length. O'Connor and Ryan include the following passage: "There are great differences in the Oedipus complex of the girl and of the boy, which I shall characterize only by saying that whereas the boy in his genital development returns to his original object, the mother, and therefore seeks female objects, with some consequent jealousy of the father and men in general, the girl to some extent has to turn away from the mother and find the object of her desires in the father and later on in other men" (AW&RI, 252). Klein's text goes on with no interruptions as follows: "I have, however, stated this in an over-simplified form, because the boy is also attracted towards the father and identifies with him; and therefore an element of homosexuality enters into normal development. The same applies to the girl, for whom, the relation to the mother, and to women in general, never loses its importance. The Oedipus complex is thus not a matter only of feelings of hate and rivalry towards one parent and love towards the other, but feelings of love and the sense of guilt also enter in connection with the rival parent. Many conflicting emotions therefore centre upon the Oedipus complex" (252).

This is only one case of the striking misappropriation of Kleinian ideas. O'Connor and Ryan seem to make it clear that, no matter how or at what cost, they need to dismantle the tenets of most previous psychoanalytic thought.[19] Their whole critique builds upon these sorts of misreadings and misapprehensions of Klein's ideas.

In their discussion of female development, they base their critique on a highly literal reading of what they call Klein's heavy reliance "on anatomical similarity and difference" (1993, 79) such as the girl's anatomical difference from her father or her difficulties in identifying with her mother because of the internal quality of her sexual organs. I have attempted to provide readings of the oedipal situation in both sexes that precisely show the aporias implicit in the Kleinian text and the complexity involved in attaining any fixed sexual position. In this respect, the collapse of heterosexuality in specific sections included in The psycho-analysis of children proves illuminating. Once again, and most importantly, a discussion of the notion of unconscious phantasy in relation to the anatomical question is a totally neglected and urgent task in O'Connor and Ryan's project.[20] Their charge against Kleinian interpretations as "ahistorical 'psychic' facts" (82), given in terms of early prelinguistic phantasies, is certainly related to the larger issue of the classical critique of Kleinians' relying too much on the inner world and virtually neglecting external reality. I have repeatedly addressed these arguments in this book.

Along the same lines, O'Connor and Ryan do not seem to tolerate the fact that "Klein assumes the existence of an 'inner world' that lies outside language" (1993, 82). The issues of the inner world (introjection, incorporation) and that of language are far too complex to address in depth here. The same applies to their alignment of Klein "with many essentialist, universalist, foundational theories" (83). To grasp part of what is at stake in these questions, I refer the reader to the debates waged during the Controversial Discussions in King and Steiner 1991.[21] I have also tried to refer to this in chapter 7.[22]

In "Envy and gratitude" ([1957] 1975), Klein once again devotes attention to the persistent issue of female homosexuality in her work based on her newly developed ideas of envy and gratitude. In this work, Klein states that if the penis is desired and not envied excessively its incorporation will be a preparation for genital receptivity, but if the envy is too intense narcissistic identification will predominate. The girl will thus want to have and be what she envies. The more the penis is envied, the more difficult it is to have it as a love object at the time when the breast is abandoned for the penis. Intense penis envy is in fact connected with envy of the breast. So there is a displacement of the wish or the envy previously experienced for the breast (on)to the penis. Hence, the foundations of both heterosexual and homosexual object choice are already laid in the oral situation, its main fixation points being at the oral stage. From this analysis of the Kleinian narrative, it is clear that in her view homosexual tendencies are a part of normal development. However, the little girl must mourn these if, in the course of her development toward adulthood, the heterosexual tendencies are eventually to predominate over the homosexual ones.

In her discussion of the Oedipus complex in the light of her new notion of envy included in *Envy and gratitude*, Klein argues that if envy toward the primal object is not excessive the infant will probably be able to work through the depressive position satisfactorily. She writes about the influence of the combined parent figure on the infant's ability to differentiate between the parents and establish good relations with each of them, which turns out to be deeply affected by the strength of the envy and the intensity of his or her oedipal jealousy. Klein makes it clear that the object of envy is "largely oral" (E&G, 198). Klein acknowledges Freud's "contribution to the understanding of envy" (199) through his idea of penis envy in women with no further comment. There are several factors that contribute to penis envy.[23] In the case of the girl, "the girl's penis-envy can be traced back to envy of the mother's breast" (199). This may have different outcomes. If envy toward the breast is strongly transferred to the father's penis, this will lead to a reinforcing of the girl's homosexual attitude. A second outcome will be that of "a sudden and abrupt turning to the penis away from the breast, because of the anxieties and the conflicts to which the oral relation gives rise" (199). In other words, heterosexuality appearing as failure or impossibility, since Klein further adds that this situation does not lead to stable relations with the object. The third and last outcome gives the picture of a "more successful" situation (Klein's words, 200), when hate and envy of the mother are not so strong and the girl turns away from her and toward the father.

It is true that along the lines of the pessimistic and negative tenor of this essay Klein argues that friendship with women and homosexuality may be based on "the need to find a good object instead of the avoided primal object" (E&G, 200). Many times these good object relations are "deceptive," since "the underlying envy towards the primal object is split off but remains operative and is liable to disturb any relations" (200). Nevertheless, it is no less true that in "Love, guilt and reparation" ([1937] 1975), Klein holds what seems to be the opposite view. When referring to the fact that homosexual tendencies play an important part in friendships between people of the same sex, Klein writes in a footnote: "The subject of homosexual love relations is a wide and very complicated one. To deal with it adequately would necessitate more space than I have at my disposal, and I restrict myself, therefore, to mentioning that much love can be put into these relationships" (331).

In the case of the boy, excessive envy of the breast is also a definitive factor in disturbances in development. Klein does not modify her previous position as far as male homosexuality is concerned; she just adds a further remark on guilt and male homosexuality, namely, that one of the sources of guilt about homosexuality is "the feeling of having turned away with hate from the mother and betrayed her by making an ally of the father's penis and of the father" (E&G, 201). Klein also states that paranoid jealousy and rivalry exist in both sexes, in both the direct and inverted Oedipus complex, and that they are based on excessive envy of the primal object, the breast.

4

Masculinities: Anxiety, Sadism, and the
Intricacies of Object-Love

In one section of "The effects of early anxiety-situations on the sexual development of the boy" ([1932] 1975c), Klein gives an account of the psychosexual development of the boy by effecting a reversal of the rhetoric of the Freudian narrative.[1] In the Kleinian scenario, the little girl no longer "is a little man" (Freud [1932] 1933, 1953, 118) and the paradigm built upon the fear of castration and the primacy of the penis suffer significant changes. Klein has already devoted a whole, autonomous chapter to the development of the girl and now, after acknowledging that analysis shows that the boy's development runs parallel with that of the girl, she extends the analogies much further.[2] "As in the girl['s case]," (EASB, 240) what is emphasized now, at these very early stages, is the oral frustration that reinforces the boy's destructive tendencies toward his mother's breast and, during the phase of maximal sadism, the attacks addressed to the inside of his mother's body.

During the feminine phase, the boy has an oral-sucking fixation on his father's penis, "just as the girl has" (240). In Klein's view, this fixation constitutes the basis of "true homosexuality in him" (240). As in melancholia, orality, and by extension introjection are the basis of homosexuality. This agrees with Freud's analysis in *Leonardo da Vinci and a memory of his childhood* ([1910] 1953), wherein he concludes that Leonardo's homosexuality went back to an excessive fixation upon his mother—ultimately upon her breast—and by displacement to the penis as an object of gratification.[3] Klein's analytic experience leads her to argue that every boy moves from an oral-sucking fixation on his mother's breast to one on his father's penis. During this feminine phase, the boy believes that his mother has his father's penis—or a number of them—incorporated in her body and develops an imaginary relation to it. Out of rivalry with his mother for the possession of the father's desired organ, he launches sadistic attacks on her body. Retaliation from his mother produces a deep anxiety in him. These early rivalry situations form the basis of his femininity complex. During the early stages of the Oedipus conflict, the boy's genital impulses lead him to take his mother's body and genitals as sexual objects. He desires to possess her and now turns his sadistic attacks against his father's penis within her. His oral position has also been frustrated by his father's penis, and his destructive impulses toward it are often much stronger than the girl's since his longing for his mother as a sexual object induces him to feel this way.

Klein's description of the boy's early anxiety situations is rich in detail and crucial for our understanding of his future development. Besides the fears the boy feels out of his rivalry with his mother, his fear of his father's dangerous internalized penis stands in the way of his maintaining a feminine position. This latter fear and the increasing strength of his genital impulses cause him to give up his identification with his mother and to fortify his heterosexual position. But if his fears are too strong he will not be able to properly overcome his feminine phase. This will be "a decisive bar to his becoming established in a heterosexual position" (EASB, 242). Furthermore, Klein stresses that if the boy's early mental life has been dominated by a fear of the combined parent figure in copulation—and the concomitant fear of being castrated by his conjoint "bad" parents—and anxiety has been excessive, it will be "more difficult to him to attain any position" (242).[4]

Aggressivity and sadism are thus at the core of the Kleinian account of the origin of desire and sexuality. In the Kleinian primal scene, there is mortal combat between the life and death drives in the guise of the combined parent figure in copulation. The first battle on behalf of the child's future development is won by the death drive. It results in oral frustration, orchestration of attacks, fear of retaliation, and the relinquishing of the child's first object of satisfaction. This relinquishing is always a loss that is internalized to different degrees. The lost object—the mother's breast—is metaphorically displaced onto the father's penis, and by extension onto any of the sexual partner's organs, which may become subject to oral fixation—can literally remain inside, incorporated, and thus produce melancholia or it can be worked through in the process of mourning.

Kleinian Primal Scenes: Rereading the Combined Parent Figure

Lewis Aron, in a new and compelling reading of the Kleinian concept of the combined parent figure, argues for a revision of the metaphor of the internalized primal scene both as a challenge to traditional notions of a unitary gender identity and as supportive to the postmodern critique of a core or unified identity.[5] Aron elaborates a deconstructive critique of gender dichotomies in his endeavor to show the necessity of notions of gender identity and gender multiplicity. Based on the early Freudian idea of the general bisexual disposition outlined in *Three essays on the theory of sexuality* ([1905] 1953) and its history in psychoanalysis, Aron claims that far from being a pathogenic phantasy of omnipotence—as it has usually been considered—the wish to fulfill symbolically the phantasy of being both sexes can be used constructively and creatively (1995). Melanie Klein introduced the concept of the combined parent figure in "Infantile anxiety situations reflected in a work of art and in the creative impulse" ([1929] 1975). Since then, its potential has barely been explored outside the post-Kleinian tradition.[6]

In a stimulating and eclectic elaboration, Aron shows in what ways the combined parent figure and the traditional primal scene can be used as metaphors to illustrate the possibility of holding two contrasting ideas in mind simultaneously without either fusing them or splitting them apart. He considers psychic bisexuality as one aspect of narcissism and the phantasy of omnipotence in human development, and he holds that the bisexual phantasy involves "having it all, to identify with and to desire both mother and father and to allow the masculine and feminine sides of our personalities to engage each other, to conjoin" (1995, 202). In Aron's view, it is paradoxical that, while we need a core gender identity—Aron does not advocate the elimination of gender as a category—we also need to preserve a "multigendered self" that preserves the fluidity of our multiple identifications. In Aron's view, the primal scene serves as an internal structure regulating both narcissism and object relations.[7]

Through the continual operation of internalization, Klein holds that the combined parent figure is established inside the child. In the passage from the paranoid-schizoid to the depressive position, and from an early stage of confusion and part-object relations, there is a progressive differentiation of the elements that make up this figure. Following Klein, Aron argues that since the development of the mind is not linear the combined parent figure is not simply replaced by the latter primal scene. Rather, both coexist and operate synchronically as crucial dimensions of experience.[8] In this sense, although Aron focuses specifically in the combined parent figure in his essay (1995), his reading of psychosexual development in Klein broadly coincides with my own.[9]

Aron claims that the combined parent figure is useful "because it does not privilege heterosexual intercourse but rather allows for, and even suggests, all sorts of sexual and aggressive arrangements: heterosexual and homosexual combinations and also nongenital sexuality" (1995, 213). The danger he identifies in using only the more "mature" primal scene lies in its possible privileging of procreative sexuality over other alternatives.[10] What Aron is aiming at in his rereading of the primal scene is to challenge stable heterosexuality and suggest in its place a more fluid view that emphasizes process, flux, difference, and multiplicity in development. In Aron's view, it is important to note that in the move from the paranoid-schizoid to the depressive position, the child should be able to identify with each parent, internalize the complex set of relations implicated in the primal scene, and thus integrate a sense of self as "bigendered" (219). The capacity for creativity may emerge on the basis of homosexual as well as heterosexual primal scenes and may be inspired by pregenital as well as genital and oedipal sexual imagery.

I see Lewis Aron's essay as an important contribution to the reading of one of the central tropes in Klein's work as well as part of a recent renewed and more balanced trend in the contemporary return to Klein. His endeavor to dismantle the reified traditional understanding of the primal scene opens up new ways to reflect upon former teleologically prescribed notions of developmental progress. We might suggest rethinking related issues such as the ideas of fixation and regression; what counts as normal or healthy and what counts as perverse; and, most broadly, the consequences of what may be thought as a new concept of psychic space (based on a range of nonnormative phantasies as the ones implicit in the Kleinian combined parent figure) in relation to its concomitant analytic space and issues of transference, countertransference, and technique in the most general sense.[11] Aron follows along the lines of the postmodern critique of gender and sexuality, which problematizes the nature of embodiment and argues for an urgent revision of the rationale underlying earlier evolutionary models of reproductive sexuality.

By means of the penetrating penis which is equated with an organ of perception, to be more precise, with the eye, the ear or a combination of the two, he wants to discover what sort of destruction has been done inside his mother by his own penis and excrements and by his father's, and to what kind of perils his penis is exposed there.—Melanie Klein

Each sex has its own ways of mastering anxiety. In the case of the boy, his initial belief in the omnipotence of his penis—an external organ "accessible to tests by reality" (EASB, 243)—imagines it endowed with destructive powers and "likens it to devouring and murderous beasts, firearms, and so on" (243). Klein writes that in child analysis it is common to come across the idea of the penis as a "magic wand" and masturbation as magic. Erection and ejaculation are seen as heightening its sadistic powers.

The primacy of the visible in the recognition of sexual difference is also present in the Kleinian narrative. At stake here is a very precarious visibility. Klein's fundamental contribution to current debates on sexualities and gender lies in her problematization of the attainment of any stable sexual position through an analysis of the influence of early anxiety situations in the development of girls and boys that does not privilege castration anxiety—that is, the primacy of the visible—as the only important one. In the case of the boy, the penis is visible as long as it is not put under too much risk—it may be cut off and shut up inside the mother's body. The girl develops an early perception of her sexual organs—clitoris and vagina. But the apparent invisibility of her genitals is not an obstacle to her mobilization of attacks on and defenses against her mother's body or to her search for pleasure by means of clitoral masturbation or by adopting a homosexual (restorative) or heterosexual position. Sadism, paradoxically, is what is most visible in this primitive sexual organization of the (death) drives.

What is crucial in the Kleinian narrative is the fact that these modes of mastering early anxiety situations are always already constructed according to social standards and expectations. In the case of the boy, Klein writes: "Both as regards the sexual act and sublimations he displaces his danger-situations into the outer world and overcomes them there through the omnipotence of his penis" (EASB, 244). The boy's phantasies of conquering his mother's body—the interior of which contains objects such as penises, excrements, and children—by copulating with her "form the basis of his attempts to conquer the external world and to master anxiety along masculine lines" (243–44). Phantasies of conquest and colonization of a feminine interior space are at the root of subsequent phantasies of the male conquest of reality.

The concentration of sadistic omnipotence in the penis is of the utmost importance for the masculine position of the boy. With this omnipotent belief in mind, the boy can pit his penis against his father's and take up the struggle against that dreaded and admired organ. The boy's hatred of his father's penis incites him to possess his mother in a genital way and to increase his libidinal desire to copulate with her. Another factor that acts as an incentive to having coitus with her—which in the girl strengthens her homosexual position—is his epistemophilic instinct, intensified as it has been by his anxiety. His penis is felt to be a privileged organ of perception that helps him find out about the destruction caused in his mother's body and about the dangers that may await his penis there.

In her section "The woman with a penis," Klein writes: "The child's belief that its mother's body contains the penis of its father leads . . . to the idea of 'the woman with a penis' " (EASB, 245).[12] Normally the boy's fear of his father's penis inside his mother decreases as his relationship to his objects develops. Since his fear of the "bad" penis is to a great extent derived from his destructive impulses against his father's penis and since the character of his imagos depends largely on the quality and quantity of his own sadism, the reduction of that sadism, and consequently of his anxiety, will lessen the severity of his superego and will thus improve the relations of his ego toward both his internalized and his real objects. Progressively, if, along with the imago of the combined parent figure, individual imagos such as that of the "good" mother are sufficiently strong, the boy's hatred of his father's penis will decrease and from then on will mostly be directed toward his real objects. As the boy's genital tendencies grow stronger and he overcomes his sadistic impulses, his phantasies of making restitution begin to gain momentum.

In the early stages of development, the child perceives the sexual act, in addition to its libidinal purposes, as a means of destroying or injuring the object. In later stages, it serves to restore the mother's body and thus to master anxiety and guilt. During the genital stage, the child attributes to his penis in copulation the function not only of giving the woman pleasure but of repairing in her all the damage that it and his father's penis have done. Now his belief in his "good" penis also involves a belief in his father's good penis.

So far in EASB, Klein has been relegating most of her interesting remarks on the issue of male homosexuality to the footnotes.[13] At this point, she introduces the idea of a restitutive kind of homosexuality, which is central to my argument. She describes it as follows: "The boy's sense of guilt towards his mother and his fear that his father's 'bad' penis may do her harm contribute in no small degree to his endeavour to restore his father's penis as well and give it back to her, and to unite the two in an amicable fashion. In certain instances this desire can become so dominating that he will relinquish his mother as a love-object and make her over to his father entirely. This situation disposes him to go over to a homosexual position; in which case his homosexuality would serve the purpose of making restitution towards his father's penis, whose function it would then be to restore his mother and give her gratification" (249). Only a few pages earlier, Klein referred to some of Felix Boehm's arguments in his essay "Homosexuality and polygamy" (1920), which corroborate these thoughts. "For Boehm, the boy's impulse to attack his father's penis inside his mother's vagina and the repression of that aggressive impulse are important factors in the adoption of homosexuality. So in these cases it is the repression of aggressive impulses rather than regression to earlier stages or fixation at a definite point that produces a restitutive kind of male homosexuality.

The Boy's Feminine Phase and Its Resolution

The difference between the sexual trends of the man and the woman necessitates, as we know, different psychological conditions of satisfaction for each and leads each to seek the fulfilment of different and mutually incompatible requirements in their relations to one another.—Melanie Klein

As a result of the boy's restitutive phantasies, the fear of his "bad" superego derived from his father decreases and he can now identify more strongly with his "good" father.[14] The final attainment of a heterosexual position depends upon the boy's having successfully overcome the early feminine phase of development. At this point, and again in a footnote, Klein provides us with one of the most important theses in EASB. She writes: "Where the boy's fear of the 'bad' penis or, not infrequently, his inability to tolerate his own sadism heighten his belief in the 'good' penis to an exaggerated degree, not only in regard to his father's penis inside his mother, but in regard to his super-ego, his attitude towards women may become quite distorted. The heterosexual act will serve first and foremost to satisfy his homosexual desires, and the womb will be nothing more than something which contains the 'good' penis" (249). The boy's excessive belief in his father's good penis, metaphorically displaced onto his now benevolent superego, causes this "quite distorted" attitude toward women. What should we make of this heterosexual but always already homosexual scenario? The aim of Klein's complex argument is fundamentally deconstructive of any stable and fully present notion of sexual positions. If, in these cases, the heterosexual act serves phantasmatically to satisfy homosexual desires, then the opposite should hold true as well. Homosexual acts may phantasmatically satisfy heterosexual desires. In the passage just quoted, Klein dares to argue that there is no guarantee—in other words, there is no reason to believe—that the specific desires underlying the sexual act with a different sex partner should be heterosexual. With these views in mind and with her emphasis on the foundational role of phantasy in human sexuality, Klein totally disrupts the system of sexual relations built upon compulsory heterosexuality. This disruptive potential of phantasy in Kleinian theory opens up new ways to start rethinking "making sex" and "being sexual" along more fluid lines and outside the matrices of power which violently dictate which sexual practices are legal and which are outside the law. Klein's advocacy of a notion of a neither terribly bad nor excessively good superego argues for the attainment of a difficult balance in psychic life among early anxiety situations, superego formation, and object relations. In all of these cases, the death drive, as manifest in sadism in its combat with the life drives—self-preservation and object love—is the motive force that sets the psychic apparatus and its machinery in motion.

By the end of the feminine phase, the boy reinforces his pride in the possession of a penis and displaces it onto intellectual activities. Klein refers to Mary Chadwick's thesis that the boy displaces his envy of the reproductive capacities of women onto the mental plane and compensates for his inability to have children with the exercise of his epistemophilic instinct.[15]

In this essay, Klein gives us one of the most dismal and negative views of heterosexual relations to be found in her whole body of work. The difference between the "sexual trends" of men and women "necessitates, as we know, different psychological conditions of satisfaction . . . and leads each to seek the fulfilment of different and mutually incompatible requirements in their relations to one another" (EASB, 250). In her form of address to her readers, Klein is using a "we" that first includes herself and second assumes that these irreconcilable differences and needs are common knowledge. Her usually detached and objective rhetoric interestingly becomes personal—all too personal?—in these sections where her deconstructive endeavors take the lead. Despite all the difficulties encountered, the man may finally be able "to be in touch" with the mental needs of the woman on the basis of his early identification with his mother. At this point, the introjection of the father's penis as love object and his good relationship with his mother will help him to understand "the woman's tendency to introject and preserve the penis" (250). Once again, the profiles of melancholia seem to have a distinctly feminine shape.

Only when the boy is able to sublimate his feminine instinctual components and surmount his feelings of envy, hatred, and anxiety toward his mother will he be able to consolidate his heterosexual position "in the stage of genital dominance" (EASB, 251). His capacity to make restitution by means of the sexual act—and his belief in his "good" penis—is threatened by his anxiety situations, among which the fear of castration is by far the most important. The penis plays a crucial role in mastering the boy's anxiety situations and is a privileged vehicle for his destructive and later creative omnipotence. Moreover, it assists in reality testing and promoting object relations. Thus, progressively it is "brought into specially close relation with the ego and is made into a representative of the ego and the conscious; while the interior of the body, the imagos and the faeces—what is invisible and unknown, that is—are compared to the unconscious" (252).

In the section "Disturbances of sexual development," Klein gives a very complex account of the path that may lead the boy to adopt homosexuality. If the boy's feminine phase has been too strongly governed by sadism and the introjection of his father's bad penis and the hostile combined parent figure in copulation run parallel to his very feeble introjection of a "good" mother, this will give rise to an excess of anxiety concerning the interior of his body. If the boy's attacks on his mother's breast and body have been too intense, so that in his imagination she has been destroyed by his father's penis and his own, he will have all the more need of a "good" penis with which to restore her. Yet it is precisely his fear on account of all this destruction that prevents him from believing in his possession of a "good" penis and sexual potency. In Klein's view, the cumulative effect of all these factors may result in his suffering from disturbances of potency in his heterosexual position or in his adoption of homosexuality.

Incestuous Brotherhood

"Adoption of homosexuality" is the longest and by far the most complex section in this essay. Homosexuality starts with the mechanism of displacement and is followed by disavowal of the boy's belief in his "bad" penis. It is through displacement that the boy locates all that is terrifying and uncanny in the interior of the woman's body. As was noted before, in the "normal" attitude, the boy's penis represents his ego and his conscious, as opposed to the contents of his body and his superego, which represent his unconscious. In the homosexual attitude, this significance is extended by means of his narcissistic choice of object to the penis of another male, and this penis now serves as a counterproof against all his fears concerning the penis inside him and the interior of his body. Thus, according to Klein one mode of mastering anxiety in homosexuality is that "the ego endeavours to deny, control or get the better of the unconscious by over-emphasizing reality and the external world and all that is tangible and perceptible to consciousness" (EASB, 260). We could say that implicit here, to a certain extent, there is a process of disavowal of the unconscious.

Klein argues that in cases in which homosexual relations occurred in early childhood they contributed to moderating the boy's feelings of hatred and fear of his father's penis and to strengthen his belief in the "good" penis. All his homosexual affairs in later life will rest on such relations. These early homosexual relations provide him with assurances. It is important to devote attention to relations with his siblings, which Klein describes in depth. Early homosexual relations with the boy's brother or "brother-substitute" prove to him that his fears of being punished— phantasies of being turned out of the house, castrated, or killed—have no foundation "since his homosexual acts had no evil consequences" (EASB, 261). In addition, he now has secret accomplices, as these sexual relations with his brother (or brother-substitute) also mean that the two of them have banded together to destroy their parents either separately or combined in copulation. In his imagination, his partner will at times take on the role of his father—with whom he jointly attacked his mother's body— or the role of his brother—who, together with himself, destroyed his father's penis inside his mother and himself. From having sadistic masturbatory phantasies in common, they derive the feeling of being in league with one another against the parents by means of the sexual act. In Klein's view, this feeling is of general importance for the sexual relations of small children and "is closely bound up with paranoic mechanisms" (261). The role played by paranoia in all infantile sexuality is thus acknowledged as not exclusively restricted to homosexuality. In other words, heterosexuality is no guarantee against paranoia. Klein foregrounds this argument when she states that the boy may adopt a heterosexual position—if he wins his mother to his side against his father—even if he has marked paranoid traits.[16] On the other hand, if his fear of his mother is too strong and his good mother-imago has not been able to develop, his phantasies of allying himself with his father against his mother and of joining with his brother against both parents will determine his adoption of a homosexual position. Thus, in Klein's view male homosexuality stems from the failure to introject a good mother-imago.

When the boy falls prey to paranoid anxiety, his love object of the same sex represents first and foremost an ally against his persecutors. Only when his feelings of hate and fear toward the bad penis do not dissipate will parallel negative feelings toward his love-object emerge and effect a paranoid reversal of the beloved person into the persecutor. These mechanisms, which Klein sees at work in paranoia, are present "to a lesser degree" into every homosexual activity (EASB, 262).

Klein's discussion of Felix Boehm's "Homosexualität und Ödipuskomplex" (1926) turns out to be central to the further elaboration of her argument. Boehm focuses on the part played by the boy's hatred of his father and his death and castration wishes directed against him in the Oedipus complex. He concludes that in performing homosexual acts an individual often has two aims: first, to make his partner impotent for the heterosexual act and keep him away from women; and, second, to castrate him so as to get possession of his penis and further increase his own sexual potency with women. Regarding the first point, in Klein's view the boy's wish to keep other men away from women is based both on a primary jealousy of his father, and on his fear of the risks his mother runs in copulating with him.

Jealousy, in the Kleinian scenario, seeks to exclude another from the source of the good. Its privileged paradigm is indeed the Oedipus complex. This dismal view obviously corresponds to Klein's version of male homosexuality in the paranoid-schizoid position. Envy is far more primitive and infinitely more destructive than jealousy since it actively seeks to spoil the good itself. By interfering with the primal split between the good and bad penis, the building up of a good object—the good penis—becomes virtually impossible in that even the good is spoiled and devalued. The boy is left alone in a world of persecutors. Jealousy, envy, and greed interfere with reparation and with the attainment—and the working through—of the depressive position.

Klein cites Freud's "Certain neurotic mechanisms in jealousy, paranoia, and homosexuality" ([1922b] 1953), where he draws attention to the fact that in some cases what contributes to a homosexual choice of object are feelings of rivalry that have been surmounted and aggressive tendencies that have been repressed. Along these lines, Klein holds that the male in the homosexual position "has made a pact in his unconscious with his father and brothers by which they shall all abstain from having intercourse with his mother (and sisters) so as to spare her and shall seek compensation from that abstention in one another" (EASB, 263). Feelings of comradeship, alliance, and sexual and social bonding underlie these early homosexual relations. The idea of the homosocial pact intended to spare their mothers and sisters from incestuous sex—which involves risks mostly derived of the "bad" sadistic quality of their penises—establishes in Klein the basis for the development of homosexuality in the paranoid-schizoid position.

With regard to Boehm's second point, Klein expresses her "full agreement" (EASB, 263). But she interestingly draws an analogy that is not present in Boehm's account. Whereas Boehm is speaking of performing homosexual acts with a same-sex partner, Klein, in an incestuous metaphor, is substituting the sexual partner for the father and the collective "women" for the mother: "The child's desire to castrate his father so as to get his penis and be potent in sexual intercourse with his mother urges him towards a homosexual position" (263). As we saw earlier in the case of heterosexuality, the homosexual position has heterosexual phantasies in its reverse. In the Kleinian scenario, there is no place for complacency about the stability of any sexual position. The workings of the death drive introduce sadism and aggressivity from the beginning of psychic life, coloring every object, and consequently every sexual, relation. Klein goes on to say that if the boy's "sadistic trends predominate, his desire to get possession of his father's penis and semen by means of the homosexual act will also in part have a heterosexual aim. For in identifying himself with his sadistic father he will have all the more power to destroy his mother by copulating with her" (263). Furthermore, Klein argues that when the boy obtains gratification of his epistemophilic instinct from homosexual activities "he employs it in part to increase his efficiency in the heterosexual position" (263).[17]

The intricacies of the Kleinian text, animated by a deconstructive impulse, pose a variety of questions and challenges for current debates on issues of sexualities and gender. In this essay on the sexual development of the boy, Klein seems to be asking if sexuality is possible at all from the vantage point of only one gendered position within a binary. As has been amply shown, the fragile, unstable, and precarious nature of any such position (homosexual or heterosexual) undermines the very possibility of stabilization, permanence, or even attainment of the positions as such, rendering them undecidable. Both homosexuality and heterosexuality are undermined by phantasies of the other. The complex interaction among introjection, projection, defense mechanisms, object relations, and the specific modes intended to master early anxiety situations, together with the entropy—sadism, aggressivity, chaos—introduced by the death drive, brings us to the complex panorama of the Kleinian (con)figuration of sexuality. Sexuality is a signifying system that avoids closure. In its constitutive incompleteness, it cannot cease to build on contingent interventions, discrete acts, and historically specific social and material practices.

In Front or Behind? A True (Melancholic) Homosexual

It would seem that for the unconscious nothing is more distant and more unfathomable than the inside of the mother's body and, still more, the inside of one's own body. —Melanie Klein

Although B's homosexual position had been established so early and so strongly, and although he consciously rejected a heterosexual one, he had always unconsciously kept the heterosexual aims in view.—Melanie Klein

In her whole body of work, Klein gives us only one case study of an adult male homosexual.[18] This is not surprising given that Klein devoted most of her efforts to theorizing and developing the technique of child analysis and therefore to analyzing children. For this reason, and following the line of thought put forward in EASB, the long and detailed analysis of her patient "Mr. B." deserves our keenest attention.

The case of Mr. B. works as a kind of appendix to or illustration of the main ideas included in the last two sections of EASB, which are devoted to disturbances of sexual development and to the boy's adoption of homosexuality. Klein describes her patient as a man in his midthirties who had been obliged to resign his post as a teacher on account of severe inhibitions and deep depressions. Although he was "unusually gifted intellectually, he suffered from severe disturbances of mental health" (EASB, 264). His fits of depression, which went back to early childhood, had recently become so acute as to sink him into a general state of severe depression. Behind his more manifest symptoms, Klein was able to elicit the presence of a profound hypochondria together with strong notions of persecution—which at times took on the character of delusions—and serious obsessional symptoms. The patient showed an extraordinary power of dissimulation, which helped him to conceal his illness.[19] This was due to his positive early object relations and strong optimistic feelings in the depths of his mind.

After more than a page of detailed description, Klein reveals that Mr. B was "a true homosexual" (EASB, 265). He completely rejected women as sexual objects, attributing to them grotesquely monstrous qualities. From a physical point of view, the shape of their bodies repelled him, especially their breasts and buttocks and their lack of a penis. Klein interprets his hatred of women's "sticking out" parts as aimed at his father's internalized and reemerging penises. The interior of the woman's body was "an infinitely and unexplorable expanse where every kind of danger and death lurked, and she herself appeared to him only as a kind of container for terrifying penises and dangerous excrements" (265–66). He regarded "her delicate skin and all her other feminine attributes" as one of the many signs of her deceitful and treacherous nature.

The patient displaced the fear caused by his father's penis onto his mother's body, together with all other things that frightened him as potential dangers. He had idealized the penis and the male sex to a very high degree. In fact, his fears about the interior of the woman's body were increased by the fact of her having no penis. In the male, "all was manifest and clearly visible and [he] concealed no secrets within himself, and was the natural and beautiful object" (EASB, 266). Klein tells us that Mr. B. also had repressed everything that had to do with the inside of his body and had concentrated his interest on all that was external and visible, especially the penis. Among his many symptoms, Klein also reported that he suffered from a "severe doubting-mania." This was in part due to an episode that went back to his childhood. In Klein's words, "when he was about five years old he had asked his nurse which she thought was worst—'in front or behind' (meaning penis or anus)—and had been very much taken aback when she had answered 'in front'" (266). Other memories associate his looking at himself—which in fact meant "looking inside himself" but had been repressed and displaced onto his "outside"—and hating his appearance, including items of clothing such as his underwear.

It is important to concentrate on one fragment of material that turns out to be central to my reading of the patient's melancholic homosexuality. According to Klein: "He also remembered when he was about eight years old standing at the top of the stairs and looking down them and hating himself and the black stockings he had on. His associations showed that the interior of his parents' house had always seemed specially gloomy to him—'dead', in fact—and that he held himself responsible for this gloominess—or rather for the destruction inside his mother's body and his own, symbolized by the gloomy house—which he had brought about by his dangerous excrements (the black stockings)" (EASB, 266–67). The connections that Klein establishes among the black stockings, excrements, and damaging effects seem to me to go beyond that. There is a highly charged term, the adjective *dead*, which is all too quickly read and tempered as *damaged*. Black is the color associated with death and mourning. This scene of the parental house is far too overdetermined for us to be able to decode it in just one (Klein's) reading. Adjectives like *black, gloomy,* and *dead*, distressingly and disquietingly paint a deadening interior landscape where not only danger but death lurk. But whose death is it? How can the subject in this scene discern what has been lost in his ego? And how, by way of his own survival as a monument to this loss, can he preserve his beloved object if not inside himself? I wish to suggest that this scenario of solitude, depressive anxiety, and the desire for symbolic reparation can act as the Kleinian primal scene of male homosexuality as fundamentally melancholic. Identifications—in this case between his mother's body and his own—emphatically operate by way of a loss, a dispossession. The subject finds no comfort in the parental house—he in fact has no home—which is felt to be both alien and terrifying. This desire for symbolic reparation born out of guilt—the subject holds himself responsible for the destruction in his mother's body and his own—marks the beginning of the depressive position, a "melancholia in statu nascendi" ([1935] 1975, 345) to use Klein's own terms. The image of this "unfathomability" that characterizes the inside of our bodies is a trope that is compulsively repeated and haunts the text. Desire is born out of this "fathom," elusive and irretrievable but always in circulation. Later in this case study the imagery of the house will recur again, taking up from the symbolics of loss the idea of the absence (or the existence) of faulty or fragile foundations in the building of the subject's homosexual position. Reparation must be previously and primarily made to the subject's own body.[20]

There is another highly significant episode in this case, that of the analysand's seduction by his elder brother. At this point, the traumatic nature of sexuality is writ large. Klein tells us that Mr. B. had two elder brothers, David, four years older than himself—and born from the father's former marriage—and Leslie, about two years his senior. Leslie had seduced the patient when he was two years old, and this was fundamental in his adoption of "a homosexual attitude." Klein writes: "Since the act of fellatio gratified his hitherto starved oral-sucking desires, this event led him to become too excessively fixated on the penis" (EASB, 267). The circumstances of the scene of seduction remain unclear since Klein does not provide us with further information.[21] Another factor was that his father—who had been rather "undemonstrative" until then—grew more affectionate toward him. The patient regarded this as a victory in his effort to turn his father's bad penis into a good one.

Mr. B. deeply admired and loved Leslie—he made him the representative of the "good" penis—and showed much disdain and contempt for David.[22] This was in part due to David's masochistic attitude and Mr. B's great mental superiority over him, which finally made him the symbol of the "bad" penis and the target of his brother's sadistic attacks. Klein's analysand never came to like David and felt guilty for his cruel and sadistic behavior toward his brother. Klein says that both of Mr. B's brothers were substitutes for his parent-imagos. In the patient's phantasy world, his relations with his imagos were just the opposite of those he had in reality. Whereas the patient loved his mother much more than his father, "he was possessed in fantasy, as we know, by imagos of the magical 'good' penis (his father) and of the terrifying mother" (EASB, 268). This is indeed one of the clearest examples in Klein's writing of phantasy's complex and subversive power to invert and overturn the categories of the real.

A number of external factors also contributed to Mr. B's adoption of homosexuality. We do not know much about the patient's mother. Of course, she was very fond of him, but, as is usually the case in analytic literature, she had "a very marked love of order and cleanliness" (EASB,

269). She was not really loving toward his father and "had an aversion to the male genital in general" (268). She was probably frigid and most likely disapproved of her youngest son's sexual desires. Unfortunately, Mr. B's mother has too many things in common with Dora's mother—from Freud's *Fragment of an analysis of a case of hysteria* ([1901, 1905] 1953). Furthermore, the seduction—as in Dora's case—was orally performed as well.[23] To put it briefly, if we recall the analysand's traumatic reaction to his nurse's condemnatory answer we can easily conclude that he had been raised in an atmosphere of feminine aversion to sex. Another factor that hindered Mr. B's establishment of a heterosexual position was the fact he had no female playmates in early childhood. No doubt, his fear of the mysterious interior of the woman's body would have been lessened if he had, for he could have satisfied his curiosity concerning female genitals much earlier. As unusual as it may appear, Klein reports that "it was not until he was about twenty years old that, on looking at a picture of a naked woman, he first consciously realized in what respect the female body differed from the male" (EASB, 269). His ignorance about sexual matters had contributed to his rejection of the female as a sexual object.

A Faulty Superego

As was mentioned earlier in this chapter, in the development of the male individual toward the establishment of a heterosexual position, the centering of his sadistic omnipotence on his penis is a very important factor. In order to do that, his ego must have acquired sufficient capacity to tolerate the sadism and anxiety that typified earlier stages of his development. Klein remarks that this capacity was small in Mr. B. His genital impulses and feelings of guilt had come to the fore very early, and they soon brought with them a good relationship with his objects and a satisfactory adaptation to reality. Nevertheless, his prematurely strengthened ego had repressed his sadistic impulses—especially those directed toward his mother—so that they could not make sufficient contact with his real objects. They remained for the most part attached to his phantastic imagos. In Klein's words, this situation was because "B's unsuccessful super-ego formation (i.e., the overstrong action of his earliest anxiety-formations) had not only led to severe disorders in his mental health, to an impairment of his sexual development and to an inhibition of his capacity to work, but was the reason why his object-relationships, while in themselves good, were at times subjected to grave disturbances" (EASB, 269). The patient was dominated by a profound fear of his bad phantastic imagos, and he believed he could not restore his mother by means of his good penis in the sexual act. His hatred of his father's penis—together with all external factors that have been discussed so far—had to be in part overcompensated for by a belief in the "good" penis, and this formed the basis of his homosexual position.

Very early Mr. B developed a great admiration for the penises of other boys, together with a feeling that his own penis was inferior and "ugly."[24] His erotic life was dominated by two types of object: one having to do with the relationship he had with his brother David and the other concerning his relationship with Leslie.[25] Apparently, both types served to gratify Mr. B's restitutive tendencies and allay his anxiety. The restorative potential of homosexuality is stressed by Klein when, referring to her patient's choice of objects of love, she states that Mr. B had no conscious sense of guilt or inferiority about his homosexual activities. He had early come to admire the penises of other boys almost to the point of "worship" (EASB, 270). It is quite obvious that the patient's faulty superego formation is fundamental in this question. Nevertheless, this is not to say that the demands of his superego were totally ineffective. In fact, Klein tells us: "The standards imposed by his super-ego upon his sexual activities were very high. In copulation he had to make good every single thing he had destroyed inside his mother" (271–72).

In his relationships with David-type partners, copulating meant restoring his father's and his brother David's penises, which he imagined as having been previously destroyed. He identified himself with his inferior and castrated object, so that his hatred of that object was also directed toward himself, and his restitution of the penis of that object implied a restitution of his own. On the other hand, in Mr. B's relationships with the Leslie type he was concerned with the "perfect" penis—proof that his own penis was perfect, too. In this relationship with the admired penis, Mr. B's sadistic impulses found an unconscious outlet, for here as well his homosexual activities signified a castration of his loved object, partly out of jealousy and partly because he wanted to get hold of his good penis so as to be able in all respects to take his father's place with his mother. Klein once again stresses instability and the near impossibility of ever attaining a fully established sexual position: "Although B's homosexual position had been established so early and so strongly, and although he consciously rejected a heterosexual one, he had always unconsciously kept the heterosexual aims in view towards which, as a small boy, he had striven so ardently in his imagination" (EASB, 271).

The analysand's crisis occurred after a series of losses in the family. First, Leslie lost his life in an accident. Then David fell ill, and while he was being nursed by Mr. B he died. In Klein's words, Leslie's death "did not break [him] down mentally" (EASB, 272). David's death was the "blow that shattered him and brought on his illness" (272). The fact that he had a strong sense of guilt toward his eldest brother and that his belief that he could restore the damaged penis had been undermined determined his abandonment of any hope that he could restore his mother's, and ultimately his own, body. This also resulted in his severe inhibition in his work and in an unsurmountable obstacle for his sublimatory tendencies. Klein relates that her patient remained in his unconscious a slave to his preoccupation with his mother's health, "although, as he said himself, she was not ill, but 'delicate' " (272). If, according to Klein, the impossibility of introjecting (i.e., identifying himself with) a good mother-imago is on the basis of male homosexuality, it is evident that in this case the patient's identifications as an ill (crippled, useless, unable to perform sex) and "delicate" (sissy, homosexual) individual back up her argument.

The impossibility of mourning his eldest brother—what he himself had lost in him—together with mourning that lost part of his body—destroyed by his sadistic attacks turned back upon himself as a consequence of an external frustration—are to be considered the cause of his melancholia. In Klein's only narrative of adult male homosexuality, the symbolics of loss and its trope of melancholia, as figured in bodies that are dispossessed by a law that inflicts violence and imposes guilt, allow us to postulate that homosexuality and melancholia appear to be inextricably linked in a heterocentric and heterosexist system of sexual difference.

The patient's continual phantasy that he would never see his mother again translated in the transference situation into his fear that he would never see his analyst again because she would be knocked down and run over by a car in a crowded street. For Klein, this was a familiar scenario, for it appeared in many of her analyses of children. The movement of cars represented the act of copulation between Mr. B's parents—in phantasy fatal to both parties—and made him prey to the fear that both he and his mother would be wrecked by his father's dangerous penis. Hence he possessed a manifest fear that she and he would be run over by a car.

Klein's narrative of Mr. B's case study is haunted by compulsive repetitions of what I have identified as melancholia and its symbolics of loss. At this point in the story, Klein tells of one of her patient's most frequent phantasies: "In contrast to his native town, which he thought of as a dark, lifeless and ruined place in spite of the fact—or because of the fact, as it became clear—that there was a lot of traffic there (i.e., continual copulation between his father and mother), he pictured an imaginary city full of life, light and beauty, and sometimes found his vision realized, though only for a short time, in the cities he visited in other countries. This far-off visionary city represented his mother once more made whole and reawakened to a new life, and also his own restored body" (EASB, 273). The former imagery of the parental house, gloomy and dead—together with his mother's body and his own brought to "ruin" by his dangerous excrements (267)—is now recast in the shape of this dark, lifeless, and ruined native place where his parents do not cease to copulate. The phantasy of excessive and continual heterosexual copulation (as figured by the parents or the cultural image repertoire at large) unveils a deficit in the cultural representation of homosexuality. His alternative is the vision of an imaginary far-off city with opposite features, which he at times had seen in foreign cities. It is highly significant that this figuration of bodies—which were dead and impossible to mourn?—reawakened to a new life, these bodies wounded and almost destroyed, could now be effectively restored in some foreign places. For the male (and female) homosexual, the diasporic operation of moving to a foreign land represents the possibility of liberation from social constraints that are most strongly regulated at home. Diaspora and exile—understood as a dispossession of one's own land—are thus fundamental conditions of homosexuality.

During the time when Mr. B was still able to work, he was engaged in writing a book in which he set down the results of his scientific researches. This book, which he had to give up writing when his inhibition in teaching grew too strong, had the same meaning for him as the beautiful city. His sublimation via creativity represented his unimpaired mother and his own restored body. Mr. B showed hypochondriacal symptoms as well, one of them being a feeling of immense emptiness. On the intellectual plane, it took the form of a complaint that things that were valuable, beautiful, and interesting to him lost their value, "wore out," and were taken away from him in some way.

For Klein, the most powerful motivating force in the patient's creative work came from his feminine position. In his unconscious, this meant that not until his body was filled with good objects could he create, that is, bring children into the world. When the analysand took up his book again after being in analysis for fourteen months, his identification with his mother came to the fore very clearly. As a small child, his infantile sexual desires could only be satisfied when he was able to change his sex and become a girl: "He remembered that when he was a small boy he longed to be a girl consciously, because he knew that his mother preferred a daughter; but, unconsciously, he could then have loved her sexually as well" (EASB, 274). At present, despite his identification with his mother, he was not able to maintain the feminine position. This was a great stumbling block standing in the way of his creative activities, which had always to some extent been inhibited. Klein argues: "As his identification with his mother and his desire to be a woman became more prominent in his analysis his inhibition in work gradually diminished" (274–75). His work in writing his book and that invested in intellectual activities in general were likened in his unconscious to restoring the inside of his body and creating children. As soon as he was able to adopt and sublimate this feminine position, his masculine components became more effective and fruitful in his work. In proportion, as his belief in his good mother grew stronger and his hypochondria and depressions became less intense, B became increasingly able to carry on with his work, and "Hand in hand with this there went a steady diminution of his homosexual impulses" (275). In this phase, as his adoration for the penis lessened he also experienced the fear that his father's "bad" internalized penis had got possession of his own and was controlling it from within. This fear had arisen very strongly in puberty, when he came to think that he could not control his penis and that it was possessed by the devil. He attributed all of its transformations, such as changes in size and the like, to this. This fear contributed to his dislike of his own penis and to his feeling that it was inferior and destructive. His phantasy that his father's "bad" penis was always present when he had sex with his mother and forced him to commit bad actions worked against Mr. B's adoption of a heterosexual position. He kept himself away from women, and not until his fears had been analyzed was he able to resume work and fortify his heterosexual position.

It is almost impossible to track the way to homosexuality. Simply put, there is no single way, not even psychoanalytically speaking, and certainly not in Klein's narrative of the Oedipus conflict. Klein posits only one prerequisite for the attainment of the normal (i.e., the most common) heterosexual position, the supremacy of the good mother-imago, which helps the boy to overcome his sadism and works against all his various anxieties. Thus, it is not the threats posed by the punishing (always already paternal at this point) superego that determine heterosexuality but rather the predominance of a good mother-imago. In male homosexuality, this good mother-imago is felt to be lost.[26] There is a foreclosure of the image of the good mother effected by social constraints, in other words, by paternal interdiction. The good mother-imago can only be "good enough," not all good.[27] Otherwise, how would the social order be able to overcome its allure?

"Mr. B." is Klein's only narrative of a true melancholic homosexual. He had neither a good mother-imago nor a "successfully" formed superego. The circumstances surrounding his childhood are self-explanatory. In her clinical report, Klein writes: "The results so far were that his deep depressions and his inhibition in work, had been almost completely removed and his obsessional symptoms and the paranoid and hypochondriacal anxiety considerably diminished. These results justify us, I think, in believing that a further period of treatment will enable him fully to establish a heterosexual position" (EASB, 276–77). Klein leaves the analysis open. She tells us that at this point her patient had to go back to America to settle his affairs but that he intended to return for further treatment (276). There is no further mention of the case in her subsequent works. There has been no effort on the part of the analytical community—as in the cases of Dora, the Wolf Man, and Schreber—to learn the whereabouts of the man or provide the last details about him. Male homosexuality as observed and analyzed by a woman is not an issue about which one makes much fuss.

Klein did not fall into the traps of the *furor curandi* and the pathologization of homosexuality by which most of her contemporaries were driven. In the genital stage, the boy's desire to restore his mother's and his own body interact and are a precondition for his attainment of sexual potency. The boy needs to believe in the "good" contents of his body, and this coincides with his belief in his capacity to love. Upon attainment of the full genital level, the boy returns in copulation to his original source of pleasure, his mother, who now gives him genital pleasure as well. Klein concludes her case study with a highly ambiguous scenario: "The anxiety and sense of guilt that are still present in him have increased and deepened and lent shape to his primary libidinal impulses as an infant at the breast, giving his attitude towards his object all that wealth and fullness of feeling which we call love" (EASB, 277–78). So the genital level of sexual organization is always already traversed by regression. To what extent can we say that the stage of partial object love is ever overcome? To what extent can full love of genitality be called whole object love when it is modeled on the pattern of the infant trying to make reparation for his or her sadistic attacks on the mother? The ambiguity comes once again to the forefront when Klein writes that the boy gives his mother "his 'wholesome' semen which shall endow her with children, restore her body and afford her oral satisfaction as well" (277). A strong sense of craving orality is reedited in full genitality. But in this case, and by displacement, the boy's penis stands in for the source of satisfaction—which will end up being the source of frustration as well. It seems as if the narrative of the circuitous route to (melancholic) male homosexuality was constantly undermined and subverted by heterosexual phantasies.

Klein attached great importance to the developing child's ability to pass successfully through predominantly homosexual and heterosexual phantasies in his or her development, this being in her view an essential background for normal sexual development. Her emphasis on the central role of phantasy in psychic life, on the idea of positions rather than phases, and on specific and individual modes of mastering anxiety situations allows a flexibility and openness—there is no such a thing as a movement forward or backward, but a constant interaction—which set sexuality free from any aprioristic teleological notion.

Nevertheless, it is crucial to acknowledge why the male homosexual position (and, as we have argued before, the feminine, feminine masochist, and female homosexual positions) is inextricably linked to melancholia from the start. What is it that gets lost in homosexuality and is always longed for? I would argue that the individual in a homosexual position needs to mourn the loss of his or her homosexual phantasy—or tendency—of a perfect relationship with the internal object (the good breast or the good penis in their phantasy versions, respectively), one that is undisturbed and unthreatened by external dangers or external persecutors. Through what I have called, inspired by Klein, the foreclosure of the image of the good mother and what it entails, the risk of being deprived of our private good internal object forever, male and female homosexuals and women and feminine masochists are particularly prone to melancholia. The Kleinian depressive position is "a melancholia in statu nascendi," that is, we may be able to work through it or not. Homosexuality is always moving on the dangerous edge between melancholia and the law, a super-egoic law whose internalization always comes as a prohibiting stance and whose intensity and cruelty are measured against the individual alone. The superego behaves with particular severity and harshness when the individual deviates from the social and moral norm determined by the patriarchal regime of compulsory heterosexuality.

5

Kleinian Melancholia

We know that painful experiences of all kinds sometimes stimulate sublimations, or even bring out quite new gifts in some people, who may take to painting, writing or other productive activities under the stress of frustrations and hardships. . . . Such enrichment is in my view gained through processes similar to those steps in mourning which we have just investigated.—Melanie Klein

In 1935, with the publication of Klein's "A contribution to the psycho-genesis of manic-depressive states" ([1935] 1975), her first major theoret-ical paper, the harmony between Klein's work and that of members of the British Psychoanalytical Society began to dissolve. Klein began to challenge major Freudian theoretical assumptions, although she argued she was only elaborating on them. Her formulation of the early Oedipus complex and early emergence of the superego—during the first year of life—together with her emphasis on pre-oedipal developmental events marked the begin-ning of a period of tension that reached its peak in the sessions known as the Controversial Discussions held at the British Psychoanalytical Society between 1941 and 1945.

"A contribution to the psychogenesis of manic-depressive states" ([1935] 1975) is a groundbreaking essay in which Klein sets out to map the territories of her new theories, bringing to the fore in a systematic way notions such as unconscious phantasy, internal objects, anxiety, aggres-sion, introjection, and projection. She explores the ego's changing rela-tionships with its internalized and external objects and the fluctuations of early psychotic paranoid and depressive anxieties. What is most remarkable is the way in which she elaborates on two interwoven theories, a theory of early development and a theory of the origin of manic depressive illness, so that this essay must also be read as a major contribution to the study of psychosis. She begins by summarizing some of her earlier findings as these are laid out in *The psycho-analysis of children*. She holds that the first year of life in the child is characterized by a phase of maximum sadism. The development of the child is governed by the mechanisms of introjection and projection. From the beginning, the ego introjects "good" and "bad" objects on the model of the mother's breast—perceived as good if satisfying and as bad if frustrating. These imagos, which are a phantasy picture of the real objects upon which they are based, become installed not only in the outside world but, by the process of incorporation, within the ego.[1] Klein states that little children pass through anxiety situations whose contents are comparable to those of psychoses in adults. One of the earliest modes of defense against the dread of persecutors—external or internal—is that of *scotomization* or denial of psychic reality. This mechanism is the basis of the most severe psychoses. Scotomization is followed by processes of expulsion and projection. Acute dread of internalized persecutors that cannot be overcome by projection forms the basis of paranoia.

In this essay, Klein deals directly with depressive states in their relation to paranoia and mania. She follows Freud and Abraham in considering that the fundamental process at work in melancholia is the loss of the loved object: "The real loss of a real object, or some similar situation having the same significance, results in the object becoming installed within the ego. Owing, however, to an excess of cannibalistic impulses in the subject, this introjection miscarries and the consequence is illness" (M-DS, 263). Melancholia is thus the aborted introjective movement brought about by an excess of sadism in the oral cannibalistic stage. The effects of the miscarriage of introjection are harbored inside as remnants, as residual by-products of a thwarted labor of love.[2] Metaphors of death and dying objects bleakly color this scenario: "Both in children and adults suffering from depression, I have discovered the dread of harbouring dying or dead objects (especially the parents) inside one and an identification of the ego with objects in this condition" (266). Throughout this essay, Klein uses *introjection* and *incorporation* interchangeably, but we must be aware that in all these cases she is referring to a failure in introjection.[3]

Early anxiety situations and defense mechanisms are crucial to ego development and the ego's relation to its objects. In her early work—

especially in *The psycho-analysis of children*—Klein postulated that the primary function of the ego was the deflection of the death drive outward, toward an external object that was then feared as a persecutor through projection. In M-DS, she begins to view the introjection of the good object as the foundation of the ego. There is no exhaustive description of the primitive ego. Nevertheless, we know that it is at first very loosely organized, still uncoordinated partly because the introjected objects are still mainly partial objects—equated at that time with feces. As the ego becomes more fully organized, its imagos will approximate reality more closely and the ego will identify more fully with "good" objects. From then on, preservation of the good object is regarded as synonymous with the survival of the ego (264).

So first there is an operation of distortion at the level of the subject's perceptive apparatus and second a corrective mimetic operation by way of resemblance. Good objects always already exist as simulacra—they exist by way of a metaphoric substitution of an originally lost good object—bad objects are primary and are born out of the child's innate aggressivity.[4] Parallel to this development in the ego there is a change in the ego's relationship with its objects, which shift from partial to whole. Klein argues that the loss of the loved object takes place precisely during that phase of development in which the ego makes the transition from partial to total incorporation of the object and that the precondition for feeling the loss of the loved object as a whole is that it be loved *as a whole*. Later, in "Notes on some schizoid mechanisms" ([1946] 1975), Klein will add that sometimes internal objects act as foreign bodies embedded in the self, and even if this is more obvious with regard to the bad objects it may also be the case with good ones "if the ego is compulsively subordinated to their preservation. When the ego serves its good internal objects excessively, they are felt as a source of danger to the self and come close to exerting a persecuting influence" (SM, 9).

With this change in the relationship with the object, new anxiety situations appear. Paranoid anxiety, with its fear that the objects sadistically destroyed would be a source of poison and danger inside the subject's body, causes the child to be profoundly mistrustful of objects while still incorporating them. This leads to a weakening of oral desires.[5] Klein argues that an important stimulus for an increase of introjection is the phantasy that the loved object may be preserved in safety inside oneself—in this case, the dangers of the inside are projected onto the external world. However, an additional anxiety that the object may be destroyed in the process of introjection leads to disturbances of the function of this mechanism.

According to Abraham's hypothesis, the expulsion of the object—characteristic of the earlier anal level—initiates the depressive mechanism. This confirms Klein's idea of the "genetic connection between paranoia and melancholia" (M-DS, 265), and it constitutes one of the central arguments of this volume. Klein goes on: "In my opinion, the paranoiac mechanism of destroying the objects (whether inside the body or in the outside world), by every means derived from oral, urethral and anal sadism, persists but still in a lesser degree and with a certain modification due to the change in the subject's relation to his objects. As I have said, the dread lest the *good* object should be expelled along with the *bad* causes the mechanisms of expulsion and projection to lose value. We know that, at this stage, the ego makes a greater use of introjection of the *good* objects as a mechanism of defence" (265). Paranoia and melancholia, in the Kleinian scenario, share the same myth of origins. This allows us to read homosexuality and its paranoid mechanisms of defense as melancholia and to read melancholia as constructed and dependent upon phantasies of homosexuality. Homosexuality as the repressed and disposable Other of psychoanalysis thus comes to occupy a privileged place in the theorization of the subject's organization of its internal world by securing a safe haven for the preservation of the good object, an object of love that is under the threat of annihilation for being abject or improper (as in deviant sexualities), or for being disputed due to rivalry (as in jealousy or envy in heterosexuality, primarily in the Oedipal scenario) and likely to be lost. In Klein's words, "The processes which subsequently become clear as the 'loss of the loved object' are determined by the subject's sense of failure (during weaning and in the periods which precede and follow it) to secure his *good, internalized* object, i.e. to possess himself of it. One reason for this failure is that he has been unable to overcome his paranoid dread of internalized persecutors" (267). In other words, an excess of paranoia leads to melancholia and melancholia is always paranoid at its origin.

Klein's views differ from those of orthodox Freudian psychoanalysis at this point. The great importance attributed to early processes of introjection leads her to conclude that "the earliest incorporated objects form the basis of the super-ego and enter into its structure" (M-DS, 267).[6] The superego of the melancholic is characterized by its relentless severity (267). And we can say that the extremely sadistic Kleinian superego is the concept that best translates the Freudian formulation "a pure culture of the death instinct" (Freud [1923] 1953, 53). Klein inscribes the origin of bad conscience in a battleground where the ego feels "prey to contradictory and impossible claims from within" (M-DS, 268) and where the persecutions and demands of bad internalized objects—and their violent attacks upon one another—and the need to fulfill the demands of the good objects and protect and placate them within the ego result in the hatred of the id.[7] She speaks of the "earliest utterances of conscience" and their association with persecution by bad objects: "The very word 'gnawing of conscience' (Gewissensbisse) testifies to the relentless 'persecution' by conscience and to the fact that it is originally conceived of as devouring its victim" (268). Conscience is thus present in a voice. It first interpellates an ego and then sets out to persecute it up to the point of devouring it. The insatiable appetite of conscience shows in the incommensurability of its demands with the precarious existence and capacities of the early ego. We may draw an analogy between the Kleinian scenario of bad conscience and the Althusserian doctrine of interpellation, where the latter comes to be restaged in an embattled intrapsychic domain where superego and id torture an ego that is born as a contradictory terrain of contending forces where good and bad objects, anxiety situations, and defense mechanisms violently interact.[8] Conscience both makes the ego and devours it. Interpellation takes an oral-cannibalistic element that renders it complicit with the violence of a law that phagocytes its subjects. Conscience is primarily and fundamentally bad conscience, and the ego is torn between the cruel demands and admonitions of both its good and bad objects. In this parable of sadomasochistic content, the ego simultaneously submits to slavery while complying with the extremely cruel demands of its objects and resists slavery through its endeavors to exert its incipient capacity of judgment (reality testing), keeping the good apart from the bad and the real away from the phantastic objects.

Klein acknowledges how difficult it is to draw a sharp line between the anxiety content and feelings of the paranoiac and those of the depressive or melancholic since they are closely linked.[9] She states that when the persecution anxiety is related to the preservation of the ego it is paranoiac in nature; when it is related to the preservation of the good internalized objects—with which the ego is identified as a whole—it is depressive.

For Klein, only when the ego has introjected the object as a whole, and has established a better relationship to the external world and to real people, is it able to realize the devastating effects of its sadism and cannibalism and to feel distressed about it. The anxiety situations that derive from the ego's confrontation with the psychic reality of its damaged good objects are at the bottom of depression and all inhibitions of work. The ego faces its good objects in a state of disintegration—in a state of dissolution in bits (M-DS, 269). The bits and fragments to which they have been reduced and the effort to put them back together are crucial for the work of sublimation. Thus, in Kleinian parlance *sublimation* means first and foremost reparation in the sense of making whole, to avoid disintegration by restoring the perfection of the primal form. In Klein's words, "The idea of perfection is, moreover, so compelling because it disproves the idea of disintegration" (270). The emphasis on the idea of the restoration of the perfect and beautiful form is no doubt one of the central tenets of Kleinian aesthetic theory and one of its major contributions to modernist discourse.[10] In this respect, it is important to note how phantasy in the psychic as much as in the aesthetic domain operates an effect of trompe l'oeil that has powerful repercussions in the specific workings of sublimation: "In some patients who had turned away from their mother in dislike or hate, or used other mechanisms to get away from her, I have found that there existed in their minds nevertheless a beautiful picture of the mother, but one which was felt to be a *picture* of her only, not her real self. The real object was felt to be unattractive—really an injured, incurable and therefore dreaded person. The beautiful picture had been dissociated from the real object but had never been given up, and played a great part in the specific ways of their sublimations" (270).[11] The vicissitudes of the visual in the numerous avant-garde and modernist cultural practices of the 1920s and 1930s—cubism, dadaism, surrealism, and *neue stijl* in art and literature—provide excellent examples against which to test the implications of Klein's insight.

The Depressive Position: A Melancholic Retreat?

In the Kleinian account of the psychogenesis of manic-depressive states, melancholia shifts progressively into depressive states and the depressive position. The ego comes to be aware of its love for a good object as a whole object with "an overwhelming feeling of guilt towards it" (M-DS, 270). Full identification with the object is based on the libidinal attachment, first to the breast and then to the whole person. It goes hand in hand with anxiety over it (fear of its disintegration) and guilt, remorse, and a sense of responsibility, "whether conscious or unconscious" (M-DS, 270). For Klein, all these emotions are among the essential elements of the feelings we call love.

In Klein's comparison between the paranoiac and the depressive—or melancholic—she further adds that, although the paranoiac has also introjected a whole and real object, he or she has not been able to achieve full identification with it. Or the individual has not been able to maintain it, mostly because the persecution anxiety is too great and it works against the full and stable introjection of a real good object. In any case, the main differences we can elicit from the comparison between the paranoiac and the depressive are best illustrated in the specific instances Klein refers to in her essay. For example, with regard to the issue of disintegration, the depressive is filled with sorrow and anxiety for the object, which he will strive to unite again into a whole, while to the paranoiac the disintegrated object is mainly a multitude of persecutors (each piece grows into a persecutor). For Abraham, these pieces were interpreted as part objects and equated with feces.[12] Klein finally argues that the depressive state is based on the paranoid state and is genetically derived from it (M-DS, 275). In a footnote she explains why she needs to introduce the notion of "position" instead of "phase." In her former work, she had described the psychotic anxieties and defense mechanisms of the child in terms of phases of development, but since they never predominate solely by themselves the term *psychotic phases* is no longer satisfactory. *Position* is a much better term, allowing differentiation between the developmental psychotic anxieties of the child and the psychoses of the adult. Thus, for Klein the depressive position arises out of a full and stable identification of the ego with its introjected object. This identification is always empathic.

Klein gives a full explanation of suicide, and the question of melancholia comes to the fore. In some cases, the phantasies underlying suicide aim to preserve the internalized good objects and that part of the ego that is identified with good objects and also aim to destroy the part of the ego that is identified with the bad objects and the id. Thus, the ego is able to unite with its loved objects. In other cases, suicidal phantasies relate to the external world and real objects. In committing suicide, the subject may want to rid itself of some real object—or the "good" object that whole world represents and with which the ego is identified—of itself or rid itself of that part of the ego that is identified with its bad objects and its id.

According to Klein, this is largely responsible for that state of mind in the melancholic who breaks off all relations with the external world.

At bottom, we perceive in the suicide of the melancholic a reaction to his or her sadistic attacks on the mother's body, the first representative of the outside world for the child. Klein concludes: "Hatred and revenge against the real (good) objects also always play an important part in such a step, but it is precisely the uncontrollable dangerous hatred, which is perpetually welling up in him, from which the melancholic by his suicide is in part struggling to preserve his real objects" (M-DS, 276–77). The Kleinian portrait of the melancholic as enraged hero is intimately bound up with reparative phantasies. The suicide of the melancholic is essentially an act of love that aims to save and preserve his or her objects, not only from the threats and dangers of the outside world but from his or her own sadism and hatred. The melancholic thus sees himself or herself as potentially dangerous, and the oxymoronic desire to die is also a desire to go on living in the good objects. Nevertheless, this desire for continuity is deceptive, as it is based on a misrecognition of the essential discontinuity between the ego and its objects and stems from a fundamentally simulacral stance, that of melancholia.

In her discussion of mania, Klein suggests that the ego seeks refuge not only from melancholia but from a paranoiac condition that it is unable to master. The ego strives to find freedom from the excessive dependence of its loved objects and at the same time finds itself pursued by its dread of bad objects and the id. Therefore, the ego must defend itself by recourse to different mechanisms. The sense of omnipotence is what first and foremost characterizes mania, and mania is based on the mechanism of denial.[13] In Klein's view, denial arises very early in development. What is denied is psychic reality, and from there the ego may proceed to deny a great deal of external reality. Specific to mania is the utilization of the sense of omnipotence for the purpose of controlling and mastering objects. The evidence of this effort shows in the ego's hyperactivity.

Manic defenses assume many forms.[14] In phantasies, maniacs kill their objects, but because they are omnipotent they can also immediately call them to life again. One of Klein's patients used the felicitous expression "keep the objects in suspended animation" (M-DS, 278), which evokes both the destruction (defense mechanism) and later resuscitation of the objects (reparative move).

As Freud noted, in mania the ego and ego-ideal come to coincide.

Klein approaches this Freudian argument from her own angle. She states that the ego incorporates the object in a cannibalistic way (the "feast," as Freud calls it in his account of mania) but denies that it feels any concern for it. Mania is characterized by an insatiable hunger for objects, and the maniac does not care if a particular object is destroyed since many others can be incorporated. For Klein, the disparagement of the object's importance and contempt for it are specific characteristics of mania. There is a partial detachment of the ego side by side with its hunger for objects. Such detachment, which is impossible to achieve in the depressive position, represents a fortification of the ego in relation to its objects, but this advance is counteracted by the same mechanisms that the ego employs in mania—denial or scotomization, omnipotence, and phantasies of mastery and control. Klein ends by referring to the three positions (paranoid, depressive, and manic) that interact in normal development.

Splitting, Ambivalence, and the Depressive Position

In The psychoanalysis of children, Klein studied the role of early anxiety situations and object relations in the development of the child and the continuous interplay between his or her actual experiences and phantasy life. Again, in "A contribution to the psychogenesis of manic-depressive states," Klein stresses the importance of external factors, especially a good relationship with the mother and the external world. In the normal course of events, between four and five months of age the ego is forced to acknowledge psychic as well as external reality to a certain degree. The infant relates to real objects and its unreal imagos, and these two kinds of object relations intermingle and color each other in the course of development. For Klein, the fact that the child comes to know its mother as a whole person—the child becomes identified with her as a whole, real, and loved person—is a crucial step in development that leads to the attainment of the depressive position. The depressive position is melancholic because it "is stimulated and reinforced by the 'loss of a loved object' which the baby experiences over and over again when the mother's breast is taken away from it, and this loss reaches its climax during weaning" (M-DS, 286).

Klein cites Radó's essay "The problem of melancholia" (1928) and differs from his conclusions in significant ways, especially in his belief that guilt becomes connected to the early experiences of the child.[15] For Klein, in the passage from the paranoid to the depressive position the infant experiences "in a lesser and milder degree" some of the feelings of guilt, remorse, pain, and the accompanying anxieties that we find fully developed in the adult melancholic. If the infant at this period of life fails to establish its loved object within, then the situation of the loss of the loved object arises in the same sense as it is found in the adult melancholic.

It is also at this stage of development that manic phantasies set in, first of controlling the breast and very soon after of controlling the internalized parents as well as the external ones, with all the characteristics of the manic position. These are used to combat the depressive position. The conflict at the core of the depressive position is that between love and uncontrollable hatred and sadism. For Klein, the more the child at this stage can develop a happy relationship with its real mother, the better it will be able to overcome the depressive position.

In the paranoid position, the good and bad objects are kept far apart in the child's mind. When at the onset of the depressive position, with the introjection of the whole and real object, good and bad come closer together, the ego must resort to splitting. Splitting is a crucial mechanism in the development of the ego's relationship with objects, in that it divides imagos into loved and hated and good and dangerous ones. It is also at this point that ambivalence sets in. It is carried out in a splitting of the imagos, and it enables the child to gain more trust and belief in his or her real and internalized objects and to direct paranoid anxieties and defenses toward bad objects. As the adaptation to the external world increases and splitting is carried out on planes that are nearer to reality, ambivalence diminishes.[16]

In the normal process of overcoming the infantile depressive position, reparation phantasies play a very important part. They are set in motion by different methods. The two most fundamental of these are the manic and obsessional defenses and mechanisms. There are two other ways in which the ego attempts to put an end to the suffering connected to the depressive position, namely, by means of a "flight to the 'good' internalized object" (the extreme result being the denial of psychic and external reality and thus psychosis) and by a flight to external "good" objects as a means of disproving all anxieties, both internal and external (the extreme result is a slavish dependence on objects and weakness of the ego). Failure to successfully work through this position may lead to the predominance of one or another of these flight mechanisms and thus to a severe psychosis or neurosis. The infantile depressive position is the central position in the child's development. The normal development of the child and his or her capacity for love rests largely on the way the ego works through this position, and this depends on the modification of early anxiety situations—which remain at work in the adult—in the changing relationships of the ego with its objects, and especially on a successful interplay between the depressive, the manic, and the obsessional positions and mechanisms (M-DS, 289).

À La Recherche de l'Objet Perdu

the encountering and overcoming of adversity of any kind entails
mental work similar to mourning.—Melanie Klein

Happily for Swann, beneath the mass of new sufferings which had entered his soul like an invading horde, there lay a natural foundation, older, more placid, and silently industrious, like the cells of an injured organ which at once set to work to repair the damaged tissues, or the muscles of a paralysed limb which tend to recover their former movements. These older, more autochtonous inhabitants of his soul absorbed all Swann's strength, for a while, in that obscure task of reparation which gives one an illusory sense of repose during convalescence, or after an operation.—Marcel Proust

"Mourning and its relation to manic-depressive states" ([1940] 1975) follows up Klein's 1935 essay. It places mourning among the phenomena of the depressive position. Klein explores mourning in depth and connects it to her work on manic-depressive states. From the point of view of her general theory of development, this essay completes the exposition of the depressive position begun in 1935. Klein reminds us that in "Mourning and melancholia" Freud points out that an essential part of the work of mourning is the testing of reality, for "in mourning time is needed for the command of reality-testing to be carried out in detail, and that when this work has been accomplished the ego will have succeeded in freeing its libido from the lost object" ([1915, 1917] 1953, 252). For Klein, there is a close connection between the testing of reality in normal mourning and early processes at work in the psyche of the child. The most important method by which the child overcomes his or her states of mourning is precisely the testing of reality.

Klein rephrases her position in M-DS by stating that the depressive position is a melancholia in statu nascendi (MM-D, 345). Again, melancholia is literally born and finds its place in the world in the space of the depressive position. But, as we know, in its birth the introjective movement miscarries and in this aborted impulse melancholia is born as a failure in the (re)productive machinery of the ego. Introjection and projection are arrested, the object becomes encysted inside the ego, and the ego is overburdened with a gallery of stranded objects.[17] This pregnant ego of the melancholic, which is blocked in a claustrophobic space with its object(s), is the site where the battle between ego and object(s) will take place.

For Klein, the first object that is mourned is the mother's breast and all that it represents, love, satisfaction, and goodness. When the child feels it as lost, he launches his or her destructive phantasies against the mother's body. Further distress about loss—now of both parents—arises out of the Oedipus situation, at the beginning also dominated by oral impulses and fears. Progressively, the circle of loved objects that are attacked in phantasy widens, owing mostly to the child's ambivalent relations to his or her brothers and sisters. Aggression gives rise to feelings of guilt and loss.

The increase of love and trust and the diminishing of fears through happy experiences help the child overcome depression and feeling of loss (mourning). They enable the child to test his or her inner reality by means of outer reality. Along with this goes the child's attempt to firmly establish his or her inner "good" objects as a means of overcoming the depressive position. The fluctuations between the depressive and the manic position are an essential part of normal development. With regard to this, it is important to note that the mechanism of splitting, whose role in the depressive position was seen in 1935 as operating in more and more realistic planes in the unification of imagos, is now seen as the "all-important process of bringing together more closely the various aspects of objects (external, internal, 'good' and 'bad', loved and hated), and thus for hatred to become actually mitigated by love" (MM-D, 349).[18]

Klein describes at length the connections between obsessional mechanisms and manic defenses in their relation to the depressive position. Obsessional mechanisms are a defense as well as a way of modifying paranoid anxieties. They are mobilized when manic defenses fail. Obsessional mechanisms and manic defenses contribute to the ego's fear that the attempted reparation failed. Klein describes the vicious circle that is repeated when reparation is contaminated by the operations of mania and obsession: "The desire to control the object, the sadistic gratification of overcoming and humiliating it, of getting the better of it, the triumph over it, may enter so strongly into the act of reparation (carried out by thought, activities or sublimations) that the 'benign' circle started by this act becomes broken. . . . As a result of the failure of the act of reparation, the ego has to resort again and again to obsessional and manic defenses" (MM-D, 351). The feeling of triumph, closely bound up with contempt and omnipotence, is a characteristic element of the manic position. It deeply disturbs the process of reparation and impedes the work of early mourning. When in the course of normal development a relative balance between love and hate is attained, and the various aspects of objects are more unified, a certain equilibrium between these mechanisms is reached and their intensity is diminished.

Klein moves on to connect the infantile depressive position with normal mourning. According to Freud and Abraham, the loss of a loved person leads to an impulse in the mourner to reinstate the lost loved object inside the ego. In Klein's view, the mourner not only reincorporates the person whom he or she has just lost but also reinstates his or her internalized good objects—ultimately the good parents. Therefore, the pain experienced in the slow process of testing reality in the work of mourning seems to be due to the necessity not only to renew links to the external world—and thus, to reexperience their loss—but at the same time and by means of this to rebuild the inner world, which is felt to be in danger of collapsing.

The intense feeling of having triumphed over the dead one by surviving is, in Klein's view, symptomatic of a mourning process gone astray. Here she differs from Freud and sees triumph as a common constituent of the final phase of mourning.[19] The transitory states of elation that occur between sorrow and distress in normal mourning are manic in character and result from the feeling of possessing the perfect loved object (idealized) inside.

When in normal mourning grief is experienced to its fullest, love for the object wells up and the mourner feels that life will go on and the lost loved object can be preserved within. In Klein's view, at this stage in mourning suffering can become productive. She concludes that any pain caused by unhappy experiences, whatever their nature, has something in common with mourning and reactivates the infantile depressive position. The ability in later life to mourn and recover from mourning is contingent upon the resolution of the depressive position in childhood. This adds up to the Kleinian notion of sublimation. Painful experiences of all kinds sometimes stimulate sublimations; they may even "bring out quite new gifts in some people" (MM-D, 360). She explicitly refers to painting, writing, and other productive activities that may be undertaken under the stress of frustrations and hardships. The "enrichment" gained through these activities has something in common with the work of mourning. Reparation and its server, sublimation, are thus crucial to overcoming states of mourning.

Klein explicitly wants to link her contribution to those of Freud and Abraham. Abraham argued that the processes at work in melancholia also operate in the work of normal mourning. In his view, the mourner succeeds in establishing the lost loved person in his or her ego, while the melancholic fails to do so. Klein adds to this by saying that when the mourner sets up the lost loved object inside, he or she is not doing so for the first time. Through the work of mourning, the subject is reinstating that object as well as his or her loved *internal* objects, which are felt to be lost. The mourner is therefore *recovering* what had already been attained in childhood. This recuperative move is essential for understanding the Kleinian stance vis-à-vis psychic development and manic-depressive states or psychosis. In this respect, psychic development is experienced as growth when the individual has been able to establish his or her good internal objects and deal with paranoid and depressive anxieties, manic defenses, and obsessional mechanisms, in brief, when the ego has used every possible resource in its effort to overcome the depressive position. All subsequent losses that threaten the precarious stability of this psychic system can be mimetically negotiated, so to speak, *as if* the individual were reinstating his or her inner objects anew but with the backup of the memory that he or she once succeeded in doing it. The opposite holds true for manic-depressive states. The violence of sadistic impulses and paranoid anxieties does not leave room for establishing good (whole) internal objects. The individual is overwhelmed by the sense that there is nothing "good" to hold on to, nothing good inside, and therefore nothing to recuperate. The feeling of emptiness and nothingness that the melancholic exhibits is due to a failure in introjection and to the infinite doubts and uncertainties that assail a subject who was unable to firmly establish his or her good internal objects.

Klein thus suggests that the psychic system is always under construction. The flexibility of her notion of "positions" that fluctuate and interact resolves in a much better way the problem of providing a model for the psychic apparatus. The Kleinian psychic system is always in flux and unsettled, always in a precarious, contingent, and transitory unfinished state.

Klein differs from Freud on the nature of the superego and the history of its individual development. She takes up Freud's concept of the super-ego and radically transforms it. By introducing her idea of a very early superego, she significantly departs from the Freudian account in which the ego-ideal (and later the superego) is seen as "heir to the Oedipus complex" (Freud [1923] 1953, 36), Klein refers to the subject's inner world of objects to give her account of the origin of the superego: "This assembly of inter-nalized [good and bad] objects becomes organized, together with the or-ganization of the ego, and in the higher strata of the mind it becomes discernible as the super-ego. Thus, the phenomenon which was recog-nized by Freud, broadly speaking as the voices and the influence of the actual parents established in the ego is, according to my findings, a com-plex object-world, which is felt by the individual, in deep layers of the unconscious, to be concretely inside himself, and for which I and some of my colleagues therefore use the term 'internalised,' or an internal (inner) world" (MM-D, 362). To some extent, the superego could be considered to function as a substitute for the subject's relationship with external objects. Klein had postulated the existence of phantasy figures—or imagos—which now could be seen as superegos and thus as substitutes for external ob-jects. She relates her findings on the early superego to the work of mourn-ing. In her view, in normal mourning the individual reintrojects and rein-states as well as the actual lost person his or her loved parents, who are felt to be "good" inner objects. When the actual loss occurs, the inner world of the mourner is destroyed in phantasy, and it is the rebuilding of this inner world that characterizes the successful work of mourning.

The resolution of the depressive position is the essential prerequisite for the development of the capacity to grieve. Failure to do so may result in depressive illness (or melancholia), mania, or paranoia. There are, how-ever, many ways (based on obsessional, manic, and paranoid defenses) in which the individual can escape the sufferings connected with the depres-sive position. All of these mechanisms are at work and can be observed in the analyses of people who fail to experience mourning.[20]

Pathological mourning involves processes of reparation of phan-tasized damage to the object that have destructive consequences. Manic and omnipotent reparation are examples of a pathological need to repair the damaged object. Klein concludes by stressing that the fundamental difference between normal and abnormal mourning and manic-depressive states is that "The manic-depressive and the person who fails in the work of mourning . . . have this in common, that they have been unable in early childhood to establish their 'internal' good objects and to feel secure in their inner world. They have never really overcome the infantile depressive position" (MM-D, 369).

I would suggest that the Kleinian depressive position can be re-thought in terms of a theoretical phantasy that unveils the open and provisional nature of a system that avoids fixity and closure. Reparation and integration are only partial outcomes, never fully achieved, which bring about various ways of living with the damage. The subject is founded upon the reproduction of a failure and the repetition of defensive strategies involving many kinds of splitting and idealization, countered by efforts toward integration and reparation under the stimulus of what is yet to come.

Oedipal Melancholia

Klein's theorization on mourning and manic-depressive states and the discovery of the centrality of the depressive position in development adds to her version of the Oedipus complex as it is laid out in *The psycho-analysis of children*. In this respect, her essay "The Oedipus complex in the light of early anxieties" summarizes her views on the question, slightly modified according to her new findings ([1945] 1975). Her major aims in this essay are to explore the relationship between the depressive position and libidinal development and to compare her conclusions about the Oedipus complex with Freud's ideas on the subject. She illustrates her views with material drawn from two patients, Richard, the boy whose analysis was published in full in *Narrative of a child psycho-analysis* ([1961] 1975), and Rita, a girl, much of whose analysis had already appeared in previous papers.[21]

Klein stresses the fusion of libido and aggression from the beginning of life and the fact that the development of the libido is at every stage vitally affected by anxiety derived from aggressiveness. Anxiety, guilt, and depressive feelings at times move the libido forward to new sources of gratification; at other times the fixation on an earlier object and aim moves it in the opposite direction through the process of regression.

The breast relationship, with its gratifying and frustrating aspects, colors the infant's early experiences. For Klein, the nucleus of the super-ego is formed by the establishment within the ego of the imagos of the mother's breast and the father's penis, which constitute the first identifications that the ego develops. Klein also stresses the constant interaction between the early stages of the positive and the inverted Oedipus complex by virtue of "this movement to and fro between the various aspects of the primary imagos" (OCEA, 409). Klein now holds that "the core of infantile depressive feelings, i.e. the child's fear of the loss of his loved objects, as a consequence of his hatred and aggression, enters into his object relations and Oedipus complex from the beginning" (410). In other words, the onset of the Oedipus complex coincides with the onset of the depressive position. In the case of the boy, Klein clearly identifies a number of early anxieties from various sources that contribute to castration fear—such as fears about the inside of his body and fear of the combined parent figure in retaliation.

In the feminine phase, the boy wants to enter his own penis, thus not into the body of the mother but into that of the father. He wants to enter father and receive a baby from him. In the Kleinian account, this is the inverted Oedipus complex, which forms the basis of homosexuality—the attempt to have children with the father as the boy phantasizes the mother does. Phantasizing the penis as beneficial is a precondition of developing a positive oedipal phase. After the breast, the penis comes to the fore as the alternative object of choice. During this phase, the boy develops oral phantasies of incorporation of the penis through the anus and his own penis. With the incorporation of the penis, the boy begins to identify with the father. This incorporation strengthens heterosexuality and moderates sadism. The element of envy of his mother is also an element in the inverted Oedipus conflict of the boy. Not until the boy is able to introject the image of his father's penis as a good and creative organ can he develop his positive Oedipus desires. When anxiety diminishes and love predominates, he strives to make reparation first to his mother and then to his father and siblings.

Klein argues that in his "Analysis of a phobia in a five-year-old boy" ([1909a] 1953), Freud "has . . . not given enough weight to the crucial role of these feelings of love [for his father], both in the development of the Oedipus conflict and in its passing. In my experience the Oedipus situation loses in power not only because the boy is afraid of the destruction of his genital by a revengeful father, but also because he is driven by feelings of love and guilt to preserve his father as an internal and external figure" (OCEA, 418). As one can easily gather from this passage, Klein's account of the boy's Oedipus conflict is radically different from Freud's. The loosening up of the Oedipal law results in possibilities other than fear of retaliation and sets up the basis for all kinds of homosocial ties and homosexual love.

In the case of the girl, the fear of having the inside of her body injured or its contents taken away constitutes her main anxiety situation. Her negative Oedipus conflict also represents her feminine characteristics. In this way, identification with and homosexual urges toward the mother, who is phantasized as having a penis inside her, are enhanced. The early Oedipal phase of oral incorporation of the father's penis is associated with genital sensations, and the girl is not only concerned about her body and vagina but about her clitoris as well. Incorporation of the penis at this stage results in homosexuality. Also, if penis envy is strong, the girl's future rivalry with men will also be strong. If penis envy is moderate, the girl will start identifying herself with her mother (whom she phantasizes as copulating with the father and producing babies). She will also be able to have babies if she succeeds in her identification. If phallic rivalry is very intense, this will result in the development of an exclusive link to the mother and hatred of the father. The mother is seen as containing all desirable objects—breast, penis, babies—and the frustration of not obtaining the rivalrous penis pushes her psychosexual behavior toward a homosexual relationship, although her homosexual wishes may become sublimated later.

Envy of the mother forms part of the girl's positive Oedipus conflict. The bisexual element in libidinal development is also explicitly underscored: "The girl's desire to possess a penis and to be a boy is an expression of her bisexuality and is as inherent a feature in girls as the desire to be a woman is in boys" (OCEA, 414). The complexity of the feminine superego is disclosed by virtue of a double-sided work of identification in her inverted Oedipus.

> She identifies herself with her father in her male position, but this identification rests on the possession of an imaginary penis. Her main identification with her father is experienced in relation to the internalized penis of her father, and this relation is based on the feminine as well as on the male position. In the feminine position she is driven by her sexual desires, and by her longing for a child, to internalize her father's penis. She is capable of complete submission to this admired internalized father, while in the male position she wishes to emulate him in all her masculine aspirations and sublimations. Thus her male identification with her father is mixed with her feminine attitude, and it is this combination which characterizes the feminine super-ego. (414)

Klein posits the existence of an imaginary object, the "imaginary penis," on the basis of which the illusion of resemblance is constructed. The feminine superego is built upon a double identification, and here Klein seems to be taking things to an even higher level of complexity, since from the above quotation we can infer that the girl's relationship with the internalized father's penis is based on a masculine as well as a feminine position. For Klein, in the course of the Oedipal phase the girl and the boy constantly vacillate between homosexual and heterosexual positions.

Interestingly, the depressive position at the onset of the Oedipus conflict, which is characterized by identifications with whole good objects, encapsulates within itself masculine and feminine identifications that add layers of complexity to the questions of desire, identification, and sexuality along the lines of the Kleinian destabilization of the binary gender system. In this essay, written after the period of the Controversial Discussions, Klein marks her main differences with Freud in an attempt to demarcate and draw a sharp line between the Kleinian and Freudian groups.

We cannot separate Klein's theory of early development from that of the origin of manic-depressive illness and psychosis in general. Mourning and melancholia are at the heart of the Kleinian project, so there is no subject without an object that is already lost. Kleinian theory is an intrinsically melancholic theory that seeks to restore, by way of every subsequent loss, a world of good internal objects in an incorporative and a reparative manner.

This is the reason why it is most suitable for the central argument of this project. In her 1946 elaboration of the concept of projective identification ([1946] 1975), this proves to be both an answer to and a refusal of the situation of object loss. It is the solution to object loss, and melancholia— paranoid in its origin for Klein—partakes of the nostalgia of an external object that was lost and an internal object that can always be lost. The ego's ability to safeguard its good objects is always uncertain—much as the perception of good and bad is uncertain. Klein will not follow Freud in his formulation of the unconscious hallucination in dreams but rather will render the hallucination conscious—as in (psychotic) delirium, understood as a movement toward the cure—by opening up another scenario of desire. For Klein, there is an Other of desire, the hallucination of the dream sparks nostalgia for the return to the breast, which is ultimately and most poignantly the return to our private phantasmatic scenarios of unrestrained infantile bliss.

6

The Death Drive and Aggression

It is the death instinct, through projection, in a sense, that creates objects and the relation to them. The organism then creates powerful, destructive, and persecutory objects.—W. W. Meissner

The importance of aggression was implicit in Freud's earlier work, but his later theories seem to have taken shape during the years of World War I, paving the way for what would eventually be his *Beyond the pleasure principle* ([1920a] 1953). Upon its publication, Freud totally revised his classification of the drives and gave equal status to aggression and libido. As a result of these ideas, an important transformation affected psychoanalysis. During the 1930s, the major emphasis was on aggression and the analysis of negative transference. As is well known, the highly speculative character of Freud's new theory and the difficulties of its clinical application were matters of much controversy. Ernest Jones in his biography of Freud acknowledges that the death drive theory has "little objective support." Nevertheless, he writes, "So far as I know, the only analysts, e.g. Melanie Klein, Karl Menninger and Herman Nunberg, who still employ the term 'death instinct' do so in a purely clinical sense which is remote from Freud's original theory. Any clinical applications he made of it were postulated after deriving the theory, not before" (1953–57, 3:277).

The real beginning of the new development in Freud's thinking should be traced back to his introduction of the concept of narcissism between 1910 and 1914 and especially to "On narcissism: An introduction" ([1914] 1953). His positing that the ego is cathected with libido—the ego is taken as or instead of an object of love—evidently came to alter his previous classification of the drives between self-preservation and sexual instincts. It seems that his concern about the need for a modification of his theory of the drives was much influenced by the pressure exerted on him by Jung, who was in favor of a concept of an all-embracing libido as a representative of mental energy in general. At the same time, Freud had to make clear that he disagreed with Adler's ego-oriented views, which were based more on a theory of social motivation than on narcissism.

Early on, Freud was convinced of an essential bipolarity in psychic life, which he felt must be reflected in the nature of the drives, so that these must belong to two great classes in permanent conflict and opposition. He justified his view clinically by stressing the universality of conflict in the psyche. There are two main hypotheses contained in Freud's last theory of the drives: first, that aggression is a drive equal and opposite to the sexual drive; and, second, that aggression originally takes the form of a self-directed death drive derived ultimately, on the homeostatic principle, from the fact that living organisms developed out of inorganic matter and there is a need to return to this primitive state. In this case, the whole body could be understood as the source of the death drive, which finally should give rise to some kind of "demand made upon the mind for work."[1] The homeostatic character of the drive was implicit in Freud's original formulation that a drive (*Trieb*) has a source, an aim, and an object.[2] An imbalance in the system is the source of the drive; the aim is to redress the imbalance and achieve homeostasis, and the object is that through which this aim may be achieved. From this point of view, unless we reject this particular formulation of *drive*, we must accept that all drives are homeostatic. Moreover, Freud suggested the notion of an externalization of the aggression to account for the effort to reconcile the demand for death coming from the soma with the conflicting demand to avoid death until the appropriate time.

Most analysts compromised with the death drive by accepting the theory of a primary instinct of aggression but rejected or ignored the self-directed aspect of the death drive theory. This was certainly not the case with Melanie Klein. She took the death drive as crucial in the psychosexual development of the individual, and it acquired a central and even founding role in her theory. She followed Freud in conceiving of aggression as a turning outward of the immediately life threatening death drive and argued that the infant felt persecuted as a consequence of the internal threat, and then, in turn, was persecuted from outside, following the externalization of the death drive. In her theory of internal objects, they were first divided into "good" and "bad" according to whether they granted satisfaction or frustration to the infant. The bad object was a frustrating object, which aroused an aggressive response and onto which aggression was projected. The aggressive element in the infant is fundamental in the development of the Kleinian theory of the paranoid-schizoid and depressive positions.

The Kleinian Death Drive and Projective Identification

"Notes on some schizoid mechanisms" ([1946] 1975) is one of Klein's most important essays. In it, she gives a detailed account of the psychic processes that occur in the first three months of life. In her previous work, she had elaborated on the depressive and paranoid positions. From now on she will call the latter the paranoid-schizoid position and will occupy herself with describing the complex fluctuations between both of them throughout life.[3] The emphasis placed on the operations of the death drive, the introduction of the mechanism of projective identification, and her research and reflections on the relations between manic-depressive states and schizophrenia position this essay at the center of many of the arguments with which I am dealing in this volume.

Klein understands the early ego's lack of cohesion as a constant fluctuation between tendencies toward integration and tendencies toward disintegration. Its most important function is that of dealing with anxiety, which "arises from the operation of the death instinct within the organism, is felt as fear of annihilation (death) and takes the form of fear of persecution" (SM, 4). Deflection of the death drive, that is, its projection outward, marks the first movement of externalization effected by the ego, and as a consequence the death drive is attached to the first external object, the mother's breast.[4]

Klein suggests that at this very early stage processes of splitting are already active; the early ego splits the object, and this may also imply some active splitting of the ego itself. These processes of splitting result in a dispersal of the destructive impulse. The vital need to deal with anxiety forces the ego to develop defense mechanisms. Splitting the object gives the infant a distinct and radically opposite image of a bad (frustrating) and good (gratifying) breast; the latter would be incorporated as the first internal good object and will act "as a focal point in the ego" (SM, 6). For Klein, there is no possibility of splitting the object without a corresponding splitting taking place within the ego.

Apart from splitting, closely connected with introjection and projection are the mechanisms of idealization and denial. Idealization is bound up with the splitting of the object, for the good aspects of the breast are exaggerated as a safeguard against the fear of the persecuting breast, and "it also springs from the power of the instinctual desires which aim at unlimited gratification and therefore create the picture of an inexhaustible and always bountiful breast—an ideal breast" (SM, 7). In infantile hallucinatory satisfaction, idealization is closely associated with denial; not only is the bad object kept apart from the good but its very existence is denied. In this early splitting, denial and omnipotence play a role similar to that of repression at a later stage of ego development.

In dealing with persecutory fear, oral, urethral, and anal desires, both libidinal and aggressive, act together. There is a predominantly oral impulse "to suck dry, bite up, scoop out and rob the mother's body of its good contents" and an urethral impulse that "expell[s] dangerous substances (excrements) out of the self and into the mother" (SM, 8). Together with these harmful excrements, split-off parts of the ego are projected into the mother.[5] Klein is about to describe the mechanism of projective identification. She writes: "These excrements and bad parts of the self are meant not only to injure but also to control and to take possession of the object. In so far as the mother comes to contain the bad parts of the self, she is not felt to be a separate individual but is felt to be the bad self. Much of the hatred against parts of the self is now directed towards the mother. This leads to a particular form of identification which establishes the prototype of an aggressive object-relation. I suggest for these processes the term 'projective identification'" (8). It is important to point out that projective identification becomes the leading defense mechanism against anxiety in the paranoid-schizoid position and that it comprises processes that build up the specific forms of narcissistic object relations characteristic of this period by equating objects with split-off and projected parts of the self.[6] If projective identification is excessive, good parts of the personality are felt to be lost and the process results in an impoverishment of the ego. It is important to note that Klein identifies the loss of the capacity to love as a further consequence of an excess in these processes: "Another consequence is a fear that the capacity to love has been lost because the loved object is felt to be loved predominantly as a representative of the self" (SM, 9).

In schizoid modes of object relations—which for Klein are narcissistic in nature—violent splitting of the self and excessive projection are combined. Since the destructive parts of the self are split off and projected, they are felt as dangerous to the loved object, and this gives rise to guilt. This movement, which to some extent implies a deflection of guilt onto others, returns and is felt as an unconscious responsibility for those who have become representatives of the aggressive part of the self. In the Kleinian system, guilt operates along the lines of the death drive.

In her attempt to relate the depressive position to the paranoid-schizoid position as the next step in development, Klein uses the trope of the "vicious circle" to describe the anomalies that may disrupt the normal course of events: "If development during the paranoid-schizoid position has not proceeded normally and the infant cannot—for internal or external reasons—cope with the impact of depressive anxieties a vicious circle arises. For if persecutory fear, and correspondingly schizoid mechanisms, are too strong, the ego is not capable of working through the depressive position. This forces the ego to regress to the paranoid-schizoid position and reinforces the earlier persecutory fears and schizoid phenomena" (SM, 15). In *Envy and gratitude* ([1957] 1975), she refers to this vicious circle again in her discussion of how the "envious super-ego" is felt to disturb or eliminate all attempts at reparation and creativeness. Guilt feelings are added to persecution as a result of the individual's own envious and de-structive impulses, and "The need for punishment, which finds satisfaction by the increased devaluation of the self, leads to a vicious circle" (E&G, 231). Here there is obviously a connection among the envious superego, guilt, and melancholia, whose condition seems to be constantly fluctuating between the paranoid-schizoid and the depressive position.

In "Notes on some schizoid mechanisms" ([1946] 1975), Klein estab-lishes in a definitive way the constant fluctuation between the paranoid-schizoid and the depressive position as part of normal development and argues that in abnormal development this interaction influences the clini-cal picture of schizophrenia and manic depressive disorders. She tenta-tively advances the idea that schizophrenia and manic depression are closely connected in development and that this is the reason why the differential diagnosis between melancholia and schizophrenia is exceed-ingly difficult.

In the appendix to this paper, Klein discusses some aspects of Freud's analysis of the Schreber case, specifically his reference to the patient's "abnormal changes in the ego" and his argument that "it is probable that processes of this kind constitute the distinctive characteristic of psychoses" (Freud 75).[7] Regarding these processes, which are at the bottom of Schreber's paranoic "world catastrophe," she suggests that it is the mechanism of the ego annihilating other parts that underlies this phantasy and that it implies a preponderance of the destructive impulse over the libido. Klein argues that if the ego and its internalized objects are felt to be in bits, anxiety states relating to an internal catastrophe do arise and excessive projection follows. Such anxiety states take the lead during the paranoid-schizoid position and form the basis of later schizophrenia.

Anxiety and Guilt at the Origin of the Subject

Guilt is at bottom nothing else but a topographical variety of anxiety.—Sigmund Freud

In one of her footnotes to "On the theory of anxiety and guilt" ([1948] 1975), Klein expands on her differences with Freud as regards the relationship between anxiety and guilt. She points out that whereas Freud aims to connect anxiety and guilt he also distinguishes between them. He refers to guilt with regard to early manifestations of "bad conscience" and writes: "This state of mind is called a 'bad conscience'; but actually it does not deserve this name, for at this stage the sense of guilt is clearly only a fear of loss of love, 'social' anxiety. In small children it can never be anything else, but in many adults, too, it has only changed to the extent that the place of the father or the two parents is taken by the larger human community. . . . A great change takes place when the authority is internalized through the establishment of a super-ego. The phenomena of conscience then reach a bigger stage. Actually, it is not until now that we should speak of conscience or a sense of guilt" ([1929, 1930] 1953, 124–25). In Freud's view the superego emerges as a sequel to the Oedipus complex; therefore, as Klein points out, the terms *conscience* and *guilt* do not apply before, in the first few years of life, anxiety is distinct from guilt.

In "Early stages of the Oedipus conflict" ([1928] 1975), Klein put forward her idea that, in both the normal and the pathological development of the child, anxiety and guilt arising during the first year of life are closely connected with processes of introjection and projection, with the first stages of the superego development and of the Oedipus complex, and that in these anxieties aggression and defenses against it are of paramount importance.

"On the theory of anxiety and guilt" ([1948] 1975) is Klein's most comprehensive essay covering her ideas on anxiety and guilt, including her agreement and differences with Freud. She points out that so far psychoanalysis had remained predominantly concerned with libido and had underrated the importance of aggression. Her own research had pivoted on understanding the relationship between aggression and anxiety. The death drive is for Klein the primary factor in the causation of anxiety, and in her conclusions to this essay she states that "it is . . . the *interaction* between aggression and libido—ultimately the fusion as well as the polarity of the two instincts—which causes anxiety and guilt" (A&G, 42). Anxiety can never be eliminated, but it may be "counteracted and kept at bay by the power of the life instinct" (42).[8]

Whereas, as we have just seen, for Freud guilt has its origin in the Oedipus complex and arises as a sequel to it ([1929, 1930] 1953), Abraham pointed out the connection among anxiety, guilt, and cannibalistic desires ([1924] 1949). Along these lines, Klein argues that anxiety has its origin in the "danger arising from the inner working of the death instinct" (A&G, 29). In her elaboration, the early superego is built up from the devouring breast (mother), to which is added the devouring penis (father). These internal figures become the representatives of the death drive. Yet the superego has another, opposite aspect, a helpful one, and it is formed by means of the internalization of the good breast and the good penis. According to Klein, "the fear of death enters from the beginning into the fear of the superego and is not, as Freud remarked, a 'final transformation' of the fear of the superego" ([1925, 1926] 1953, 140). For Klein, the primary danger situation arising from the activity of the death drive within is felt by the infant as attack and persecution. The frustrating (bad) external breast becomes, owing to projection, the external representative of the death drive; through introjection, it reinforces the primary internal danger situation, and the ego feels urged to deflect this inner activity of the death drive into the external world. Nevertheless, the activity of the death drive cannot be considered apart from the simultaneous activity of the life drives. When the libido attaches itself to the external object and the gratifying (good) breast is felt to be the representative of the life drive, the latter is introjected. The ego is the site of a constant struggle between the life and death drives.

Klein discusses at length the relationship between guilt and anxiety. She distinguishes between persecutory and depressive anxiety. Both forms of anxiety were described in her "A contribution to the psychogenesis of manic-depressive states" ([1935] 1975), and now Klein moves on to add that "anxiety and guilt already play some part in the infant's earliest object-relation, i.e. in his relation to his mother's breast" (A&G, 34). She is thus also positing a theory of early anxiety and guilt consonant with her previous work on the early superego and the Oedipus conflict. She problematizes even more her already complex view of the positions by claiming that during the paranoid-schizoid position, when the ego is overwhelmed with persecutory anxiety, "splitting processes are never fully effective" and there appear to be "transitory states of integration . . . in which the cleavage between the good and bad breast is less marked" (34). In such states of integration, some measure of synthesis between love and hatred in relation to part objects comes about.

This obviously affects and modifies the depressive position to a certain extent. Klein argues that persecutory anxiety still plays a part in the depressive position, but it lessens in quantity as depressive anxiety takes the lead. Depressive anxiety, guilt, and the urge to make reparation are experienced simultaneously. Klein defines *guilt* as being intertwined with the other two elements: "The feeling that the harm done to the loved object is caused by the subject's aggressive impulses I take to be the essence of guilt. . . . The urge to undo or repair this harm results from the feeling that the subject has caused it, i.e. from guilt. The reparative tendency can, therefore, be considered as a consequence of the sense of guilt" (A&G, 36). She notes that it seems probable that depressive anxiety, guilt, and the reparative tendency are only experienced when feelings of love for the object predominate over destructive impulses. In her own words, "Guilt inextricably is bound up with anxiety (more exactly, with a specific form of it, depressive anxiety); it leads to the reparative tendency and arises during the first few months of life, in connection with the earliest stages of the super-ego" (38).

Klein agrees with Freud on the impossibility of drawing a sharp distinction between objective and neurotic anxiety.[9] In her view, objective anxiety would correspond to the infant's fear of loss of the mother out of its sense of dependence on her for survival. Neurotic anxiety would have to do with the infant's perception that the loved mother—indispensable as an external and internal good object—has been destroyed (or is in danger of being destroyed) by its sadistic impulses and she will never return. For Klein, the interaction between external and internal danger situations persists throughout life.

"On the theory of anxiety and guilt" constitutes one of the clearest instances in Klein's work in which the death drive appears throughout the text as the ever present and primary factor in the causation of anxiety. In the Kleinian narrative, guilt arises out of the subject's own aggression; it first appears in the paranoid-schizoid position and, most importantly, triggers the urge to repair in the depressive position. There is a very early sense of guilt, a precocious sense of guilt in Klein, which, consonant with her notion of the death drive, colors the infant's psychic development. Whereas anxiety poses a threat, this is just the threshold of guilt. There is no psychic subject without its quota of guilt. The prospects for acquitting oneself of such a guilt rest on one's complex negotiations in working through the depressive position.

I want to argue that in melancholia the introjection of the lost object of love comes as a result of the Oedipus conflict in its focal position as psychic catalyst and social device—as melancholic apparatus. How can we account for the fact that melancholia (depression in its present form) affects some individuals—especially women and deviant subjects—and not others? We need to find the answers to these questions in a space between the psychic and the social, where both the psychic and the social find their Others wanting. Klein gives us an important vantage point from which to reflect on these issues in her theory of the positions and her reluctance to adopt a structural view of the psyche inscribed in a teleological developmental model. Kleinian theory is a melancholic narrative of the constitution of the sexual subject and, by extension, of the social subject. There is an introjection of the lost object of love (which is nothing but a reedition of the introjection of the first loved and lost object—the breast, the mother) and a harboring of the object inside the ego. At best, melancholia can be worked through into mourning with the relinquishment of the object. But is this possible at all in the Kleinian scenario? At the base of Klein's notion of the depressive position there is the fact that any subsequent losses will shake the already fragile constitution of the ego by making it reinstate its good internal objects, which are felt to be under threat. The depressive position is a *remembrance of things past*. Is there a way in which the subject can free itself from the burden of the past? Is there a way in which the subject as the victim of its own aggression can be set free—radically and essentially free of guilt—in the Kleinian account?

Following her arguments in "On the theory of anxiety and guilt" ([1948] 1975), in *Envy and gratitude* ([1957] 1975), Klein argues that one of the consequences of excessive envy is the early onset of guilt. She writes that "one of the deepest sources of guilt is always linked with the envy of the feeding breast, and with the feeling of having spoilt its goodness by envious attacks" (E&G, 195). In this work, Klein identifies the devaluation of the self—characteristic of the melancholic—as a defense particular to depressive types, and she establishes that one of the deepest roots of this defense is guilt and unhappiness over not having been able to preserve the good object because of envy (218).

Klein adds some further remarks on the superego in her "On the development of mental functioning" ([1958] 1975). She introduces one more aspect to her already rich and complex account of splitting processes. In this essay, she suggests that the superego develops in a state of fusion together with the life and death drives. Thus, "the splitting of the ego, by which the super-ego is formed, comes about as a consequence of conflict in the ego, engendered by the polarity of the two instincts" (DMF, 240). She reports that in her analysis of very young children since the 1920s she had come across "a very early and savage super-ego," (241) and discovered the ways in which children introjected their parents in a phantastic way as terrifying or idealized objects. In her view, these terrifying objects, "are split off in a manner different from that by which the super-ego is formed, and are relegated to the deeper layers of the unconscious" (241). Klein differentiates between two kinds of splitting, one in which the fusion of the life and death drives is in ascendance and another that is carried out predominantly through fusion of the two drives. In her view, during the depressive position, together with the increase in the feelings of guilt toward the damaged love object and the ego's urge to make reparation, "This relation to the loved injured object goes on to form an important element in the super-ego" (242). During the latency period, an important gap emerges between the "organized" part of the superego and its "unconscious part," which is felt to be separated.[10]

Klein goes on to draw a topography of the psyche that is mobile and resists any fixed structure. In addition to the life and death drives, she describes an unconscious that "consists of the unconscious ego and soon of the unconscious super-ego. It is part of this concept that I regard the id as identical with the two instincts" (DMF, 243). It is an unconscious in which, contrary to the Freudian view, splitting mechanisms are prior to repression. In fact, "The nature of splitting determines the nature of repression" (244). Klein concludes that the ego, from the beginning of life, has a capacity not only to split but to integrate itself. Integration depends on the preponderance of the life drive and implies in some measure the acceptance by the ego of the working of the death drive. The ego may achieve this integration through its earliest object relations, and it is on the basis of the breast—on which the life and death drives are projected—as first object, internalized through introjection, that the psychic subject comes into being. The ego is a permanent site of struggle between representatives of the life and death drives. Its level of equilibrium is fragile and contingent, and it depends on a multiplicity of internal and external factors. Klein's interest in psychoses, especially manic depression and schizophrenia, shows in her nuanced and detailed descriptions of such mechanisms as splitting, scotomization, denial, and projective identification.

A Lonely Superego

Klein is undeniably the theorist of melancholia. Melancholia is dangerously placed in between neurosis and psychosis. As we saw earlier, failure to work through the depressive position may result in melancholia, mania, or paranoia. Since Klein also aims to posit a theory of love and a theory of the passions—envy, hate, gratitude, jealousy—the near impossibility of ever achieving a feeling of integration and other love that permeates her writing results in her latest thoughts on loneliness.

"On the sense of loneliness" ([1963] 1975) is a posthumously published and unfinished essay in which Kleinian melancholia is even more present, though in different ways, than in her previous work. Klein sets out to explore what she calls the inner sense of loneliness, "the sense of being alone regardless of external circumstances, of feeling lonely even when among friends or receiving love" (SL, 300). It is important to note that Klein places at the core of this inner sense of loneliness a longing for the intimate, earliest relationship with the mother, "the most complete experience of being understood . . . essentially linked to the preverbal stage" (301).[11] This, in her view, contributes to the sense of loneliness and derives from the depressive feeling of an "irretrievable loss" (301).

Paranoid and depressive anxieties that are never entirely overcome are at the root of the sense of loneliness. Crucial to my main arguments is the fact that Klein identifies and explains why loneliness is generally understood to derive from the conviction that there is no person or group to which one belongs. This not belonging is spelled out in terms of projective identification. Since total and permanent integration of the ego is never possible, some of its split-off parts are projected into other people and contribute to the feeling that one is not in full possession of one's self, that one does not fully belong to oneself or, therefore, to anybody else: "The lost parts too, are felt to be lonely" (SL, 302).[12] In the schizophrenic, this sense of loneliness is exacerbated, since his or her ego, through its multiple splittings and projections, is weakened and felt as fragmented. The fragility of an ego that cannot rely on any external or internal good object is bound up with loneliness, for it increases the feeling that the individual is left alone "with his misery" (303).

The prevalence of depressive anxiety results in loneliness. On the manic depressive's way toward the depressive position, the object is experienced more as a whole, but the feelings of guilt bound up with paranoid mechanisms are prevalent. The manic depressive longs to have the good object safely inside, protected and preserved. But he or she feels unable to do so, as the capacity for making reparation is still uncertain. Finally, the individual succumbs to the threat of his or her destructive impulses. Klein argues that the longing to overcome these difficulties and work through the depressive position results in a feeling of loneliness. Moreover, in extreme cases this expresses itself in a tendency toward suicide.

In her discussion of further difficulties in integration, Klein also acknowledges the importance of the complex ways in which male and female elements appear in both sexes under the sway of maternal and paternal identifications.[13] Here it is the superego that complicates things further and throws the ego into confusion with its almost impossible demands. Klein seems to suggest that the harsher the superego the more difficult it will be to come to terms with the labor of integration.

At the end of her career, as was certainly the case with Freud, Klein has a brilliant insight into one of the pillars on which her theory rests, her ongoing reflection on mourning, melancholia, and manic-depression.[14] In SL, she seems to go beyond her previous positions, giving us an almost subversive reading of her ideas on the superego.

> These identifications [with both parents] vary in strength and also in quality, depending on whether admiration or envy is the more prevalent. Part of the desire for integration in the young child is the urge to integrate these different aspects of the personality. In addition, the super-ego makes the conflicting demand for identification with both parents, prompted by the need to make reparation for early desires to

rob each of them and expressing the wish to keep them alive internally. If the element of guilt is predominant it will hamper the integration of these identifications. If, however, these identifications are satisfactorily achieved they become a source of enrichment and a basis for the development of a variety of gifts and capacities. (306)

It is the superego that enters into the picture with the difficult and almost melancholic demand to preserve the identifications with both parents inside the ego. Since guilt arises directly from the superego, how is the subject to make the difficult transit of acquitting itself of guilt and embracing a multiplicity of identifications? Is it not the case that in order to keep and preserve all its possible identifications the subject must deceive the superego and do this in hiding, by resorting to perversion in the most general sense? What seems to be at stake here is an opening up and acknowledging of the complex ways in which the subject assumes its identifications—basically, but not only, same sex or other sex—and how this becomes entangled in and complicated by the question of desire.

Klein also argues that there is a link between loneliness and the inability to sufficiently integrate the good object as well as those parts of the self that are felt to be inaccessible. All the factors that Klein lists as mitigators of loneliness—such as successful internalization of the good object, gratitude and tolerance, among others—never entirely eliminate it, and they are likely to be used as defenses. As she herself admits, Klein merely touches upon the importance of the superego in connection with all these issues. In the penultimate paragraph of this "unfinished" essay, she writes: "A harsh super-ego can never be felt to forgive destructive impulses; in fact, it demands that they should not exist. Although the super-ego is built up largely from a split-off part of the ego on to which impulses are projected, it is also inevitably influenced by the introjection of the personalities of the actual parents and of their relation to the child. The harsher the super-ego, the greater will be the loneliness, because its severe demands increase depressive and paranoid anxieties" (SL, 313).[15]

We may read this harsh and relentless Kleinian superego as an almost paranoid agency of surveillance, which does not only deny forgiveness but instead opts for disavowal. Destructive impulses exist throughout the world, but the superego obsessively demands that "they should not exist." So, by definition, this latter Kleinian superego can be best described as a paranoid and policing agency, which, by way of its own denial, punishes an ego already under suspicion of being responsible for such destruction.

The superego can never forgive, but it can deny. It inhabits the space of the paranoid-schizoid position. The ego finds itself in a nonplace; it is the masochistic victim of the attacks launched by the punitive agency. Feelings of loneliness, melancholia, and the impossibility of ever working through the depressive position increase progressively with the superego's harsher demands. How can the ego be watched by a milder superego if this change would come as a result of a move toward the depressive position (and this, in its turn, would very much depend on the introjection of the personalities of the actual parents)? Klein's legacy in this essay is a melancholic statement on the impossibility of ever achieving integration. The fragility of the ego is more present than ever before. This primary good internal object, which was lost, will always remain inexorably so. Attempts at substitution are doomed to fail. The feeling of not belonging—to a person, a group, or even oneself—brilliantly described by Klein in this essay, is parallel to the feeling of not belonging of the melancholic, of his or her retreat from the world. Why is it that in the field of the social, within the frame of the large group, the melancholic feels so excluded? The retreat to an inner world where the lost object of love is harbored has everything to do with the impossibility of bearing the anxieties that derive from the social in the subject's paranoid-schizoid position. The projection of aggression and violence—in overt as well as more subtle ways—into or onto others is a feature of our present highly prejudiced societies. Xenophobia, homophobia, racism, and class and social prejudices are paranoid defenses articulated on the basis of hatred and projection of our own rejected and devalued split-off parts.

At the core of Kleinian theory, there is a potential for understanding and resignification of what counts as a psychic and social space where the subject may be able to live. The unending and never quite fully achieved task of integration, in the process of recomposing the subject and setting it free from excessive guilt, is both a personal and a social project. Reading and rereading Klein, in the light of the turbulence and concerns of our own times, leaves the door open for future possibilities of change. The dystopia at the center of the Kleinian account of the child's early aggressive relationship with the mother gives us space for thought as to what taking an oppositional stance even to where we feel we most intimately belong may mean. But dystopia and utopia, as opposites, are too close for us to be able to think of one without the other. In a terrain of permanent oscillation between neurosis and psychosis, melancholia and the Kleinian depressive position signal the impossibility of their practical resolution. In this movable and changing force field, the strivings for integration of our selves and those of others sound like a felicitous promise that holds no guarantees, although it may be worth the effort to assume the risk.

Melancholia, Performativity, and the Death Drive

Freud's discussion of melancholia in "Mourning and melancholia" ([1915, 1917] 1953) provides the context for Judith Butler's persuasive argument about the necessity of a melancholic identification for the process whereby the gendered character of the ego is assumed. Butler understands "gendered character of the ego" to mean the influence upon the ego of the prevalence of a heterosexual matrix in the construction of gender as it emerges in many of Freud's texts as well as in cultural forms that have absorbed heterosexuality as their naturalized cultural norm (1990a, 57–65).

Butler reminds us that in The ego and the id ([1923] 1953), Freud makes room for the notion that melancholic identification may be a prerequisite for letting the object go, and giving up the object becomes possible on condition of a melancholic incorporation. This incorporation is also a way to disavow that loss. Butler claims that "masculine" and "feminine" positions are produced through melancholic identification, that they are established "in part through prohibitions that demand the loss of certain sexual attachments and demand as well that those losses not be avowed and not be grieved" (1990a, 168). If the assumptions of femininity and masculinity proceed through the accomplishment of heterosexuality, Butler suggests that we might understand the force of this accomplishment as "the preemption of the possibility of homosexual attachment, a certain foreclosure of possibility that produces a domain of heterosexuality understood as unlivable passion and ungrievable loss" (168).

The Oedipal conflict presumes the heterosexualization of desire and is produced by enforcing the prohibition of homosexuality, even prior to implementing the prohibition of incest. Heterosexuality thus enforces the loss of homosexual objects and aims, which is foreclosed from the start.[16] According to Butler, we can expect a culturally prevalent form of melancholia, which signals the internalization of the "ungrieved and ungrievable homosexual cathexis" (1990a, 171). In the absence of a contemporary public discourse through which such losses might be acknowledged, named, and mourned, melancholia has important consequences. Butler specifically refers to contemporary conditions of grief over the loss by AIDS of so many gay men and suggests that the cultural "unreality" of these losses may be attributable to the foreclosed status of homosexual love as that which "never was" and so "never was lost." She uncovers the blind spots of our culture of gender melancholy in which, "In opposition to a conception of sexuality that is said to 'express' a gender, gender itself is here understood to be composed of precisely what remains inarticulate in sexuality" (172).

Butler documents and discusses the issue of homosexual desire as a source of guilt in Freud's texts, underscoring that in melancholia the superego can become "a gathering place for the death instincts" (1990a, 173). She writes: "Where melancholy is the refusal of grief, it is also always the incorporation of loss, the miming of the death it cannot mourn. In this sense, the incorporation of death draws on the death instincts such that we might well wonder whether the two are separable from one another, either analytically or phenomenologically" (174). This is a crucial point of convergence with several of the arguments I have put forward in this volume. If the superego of the melancholic is "a pure culture of the death instinct" (Freud [1923] 1953, 53), reading Klein's and Butler's views together would lead us to reflect upon the forms of violence that are culturally enforced on a macrolevel and those that are enforced on a microlevel. The latter show on the first grid of cultural semiosis, that of the infant in relation to the mother, who is sadistically attacked, destroyed, and devalued in his or her finite and extinguishable condition of frustrating, ungiving, and selfish breast. In the conflictual relationship between the infant and the mother, and later the parental couple, in the passage from the paranoid-schizoid to the depressive position, and prior to the onset of the Oedipal conflict, sexuality is felt as a loss, disoriented and troubled. The value of Klein's insights with regard to the issue of the achievement of any sexual position lies precisely in her effort to show the constant interaction between pregenital and genital impulses and tendencies and in her resistance to the possibility of ever attaining a stable and fixed sexual position. Her exploration of the workings of the death drive and her crucial work on mourning, melancholia, and manic depression have authoritatively proved how the capacity for mourning and its opposite, melancholia, shape the ego's development through a complex narrative made up of the phantasies that constitute it. These narratives, as much as the development of the ego, eschew any notion of teleology—in the constant ebb and flow of moving forward and backward—in the history of the ego. Consequently, the history of the subject and its sexuality is shaped through constant negotiation, always provisional and subject to change.

In her important discussion of gender melancholia, in the context of her theory of gender performativity, Judith Butler refers to the example of the drag performance to further illustrate her point: "What it [drag performance] does suggest is that the performance allegorizes a loss it cannot grieve, allegorizes the incorporative fantasy of melancholia whereby an object is phantasmatically taken in or on as a way of refusing to let it go. Gender itself might be understood as the 'acting out' of unresolved grief" (1990a, 176). In Butler's view, drag allegorizes heterosexual melancholy, the melancholy by means of which masculine and feminine genders are formed from their respective refusals to grieve same-sex possibilities of love by preserving them through the heightening of strong masculine or feminine identifications: "Indeed, it may be, but need not be, that what constitutes the *sexually* unperformable is performed instead as *gender identification*" (177).[17] For Butler, what is most apparently performed as gender is the symptom of a pervasive disavowal. She briefly touches on the issue of suicide and argues that the melancholic effects of the public proscription of losses can achieve suicidal proportions.

But we may as well consider that delusions, hallucinations, and "acting out" are the first step in and the precondition to the cure of psychosis, the first step in the subject's own private battle with manic depression, paranoia, or schizophrenia. If acting out is in itself the first step on the way to the cure of the melancholic, breaking the long silence of noncommunication, of the absence of speech and movement, we may as well consider the performative episode as an attempt to resolve the melancholia of gender, one with no guarantees. For there can be no mourning without the acknowledgment of what was lost.[18] In my view, this state of melancholia has to do with the impossibility of mourning all the tendencies the subject had to relinquish in his or her previous history in order to become what he or she is at the moment, in order to enjoy and/or suffer his or her present sexuality. An infant no longer, the "mature" individual has had to abandon his or her "polymorphous perverse sexuality" and in so doing, must mime, reproduce, and replicate socially sanctioned behaviors and practices. In the absence—or social abjection—of alternative models, of alternative and nonrepressive ways of living sexuality, the individual is doomed to either compulsively repeat or be socially massacred and erased.

The Kleinian version of these facts would necessarily consider the vicissitudes of the passage from the paranoid-schizoid to the depressive position and the need to secure good internal objects as a precondition of it. When the subject is entrapped in the vicious circle of aggression, envy, and fear of retaliation, there is no easy way to break free. Paranoid-schizoid morality, with its concomitant manic and obsessional defenses, gives a perfect view of the psychic and social enforcement of post-oedipal sexuality, always already heterosexual in our cultural organization in the West.

What seems to me most important in Butler's arguments for future work on melancholia, and in a wider sense for sexualities and gender at the present conjuncture, is precisely her suggestion that we rethink melancholy within homosexuality and in the context of a politics of identity that may be able to operate in terms other than those of the logic of mutual exclusion by which heterosexism reproduces itself. I also believe that we must rethink the role of melancholy in the constitution of the subject, not only in psychoanalytical terms but at the crossroads of psychoanalysis and politics. For not until we are able to uncover the social and political implications of the melancholization (or, in more general and current terms, depression) of some subjects and not others will we be fully able to understand melancholia as a contemporary culture of the death drive.

Melanie Klein and Luce Irigaray: The Role of the Death Drive in New Symbolic Economies

And I have suffered the violence of your passions so many times that often peaceful serenity tries me. I am lifeless but deprived of yet living my death. Indefinitely in death. A mourning veil into which you endlessly transfigure me so as to make yourself immortal. Dwelling in death without every dying, I keep for you the dream—of being able to overcome your body. And this ideal—not to feel life passing by. Neither to suffer from nor even to imagine the matter from which life is made, and unmade. And to descend into the depths of your existence to ask you the question of your sustenance.—Luce Irigaray

The question Irigaray negotiates is the tension between the death drive as destructive and the death drive as creative; or between eros as thanatos and thanatos as eros.—Margaret Whitford

In her essay "Reading Irigaray in the nineties" (1994b),[19] Margaret Whitford briefly identifies what she will engage in depth later in her study of

Irigaray's images—particularly the utopian ones—in "Irigaray, Utopia, and the Death Drive" (1994a), as a "difficulty" that Irigaray, and perhaps feminism in general, have produced for themselves (1994b, 29). Whitford thus undertakes her discussion in terms of images, in terms of how Irigaray envisions her feminist philosophical project, which is one for the future.

Irigaray argues that there is a patriarchal death drive, that patriarchy has been constructed on a sacrifice (an originary matricide), and that we need to bring the mother into symbolic existence. Nevertheless, Whitford remarks, it seems paradoxical that Irigaray also comes dangerously close to suggesting that there might be a culture without sacrifice, and her recent work, with her emphasis on love, explicitly moves in this direction (Whitford 1994b, 29). Whitford seems too close to several of the questions on aggressivity, violence, and the death drive that have been raised through a rereading of Klein in this project. What is at stake for Whitford is exploring, understanding, and identifying the locus of violence. She writes: "It is easier to attribute violence to an *other* (like patriarchy) than to consider the implications of the inevitable violence at the heart of identity, which brings it closer to home" (29). This is no doubt one of the main issues at stake in Kleinian theory as well.

Whitford aptly links these questions to the larger picture of feminism as critique and feminism as construction. The issue of violence is seldom addressed, and in her view Irigaray's earlier work, from *Speculum of the other woman* ([1974] 1985) to *An ethics of sexual difference* ([1984] 1993), provides ample resources to start us thinking about "the kind of alibi that patriarchal violence offers for feminism as critique, and the kind of difficulties that might lie in the way of fundamental symbolic reorganizations (of which the conflicts engendered by differences between women is only the most obvious example)" (1994b, 29). In "Irigaray, utopia, and the death drive" (1994a), Whitford uncovers some of the ambiguities inherent in the concept of the death drive.[20]

Irigaray rereads Lacanian formulations in *Le temps de la différence* (1989). Reinterpreting Lacan's three registers in terms of sexual difference, she diagnoses a failure to sublimate owing to the condition of woman as Other: "Destruction [is] at work in the life drives themselves, insofar as they fail to respect the other, and in particular the other of sexual difference. Instead of being in the service of creation or recreation of human forms, [eroticism] serves destruction or the loss of identity in fusion" (109–11). For Irigaray, psychoanalytic theories "describe and perpetuate an uncivilized state" (1992, 209), and we are living in "a primitive chaos" (1989, 104). She moves on to talk about love as a philosophical issue. Whitford writes: "The point of civilization is in part to tame the destructive energies of eros (J'aime à toi, 212); Aphrodite is love sublimated, the union of spiritual and carnal, the death drive mediated by the symbolic. . . . While the male universal is governed by death, Irigaray wishes to replace this with eros—life or love" (1994a, 392).

For Whitford, there is a turning point in Irigaray's work when the image of nuptials or amorous exchange begins to emerge more strongly. This corresponds to the idea that *each* sex should have access to life and to death.[21] It is basically an image without sacrifice, an image of fertility, an image that stands for relations between men and women at the level of sexuality or at the level of the polis. Her quote from Irigaray is most telling: "A sexual or carnal ethics would demand that both angel and body be found together. This is a world that must be constructed or reconstructed. A genesis of love between the sexes has yet to come about in all dimensions, from the smallest to the greatest, from the most intimate, to the most political" (Irigaray 1992, 107). Whitford remarks that this image of nuptials is explicitly linked to the problematics of life and death.

According to Whitford, in Irigaray's recent work the idea emerges that we live in a dangerous epoch for women. In her view, "The dangers in feminism, as Irigaray sees them, lie in a politics that is heedless of the functioning of the patriarchal death drive. Such a politics risks an escalation and counterescalation of violence that leaves the sacrificial foundation untouched" (1994a, 394). She sees Irigaray's project as involved in a new symbolization, in which the death drive is bound with eros. In J'aime à toi, Irigaray understands Eros to be an "unbinding" force, and Whitford believes this is because Eros remains "primitive, 'uncivilized,' unsublimated, a purely private affair, when it should be a civil and social recognition of two generic identities" (394).

When Whitford contends that Irigaray negotiates the tension between the death drive as destructive and the death drive as creative, or between Eros as Thanatos and Thanatos as Eros, we come all too close to Melanie Klein's ideas on the death drive in its multiple manifestations: anxiety, aggression, guilt, and paranoid-schizoid and depressive defenses. Klein writes that a certain degree of anxiety—and the like—is necessary in normal development. The death drive read as stasis and Klein's image of the "vicious circle" are fundamentally the same. They are a circular movement that translates into immobility, a stasis that becomes reified, so to speak, solidified in circles of pure pain.[22] For Whitford, Irigaray's images of utopias can be understood as attempts to bind the death drive in a stable imaginary formation. Nevertheless, she warns that any stable imaginary formation is itself implicated in the death drive in its sense as stasis, which makes any image problematic. She believes the problem is how to keep the space open, to hold the tension, without succumbing to either fixation or uncontrolled and endless disruption (1994a, 394). Stability immobilizes, but perpetual disruption is immobilizing and also disruptive.

In Whitford's own terms, the problem for feminism is that it is "destined to remain contestatory—feminism as critique—or can it legitimately move to a more constructive moment?" (1994a, 395). There are no definitive answers for these questions, as "identity is both necessary and violent" (395). Whitford sees continuity in the evolution of Irigaray's work. In her later work, violence is located in patriarchy, but as we know from her earlier work she is aware that violence also comes from inside ourselves. This continuity in Irigaray's thinking, in Whitford's view, "is provided at least in part by the need to address the death drive in its destructive as well as creative potential" (395).

We may raise similar questions in the terrain of Kleinian theory. To a large extent, I have been trying to engage Klein's representation of the death drive and melancholia in terms of failed narratives, of a narrativization that traces the sinuous paths the individual psyche may take in its development from infancy into adulthood. Phantasy and space are fundamental categories in my approach to the foundation, construction, and reconstruction (re-creation) of this psyche, which is no longer built upon a structural model.

Given Whitford's insight, we may rethink these questions in terms of images, in terms of a rhetoric of the image that in Klein is mobile and in flux and cannot easily be apprehended. The complex Kleinian syntax of introjections and projections, in its very inability to attain closure, may allow us to link the Kleinian to the Irigarayan image. Paranoid-schizoid and depressive images are overlaid in a rich texture of phantasies that finally, in Klein's later work, are resolved in reparation, in the healing of open wounds, and in the destruction and dereliction that we ourselves have caused. Splitting, scotomization, and mania give way to the melancholic landscapes of depression. In the remainders, in the interstices of all these ruins, the subject strives to make repairs out of love for the damaged object. The utopian images of bliss, harmony, and reunion in Irigaray intimately connect here with the melancholic longings for a peaceful state in which we, as subjects, may come to terms with the shadows of our troubled and most turbulent interior landscapes.

A Positional Ethics

In its broadest terms, the psychoanalytic world-view is constituted by a commitment to rational understanding of the self and to such freedom of choice as can be furthered by this.—Michael Rustin

In view of our previous reflections, we may wonder whether or not there are alternative ways inside the Kleinian oeuvre and its tradition to read *reparation* and *guilt* differently. It seems to me that one of the most positive insights Kleinian thinking can offer is precisely the opening up of a vast array of possibilities through which the individual can negotiate his or her liberation from guilt and freedom of choice in a space where no position is ever completely established and therefore no ontological or epistemological assumptions can be granted. The Kleinian oeuvre offers the possibility of our playing different roles in different scenarios and circumstances. As Graham Dawson has remarked, "the really radical potential of Kleinian theory lies in its conception of the reciprocal contingency of psychic life upon social contradictions. It brings the full range of complex, conflictual social relations into dynamic interaction with the struggle for greater psychic wholeness and integrity, not as a once-and-for-all process occurring in infancy, but as an ongoing process throughout all social life" (1994, 42–43).

Klein deeply explored the development of moral capacities in the child. With her bold elaboration and ardent defense of her ideas as they were exposed during the Controversial Discussions, she showed that in a rapidly changing world in which there are continuous differences between lived experiences and points of view there is no reason to believe that psychoanalysis should make room only for one ontological, ethical, or aesthetic standpoint.

In the context of the evolution of Kleinian thinking up to the present, the central importance of the ethical and moral stance in psychoanalysis has been stressed in the Kleinian tradition by Michael Rustin, among others. He claims that "The relation between psychoanalytic knowledge and human interests therefore consists in the fact that psychoanalysis is a ground, a legitimation and a consequence of certain definitions of purposes, in what might be thought of as a virtuous circle of reasoning. It begins from a point (or points) of view regarding human nature and possibility, but then provides evidence and justification of its plausibility and claims. The density and richness of psychoanalytic accounts of human motivation have made it, in fact, into an exemplary form of moral reasoning" (1991, 142).

Kleinian analyst Roger Money-Kyrle, in his essay "Towards a common aim: A psychoanalytical contribution to ethics" (1944) sets himself up to explore to what extent, if at all, psychoanalysis can contribute to the central and unsolved problem of ethics, "the choice of ends" (106), and so be as effective in society as it has been in helping individuals. His analysis is pervaded with the climate of paranoia and social tension produced by World War II and the threat of the extension of nazism. According to him, "the most conspicuous feature in their [the Nazis'] unconscious make-up appears to be a kind of sadistic phallic worship, the surrender to the 'bad' phallic deity symbolized by a loud-voiced but probably impotent fanatic" (112). Money-Kyrle strives to find a common pattern of ethical values valid for "normal" individuals and defines normality as "an optimum freedom of neurosis" (106), acknowledging that "there is no reason to suppose that two different individuals would approach the same normality" (106–7). Following Klein, he identifies as a positive characteristic of normality freedom from excessive unconscious anxiety by virtue of having a less distorted unconscious picture of the world.

The origin of morality is closely connected to the sense of guilt, which, understood in Kleinian terms, is "the peculiar blend of anxiety and despair that follows aggressive acts or phantasies against a loved object" (Money-Kyrle 1944, 110). There exist at least three general forms of morality: negative morality, which aims at the avoidance of a repetition of aggression against the loved object or its symbols; positive morality, which aims at the reparation of the damage done; and aggressive morality, which aims at the defense of the loved object against a threat by a third party.

Money-Kyrle manages to enunciate three fundamental principles of primary morality: "It is bad (i.e., it arouses guilt) to injure or threaten a good object; it is good to love, repair and defend a good object; it is also good to hate, attack or destroy a bad object, that is, any thing or person that threatens to destroy a good one" (1944, 111). In his view, it is obvious that the developed morality of the adult is relative and different in different societies and in different individuals in the same society. His assessment of the Kleinian contribution to the issue of ethics underscores that the super-ego is no longer "a single personality. It is a collection of many, often mutually incompatible personalities and part objects, and many relation-ships, including different forms of tension, can and do subsist between its various members and the ego" (117). Guilt, therefore, is not the result of all sorts of tension between ego and superego but only of aggression against loved objects, external or internal. This is what Money-Kyrle calls "the first law of primary morality—it is bad, that is, it arouses guilt, to attack or threaten a good object" (117). In the Kleinian sense, guilt is thus defined in a wider sense, which confronts us "with a great variety of consciences" (117). This new theory of guilt may lead us to a universal system of ethics, according to which there is "only one type of conscience; and the man who deserts and persecutes his good objects does so from fear, and not because of, but in spite of his guilt" (117).

Money-Kyrle explains this in a most awkward way by reducing the multiple possibilities opened up by the Kleinian insight into "a great vari-ety of consciences" to only one type of conscience. We gather that for the sake of simplicity he means one pattern of "bad" conscience, namely, the opposite of reparative morality. If we follow the implications of Kleinian thought, this paranoid-schizoid form of morality may as well offer many variants depending on the amount of anxiety, the degree of disintegration of the early ego, and the defense mechanisms displayed.

In the Kleinian elaboration, the internal object in the depressive posi-tion is felt to be damaged, the result of an injury, an attack, the focus of violence or aggression. This damaged internal object is what generates the ambivalent tone of the depressive position. The achievement of the depres-sive position aims to sustain the feelings of concern without always revert-ing to paranoid fears. Reparation strives to reinstate or repair the object that has been damaged or destroyed.

I believe that the concept of projective identification must also be considered as an important Kleinian contribution to an understanding of ethics. Whereas projective identification can be read as a mechanism of defense, it is also a crucial element in making emotional contact with others and it may function as a form of communication. Projective identi-fication is the basis of empathy, which, as Robert Hinshelwood has re-marked, "occurs without serious distortions to the identity of either the subject or the object. In this case the violence of the primitive forms has been so attenuated that it has been brought under the control of impulses of love and concern" (1994, 133).

The forms of love that arise from the phantasies of the depressive position elicit concern and a deep sense of grief. In the intricate and complex interactions of love with hate, aggression and fear, Klein delineates a "positional" ethics in which individual perspectives and situations place concern and altruism at center stage. Aggression toward the object lurks on a horizon that can never do without opposition and antagonism, a horizon where there is no place for complacency. I believe that a Kleinian ethics of care, gratitude, and appreciation of the other qua other opens up new avenues of generosity that are yet to be explored and exercised.

7

The Setting (Up) of Phantasy

When external reality is thus called "objective" reality, this makes an implicit assumption which denies to psychical reality its *own objectivity as a mental fact.*—Susan Isaacs

Susan Isaacs's "The nature and function of phantasy" ([1952] 1983) is taken to be the Kleinian position statement on unconscious phantasy.[1] It is a splendid essay in which theory is in constant dialogue with clinical material. In her chapter notes, she provides a wealth of detail that illustrates the ambitious scientific scope of her project. Since the time of the Controversial Discussions, much attention has been paid to the implications that derive from the concept of unconscious phantasy from a variety of perspectives. As Riccardo Steiner writes in the published edition of the "Controversies," the "notion of unconscious phantasy is probably the major theoretical theme of all the Scientific Discussions" (King and Steiner 1991, 242).

In her essay, Isaacs suggested that unconscious phantasy is the mental expression Freud referred to in his comment, "We suppose that it [the id] is somewhere in direct contact with somatic processes and takes over from them instinctual needs and gives them mental expression" (Freud [1932, 1933b] 1953, 98, quoted in Isaacs [1952] 1983).[2] In the Kleinians' view, unconscious phantasies are the mental representations of instinct and somatic and psychic experience, and they underlie every mental process.

Isaacs is concerned with the definition of *phantasy*, "with the nature and function of phantasy as a whole, and its place in the mental life" ([1952] 1983, 68), and never with its particular content; her concern is rather "with describing the *series of facts* which the use of the term helps us to identify, to organize and to relate to other significant series of facts" (67–68). Isaacs thus aims to define and describe the *structuring* function of phantasy in psychic life.[3]

From studies of early mental development and observation of infant behavior, Isaacs reminds us that many intellectual processes in the child are expressed in action long before they can be put into words.[4] She claims that the principle of genetic continuity is a fundamental epistemological instrument that allows us to look at processes and behaviors in development (this shows in the particular instance of speech development). This principle of genetic continuity clearly suggests that phantasies are active in the child along with the impulses from which they arise.

Melanie Klein, in her analytic work with young children, developed her technique—the so called analytic play technique—by using children's play with material objects, their games, their bodily activities in relation to the analyst, and their talk about what they were doing or what had been happening to them in their external lives. Klein showed how in the child's relationship with the analyst—as with the adult's—the phantasies arising in the earliest situations of life were repeated and acted out in the clearest and most dramatic manner. In this respect, Isaacs points out that the patient's relationship with the analyst is almost entirely one of unconscious phantasy. Transference is thus the appropriate scene for the enactment of unconscious phantasy and a privileged place in which to gain an understanding of the particular character of the phantasies at work in particular situations and their influence on other mental processes.

For Isaacs, phantasy essentially connotes unconscious mental content, which may or may not become conscious, and it is the "mental expression" or psychic representative of instinct ([1952] 1983, 83). The Freudian discovery of dynamic psychic reality, with its own laws and characteristics different from those of the external world, was crucial for further analytical developments. In Kleinian as much as in Freudian theory, unconscious phantasy is fully active in the neurotic as well as the normal individual.

Phantasy is also a means of defense against anxieties, a means of controlling and inhibiting instinctual urges, and an expression of reparative wishes. Isaacs remarks that even when the relationship between phantasy and wish fulfillment has been emphasized the Kleinian group has proved that most phantasies (like symptoms) serve various purposes in addition to wish fulfillment: denial, reassurance, omnipotent control, and reparation, among others. For the Kleinians, the child's attempt to find symbolic expressions of his or her unconscious phantasies in the external world forms the basis of what he or she learns about reality. In this respect, Hanna Segal has emphasized the way in which this process is similar to what Freud means by reality testing. Thinking, she says, evolves from unconscious phantasy via reality testing (1980, 100).

Bodies in Phantasy

The ego is first and foremost a body-ego.—Sigmund Freud

We need to know more about what "the body" means in unconscious phantasy, and to consider the various studies made by neurologists and general psychologists of the "body-schema." On this view, the unconscious body-schema or "phantasy of the body" plays a great part in many neuroses and in all psychoses, particularly in all forms of hypochondriasis.—Susan Isaacs

Isaacs's "The nature and function of phantasy" ([1952] 1983) presents us with a notion of phantasy that finds in the body its material grounding. It is expressed through the individual's specific material needs and practices and has no existence apart from them. Phantasy only takes shape in its embodied form and never emerges in an abstract vacuum: "Although themselves psychic phenomena, phantasies are primarily about bodily aims, pains and pleasures, directed to objects of some kind" (99). Phantasy has real material effects: "It is a true mental function and it has real effects, not only in the inner world of the individual but also in the external world of the subject's bodily development and behaviour, and hence of other people's minds and bodies" (99).

Isaacs talks about a tissue of phantasies, "which take specific form in conjunction with the cathexis of particular bodily zones. Moreover, they rise and fall in complicated patterns according to the rise and fall and modulation of the primary instinct-impulses which they express. The world of phantasy shows the same protean and kaleidoscopic changes as the contents of a dream" ([1952] 1983, 83–84). These changes occur partly in response to external stimulation and partly as a result of the interplay between the primary instinctual urges themselves. There is a patterning of phantasies, which constitutes what appears to be the musical score of the subject's internal world. Phantasy closely follows and expresses the notes coming from the drives, and it is attuned to and changes according to external and internal factors, as in the performance of a musical piece.

Since from the beginning of life the infant is overwhelmed with wishes and impulses, these tend to be felt as actually fulfilling themselves, whether with an external or an internal object. The first and most primitive oral impulse and desire is that of the mother's breast. Progressively in development, the child learns to distinguish between external facts and feelings about them. This omnipotent character of early wishes and feelings is in accord with Freud's views about hallucinatory satisfaction in the infant. Implicit in Isaacs's argument is thus the fact that hallucinatory wish fulfillment is a manic defense mechanism against the prospect of frustration and object loss. Desire is also experienced as "a specific phantasy" (Isaacs [1952] 1983, 84) which translates, according to its intensity, into "I want to suck the nipple" or "I want to eat her [my mother] all up" (84).

From Freud's notion of "satisfaction by hallucination," Isaacs points out that the infant first hallucinates the nipple, then the breast, and then the mother as a whole person.[5] She writes the infant "hallucinates the nipple or the breast in order to enjoy it" ([1952] 1983, 86). Apparently, hallucination works best at times of less intense instinctual tension. When the infant feels frustration, it strives to incorporate the breast and keep it there as a source of satisfaction. For a time, satisfaction will be omnipotently fulfilled in hallucination, but if frustration continues rage and aggressive feelings and phantasies will dominate the mind. Isaacs and the Kleinian group are therefore suggesting that incorporation originates in frustration. In relation to our argument, melancholia as an incorporative mechanism has its origin in frustration, in the impossibility of ever satisfying desire, and seeks refuge in an internal world in which the lost/frustrating object is preserved and embalmed inside the subject's ego.

Isaacs points out that when in "Instincts and their vicissitudes" Freud writes of introjection, his concept accords with the Kleinians' idea of the activity of unconscious phantasy in the earliest phases of life.[6] For Isaacs, the first phantasized wish fulfillment, the first hallucination, is bound up with sensation. It gives rise both to pleasurable and unpleasurable sensory experiences. The earliest phantasies are internal; they spring from bodily impulses and are interwoven with bodily sensations and affects ([1952] 1983, 93). They begin to build up the first memories, and progressively external reality is "woven into the texture of phantasy" (93). Phantasies are not grounded on an articulated knowledge of the external world, however;

their source is internal, in the instinctual impulses. Phantasy and drive are thus inextricably linked. In the Kleinians' view, there is knowledge that is "*inherent* in bodily impulses as a vehicle of instinct, in the *aim* of instinct, in the excitation of the organ" (94). This inherent somatic knowledge of the body is colored by the workings of the drive, which by virtue of the mechanisms of introjection and projection is translated into pleasurable or unpleasurable experiences.

The infant has very few resources at its command for expressing either love or hate; therefore, it has to use all of its bodily products and activities as means of expressing profound and overwhelming wishes and emotions, Isaacs remarks: "His urine and faeces may be either good or bad in his phantasy, according to his intentions at the moment of voiding and the way (including at a later period the time and place) in which they are produced" ([1952] 1983, 95). The earliest and most rudimentary phantasies are characterized by those qualities that Freud described as belonging to the primary process, namely, lack of coordination of impulse, lack of a sense of time, and lack of contradiction and negation.

Isaacs wants to make clear the distinction between the phantasy of incorporation and the mechanism of introjection. By introjection and projection, the Kleinians are referring to mechanisms or methods of functioning in mental life. Isaacs defines them as follows: "They refer to such facts as that ideas, impressions and influences are taken into the self and become part of it; or that aspects of elements of the self are often disowned and attributed to some person or group of persons, or some part of the external world. . . . Now these mental mechanisms are intimately related to certain pervasive phantasies. The phantasy of incorporating (devouring, absorbing, etc.) loved and hated objects" ([1952] 1983, 98–99). For the Kleinians, phantasy is the operative link between instinct and ego mechanism (99).

Isaacs's definition of *drive* is also paradigmatic of the Kleinians' adherence to the Freudian notion of the drives. She is concerned with spelling it out clearly: "An instinct is conceived as a border-line psycho-somatic process. It has a bodily aim, directed to concrete external objects. It has a representative in the mind which we call a 'phantasy.' Human activities derive from instinctual urges; it is only through the phantasy of what would fulfill our instinctual needs that we are enabled to attempt to realize them in external reality" ([1952] 1983, 99).

Isaacs reminds us that in his essay "Negation" ([1925a] 1953) Freud discussed the relationship between oral phantasies of incorporation and early processes of introjection. He argued that the intellectual functions of judgment and reality testing "are derived from the interplay of the primary instinctual impulses and rest upon the mechanism of introjection" (239). Referring to that aspect of judgment that attributes or denies a particular property to a thing, Freud writes: "Expressed in the language of the oldest, that is, of the oral instinctual impulses, the alternative runs thus: 'I should like to take this into me and keep that out of me.' That is to say, it is to be either inside me or outside me" (237). Isaacs remarks that the wish thus formulated is the same thing as a phantasy. In the Kleinians' view, in "Negation" Freud is formulating the subjective aspect of the mechanism of introjection (or projection): "*Thus phantasy is the link between the id impulse and the ego mechanism, the means by which one is transmuted into the other*" (Isaacs [1952] 1983, 104). Isaacs argues that what is introjected is an image, or "imago"; she scrupulously defines *imago* as, "a) 'imago' refers to an *unconscious* image; b) 'imago' usually refers to a person or part of a person, the earliest objects, while 'image' may be of any object or situation, human or otherwise; and c) 'imago' includes all the somatic and emotional elements in the subject's relation to the imaged person, the bodily links in unconscious phantasy with the id, the phantasy of incorporation which underlies the process of introjection; whereas in the 'image' the somatic and much of the emotional elements are largely repressed" (106). It is clear that unconscious phantasy underlies even the earliest psychic mechanisms. Its psychic constitutive and archaic character mediates between the soma and the outer world; it works at establishing boundaries—inside/ outside—and at organizing sensory experience.

Isaacs remarks that the external world forces itself upon the attention of the child early and continuously, for "experiences during the first twenty-four hours must already evoke the first mental activity, and provide material for both phantasy and memory" ([1952] 1983, 107). The psyche of the infant deals with external and instinctual impulses by means of introjection and projection, and the Kleinians conclude with Freud that the disappointment of hallucinatory satisfaction is the first spur to some degree of adaptation to reality (108).

It is most interesting that Isaacs considers phantasy thinking and reality thinking not only as distinct mental processes—when fully developed—but also as "different modes of obtaining satisfaction" ([1952] 1983, 108). In her view, reality thinking cannot operate without concurrent and supporting unconscious phantasies (109). Melancholia, in this respect, can be thought of as a particular mode of obtaining satisfaction supported by the phantasy of incorporation and effected by the mechanism of introjection.

In her papers "Early analysis" ([1923] 1975a) and "The importance of symbol-formation in the development of the ego" ([1930] 1975), Klein took up Ferenczi's view that primary identification, which is the forerunner of symbolism, arises out of the baby's endeavor to rediscover in every object his or her own organs and their functioning.[7] She showed how the primary symbolic function of external objects enables phantasy to be elaborated by the ego, allows sublimations to develop—in play and manipulation—and builds a bridge from the inner world to interest in the outer world. Early learning is based upon the oral impulses. Isaacs refers to a number of conscious metaphors through which we represent unconscious psychic reality: "In our view, reality-thinking cannot operate without concurrent and supporting unconscious phantasies; e.g. we continue to 'take things in' with our ears, to 'devour' with our eyes, to 'read, mark, learn and inwardly digest,' throughout life" ([1952] 1983, 109). Primary objects are invested with oral libido, and perception and intelligence draw upon this source of libido for their life and growth.

Laplanche and Pontalis subscribe to much of Susan Isaacs's thesis. Since phantasy is the direct expression of a drive and both drive and phantasy are inseparable from their object, they conclude that "One is therefore obliged to provide every mental operation with an underlying phantasy which can itself be reduced on principle to an instinctual aim" ([1964] 1986, 24). In their view, originary phantasies are associated to autoeroticism in the young child, a moment when sexuality moves into the field of phantasy. Autoerotic satisfaction is the product of the activity of partial drives, which are closely linked to the excitation of specific erogenous zones. It is not part of a "global pleasure" but of a "fragmented pleasure, an organ pleasure [Organlust] and strictly localized" (26). It is at this moment that phantasy mediates between the source and aim of pleasure, even though the object of pleasure has been lost. Phantasy plays a crucial role in compensating for this loss. Laplanche and Pontalis insist that the structural character of phantasy acts as the setting of desire: "In fantasy the subject does not pursue the object or its sign: he appears caught up himself in the sequence of images. He forms no representation of the desired object, but is himself represented as participating in the scene although, in the earliest forms of fantasy, he cannot be assigned any fixed place in it" (26). In their view, desire is not merely a part of the drives; it is articulated logically into the fantasy structure, and therefore it is "a favored spot for the most primitive defense reactions" (27). The subject does not appear to be in control of the phantasy as if it were a narrative but as if it were desubjectivized in "the very syntax of the sequence in question" (26).

Literal(ly) Klein

Mary Jacobus, in an intelligent reading of Klein's "The importance of symbol-formation in the development of the ego" ([1930] 1975), with Lacan and Kristeva, begins by saying that Klein moves "with untroubled literalness" (1990, 161) between phantasy and its objects in an essay that resists the Lacanian language-based account of the relations between sexuality and subjectivity. Jacobus takes the case study of Klein's patient Dick as that of a borderline case, "between the regressive and the 'premature,' the literal and the metaphorical, or instinct and signification" (162), which shows a simultaneous failure to develop in the sphere of object relations and language.

After showing the main arguments of Lacan's critique of Klein in the section "Discourse analysis and ego analysis" in *Seminar I*, based on what Lacan's claims to be her "brutal," literal-minded application of her patient's Oedipus complex, Jacobus argues that we could speculate that it is the troubling presence of Kleinian object relations that Lacanian theory is reluctant to acknowledge.[8]

Taking into account the conflictual relation that the notion of projective identification introduces, a "confused category of identification" in Jacobus's own words, and one that problematizes the process of differentiation between self and other, she further refers to Klein's "The origins of transference" ([1952] 1975c), a paper in which Klein reminds her readers that Freud in *The ego and the id* argued that the first and most important identification was that with the father of personal prehistory. In a footnote, Klein goes on to claim that in Freud "these first identifications . . . are a direct and immediate identification which takes place earlier than any object cathexis. This suggestion seems to imply that introjection even precedes object-relations" (*OT*, 52). Klein points to the oscillation in Freud's views on the issue.

Jacobus reads Kristeva reading the apparent equivocations of Freud when Kristeva writes of "incorporating and introjecting, orality's function . . . the essential substratum of what constitutes man's being, namely *language*" ([1987] 1989, 26). In the chapter "Freud and Love," Kristeva introduces what she calls a "Third Party," or the archaic inscription of the father, which "seems to me a way of modifying the fantasy of a phallic mother playing at the phallus game all by herself, all by herself, alone and complete, in the back room of Kleinism and post-Kleinism" (44).[9] She argues that it is on the borderline between the psychic and the somatic where transference love appears and where the analyst as empathizer accompanies the subject in a regression to his or her most primitive object relations in an attempt to decipher a discourse that exists at the very limits of the appearance of language. She further claims that we should view little Dick's oral incorporation as primary identification. Jacobus herself suggests that we could redefine this identification as the "heterogeneity" of metaphor (1990, 177). She claims that nothing can ever be really "literal"— even for Dick, or for Melanie Klein. In her view, the Lacanian insistence on the agency of the letter in the unconscious becomes for Kristeva "the heterogeneous drift that links drives and signs in the metaphoric structures of transferential discourse. Klein's 'Premature *empathy*' (*Einfühlung*)— what might be called 'pathetic phallacy'—represents the first positing of the subject-in-language, or a founding figural moment, by means of a misplaced identification; it is less a matter of naming (as Lacan has argued) than of misnaming" (178).[10]

Jacobus deliberately reads that moment in "The importance of symbol formation in the development of the ego" when little Dick sees pencil shavings on Klein's lap with a Kristevan turn, for "in abjecting the mother, I (mis)identify or metaphorise myself" (1990, 178).[11] For Jacobus, whereas the Lacanian reading "brutalises" (178) Klein, the Kristevan reading has an empathetic feel.

Jacobus herself, in her pointing to the impossibility of doing a literal reading of Klein, seems to be moving on the borders of one more language-oriented critique of Klein and one that puts into question the very concept of unconscious phantasy at the root of Klein's thought. Jacobus, I believe, comes very close to Abraham and Torok's reading of the collapse of the notions of introjection and incorporation in Klein, drawing from Ferenczi's 1912 definition of introjection. She most graphically concludes: "I'll end by suggesting that rather than eating Klein's words, we might chew on the play of metaphor which little Dick's unspeakable slip . . .

inscribes in the 'literal' of Klein's lines" (1990, 179). Jacobus only touches on the subject of projective identification in passing. Unfortunately, she does not expand on the implications of a possible reading, of a grafting of this later notion in this early Kleinian text. And while this would have added an extra level of complexity to the possibility of differentiating between introjection, incorporation, and identification it would also have proved that this deconstructive potential to destabilize the capacities of perception, phantasy, and language is at the core of Kleinian theory itself.

Reading Phantasy

If . . . phantasy be the "language" of these primary instinctual impulses, it can be assumed that phantasy enters into the earliest development of the ego in its relation to reality, and supports the testing of reality and the development of knowledge of the external world—Susan Isaacs

As has been noted, phantasies are active in the mind long before language has developed. Freud remarked that words belong to the conscious mind. When writing about visual memory, he argued that it approximated unconscious processes more than thinking in words and it was ontogenetically and phylogenetically older than the latter ([1923] 1953, 21). Isaacs reminds us that hysterical conversion symptoms are perhaps the most convincing evidence of the activity of phantasy without words, where every detail of the symptoms turns out to have a specific meaning. The hysteric reverts to a preverbal language and makes use of sensations, postures, gestures, and organic processes to express emotions and unconscious wishes or beliefs, that is, unconscious phantasies.

It is my aim in this section to focus on the reading of two brief case studies reported by Isaacs and interspersed with her material, which, to my knowledge, have not yet received any critical response.[12] These are the only two case studies that Isaacs uses to illustrate her argument, and, interestingly enough, both narrate a perfectly perverse scenario of a fetishistic and melancholic homosexual kind.

The first is the story of a twenty-month-old girl with poor speech development. Since the story is very brief, I think it is worth quoting it completely. Isaacs reports that the girl once

> saw a shoe of her mother's from which the sole had come loose and
> was flapping about. The child was horrified, and screamed with ter-

ror. For about a week she would shrink away and scream if she saw her mother wearing any shoes at all, and for some time could only tolerate her mother's wearing a pair of brightly coloured house shoes. The particular offending pair was not worn for several months. The child gradually forgot about the terror, and let her mother wear any sort of shoes. At two years and eleven months, however (fifteen months later), she suddenly said to her mother in a frightened voice, "Where are Mummy's broken shoes?", her mother hastily said, fearing another screaming attack, that she had sent them away, and the child then commented, "They might have eaten me right up." ([1952] 1983, 90–91)

Isaacs uses the story to show that phantasies predate words. She reads the shoe as a "threatening mouth," following the child's own later perception. As readers of analytic literature, this analysis leaves us wanting. Isaacs does not wish to say one word or devote one section of her rather long essay to the issue of phantasy and perversion or to the role of phantasy in perverse scenarios, even when the only two case studies she narrates are in themselves perverse.

The story just quoted is clearly one of infantile shoe fetishism, with a girl as its protagonist, in which a reversal is effected. Even when the fetish does not provide access to pleasure, it contains anxiety as a screen for the projection of the subject's agonizing state. It is a story about the prohibition imposed by the early positive Oedipus complex on the girl, who is denied direct access to the body of the mother. Access to the body of the mother must be mediated. In other words, the body of the mother must be relinquished as an object of love and a move toward the father must be effected. In our case, the little girl wants to keep her idyll with her mother through the fetish, which comes to substitute for her unattainable breast—at this stage—and by extension her genitals. But the girl's oral-sadistic anxiety comes from the frustration imposed by the Oedipal law and is addressed toward a pair of damaged shoes worn by her mother. The fetish in this case is lived as a potential threat that can devour the girl and strip her of the contents of her body and her genitals. In the frame of the story, the omnipotence of the girl's manic defenses at their height prevents the mother from wearing any sort of shoes for some time. Fifteen months later the girl puts her frightening experience into words. Following closely Melanie Klein's remarks in *The psycho-analysis of children*, we can conclude that the phantasy of the threatening mouth is a cannibalistic oral phantasy of strong sadistic proportions. With reference to Klein's formulation in "Notes on some schizoid mechanisms" ([1946] 1975), through projective identification, the girl projects onto the shoe her own sadistic and destructive impulses, which in turn serves to ward off the fear of potential fragmentation and disintegration of the interior of her body.

The desire for the mother's body is oedipally foreclosed, and the only available way to master anxiety comes through the fetish, which is lived as a threat but finally operates as the very instrument that satisfies the daughter's illicit desire for her mother. The fetish may work both as an antidote against homosexuality and, by means of the mechanism of disavowal, as an effective defense against the enforcement of the oedipal law.

The second case study, on which I would like to dwell on for some time, concerns an adolescent boy who came to Isaacs for treatment because he was experiencing serious difficulties in his home and school life. The patient was a sixteen year old who, among other symptoms, showed "very obvious lying of a sort that was certain to be found out, aggressive behaviour, and a wild untidiness in dress" ([1952] 1983, 102). In Isaacs's words, his "conduct and attitude . . . were those of a social outcast" (102). At the beginning of the analysis, "he had been lonely and miserable and entirely without friends" (102). Isaacs places much emphasis on the fact that her patient was unable to live up to his family traditions. As the analysis progressed, he was able to join the Air Force—after the outbreak of war—and he built an excellent reputation "but always refused to accept a commission" (102). Even when the analysis resulted in a substantial improvement—he was able to maintain steady friendships and was very much liked in the army—he was unable to live up to the social traditions of his family, in which there were many distinguished officers.

Isaacs reports that her patient had a rich phantasy life and that "dominant amongst all other of his phantasies was that the only way of overcoming his aggressiveness towards his younger brother (ultimately, his father) was to renounce all ambition in their favour" ([1952] 1983, 102). The patient felt that it was impossible for both him and his younger brother to be loved and admired by his mother and father. Isaacs puts it this way: "In bodily terms, it was impossible for them both, himself and his younger brother (ultimately himself and his father), to be potent" (102). The patient had phantasized that had he orally incorporated—by means of sucking, swallowing, and possessing it—his father's genital from his mother then the good genital would have been destroyed and his younger brother would have been deprived of it. He would never grow up and become potent; he would never even exist. He opted for renouncing everything in favor of his younger brother (ultimately of his father), and this way he was able to master his aggressivity and fear of his parents.

In Isaacs's interpretation, the analysand had come to be persuaded that there is only one good object of a kind—the good breast, the good mother, the good father's penis—and if one person has this ideal object another must suffer its loss and thus become dangerous to the possessor. Finally, Isaacs ends by saying that this kind of phantasy is widely found, although it usually becomes modified and counterbalanced during development, so that it plays a far less dominant part in life. In the section "Instinct, Phantasy, and Mechanism" which I would argue is the central one in her essay, Isaacs accords a privileged space to the previous story, which is strategically placed between Richard III's soliloquy in Shakespeare and the comments on it in Freud's 1916 "Some character-types met with in psycho-analytic work," which he devotes to the study of "exceptions" in character—people who consider themselves as such.[13] What seems to me most interesting of all is the fact that right after the case study Isaacs selects a remark by Freud: "Richard is an enormously magnified representation of something we may all discover in ourselves" (quoted in Isaacs [1952] 1983, 103). In one of her chapter notes, Isaacs quotes Freud's passage at length. Freud suggests that in Richard's soliloquy there is no mere defiance on account of his physical deformity and that it shows an unconscious argument (or phantasy) that runs as follows: " 'Nature has done me a grievous wrong in denying me the beauty of form which wins human love. Life owes me reparation for this, and I will see that I get it. I have a right to be an exception, to overstep those bounds by which others let themselves be circumscribed. I may do wrong myself, since wrong has been done to me' " ([1916] 1953, 314–15). Apart from the specific contents of the phantasy in Richard III, we may ask what is behind Isaacs's overt allusion to the Freudian remark? The insertion of the case study at this specific place in the essay seems to be a wink at her readers as to how we may all discover in ourselves this physical deformity, these "congenital and infantile disadvantages" ([1916] 1953, 318), in other words, these (repressed) homosexual tendencies. There is nothing exceptional about it.

At the same time, in the context of her discussion of phantasies of incorporation, Isaacs seems to overlook several issues in this case that are central to my argument. Throughout her narrative, Isaacs equates brother and father in her discussion of the case. In this narrative, the mother provides the scenario in which the oedipal rivalry is played out. The "father as rival brother" struggles for the possession of the mother, who harbors the good penis inside. Renunciation of the desired object in favor of the father-brother guarantees survival. The phantasy of incorporation of the good penis would otherwise arouse feelings of fear and guilt and would mobilize paranoid defense mechanisms. The good penis is thus kept as a relic inside the body of the mother. In this narrative, brotherly love is not without cost, but it also grants some rewards. All the brothers will have a share of potency, and thus they will have a share of existence. This rivalry that later is resolved in an empathic homosocial link paves the way for the possibility of identifications and desires that allow room for the emergence of male homosexual love.

Throughout the story, Isaacs overemphasizes matters of social expectations and social recognition in her description of her analysand's problems. She remarks that his "conduct and attitude . . . were those of a social outcast" ([1952] 1983, 102); that "he could not follow the normal course of events for those in his social circumstances" (102); that even when he "built up an excellent reputation [in the Air Force, he] always refused to accept a commission" (102); and that "he was quite unable to live up to the social traditions of his family, in which there were distinguished officers" (120). Nevertheless, she never investigates in depth those "complex causes of external circumstances and internal response" (120) that determined his illness.

Let us remind ourselves that at the beginning of the analysis that the analysand "had been lonely and miserable and entirely without friends" ([1952] 1983, 120). This is a story with an obvious melancholic subtext. Isaacs provides no analytic material concerning the relationship between her patient and his younger brother and between him and both parents. Too many details are left out of the story. And what is it that gets lost and has to be incorporated in order to preserve it? Is it not the case that the paternal superego, with its prohibition on incest and homosexuality, is what is incorporated and melancholizes the subject? A Kleinian reading would point to the foreclosure of the image of the good mother—whose loss cannot be mourned—and incorporation of all that is bad (breast, penis, excrement) as the complex cause of melancholia.

In the context of Isaacs's case study, we have a homosexual in the military after the outbreak of World War II. It is not hard to imagine the incredible amount of anxiety the patient endured in repressing and hiding his sexuality in a most homophobic context, in an institution where manhood has to be proved through innumerable acts of violence, sadism, and aggressivity. Is there an exit to melancholia, a way out of the paranoid-schizoid position when the external world is unequivocally entrenched at its very limits?

An Aesthetics of Phantasy?

The external physical world is in fact libidinized largely through
the process of symbol-formation.—Susan Isaacs

There can be no aesthetic pleasure without perfect form.—Hanna Segal

Freud linked the desire to know to childhood curiosity about sex, particularly to that associated to the primal scene. Intellectual activity is thus a form of libidinal sublimation that can be inhibited by anxiety, with castration anxiety being its most recurrent mode. The Kleinian position acknowledges from early on the role of symbolization in achieving both differentiation and relationship to the experiences of the self and others. The relationship between the origins of symbol formation and the containment of anxiety (separation, disintegration, loss) is critical in the development of the subject. Definite states of the internal world will give rise to different forms of symbolization.

In her early writings, Klein links the epistemophilic impulse to sadism, with the desire to appropriate the mother's body and its contents. This origin of the desire to know in an aggressive impulse toward the body of the mother ultimately makes intellectual development dependent on the integration of aggression. All knowledge acquired from the outside world stems from the symbolic equation of a phantasized internal object and an external one.[14] In normal development, internal phantasies are modified when they come into contact with reality.

Originally, the symbolic connection between internal object and external reality is concrete. Gradually, as phantasy is modified through contact with external reality, the symbolism is loosened and becomes more abstract. Not only can the mother's body represent an inner object; virtually any outer object can do so as well. The original symbolic equation collapses, and the elements of the equation that are not identical stand at large in some sort of metaphoric relation. So one element may represent another because the elements resemble each other in significant ways without being identical. In other words, an internal object may come to stand for a number of external objects and vice versa.

Some Kleinians have expressed the relationship between the rigid and loose symbolic equations in terms of projective identification. In the rigid symbolic equation, there is a projection of mental states into the symbol. The symbol becomes a container, and the relationship established is one of omnipotence and total control. Progressively, a degree of acceptance of the separation of symbol and the thing symbolized is reached. Projective identification still operates, but it no longer seeks fusion and total control. Far from that, the collapse of the symbolic equation requires that the subject mourn the loss of identity between symbol and thing.[15] The individual must mourn the loss of a world in which every object is an extension of the mother's body. Therefore, in the Kleinian account mourning is not only necessary for emotional health; it is also necessary for mature thought.

In Hanna Segal's view, the process of symbolization requires a three-term relationship—ego, object, and symbol.[16] The formation of the symbol develops in the course of the transition from the paranoid-schizoid to the depressive position. In the course of normal development, in the paranoid-schizoid position the concept of absence barely exists. This primal Kleinian world of object relations is overpopulated with all kinds of beneficial and malevolent part objects. The early symbols are formed by means of projective identification, resulting in the formation of symbolic equations. Segal expanded on the notion of symbolic equation to denote the early symbols, which differ profoundly from those formed later. In her view, the early symbols are not experienced as symbols or substitutes but as the original object itself. In the course of development, disturbances in ego-object differentiation may lead to disturbances in differentiation between the symbol and the symbolized object. This explains why the symbolic equation lies at the root of the concrete thought characteristic of the psychoses (1957, 393). For Segal, excessive projective identification equates the object with the projected part of the subject, leading to what has been called a "concrete identificate" (Sohn 1985, 205), treating the symbol not only as though it were the original object but also, and predominantly, as part of oneself.

In the depressive position there is a greater degree of differentiation and separation between ego and object, and after repeated experiences of loss, reunion, and re-creation a good object is reliably installed in the ego.

The symbol is then used to overcome a loss that has been accepted because the ego has become capable of giving up the object and mourning for it. According to Segal, this is experienced as a creation of the ego. However, this stage is not irreversible because symbolism may revert in moments of regression to a concrete form, even in nonpsychotic individuals.[17]

Hanna Segal understands phantasy as a wishful hypothesis that is constantly compared to reality (1964, 1980). If the phantasy is omnipotent, desire disappears and phantasy becomes a delusion. But in the more normal infant there is a capacity to perceive a reality different from the phantasy. In her view, forming a picture of the real object and differentiating it from the hallucinated one, noting its real characteristics, both good and bad, can lead to a wish to obtain as much satisfaction from the object as possible. A rational action thus must be based on the recognition of reality.

Segal developed a Kleinian inspired aesthetic theory. In "A psychoanalytical approach to aesthetics" (1952), she argues that art is an expression of the depressive position. It is guilt, as a result of the subject's own hatred and aggression, that gives rise to the need to restore and re-create. I think it is important to note that in both Klein's and Segal's accounts, even when the depressive position is central in creativity, creativeness is not fully exhausted in it. The possibility of creating in the paranoid-schizoid position or in the difficult transit and negotiation between both positions is not foreclosed. Following the insight on early guilt in Klein's "On the theory of anxiety and guilt" ([1948] 1975), Segal writes: "Feelings of guilt probably play a role before the depressive position is fully established; they already exist in relation to the part object, and they contribute to later sublimation; but they are then simpler impulses acting in a predominantly paranoid setting, isolated and unintegrated" (1952, 198).

The picture of integration and cohesion that Segal is aiming at in her work on art as a result from the depressive position is undermined by her (and Klein's) own assumptions on the provisionality and instability of any position as such and, I would argue, by the very definition of *position* in Klein's work.[18] How, then, can we account for the disruption, instability, revolt, anger, and dissent present in much art, certainly in the avant-garde movements of the 1920s and 1930s, especially in dadaism, surrealism, and several modernisms?

Segal points out that in the unconscious of all artists there is an acute awareness that all creation is the re-creation of a once loved and once whole but now ruined and lost object, a ruined internal world and self. For

Klein, the mourner is not only deprived of the lost object but also fears the loss of his or her internal good objects, with which the loved person—or the "ideal" in the most general sense—was identified. Mourning thus reinstates the individual's internal objects, becoming once again convinced of their presence via creative phantasies. For Segal, Marcel Proust epitomizes the aesthetic attitude. In the Proustian universe, only the lost past and the lost or dead object can be made into a work of art.

Segal uses Dilthey's term *nach-erleben* (to reexperience) to describe the process by means of which the re-creation and restoration of lost loved objects help reinstate our internal objects. Art implies destruction, loss, and restoration. The creative act is a successful act of mourning. She argues that the death drive (understood as aggression, rage, and hatred) is denied less in great art than in any other human activity. Art is the field in which Eros and Thanatos play out their eternal struggle. Eros, for Segal, must be viewed not only as the desire for gratification but as an expression of the desire to make reparation. Nevertheless, the reparation that Kleinian aesthetics propounds is ultimately an internal, symbolic act that has nothing to do with the repair of actual people or objects.

Aesthetic pleasure is also experienced by the artist's public, and this vicarious pleasure in Segal's view operates as a kind of unconscious reliving of the creator's state of mind based on identification. In her brief discussion of classical tragedy—*Oedipus Rex*—she distinguishes two essential factors that make it successful as a tragedy, namely, "the unshrinking expression of the full horror of the depressive position and the achievement of an impression of wholeness and harmony" (1952, 204). She wonders whether this tragic element is essential to any aesthetic experience and attempts to explain it in terms of the death drive. The artist must acknowledge the death drive, in both its aggressive and self-destructive aspects, and accept the reality of death of the object and the self if he or she wants to realize and symbolically express depression. In Segal's words, "The achievement of the artist is in giving the fullest expression to the conflict and the union between [the death and life instincts]" (204).

I would like to call attention to yet another interesting twist in Segal's 1952 essay. When she writes about the pleasures experienced by the public in the apprehension of a work of art, she discusses the common reactions to the new in the form of resistance and rejection or idealization and admiration: "These prevalent reactions of the public are, I think, manifestations of a manic defence against the depressive anxieties stirred by art. The artists find ever new ways of revealing a repressed and denied depression. The public use against it all their powers of defence until they find the courage to follow the new artist into the depths of his depression, and eventually to share his triumphs" (206). Whereas she wants to emphasize the role that manic defenses play in these attitudes in order to abandon them in favor of what seems to be a more realistic assessment, she finally succumbs and endorses an especially manic view of our apprehension of art.

It would be crucial to be able to distinguish between creative acts and phantasized reparation, but this is difficult to grasp in the Kleinian account. As C. Fred Alford sees the problem: "The artistic representation acknowledges the external world, even as it goes on to create another one. In creating another world of perfect wholeness and reconciliation, art calls attention to the contrast between this perfect world and its damaged, fragmented, empirical counterpart. It is in this contrast between fantasy and reality that the emancipatory power of art resides" (1989, 116). For Alford, whereas art need not terminate in premature catharsis, reparation in phantasy most likely will.

As far as projective identification is concerned, when considering how art can confront the meaninglessness of existence, Alford, siding with Klein, puts it this way: "The world possesses a surfeit of meaning, the result of projective identification, in which we make the world like us in order to make a home in it. Rather than find ourselves thrown into a world already void of meaning, we empty it ourselves via our envy, greed, and hatred, taking from the world all the goodness that might make it a decent home for humanity" (1989, 129). Alford remarks that beneath the terror of meaninglessness lies humanity's terror at its own irrational aggression. The real tragedy is that it is the individual who makes the world an empty, unresponsive place.

Alford remarks that the Kleinian account suggests that the problem of integrating our love and hate is so profound—and so constitutive of reality—that it will remain a severe problem in any imaginable society, even though it may take different forms. He maintains that one of the reasons why Klein's account is tragic is because there is no redemption. A Kleinian perspective holds out little hope for individual transformation on the basis of the importance granted to the death drive and aggressivity. Nevertheless, in Alford's words, "It finds in human nature as it is currently constituted cause for hope—a hope, to be sure, that remains tragically unfulfilled, especially in the large group" (1989, 136).

By 1907, when Freud wrote "Creative writers and day-dreaming" ([1907, 1908] 1953), the predominance of phantasy over memory (connected to real events in the subject's life) seemed to be firmly established. Once Freud abandoned the seduction theory, external yielded to psychic reality. In *The interpretation of dreams* ([1900] 1953, 492–93), Freud mentions the importance of daydreams (*Tagträume*), which he relates to unconscious phantasies without making any distinction between the two: "There are unconscious ones in great numbers, which have to remain unconscious on account of their content and their origin from repressed material" (492).

The idea of unconscious phantasy as an analogue of daydreaming confronts us with an interesting notion: a daydream is an elaborate, essentially *verbal* and representational production, *visual* in nature, implying a highly developed level of psychical functioning. At the same time, the experience of satisfaction introduced by Laplanche and Pontalis ([1967] 1973) implies the search for a *perceptual identity*. After all, phantasy is for Freud a wishful phantasy (*Wunschphantasie*), so that the wish is defined for us as based on the impulse to repeat the experience of satisfaction.

Analyst Janine Chasseguet-Smirgel (1995) holds that the search for perceptual identity suggests that the origin of the most primitive phantasies (whether or not hallucinatory in form) lies in somatic sensations and that the hallucinatory fulfillment of the wish repeats the experience of a full mouth or a warm womb and is not a visual hallucination of an object (the breast): "In other words, the level here is a preverbal one, in which objects do not yet exist as such and are at any rate not sufficiently distinct from the subject to give rise to a visual hallucination. The latter presupposes the prior overall apprehension of an object at a distance from the subject" (111).

Chasseguet-Smirgel understands these unconscious phantasies that are initially connected with bodily sensations and not attached to words and visual representations as "primary matrices of phantasies" (1995, 111). In line with the Kleinians, she understands the unconscious as "consist[ing] essentially of object relations" (111). In her account, physical activity is deemed to comprise a set of phantasies about relations with objects, while perception is experienced as the incorporation of objects. Thoughts themselves are identified with objects from the very beginning of life. She acknowledges that it is impossible to accept this immediacy of object relations while maintaining the belief in the existence of a brief phase of primary narcissism from which the child emerges gradually into the acknowledgment of the existence of an object separate from him or herself. However, she believes that "we are bound to suppose that the beginnings of phantasy activity have to do primarily with coenaesthetic experiences closely associated with the instincts and their biological substrates, the matrices of more elaborate future phantasies and imaginings, which are both visual and verbal in nature" (111–12).

For Chasseguet-Smirgel, it is quite clear that not only Melanie Klein but also Freud considered that there is an innate knowledge of the breast and sexuality (objects suitable for satisfying the self-preservative drives and the sexual drives). In "The Wolf Man" ([1914] 1918), Freud postulates the existence in man of an *instinctive* knowledge similar to that of animals, which forms the *nucleus* of the *unconscious*, a primitive kind of mental activity that would later be dethroned and overlaid with human reason. Freud takes it that instinctive knowledge of this kind was involved when the child witnessed the primal scene at the age of eighteen months. Chasseguet-Smirgel writes: "Even if this is inconsistent with many of Freud's other statements (some of them even included in the account of the Wolf Man's treatment) concerning ignorance of the vagina in both sexes until puberty, the idea of instinctive knowledge nevertheless indicates the possible existence of early phantasy activity" (1995, 112). In her view, psychotics return to the somatic matrix of phantasy, that is, to a narcissistic phase prior to subject-object differentiation. She puts it this way: "This is merely another way of saying that delusion, which incorporates these primitive sensations in the web of meanings that also includes objects, does indeed constitute an attempt to re-establish the links of object relations" (113).

When Chasseguet-Smirgel turns to the part played by narcissism in creation by citing Freud's conception of the ego-ideal (Freud [1914] 1953) as a substitute for primary narcissistic perfection, the ego-ideal becomes the heir to narcissism because "man has here again shown himself incapable of giving up a satisfaction he had once enjoyed. He is not willing to forgo the narcissistic perfection of his childhood; . . . What he projects before him as his ideal is the substitute for the lost narcissism of his childhood in which he was his own ideal" (94).

Chasseguet-Smirgel ([1975] 1985, 1984) has emphasized the importance of the part played by the ego-ideal in the process of identification. In *Creativity and perversion* (1984), she summarized it as follows.

From this point onwards there will be a gap, a rift between the ego and its ideal. The ego will aim at stitching the two gaping sides of the wound which is henceforth its characteristic. Union with the first object in which the lost narcissistic perfection has been vested will become one way by which to retrieve its initial narcissism. As may be supposed, the narcissistic state is fantasized as identical in nature to the fusion between the infant and its mother on the model of the intra-uterine situation. . . . I believe that the incestuous wish rests upon narcissistic motivations: the desire to re-experience that time when the ego and the non-ego were merged. . . . In normal cases, nostalgia for primary narcissism when the child himself constituted his own ideal, pushes the subject to project his narcissism ahead of him onto his oedipal father. Nostalgia for primary narcissism may, however, lead . . . to avoid[ance] of the whole process. Forward projection of narcissism by the subject in the form of the ego-ideal is . . . in conformity with the reality principle, which leads to maturation and development. (27–28)

This led her to distinguish two paths. The first is "the short path: merging with the mother will take place here and now, without the need for evolution and growing up. Thus the long path which leads the subject to the Oedipus complex and genitality must be seen as opposed to the short path which maintains the subject fixed in pregenitality. These two paths define different forms of the ego-ideal" (1984, 28). On the basis of this conception of the ego-ideal, Chasseguet-Smirgel ([1975] 1985, 1984) concluded that there are two forms of creative activities or processes: one that integrates all the stages of development and all the obstacles it has met with, finding its satisfaction in the search for truth; and one that circumvents obstacles, masks the faults and disguises the pregenital character of the ego and the work that reflects it. This second form of the creative process is attributed to the pervert, although "not all the creations of perverse subjects are in fact false" (1995, 118). She goes on to note that some of them "can become the searing expression of their struggle against the lie that pervades their sexual behavior (Marcel Proust, for example . . .)" (118). Nonetheless, she argues that "some perverse productions remain a model for anyone wishing to understand the sleight of hand at work in the creative process" (118). Her essentializing arguments show in statements such as "The natural hypothesis is that an 'authentic' work of art is an approach from a certain aspect to a *truth* and that the satisfaction its creator derives from it (which is subsequently shared by its reader, listener or viewer) results from the sense of a *match* between that which seeks expression and the work created, even if both give rise to anxiety, pain, or even horror" (118). She argues that, although "false" creation may exert a certain fascination—whereas an "authentic" work seldom fascinates—"The aesthetic emotion it arouses is similar to that which may accrue from the discovery of the truth, which, in the words of the French proverb, 'Toute vérité n'est pas bonne à dire,' is not always suitable for telling (or for hearing). The aesthetic emotion is not then a bonus of pleasure or the result of a seduction (as it may be in the case of an inauthentic work) but is a matter of the work's very essence" (120).

We may wonder what counts as true or false in Chasseguet-Smirgel's elaborations. And what is at stake when she invokes Proust as an emblem of the struggle against the lie of homosexuality? Who and from what position of power can determine of what the "sleight of hand" at work in the creative process consists? Why is there an aversion to being seduced by a work of art? How can one define the essence of a work of art? Beneath the facade of an apparently balanced, democratic, and redemptive description of the beneficial operations of the work of art on its beholders it is not difficult to discern the blind spots of a theory that lays claim to oedipal genitality as the necessary precondition of "healthy" creativity.

The conclusion to be drawn to all this seems to be that only perversion can lure and seduce us into "(false) perception"—into the delusions of perverse sexuality?—whereas the authentic work of art will not entice us in any way but rather will give us access to a truth that might better remain undisclosed, since who may be in the privileged position of telling and receiving such a truth? Chasseguet-Smirgel's account of the workings of creativity takes us back more than two decades before the poststructuralist debates on the death of the author and well before postmodern debates on gender and sexuality.[19] How can we, if at all, assess the validity of her claims from present perspectives? Is there a way in which we can reflect on phantasy, sexuality, melancholia, and creativity while avoiding essentialist pitfalls and elaborating from a more radical philosophical and psychoanalytic perspective? Part of the aim of this volume is to give some answers, even if provisional, to these questions from a radical rereading of the Kleinian oeuvre. Klein's and Segal's insights on unconscious phantasy, symbol formation, sublimation, and creativity open up ways to rethink aesthetics and sexuality by questioning such notions as truth, resemblance, and representation. As I will attempt to show in my reading of modernist texts, their contributions prove especially fruitful when they address mourning, melancholia, and the thematics of object loss, the tenets upon which Kleinian psychoanalysis is constructed.

The Death Drive, Phantasy, and Reparation

It could perhaps be said that the only way we ever experience death (as distinct from dying) is in a change in the mode of a relation.—Leo Bersani

The thesis that Leo Bersani puts forward in *The culture of redemption* (1990) seeks to counter what he sees as the crucial assumption of those commonly held ideological and aesthetic views that argue "that a certain type of repetition of experience in art repairs inherently damaged or valueless experience" (1). According to Bersani, views on the beneficently reconstructive function of art in culture depend on a devaluation of both historical experience and of art. His claims are for a vision of art unavailable for legitimizing plots such as those that seek to exercise "the tyranny of the self in the prestigious form of legitimate cultural authority" (4). He argues for a reading of sexuality in very diverse texts and writers as a "primary, hygienic practice of nonviolence" (4) and as a kind of biological protection against the tyrannies of the self understood as an "ethical ideal" and a sanction for violence.

In his essay, "Death and literary authority: Marcel Proust and Melanie Klein," Bersani reads together the "mortuary aesthetic" (1990, 7) of Proust's *Remembrance of things past* ([1914–19] 1981) and Melanie Klein's views on sublimation in part of her work. Proust, probably more than any major artist, embodies the tendency to think of cultural symbolizations as essentially reparative. For Proust, art depends on death; the artist can possess others only when they are dead, "only then is nothing opposed to our image of them" (Bersani 1990, 8). In Bersani's own terms, this translates into the fact that the posthumous possession of others is always "an unprecedented self-possession" (8). In Proust, "Experience destroys; art restores" (14).

In view of her later work, Bersani sees in Klein's early work, especially in her essay "Early analysis" ([1923] 1975a) some very "non-Kleinian" answers to the question of how cultural activities are invested with sexual interests. In "Early analysis," Klein discusses the role of anxiety in the "neurotic inhibitions of talent" (77). Here Bersani remarks that Klein equates " 'the capacity to sublimate' with 'the capacity to empty superfluous libido [*before*, it is implied, either fixation or repression] in a cathexis of ego-tendencies" (1990, 16).

In what Bersani reads as Klein's movement from identification to symbolism in "Early analysis," identification produces pleasure.[20] In this view, "the symbolizing pleasure would be nothing more than a compulsive substitute for the frightening or forbidden original pleasures" (1990, 17). Bersani sees that the originality of the first Kleinian insight in this essay begins to dissipate when in specific instances of symbol formation she seems to be describing symptom formation. For Bersani, central to EA is Klein's assumption of a certain quantity of "superfluous" or "suspended" libido. He reads it as a moment in the individual's history of uncertainty about the fate of sexual energy when "it is as if sexual excitement exceeded the representations attached to it and therefore became greedily, even promiscuously, available to *other* scenes and *other* activities" (17). In Bersani's view, this displacement of libido can be called symbol formation only if the objects and activities effected by it *"act symbolically without symbolizing anything external to them"* (17).

What I wish to emphasize in Bersani's arguments is his contention that the Kleinian idea that pleasurable situations (experienced or phantasized) are "given play in an ego-tendency . . . [and] the fixations are divested of their sexual character" (EA, 87–88) means that the ego tendencies in question can no longer be considered symbolic—in the analytic sense—and would result in a "nonallusive or nonreferential symbol" (1990, 18). Bersani writes: "Thus the most varied ego interests would represent symbolically not specific sexual fantasies but the very process by which human interests and behavior are *sexually moved*. From this perspective, sublimation can no longer be described (as it usually has been) in terms of a drive whose aim has been changed or displaced, for the drive in question would be, precisely, an aimless one, a kind of floating signifier of sexual energy. Sublimation would describe the fate of sexual energies detached from sexual desires" (18).

Bersani accurately points out that the view of sublimation as coextensive with sexuality occupies a marginal place in Kleinian thought. He describes her most extensive view on sublimation as "the infant's most sophisticated defense against its own aggressions" (1990, 19). In this way, it becomes symbolic reparation. According to this version, as it is developed in "The importance of symbol-formation in the development of the ego" ([1930] 1975), Klein writes, "not only does symbolism come to be the foundation of all phantasy and sublimation, but, more than that, it is the basis of the subject's relation to the outside world and to reality in general" (221).

Bersani thus sees two different versions of sublimation in Klein, and he remarks that according to the latter "the ego's 'new' object relations are, by definition, new relations to old fantasy objects. Originally the ego is involved in a relation to a real other body (the mother's) but, curiously enough, as the ego develops, its relations become more spectral or fantasmatic. The objects and interests that symbolically represent the subject's early relation to the world of objects are restitutive repetitions of those early relations, which means that they fantasmatically recreate what was already a fantasmatic remodelling of the world. These new sublimations are, as it were, at two removes from any real objects; they are fantasy reparations of fantasy destructions" (1990, 20).

From the Kleinian account, Bersani assumes a relationship with a "real other body," which seems to me entirely problematic since within the Kleinian notion of unconscious phantasy this is a contradiction in terms. There is no way in which we can posit a primary relation to a "real other body." This original body is always already tainted by the infant's perception of it, and there is no perception without a phantasy since there is no perception without an initial movement of introjection. Phantasy covers everything, and this spectral character, which Bersani sees as gradually increasing, is there from the start. The Kleinian approach presupposes that our perception of the external world is always and irreducibly enmeshed in unconscious phantasy. Furthermore, we cannot draw a line in the Kleinian system between real and phantasy reparation, as in the case of obsessional or manic reparation, to mention but two examples.

Bersani acknowledges that his aim "is neither to deny nor defend the validity of this [Proust's and Klein's later] theory of sublimation" (1990, 21). He reminds us that Jean Laplanche suggested that sublimation has two modes of operation: first, as the investment of ego interests with a kind of floating or suspended sexual energy (equivalent to Klein's early view); and, second, as the other corresponding to the appropriation of the entire cultural field as "substitute objects" for the desired and feared objects or as a repository of more or less socially useful activities in which the aims of sexuality can be symbolically deflected.

Bersani sees a theoretical shift in Freud analogous to that of Klein, which has to do with the development of the structural theory of the ego laid out in Freud's *The ego and the id*, which would give us a notion of sublimation.[21] As Bersani accurately points out, "sublimation would be a relation to objects that is structurally determined by the already established relations among those internalized and lost objects which make up an ego and a superego" (1990, 22). He argues that both Freudian and particularly Kleinian views on sublimation give us diminished views of both sexuality and cultural imagination since in both systems the forms of culture are ultimately "regressive attempts to make up for failed experience" (22). Bersani translates this into a stance in which "Claims for the high morality of art may conceal a deep horror of life. . . . Everything can be made up, can be made over again, and the absolute singularity of human experience—the source of both its tragedy and its beauty—is thus dissipated in the trivializing nobility of a redemption through art" (22).

Bersani is quite right in disclosing the hidden agenda that lurks behind claims for the redemptive power of various forms of cultural production and would probably agree with the fact that this does not apply to all art but rather to a modern and elitist conception of "high" art as opposed to the diverse and rich manifestations of popular culture. I would subscribe to his warning and his critique of the perils of falling into the delusion that art may redeem the subject from anything, certainly not from the potentially unlimited paths sexuality may take. Nevertheless, I must object to his assigning to Klein—even more than to Freud, as he contends (1990, 22)—what he reads as a view of art as fundamentally made of "spectral repetitions . . . presented as a goal of normative development" (22).[22] It is certainly true that in Klein's ideas on sublimation and reparation from her early to her latter work, including her last essay, "On the sense of loneliness" ([1963] 1975)—one of her most important pieces in my view—she sees art as an outcome of depressive anxiety and a product of the depressive position.[23] The impulse to make reparation for the damage caused by the ego's aggression and destructive impulses arises when the object is both felt as whole and injured, and guilt and concern urge the ego to repair the damage.[24]

But let me remind you of the deconstructive efforts Klein undertakes, the subversion of any normative teleology implicit in her theory of the fragility of the paranoid-schizoid and depressive positions I am attempting to show in this book. The impossibility of ever working through the depressive position and the falling back into circles of sadism and aggressivity, with their specific modes of paranoid-schizoid defenses, are explicit in most of Klein's later work.

A consideration of projective identification from its formulation in Klein's "Notes on some schizoid mechanisms" ([1946] 1975) would probably help us to further problematize and add complexity to the apparently unproblematic Kleinian endorsement of what, in her time, was the omnipresent modernist aesthetics of the culture of redemption. Through projective identification, the subject may find an illusory repository of meaning, a repository of signs ready to be used, apprehended, and appropriated. This reappropriative move, which is always the result of a former projection, deludes the subject into a phantasy of plenitude in its engagement in the construction of a world of objects and artifacts that makes him or her forget the emptiness, the state of permanent loss and dereliction, of the inner world. Projective identification, which, as I have argued, is a melancholic mechanism, deludes us into believing that our fabrications will fill in the losses that constitute our personal histories. Art is a product of the depressive position, and the depressive position is a melancholia in statu nascendi that cannot easily be turned into mourning. In this reading of the Kleinian depressive position and the disruptive character of a world made out of too much projection, an almost paranoid state, art finds itself at a loss. Art cannot bridge the gap between sadism and melancholia because art by itself cannot be a substitute for anything. Art cannot repair because reparation is always yet to come.

To conclude, I would like to argue that the melancholic's cultural productions are fractured. There is an inherent inability to symbolize, to draw the boundary between the literal and the nonliteral. The result of this is the excessive (modernist) concern for the form, which is conceived of not only as an extension of the content but as the content itself. Thus, I would argue, there is an emphasis on the literalization of the form that is figured in the elusiveness of empty tropes such as the image of the frame with nothing inside, the hysterical overacting of masquerade, the traumatic repetition of an enigmatic scene, or the paranoid splitting and metonymic exchange of spare parts. The tropology of modernist melancholic cultural productions is certainly very wide. In this project, I will explore the implications of a Kleinian object-relations theory of reading for modernist texts in which melancholia emerges as a fictional (or visual) mode of mastering anxiety (the anxiety of object loss) by way of a transformation of the workings of the death drive and its constitutive role in the construction of sexualities.

From a Kleinian perspective that understands symbolization as the primary instrument of psychic growth and development, I want to suggest that melancholia is a specific form or mode of symbolization that corresponds to a state of intense internalization and has a specific relationship with both neurotic and psychotic states.[25] I would argue that melancholia plays an essential role in the construction of modern(ist) sexualities, especially those that are seen as nonnormative or deviant. The psychic and social failure inherent in the individual's inability to live love in the open and/or to negotiate losses in a nontraumatic way manifests itself in a variety of discourses, which range from public to private and are as evident in literary texts and art as in the competing professionalized and institutionalized discourses of law, politics, psychiatry, psychoanalysis, religion, and morality—to name but a few—whose conflictual interactions result in the specific historical and ideological configuration I am calling "modernisms."

PART TWO

8

Modernist Cultures of the Death Drive

Melancholy betrays the world for the sake of knowledge. But in its tenacious self-absorption it embraces dead objects in its contemplation, in order to rescue them.
—Walter Benjamin

The classic theorization of melancholia portrays the melancholic as an essentially inhibited and passive individual who broods in isolation for something that is irretrievably lost. For Freud, melancholia always indicates a pathological inhibition accompanied by an instinctual impoverishment that gradually becomes strengthened as thinking is sharpened. This sort of equilibrium between the somatic and the psychic becomes decentered on behalf of the work of intellect and imagination, which should be continued nonstop. With this in mind, I will attempt to leave melancholia in the most possible open terrain for definition. Instead of trying to reduce the imaginative activity of the melancholic to the delirious thematics of psychosis—a decision that is not always tenable, especially in the cases of creative subjects—I will endeavor to question the melancholic activity in the context in which it takes place. I might suggest that, like the obsessional, the melancholic can neither overcome the avalanche of ideas that assaults him or her nor assume any of them through the choice of a project in the short run. His or her ideas, which differ in this sense from those of the obsessive, are not worthy of consideration since their selection can only be partial and consequently devoid of value. As a mode of deepened subjectivity, as the reaction between a mournful world and one's subjective concentration, melancholia provides structure by virtue of which the relationship between sociality and subjectivity can become clearer.

Wolf Lepenies finds in the figure of the melancholic a specific category of social rebellion. He identifies melancholia as the simultaneous rejection of both the means and the ends of socially sanctioned behavior ([1969] 1992). In line with Robert Merton's (1968) ideas, Lepenies writes about melancholia as a retreat from and a total rejection of society due not only to the repression by way of social norms and interdictions but also to the total effect of society, which the melancholic experiences as a threat and as potentially suffocating.[1] In their view, what Freud referred to as a "mental constellation of revolt" ([1915, 1917] 1953, 248), is a passive one. Persuaded of the futility of all action, the melancholic retires to his or her own interiority to brood and meditate upon the very conditions of the impossibility of actions themselves. Lepenies writes of the *Zurückgezogenheit*, or retreat into interiority, characterized by nostalgia for the past and apathy toward the present. For Lepenies, the "melancholy disease" appears in a historical conjuncture when the subject is closed off from meaningful modes of self-expression ([1969] 1992). The melancholic *acedia*, his or her indifference and apathy, is thus linked to the impossibility of future significant action.

Lepenies writes of an inability to act at the crux of the melancholic's affliction, and the range of responses to this radical impotence constitutes the spectrum of affective and cognitive states of melancholia. In Lepenies's argument, melancholia may show up at the individual or group level, but in both cases its features comprise a gloomy discourse about the impossibility of action and the meaninglessness of existence ([1969] 1992).

If melancholia, in Lepenies's analysis, arises in specific sociohistorical conjunctures, when the ability to act has been compromised or aborted, it seems that one of the urgent tasks in a critical engagement with melancholia, both in the past and today, is to raise the question of to what extent the enforced conditions that deprive individuals or groups of their ability to act produce melancholia. It is my contention that melancholia is generated by what I call "cultures of the death drive," a variety of forces that produce melancholia, a malaise affecting the "privileged" victims of a new urban, industrialized, and capitalist world order: women, lesbians, gay men, blacks, Jews, ethnic minorities, and in general those who suffered the consequences of deterritorialization and diaspora after the wars. Subsequent losses, as Klein observes, reactivate the primitive paranoid-schizoid position. They are negotiated mimetically, and it is difficult to break the circle of aggression, fear of retaliation and defense that originates at this point.

I want to suggest that in melancholia a phantasy of dispossession of both a social and a psychic space is at work. Reality is perceived as an object-destructive space. The phantasy repertoire generated by the large group contributes to it, operating in the Kleinian paranoid-schizoid position. Cultural, social, historical, political, and psychosexual factors bear on the production of individuals who are prone to melancholia. One of the conclusions of this study is that women, feminine masochists, lesbians, and gay men are more prone to melancholia. To engage in a psychoanalytical and textual inquiry into the reasons why these heterogeneous groups are privileged victims of modernist melancholia is one of my aims. Kleinian melancholia is embedded in Klein's general relational view of the subject and, far from being a flight back to the narcissistic organization suggested by Freud, marks a specific mode of object relations, as I will endeavor to demonstrate.

Psychoanalyses, Modernisms

Virginia Woolf's famous statement "On or about December 1910 human nature changed" (1924, 4) provides a sense of the significant transformations and new developments that were occurring shortly after the turn of the century. Developments in the domains of art, literature, philosophy, psychoanalysis, and the humanities were matched with substantial advances in science, technology, and communications. This rapid pace of progress brought about important changes in the lives of those who went through one of the most exciting and complex periods in contemporary history in the West. Modernism emerges as a cosmopolitan and international movement across national borders, and it flourishes in the metropolitan centers associated with it. Raymond Williams has noted that the modernist centers of Paris, London, Berlin, and New York represent "the imperial and capitalist metropolis as a specific historical form, at different stages" (1989, 47). He cautions that in our approach to modernism we should be aware of the peripheral in its constitutive role in these cultural centers. He argues that our current concerns should involve "looking, from time to time, from outside the metropolis: from the deprived hinterlands, where different forces are moving and from the poor world which has always been peripheral to metropolitan systems. This need involve no reduction of the importance of the major artistic and literary works which were shaped within metropolitan perceptions. But one level certainly has to be challenged: the metropolitan interpretation of its own processes as universal" (47).

Simultaneously, the redefinition of spaces radically changed social and personal relations. Modernism was a diasporic movement, a movement of nomads and exiles in which every individual could potentially feel at home anywhere. Big cities provided the freedom of anonymity and indifference that enabled alternative relations outside the home, in the midst of intellectual communities, and in salons and cafés. The emergence of an independent urban lifestyle was determinant in the modernist undertaking of creative enterprises that otherwise would have been impossible.

Psychoanalysis also disseminated as a migrant movement, with Vienna, Berlin, Zurich, and Budapest as its main original centers. As was the case with modernism, psychoanalysis thrived in exile during the years of the rise of nazism prior to World War II. It is precisely the period from 1927 onward, when Melanie Klein moved to London in response to Ernest Jones's invitation and Freud went into exile (in 1938 after the German invasion of Austria), that interests me, although my study has no strict temporal demarcation. The difficulties inherent in assigning temporal boundaries to different modernisms, or in demarcating stages or phases in the evolution of the changes in Melanie Klein's thought prior to the schism brought about by the Controversial Discussions, are not major areas of concern in my study of modernist melancholia.[2] One of the aims of this book is to explore melancholia as one of the main tenets of Kleinian theory and to see in what ways modernism arises at the crossroads of what I am calling cultures of the death drive in a variety of texts and in the visual arts. Is it possible to read melancholia from a Kleinian perspective in modernist texts? To what extent is the whole Kleinian oeuvre shaped by her theorization of melancholia, and how can modernist discourses and cultures of the death drive enhance this dimension of her thought? To what extent does the embeddedness of melancholia in modernist cultural productions permeate and refashion psychoanalytical ideas on these issues?

Judith M. Hughes (1989) remarks that Klein, Fairbairn, and Winnicott stand as prime examples of independence, "prospering under the protection of the English Channel" (8). She writes: "Though Melanie Klein received her psychoanalytic training on the Continent she was not analysed by Freud, she did not belong to the circle around him, she never practiced in Vienna—and it was in England that she flourished and her theory grew luxuriant. . . . Still more, not one of three [Klein, Fairbairn, and Winnicott] came to psychoanalysis with a conventional psychiatric background. In short, they were on the fringe, so to speak, and this fringe location may well have lessened their commitment to Freudian solutions and prompted a readiness to entertain alternatives" (8–9). Klein holds to her independence, gained outside the mainstream psychoanalytic community; her migrant condition across countries and languages grants her a privileged, albeit marginal, place from which to view the Freudian elaboration with fresh eyes.[3] Psychoanalysis shares with modernism the sense of intellectual community across frontiers and disciplines (medical versus lay analysts). There was a dimension of modernism to which Freud was intellectually attracted. Certain ways of thinking about culture, particularly as they were shaped by social contract theory, were pervasive in different forms of social and intellectual production. The discovery of the unconscious and Freud's new science challenged commonly held ideas and assumptions about the human psyche, sexuality, and normalcy versus pathology and added layers of complexity to thinking about a social dimension informed by all this. It is difficult to try to equate the father figure of Freud with those of the fathers of modernism, Ezra Pound and T. S. Eliot, although they share some common features. The three of them held indisputable leadership in their new movements, they sanctioned what should or should not be done and how, they had close alliances with some members of their groups and confrontations with others, they exercised their patronage for many years, they were mobile and disseminated their credos across nations and continents, and they took to the limit their sense of commitment to the "new" (in science and the arts). Their entrepreneurial personalities enabled them to create new discursive fields with profound repercussions in twentieth-century intellectual history. Moreover, psychoanalysis canonized Freud as much as high modernism canonized Pound and Eliot and their works in a simultaneous process of marginalization of other positions. The institutionalization of modernism and its accession to cultural legitimacy may be fixed in 1922 with the founding of The Criterion and the circulation of texts and ideas for a new epoch.[4] The process of the institutionalization of psychoanalysis was complex due to its circuitous history of allegiances and schisms, of discipleship and heresy. We may take the foundation of the International Psychoanalytic Association in 1910 as the sign that gives public visibility and marks the spread of psychoanalytical ideas around the world. A decade later, Ernest Jones sent to press the first issue of the first psychoanalytic review published in English, The International Journal of Psycho-analysis.

Writers and analysts themselves, together with critics and historians, have participated in the construction of various hegemonic orthodoxies.

Freudianism and high modernism find alternative voices and alternative ways to approach the psyche, its patterns of relation, and the processes involved in creativity. In a different voice, dadaism and surrealism advocated that the unpredictable and the unconscious (atemporal) precipitate the unexpected into history. From the institutional borders of modernism, Melanie Klein and the writers whose works I have examined yield a vast array of responses to the challenges posed by the first decades of the twentieth century.

Modernism participates in the transition from a reliance on philosophy to a reliance on psychology to produce knowledge about the human mind. By the time modernism came of age, the ego, under the scrutiny of psychoanalysis and the social sciences, became an extremely individualized and autonomized entity largely because of capitalist policies and the worldview attached to them. At times, modernism has allied itself with either a psychology of the unconscious or a more empiricist behaviorism—after J. B. Watson's *Behaviorism* (1924)—both of them radically antagonistic. Modernist writers incorporate ideas from William James, Sigmund Freud, the gestaltists, and even the behaviorists to validate such techniques as the stream of consciousness and visual abstraction or ideas concerning poetic language, the link between psychic mechanisms, art and pathology, and the relationship between personality and creativity.

Modernism is constituted by a variety of aesthetic practices that are not built upon any coherent shared philosophical system—the plural *modernisms* thus seems more accurate within the scope of this volume. It envisions the improvement of human life based on values derived from art, introducing notions of genius, self-expression, and inspiration as instruments of world change. Early modernism is characterized by a belief in material, social, and intellectual progress coincident with modernity. The function of embodying meaning is transferred to art, which provides a unique aesthetic experience that simultaneously authenticates its value and its insights. Transcendence is now understood to manifest itself in harmonious visual and literary forms, music, poetry, and metaphor in language.

Freedom from mimesis separates modernism from both impressionism and naturalism and their claims to exactitude of representation. Modernism produces critical formalism, and eventually formalism comes to be its most essential feature. Notions of the impersonality of art gradually emerge, and even in early modernism art translates the artist's psychological processes rather than expressing a personality that precedes the experience of these processes (as in romanticism). From early on, modernism maintained an ethical ideal, understood as an ethical commitment on the part of the artist and exercised through an aesthetic, in a society whose shared ethical bonds were being replaced with political and economic structures that no longer functioned as a universal ethics, a society that now adhered to a utilitarian credo. The human ethical dilemma is central in modernist writing. Humanity is felt to be insignificant, lost, abandoned, or ineffectual, as in the narratives of Joyce, Woolf, Kafka, and Musil. Subjectivity comes to be the battleground where meaning is produced. Moral decision making is ineluctable, and the writer and the fictional character face significant choices with no resources other than psychological insight. The relativity of ethics in a world of chaos makes them intuit their errors and even sense the futility of taking action. Knowing that one's personal behavior or actions might not matter in the grand scheme of things fuels a reflection upon the extent and limits of personal freedom as a source of both grandeur and human insignificance. The modernist artist must face the ultimate meaningless and absurdity of the human world.

The aesthetic ideal in modernism understands art not as retreat from reality but as a means of mastering the dilemmas of daily existence. The artist's individual vision of the world is a response that actively seeks to intervene rather than being passively subsumed by the regular course of events. And since mortality and time cannot be transcended the modernist escape from religious orthodoxy and a morality grounded in the theological imperative goes hand in hand with the abandonment of both an art and a politics whose subject matter had historically been determined by these orthodoxies. This liberates humanity and opens up new ways for a reflection on its goals, limits, and future possibilities.

Politics and Modernisms

By the end of the nineteenth century, modernism has emerged to impede or prevent modernity from proceeding along the path dictated solely by empiricist principles. The consequences of these principles will appear to be the bleak economic dominance of urbanized, industrialized capitalism. . . . Modernist art forms will decorate all contemporary life by the midtwentieth century, but the original modernist aspiration for the art fails. Modernism may even be said to have had the opposite effect of that intended: rather than liberating people from the economy, it helped liberate them only to participate more fully in the economy.—Art Berman

In "Modernity and revolution" ([1984] 1988), Perry Anderson describes modernism as a "cultural force field 'triangulated by three decisive [historical] coordinates': the codification and institutionalization of a highly formalized academicism in the visual and other arts; the emergence of the key technologies of the second industrial revolution (telephone, radio, automobile, etc.); and the imaginative proximity of social revolution" (324–25). The most significant political factor was the defeat of Germany in World War I. After the war, empiricism flourished under the form of logical positivism in England and in the Bauhaus of the Weimar Republic, and all of this paralleled the turn to high modernist literature in the 1920s.

Together with the successes of the cultural and intellectual products of empiricist modernity came the urge for economic colonization and imperialist policies.[5] The spirit of Locke's writings inspired the forms of government established in the former British colonies in America, and empiricism, democracy, and capitalism came to work almost in unison. The increase of urban industrialism and technology was accompanied by an increase in poverty, bad working conditions, alienation, and social malaise. Modernism is a movement that remains rooted in capitalist democracies, where art is considered to have an intrinsic value that readily translates into a market value.[6]

Modernist politics basically takes two conflicting paths, a progressive and a conservative way of looking at society and at the potential of modern times. The ideological battle between socialism and capitalism after the Russian Revolution and the subsequent advent of fascism were major influences in literature and art during the period. We can identify the aesthetic Right (traditionalism and formalism) and the aesthetic Left (avant-gardism and bohemianism), but it would be highly problematical to try to equate them with the political Right and Left.[7] Throughout the 1930s, many critics associated the attacks of visual artists on tradition with bolshevik communism or anarchy, and they proscribed many works of art on political grounds. In the Anglo-American sphere, literary (high) modernism evolved on the Right, encouraged by the anxiety and terror associated to the Russian Revolution.

Modernism endeavors to use the aesthetic experience to enhance the freedom that is an essential component of an individualized personality. The freedoms of imagination, sex, experimentation and movement across frontiers were a product of the Roaring Twenties, with the hiatus of the economic depression during the thirties. During the transition to formalism in the 1920s, high modernist writers—Eliot and Pound explicitly—were in search of aesthetic structures whose formal internal relationships could be permanent and noncontingent and therefore not subject to the ups and downs of history. By the mid-1930s, the fascist Right had repudiated modernism as decisively as did the orthodox socialist Left. After World War II, modernist literary formalism allied itself with the Right. The ideology of the aesthetic Right in high literary modernism holds that there is a sense of a unified tradition in the West and that the institutions of culture embody enduring truths—which can be discovered by objective science—and values. In the domain of the arts, truths related to human nature foster enduring and permanent human values that will constitute their legacy for the future. Moreover, the artwork belongs to a tradition separate from social and political history and art history has its own internal causation, autonomous and self-explanatory.

The modernist avant-garde project seeks to undermine middle-class capitalist values in Europe and America. The aesthetic Left is concerned with an unfinished project for liberation. Human values are in a continuing process of emergence; they are subject to change and radically unfinished. The Left echoes voices of frustration, injustice, disillusionment, and alienation. It believes that modernity has corrupted the middle classes through technology, commodification, and an emphasis on consumption. Its adherents argue that common experience can be enhanced through art and call for radical and fundamental changes in art and in society at large. Finally, they have confidence in social revolution.[8] It should be stressed, however, that most modernist artists tended to adopt individual rather than consistent politically aligned positions. Many of them were active on a number of fronts, including the working out of oppositional ideological stances. Many were involved in pacifism, suffragism, and the defense of freedom of expression and individual and collective rights.

In modernist writing, melancholia takes on a specific political dimension. It is important to make a distinction between the politics effected and produced by melancholia and the notion of a melancholic politics. In the first case, the possibilities for political action in the hands of intellectuals are felt to be substantially curtailed or totally suffocated. The image of the politically detached writer or artist in an ivory tower is a product of the emergent professionalization that took place during the early decades of the twentieth century and ultimately a result of the marketplace. Alternatively, the image of the bohemian or avant-garde artist radically engaged in his or her art—which is not designed for the market in any straightforward manner—suffers the blows of repressive policies and censorship. Second, the traditional links between melancholia and passivity (acedia, *tedium vitae*, spleen) assume modernist forms. The political effects of creativity along the lines of strictly prescribed forms, canons, and styles—imagism, vorticism, and high modernism in its most general sense—inherently negate the artist's intention, that is, his or her phantasies of effective social intervention. The atmosphere of meaninglessness apparent in so many modernist texts translates at times into resignation or endless search. This gives rise to a melancholy politics, which ultimately results in a reluctant collaboration with the very forces modernism seeks to oppose.

Boundaries of Self, Language, Objects

In literature, the self becomes fragmented. In principle, it is a self predicated as autonomous, but its autonomy comes to be undermined by the rigors of rationality, which lead it toward the deterministic worldview of empirical science. The self also depends on a notion of otherness in order to come into being and to be able to assert its entity. The loss of the self's sense of unity and of its capacity for effective action haunts modernist literature. This goes along with an ethics of impersonality very distant from the romantic cult of the self. The fragmentation of the self from within renders it a site where disperse and discrete subjective events—perceptions, emotions, memories—are enacted independently. In its most extreme form, this dissolution of the self results in a cold objectivism that casts its disengaged gaze upon the world.[9] Ultimately, the modernist artist needs a selfhood to place in opposition to society and the economic system. Human consciousness lies between and connects the material and immaterial, and language permeates all human activity. Ezra Pound's exhortation to "make it new" ([1934] 1968, 9) together with the valuation of originality in avant-garde discourse are conflated with a cult of the difficult and the obscure.[10] His emphasis on technical and formal experimentation is epitomized in the statement, "I believe in technique as the test of man's sincerity" (9). The desire to escape conventional language and explore new territories of expression is present in both early and high modernism. This exploration of the new often resulted in a considerable degree of obscurity, in a reflection on the inadequacy of language to give an account of human existence, and even in a refusal to convey frustration and anger through the conventional and contaminated channels of expression at hand. A negativistic worldview goes hand in hand with a negativistic view of language. Modernism moves toward a radical exploration of the possibilities inherent in language, and literature and the visual arts exhibit an explosion of styles, trends, and movements unprecedented in literary and art history.

In modernism, a variety of degrees of linguistic self-consciousness alternate with various degrees of alienation. The inward movement of consciousness comes to deny the reality and value of the external world or else the world exhibits a radical materiality, which, in its literalness, is devoid of meaning. Art provides an alternative between extreme rationality and utter alienation.

One of the main concerns of modernism pivots around the question of the object. The object is understood as a battleground where crises of meaning and artistic validity are resolved and as commodity fetish. In the difficult transit from the aesthetic ideal of early modernism to the growing demands of a mass consumption society, art and its materialization in the objet d'art is seen as necessary.

One of the tenets of imagism was the "direct treatment of the 'thing' whether subjective or objective." In this, Pound clearly advocates the use of "no word that does not contribute to the presentation" ([1934] 1968, 3). The poetic, pictorial, and narrative approach to the object shifts from the predominance of its embodiment of desire to that of ethical responsibility to society. In literary and artistic representation, there is also an increasing concern with the domination of the object world, which parallels a similar trend in continental philosophy (notably in the work of Adorno and other members of the Frankfurt School). Modernist narratives converge as never before in moments when writers show particular affection for the physical thing. Moreover, the primacy of the artist's view over external reality, which comes to be devoid of meaning, leads to his or her sovereignty over objects. Objects are perceived to be subordinate to the perceiving subject, whereby they acquire meaning. But the opposite effect may also occur, for the artist is an observer of external reality and objects and ultimately there is no guarantee of meaning. As Louis A. Sass has noted, "the objects of human experience are reified, transformed into opaque or intransitive entities that can do no more than manifest their own mere presence (when the objects in question are *subjective* phenomena, they seem incapable of referring to a transcendent external world—one experiences experience, as it were; when they are 'objective' things,' they seem unable to evoke or convey human significance or value—one perceives meaningless bits of matter)" (1992, 33).

Modernisms and the Politics of Exclusion

Modernism is an extremely time-conscious movement, which, together with its valuation of a sense of "nowness," manifests a sense of historical impasse in its difficult balance between the demands of the present and its confrontation with the past.[11] The modernist politics of canonicity is founded on parallel exclusionary practices that result in an oppositional rhetoric in our current critical discourses on modernism.

Peter Bürger (1984) argues that the project of the historical avant-garde was inherently political. In their critique of the autonomy of art in bourgeois societies, he sees their attempt to "organize a new life praxis from a basis in art" (49). Bürger is interested in considering art as an institution, understood as a "productive and distributive apparatus" and "the ideas about art that prevail at a given time and that determine the reception of works" (22).

Shari Benstock (1990) has also noted that modernism constructed itself on a political agenda of exclusion. She identifies two main trends in modernism. The first is "the urge towards polarities and oppositions (the proclamation of an adversary culture); the second is the effort to separate art from history (the proclamation of artistic autonomy). In fact, these pulsations are the same, and they lead to high modernism, which justifies continuity and exclusivity, in literary traditions. A different kind of modernism, what I call avant-garde modernism (the excluded Other), announces itself as a rupture, a break with the past, and marks a cultural historical shift" (186). Benstock underlines the fact that even though texts that belong to avant-garde modernism are sometimes written by "high modernists" (Finnegans wake, Pisan cantos) more often avant-garde works are excluded by high modernism.

Andreas Huyssen has argued that modernism operates under the sign of its anxiety (1986, vii) and Benstock states that "Fear of contamination is the founding premise of modernism" (1990, 186). It is my contention that high modernism is essentially phobic (fear of contamination, anxiety, fear of alternative sexualities and political radicalism), and Klein's work on phobias and manic depression, in that she radically innovates, is fundamental for my understanding of different modernisms.[12] The phobias that assail modernism are present in a variety of responses to anxiety situations that put to the test the spirit of the times. They are manifest in defense mechanisms against the potential threat of the new, against social transformations and artistic experimentation, against a direct political confrontation that may lead to another world war, against the challenges that science and technology may pose to the individual, and against the new lifestyles informed and derived from all of this. The history of modernist canonization has been blind to the cultural, literary, and artistic production of women, lesbians, gay men, and racialized and stigmatized Others. By recourse to Klein and her ongoing reflection on the death drive, melancholia, and manic depression and through an analysis of the cultural productions of these abject Others, we may gain a better understanding of the circles of aggression and retaliation as well as of the chances of breaking up these circles in the dynamics of modernism.

Sexuality and Its Discontents

What is obscenity? What is literature? What is the difference
between the subject and the treatment?—Virginia Woolf

The 1895 Oscar Wilde trials had enormous repercussions in the construction of the figure of the modern homosexual. Writing about the beginnings of the figure of the queer in cultural history, Alan Sinfield has aptly remarked: "The sexologists and the boy-love advocates made the masculine/feminine binary structure even more central and necessary while, at the same time, doing little to clarify its confusions. The Wilde trials exploded in the midst of all this urgent ideological work. As a consequence, the entire, vaguely disconcerting nexus of effeminacy, leisured idleness, immorality, luxury, insouciance, decadence and aestheticism, which Wilde was perceived as instantiating, was transformed into a brilliantly precise image" (1994, 118).[13] Sinfield holds that the notion of "effeminacy" was a contested construct and addressed a far wider range of concerns than sexual orientation. Gay men did not think of themselves as women trapped in men's bodies until the sexologists began popularizing this theory in the 1860s. Heinrich Ulrichs, Richard von Krafft-Ebing, and Havelock Ellis were instrumental in creating a new discourse on male and female homosexuality. We must also note the influence of Otto Weininger's misogynist and antisemitic Sex and character (1908) in the wake of a series of late-nineteenth-century views that endeavor to place "genius" within an almost paranoid discourse of physiology.[14] Weininger held that "the man of genius possesses, like everything else, the complete female in himself; but the woman herself is only a part of the Universe, and the part can never be the whole; femaleness can never include genius. . . . A female genius is a contradiction in terms, for genius is simply intensified, perfectly developed, universally conscious maleness" (189).

In Sinfield's view, a queer identity began to coalesce around Wilde in Robert Hichens's novel The green carnation ([1894] 1929)—the emblem of Wilde and his circle—but there is something significant missing in it, and this is the material consideration that at this point the image of the queer as a leisured, effeminate, aesthetic dandy "was discovered in same-sex practices, underwritten by money, with lower-class boys" (Sinfield 1994, 121).[15] The queer came to be a totally unacceptable figure, and after the trials effeminacy was conceived as a product of these men's class and disoluteness. This complicated the question of developing a concept of the homosexual in a way that would not be contaminated by a pure culture of the death drive. The figure of the homosexual was dangerous for the social order, morally despicable, intrinsically corrupt, and potentially infectious (through venereal diseases). The English society homophobic response stigmatized homosexuals, but the occasion of the Wilde trials enabled the appearance and circulation of a public discourse on homosexuality.[16]

The fin de siècle aesthetics of Oscar Wilde and Aubrey Beardsley widely circulated in the bohemian circles of Greenwich Village from 1912 to 1920. Many early modernist writers continued the literary and visual styles of symbolism, decadentism, and aestheticism of the late nineteenth century. This re-creation of earlier styles has in itself a strategic importance that can only be understood within the context of emerging discourses on deviant sexualities. The discourses on inversion, queerness, and camp intersect and overlap in ways that both enrich and problematize our current understanding of the sexual styles of modernism.

The effect of the Wilde trials was comparable to that of the obscenity trials of Radclyffe Hall's The well of loneliness (1928) for lesbianism. Hall's novel was first published in England by Jonathan Cape in July 1928, and a few months later it was withdrawn under obscenity charges and taken to court. As is well-known, Virginia Woolf and several other highly reputable writers (such as E. M. Forster and Desmond MacCarthy) appeared in court basically to support freedom of expression and oppose the trials, in a word, to oppose the enforcement of external morality and the interference of the law in the province of literature. Coincident with the hearings, Woolf and Forster wrote a letter to the editor of the *Nation and Atheneum* in which their major intellectual objection was to the hindrance posed to the "free mind" that both considered essential to their work as writers.

It is well known that Hall's novel avoids explicit descriptions of sex under a facade of decorum and seeks to make a plea for the repressed and marginalized status of lesbianism. Through the image of Stephen Gordon, the archetype of the "mannish lesbian," Hall was largely following the script of Havelock Ellis's ideas on inversion—as an inborn constitutional abnormality—but, due in part to the notoriety of the trials, lesbianism gained wide currency in the late 1920s.[17]

(Homo)phobic modernism translates fear of alternative sexualities and shows up as repression. But it is no less true that many writers's responses to contemporary discourses on sexuality managed to subvert the moral, legal, and aesthetic premises on which censorship was operating. As Adam Parkes has noted, "Where public discourses block the route, modernism takes another path, which, though indirect and sometimes barely perceptible, disturbs discursive conventions more radically than a more direct or polemical approach. Locating obscenity at the level of formal and stylistic experiment, modernism dramatizes crucial questions relating to literary censorship, suggesting subversions and transformations that even Wilde might not have imagined" (1996, 19).

It is indisputable that during modernism censorship and repression in the widest possible sense operated more strongly than ever before. The trials of Radclyffe Hall, James Joyce, and D. H. Lawrence, to name but a few, illustrate a culture threatened by anxieties and fears, which are the product of its own aggressive and retaliatory phantasies against its Others. In the political and legal rhetoric of the times, these Others appear as "enemies," potential threats to the stability, uniformity, and continuity of the system. Issues of artistic and literary representation became entangled in a complex web, with moral and political questions and the meaning of the text, in the hands of judges and legislators and detached from its inherent formal and stylistic features taken to be unidimensional.[18]

Unnatural Rights

Marianne DeKoven has posited a profound connection between the historical emergence of late-nineteenth-century feminist and socialist movements and the development of modernist literature. She argues that "Modernist writing is 'rich and strange,' its greatness lies in its density and its estranging dislocations" (1991, 3). Between 1905 and 1914, the militant Women's Social and Political Union, under the leadership of Christabel and Emmeline Pankhurst, was a serious political force in both peaceful and militant terms. It produced pageants, marches, posters, and banners for display at demonstrations and used these and other more subversive strategies involving direct action (interruptions of male speeches and boycotts of legal initiatives that perpetuated discrimination) to publicize its ideas and their campaigns.[19] The women's movement, initiated by suffragettes, moved far beyond the question of the right to vote to include a vast array of issues that broadened the original battle over democracy. Women's discussion circles endeavored to publicize their ideas and political positions in written form by publishing their own magazines and books outside commercial channels.

The Free Woman, the New Freewoman, and Time and Tide were among the first magazines published in Britain by women who were ideologically close to the ideals of Fabian socialism and more radical anarchist positions.[20] They gradually introduced into their discussions issues of sexuality, women's lack of economic independence, motherhood, and the constrictions imposed upon women by a patriarchal culture. In America, the Little Review (founded by Margaret Anderson in Chicago in 1914) gathered writers and activists (Barnes, Mina Loy, and Emma Goldmann) mostly around women's issues and cultural criticism.

Margaret Sanger, the birth control advocate, was also an assiduous figure in Greenwich Village. In 1915, Sanger coined the term birth-control, and in 1920 she published Woman and the New Race, in which she presents "the revolt of woman against sex servitude" as the "most far-reaching social development of modern times" ([1921] 1969, 1).[21] She advocates voluntary motherhood and stresses the benefits of limiting reproduction—benefits for women, families, and "the race" as a whole. Woman and the new race criticizes traditional ideas concerning motherhood; "encouraging . . . large families" is, for Sanger, a "serious evil" (57). Furthermore, since men oppose contraception—as individuals and through patriarchal institutions—she believes it is up to women to assume responsibility for limiting reproduction (96).

In 1928, Sanger published Motherhood in bondage, a book that expands upon a chapter of the earlier work, in which Sanger gathered letters from women describing their situations and pleading for birth control information. The text consists mainly of letters, organized according to different aspects of "enforced maternity" ([1928] 1956, xi). Sanger wrote an introduction and conclusion for this volume, along with an introductory commentary for each chapter, but the voices in the text are a testimony to what she called "the confessions of enslaved mothers' cries from the inferno of maternity" (60, xi). Sanger's avowed purpose is to reveal "the tragedies concealed in our social system" (xii). She blames women's enslavement on church, state, the medical profession, tyrannical husbands, and passive wives, but most importantly she explicitly challenges all that is considered to be normative in sexuality and reproduction by revealing its socially constructed nature.

As paradoxical as it may appear, the late-nineteenth-century decline in U.S. and British fertility was accompanied by a backlash. Precisely at the moment when the practice of birth control was clearly on the rise, there was also greater emphasis on women's maternal role, opposition of the medical profession to contraception, and increased legal obstruction to the circulation of family-planning information. Condemnation of family planning drew its inspiration from Darwinist social theory, with its emphasis on rigid sex roles as characteristic of human evolution and as necessary for the production of superior offspring. Contraception was presented as a threat to the centrality of the female's reproductive role, potentially leading to women's becoming more and more concerned with sex rather than mothering. Childbearing and maternity practices were also under the sway of a pure culture of the death drive.

Cosmopolitan Modernisms

Modernism is a cosmopolitan urban movement that in many respects takes its distinctive features from the cities where it flourishes. In London, the Bloomsbury group members saw themselves as part of a movement opposed to the institutions of British culture. As Raymond Williams has suggested, Bloomsbury's commitment to a public sphere, and to some extent to social action, distinguished it from the ideologies of high modernism. In his essay "The Bloomsbury fraction" (1980), Williams describes Bloomsbury as a class fraction that is anomalous within the English elite. Its members' open critique of the establishment and sexual tolerance is, in his view, their most important feature of dissent. Bloomsbury was instrumental in reshaping the British ruling ideology during a time of cultural crisis.

Williams argues that the Bloomsbury Group can be "separated out as a distinct formation on the basis of . . . [its] social and intellectual critique, and the ambiguity of the position of women" or "the specific contradiction between the presence of highly intelligent and intellectual women, within these families, and their relative exclusion from the dominant and normative male institutions" (162). Bloomsbury also constituted an important platform for pacifism. Virginia Woolf, Vanessa Bell, Lytton Strachey, Clive Bell, and Duncan Grant, among others, were deeply committed to the pacifist cause both in their public role as intellectuals and in their private lives as conscientious objectors, among their friends, and in their relationships.

In New York, the circles of the Theatre Guild and the Provincetown Players in Greenwich Village and a rich and emergent African American culture in Harlem were interesting participants in the development of a genuine bohemian modernism. In Harlem, the intellectual and artistic milieu flourished in a variety of styles, from Jazz Age life to progressive magazines, from poetry to photography and film, together with a revival of autochthonous African American arts. In a similar vein to that of European salons, gatherings of artists were common in the cultural atmosphere of Harlem. Carl van Vechten's soirees were well known as stimulating meetings that brought together black and white artists, musicians, and writers who exchanged views on virtually everything.[22] In the context of black modernism, the Harlem Renaissance is indisputably at the center of the African American literary and artistic scene of the 1920s.

In Paris, Natalie C. Barney established her salon at 20 rue Jacob. In her "Academie des Femmes," she was host to the gatherings of many writers and artists, particularly lesbians. Gertrude Stein, Romaine Brooks, Radclyffe Hall, Janet Flanner, Solita Solano, Anna Wickham, and Colette joined the circle. These literary soirees also included male writers such as Pound, Joyce, and Ford Madox Ford. Gertrude Stein in the rue de Fleurus also gathered around her artists and intellectuals from Picasso to Fitzgerald. Peggy Guggenheim became the patron of many American women in their European journeys, providing them with financial support at her British estates of Hayford Hall, Warblington, and Yew Tree Cottage. Djuna Barnes, Emily Holmes Coleman, Kay Boyle, and Antonia White were among her guests.

We must abandon the attempt to look behind literature's statements for the other discourse of which it is the distorted and deformed expression, and which constitutes its authentic meaning. For if literature does deal with truth, the truth in question has no value other than that conferred upon it by literature. It is the truth of its style. Literature establishes a real stylistics of depth rather than a metaphysics, and stylistics is in itself a partial substitute for philosophy—Pierre Macherey

Through mutual misunderstandings introduced by the "letter" . . . literature explores the realm within which the entire human journey unfolds—the realm of trickery. It works within this trickery; it traces there a "truth" which is not the opposite of error, but, within the lie itself, is the symbolization of the impossibility at play.—Michel De Certeau

In his classic essay, "Spatial form in modern literature," Joseph Frank argues that modernist fiction makes a deliberate attempt to deny its own temporality and approach the condition of the poetic image defined by Ezra Pound as "that which presents an intellectual and emotional complex in an instant of time" (Frank [1963] 1968, 9). In order to achieve this, writers used a number of strategies to draw attention away from the intrinsic temporality of language and human action, among which we can include the use of mythic structures as organizing principles (as in Joyce's *Ulysses*), the movement from perspective to perspective instead of from event to event (as in Woolf's *The waves*), and the use of metaphoric images as leitmotives to draw together separate moments and thereby efface the time that has elapsed between them (as in Barnes's *Nightwood*).

In modernism, aesthetic form takes precedence over content, but both of them are understood as intimately linked and almost indistinguishable. The content of the work of art is the content of the psyche, and the form of the work of art is equivalent to the form of the psyche.[23] Creativity requires formal investigation and innovation. In formalism, meaning is both communicated and produced by the medium. Form in art is the sensory organization of matter abstracted as a category or pattern from its existence in time. Literary and art history are conceived as autonomous and self-contained; they are distinct from social and political history.

Modernism values and places aesthetic and psychological truth above all other potentially apprehended truths. Form is the truth about the artwork. This does not mean that truth is contained in the form (as if it were a message conveyed by means of form). Rather, it is equivalent to the form.

Moreover, the truths of art yield meaning as much as language yields meaning, through a contingent, arbitrary, and ever-changing repertoire of signifiers. Formalism assumes that the more powerful the connection between the formal sensory properties of the artwork and basic psychic mechanisms the better the artwork is.[24] Artists must produce the aesthetic effect by virtue of their unique abilities rather than by imitation. Copying and mimetic resemblance are proscribed. There is also a strong element of self-referentiality at work in modernism: the work of art focuses upon itself by concentrating on its own language, structure, and materiality and by displaying the artistic processes involved in its creation.

Modernism displaces the presumed objective detachment of impressionism and literary naturalism and maintains that the expression of artistic form is personal and unique. Artistic form is taken as evidence of a universal transcendent impulse toward form itself. But the notion of "truth" is far from being stable and immutable; there is instead a proliferation of "truths" (which correspond to the artists' distinctive visions) that deserve their name because of their creative authenticity, not because of their putative correspondence with reality. Modernist truth is not a revelation about things but a disclosure about the artist, and art is a disclosure by way of confession. Visual modernism distinguishes itself by means of a juxtaposition of shapes defined by their formal properties, with mimetic representation no longer a concern. In literature, metaphor explodes and emerges in a rich sensory display.

The Concreteness of the Form

Narrative is not merely a neutral discursive form that may or may not be used to represent real events in their aspect as developmental processes but rather entails ontological and epistemic choices with distinct ideological and even specifically political implications. . . . narrative discourse, far from being a neutral medium for the representation of historical events and processes, is the very stuff of a mythical view of reality, a conceptual or pseudoconceptual "content" which, when used to represent real events, endows them with an illusory coherence and charges them with the kinds of meanings more characteristic of oneiric than of waking thought.—Hayden White

Hayden White has formulated the relationship between meaning to structure (in historical representation) by means of the phrase "the content of the form." In his words, "narrative, far from being merely a kind of discourse that can be filled with different contents, real or imaginary as the case may be, already possesses a content prior to any given actualization of it in speech or writing" (1987, xi). He points to the rejection of narrative in literary modernism, which goes hand in hand with the general perception in our time that real life "can never be truthfully represented as having the kind of formal coherency met with in the conventional, well-made or fabulistic story" (ix). When trying to specify the distinction between real and imaginary events in the context of modern discussions of both history and fiction, White points out that this very distinction "presupposes a notion of reality in which 'the true' is identified with 'the real' only insofar as it can be shown to possess the character of narrativity" (6).[25]

In his important discussion of the role of form in historical discourse, White puts forward a crucial argument that can be extrapolated to the literary domain: "When the reader recognizes the story being told in a historical narrative as a specific kind of story—for example, as an epic, romance, tragedy, comedy, or farce—he can be said to have comprehended the meaning produced by the discourse. This comprehension is nothing other than the recognition of the form of the narrative" (1987, 43). This labor of recognition, I would argue, is problematized in complex ways in modernist narratives, where there is a proliferation of forms that are deliberately confounded and mixed and whose boundaries blur with recourse to strategies of montage, collage, pasting, and hybridization. In this respect, Celeste Schenck has persuasively suggested that genres "might be more usefully conceived as overdetermined loci of contention and conflict than as ideal literary types that transcendentally precede and predetermine a literary work" (1989, 282). The crisis of genre during modernism resonates not only with problems of literary history and institutions but with wider ideological, social, political, and legal issues and concerns.

The lyrical novel, and to some extent the long poem, the rise of new modes of biography and autobiography, and the poetical drama, make it hard for the reader to immediately recognize the form that is printed on the page. This fusion and confusion of forms and the rise of mixed genres testify to a profound problem with boundaries, with the clear distinction between inside and outside, which I want to suggest also diffusely delineates, in the psychic terrain, the profiles of neuroses and psychoses. In borderline pathologies such as melancholia, this is manifest in the impossibility of ever securing the space where the psychic and the social converge. The space of melancholia is an uncertain space, whose form is drawn and redrawn until it becomes reified and solidified and whose content is disseminated and redistributed in virtually endless ways in its interior landscapes. The collapse of the container-contained relationship is at the core of melancholia and its representations in modernist discourse.[26]

In "The Oedipus complex in the light of early anxieties" ([1945] 1975), Klein points out the enormous difficulty one encounters in expressing a young child's feelings and phantasies in adult language. She emphasizes the primacy of content over form in her description: "All descriptions of early unconscious phantasies—and of that matter of unconscious phantasies in general—can therefore only be considered as pointers to the contents rather than to the form of such phantasies" (*OCEA*, 409). Klein acknowledges the difficulties implicit in any attempt to capture the form. This notwithstanding, the elusiveness of the form acquires potential shape under various metaphoric tropologies of space in the fluctuation between positions. In the movements of introjection and projection, Klein orchestrates a dynamics of form that sets up the limits of psychic space, inside and out, while showing through the workings of phantasy the impossibility of delineating a stable and fixed boundary.

Klein provides us with a drama in which positions change without ever becoming reified. In this respect, Donald Meltzer (1978) has compared unconscious phantasy to a theater in which meaning and significance are first generated and only then projected onto the external world. The world is basically seen as empty and formless, a screen for the projection of unconscious phantasies.[27] Unconscious phantasy could thus be understood as some sort of structuring principle that gives shape to the individual's inner drama and transforms it into a particular and contingent configuration.

Phantasies of an ideal object as the source of goodness (based on satisfaction) and a bad object as the source of evil (based on frustration) are in the mode of the paranoid-schizoid position. In the mode of the depressive position, the object can be felt to exist but be absent or lost. Frustration is experienced as arising within the self as a consequence of something missing. As Ronald Britton has remarked, when the absence of the object is recognized, the place the object originally occupied is experienced as space: "If this space is felt to contain the promise of the return of the object, it is felt to be benign. . . . If in contrast to this benign expectancy it is believed that the space itself eliminates good objects . . . it is felt to be a malignant space. The belief in benign space depends ultimately on the love for the object surviving its absence, thus a place is kept for the object's 'second coming.' In contrast, malignant space arises when the idea of the object continuing to exist in its absence cannot be tolerated because it causes too much suffering. The object, therefore, is in phantasy, annihilated" (1995, 91). Britton argues that in its clinical manifestations this gives rise to a terror of space, external or internal; it leads to obsessive manipulation of space and time in order to eliminate the danger of gaps appearing in the external world, and it also promotes compulsive space-filling mental activity so as to eradicate gaps in psychic space.

The Kleinian notion of spatialization in the paranoid-schizoid and depressive positions, in its constant oscillation, suggests a range of different forms that the individual's inner landscapes may take, from an embattled struggle in which sadism is at its height to a derelict space in ruins, where fragments become intelligible as integral parts of larger structures.

Modernist art and literature, with their emphasis on spatialization and the relevance of forms, reveal a troubled aesthetic state pervaded with melancholia.[28] Klein's work is a special kind of aesthetic text that aims to explore the distinctive effects of human sexuality on the general production and articulation of forms and to which we might apply what Pierre Macherey has stated about literature, that [it] "establishes a real stylistics of depth rather than a metaphysics" ([1990] 1995, 132). Within the failures and radical incompleteness of sexuality and language, Klein echoes a modernist concern with the precarious and contingent character of the analytic vocabularies available and more widely with the nature of representational discourse itself.

The (Im)morality of Loss: Melancholia and the Political

Melancholia is an epochal sign in modernism. After the golden age of melancholy in the Renaissance, modernism appears with a revival of the melancholic affliction in a specific historical conjuncture after World War I and under the scrutiny of psychoanalysis. Melancholia considered as pathological grief may also be read as a mourner's response to loss that is not socially acceptable or socially understood, and it is therefore hard to tolerate or explain. Though neither Freud nor Klein say it explicitly, implicit in their views on mourning, melancholia, and manic depression is the notion that in cases of mourning or "normal" grief there is a consonance between how the mourner understands his or her loss and how that loss is understood—

and responded to—by others. In line with Martha Fowlkes's arguments in "The morality of loss" (1991), I argue that that very consonance is a necessary precondition for the development of normal, as distinct from pathological, grief.

As Fowlkes has aptly remarked, "The experiences of loss and mourning are not only individual and intrapsychic experiences; they are also embedded in a social and relational matrix" (1991, 529–30). In Kleinian terms, loss requires reinstatement of our good internal objects. In more general terms, we may say that loss requires a reworking of the view of the self that will include changes in life circumstances and will eventually lead to questioning and revision of the individual's major assumptions about the world. As Fowlkes has pointed out, all too often the social is underestimated in the effective resolution of grief and its outcome is entirely attributed to the individual psyche. Fowlkes's insight into the social construction of mourning and melancholia is crucial and comes to illuminate some of the issues I am dealing with in considering in what ways modernist cultures of the death drive produce melancholia. She writes: "Grief, like illness, is a form of deviance from a state of normality and normative criteria are operative in the definition of both. . . . the right to grieve is conferred (or not) on the mourner in consequence of the social approbation that is conferred (or not) on the loss. Social confirmation on the right to grieve is essential for setting into motion the process by which grief can be overcome and the mourner restored to a state of non-mourning" (533–34). The prototypical loss where personal relationships are concerned is the death of a member of one's family. Fowlkes explicitly notes that non-family losses will not elicit the ritualized expressions of sympathy that automatically accompany the loss of a family member. Thus, "no matter how many or how meaningful our extra-familial attachments to others, they are privatized, individually negotiated and lacking the moral imprimatur of the love normatively associated with formalized family ties" (535–36).[29] Fowlkes endorses the constructionist argument when she states that "Stigmatized loss [i.e., illegitimate social loss], shrouded in secrecy or shame leaves the mourner either scandalized by or destitute in grief. When an individual mourner is caught in melancholia we would do well to attend to the morality of the love and the loss at issue. If social regard for the meaning of the loss is inadequate or withheld, we must consider the possibility that mourning itself may manifest a depressive loss of individual self-regard. This loss may be more accurately interpreted as a social—than a self—construction" (550).

I subscribe to Fowlkes's lucid analysis, and I believe that uncovering the social causes that induce depression or melancholia is an urgent task if we want to understand a psychic dynamic that is not divorced from its social and material foundations, from its specific grounding in history, and from its complex implications at a larger than individual level. It is my contention that Kleinian theory and post-Kleinian developments, with their valuable insights into individual and group dynamics and their elaboration of the paranoid-schizoid and depressive positions, of projective identification and defense mechanisms, can help us gain a better understanding of melancholia and related pathologies not only today but also at a time contemporaneous with Klein's first formulations.[30]

The instability and the challenge to traditional family values and ties in the lives of many modernist writers and artists testifies to the difficulties they should encounter in coming to terms with their losses. Virginia Woolf's life was fraught with the sorrow brought about by the loss of her mother and several of her closest family members (Stella, Thoby, her father, and her nephew Julian). But, parallel to these familiar losses, her lifelong friends and other intimate relationships were irretrievably lost with the passage of time. Djuna Barnes sank into a period of depression after her nine-year relationship with Thelma Wood came to an end. Lytton Strachey, in his complex web of relationships, was constantly oscillating between periods of relative stability and melancholia that often coincided with his breakups with his partners. Countee Cullen painfully negotiated his uncongenial public image after the failure of his marriage to Yolande DuBois. His attachments to other men were perilously compromised due to external circumstances. These and many other modernist writers were the targets of different cultures of the death drive at work in the period between the two world wars.

Virginia Woolf, in a splendid melancholic move, endeavors to escape from what in A room of one's own ([1929] 1957) she identifies as the shadow of the "I" falling across the page in so many of her contemporaries, to a writing space closer to melancholia, where the shadow of the object, in its materiality, its solidity, and its corporeality, falls upon the ego.[31] Virginia Woolf's writing and the texts of many modernist writers place themselves on a difficult ridge, negotiating their losses in the absence of any secure good internal object or perilously fluctuating on the verge of risking their good internal objects forever.

9

Framing the Fetish: To the Lighthouse—
Ceci n'est pas un Roman

For it was not knowledge but unity that she desired, not inscriptions on tablets, nothing that could be written in any language known to men, but intimacy itself, which is knowledge, she had thought, leaning her head on Mrs. Ramsay's knee.—Virginia Woolf

I meant *nothing* by The Lighthouse. One has to have a central line down the middle of the book to hold the design together.—Virginia Woolf

Of the three powers which may dispute the basic position of science, religion alone is to be taken seriously as an enemy. Art is almost always harmless and beneficent; it does not seek to be anything but an illusion.—Sigmund Freud

Woolf: Between Cézanne and Magritte

The relationship between art critic and Bloomsbury luminary Roger Fry and Paul Cézanne was very intense.[1] It was about 1905, when Roger Fry was preparing his book on abstraction, that he came to a full and overwhelming appreciation of the French painter. In November 1910, Fry's long-cherished project crystallized in the opening of the exhibition Manet and the Post-Impressionists at the Graffton Gallery in London. It was designed to give the British public its first look at the works of Cézanne, Van Gogh, Matisse, Picasso, and those painters who since the 1870s had profoundly transformed European art. Years later, Virginia Woolf saw the spirit of the modern era as emanating from that exhibition when she wrote in her essay on the genesis of the modern novel, *Mr. Bennett and Mrs. Brown,* "On or about December 1910 human nature changed" (1924, 4). The exhibition made the public aware of the gulf that had opened between its assumptions and the preoccupations of modern artists.

The central thesis in Roger Fry's *Vision and design* ([1920] 1924) is that vision is subordinate to design and the all-important element is form. In his essay "The double nature of painting" ([1933] 1969) Fry pointed out that music and architecture could be abstract in a way that poetry and painting could not; he discussed the limitations of two-dimensional surfaces, arguing that one could not construct either volume or space on a canvas without having recourse to representation. In 1917, Woolf wrote of a discussion between Roger Fry and Clive Bell on literature and aesthetics with the illusion of a young intellect open to learning and inquire: "Roger asked me if I founded my writing upon texture or structure; I connected structure with plot, and therefore said 'texture.' Then we discussed the meaning of structure in painting and writing" (quoted in Lee 1992, 79). Woolf passionately engaged in discussions with Fry, who soon became one of her best friends.

Mary Ann Caws has remarked that Woolf was totally seized by sight: "So Virginia was seized by sight. A large part of the charm of her diaries, her letters, and her fiction comes from the quite extraordinary vividness of her vision. If Vanessa was, as she called her, a poet in color, she herself was supremely that" (1990, 35). Virginia Woolf's and Vanessa Bell's styles have sometimes been compared to that of Cézanne's paintings.[2] In *To the lighthouse*, Lily Briscoe's perception of colors, shapes, and their materialization into objects, masses, or landscapes owes much to Cézanne and Roger Fry's appreciation of the French painter. In Fry's view, for Cézanne reality lay always behind a veil of appearance. Cézanne "gave himself up entirely to this desperate search for the reality hidden beneath the veil of appearance, this reality which he had to draw forth and render apparent" (1927, 38).[3] Something similar could probably be said of Lily's uncertain image of Mrs. Ramsay.

In 1927, Virginia Woolf published *To the lighthouse*, only two years after René Magritte painted the first in his series of paintings *La Trahison des Images*. Melanie Klein had already published her first psychoanalytic essays as well. In 1928, Klein published "Early stages of the Oedipus conflict," one of her most important works.

In this chapter, I want to venture something that may initially sound discordant and even far-fetched: the proximity of Woolf to the Belgian surrealist painter René Magritte in a reading across disciplines from literature to art to psychoanalysis. My emphasis will be on the critiques of the representational apparatuses (language and the image) that Woolf and Magritte so powerfully effect and their radical modernist critique of form and by extension of genre. It is my contention that in *To the lighthouse* Woolf, by transgressing the boundaries between fiction and life and the generic boundaries between narrative and lyrical discourse, embarks on a project that aims to explore the irreducible elegiac dimension of signification. Magritte, animated by the surrealist impulse, totally dismantles any attachment to taxonomies of genre painting. My reading of *To the lighthouse* will focus on the melancholic nature of the fetish through a Kleinian lens. My readings of Magritte's art will go hand in hand with readings of diverse fictional and analytical materials ranging from Lily Briscoe's canvas in *To the lighthouse* to Melanie Klein's discussions of her patient Richard's drawings and the paintings of one of Paula Heimann's analysands, as reported in clinical papers. In the errancy of a triple modernist dialogue from text to canvas to psychoanalysis, I will endeavor to reflect on melancholia and its vicissitudes within the triptych that Woolf designs and suggests to her readers in *To the lighthouse*.[4]

The Empty Frame

In *To the lighthouse*, Lily Briscoe painfully comes to know that the affirmation of any identity goes through a social game defined by an Other; this precocious fragment of truth comes under the guise of an ideal model that prevents the emergence of any other model, especially that of the subject's own image. Lily is torn, facing the alternative of building an identity that is molded on an Other's features or social values. Lily as melancholic exhibits emblematic symptoms: hypertrophied memory, fixation on the arrangement of fragmented experience, obsession with time, depression, contradictory behavior, and self-absorption. The melancholic preserves her artificial "external scenic constructions" before coming to use aesthetically the elements that surround her and invest them with affect. But how can Lily Briscoe explore and claim an aesthetics of her own? How can she authorize her experiments in technique? Bridget Elliott and Jo-Ann Wallace have pointed out Lily's status as an amateur, which, as they argue, is implied rather than described in the novel.[5] In their view, Lily is clearly positioned outside of the two economies which marked, for Woolf, the space in which she negotiated her professional identity: the sexual (represented here by marriage) and the economic (represented by professionalism)" (1994, 75).

Lily epitomizes the anxieties and melancholia of the young female modernist artist, who can easily fall into an emptiness that has no borders or frames. The question of the absence of the frame and the evanescence of form is at the core of melancholia.[6] As Marie-Claude Lambotte (1993) has observed, in the absence of an inner structuring in which the dynamics of form and content is inscribed, and where form, understood as the first morphogenetic reference to the human body, has yielded its place to a deceitful projection of the ego, the melancholic wanders in a space whose artificial boundaries change as much as the models that he or she desperately clings to and borrows an identity from. The melancholic harbors a feeling of emptiness that translates into an absence of frame, a confusion of bodily boundaries and the threatening possibility of a plunge into emptiness. This emptiness, in Lambotte's words, is characterized as "The progressive withdrawal of sensations and feelings, as if things and beings would no longer have any effect on the individual, and as if, in turn, the individual would no longer desire anything. . . . Everything becomes faint, dull, and to the so often described impression of loss of vitality that the melancholic subject experiences, the stranger one of being inhabited by the emptiness, of transmitting the emptiness, is added, in such a way that the body becomes transparent and that the limits of the inside and the outside tend to blur" (261). Lambotte interestingly observes that, in the absence of sensory reactions, the melancholic experiences his or her body "as a kind of impersonal ectoplasm that one drags behind" (261). The melancholic remains anchored to a sort of "white fixation" that deprives him or her of the sense of sight. When considering the loss of mental vision, Jules Cotard stated in 1884 that "It would have to be studied if there is anything analogous to a loss of mental vision, a diminutive of this symptom in the melancholics who complain of no longer being able to see objects but confusedly, of no longer being able to recognize them, and who feel separated, as if by a veil, from objective reality. . . . As interesting as the loss of mental vision, it would be to approach the alteration of affective feelings" (quoted in Lambotte 1993, 264). For Lambotte, the melancholic feeling of general indifference is linked to the vicissitudes of the scopic drive and to the narcissistic constitution that derives from it. From a Lacanian viewpoint, Lambotte concludes that the problems derived from the internalization of a boundary between an inside and an outside are crucial in the constitution of the melancholic subject, since his or her relationship with an Other exhibits what she describes as the "traumatic paradigm of a first contact with the outside" (268). She traces the problem back to the subject's failure to introject a *regard* and surrendering to a negativism of the drives (*négativisme pulsionnel*) that makes the subject rule out all of his or her chances in the world: "It is not that he has not been able to distinguish an inside and an outside, but rather that he has not been able to discern, within this outside, the pleasurable from the non pleasurable objects, in such a way that the first ones would correspond to the I-subject and the second ones to the outside world. For the melancholic subject, then, it would appear, that the objects from the outside world lay within some sort of generalized indifferentiation" (271).[7]

Following the Kleinian elaboration, Lambotte goes on to argue that "the imaginary dissociation I-pleasure and outside world-displeasure, according to which the good objects are incorporated and the bad objects are rejected, has only been able to operate imperfectly—and which confirms the fundamental ambivalence that characterizes the attempts at investment in such a subject—and, on the other hand, that the repression of instincts has occurred too early, learning only out of an internal control that, for the melancholic subject, will become more and more cruel" (1993, 275). This generalized lack of differentiation, the troubled perception of bodily boundaries, the absence of frame, and the problems associated with the sense of sight will be the focus of my argument in this chapter.

Scopic Regimes

Magritte's images surely do probe our capacity for tolerating epistemological uncertainty, emotional ambiguity, and the lure of forbidden knowledge, especially knowledge by forbidden *looking*, all these abstractions must be linked with the exigencies of development and the aftermath of childhood trauma.—Ellen Handler Spitz

It seems that both Woolf and Magritte set out to explore the limits of representation and language as guarantor of communication and meaning. In reading Woolf and Magritte with Klein, I will attempt to invoke the images of the past that are preserved and stored in their art, and I will try to interrogate the psychic dynamics they exhibit in an analysis of their recurrent obsessions with seeing, knowing, and capturing experience.

Ellen Handler Spitz has read some of Magritte's best-known paintings with the underlying hypothesis that his art translates a state of bereavement coincident with the early and tragic death of his mother. In Spitz's words, his cold canvases, "in all their horror, catch and hold. The circumstances of Magritte's early life—particularly its nodal point of sudden, dramatic, self-inflicted parental death—shortcircuited a normally protracted path of separation. Thus, his gallery of bizarre women can be read as figuring the gamut of emotions a child may have and continue to feel toward an untimely maternal bereavement" (1994, 10). Magritte's images, in their hieratic aloofness are signs of his lifelong struggle with the loss of his mother.

There are some uncanny coincidences between Virginia Woolf and René Magritte's life stories. In 1895, Julia Stephen, Woolf's mother, died when her daughter was only thirteen. It was at this time that Virginia first suffered symptoms of melancholia and manic depression, which were to plague her throughout her life. In the spring of 1912, the mother of the future surrealist artist René Magritte committed suicide by drowning herself in the river Sambre in Belgium. Magritte was also thirteen at the time. Martha Wolfenstein tropes Magritte's loss with a melancholic Freudian figure when she argues that his trauma persists in his art like "an everbleeding wound" (quoted in Spitz 1994, 26).[8] Spitz remarks that after surveying forty years of his paintings "one senses a driven, repetitive quality—emblematic of concepts that continue to seethe and boil. Sophisticated surrealist agendas fuse with an archaic inner splitting: a young person's need and wish and hope, perhaps, for his mother's return and the implacable intellectual knowledge that she could, in fact, never return" (26–27). It is unlikely that he would have been able to mourn his mother at that time. Mary M. Gedo brings us even closer to an understanding of an underlying current in Woolf and Magritte's lifelines when she argues that the history of Magritte's adolescence suggests that he must have veered dangerously close to psychosis in the years immediately following his mother's death (1994, 180).

If we think about Lily Briscoe's and of some of Magritte's canvases, it is not difficult to identify their proximity, their near contiguity. In Spitz's words, Magritte's images "strive on many levels to deny its occurrence, to touch and hide its sadness, to recapture states associated with it, to mark and disavow its absence, to create substitutes while simultaneously devaluing them, to vent and contain rage, to doubt any project of reparation, to replay the shattering moments of final trauma, and, encompassing all of these postures, to comment darkly on art, on vision, and on the entrapment that constitutes human life" (1994, 11). How can we comment on Lily Briscoe's canvas and avoid a direct allusion to bereavement, to the impasse of creativity and the rage associated with it, to the shattering character of sexuality, to the difficult (almost impossible) task of separation, and to Woolf's metacommentary on art? Woolf's and Magritte's projects interrogate art as representation, challenging its boundaries, power, and functions head on, a crucial issue at stake for all modernist intellectuals and artists.

In Lily Briscoe's canvas, we witness a painting project that restages and denies the trauma that produced it. *To the lighthouse* enacts the drama of separation-individuation. Lily, unable to relinquish the past, is doomed to look in both directions (past and present) and to live in a state in which psychic borders are movable and fragile. We may read the structure of Woolf's novel as a triptych, painted with the colors of life and death, in which each compartment conveys in visual terms the discrete, post-Impressionist, and at times unintelligible component of a dream sequence. Lily Briscoe's unfinished painting operates an undoing, an incompletion, and a defamiliarization of what we thought we could recognize in ourselves; of what a quick glance at the familiar canvas of our personal histories told us that certain faces, gestures and movements had stood for; and of what we had thought we knew to be ourselves, the rule of such recognitions and substitutions in some sort of transcendental synthesis between pure abstraction and pure figurality.

Both Woolf and Magritte are fascinated with the problem of frames. Their enclosed spaces contain windows, curtains, and images that are held upon the scaffolding that contains them. Magritte was obsessed with both theatrical and symbolic curtains. The attempt to investigate the problems of the relations between inner and outer space are thus foregrounded. What does the window have to offer in Woolf and Magritte? In the latter, the window at times seems to open up a possible way to escape the inwardness and obsession that storm his psyche.[9] In Woolf, frames are labile. Far from suggesting fixity, they evoke some sense of unsettlement. In this respect, C. Ruth Miller has argued: "Still the frames in her writings and her exploration of the principles of framing reveal the extent to which she anticipated the contemporary interest in the threat that the marginal poses to the integrity of the centre" (1988, ix).

Ellen H. Spitz has pointed out Magritte's obsession with blocked looking, with blindness and invisibility. In his imagery, we find heads that are covered or turned away, eyes that are closed or occluded (as by an apple), and pictures in which the inability to see or be seen is placed at center stage.[10] Spitz relates Magritte's adherence to conventional means of pictorial representation rather than exploring abstraction. In her view, "These limitations bespeak a species of willed blindness, a protective failure to see" (1994, 20). With regard to this sense of generalized inability or impotence, stillness and immobility also signal the threshold of action that is figured in its utter impossibility.

It is important to note that the apparent movement toward the lighthouse in Woolf's novel is always aborted, and the strenuous efforts to set off for it result in immobility and frustration. Rachel Bowlby has emphasized this stasis, this sense of absence of progression within the novel, as an alternative to the steady linearity of the masculine sense of history: "The eventual arrival at the lighthouse, and the eventual completion or composition of Lily Briscoe's picture of James and Mrs. Ramsay, are so belated in the novel as to put in question the very progression of which their achievement appears, at length, as a kind of formal culmination. This is no Z at the end of the alphabet, but rather the discovery of a different kind of line, contrary to the 'doomed expedition' ordained for the forward march of masculine history" (1988, 79).

Crucial for our understanding and imbrication of Woolf's and Magritte's art is to consider the latter's painting The Spirit of Geometry (L'Esprit de la Géométrie).[11] The painting presents us with an unusual motherhood scene in which the heads of the mother and the child have been transposed from one body to another, effecting the subsequent reversal of roles (fig. 1). Magritte seems to be suggesting that mother and child are equally dependent on each other. As Spitz views the scene: "A coldness pervades the canvas, a forbidding air that contrasts dramatically with the tender tradition of mother-child images in Western art . . . The reversal of heads takes on an added meaning, for, with Mary and baby Jesus, it is the mother who must one day watch as her son dies a horibble and untimely death. . . . In the artist's [Magritte] own life, it was he, the son, who had to witness and bear the unforeseen demise of his mother" (1994, 24).

In works from his first surrealist phase, Magritte explored another troubling aspect of his childhood, what Mary M. Gedo has called his sense of "oneness with his mother" (1994, 196). She writes: "The vivid imagery in several pictures suggests that the artist may have been involved in a psychological fusion with the mother so profound that he must frequently have experienced difficulty in separating his emotions and reactions from hers. In order to investigate this novel theme, Magritte made clever original

Figure 1. René Magritte, *The Spirit of Geometry* (*L'Esprit de la Géométrie*), 1936 or 1937. (Tate Gallery, London.) © Succession René Magritte, VEGAP, 2002.

adaptations of the Surrealist penchant for producing twin or double im-ages, creating a series of pictures featuring androgynous beings whose ambiguous sexual identity may reflect the fact that Magritte's mother-child merger required him to cross sexual lines as in his canvas *He Doesn't Speak, He Isn't Speaking* (1926)" (196). Gedo has also pointed out that the nature of Magritte's imagery—especially his frequent use of anthrophomorphized objects to represent female figures—suggests that "his sexual require-ments may have involved fetishism" (286).

These phantasies of fusion and merger with the mother are also at the center of Woolf's imaginary in *To the lighthouse*, together with phantasies of love between women—even though Mrs. Ramsay has been called a "surro-gate mother" by many critics, we must acknowledge that ultimately she is not Lily's biological mother—outside the domain of patriarchal law. Her aesthetic, epistemological, and emotional exploration of this mother/lover figure in its fetishized version will guide my reading of Woolf's narrative.

One must keep on looking without for a second relaxing the intensity of emotion, the determination not to be put off, not to be bamboozled. One must hold the scene—so—in a vise and let nothing come in and spoil it.—Virginia Woolf

Always, Mrs. Ramsay felt, one helped oneself out of solitude reluctantly by laying hold of some little odd or end, some sound, some sight.—Virginia Woolf

My second quotation marks the opening lines of the last two paragraphs of section eleven, almost in the symmetrical midst of "The Window," with Mrs. Ramsay's intense rapture when caressed by a stroke of light coming from the lighthouse. This is the only explicit scene in *To the lighthouse* in which Mrs. Ramsay's sexuality explodes in an uncontrollable *jouissance*. Woolf writes: "watching it with fascination, hypnotised, as if it were stroking with its silver fingers some sealed vessel in her brain whose bursting would flood her with delight, she had known happiness, exquisite happiness, intense happiness, and it silvered the rough waves a little more brightly, as daylight faded, and the blue went out of the sea and it rolled in waves of pure lemon which curved and swelled and broke upon the beach and the ecstasy burst in her eyes and waves of pure delight raced over the floor of her mind and she felt, It is enough! It is enough!" (65). This bursting of the brain and this flood of delight are Woolf's metaphors to represent the unpresentable, feminine sexuality outside the domain of the phallus, whole, autonomous, and aroused with its pleasures. The stroke of light from the lighthouse has an allure that Mrs. Ramsay does not want to resist, but the intensity of her rapture is such that at times "she would not let herself look at it" (68).

In fetishism, a presence (the fetish object or a fetishistic phantasy) is employed as a screen for an absence that would otherwise arouse anxiety. In Freud, specifically, the fear of loss of the love of the object may serve as a screen for castration anxiety. In a footnote added to *Three essays on the theory of sexuality* ([1905] 1953) in 1920, Freud modified his former understanding of the fetish as an infantile perception of the absence of the female genitals and stated that fetishism functions like a screen memory: "Behind the first recollection of the fetish's appearance there lies a submerged and forgotten phase of sexual development. The fetish, like a 'screen-memory,' represents this [forgotten] phase and is thus a remnant and precipitate of it" (154).

In 1899, Freud coined the term *screen memory*, whereby he refers to apparently trivial relics of the past that are remembered in place of events that would be traumatic if brought to mind. Thus, the fetish and the screen memory manifest analogous functions. In both of them, the modes of representation are similar. Like the fetish, the screen memory is vivid and concrete and foregrounds an element or image of bright intensity. Susan Isaacs further elucidated the notion of screen memory in her discussion of unconscious phantasy, arguing that "The visual element in perception slowly increases, becoming suffused with tactile experience and spatially differentiated. The early visual images remain largely 'eidetic' in quality— probably up to three or four years of age. They are intensely vivid, concrete and often confused with perceptions. Moreover, they remain for long intimately associated with somatic responses: they are very closely linked with emotions and tend to immediate action" ([1952] 1983, 105).

Characteristic of fetishism is that one part should be used to represent a whole. In To the lighthouse, this metonymic and virtually infinite displacement that the fetish performs is present at times in its modality of fetish object or in that of screen memory. The fetish provides an alternative way to access pleasure by way of a detour, a deviation. In its operations, the terms of absence and presence are reversible, and this is what grants the fetish its striking versatility.

Spitz's reflections on the image in Magritte show similarities to the idea of the fetish as screen image in Woolf. She writes that "the image condenses a temptation to merge and to regress with a powerful imperative to ward off that temptation, to fight it by attacking it at its source, to insist with strenuous hostility on sharp boundaries, on the maintenance of differentiation and distinction" (1994, 33). The vividness of the screen memory exhibits this quality of detachment and sharp boundaries, which places the subject as if facing the mirror of its past selves. In the complex interaction between memories and phantasies, the ubiquitous conflicts over looking, composition, bodies, and narratives are performed.

There is a strong element of orality at the origin of the fetish. The oral character of the fetish is present in To the lighthouse. Lily's painting bespeaks an oscillation between oral and visual experience that shows in a language that discloses visual greed. The pleasures associated with taking in objects are manifest, and there is a clear displacement at work from the urge to incorporate orally to the voracity of the visual.

An important element of orality is present in Magritte's painting, most notably as oral aggression or oral erotism. In the latter, Spitz has

Figure 2. René Magritte, *Girl Eating a Bird* (*Jeune Fille Mangeant un oiseau*), 1927. (Kunstsammlung Nordrhein-Westfalen, Dusseldorf.) © Succession René Magritte, VEGAP, 2002.

emphasized the many different versions of the *Girl Eating Bird* (*Jeune fille Mangeant un Oiseau*) painted between 1927 and 1945, all of which are variations on the theme of a little girl calmly devouring a live bird (fig. 2). Magritte's *Girl Eating Bird* can certainly be placed among his most disturbing works. Spitz focuses on the element of sadistic oral aggression and argues: "Oral aggression, usually displaced to the eyes, is here returned to the mouth, and it is our eyes as spectators, that are made, by projective identification to witness it. . . . from a Kleinian perspective: the internalized persecutory object, the mother, despite (and because of) her death, continues to feed on the living child" (1994, 53–54).

My understanding of the symbolic equation in relation to melancholia in the section on phantasy in this book can best be illustrated with instances from Woolf and Magritte. In Magritte's painting *Evening Falls* (*Le Soir qui Tombe*) of 1964 (fig. 3), the symbolic equation is present in a metapictorial commentary. As the sun sets, the glass window through which we view it cracks into smithereens and the fall of evening results in the actual fragmentation and disintegration of the image. The relationship between words and things materializes in the literalization of its title.[12]

Figure 3. René Magritte, *Evening Falls* (*Le Soir qui Tombe*), 1964. (Menill Collection, Houston.) © Succession René Magritte, VEGAP, 2002.

Both Woolf and Magritte seek to interrogate and problematize relations of distance, perspective, dimension, and inner and outer boundaries. Woolf's involvement with the symbolic equation is manifest in *To the lighthouse*, as I will attempt to show later in this chapter.

It is my contention that Lily Briscoe's and Woolf's obsessions with the lighthouse can be read together with Magritte's compositions of dark and apparently empty houses that explode into light in the middle of the day. Magritte's variations on *The Empire of Light* (or sometimes *The Dominion of Light*) are oxymoronic since they depict the dark silhouettes of these houses in a deserted nocturnal scenario with lamplight, and right on top of them the sky shows a deep blue with white clouds (fig. 4).

Biographers and critics have pointed out that Magritte scarcely ever spoke about his mother's death. The body of his mother was apparently found with her face covered by her nightdress. It was never known whether

Figure 4. René Magritte, *The Dominion of Light*
(*L'Empire des Lumières*), 1954. (Musées Royaux
des Beaux-Arts de Belgique, Brussels.)
© Succession René Magritte, VEGAP, 2002.

she had hidden her eyes with it in order not to see the death she had chosen
or whether the current of the river had veiled her thus. Magritte's fantasy
about his mother's death has many echoes in his paintings. Several evoke
death by water, and there are numerous instances of faces that are concealed or absent.[13] In any case, Régina Magritte's absence from her home
was noticed, and the search for her begun, in the middle of the night.[14] The
series of paintings *The Empire of Light* surely evokes this moment of terror
and fright, of uncertainty and the premonition of death.[15]

In *To the lighthouse*, the lighthouse marks the felicitous encounter of
the errant mariner with the light that eventually will bring him safely
to port. The lighthouse keeps us from getting lost, saves us when we are
lost, and prevents us from losing sight of land. It is a symbol of security,
of shelter and warmth, that rescues us from the potential abyss of darkness, from the perils of the night. But we may also try to decompose and

deconstruct the lighthouse into a lit house, a house well lit or a house in flames. In Magritte, the eerie images of his lit houses at night do not convey the security or comfort that we might expect. Rather, they uncannily suggest that something terrible has happened or is about to happen. We perceive these houses as mere silhouettes, as frames for the enactment of that flash when something ineluctably occurred.

Phantasy and Trompe l'Oeil

We are likely to observe an obsessional aspect of art within the broad compulsion to repair and to integrate what has been threatened, scattered, or destroyed. Indeed, it is a narrower compulsive element . . . that bestows on much art a quality of urgency and inevitability.—Adrian Stokes

In his contribution to the Controversial Discussions on the issue of phantasy, Adrian Stephen, analyst and brother of Virginia Woolf, siding with the Kleinians, remarked that in his discussion of aims and objects of the drives at the beginning of *Three essays on sexuality*, Freud is thinking of cases in which the object is concrete—such as food—but "he would certainly have agreed, as I suppose we all should, that the object may be imaginary or, if you like, phantastic" (Isaacs [1952] 1983, 119). He further agreed on the unseparability of phantasy and drive: "The phantasy and the impulse to get pleasure are not two separate psychic entities, though it may be useful sometimes to separate them conceptually; they are two aspects of one psychic process" (120). In this passage, Stephen is clearly veering the discussion toward the fetish.

In *To the lighthouse*, Lily has been haunted by the living image of Mrs. Ramsay after her death. She is certain that the vision will come to her at any time, anywhere. This vision had been part "of the fields of death," so it should also be perpetually remade. Its nature comes very close to that of trompe l'oeil since Lily herself describes it as "some trick of the painter's eye" (181).

The fetish (or the simulacrum) is ultimately linked to the notion of trompe l'oeil.[16] Trompe l'oeil raises crucial questions on visual and pictorial representation—on the reality (presence) of the object—and on scopic pleasures. It also allows us to interrogate the issue of representation in psychoanalysis.[17] Trompe l'oeil substitutes figuration (*Darstellung*) for representation (*Vorstellung*); it is a sort of figuration of the unrepresentable.

Whereas in painting the technique and craft strive to eliminate the distance between object and representation, trompe l'oeil, in its power of imitation on the verge of pictorial representation, manages to remove all symbolic power from separation and absence. It subverts limits. It separates the painted object from the representational level in order to "render" it to the world of material objects. But for this detachment to take place there must be a relation of content-form, container-contained, and presence-absence simultaneously invoked and subverted. In order to be successful, the trompe l'oeil effect needs to both rehearse and disavow a limit. On the grounds of an interrogation of the false, it radically questions the so-called true, objectivation, or reification. Trompe l'oeil poses a threat of disappearance, a sinking background, a collapse of the holding structure, and an emptiness of the image as much as it attempts to restore a surface for the look and a surface with its frame.

Magritte opposed the classic concept of trompe l'oeil in painting. He wrote in 1946 that "if the images are precise, in formal terms, the more precise they are, the more perfect the trompe l'oeil, THE GREATER THE DECEPTION." In 1963, he added, "Trompe l'oeil (if indeed there is such a thing) does not belong to the realm of painting. It is rather a 'playful physics'?" (quoted in Foucault [1968] 1983, 62). Read attentively, these lines give evidence of some of the problems of the limits of the canvas and its relation to the frame or the container-contained relationship. It is not difficult to detect a deep anxiety underlying Magritte's statements between the abstract and the concrete, symbolization and literalization, and representation and physicality. Magritte's paintings show his tortured appreciation of objects in their volumes and shapes, in their corporeality, frozen in space.

It appears that Magritte never thought of himself as an artist but as a thinker who communicated by means of paint. He was well read in philosophy (Hegel, Heidegger, Sartre, Foucault), and after experimenting with different styles in his painting the discovery of Giorgio De Chirico constituted for him a unique experience that profoundly unsettled his former ideas about art. As James Harkness has remarked, "In paintings such as De Chirico's The Song of Love Magritte claimed to have realized 'the ascendancy of poetry over painting . . . for the fact was that Magritte very early grew bored with painting as an end in itself'" (Foucault [1968] 1983, 2).

In his Manifesto of surrealism (1924), Breton defined the surreal as that beyond all control of reason, under the guise of the accidental or haphazard, of that concerned with chance and the absurd, as in the domain of dreams. Surrealism defamiliarizes all that we grasp through the senses, our previous assumptions about external reality and ourselves, and our reliance on language. It manipulates our closeness to and distance from objects, our sense of perspective, and forces us to confront them with a new and dislocated perception of experience.

An Uncanny Light

The most extraordinary case seemed to me to be one in which a young man had exalted a certain sort of "shine on the nose" into a fetishistic precondition.—Sigmund Freud

Why should we not be illuminated by the light of our *jouissance?* Which casts a different light on things, on their contours, their spacing and their timing. It brings them back into the world, and reshapes them according to a perception foreign to the rigour of the day, which makes colder distinctions. For sight is no longer our only guide. Seeing within an expanse which is dazzling and palpable, odorous and audible. A night of sensation where everything lives together, permitting co-existence without violence.
—Luce Irigaray

Melitta Sperling's (1963) and Phyllis Greenacre's (1953, 1968) ideas on fetishism prove illuminating to my understanding of the fetish in *To the lighthouse.* Sperling argues that separation anxiety due to the loss of the pre-oedipally gratifying mother is of greater importance than castration anxiety and that the childhood fetish represents a (pathological) defense against separation from the mother on the pre-oedipal (oral and anal) levels. Greenacre (1968) holds that early disturbances in the mother-child relationship severely impair object relations, and she underscores the weakness of the body and self-images as important manifestations of it. In Greenacre's view, the fetish is constituted in an attempt to restore the integrity of the mother's body and one's own. Crucial also to my discussion are some previous arguments laid out in Susan Isaacs's "The nature and function of phantasy" ([1952] 1983). I would like to extend these arguments beyond the actual stages of pregenitality in order to problematize the traditional chronological location of the fetish in a pregenital organization. Following Klein's elaboration on the radical inability to ever attain one definite position in development, and the fluctuation between paranoid-schizoid and depressive modes of relations, I want to suggest that the overdetermination of the fetish and its constant and shifting operations of displacement, its essentially mobile nature, problematize and eschew the creation of concrete chronological boundaries. It is at this point that Kleinian theory infuses its radical potential into psychoanalysis by overturning and discarding pathologized notions such as fixation, arrested development, or regression and allowing us to read and interpret them differently. Sperling's emphasis on the question of "relations" in her notion of "fetishistic object relations" and her refusal to locate the fetish on a specific site (part of the body, quality, gesture, or posture, among other features) allow the necessary flexibility that the elusive and always displaced nature of the fetish requires.

In a much quoted passage from "A Sketch of the Past," Woolf, in her retrospective vision of *To the lighthouse*, stated: "I suppose I did for myself what psycho-analysts do for their patients. I expressed some very long felt and deeply felt emotion. And in expressing it I explained it and then laid it to rest" (1985, 81).

To the lighthouse is a composite canvas. It can be read as a triptych traversed by different tonalities and different subjects, from the vicissitudes of the bourgeois family structure and the differences derived from the sexual division of labor, to the ravages of time in personal and historical narratives, to a meditation upon the anxieties that afflict the subject (the woman artist) on her way to individuation, independence, freedom, and creativity. My focus will not be on the oppositional dynamics between the sexes that dominate the first part of the novel or on the oedipal scenario that informs the relations between parents and children within the Ramsay family.[18] I am interested in reading Woolf with Klein and object relations theory, and my approach will gradually shift, like the eye of a camera, to the third section of the triptych, where the anxieties that assail Lily Briscoe and melancholia emerge in full force. Reading Woolf with Klein and psychoanalytical literary and art theory, I will endeavor to show in what ways their insights intersect, overlap, and sometimes oppose each other. They critically contribute to what I understand to be a modernist composite of prisms of meaning into the multidimensional space of the written page. In the hybridity of genres, from Woolf's own problematization of boundaries between the novel and lyrical narrative and the elegy to Klein's clinical and literary or more autobiographical papers and Magritte's condensation of philosophy into image, I will move among the three domains, which, in my view, triply constitute the complex triptych of *To the lighthouse*.

Woolf's novel exhibits an almost psychotic obsession with the sense of sight, from seeing to not seeing to being caught in the act of looking, from voyeurism to scopophilia, from eyes to water and all sort of surfaces on which light may be reflected. In "Fetishism" ([1927] 1953), Freud reports the case of a young man who was sexually aroused by a certain "shine on the nose." He explains this as a case of confusion of tongues in which the patient forgets his native English almost completely when he moves to Germany. According to Freud, "The fetish, which originated from his earliest childhood, had to be understood in English, not German. The 'shine on the nose' [in German, *Glanz auf der Nose*]—was in reality a 'glance at the nose.' The nose was thus the fetish, which incidentally, he endowed at will with the luminous shine which was not perceptible to others" (152). In the Freudian account, the phallic subtext (Glanz/glans) of the fetish cannot possibly pass unnoticed.

In *To the lighthouse*, Woolf writes of a light that shines, which is also simultaneously a light that blinds and thus connotes its opposite, darkness. In both the radiance and the extinguishing of light, we may observe a pattern that shifts from mania to melancholia, always on the border of manic depression. But let us follow the path to Lily's creativity, to her production of her painting, which is in itself a play of light and shadow, of colors, tonalities, and shades.

In *To the lighthouse*, Mrs. Ramsay sits in the window, which opens on the terrace, and watches the men talk and her children play. She beholds the waves beating on the beach and the gleam of the lighthouse. The beating of the waves and the rustle of conversation—all sounds have a rhythmical quality. For Lily, Mrs. Ramsay epitomizes a perfect feminine shape, "an august shape; the shape of a dome" (51). Mrs. Ramsay has the wisdom that allows her to recognize differences among people without having to theorize about them: "It seemed to her such nonsense—inventing differences, when people, heaven knows, were different enough without that" (8). She mocks the male impulse to classify and taxonomize differences in order to posit them as insurmountable obstacles to understanding and communication. Mrs. Ramsay has the daily experience of watching rich and poor, high and low, and this brilliant intuition of the irreducible differences among individuals nourishes her love of knowledge and will probably cause her to become "what with her untrained mind she greatly admired, an investigator, elucidating the social problem" (9). The lighthouse, in Mrs. Ramsay's words, appears as a wonderful vision, aloof and sober, splendid in its majestic stillness: " 'Oh, how beautiful!' For the great plateful of blue water was before her; the hoary Lighthouse, distant, austere, in the midst" (12).

In the section entitled "To the Lighthouse," Mr. Ramsay, in his interior monologue, confesses his incapacity to understand women's minds: "He thought, women are always like that; the vagueness of their minds is hopeless; it was a thing he had never been able to understand; but so it was" (167). Pierre Bourdieu sees in the paternal figure of Mr. Ramsay, a man "surprised in flagrante delicto of childishness" (1990b, 22).[19] He sees himself as a failure for not having achieved the ideal of masculinity and paternity that he must represent. In his discourse, Mr. Ramsay proceeds from the phantasies of the infantile world (invoking adventure and heroism) to those of the *libido academica* (in his anxieties about his reputation and future influence as a philosopher). For Bourdieu, there is a sense of *illusio* at the basis of masculinity whose expression is essentially "postural." This, he argues, "lies at the basis of all forms of *libido dominandi*" (23). But at the same time Mr. Ramsay is a child who plays the man. In a word, "it is because he is designated too early, especially by the rites of institution, as dominant, and endowed, because of this, with the *libido dominandi*, that he has the double-edged privilege of devoting himself to the domination games, and that these games are in fact reserved to him" (24).[20]

The narrative voice announces that Mrs. Ramsay "had the whole of the other sex under her protection" (*To the lighthouse*, 6). For Mrs. Ramsay did feel passionately in her nurturing role at home, in hospitals, and in her charitable missions. Rachel Bowlby has also seen the child in Mr. Ramsay's relationship with his wife. This relationship

> suggests the man's wish to return to the position of the child in relation to a woman like his mother. According to Freud, it is in so far as she identifies with her mother that the woman: "acquires her attractiveness to a man, whose Oedipus attachment to his mother it kindles into passion. How often it happens, however, that it is only his son who obtains what he himself aspired to! One gets an impression that a man's love and a woman's are a phase apart psychologically" (*Femininity*). . . . Mr. Ramsay attempts to recover, with another woman, the relation of dependence and centrality in which he once stood, to his own mother: after receiving the sympathy he claims from his wife, he is "like a child who drops off satisfied." (1988, 68)

We can also approach Mr. Ramsay's relationship with his wife from a different angle through Klein. Woolf writes: "Filled with her words, like a child who drops off satisfied, he said, at last, looking at her with humble gratitude, restored, renewed, that he would take a turn" (38). In this scene, Mr. Ramsay is filled with nourishment from Mrs. Ramsay's good breast, and, satisfied, he corresponds with gratitude. But Mr. Ramsay learned of gratitude through his infantile experience of his good internal object, his mother's good breast. As much as the almost perfect dream of mother-child symbiosis is totally dismantled in Kleinian theory, the happy and harmonious relationship between the sexes is also undermined. Mrs. Ramsay can only be herself in solitude, in her private, lonely, and meditative contemplation of life: "There it was before her—life. Life, she thought—but she did not finish her thought. She took a look at life, for she had a clear sense of it there, something real, something private, which she shared neither with her children nor with her husband" (59).[21] Mrs. Ramsay's resplendent beauty can even alleviate mourning.[22]

In "The Window," Lily has her first experience of rapture with a beam of sunlight: "this 'rapture,' this silent stare, for which she felt intense gratitude; for nothing so solaced her, eased her of the perplexity of life, and miraculously raised its burdens, as this sublime power, this heavenly gift, and one would no more disturb it, while it lasted, than break up the shaft of sunlight, lying level across the floor" (48). In a synaesthetic confusion of the senses, Lily finds pleasure in the fetishistic and scopophilic exchange of silent stares between this "shaft" of sunlight and her own eyes. This splitting of the shaft of sunlight is a projection of Lily's split ego, and her fetishistic pleasure both traverses and disavows castration. Lily, in her inflamed ecstasy, "saw the colour burning on a framework of steel; the light of a butterfly's wing lying upon the arches of a cathedral" (48), but all this collapses into her canvas, and only a few random marks remain. According to Klein, the anxieties that characterize women's psychosexual evolution have to do with a sense of deprivation, of being robbed of the contents of their bodies. In To the lighthouse, Charles Tansley's insistent misogynist chant, "Women can't paint, women can't write," is repeated with the same monotonous intensity as the death drive. Lily's anxieties find some alleviation in her chance to look without being made the object of the (male) gaze, in her recourse to the fetish, which in the novel is a fetish of light.

In the solitude of Mrs. Ramsay's meditation upon her private self, metaphors of sinking and darkness pervade the text. Thus, "one shrunk with a sense of solemnity, to being oneself, a wedge-shaped core of darkness, something invisible to others. . . . Beneath it is all dark, it is all spreading, it is unfathomably deep; but now and again we rise to the surface and that is what you see us by" (62). The Kleinian metaphors about our physical bodies come to mind.[23] This trope that attributes to water an unfathomably deep quality is almost obsessively repeated, and by the end of the novel it reappears when Lily is alone, looking at the sea and remembering those times when life was most vivid. She now meditates melancholically, immersed in her cogitations: "She seemed to be standing up to the lips in some substance, to move and float and sink in it, yes for these waters were unfathomably deep" (192). In the absence of light, the subject descends into her abyss of darkness, shrinks into her self. There is always something of us that is lost by others and something of us lost to others. In this melancholic descent into the self, into its unfathomable depths, darkness produces the same effect as intense light; it blinds. It is the impossibility of recognizing these losses, of reaching into these depths, that produces a split ego, parts of which rise to the surface while others remain beneath the waters.

Lily's dream of unity with Mrs. Ramsay is disturbed by (man-made) language and the epistemological claims that men impose on their objects of study and even on their objects of love. Woolf's rhetoric phantasizes a remote place where sacred tablets are kept secretly, holding the promise that if one could spell them out they would teach everything: "What art was there, known to love or cunning, by which one pressed through into those secret chambers? What device for becoming, like waters poured into one jar, inextricably the same, one with the object one adored?" (51). Only those initiated into the art of deciphering those signs will ever enjoy their prophetic exhortation. The unraveling of these inscriptions promises the ideal fusion of lovers, of form and content, and the dissolution of boundaries between container and contained.

In her first attempt, Lily has painted a "triangular purple shape" (52), to the eyes of William Bankes, unrecognizable as a human shape. But Lily had made "no attempt at likeness" (52) in her portrait of Mrs. Ramsay and James, mother and child. William Bankes evokes the religious quality of motherhood in art and would like to have the canvas explained. For Lily, a picture must be a "tribute" (53), and the main problem with her painting is now "how to connect this mass on the right hand with that on the left" (53). Elizabeth Abel has argued that Lily's "position, more importantly, dissociates her art from the aesthetic of verisimilitude: painting, she insists at this stage of her work, is to be an autotelic whole, freed from the claims of representation and assessable by purely formal criteria. Making 'no attempt at likeness' and insisting on the formal relations of masses, lights, and shadows, Lily's echoes Fry's belief that 'our reaction to a work of art is a reaction to a relation and not to sensations or objects or persons or events,' that the aesthetic effect arises from 'self-contained, self-sufficing' structures which are 'not to be valued by their reference to what lies outside'" (1989, 72).

In Lily's mind, the unity of the composition must be preserved, and breaking the vacancy in the foreground with an object (James?) risks the loss of that unity. This anxiety about having a sense of completeness or wholeness broken has to do with primitive anxieties linked to attacks by bad internal objects and the chaos this brings about. Interestingly, what may disrupt the unity of the composition is the image of the child, in a reverse reading of the oedipal ideal of completion of a "woman with child."

Mrs. Ramsay is not a perfect shape to be admired, an object of desire. By the end of "The Window," she has become a desiring subject with more intensity than ever before: "she wanted something more, though she did not know, could not think what it was that she wanted" (117). In the description of Mr. and Mrs. Ramsay's impasse of communication, the narrative voice utters: "She [Mrs. Ramsay] could feel his mind like a raised hand shadowing her mind" (123). Here we have a metaphoric instance of the production of melancholia in women, and in this and other countless cases we can understand why in the general atmosphere of melancholia that pervades To the lighthouse Lily and Mrs. Ramsay are "most melancholic."

Projective identification is also at work in Mrs. Ramsay's sense of emptying her mind when sitting alone, in a moment that Woolf describes as "losing personality," a moment outside of time, absorbed in eternity, so "pausing there she looked out to meet the stroke of the Lighthouse, the long steady stroke, the last of the three, which was her stroke, for watching them in this mood always at this hour one could not help attaching oneself to one thing especially of the things one saw; and this thing, the long steady stroke, was her stroke. Often she found herself sitting and looking, sitting and looking with her work in her hands until she became the thing she looked at—that light, for example" (63). Mrs. Ramsay's pleasure passes through contemplation, projection, and introjective identification with the fetish of light. The evacuation of emotions and feelings in melancholia make the subject feel that inanimate objects express one's own self. As it is the case with Mr. Ramsay, "inanimate things . . . felt they expressed one; felt they became one, felt they knew one, in a sense were one" (63).

By the end of "The Window," Lily thinks, in consonance with Klein's later insight in *The psycho-analysis of children* ([1932] 1975e): "Human relations were all like that, she thought, and the worst . . . were between men and women" (92).[24] In the memorable scene at the party, Lily tries to find a reason for her sudden exhilaration and compares it to a previous moment, "when solidity suddenly vanished . . . now the same effect was got by the many candles in the sparely furnished room, and the uncurtained windows, and the bright mask-like look of faces seen by candlelight" (98). This spectral vision, when Lily feels that "weight was taken off them" (98), foretells Mrs. Ramsay's bitter ironies about heterosexual love, for "what could be more serious than the love of man for woman, what more commanding, more impressive, bearing in its bosom the seeds of death" (100). It is important to note that throughout the novel the solidity of objects is almost the only material quality one can apprehend. In the "Time Passes" section, where the ravages of time are most intensely felt, solidity is longed for, and even mourned, in the quest of the narrative voice for "something alien to the processes of domestic life, single, hard, bright, like a diamond in the sand, which would render the possessor secure" (132). This is ultimately a scene in which Mrs. Ramsay's powers are equated with those of a sorceress, who puts a spell on them all (101), with something uncannily frightening about her.

After the dinner party, Mrs. Ramsay pauses, and in a fleeting and vanishing look she stares at what is already irreducibly past: "With her foot on the threshold she waited a moment longer in a scene which was vanishing even as she looked, and then as she moved and took Minta's arm and left the room, it changed, it shaped itself differently; it had become, she knew, giving one last look at it over her shoulder, already the past" (111). The past is figured as threshold, and Mrs. Ramsay's look, like the look of a camera, captures this scene in its changing nature, in its transformations. Mrs. Ramsay's look frames the past as still life, since the past as *nature morte* is a subject to be framed in order to store it in our memories as dead. But Mrs. Ramsay harbors the hope that there is a way to undo this implacable and devouring work of the past, which entails defying it by being woven into the hearts of her loved ones.

In "Time Passes," The Ramsays' many losses are verbalized. Prue died of some illness connected with childbirth, Andrew was killed during the war, and Mrs. Ramsay "died rather suddenly" (128), but the circumstances of her death remain parenthetical and unexplained.[25] At this point, the stroke of light from the lighthouse is the only remainder of those moments of happiness lost forever: "When darkness fell, the stroke of the Lighthouse . . . came now in the softer light of spring mixed with moonlight gliding gently as if it laid its caress and lingered stealthily and looked and came lovingly again. But in the very lull of this loving caress, as the long stroke leant upon the bed, the rock was rent asunder; another fold of the shawl loosened; there it hung, and swayed" (133). The ideal of sharing, and thus codependence and wholeness, is shattered like a reflection on a broken mirror.[26]

Only the alleviating function of the fetish comes to rescue the subject from a universe in wrack and ruin. The Ramsays' family house is now in a state of total dereliction, and "Only the Lighthouse beam entered the rooms for a moment" (138). The narrative voice identifies some "force" at work that spares the house from plunging into the depths of darkness, a force "not highly conscious; something that leered, something that lurched; something not inspired to go about its work with dignified ritual or solemn chanting" (139). In this instance, the fetish of light works in the service of the life drives, in its attempt to irradiate warmth and infuse vitality into the coldness and almost inert quality of the house, anthropomorphized as a living organism. A profusion of domestic sounds comes to be heard anew. The war is over, and Lily and the Ramsays return to the house. This period of loss and intense distress is figured as both a personal and a historical nightmare that Lily has to endure. And "The Lighthouse" opens after two significant lines that once again allude to Lily's restored sense of sight, to her eyes wide open and her awakening: "Her eyes opened wide. Here she was again, she thought, sitting bolt upright in bed. Awake" (143).

"The Lighthouse," the third section of Woolf's novel, opens with an image of Lily caught in the maze of language and the numbness of aborted feelings and emotions. Lily's portrait contains an almost perfect replica of melancholia: loneliness, stillness, a generalized inhibition, and a sense of meaninglessness. Lily, in her solitude, repeats words, absorbed in their incantatory sound, which evokes nothing, devoid of all meaning, empty. And this section opens with a far-reaching question that aims to address the rhetorical character of all questions, even more anxiously acute in the case of the melancholic: "What does it mean then, what can it all mean? Lily Briscoe asked herself, wondering whether, since she had been left alone, it behooved her to go to the kitchen to fetch another cup of coffee or wait there. What does it mean?—a catchword that was, caught up from some book, fitting her thought loosely, for she could not, this first morning with the Ramsays, contract her feelings, could only make a phrase resound to cover the blankness of her mind until these vapours had shrunk. For really, what did she feel, come back after all these years and Mrs. Ramsay dead? Nothing, nothing—nothing that she could express at all" (145).[27] Language speaks Lily. This sense of dissociation of the subject from her own words gives ample evidence of the splitting of Lily's ego. Her mind is blank, and all significant sensory and emotional experiences have been evacuated, projected onto a now blank world.

It is crucial to note that in this section, more than ever before, Woolf's rhetoric is tainted with the chiaroscuro conventions of the literary and psychoanalytic discourses on melancholia. The contrast of light and shadow is played out in the continuous struggle between self-preservative instincts and the death drive. Lily arrives at the Ramsays' house at night, "when it was all mysterious, dark" (145). The gloomy atmosphere that surrounds Lily throughout this section is entirely a projection of her own turbulent inner state: "It was all dry: all withered: all spent" (150). The supremacy of thought over action is also a relevant feature in melancholia. And we learn that both Lily and Mr. Carmichael, the poet, share "Some notion . . . about the ineffectiveness of action, the supremacy of thought" (196).

The expedition to the lighthouse is finally going to take place. Lily feels in a state of estrangement, for "all seemed strangers to her. She had no attachments here, she felt, no relations with it, anything might happen, and whatever did happen, a step outside, a voice calling . . . was a question, as if the link that usually bound things together had been cut, and they floated up here, down there, off, anyhow. . . . It was a beautiful still day" (146). This dangling and suspended state of chaos shows in a phantasy of obsessive questioning and interpellation. Because Lily, in her paranoid-schizoid state, feels morbidly under the surveillance of others, especially Mr. Ramsay, she must strive to escape "his demand on her" (147).

In this interior monologue, Lily shifts and capsizes in the waters of her passionate engagement with a past and a body forever lost. The collapse of the referential function of language shows in the emergence of the symbolic equation, in its desperate and urgent frenzy to unite words with things, to literalize experience on the border of psychosis. Lily is prey to a hallucinatory episode of writing on the wall: "and like everything else this strange morning the words became symbols, wrote themselves all over the grey-green walls. If only she could put them together, she felt, write them out in some sentence, then she would have got at the truth of things" (147).[28] This inability to bind or put two things together in the mind refers us to Klein and further to Bion's elaborations on the combined parent figure (Bion 1962a,b). Bion specifically described learning and knowing as activities that entail bringing things together in the mind: bringing together preconceptions (anticipations) with things as they actually are, bringing one idea together with another, adding things up. He likened such activities to the parents' coming together in their sexuality.[29] Bion considered that things linked together in the mind may create reactions similar to parents linking together sexually. The experience of things coming together in the mind would thus be some sort of version of the internalized combined parent figure. In this arena, the death drive, under the form of tensions and aggression, emerges in thought disorders based on disturbances in the coupling of ideas.

Since in *To the lighthouse* this binding of things together has so much to do with seeing them, with perceiving these things first as separate entities and later as parts that may compose a whole, it is clear that perception, and specifically seeing, has to do with the trauma of sexual difference. In Freud, seeing is indisputably related to the primal scene and the parents' roles in copulation. In Klein, the first sadistic phantasy of the combined parent figure horrifies the child, and this may progressively evolve into an image of peace and harmony when sadism and paranoid-schizoid defenses cease to be at their height. In Woolf, the blockage of sight results also from an interdiction that has to do with paternal heterosexual copulation. Thus, in the first section of the novel Lily and William Bankes are caught furtively looking at Mr. and Mrs. Ramsay: "Mr. Ramsay glared at them. He glared at them without seeming to see them. That made them both vaguely uncomfortable. Together they had seen a thing they had not been meant to see. They had encroached upon a privacy" (18). Lily promptly feels the need to take her eyes off the scene and go back to her painting.

In the final section, Lily decides to resume her painting, and her obsession with light, with the light coming from the lighthouse, with that reflected on the surfaces of furniture and walls, and with the specter of light she needs to create the different colors for her canvas, shows in what I would call a fetishistic object relation, the fetish materialized in a certain glow of uncanny light. But Lily is unable to paint or do anything with Mr. Ramsay "bearing down on her" (148). Her anxieties over his persistent demands are also channeled through the sense of sight. Lily, in her obsessive ruminations, wonders: "Did she not see what he wanted from her?" (151). This impaired sense of sight extends into an impairment of her creative capacities and a generalized inhibition.

Throughout this section, Mr. Ramsay's grief, manifested in his strenuous impositions on others, is so excessive that it borders on mania: "All Lily wished was that this enormous flood of grief, this insatiable hunger for sympathy, this demand that she should surrender herself up to him entirely, and even so he had sorrows enough to keep her supplied for ever, should leave her, should be diverted (she kept looking at the house, hoping for an interruption) before it swept her down in its flow" (151). And it is Mr. Ramsay's gaze that depletes the world of energy, of color and vitality, until "the whole horizon seemed swept bare of objects to talk about" (152). Mr. Ramsay's gaze phagocytes objects in his passage from melancholia to mania.

On a wonderful night, starlit, in the subtle radiance emanating from a black sky, Lily, in her melancholic rapture, falls asleep. This suspension of consciousness is accompanied by the fetishistic glitter of several dim lights: "Then, being tired, her mind still rising and falling with the sea, the taste and smell that places have after long absence possessing her, the candles wavering in her eyes, she had lost herself and gone under" (149). And this time, Lily poses another rhetorical, albeit indirect, question, "The question was of some relation between those masses. She had borne it in her mind all these years. It seemed as if the solution had come to her: she knew now what she wanted to do" (147–48). This problem with masses constitutes a true stumbling block for Lily. Gradually, it becomes more dramatic, producing more anxiety and conveying a claustrophobic sense of entrapment. Lily undertakes her painting aggressively, assailed by anxiety and a paranoid-schizoid reaction of hostility and defense. Tansley's misogynist remarks come to her mind, and the compulsion to repeat makes her engage in a vicious circle of introjections and projections. She "murmurs monotonously, anxiously considering what her plan of attack should be. For the mass loomed before her; it protruded; she felt it pressing on her eyeballs" (159). This rhetoric of attack and aggression reemerges throughout this last section, and it clearly alludes to the effects of the death drive in the psychosexual, emotional, and intellectual organization of the subject.[30]

The terror that the empty canvas poses for Lily is equated with a white stare, with the blindness emanating from the blank surface that is ready to capture and freeze life: "She looked blankly at the canvas, with its uncom-promising white stare; from the canvas to the garden" (157). The act of creation is simultaneously an act that defies death and produces death by annihilating life, by framing, incorporating, and embalming those already lost objects of life. Lily gives birth to her painting, and her painting gives birth to Lily in an uncertain and immensely painful moment, as "she seemed like an unborn soul, a soul reft of body, hesitating on some windy pinnacle and exposed without protection to all the blasts of doubt" (158). Interestingly, it is Lily's body that is lost, and this phantasy of disposses-sion of the body will be compensated for through the mediating role of the fetish. Susan Isaacs argues that there is an element of visuality that effects a repression of the body.

> During the period of development when the visual elements in percep-tion (and in corresponding images) begin to predominate over the so-matic, becoming differentiated and spatially integrated, and thus mak-ing clearer the distinction between the inner and the outer worlds, the concrete bodily elements in the total experience of perceiving (and phantasying) largely undergo *repression*. The visual, externally referred elements in phantasy become relatively de-emotionalized, desexual-ized, independent, in consciousness of bodily ties. They become "im-ages" in the narrower sense, representations "in the mind" (but not, consciously, incorporations in the body) of external objects recog-nized to be such. It is "realized" that the objects are outside the mind, but their images are "in the mind." ([1952] 1983, 105)

Through the specter of light that traverses the window panes and the colors of her palette, Lily will be able to create, (re)create, and retrieve her self "reft of body."

Lily endeavors to capture the emotions of the body and the sense of emptiness in words, but the incommensurability of this experience pushes her to revert to painting. In an almost surreal vision, the space around her diffuses and becomes "like curves and arabesques flourishing round a centre of complete emptiness." The whole world dissolves into "a pool of thought, a deep basin of reality" (179). Woolf splendidly mimics the dead-ening movement of the death drive with her emphasis on repetition and with the rhythm evoked by this passage: "To want and not to have, sent all up her body a hardness, a hollowness, a strain. And then to want and not to have—to want and want—how that wrung the heart, and wrung it again and again!" (178). Woolf aims to trace the movement of desire, its endless displacement and unsatisfiability.

Lily has a totally insecure sense of her bodily boundaries. I would argue that this sense has been severely disturbed as a result of her melancholia. Substances, objects, and physical (inanimate) elements assail her body. The feelings associated with this range from asphyxia to engulfment, dissolution, suspension, blindness, and stillness. There is virtually nothing that can contain her body, and even the air would do, facing her sense of fragmentation and disintegration. In the scene in which Lily, thinking of Mrs. Ramsay, looks at the sea and is disturbed by the vision of Mr. Ramsay's boat, it seems, "as if the air were a fine gauze which held things together and kept them softly in its mesh, only gently swaying them this way and that" (182).

And Lily must face again a remaining problem, that of space, which is always a problem of distance, of location of the viewer, and of segmentation and division. The problem with her painting is ultimately a problem of vision, and of light and darkness, and Lily moves from that unrecognizable object—that mass upon which the whole picture is poised—to the "extreme obscurity of human relationships" (171). Lily's canvas wants to be both a tribute to and an exploration of her past; she dips into her colors as she dips into her past. Woolf graphically describes her journey with a metaphor that connotes excavation and the darkness associated to it: "She went on tunnelling her way into her picture, into the past" (173). This process of excavation goes deep into the layers of her self; it is simultaneously a psychoanalytical search for origins and a melancholic tracing of the subject's many losses. The poignant anxiety about loss and the ambiguities of reparation are conveyed by Lily's strenuous, albeit failed, attempts to paint unencumbered from the burden of her past. But there is a sense of obstruction that blocks Lily's way into her painting and her past. Her internal objects weigh her down, and she finds herself melancholically embarrassed by them. The physicality of her lost objects is figured in the physicality of the corpses that dwell in her past: "But the dead, thought Lily, encountering some obstacle in her design which made her pause and ponder, stepping back a foot or so, oh, the dead!" (174).

It is interesting to note that there is a moment of fixity in the midst of the Ramsays' excursion to the lighthouse, a moment when everything seems to come to a halt, which coincides with James's greatest tension of oedipal rivalry with his father. At that time, the lighthouse, in its majestic fixity, uncannily acquires the appearance of a cyclops, the projection of James's terror and hatred of his father: "The Lighthouse was then a silvery, misty-looking tower with a yellow eye, that opened suddenly, and softly in the evening" (186). And in this frightening delirium of appearances James acknowledges the ambivalence implicit in perception, moving between the borders of the paranoid-schizoid and the depressive mode of object relations: "No, the other was also the Lighthouse. For nothing was simply one thing. The other Lighthouse was true too" (186). For "The Lighthouse" is also a lesson in the forms of resistance to the tyranny of the father and the dead. It is a lesson in the strategies and ruses the subject may deploy to resist oedipalization and reification into a daughter's or a son's role. James believes that he must resist and fight his father, "For they [James and Cam] must fight tyranny to the death" (168). And Cam, endowed with the wisdom of the daughter, launches her irony at her brother's supposed knowledge: "James the lawgiver, with the tablets of eternal wisdom laid open on his knee . . . said, Resist him. Fight him" (168). Cam, more versed in the practicalities of daily existence, mistrusts his idealism and his belligerent hope for liberation from the law.

By the end of the novel, Lily meditates upon the sense of repetition in the Ramsays' lives and in her own.[31] In a delirium of hallucination, she can discern that "the window at which she was looking was whitened by some light stuff behind it" (201), and Mrs. Ramsay appears, sitting as she used to in "some wave of white" (202). Once again, Lily is able to regain her pleasure in a rapture of light. She wishes to be on a level with ordinary experience, to perceive objects qua objects, "to feel simply that's a chair, that's a table, and yet at the same time, It's a miracle, it's an ecstasy" (202). She cannot put her easel aside since her mind is totally full of what she is thinking and seeing.

At this point, Lily's heightened creativity is accompanied by a heightened anxiety. She can only free herself from her anxiety and assuage her melancholia by recourse to the fetish. Beneath a surface of conventional femininity, her socially forbidden and dangerous "masculine ambitions" lie. Lily has trespassed upon the field of art; she has violated the interdiction "Women can't paint, women can't write" and will have to pay a high price for it. As I have argued, for Klein the highest anxiety situation in the girl has to do with having the inside of her body stripped of its contents by a retaliating mother. And the mother (or the breast) is the figure toward which the girl expresses extreme ambivalence in the passage from the paranoid-schizoid to the depressive position. Among the anxieties related to object loss, the pre-oedipal crises brought about by absences of the mother and the further oedipal crises within the phantasy triangle of the primal scene attribute these absences of the mother to the third element, which breaks up the exclusivity of the original dyadic bond.

In *To the lighthouse*, the mother, in the figure of Mrs. Ramsay, is either possessed by others or irretrievably lost. The recurrent scenario of Lily's emptiness, dissolution of bodily boundaries, and melancholia has to do with the foreclosure of the image of a good mother (breast) that may satiate her and consequently with the foreclosure of a domain of love between women outside the tyrannical logic of the excluded middle. Teresa de Lauretis has aptly argued that "if indeed any number of fetish objects, images or signs can lure and signify lesbian desire, the (lost) object which they displace and resignify in many different ways is always the female body itself. Thus perverse desire is indeed 'cut off' from its original object (the breast with milk, the mother's body) and moves on to other images/objects/ signs, but the latter do refer metonymically to one and the same instance, the female body itself, a loss of her body-ego. The fantasy of castration reinscribes this law in the paternal law that prohibits her access not only to the mother but to the female body in herself and in other women" (1994a, 243). The screening function of the fetish of light is a melancholic strategy that rescues Lily from excessive splitting and disintegration.[32]

The Ramsays' arrival at the lighthouse parallels Lily's intense work on her canvas. She observes "its attempt at something" and sees how its blurred quality dissipates into a second of clarity. Exhausted, Lily finishes her painting: "I have had my vision" (209). Out of fear of the total loss of the mother, Lily's final figuration of Mrs. Ramsay in her painting, by recourse to the mediating role of the fetish, rises from diffuseness "with a sudden intensity, as if she saw it clear for a second" (209). And Lily, in the extreme fatigue of her strenuous work of melancholia, hallucinates another scene, which, in her almost manic-depressive delirium, rescues the mother/lover in an ardent rapture of light.

But the beam of light in *To the lighthouse* may be both beneficial and destructive. It is through Bion's metaphors that we can best understand this damaging effect of light in the work of the analyst and, by extension, I would argue, in the work of the writer, haunted by the sounds and rhythms of the words that populate his or her mind. Wilfred Bion, in his work with psychotic patients, came across the obvious analytic difficulties of the inability to communicate verbally or at the very best to communicate in states of apparent hallucination or delusion. He held that in order to make any progress with these patients it was necessary to empty the mind of theoretical preconceptions, which became under these conditions merely defenses against what had to be experienced in feeling before it could be experienced in thought. He urged this technical requirement of a wholly receptive mind, working without preconceptions in the most literal sense, when he called on analysts to empty their minds of memory and desire during analysis: "Memory and desire are 'illuminations' that destroy the analyst's capacity for observation as a leakage of light into a camera might destroy the value of the film being exposed" ([1970] 1977, 69). This ideal of total receptivity (which is compared to the aesthetic idea of "negative capability") finds its concomitant version in the figure of the artist facing his or her creation. In Lily Briscoe, the effusion of light enables her to perceive, mix her colors, and paint, but an excess of light brings her close to a deadly jouissance.

Ceci n'est pas un Roman

I am making up To the Lighthouse—the sea is to be heard all through it. I have an idea that I will invent a new name for my books to supplant "novel." A new —— by Virginia Woolf. But what? Elegy?—Virginia Woolf

Magritte's concerns were opposed to those of painterly aestheticism from the beginning of his career. Both Magritte and Foucault were fascinated with what in The order of things ([1966] 1970) the French philosopher called "heterotopias."[33] Heterotopia has an inherent dimension as a critique of language provided by its disruptive potential of syntax and syntagmatic relations in the most general sense. And in this respect Magritte's disturbing images overturn the principle of resemblance, since they do not really resemble anything whose presence might be taken as their model or origin.

For Foucault, Magritte totally dissociated similitude from resemblance. This is one of the crucial arguments of the French philosopher in The order of things. In his view, resemblance "has a 'model,' an original element that orders and hierarchizes the increasingly less faithful copies that can be struck from it. Resemblance presupposes a primary reference that prescribes and classes. The similar develops in series that have neither beginning nor end, that can be followed in one direction as easily as in another, that obey no hierarchy, but propagate themselves from small differences among small differences. Resemblance serves representation, which rules over it; similitude serves repetition, which ranges across it. Resemblance predicates itself upon a model it must return to and reveal; similitude circulates the simulacrum as an indefinite and reversible relation of the similar to the similar" ([1966] 1970, 44). The model in the principle of resemblance is taken to be ontologically superior to its copies, which submissively replicate it. In similitude, the whole notion of model is erased. Classical painting, from perspective to trompe l'oeil attempted to identify images with the "models" that inspired them. Magritte's strategies largely consist of subverting the tyranny of the familiar image by showing it in an impossible or absurd conjunction. He also undermines discourse by using it against itself, in his insistence on literalism, and in his painted words and his titles. Magritte explodes mimesis and disrupts both classical figuration and discourse. His project partakes of the intellectual atmosphere of representational crises in modernism.

The first version of *Ceci n'est pas une Pipe* was painted by Magritte in 1929. It shows a pipe and an artificial script underneath written in calligraphic style. The other version in which Foucault is interested depicts "The same pipe, same statement, same handwriting. But instead of being juxtaposed in neutral, limitless, unspecified space, the text and the figure are set within a frame. The frame itself is placed upon an easel, and the latter in turn upon the clearly visible slats of the floor. Above everything, a pipe exactly like the one in the picture, but much larger" (Foucault [1968] 1983, 15).[34] Both versions disconcert us, the first with its simplicity and the second with a *crescendo* of ambiguities.[35] Foucault reads the words on the surface of the canvas as "words drawing words; at the surface of the image, they form the reflection of a sentence saying that this is not a pipe. The image of a text" (23). In his view, *Ceci n'est pas une Pipe* "exemplifies the penetration of discourse into the form of things; it reveals discourse's ambiguous power to deny and to redouble" (37).

Foucault has reflected upon the nonrelation, or at least the problematic relation, between Magritte's paintings and their titles.[36] If, as Foucault has stated, Magritte names his paintings in order to focus attention on the very act of naming ([1968] 1983, 36), how can we approach Virginia Woolf's use of the title *To the lighthouse* in relation to what we as readers know after having read the text? Is it not the case that Woolf performs a similar operation and announces that she is going to write a poem (an elegy or an ode) and in a transgressive act writes a novel instead? And what is in the quality of the novel's prose that refers us to a poem?

Foucault's rhetoric turns melancholic when he refers to Magritte's transformations of the old space of representation, which "rule[s], but only at the surface, no more than a polished stone, bearing words and shapes: beneath nothing. It is a gravestone" ([1968] 1983, 41). In his discussion of some of Magritte's paintings that include masses,[37] he underscores that the form of the object is elided and the name superimposed on the mass. We face "the mass that casts a shadow and the name that designates it" (40). What Foucault understands as the word assuming the solidity of an object (41) is what I have called the symbolic equation. This materializes in Magritte in many instances. The one referred to by Foucault is the painting *L'Usage de la Parole* (1932), in which the word *sirène* is written in reference to a huge upraised finger emerging from the floor, which is crowned with one of the bells so recurrent in Magritte's work.

For Foucault, resemblance and affirmation cannot be dissociated. In his view, *Ceci n'est pas une Pipe*, subverts affirmation by recourse to the simulacrum: "Each element of 'this is not a pipe' could hold an apparently negative discourse—because it denies along with resemblance, the assertion of reality resemblance conveys—but one that is basically affirmative: the affirmation of the simulacrum, affirmation of the element within the network of the similar" ([1968] 1983, 47). The plays of similitude in Magritte establish metamorphoses that hold back affirmation of identity but in many cases, by virtue of proportions, guarantee analogy.[38]

It is my contention that *To the lighthouse* operates on principles similar to those that Magritte employs in his nonaffirmative paintings. Woolf defamiliarizes the genre of the "novel" by giving to her narrative the title of a poem and simultaneously explodes the scope of the poem into a long lyrical meditation on loss, death, and art.

The melancholic nature of Woolf's texts turn writing into a privileged space in which to experiment with variations on the genre of elegy. The basic structure of the elegy consists of a substitution of an aesthetic object for whatever has been lost. At times, the elegist/mourner enlarges grief so that the world seems to participate in it, a grief objectified and heightened until it is purged.[39] In *To the lighthouse*, Woolf devises a grief practice that comes close to the Kleinian theorization on mourning, melancholia, and manic-depressive states.

In order to complete the work of mourning, some distance, some sense of detachment from the lost object, is needed. This is also the case with literary and artistic production concerned with separation, loss, and death. In melancholia, there is no such distance since the subject sinks into confusion, being caught in the anxieties arising from an external object that was lost and an internal object that can always be lost. The pictorial sense of perspective is also lost. And, since melancholia marks the radical irresolution of the depressive position, *To the lighthouse* as melancholic text draws the repeated and repeatable transit between paranoid-schizoid and depressive modes of object relations. Thus, Woolf deludes us with her title *To the lighthouse* since this is not a poem or an elegy. She simultaneously undertakes a different project from that of a novel. What is Woolf, ultimately, framing for us?

In my reading, Woolf's attempts to replace the lost object of love with the aesthetic object of Lily's canvas, or with her own writing, fail since the image of the good mother cannot be either restored or retrieved. Lily's second of clarity, this second of "sudden intensity," operates in the mode of a hallucination, a screen memory, or a fetish of light that melancholically covers what is lost and already introjected.[40] However, the intrinsic mobility and substitutability of the fetish allows for the projection of loss onto different surfaces. Lily's canvas frames the fetish outside the domain of perspective and within the lyrical internal movement of Woolf's writing.

Drawing the Mother's Internal Empire

Painters often express the feeling that their hands are only the instruments of something within them that directs their activity. But the tone of this feeling varies greatly, and indicates whether this invisible force (their internal objects) is beneficial, in harmony with the artist's personality, or persecutory.—Paula Heimann

If persecutory fears are very strong, and for this reason (among others) the infant cannot work through the paranoid-schizoid position, the working through of the depressive position is in turn impeded. This failure may lead to a regressive reinforcing of persecutory fears and strengthen the fixation-points for severe psychoses.—Melanie Klein

many families had lost their dearest . . . but every one had lost some one these years.—Virginia Woolf

"The Oedipus complex in the light of early anxieties" ([1945] 1975), is Klein's definitive statement on the Oedipus complex and a summary of her major findings and arguments in her departure from Freud. In this essay,

Klein gathers together material from two previous cases, those described in her *Narrative of a child psycho-analysis* ([1961] 1975)—better known as the ten-year-old Richard case—and *The psycho-analysis of children* ([1932] 1975e)—her analysis of two-year-old Rita. I am particularly interested in Klein's analysis of the series of drawings that Richard produced during the course of the analysis since Klein's assessment of these pieces of infantile art runs parallel to her changing ideas on the onset of the Oedipus complex. From this point on, Klein moves away from her former postulate, which placed the release of the first oedipal impulses upon the oral frustration of weaning, and holds instead that the onset of the Oedipus complex coincides with the onset of the depressive position. This has been widely discussed earlier in this book, where I emphasize the nature of Oedipus as melancholic apparatus.[41]

I want to suggest that we can read Klein's "The Oedipus complex in the light of early anxieties" together with Woolf's *To the lighthouse* and Heimann's "A contribution to the problem of sublimation and its relation to processes of internalization" (1942) in an attempt to reflect upon modernist art and creativity in the context of the Kleinian idea of the fluctuation between the paranoid-schizoid and depressive positions and melancholia. Is it possible at all to read Lily Briscoe's canvas in its emptiness and its subsequent crises in representation as a melancholic reverberation that challenges the achievement of the depressive position? To what extent can we read Klein's concept of the depressive position as a theoretical phantasy, a utopian asymptotic boundary that we constantly strive but fail to reach? In an attempt to explore the specificity of the work of melancholia, painting and writing as potentially restorative activities will guide us in our inquiry into this kind of labor, its differences, and its dissimilarities to the work of mourning. What is the product of the work of melancholia and how can we apprehend the consequences that this almost muted labor has in the psychic economy of the subject?

In *OCEA*, the specific oral character of Richard's drawings is present from the start. He draws using crayons in four different colors, black, blue, purple, and red, which symbolize his father, mother, brother, and himself, respectively. Klein remarks that Richard's interest in the events of the war played an important part in his associations, and his drawings came to represent an empire under siege: "The pattern represented an empire, the different sections standing for different countries. . . . He often looked up on the map the countries which Hitler had subjugated, and the connections between the countries on the maps and his own empire drawings was evident. The empire drawings represented his mother, who was being invaded and attacked. His father usually appeared as the enemy; Richard and his brother figured in the drawings in various rôles, sometimes as allies of his mother, sometimes as allies of his father" (373). Richard's drawings, though superficially similar, varied greatly in detail, and his main mode of composition seemed to be improvisation, "He did not start out with any deliberate plan and was often surprised to see the finished picture" (373). Klein sets herself up to analyze certain anxieties that would come more strongly to the fore as represented in seven drawings produced in the course of six analytic hours. She examines such recurring motifs in Richard's drawings as the bumping of one ship against another, which turned out to symbolize sexual intercourse. The destructiveness inherent in it was linked to its oral-sadistic character.[42] Richard showed enormous anxiety about his aggression toward his mother, and a sense of guilt and fear related to this destructive phantasy molded his emotional life. Crucial in Klein's analysis is the description of the mechanism of splitting: "The early splitting of the mother figure into a good and a bad 'breast mother' . . . developed further into a division between the 'breast mother' who was 'good' and the 'genital mother' who was 'bad' " (377). Richard manages to draw paranoid-schizoid landscapes where he defends himself against the fear of being attacked by his rivals (father and brother), by strategically arranging his fleet of battleships in a row lengthwise and in order of age so as to give the impression that harmony and peace reign in the family. Thus, he manages to hide his jealousy and hatred. He also deals with ambivalence, anxiety, and guilt in his drawings. In the second drawing that Klein examines, Richard has divided the "empire" in two: in the West, there were countries belonging to everybody, while the East does not contain anything of his mother but only himself, his father, and his brother. In Klein's reading, this drawing expressed "the division into the endangered bad mother (the genital mother) and the loved and safe mother (the breast mother)" (379). She concludes that Richard could achieve relative stability only on a predominantly pregenital level. The genital organization could not be sufficiently stabilized, and the interplay between the phenomena of fixation and regression was present at every step of his development. In another drawing, we find a combination of motifs (plants, starfish, ships, and fish) that show that the positive Oedipus situation has come more fully to the fore. Richard does not identify with the role of the baby anymore and comes to be represented differently. His triumph over his father transforms the father into a baby, and his space is substantially reduced in the drawings.

Progressively, Richard develops hypochondriacal anxiety and draws what he calls a "very horrid bird" onto which he projects parts of himself. The bird stands for a greedy and destructive mother, but, interestingly, the drawing shows two sharply differentiated sections, one totally blue, coinciding with the "good" aspects of the mother, and one painted with mixed colors, representing her "bad" aspects. Richard is now more able to face external reality and recognizes the fact that his mother has frustrated him and therefore aroused his hatred. In Richard's last two drawings, Klein sees manifest the process of internalization of his objects, from the threatening moment of internalization of the combined parent figure (attacking him from within) to the growing perception of the internalization of his good mother, which comes to coincide with his external mother.

Richard's drawings evolve from the spread of an undifferentiated space on the page, to represent the mother, to the compartmentalization and splitting into a good (breast) and a bad (genital) mother, the internalization of the terrifying combined parent figure, and finally that of the good mother. Klein concludes that Richard's failure to establish the genital position securely was largely caused by his inability to deal with early anxiety situations in his development. She writes: "The great part which the bad breast played in Richard's emotional life was connected with his unsatisfactory feeding period and the strong oral—urethral—and anal-sadistic impulses and phantasies which it stimulated" (OCEA, 392). By the end of the analysis, Richard was able to link his feelings of love and hatred, to strengthen his genital position and experience his oedipal desires, and to trust his own constructive and reparative tendencies as well as his internal and external objects.

In light of Klein's analysis and what concerns us here, I want to suggest that Richard's surprise at the recognition of his drawings has to do with his separation anxiety and lack of confidence in his potential. His precarious achievement of the genital position is just a step toward an integration that remains an uncertain project in the horizon. As we have discussed, in Klein's view castration fear is not the only factor that determines the repression of the Oedipus complex in the boy. In the case of the girl, since the pre-oedipal and early stages of the Oedipus conflict mark "a period of fluctuation between desires directed towards the mother and father in all libidinal positions, there is no doubt in my mind as to the far-reaching and lasting influence of every facet of the relation to the mother upon the relation to the father" (OCEA, 418). Ultimately, Richard and Lily Briscoe, in their different formulations, strive to inquire into the meaning of life: "What was the meaning of life? That was all—a simple question; one that tended to close in on one with years. The great revelation had never come. The great revelation perhaps never did come" (To the lighthouse, 161). And the enigma of the meaning of life is intrinsically related to that of the origin of signification and to the maternal body as the site where semiosis emerges in the contrast and opposition between mother and child, both of them minimal and complex units within the signifying chain.

Along the lines of Richard's analysis, the issue of war is also omnipresent in the work of Woolf and Magritte. We could probably say that they share what Ellen H. Spitz has written about the latter's work: "for Magritte the most compelling agendas are never those of external war and politics but rather the internal battlegrounds of memory, fantasy and desire, where strife is equally intense but, paradoxically, both more and less possible to control. For Magritte, it is not at Verdun or in the trenches but rather internally, behind the apple, that the 'great war' is continually being fought" (1994, 48). Spitz is specifically alluding here to one of Magritte's best-known pictures, The Great War (1964), which shows the head of a man with a bowler-hat whose eyes are hidden behind a great apple. Whereas the title overtly refers to World War I, apparently Magritte denied this and remarked that it had strictly to do with "the eternal struggle between the gaze and objects" (quoted in Spitz 1994, 48). Apart from the apple as a symbol of forbidden knowledge, Spitz notes its double function as the object behind which the figure hides and that which blinds him.

In the second section of To the lighthouse, "Time Passes," there are fleeting allusions to the war. Andrew Ramsay is killed in France during the war, and the narrative voice echoes confusion and chaos raising rhetorical questions: "Were they allies? Were they enemies? How long would they endure?" (126). By the end of "Time Passes," peace has been restored and the nightmare of history dissolves into the now placid image of Lily's dream.

In "Love, guilt, and reparation" ([1937] 1975), Klein puts forward her idea that gradually in life anything that is felt to dispense goodness and beauty and that produces pleasure and satisfaction in the most general sense can take the place of the ever-bountiful breast, and of the whole mother, in the unconscious. Interests and activities result from a met-onymic displacement that operates by literally "put[ing into them] some of the love that originally belonged to people" (333). In this context of repara-tive phantasies, Klein discusses Keats's sonnet "On First Looking into Chapman's Homer" to illustrate her arguments and provides a melan-cholic oedipal reading of it. The poem is about the pleasure one experi-ences in enjoying a great work of art. In it, the world stands for art and the activities described range from science to the exploration of new territo-ries. The appreciation of beauty derives from "the realms of gold," which for Klein stand for "the loved mother, and the longing with which these lands are approached is derived from our longings for her" (LGR, 335). Klein suggests that "the 'deep-browed Homer' who rules over the land of poetry stands for the admired and powerful father, whose example the son (Keats) follows when he too enters the country of his desire (art, beauty, the world—ultimately, his mother)" (335). Klein makes an analogy with sculp-ture that can be extrapolated into the wider domain of the arts: "the sculp-tor who puts life into his object of art, whether or not it represents a person, is unconsciously restoring and recreating the early loved people, whom he has in phantasy destroyed" (LGR, 335).[43] In this fragment, Klein does not make any claims about the representational nature of art. In this sense, her postulates are close to the formal credo of modernism. In this mise en abîme of the scene of reading there is something that gets lost, the thing itself, the bodies of our loved ones in our constant re-creations and reeditions, and this is intrinsic to the nature of language, which exhibits the inherent melancholic dimension of all signification.[44]

What may allow us to relate Keats's, Klein's and Woolf's (Lily Bris-coe's) ideas on art is precisely the quality of permanence that they all underscore. In To the lighthouse, Lily recognizes this epiphanic atemporal moment of revelation when shape emerges out of chaos: "(as in another sphere) Lily herself tried to make of the moment something permanent)—this was of the nature of a revelation. In the midst of chaos there was shape; this eternal passing and flowing . . . was struck into stability" (161). But art and beauty share a horrendous quality; they freeze life: "Beauty had this penalty—it came too readily, it came too completely. It stilled life—froze it" (177). Also, by the end of the second section, "The Window," Mrs. Ramsay, in her reverie—"asleep in broad daylight" (121)—engages in a passionate memory of reading and brings to her mind, with immense autoerotic pleasure, the thing itself, the sonnet: "and so reading she was ascending, she felt, on to the top, on to the summit. How satisfying! How restful! All the odds and ends of the day stuck to this magnet; her mind felt swept, felt clean. And then there it was, suddenly entire; she held it in her hands, beautiful and reasonable, clear and complete, the essence sucked out of life and held rounded here—the sonnet" (121). This sense of the completeness and roundness of the sonnet is equated with the wholeness and autonomy of feminine sexuality, even when, as in this passage, it is under the scrutiny of the male (Mr. Ramsay's) gaze.[45]

Reparation or Aggression?

The problem of space remained, she thought, taking up her brush again. It glared at her. The whole mass of the picture was poised upon that weight. . . . And she began to lay on a red, a grey, and she began to model her way into the hollow there.—Virginia Woolf

In "Infantile anxiety-situations reflected in a work of art and the creative impulse" ([1929] 1975), Klein briefly discusses a musical piece and a literary story to illustrate her ideas on early anxiety situations in development.[46] The materials come from the libretto of Ravel's opera *Das Zauberwort* (The Magic Word) and from an essay written by Karin Michaelis on the beginnings in art of her friend, the painter Ruth Kjär. This last piece is more interesting for my purposes, since it deals with a woman painter and connects us directly to Woolf's Lily Briscoe.

Klein reports that Karin Michaelis, in her essay "The Empty Space" writes about the development of her friend, the painter Ruth Kjär. She describes her as a woman who "possessed remarkable artistic feeling . . . but she had no pronounced creative talent" (Klein, IASWA, 215). She suffered from fits of deep depression that Michaelis records in terms of severe melancholia: "There was only one dark spot in her life. In the midst of the happiness which was natural to her, and seemed so untroubled, she would suddenly be plunged into the deepest melancholy. A melancholy that was suicidal. If she tried to account for this, she would say something to this effect: 'There is an empty space in me, which I can never fill!' " (215). As the story goes, Kjär married, and she seemed happy until her melancholy state recurred. This was triggered by the removal and sale of a picture that used to hang on one of the walls of her home. Michaelis writes: "This left an empty space on the wall, which in some inexplicable way seemed to coincide with the empty space within her" (215). Kjär finally decided to paint something by herself that might cover up that emptiness. Seized by an irrepressible impulse to create, she managed to paint a picture that surprised everybody with her talent and skills. Michaelis describes Kjär's feverish state in the frenzy of creation as an apotheosis of ecstasy: "She was on fire, devoured by an ardour within. She must prove to herself that the divine sensation, the unspeakable sense of happiness that she had felt could be repeated" (216). As the story goes, Kjär continued on to a successful painting career.

This feeling of an empty space that Klein promptly translates into a feeling of something lacking in her body originates in the most profound anxiety situation experienced by girls, the phantasy of being robbed of the contents of their bodies and that their bodies would be destroyed or mutilated by their mothers. Klein moves on to consider the sort of pictures that Kjär painted. Apart from her peculiar first painting, a life-sized figure of a naked Negress and one picture of flowers, she observes that "she had confined herself to portraits" (IASWA, 217).[47] Michaelis comments on her two last works, a portrait of an old woman—"bearing the mark of years and disillusionments" (217)—and a portrait of her Irish-Canadian mother, which has an uncanny quality in Michaelis's description and it is worth quoting: "This lady has a long time before her before she must put her lips to the cup of renunciation. Slim, imperious, challenging, she stands there with a moonlight-coloured shawl draped over her shoulders: she has the effect of a magnificent woman of primitive times, who could any day engage in a combat with the children of the desert with her naked hands. What a chin! What force there is in the haughty gaze!" (217).

By the end of her analysis, Klein writes: "It is obvious that the desire to make reparation, to make good the injury psychologically done to the mother and also to restore herself was at the bottom of the compelling urge to paint these portraits of her relatives. That of the old woman, on the threshold of death, seems to be the expression of the primary, sadistic desire to destroy. The daughter's wish to destroy her mother, to see her old, worn-out, marred, is the cause of the need to represent her in full possession of her strength and beauty. By so doing the daughter can allay her own anxiety and can endeavour to restore her mother and make her new through the portrait" (IASWA, 218). It is most interesting that Klein does not say a single word about the violence implicit in Kjär's last portrait of her mother. How can we read this new image of her mother without paying attention to the signs of aggression exhibited by this terrible effigy? Is it not the case that this attempt at reparation can be read as a reverse movement to the paranoid-schizoid position? If not, what are we to make of this atavistic mother ready to "engage in combat with the children of the desert with her naked hands"? Michaelis's adjectives and Klein's apparent over-looking of this issue are too symptomatic to pass without notice. The eerie quality of this portrait approaches the surreal/hyperreal quality of many of Magritte's paintings. Michaelis's highly charged description is colored with the sand tonalities of the desert, which are evocative of the coloration of the naked human body. The desert, in its barren, forlorn, desert-ed connotation, alludes to the melancholy state of mother-child(ren) separa-tion, and the mother's naked hands, bare, empty and already absent, strive to return to this previous and premelancholic stage of combat, aggression, and retaliation. For what can be more painful than bearing your once full hands (and arms, and womb) empty? What can be more distressing than being ejected into the world, dislodged and abandoned forever to your fate? This almost hyperreal portrait of Kjär's mother reaches us with the un-canny and repulsive quality of some of Magritte's canvases.

It is important to note that in the melancholic rhetoric of Klein's essay she explicitly refers to Kjär's activity as involving "confination" when she writes that "she had confined herself to portraits" (IASWA, 217). This con-fination connotes entrapment, enclosure, limitation, and ultimately "con-finement" and marks the space where children are born, where a new being (artwork?) comes to life. The oxymoronic quality of the portrait gathers simultaneously within itself life drives and death drives. Whereas it memorializes and thus preserves for the future, it also brings to mind the deadening quality of the image it portrays, always already dead or lost forever.

In Kjär's last portrait of her mother, we can identify this protracted and conflictual state of separation anxiety and the melancholia attached to it. The purported reparation that creativity brings about finds itself at a loss. The depressive position figures as a phantasy whose achievement can never be guaranteed, and the lesson we draw out from this "instructive" moment may be that to learn how to live in this constant unstability, to endure and simultaneously resist paranoid-schizoid episodes, is the best as we can expect in this ever changing drama of positions.[48]

The foreclosure of the image of the good mother as a crucial condition for melancholia is conspicuous in this instance, among others. In Richard's drawings, Klein also perceives the splitting of the mother into a good and a bad one as a precondition to the further ambivalence arising from considering her good and bad aspects as coextensive: "The division of the empire also expressed his wish to keep the dangerous Daddy away from Mummy and to protect her against him; but it also meant that Mummy was divided into a bad Mother, the east, full of dangerous male genitals, and into a good and peaceful Mother" (NChP, 197).

Klein argues that in the analysis of children it is very common to find that drawing and painting are used as a means of restoring people. In "Mourning and its relation to manic-depressive states" ([1940] 1975) she writes: "We know that painful experiences of all kinds sometimes stimulate sublimations, or even bring out quite new gifts in some people, who may take to painting, writing or other productive activities under the stress of frustrations and hardships. Others become more productive in a different way—more capable of appreciating people and things, more tolerant in their relation to others—they become wiser. Such enrichment is in my view gained through processes similar to those steps in mourning which we have just investigated" (MM-D, 360). In all the cases we have approached thus far, Lily Briscoe, Ruth Kjär, and René Magritte—and Richard in a different way—paint scenes and portraits. With regard to the question of portrait painting, generously understood, it is interesting to consider Magritte's 1951 *Perspective: Madame Récamier by David*, a metacommentary on Jacques-Louis David's 1799 portrait of Madame Récamier (fig. 5). The painting represents some sort of anthropomorphized coffin bent in the middle as if it were sitting on a chaise longue; hanging underneath it is a white sheet, which probably represents a shroud. In Spitz's reading, she sees Magritte engaging in a subversive exercise in deception. Magritte "is saying . . . You thought you understood that a portrait is made to preserve a beloved person, the object of one's affections, through time, to keep her alive, as it were. Perhaps it works just the other way around. Perhaps, he says through this image, to paint a portrait or to gaze at one is not to keep the beloved alive but maybe, to the contrary, to kill her again and again. For, in looking at David's original painting, we are inevitably reminded not only that Madame Récamier was once beautiful but that her beauty was now utterly vanished since she is, in fact, dead" (1994, 53).[49] Spitz goes on to argue that Magritte's *Perspective: Madame Récamier by David* questions the reparative potential of art: "Questioning the reparative value of art, this image suggests, in a manner that betrays both depression and manic

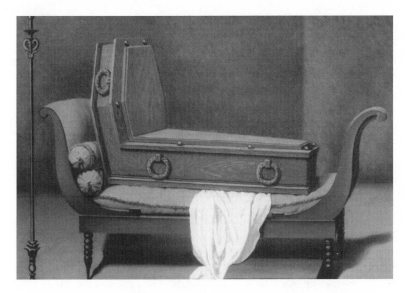

Figure 5. René Magritte, *Perspective: Madame Récamier by David* (*Perspective:
Madame Récamier de David*), 1952. (Private collection.)
© Succession René Magritte, VEGAP, 2002.

denial, that to depict an object may not be to preserve it but, rather, re-
petitively, to hurt and even to destroy it. And the larger fear here—the fear
of doing damage to the person and thing one loves most—is the same fear
that causes an averting of the eyes, a turning of the head" (53).

If we go back to Bloomsbury and consider the genre of portrait painting, we should remember that it played an important part in Vanessa Bell's
art. Bell painted most of her portraits for her friends and relatives. Since
she was far from being a fashionable portrait painter, she was able to
experiment with the genre. Bridget Elliott and Jo-Ann Wallace have described Bell's execution of her portraits in ways that are significant for my
argument. They summarize the position of critics as far as Bell's portraits
of women are concerned by saying that she would paint women with
"curiously featureless and dissolving faces."[50] They argue that "While undoubtedly the stress on the surfaces and the self-conscious reference to her
own art take up the formalist concerns of Post-Impressionism, such pictures also emphasize (whether intentionally or not) the painter's problematic role in the representation of femininity, which in turn raises questions
about the stability of sexual categories and gendered identities" (1994, 61).
To the lighthouse shows Lily Briscoe's attempt to portray Mrs. Ramsay. In her

pictorial poetics of figuration, she resorts to terms that are nonrepresentational and mark the failure of representation, since representation is founded upon the loss of that which cannot be represented: "She must try to get hold of something that evaded her. It evaded her when she thought of Mrs. Ramsay; it evaded her now when she thought of her picture. Phrases came. Visions came. Beautiful phrases. But what she wished to get hold of was that very jar on the nerves, the thing itself before it has been made anything" (193). Mrs. Ramsay's elusiveness simultaneously marks the absence of a space for the representation of love between women and the melancholic burden of lost and dead objects inherent in language.

Designs, Frames and Phantasies

Paula Heimann, in her essay "A contribution to the problem of sublimation and its relation to processes of internalization" (1942) narrates a case story of one of her female analysands, a painter in her early thirties who suffered from depressions, inhibitions in her creative work, disturbances in her sexual life, and an addiction to morphine.[51] She describes her as having strong paranoid phantasies of being possessed and inhabited by devils, which made her develop anorexia.[52] She was also prone to feelings of unworthiness and suicidal states of despair. It is obvious that these features compose a perfect portrait of the state between melancholia and manic depression. The patient grew aware of the obsessive element in her painting, and a compulsion to repeat and reproduce scenes from her childhood threatened her with the terrifying sense that "she would not attain the full range of a boundless territory in which to develop herself" (13). Heimann relates that as the analysis moved forward she "gradually developed into a desire to express herself and to *improve* her internal objects as distinguished from a compulsion to save them from unutterable destruction" (13). She gained the internal freedom and independence that Heimann considers to be an essential condition for successful sublimation, and her restorative impulses emerged. Heimann goes on to say that the anxieties relating to bad—or good—internal objects that interfere with the subject's internal freedom are bound to arise when the internalized parents are felt as foreign bodies embedded in the self.

The extraneous character that the internal object may take can be overcome through the process of assimilation. Thus, the subject can absorb the qualities of his or her internal objects that are suitable and adequate. Heimann concludes by saying that love and hate urge the subject to strive for sublimation and that internal freedom—which does not abolish conflicts—enables him or her to enlarge and unfold the ego in sublimation.

By the end of the analysis, Heimann reports that her patient felt happier than ever before. Her disturbances had been overcome to a large extent, and she had married a man "with whom she has a satisfactory relationship in many respects although full sexual gratification has not yet developed" (1942, 9). It is interesting to note how the three women painters we have been discussing exhibit this pattern of sexual inhibition or dissatisfaction in their relationships with men. Kjär sinks into her deep melancholic state shortly after her marriage, and Lily Briscoe does not even remotely relate sexual plenitude with the male sex.

Heimann describes what her patient used to call "the design" as some sort of experience of the connection among things that emerged under different shapes, from her good parents joined together in harmony to the moment when interpretations in analysis combined fragments of her associations and "made her feel that these associations were not accidental and senseless but had a deep meaning through which she could appreciate the whole context of the processes in her mind—then she would say: 'That fits into the design' " (1942, 10). It is worth noting the obsession that all three women—Heimann's analysand, Ruth Kjär in Michaelis's story and Klein's essay, and Lily Briscoe—exhibit over the question of the frame, under different guises, as design, empty space, or empty canvas. This obsession with form, with the containment of experience in a shape that may spare them from psychotic delirium, has to do with the problem of boundaries, which is at the core of melancholia and ultimately has to do with the fluctuation between the paranoid-schizoid and the depressive position.

Heimann's analysand, in a similar way to Lily Briscoe's vision at the end of To the lighthouse, actually sees her "design," and this epiphanic moment is also associated with light, illumination, and plenitude: "After an hour, for instance, in which light had been thrown on some important factors in her life, she would experience a blissful state of happiness, about which she said: 'I saw my design. It came into me.' This made her love me so much that she wanted to rush to me and to give me all her possessions" (1942, 10). This sense of momentary elation is accompanied by a sudden welling up of love and generosity. It is as if the patient needs to rid herself of the encumbrance of her internal objects. This process of expulsion proves telling in the actual pattern of the analysand's giving of love.

Heimann reads the design as "represent[ing] love and creativeness. It was the principle which binds together, and which turns chaos into cosmos. It was an ideal of perfection" (10). It is my contention that the inability the subject experiences when attempting to match this ideal mold of perfection, of faultless containment, translates into inhibition, impotence, and melancholia.[53]

The connections between the anxieties underlying Heimann's analysand and Woolf's Lily Briscoe are telling, extend far beyond what one would anticipate, and reveal an astonishing intertextual flow. Heimann's Kleinian elaboration illustrates part of the complex psychosexual and creative problem figured in Lily Briscoe—and by extension in other women—and Lily, and Woolf herself, contemporaneously dramatize some of the central issues on which Klein focuses in her departure from Freud. As I have mentioned, it is precisely during the first decades of the twentieth century and coincident with modernism, that women are becoming more visible than ever before, active in politics and in the workplace, engaged in professional careers, entering universities, and producing goods, from commodities to works of art. Woolf and Klein are themselves paradigmatic in their own professional activities. The anxieties generated by different cultures of the death drive are then felt in full force, and Woolf and Klein elaborate their particular responses in their writings. An atmosphere of melancholia permeates most of their works, and it can be intertextually read from narratives to essays and from clinical papers to personal (auto)biographies. It is crucial to read Woolf and Klein dialogically and Klein with Woolf, Heimann, Isaacs, and Riviere. As I am attempting to show, Woolfian fiction illuminates Kleinian theory and Kleinian theory receives nurturing inspiration from Woolf and other contemporary writers and artists.[54] In this osmotic movement, modernist cultural productions both enrich and problematize each other.

If we go back to Heimann's text it is important to note the similarities it exhibits with specific passages from To the lighthouse. Thus, it is intriguing to read Heimann's account of her patient's "devil phantasies" (phantasies about her bad internal objects) and how they affected her life and work: "The devils represented the objects of her instinctual drives, both libidinal and aggressive . . . [they] were a cover for her own sadistic and destructive impulses, which she disowned and personified in them" (1942, 11). Heimann goes on to say that it was through the analysis of her patient's devil phantasies that her childhood history was recaptured. Her earliest oral anxieties relating to the breast and the penis are the focus of her work.

Let us also remember that when Heimann's analysand went through her period of deepest depression she was mainly drawing from a model: "These drawings showed strong, but rather gross and coarse lines. Without laying claim to an expert understanding of this matter I would say that they definitely showed talent, but perhaps hardly more than that" (1942, 9). On her way to progressive improvement, she proceeded from drawing to painting. First, she attempted to restore her destroyed internal objects, and her paintings showed very few objects and "an absence of elaboration, differentiation, and movement" (12). Heimann even writes of a process of translation in her patient's passage from the rhetoric of a "devil-language" to painting different scenes, from Victorian family scenes to a variety of subjects and events, more differentiated and invested with more life and movement.

In *To the lighthouse*, Woolf writes that: "it was when she took her brush in hand that the whole thing changed. It was in that moment's flight between the picture and her canvas that the demons set on her who often brought her to the verge of tears and made this passage from conception to work as dreadful as any down a dark passage for a child" (19). Is it not the case that we to some extent could predicate Lily's situation on what Heimann says of her patient, namely, that "Severe depression, the feelings of absolute unworthiness and suicidal states of despair ensued from this situation of having active devils inside her" (12).[55]

In the section "The Window," in which Woolf sets out to narrate Lily's anxieties about creation, she describes her violent combat with the bad internal objects that want to deprive her of her sense of sight and consequently of what she is able to re-create in her paintings. Thus, "she often felt herself—struggling against terrific odds to maintain her courage; to say: 'But this is what I see; this is what I see,' and so to clasp some miserable remnant of her vision to her breast, which a thousand forces did their best to pluck from her. And it was too, in that chill and windy way, as she began to paint, that there forced themselves upon her other things, her own inadequacy, her insignificance" (19). This passage clearly shows those early anxiety situations that, according to Klein, are most common in the girl, such as having the inside of her body injured and stripped of its contents. In this case, the fear underlying this anxiety may well be related to her having her eyes hollowed out and made blind. These bad internal objects also repress Lily's impulse to reveal her love to Mrs. Ramsay and explicitly foreclose a certain space of love between women.[56]

Strong paranoid anxieties are also present in Lily's horror at having her picture inquisitively viewed by others. She "kept a feeler on her sur-roundings lest some one should creep up, and suddenly she should find her picture looked at" (17). We can perceive a strong sense of shame and insecurity about the disclosure of her creation that relates to a similar sense about her own body. Lily sinks into the abyss of creation, painting her canvas and fashioning her self. Art and life, in their constant flow between construction and deconstruction, result in melancholic agony. Her "thirty-three years, the deposit of each day's living mixed with something more secret than she had ever spoken or shown in the course of all those days was an agony" (52). Lily's as much as Magritte's canvases eschew all symbolism; they are not conceived of to be penetrated by the gaze.[57]

Interestingly, in Heimann's account her patient achieves a distinctive style and even "made her name by [these pictures]" (13) in the artistic world, but the death drive interfering with its obsessional component compelled her to repeat and repeat these scenes and motives and an in-creasing feeling of restriction of her self-expression emerged. Heimann's analysand strives to attain the freedom of a potentially "boundless" space. Heimann explicitly tropes her patient's melancholia and her separation anxiety to the vicissitudes of bonding, boundaries and subjection to a definite form.[58] What is it that the "form as mold," as container, both holds and supports and simultaneously threatens the individual? How is it that being a subject implies acquiring a certain psychic and physical form and at the same time, in its very constitution, gains subjectivity by being sub-jected to the tyranny of forms (social, family, cultural, and institutional)? Heimann sees the crucial step on her patient's way to recovery in her impulse to struggle to do something for herself and not only restore her objects out of love and freedom from compulsive necessity.

We can certainly trace many striking similarities among Lily Briscoe, Ruth Kjär, and Heimann's analysand. When Ruth Kjär's melancholia re-curs, Michaelis writes: "The accursed empty space was once more empty" (quoted in IASWA, 215). There is also a sense of bitter scorn and ridicule that elicits guilt and shame: "The empty space grinned hideously down at her" (215). This feeling of shame is also present in Heimann's patient: "It turned out then that even the humour of her father, which she had valued so highly, had a very bad aspect; for he had treated her as a funny little thing and refused to take her seriously" (1942, 9).

The method of composition based on improvisation also links Lily Briscoe and Ruth Kjär; the latter "stood before the empty wall with a piece of black chalk in her hand and made strokes at random as they came into her head" (IASWA, 216). By the time Heimann observes a dramatic improvement in her patient, she sees a parallel advance in color and composition: "During this period her internal objects (previously represented by the devils) appeared frequently in the form of artistic problems. Her interest was thus not only more objective, but far richer and comprehending far more varied details. Her internal conflicts were objectified in terms of aesthetic and technical problems. Instead of suffering from the torments of a devilish father and mother, she struggled with the problems of 'human interest' and 'aesthetic interest' in painting" (1942, 13). Heimann italicizes in her text two key terms, internal freedom and *independence*, which are in her view an essential condition for successful sublimation. If guilt and anxiety are too strong, they interfere with the successful functioning of the impulse to restore.[59]

The underlying Victorian subplot cannot be overlooked in our reading of Woolf with Klein and Heimann. Thus, for instance, Heimann's patient felt for a time compelled to paint Victorian family scenes, to paint "in a Victorian fashion" (1942, 16). Klein's retelling of Ruth Kjär's story shows many elements, rituals, and Victorian conventions distinctive of the haute bourgeoisie. And Lily Briscoe beholds a Victorian scenario in the Ramsay family and its circle. In this respect, Elliott and Wallace have remarked that Lily—as an alter ego, as much as Woolf herself—is located very explicitly "as a product of late Victorian England, as the daughter of an educated man, who was herself denied formal education or training, and as 'redundant' in a marriage market. Lily's vocation is unrecognized and her social, like her professional, identity is constituted by lack" (1994, 75).[60]

Heimann tropes the anxieties involved in the process of creation in terms of "giving birth": "My patient could not enjoy the symbolic intercourse with her crayons nor give birth to a child-picture, because her fear and guilt about her aging and deprived mother were too intense" (1942, 16). She reports that her patient was compelled to paint Victorian family scenes "by an internal Victorian mother" (16), and, despite the fact that she becomes aware that there is something wrong with her drawings, "she did not know what it was. She did not know her own creation" (16). Even when Heimann does not directly address the issue of the superego, in a footnote she attributes her patient's misrecognition of her work to it: "It will be seen that these phenomena are such as are usually described as due to the superego" (16). It is clear that Heimann is following the evolution in Klein's thinking. Even when she explicitly refers her readers to *The psycho-analysis of children* ([1932] 1975e), after 1940 ("Mourning and its relation to manic-depressive states"), Klein is ready to introduce her idea of a superego that shares both maternal and paternal traits.

Heimann's essay is a manifesto on freedom. In her view, assimilation "contributes to the setting free of forces which the subject can employ for his own benefit in a free choice of activity and for the development of his talents. This will result in an increase of productive capacities directed towards actual reality and aiming at a truer expression of the self and in an increase of the gratification experienced through his sublimatory activities" (1942, 16–17). Her exultant rhetoric of freedom contributes in an important way to the Kleinian group's efforts to eschew widely held ideas about stasis and fixation in psychosexual development: "The internal freedom to which I refer is a relative, not an absolute fact; it does not abolish conflicts, but it enables the subject to enlarge and unfold his ego in his sublimations" (17). What Heimann almost programmatically discloses here has crucial implications in the questioning of ever unraveling melancholia, or the work of mourning, and by extension any psychic work. In its contingency and precarious stability, Heimann lays out new avenues for sublimation.

> I contend that the anxieties resulting from a compulsion to look after the good internal objects, to preserve them in a good condition, to subordinate all activities to their well-being and to watch them constantly also constitutes a danger to the success of a sublimation. The anxieties relating to bad and good internal objects which interfere with the subject's internal freedom are bound to arise when the internalized parents are felt as foreign bodies embedded in the self. I think that the independence which is an important factor in successful sublimation and productive activity is achieved through a process which I like to call the "assimilation" of the internal objects, by which the subject acquires and absorbs those qualities of his internal parents which are suitable and adequate to him. (16)

This process of assimilation, which consists mainly of the "absorption" of good qualities, is a vampiristic exercise. When the internal objects become more human, "less like monsters, less like saints. . . . These assume more the character which the external parents had and the subject in his phantasy feels he is creating his parents rather than swallowing them—the child is father to the man—and with this diminution of greed he acquires the right to absorb their good qualities" (16). But in the end how can we move from the melancholia of introjection to the work of mourning of parturition?

Irreparable Melancholia

And the greater tolerance enabled her to react with less anxiety towards aggressive situations and to avoid the vicious circle in which aggressiveness increases anxiety and anxiety increases aggressiveness.—Paula Heimann

Let us for a moment phantasize about Virginia Woolf's need to exorcise the ghost of her parents and set herself free from their haunting presence in *To the lighthouse*. Let us consider the idea that Woolf, as she herself declared in "A sketch of the past," writes her novel as a memorial to her lost parents, a ritual of bereavement. Woolf performs at least a double activity, writing a lyrical narrative and painting a picture that probably aims to preserve in the medium of art their imperturbable image. And let us be suspicious of the reparative potential of these activities and hypothesize that maybe Woolf's hidden wish was not to protect and preserve her good internal objects but in their absence (insecure, not sufficiently established or threatened) to defend herself by attacking lest her own life be placed at risk. In other words, we might attempt to read inversely the Kleinian developmental plot from the paranoid-schizoid to the depressive position and traverse it, so to speak, backward, in a persistent impulse toward the paranoid-schizoid domain. Let us interrogate to what extent Woolf herself questions the reparative quality of art by presenting instead a *Künstlerroman* about the failures of the artist and the fault lines of the artistic career and the artistic paradigm in modernism. I specifically want to suggest that Lily Briscoe sets out on an unrealizable journey to the lighthouse and a quest for her own personal style, of her maturity in art, to find herself wanting. Woolf's lyrical meditation is a blunt account of how on our way to personal expression, in our search for a distinctive voice or a particular style, we may easily move backward to the paranoid-schizoid mode of relations.

How can we possibly describe Lily's achievement? We may get a glimpse of the measure of her melancholic happiness in her vision by the end of the novel. But what can assure Lily that this is not a delusion, a hallucination? How can we discern between the high quality of vision, of that quasi-mystical modernist epiphanic moment, and the psychotic delirium of hallucination? In this avalanche of epistemological uncertainties, Lily opts for painting the human figure. Mrs. Ramsay's body surely materializes in one of the masses that have captured Lily's attention for so long. And maybe what Lily—and Woolf—most secretly desire is to "lay [her] to rest" (Woolf 1985, 81), to bury her forever, and by doing so aggressively pour guilt over the canvas/narrative and close that embattled chapter in their childhoods and formative beginnings. Lily's quest leaves all the "windows" open, all possible chances to start anew, with no guarantees. The Kleinian trope of the vicious circle of introjection and projection is repeated ad infinitum. Where does the work of the artist start in the midst of this chaos, and how can we find and secure our good internal object? Echoing Lily Briscoe, we may launch one last desperate query: where is the labor of melancholia to be closed and how can we begin the work of mourning?

Ultimately, it may also be important to reflect on the suspension of temporal boundaries that To the lighthouse invites us to take and see, in the collapse of the difference between Lily Briscoe's painting and any painting stored in an attic or hanging in a museum today, to what extent life and death are problematized in the domain of art? How can the failed achievement of Lily not be remembered and invoked forever by future generations of readers and critics? To what extent is this melancholic labor telling us of a deeper melancholia that may have to do with reading and writing as entombments, as memorials to all the cultural and emotional losses of our pasts?

10

Funereal Rites: Melancholia, Masquerade, and the Art of Biography in Lytton Strachey

Uninterpreted truth is as useless as buried gold; and art is the great interpreter. It alone can unify a vast multitude of facts into a significant whole, clarifying, accentuating, suppressing, and lighting up the dark places with the torch of the imagination. More than that, it can throw over the historian's materials the glamour of a personal revelation, and display before the reader great issues and catastrophes as they appear, not to his own short sight, but to the penetrating vision of the most soaring of human spirits. . . . Indeed, every history worthy of the name is, in its own way, as personal as poetry, and its value ultimately depends upon the force and the quality of the character behind it.—Lytton Strachey

The historical narrative . . . reveals to us a world that is putatively "finished," done with, over, and yet not dissolved, not falling apart. In this world, reality wears the mask of meaning, the completeness and fullness of which we can only imagine, never experience. Insofar as historical stories can be completed, can be given narrative closure, can be shown to have had a plot all along, they give to reality the odor of the ideal. This is why the plot of a historical narrative is always an embarrassment and has to be presented as "found" in the events rather than put there by narrative techniques.—Hayden White

In "The new biography" ([1927] 1958), Woolf declared that the modern biographer needed to weld together the "granite" of truth and the "rainbow" of personality, but she warned, "Truth of fact and truth of fiction are incompatible." And in "The art of biography" ([1942] 1967) she argued that Lytton Strachey's "tragic history," *Elizabeth and Essex* ([1928] 1948), daringly mixed invented facts with verified ones. Yet in *Orlando* (1928) granite is contiguous to rainbow and truth comes all too close to the artifice of fiction. Woolf transgresses the line between reality and representation, and in this open love letter to Vita Sackville-West she necessarily turns fact into fiction; otherwise the book, like Radclyffe Hall's *The well of loneliness*, might well have been banned.

And yet, in the wake of Woolf's reflection, we may wonder what the history of the individual has to do with the issue of historical truth. What is the relationship between the truth in (auto)biographical narration and the truth in historical narration? In "Mourning and melancholia," Freud raises a question under the guise of an enigma: "We only wonder why a man has to be ill before he can be accessible to a truth of this kind" ([1915, 1917] 1953, 246). The question mark is dropped in order to leave unmarked a question that is not a real question, since no answer can satisfactorily respond to it. It is a question that undoes itself in its very formulation, in the impossibility of ever coming up with an adequate answer.

My aim in this chapter is to read Lytton Strachey's *Elizabeth and Essex* at the crossroads of history, biography, and personal narrative. My claim is to reflect upon the writing of biography as a melancholic exercise and upon the innovations that Strachey contributes to this genre as intrinsic to his ethics, his worldview, and his sexuality. I will attempt to explore to what extent we can think of Strachey's biographical method as one that is always already autobiographical and how shaping other people's lives expresses a desire to be able to shape one's own.[1] Strachey's concern with form, specifically with the forms of the complicated genre of biography, in a permanent oscillation between history and fiction, crude facts and emotional details, partakes of the general modernist concern with form that we have examined in previous chapters.[2] In Strachey, biography is essentially a melancholic projective enterprise, and in the complex syntax of projection, introjection, and projective identification his writing and his "persona" acquire their singular configurations. Following Melanie Klein's theorization on melancholia and the paranoid-schizoid mode of object relations and Joan Riviere's main psychoanalytic contribution in her essay "Womanliness as a masquerade" (1929), I will show how melancholia can be read in Strachey's texts and how he negotiates his masculinity and effeminacy by recourse to the masquerade, a masquerade of masculinity that ultimately reveals the instability of gender categories in the collapse of the binary and the always putative ascription of feminine and masculine attributes and qualities to individuals. In *Elizabeth and Essex*, Strachey seems to be arguing that the forcing of prescribed identities onto individuals negates the truth of their lives. This fragment of truth that, as Freud reminds us, has so much to do with melancholia emerges in both a psychic and a writerly economy that finds cannibalistic nourishment in lost and dead objects.[3]

The issues dramatized in Strachey's *Elizabeth and Essex* foreground a crisis in the representation of history or in the relation of art to the real world. The problem exposed by the failure to fully apprehend the intricacies of the characters of personalities from the past involves a suspension of mastery and a relinquishing of authority. Strachey tries to introduce a notion of "history as process," whose product is always provisional, fragmented and partial. Here, history is nonaffirmative; it is composed of heteroclite materials and always on the point of veering toward fiction.

In *Elizabeth and Essex*, *and* is a copulative. It adds up. Its effect is cumulative and aggregative. But simultaneously it produces juxtaposition, dissemination, independence, and autonomy. We are faced with two characters that do not fit together but rather side by side. The two of them in the binary have independent existences, and their ways intersect in the syntax of fusion and interruption that dictates the designs of the court.

Biography and Melancholia

"And what in your opinion, Monsieur Strachey, is the most important thing in the world?" . . . There was a long silence. Then from the sleeping beard of Strachey issued a tiny falsetto voice: "Passion," he said finally with suave nonchalance.—André Maurois

Could not biography produce something of the intensity of poetry, something of the excitement of drama, and yet keep also the peculiar virtue that belongs to fact—its suggestive reality, its own proper creativeness? . . . Queen Elizabeth seemed to lend herself perfectly to the experiment . . . to the making of a book that combined the advantages of both worlds, that gave the artist freedom to invent, but helped his invention with the support of facts—a book that was not only a biography but also a work of art.—Virginia Woolf

The last epigraph was written by Woolf in "The art of biography" ([1942] 1967) six years after Strachey's death. In this piece, Woolf contrasts *Queen Victoria* with *Elizabeth and Essex* to show what biography can and cannot do. In Woolf's view, in the former Strachey treated biography as a craft and "submitted to its limitations," whereas in the latter he treated biography as an art and "flouted its limitations" (223). Woolf's rhetoric reveals her own personal anxiety over the balance between masochistic submission to the law of genre and the almost manic liberation from constraints that might be imposed upon her creativity and by extension her sexuality. So Woolf believed that she and Strachey shared a sense of fierce opposition to all social or literary constraints upon the individual, but at the same time they were ambivalent as to their private responses in the execution of their works and their personal ways of living their sexualities.

In *Eminent Victorians* (1918), Strachey developed a new concept of biography, distancing himself from those who have written colossal two-volume Victorian biographies. At this time, he was much influenced by Dostoyevsky, whose novels he had been reading and reviewing as they appeared in Constance Garnett's translations.[4] He was greatly impressed by the Russian novelist's fine psychological insight and his conception of human beings as highly complex, a mixture of many heteroclite elements.

Strachey's preface to *Eminent Victorians* (1918) is his most important statement in his conception of biography. In his view, the basis of all good biography must be the humanistic respect for men, in their singularity, in their differences from one another, in their individuality, and in their personal and lived experiences. For Strachey, each individual carries a secret within him or her, and the task of the biographer consists in unveiling and discerning what it might be. In the preface, Strachey writes: "Human beings are too important to be treated as mere symptoms of the past. They have a value which is independent of any temporal process—which is eternal, and must be felt for its own sake" (8). In Strachey's view, only art could make imaginary characters live before us, and it could also make real people who had once lived become alive again. History and biography were thus art, which he described as "the most delicate and humane of all the branches of the art of writing" (8). Charles R. Sanders, in his discussion of Strachey's new ideas on biography and the writing of history has remarked: "To him [Strachey], true history and true biography must be art. And to be art they must deal with facts as they were interpreted and at times even transmuted by the imagination. Imaginative refraction, with its readjustment of line and its addition of color, was far different from mere willful distortion of fact" (1957, 208).[5] According to Sanders, Strachey wrote history "for the sake of its appeal to the imagination." Both history and biography were drama for him, "with a story which marched, proudly and vigorously, and in which all the details were vivid, alive, significant" (208). Apparently, Thucydides was a model for Strachey due to his absolute mastery of order, brevity, vividness of detail, and significant selection of materials.

In most of his writings, Strachey is obsessed with bringing back to life lost bodies from his cultural past. He is concerned with techniques of awakening, resuscitation, and re-creation: "No study of a man can be successful until it is vital; a portrait-painter who cannot make his subject live has very little reason for putting brush to canvas."[6] Biographical research unearths significant materials about those lives of the past. Strachey is much more interested in the subject of biography than in the actual facts. We might venture that his generative anxieties have to do not with producing new life but with reanimating the dead.[7] Life in decay horrifies him. I would suggest that he sticks to an ecological imperative that is about recycling and avoiding waste. How can we get nourishment from these bodies of the past? What can we learn from them? Where does this epistemophilic drive lead us? If biography is a necrophilic practice, its cannibalistic urges can only be satiated in the omophagic feast. This involves a ritual of melancholia, introjection at its highest.

It is precisely the inability to digest or metabolize that Strachey was critiquing in the English biographical tradition: "Those two fat volumes, with which it is our custom to commemorate the dead—who does not know them, with their ill-digested masses of material, their slipshod style, their tone of tedious panegyric, their lamentable lack of selection, of detachment, of design? They are as familiar as the cortège of the undertaker, and wear the same air of slow, funereal barbarism" (1918, 8). Strachey's funereal practices were diametrically opposed to the former ones, since what he was aiming at involved a difficulty and risky operation, that of infusing new life into dead bodies. We can also infer from the obsessional character of his biographical practices a sense of manic denial that has to do with the propagation of life in a cycle that eschews decay. Strachey, too sensitive to the appreciation of beauty, abhors old age, the fading away of physical and intellectual faculties, degeneration, and death. Through his biographical work, he counters death with supreme mastery and displays phobic mechanisms for which he compensates with manic defenses.

Besides, biography should be brief—avoiding redundancy—and the biographer should maintain his own freedom of spirit: "It is not his business to be complimentary; it is his business to lay bare the facts of the case, as he understands them" (1918, 9). He acknowledges that his aim in Eminent Victorians has been to lay bare the facts, "dispassionately, impartially and without ulterior intentions." We can also see here that Strachey was obsessed with nudity, with "laying bare the facts" about the bodies of his historical characters, with looking beneath their clothes. This obsession can be traced in the opening pages of *Elizabeth and Essex* when Strachey announces his purpose to give a "vision" of Elizabeth that does not suffer from the "deceit" characteristic of posterity, "from her visible aspect to the profundities of her being" ([1928] 1948, 10), an almost irreverent vision that we can see "below the robes" (11).[8] Simultaneously, this avowed dispassionate and impartial laying bare the facts should probably be read as its opposite. In all of Strachey's writings, passions (love, hate, jealousy, envy) are dominant. In this, he is very close to Melanie Klein's elaborations.

Apparently, Strachey found in Racine some of the qualities he admired most in biography: an acute sense of reality, selection according to true judgment, and fine psychological insight.[9] When Strachey writes about the French playwright, there is an uncanny quality of identification at work: "When Racine is most himself, when he is seizing upon a state of mind and depicting it with all its twistings and vibrations, he writes with a directness which is indeed naked, and his sentences, refined to the utmost point of significance, flash out like swords, stroke upon stroke, swift, certain, irresistible" (1922). Strachey bluntly rejects the imposition of "artistry," which may clothe its objects and cover their splendid nakedness. He venerates those naked bodies and seeks to invest them with "something of the palpable reality of life."[10]

In July 1927, Virginia Woolf began to conceptualize "a biography beginning in the year 1500 and continuing to the present day, called Orlando: Vita; only with a change about from one sex to another" (1977–84). Writing of Orlando, Woolf told Sackville-West that "it sprung upon me how I could revolutionise biography in a night."[11] Woolf conceived of *Orlando* as a new kind of biography, of which she says, in another context, it is "not fiction because it has the substance, the reality of truth. It is not biography because it has the freedom, the artistry of fiction" ([1942] 1967, 232).[12]

Michael Holroyd has placed a personal experience at the center of Strachey's *Elizabeth and Essex* and thus has compared it to Woolf's *Orlando*. Strachey's love affair with Roger Senhouse and Woolf's with Vita Sackville-West were "transferred to the page as self-projected dreaming" (1994, 605). In his view, both were experimenting with ways of leaving the conventionality of Victorian manners and mingling gender and time, "challenging public taste with deviant phantasy" (606).[13] What is so at stake in *Elizabeth and Essex* that we may refer to it as "deviant phantasy"? What does this deviance have to do with the textualization of sexuality that Strachey effects in his narrative? And what is Strachey channeling through this tragedy in his fidelity to or his distortion of facts, in the interplay between his projections and the muffled echoes of these figures from his remotest past?

Holroyd has suggested different patterns of phantasies at work in Strachey's love relationships.[14] It is interesting to note that in the case of Roger Senhouse he believes that Strachey "stepped into a wish-fulfilment world where both of them could adopt fictitious identities and play out vicarious roles" (1994, 581). They might impersonate David and Absalom, Nero and his slave, or a parent and a child in their almost inexhaustible repertoire. Holroyd maintains that Lytton's feeling "that he could be absorbed into a multitude of imaginary-historical scenes and forms and places added to his life an unexplored enchanted territory, into which he might be carried almost at will" (582). Strachey and Senhouse thus seemed to live in some sort of "as if" world where their shared literary and musical tastes were cathected in a privately encoded way.

Whose (Hi)story?

A generalized, colorless, unimaginative view of things is admirable when one is considering the law of causality, but one needs something else if one has to describe Queen Elizabeth.—Lytton Strachey

Elizabeth and Essex was first published with omissions in the *Ladies' Home Journal* from September to December 1928 and in England as a book in December of that year. The story soon enjoyed the status of a best-seller, setting an unparalleled record in the production and distribution of a nonfiction book in Britain and the United States.[15] It is important to note that when *Elizabeth and Essex* first appeared it was immediately recognized by scholars in Elizabethan history and literature as a "tragical-historical drama."[16] Strachey's contemporary, historian G. M. Trevelyan, had positively assessed the importance of his work in connecting history to literature and thus interesting the public in historical themes. Strachey's background in Elizabethan literature and culture was impressive. He had eagerly read the prose, poetry, and drama of the age of Queen Elizabeth since childhood, and later, during the early years of his literary career, he reviewed countless books on the Elizabethan period for the *Spectator* and other journals. Even when Trevelyan cautioned against relying too much on novelists for historical interpretation, he still praised Strachey's achievements in *Queen Victoria* and especially *Elizabeth and Essex*. In a letter to Strachey, he wrote, "It is much your greatest work. And its success bears out my theory as against your own—or what used to be your view. You used to tell me that your strength was satire and satire alone, so you must choose people you did not much like in order to satirize them. I thought the argument bad then, and now the time gives proof of it. Your best book has been written about people to whom you are spiritually akin—far more akin than to the Victorians. And it is not a piece of satire but a piece of life" (quoted in Holroyd 1994, 614). Trevelyan, as a professional historian, was moved at seeing a fragment of the past resuscitated and brought to life between the lines of a new narrative. The libidinal vibration that this type of spiritualistic medium work grants the historian is displaced onto a personal terrain, where introjective identification dominates the scene. This passage raises important questions. What is implicit in Trevelyan's idea of Strachey's masterwork in which history shows as a "piece of life" only when he is "akin" to his characters? Which kind of identification, if any, is implicit in historical research and, most importantly, in the writing of history? Is it that the reverberations of this past brought to life signal the return of the repressed?

Furthermore, Trevelyan seems to point to a hidden animistic notion that implies that all objects of inquiry possess a natural life or vitality.[17] Even when he is far from implying that history shares a quasi-religious sort of knowledge, he may be closer to a fetishistic notion of existence preserved in writing and cast in an embodied form. The historian, by virtue of his or her supernatural agencies, brings back to life the voices and bodies of the past and simultaneously, invested as he or she is with power, is able to produce a knowledge to which only those who are initiated (or "playing the game") may have access. Literature and the literary text as privileged sites where transference operates should thus be one step closer to ordinary life. Strachey romantically believed that great individual personalities influence and even determine the historical course of action. The motive force of history had more to do with passions and human confrontation than with other forces or circumstances. Passions and emotions are also at the core of the Kleinian theorization.

Here I aim to explore what it means for a man like Strachey to construct "biographies" of so many canonical figures in the English national past and what that might have to do with a question of gay men and representation in general and with each of the two "subjects"—the "biographer" and the "subject" spoken about—and their particular phantasmatic spaces. My exploration also points to how this method of writing the self binds itself to history, becomes an insertion into history. A kind of doubleness is needed to produce the self, that is, Strachey needs his characters to represent himself and vice versa. This parallels the conundrum of language for gay men in which the only way to represent oneself is through a doubled otherness. In other words, if language inscribes absence and loss in the play of signification, if naming is predicated upon a loss and gay men occupy a reified space in culture, then the homosexual himself is always detached and dis-located in the very act of fixation and estrangement that this operation entails.

These issues must also be considered against the backdrop of the public scrutiny of the "subjects" of gender, relationships, homosexuality, and inheritance in both the genres of biography and the novel and in Strachey's world. These public/private and fact/fiction splits are profoundly interwoven in any consideration of Strachey's narratives. If we take the perspective of reading unconscious phantasy in the text of biography, Strachey's public and open narrative to Senhouse necessarily had to be some sort of tale, it had to be emplotted in a specific way, and it necessarily had to turn "fact" into "fiction."[18] Without the phantasmatic elements of "unnatural" time (chronologically remote) and "unnatural" sexual relationships (changing rather unremarkably regarding Strachey's changing identifications), the reception of the book and the readers' reactions to Strachey would probably have been totally different.

Confusion of Bodies

I am but one body, naturally considered though by [God's] permission
a Body Politic to govern.—Queen Elizabeth I

Upon the life of Elizabeth hung the whole structure of the State.—Lytton Strachey

Lytton dedicated *Elizabeth and Essex* to James and Alix Strachey, who were already established as highly reputed translators of Freud. After 1924, when the Hogarth Press began publishing translations of Freud, Lytton's interest in psychoanalysis increased and he began reading and discussing Freud's work with James and Alix. Holroyd sees Strachey's *Elizabeth and Essex* as "adding a stream of unconscious inevitability to the mood of sixteenth-century superstitious fatalism" (1994, 610). In this sense, one of the important Freudian arguments that Strachey uses to explain Elizabeth's attitude toward Essex and other men is the underlying oedipal narrative of the father-daughter relationship between Elizabeth and Henry VIII. As Charles R. Sanders has observed, preserved among Strachey's manuscripts is a work called *Essex: A Tragedy*, which was written in blank verse some years before the composition of his narrative. Thus, it should not surprise us that when *Elizabeth and Essex* was published "it was discovered that it flowed quite easily into the dramatic mold" (1957, 97). Sanders sees this work as a tragedy with a cathartic effect.[19]

Michael Holroyd has remarked that passion is the supreme motive in *Elizabeth and Essex*. Martin Kallich believes that the sexual motive is the main force he relies on to explain the personality traits of his characters (1961, 21). He has traced the influence of Freud and the Freudian climate of the times in Strachey's long biographies.[20] The discussion of Freudianism became central in intellectual circles in the second and third decades of the twentieth century. Its allure in Bloomsbury came from its aura of a new psychology that encouraged freedom from social and moral constraints. *Elizabeth and Essex*, published in 1928, marks in Kallich's view a certain climax in Strachey's development as a biographer. He "consciously and deliberately adopted Freudian theses and experimented with imaginative psychoanalysis" (102). In Kallich's Freudian reading, the crux of this narrative is Elizabeth's hysteria, the result of abuse and seduction during her childhood. It is manifest in her abnormal sexuality, which shows itself in neurotic frigidity and masculine tendencies.[21]

In this chapter, I want to go back to the Bloomsbury of the Strachey family and suggest a Kleinian reading of *Elizabeth and Essex* that should not be too far from Lytton Strachey's ideas, atmosphere, and influences. We know that Strachey sent Freud a copy of *Elizabeth and Essex* and that the latter substantially agreed with the personality analysis it contained. Nonetheless, Strachey never mentioned Freud by name in any of his seven published works. At this point, I would like to speculate on the possible, albeit indirect, influence of Melanie Klein in Strachey through James and Alix Strachey. This must remain in the field of intellectual, or even fictional speculation, since there is no feasible way to prove my arguments. What if the Stracheys, contaminated as they were at the time with various psychoanalytical ideas, would have talked and argued about the new developments that Klein was introducing in England? What if Klein would have been a haunting presence in the Strachey's conversations and nascent analytical concerns? As we have seen in previous sections of this book, Klein arrived in London in 1925, and she gave her first lecture in Adrian and Karin Stephen's home in Bloomsbury.[22] Klein had begun her career writing in her native German, and it was precisely Alix Strachey who was in charge of the English translation of *The psycho-analysis of children*. Adrian Stephen, Joan Riviere, Susan Isaacs, Paula Heimann, and the Stracheys were closest to the Kleinian circle from the beginning. It is interesting to note, though, that when conflicts arose and years later the Controversial Discussions reached their climax the members of the Bloomsbury Group remained undefined and disengaged, finding themselves in the middle group.

Why not, then, a Kleinian reading of Strachey's narratives? I want to suggest that it is the concept of masquerade, coined by Joan Riviere and thus a product of the Kleinian group, that is at stake in the complex play of identifications in *Elizabeth and Essex*. Riviere's and Klein's arguments on masquerade—as developed in *The psycho-analysis of children*—seem to me to be crucial for an understanding of the textual and psychic dynamics among Elizabeth, Essex, and Strachey as the main characters in this drama.

Strachey, in his preface to *Eminent Victorians*, wrote that the wise biographer "will attack his subject in unexpected places; he will fall upon the flank, or the rear; he will shoot a sudden revealing searchlight into obscure recesses, hitherto undivined. He will row out over that great ocean of material, and lower down into it, here and there, a little bucket, which will bring up to the light of day some characteristic specimen, from those far depths, to be examined with a careful curiosity" (1918, vii). Here, interestingly, Strachey's metaphors have important analytic resonances. First, the biographer is in a sadistic position of attack. Epistemophilia is his main ally and also his main risk. The biographer comes to perform a function akin to that of the analyst in the singularity of his or her quasi-speleological quest. The darkness of the ocean of material into which he or she must plunge will eventually become illuminated in a transferential working through. But Strachey's programmatics in this passage call for another reading. In this "attack[ing] his subject in unexpected places" such as "the flank or the rear," he aligns himself with decadent sensitivity and aesthetics and with homoeroticism and the tradition inaugurated by Wilde in the last two decades of the nineteenth century. The Wildean process and his prosecution under charges of sodomy brought to light central issues concerning the figure of the modern homosexual. As I have argued, issues of class and conflicts over gender in the emerging debate on sexual inversion (Ellis, Krafft-Ebing, Ulrich) enable the emergence of the "homosexual as effeminate."[23]

As Alan Sinfield has noted, Lytton Strachey "blatantly accepted the Wildean stereotype for himself" (1994, 141). As is the case with the aestheticized dandy, Strachey was horrified with decay and death, and in this sense the drama he enacts in his biographical writing is not far from that exposed by Wilde in The picture of Dorian Gray. Dorian comes to prefigure the image of the homosexual cast in the domain of art in the uncanny transference of bodily decline and decomposition to the canvas while its subject remains unchanged. Dorian is led along this way by Lord Henry Wotton, who declares something close to Strachey's own aphorisms: "Being natural is simply a pose, and the most irritating pose I know" ([1890] 1981, 4). This pose, under the guise of mask, under the signs exhibited by a specific style (dandy, camp, drag), has as its obvious underlying subtext the pose of the sodomite and in the case of Strachey shows in a particular "attack . . . on the rear." Strachey is going to traverse a thus far inscrutable and obscure geography, fiercely maintaining his freedom and independence in his point of view. He will be interested mainly in the "quality of the character behind [every history]," and this he will undertake with successive attacks "in unexpected places." Strachey's melancholic character and his obsessive preoccupation with himself and the lost bodies of the past, in a distinctive style, will shape his peculiar approach to biography and history. History and biography as melancholic genres thus come to be doubly melancholic in Strachey's idiosyncratic sexual and political interventions. Situated at the crossroads of a social, literary, psychosexual, and judicial discourse that sanctions the legitimacy of individual practices, Strachey will effect a powerful reversal in the traditional approach to writing (and living) "appropriate" lives.

How is Strachey going to approach and counter the specific path imposed on the body through Victorian disciplinary discourses? Which strategies will he use to deconstruct the Victorian doctrine of austerity, industriousness, and achievement as parameters within which to assess a life? What alternatives will he explore with his new attitude of relinquishing the "eminence" of authority in his lives? The struggles of nineteenth-century writers would seem to indicate that rhetoric cannot defuse anxiety, although it provides some pleasurable distractions. This may be the reason why the decadent artists leaned so heavily on irony as a rhetorical mode.

Along these lines, Strachey's ironic self-consciousness builds ambiguity into rhetoric; the layered structure of meaning in his texts embodies signifiers of same-sex desire while deflecting the uncertainty of adequate or appropriate signification through its multiplicity.

Surveillance and Paranoia

The belief in the mind of the questioner became a statement in the mouth of the questioned.—Lytton Strachey

In the opening pages of *Elizabeth and Essex*, Strachey's penetrative impulses are conveyed by way of an irreverent and almost obscene metaphor. He writes: "More valuable than descriptions, but what perhaps is unattainable, would be some means by which the modern mind might reach to an imaginative comprehension of those beings of three centuries ago—might move with ease among their familiar essential feelings—might touch, or dream that it touches (for such dreams are the stuff of history) the very 'pulse of the machine.' But the path seems closed to us. By what art are we to worm our way into those strange spirits, those even stranger bodies?" ([1928] 1948, 8). He is also led by a reconstructive endeavor always centered on rescuing human beings from the ravages of time, not content with having "exterior visions" (8) of the Elizabethans that, as he argues, we do not truly understand. Why this insistence on shattering the surface and reaching some core buried deep within the psyche? What does Strachey's biographical project have to do with penetration, sadism, and the slow, deviant, and insidious workings of the death drive?

In Charles R. Sanders's view, the *Elizabeth and Essex* narrative/tragedy thrives on conflict; on the clash of rivals who struggle to win the queen's favor; on the confrontation between Elizabeth and Essex, who are both lovers and violent antagonists; and on what he understands as "the inner struggle—the debate of the mind with itself—which goes on in Elizabeth, Essex, Cecil and Bacon" (242). Strachey's personal elaboration of this debate, which concerns the inner world, shows in exquisite detail in his characters' mental processes, which come very close to the soliloquies of Shakespearean drama.[24]

In *Elizabeth and Essex*, Strachey presents us with a brutal and insensitive picture of the Elizabethan age. He describes in the goriest detail the execution of Essex and the hanging, castrating, drawing, and quartering of

Dr. Ruy Lopez—the Jewish doctor who had been at the service of the queen for so many years: "A vast crowd was assembled to enjoy the spectacle" (89).[25]

In *Discipline and punish*, Michel Foucault registers the changing practices in rituals of execution that progressively result in the disappearance of torture as a public spectacle and the elimination of pain. He records a very similar scene to the one on which we are focusing and reflects on the new morality that accompanies the act of punishment. He writes: "There are no longer any of those executions in which the condemned man was dragged along on a hurdle (to prevent his head smashing against the cobblestones), in which his belly was opened up, his entrails quickly ripped out, so that he had time to see them, with his own eyes, being thrown on the fire; in which he was finally decapitated and his body quartered" ([1975] 1995, 12). By the end of the eighteenth century and the beginning of the nineteenth, the spectacle of punishment was in decline, and it gradually became the most hidden part of the penal process.[26] In Elizabethan England, disembowelment was a punishment reserved for the crimes of high treason and regicide.

As Gabriel Merle has noted, in the Elizabethan age "To be suspicious was in itself a crime. The State trials were nothing but a formality, the verdict was known in advance" (1980, 618). And, in Strachey's own words, "In the domain of treason, under Elizabeth, the reign of law, was, in effect, superseded, and its place was taken by a reign of terror" ([1928] 1948, 78). At this point, the text can read as an excerpt from *Discipline and punish*: "Who could disentangle among his [the prisoner's] statements the parts of veracity and fear, the desire to placate his questioners, the instinct to incriminate others, the impulse to avoid, by some random affirmation, the dislocation of an arm or a leg? Only one thing was plain about such evidence: it would always be possible to give it to whatever interpretation the prosecutors might desire. The Government could prove anything" ([1928] 1948, 79). This is a system in which "truth was forced from [individuals]" (81), a paranoid-schizoid regime of surveillance and punishment. Furthermore, whereas violence is not an intrinsic element of tragedy, in *Elizabeth and Essex*, violence pervades the text.[27] Elizabeth implements torture as punishment, and horrendous and painful deaths ensue. King Philip II of Spain burns heretics. The spectacle of death (even those of monarchs) exhibits an irrepressible and spasmodic violence. Imprisonment and punishments such as mutilation (cutting off the ears, hands, or other parts of the body) were common disciplinary practices. In *Elizabeth and Essex*, Strachey shows history to be a web of power generated through and maintained by specifically gendered and racialized sexual oppression. We should be concerned with the ways in which Strachey negotiates the results of his characters' confrontations with the violence of their histories.

Usurping the Story

I am acquainted with all your earlier publications, and have read them with great enjoyment. But the enjoyment was essentially an aesthetic one. This time you have moved me deeply, for you yourself have reached greater depths. You are aware of what other historians so easily overlook—that it is impossible to understand the past with certainty, because we cannot divine men's motives and the essence of their minds and so cannot interpret their actions. . . . with regard to the people of past times we are in the same position as with dreams to which we have been given no associations. . . . As a historian, then, you show that you are steeped in the spirit of psychoanalysis. And with reservations such as these, you have approached one of the most remarkable figures in your country's history, you have known how to trace back her character to the impressions of her childhood, you have touched upon her most hidden motives with equal boldness and discretion, and it is very possible that you have succeeded in making a correct reconstruction of what actually occurred.—Letter from Freud to Strachey

Strachey's main point was that to be mastered by the facts was
not to write biography.—Charles R. Sanders

In his extensive discussion of Strachey's ideas on biography (1957, 210), Charles R. Sanders penned the sentence just quoted. He argues that Strachey would probably have agreed that the biographer who has achieved art at the expense of the facts has failed. On the whole, his assessment is that Strachey's felicitous accomplishments as a biographer far outweigh his failures.[28]

It is my contention that Strachey's surface of feeble and refined aesthete desperately in search of masochistic love with athletic men who could dominate and violently penetrate him, is countered in his texts with his personal sadistic impulse to penetrate other objects, master them in epistemophilic delirium and thus be the narrator of a story that comes to be his own. There is a sadistic streak at the heart of this apparent masochistic exercise. In any case, far from any psychobiographical approach, my aim in this chapter is to disentangle Strachey's melancholic narratives from his own melancholia and reflect upon the issues of object loss, introjective identification and masquerade in the complex negotiations exhibited by his poetics. *Elizabeth and Essex* is Strachey's most personal biography. John Ferns shares this same idea and argues that in this piece Strachey articulates his elements into an artistic whole "through the use of poetic prose" (1988, 90) as *Elizabeth and Essex* "is the [biographical study] into which Strachey put most of himself, and this is the reason that he attempted to introduce a poetic prose that would allow for a fuller expression of feeling than the ironic Voltairean prose of *Eminent Victorians* and *Queen Victoria*" (101–2).

The impact and triumph of a prelude of rationality over the romantic, feudal, and courtly love aesthetic of a way of life doomed to disappear in Elizabethan England is what is at stake in *Elizabeth and Essex*. It is crucial to note that in the opening pages of the narrative Strachey re-creates the baroque atmosphere of the age in an oxymoronic rhetoric that shocks and intrigues: "How is it possible to give a coherent account of their subtlety and their *naïveté*, their delicacy and their brutality, their piety and their lust?" (9). Strachey raises totally relevant questions, similar to the ones we may raise today in our enquiries about the past. His concerns are both epistemological and archaeological, having to do with the sort of "mental fabric" that paradoxically "had for its warp the habits of filth and savagery of sixteenth-century London and for its woof an impassioned familiarity with the splendour of *Tamburlaine* and the exquisiteness of *Venus and Adonis*" (9). Strachey's interest lies in narrating a story in which "politics gave way to lovemaking" (162) and in a reflection upon love, aggression, and melancholia.

Strachey's cast of characters is full of typically divided personalities. In the history of Essex, Strachey perceives "the spectral agony of an abolished world" (2). Essex is a man of action who is seized at times with deep melancholia.[29] In the narrative, he takes a line of oppositional action, one through which he sadistically enters the vicious circle of projection and introjection in his relationship with Elizabeth. "I know," he writes, "I shall never do her service but against her will" (98).

The revenge motive is also crucial in *Elizabeth and Essex*. In 1928, just after its publication, G. B. Harrison, a scholar in the field of Elizabethan history and literature, remarked that Essex was not a convincing character since Strachey had overlooked one of his most important personality traits: "Essex was over-sensitive to laughter; and he often made himself ridiculous." Far from having destroyed Dr. Lopez out of patriotism, he acted out of revenge.[30] Aggression and retaliation are clearly identifiable trends throughout the narrative.

Elizabeth was "a fascinating spectacle" (17). She represented the embodiment of the spirit of the baroque, since, as Strachey remarks, "it is the incongruity between their structure and their ornament that best accounts for the mystery of the Elizabethans" (10) and, in the case of the queen, "every part of her was permeated by the bewildering discordances between the real and the apparent" (10). By the end of the narrative, Essex has learned a painful lesson about his queen, that she "was merely an incredibly elaborate façade, and that all within was iron" (260). At the core of the spirit of the baroque lies something that in Kleinian terms we might call the conflict between unconscious phantasy and external reality, whether it is a reality putatively ascribed to the individual or to any other object, discourse or institution.

Elizabeth's character is enormously complex, and her portrait, in Strachey's hands, corresponds to the traits of profound melancholia.[31] She was virtually unable to make decisions and procrastinated on account of her irresolute character—at times, her inability to decide reached a state of paralysis—and she gathered feminine (sinuosity, vacillation) and masculine (vigor, pertinacity) traits within herself. Crucial in this portrait of the queen was precisely this oscillation between genders. Strachey describes Elizabeth as being "something more" than a woman and a master of deception: "She gazed at the little beings around her, and smiled to think that, though she might be their Mistress in one sense, in another it could never be so—that the very reverse might almost be said to be the case . . . [that] she might have fancied herself, in some half-conscious day-dream, possessed of something of that pagan masculinity" (28). In this avalanche of paradoxes, it is also important to note that Elizabeth hated war, "for the best of all reasons—its wastefulness" (14), and that she kept the peace in England for thirty years.[32] The philosophy of Elizabeth's policy shows in a perpetual postponement of action.[33] Her psychosexual portrait is that of a hysteric, and Strachey's account corresponds to the Freudian narrative. Among the important motives that might have determined her "morbid symptoms" are the facts that her father had her mother beheaded when Elizabeth was under three years of age and the flirtatious and possibly abusive behavior of Thomas Seymour, the second husband of her stepmother, Catherine Parr. When Elizabeth came to the throne, after countless delays and indecisions, speculations as to the most suitable candidate to become her husband turned into speculations about the queen's sexuality, her inveterate chastity. Elizabeth did not want to compromise her power, but in any case Strachey gives us the opposite view of the supposedly inhibited sexuality of the queen: "Nature had implanted in her an amorousness so irrepressible as to be always obvious and sometimes scandalous. She was filled with delicious agitation by the glorious figures of men" (22). Elizabeth was enveloped in an atmosphere of personal worship that she herself fostered. Moreover, she was extremely self-conscious about her personal image and she had a passion for dress and ornament.

In *Elizabeth and Essex*, Strachey presents us with the sombre landscape of the last decade of Elizabeth's reign, when social malaise was at its height due to generalized hardship and discontent with the corrupt atmosphere of the court. Elizabeth had given lucrative monopolies to many of her favorites. Roger Devereux, earl of Essex, was the last in a long line of men who enjoyed privileged economic (and at times sexual) treatment from the queen.[34] After the detailed narration of the battles fought against the Spanish Armada, the climax of the text comes with the confrontation with Irish rebel forces led by the earl of Tyrone. Essex had undertaken to defeat the Irish, but in a difficult moment of vacillation he returns to England against the queen's orders and violently argues with her in public. His attempts to raise an insurrection fail, and finally he is tried for treason and executed in 1601.

When the narrative opens, Elizabeth "was fifty-three, and he was not yet twenty: a dangerous concatenation of ages" (5). When Essex begins to serve the queen on military missions, after the second attack on the Spanish Armada, he returns triumphant and gains her first economic and political favors. The queen learns that Essex is married, and after an initial reaction of disappointment and rage she "remembered that the relations between herself and her servant were unique and had nothing to do with a futile domesticity" (37). It is true that the relationship between Elizabeth and Essex—like those of Strachey's own life—was far from conventional.

Elizabeth sadistically embraces power and even at times risk: "She relished everything—the diminution of risks and the domination of them" (183).[35] In the paranoid context of Elizabeth's court, where everybody had the feeling that they would sooner or later fall prey to the design that had been plotted against them, strategies of splitting, scotomization, and denial are frequent and characteristic of a paranoid-schizoid mode of object relations.[36] In this respect, as a part of his struggle for power against his adversaries, when Essex is appointed minister and takes on the privileges of a statesman he tries by every possible means to have his protégé, Francis Bacon, assume the post of attorney general: "Essex, seven years his junior, had been, from the first moment of their meeting, fascinated by the intellectual splendour of the elder man. His enthusiastic nature leapt out to welcome that scintillating wisdom and that profound wit. He saw that he was in the presence of greatness" (49–50). The homosocial undercurrent is present in the stormy relationship between these two men, a relationship that in the end is facilitated by the physical body and the "body politic" of a woman.[37] Elizabeth, an artful master in a variety of tactics, discusses with Essex the qualifications of Bacon and delays her decision. This fuels anxiety, and a deadening passion arises out of the ruses and impositions of a severe superegoic law: "At moments flirtations gave way to passion. More than once that winter, the young man [Essex], suddenly sulky, disappeared, without a word of warning, from the Court. A blackness and a void descended upon Elizabeth; she could not conceal her agitation; and then, as suddenly, he would return, to be overwhelmed with scornful reproaches and resounding oaths" (56). The atmosphere of this passage shows the frightening and extremely cruel nature of the sanctions imposed by the superego of the melancholic. Strachey's rhetoric of darkness and absence (void, disappearance) and the element of arrested movement in the language of flirtation, passion, and agitation evoke a sadomasochistic vicious circle in which projection gives way to introjection, and vice versa, resulting in the impossibility of action or denouement. The enraged stillness of melancholia shows in these two figures. The context of the narrative presents us with a geographical space that needs an Other in order to assert its limits and claim its laws. The geographical space of Elizabethan England is paranoid-schizoid, it is in the hands of a paranoid leader who needs enemies as scapegoats in order to orchestrate her machinations.

Essex sets himself up as the leader of the anti-Spanish party in England and consequently as an emblem of patriotism. His commitment to fight the country's monstrous Catholic adversary makes him prey of paranoid delirium. In Essex, Strachey diagnoses symptoms of an anti-Spanish obsession that leads him to see "plots and spies everywhere" (75). But he also, symptomatically, sees himself as "Pressed and harassed on every side by the labours of military organization" (100). Paranoia appears all too close to the homosocial organization of the military, and Essex seems to be presenting Strachey's own arguments against military conscription and in favor of conscientious objection.

Military, sexual and "intellectual" triumph was always a manic quality in *Elizabeth and Essex*. Victories in battle, bed, and wit share an excessive rhetoric of glory and the vanquishing of the Others that the subject needs to dominate, humiliate and degrade.[38] The death drive, allied with sadism in full force, colors a melancholic picture of lost bodies that were loved, or maybe hated, and then tortured and vanquished. How can we speak of love in a paranoid-schizoid regime of terror, aggression and fear of retaliation? How can we speak of love in the midst of an endemic melancholia that, in the orgy of the cannibalistic feast, devours its objects?

Yet implicit in Strachey's rhetoric there is a fascination with the figure of Essex. He writes of "Essex, who was always in a hurry or a dream. . . . His spirit, wayward, melancholy, and splendid, belonged to the Renaissance—the English Renaissance, in which the conflicting currents of ambition, learning, religion, and lasciviousness were so subtly intervoled. . . . He could not resist the mysterious dominations of moods—intense, absorbing, and utterly at variance with one another" (120–23). Essex reads poetry (Spenser), daydreams, meditates in solitude, and is overwhelmed with contradictory emotions, a perfect melancholic character. He is "a romantic—passionate, restless, confused," who at times "shut his eyes to what was obvious" (178). His inflamed epistolary style explodes within the generic conventions of courtly love to expose a totally oedipal melancholia: "I humbly kiss your royal fair hands . . . and pour out my soul in passionate jealous wishes for all true joys to the dear heart of your Majesty, which must know me to be your Majesty's humblest and devoutest vassal, Essex" (134). Desire titillates against a backdrop of detached passion (at a distance, doomed to fail) and jealous possession (to be inside, joyfully introjected into the lover's heart). What are we to make of this detached but inflamed and hectic passivity, of this inability to relate "in the flesh"? Is it not the case that these perverse object relations are but another sign of melancholia?

After the collapse of the Azores expedition, Essex is devastated and decides to retire in order to rest his "sick body and troubled mind" (149). Once again, it is in his letters, in his writing, that we discover the oedipal quality of his love for Elizabeth: "Most dear lady . . . your kind and often sending is able either to preserve a sick man, or rather to raise a man that were more than half dead to life again. . . . If your Majesty do in the sweetness of your own heart nourish the one, and in the justness of love free me from the tyranny of the other, you shall ever make me happy" (150). At this point, Elizabeth is phantasized as the good breast (mother) who should be able to nourish and comfort Essex in his troubled state. The good breast can restore us to life in a prelapsarian moment when the death drive has not yet been introjected.

Relations between Elizabeth and Essex deteriorate after the failure of the last British expedition against the Armada. When Essex returns empty-handed from the Azores, Strachey ironically writes that "mutual confidence had departed" (184). To regain the confidence of the queen, Essex needs a victory in the Irish campaign. Strachey tropes Essex's melancholic state in the dissolution of the boundaries between the real and the unreal, reality and phantasy, fiction and fact. He "began . . . to catch the surrounding infection, to lose the solid sense of things, and to grow confused over what was fancy and what was fact" (201). This is in itself a self-conscious mise en abyme of Strachey's own universe of writing. In the infectious profession of the writer, the persistent contamination between fact and fiction produces effects with important generic and even psychic and social consequences. What is at stake in Strachey's insistent problematization of the boundaries between reality and phantasy, between biography and fiction, when the solidity of the limit begins to collapse? Why is it precisely at this moment that Essex, in a painfully melancholic epistle, raises the question of how to "ransom" himself, "my soul, I mean, out of this hateful prison of my body" (209), and longs for death? What in the nature of writing precludes a space for the living body and preserves one for the dead or already lost?

The Irish episode is crucial in the design of *Elizabeth and Essex*. Strachey addresses here and in its aftermath all the questions that have been troubling him throughout the narrative. The crescendo of inevitability preempts the catastrophic end of the narrative and the tragic fate of Essex. Essex is now prey to an enormous anxiety, which paralyzes him. His constant meditative and now "hysterical" mood is an evident sign of the inhibition and paralyzing effects of melancholia.[39] Essex refuses to give battle when he confronts the Irish army. He feels impotent and humiliated (210) and returns home. The only encounter between Elizabeth and Essex divested of their courtly clothes and ornaments takes place now. And Strachey lingers over a scene in which the struggle over power is once again the leading motive. Elizabeth's paranoid state shifts from terror to dissimulation, from dangerous pleasure to obsessive calculation. Finally, she feels that she is in command again: "Essex was now completely at her mercy. She could decide at her leisure what she would do with him" (215). As Elizabeth begins her ritual of hesitation and doubt, she finds in Bacon her ideal adviser. As noted earlier, the homosocial link between Essex and Bacon is present throughout the narrative. When the fate of Essex is not yet clear, Bacon sends him an explicitly homoerotic letter: "I am more yours than any man's and more yours than any man" (214). Later, facing the possibility of increased power and prerogatives, he decides that "it would be futile to spoil his own chances of fortune by adhering to a hopeless cause" (219). Bacon's reaction leads us to believe that Essex's behavior violates their secret pact. His is a crime that may be situated in what I have earlier called the Kleinian sphere of incestuous brotherhood.[40] As Klein remarked in The psycho-analysis of children ([1932] 1975e), at a certain stage in the paranoid-schizoid position the boy feels that his father's and brothers' dangerous penises are sadistically inside his mother's body inflicting pain. In her view, the homosocial pact in the paranoid-schizoid position is intended to spare the subject's mother (and sisters) from the aggression launched by the "bad" sadistic quality of his father's and brothers' penises.

In the judicial proceedings against Essex, Bacon will take up "the rôle of intermediary between the Queen and the Earl" (229). Strachey's rhetoric shows more explicitly than ever before the confusion of genders and the qualities associated with them, questioning such central notions as passivity and activity in the Freudian elaboration. In the following passage, passivity is attributed to a man, Robert Cecil, one of Essex's enemies: "But passivity may be a kind of action—may, in fact, at moments prove more full of consequence than action itself. Only a still, disillusioned man could understand this; it was hidden from the hasty children of vigour and hope" (221). I take this as a crucial statement that may come directly from Strachey himself and entirely discloses and questions his own psychic economy. These "hasty children of vigour and hope" sound familiar to those who have read Strachey's poetry and personal letters. This can be read as a complicitous wink to his readers and a meditation in a loud voice. How can we distinguish passivity from activity in love? Is there a way to think of masochistic pleasure as independent of sadism? How can we ascertain that the appearance of passivity in the melancholic is not, in itself, strenuous mental action?

The denouement comes with hatred and a strong desire for retaliation. Elizabeth is a dreadful, retaliatory mother—"Essex was a naughty boy, who had misbehaved" (227)—who no longer trusts Essex's letters even when Strachey tells us that she found "those words impossible to resist" (231). Her anger explodes in a manic outburst. Essex is proclaimed a traitor. His failed attempt to raise an insurrection finally gets him confined to the Tower to await trial. Bacon will be one of his accusers, and Essex will be found guilty of a deliberate conspiracy.[41] The trial is the occasion for the confrontation of these two diametrically opposed personalities. Essex was "loved and hated—he was a devoted servant and an angry rebel—all at once" (248). Bacon "could never have comprehended a psychology that was dominated by emotion instead of reason" (249). After the verdict is announced, scenes of weakness and humiliation follow, and Essex, seized by anxiety and horror, confesses his guilt in planning the insurrection. Elizabeth is absorbed in a deadly jouissance; the compulsion to repeat and the death drive now provide some leeway for sadomasochistic enjoyment. She "allowed herself to float deliciously down the stream of her desires. But not for long. She could not dwell infinitely among imaginations; her sense of fact crept forward . . . with relentless fingers it picked to pieces the rosy palaces of unreality. . . . She saw plainly that she could never trust him, that the future would always repeat the past, that, whatever the feelings might be, his would remain divided, dangerous, profoundly intractable, and that, if this catastrophe were exorcised, another, even worse, would follow in its place" (256). Her paranoid-schizoid state shows in splitting, manic denial, and an increase in projection. She projects into Essex her devalued split parts.

The queen indulges in an agony of triumph. Identified with her father, she has been condemned to repeat his ghastly actions—"her father's destiny, by some intimate dispensation, was repeated in hers" (258). Strachey meditates in Kleinian terms at this point: "Was it her murdered mother who had finally emerged?" (258). In "Notes on some schizoid mechanisms," Klein had suggested that "From the beginning the destructive impulse is turned against the object and is first expressed in phantasied oral-sadistic attacks on the mother's breast, which soon develop into onslaughts on her body by all sadistic means. The persecutory fears arising form the infant's oral-sadistic impulses to put his excrements into her . . . are of great importance for the development of paranoia and schizophrenia" ([1946] 1975, 2). At this point in the narrative, Elizabeth's retaliatory nature turns all her sadistic potential against Essex as a representative of the murderous sex.

The narrative closes with a scene of what we may call imperialist surveillance. The spectacle of Essex's execution is viewed by Walter Raleigh, "the ominous prophet of imperialism" (261). Strachey lingers over the description of the ritual of the execution, and his rhetoric foregrounds the violence that is perpetrated against this man who now confesses that he "had bestowed his youth in wantonness, lust and uncleanness" (261–62) and blames himself for an "infectious sin" (262). This now infectious crime is never named, so that the examination of the Elizabethan scene of judicial and criminal justice—and by extension the Victorian disciplinary regimes—is read against itself.[42]

Elizabeth, in silence, sinks into "moody melancholy" (271), and it is precisely in the frenzy of her paranoid-schizoid state that she needs to restore the image of the good mother. She unwillingly takes up again "the cares and troubles of [the] crown," arguing that "for my own part, were it not for conscience' sake to discharge the duty that God had laid upon me, and to maintain His glory, and keep you in safety, in my own disposition I should be willing to resign the place I hold to any other, and glad to be freed of the glory with the labours" (275). But how can she restore the image of the good mother when she is immersed in melancholia? Is there a way to reconcile the demands of Elizabeth's paternal superego with the lost and foreclosed image of her good mother?

Strachey's narrative can be read as a story with two endings. In my view, he suggests two ways of closing the story. One is the actual final scene of the narrative. The other is the scene in section 16 in which Bacon is asked to give an account of the facts surrounding Essex's trial and execution. This second scene is the one in which Strachey self-consciously resigns his fabulistic power and passes it on to historians and legislators. He parodically reflects upon the intimate links between narrative and the law, between narrative and forms of authority, for "it was determined to print and publish a narrative of the circumstances, with extracts from the official evidence attached. Obviously Bacon was the man to carry out the work; he was instructed to do so; his labours were submitted to the correction of the Queen and Council; and the 'Declarations of the Practices and Treasons of Robert Late Earl of Essex and his Complices . . . together with the very Confessions, and other parts of the Evidences themselves, word for word taken out of the Originals' was the result. The tract was written with brevity and clarity . . . and there was only one actually false statement of fact" (266). Strachey reflects on the boundaries between fact and fiction, phantasy and the law, the licit and the illicit, and truth and falsity. He takes up a parodical and critical stance that can be read against the backdrop of the debates on censorship that were taking place in Edwardian England.

The last section of *Elizabeth and Essex* exudes a mixture of melancholia, mania, and manic depression in the scenes approaching the death of Elizabeth. Her manic triumph has only brought her "solitude and ruin," and she remembers Essex "with deep sighs and mourning gestures," compulsively repeating his name. She moves from the repetition of the rituals of bereavement to psychotic states of delusion, which are manifested in her speech. Elizabeth exhibits physical weakness and a "profound depression of mind" (278). Up to the last moment, she "fights" death with enormous tenacity. Strachey's wealth in the gloomy description of a court immersed in an atmosphere of "hysterical nightmare" has an almost surreal quality. Elizabeth's imposing presence and her desire to exert power remain unflinching until the end. After her death, as elusive to her courtiers as ever, "a haggard husk was all that was left of Queen Elizabeth" (280). Strachey splendidly opposes the spectacle of the sovereign's death to the implacable continuity of the life drives in the pressures that the body politic imposes on its subjects.

Lord Cecil and Elizabeth's councillors were hard pressed to choose a successor to the throne, but everything has been arranged and "The momentuous transition would come now with exquisite facility" (280). In the closing paragraph of the narrative, Strachey describes a scene of writing: "As the [secretary's] hand moved, the mind moved too, ranging sadly over the vicissitudes of mortal beings, reflecting upon the revolutions of kingdoms, and dreaming, with quiet clarity, of what the hours, even then, were bringing—the union of two nations—the triumph of the new rulers success, power, and riches—a name in after-ages—a noble lineage—a great House" (280). Ultimately, writing is all that remains. This passage shows an uncanny proximity with Strachey's own melancholic state of mind. Life is a succession of losses, and death is merely its epitome. Strachey's style is painfully broken with a staccato rhythm interspersed with excessive hyphenation. As Gabriel Merle has acutely noted, Strachey's frequent use of hyphens in his writing "contributes to weakening the discourse." It is frequent in *Eminent Victorians*, and in *Elizabeth and Essex* he believes it is especially remarkable in its last page, "which is, perhaps, a self-parody" (1980, 756). Following Merle's suggestion, we may think of Strachey's last defiant act in *Elizabeth and Essex* as an act of writing that melancholically seeks to retrieve his lost good internal objects, those moments of happiness in his childhood and adolescence, his first loves. What is Strachey, ultimately, self-parodying? How can we tell? Is this simply a parody of the scene of writing? Recollections, screen memories glimpsed "with quiet clarity," and traces of the past all remain subsumed under the sway of the death drive, within the ego's vertiginous turmoil. Writing, with its burden of irretrievable lost objects, extends its triumphant gaze in the end.

Melancholia, Effeminacy, and Mask-erade

You seem, on the whole to imagine yourself as Elizabeth, but I see from the
pictures that it is Essex whom you have got up as yourself.—John Maynard Keynes

Strachey's Elizabethanism is a personal evocation peopled with extravagant phantoms which act out the instincts that four hundred years later had receded into our subconscious—a never-never-again land with which we were connected by residual memories and in whose strange atmosphere we are invited triumphantly to lose ourselves. —Michael Holroyd

Holroyd's rhetoric, quoted in the epigraph, shifts from the abandonment of melancholia to the triumphant state of mania in a phantasmatic scenario that lays claim to some sort of collective subconscious populated with ghosts in whose memories one can become lost. The megalomaniacal element in Holroyd's understanding of the enterprise that Strachey undertakes seems to me both apt and entirely problematic. In Strachey's appropriation of his characters' stories, one can see how his use of strategies of supplantation, impersonation, and passing[43] dangerously works both ways, in the sense that he both fashions his characters' lives and actions and, in a parallel way, is fashioned by them in the transferential space of the narrative. Both projective and introjective identification are at work.

In the Kleinian psychoanalytic context, Joan Riviere published her most important piece of writing, "Womanliness as a masquerade," in 1929. This essay was a product of the work accomplished and debates held during the 1920s on sexual difference and female sexuality. Riviere postulates that there is no difference between "genuine womanliness" and the masquerade. She finds, however, that women put on the womanly mask in order to hide their masculine strivings, that is, their phallic masquerade (35–44).

Mary Ann Doane has shown, using Joan Riviere's work, that "masquerade . . . constitutes an acknowledgement that it is femininity itself which is constructed as mask—as the decorative layer which conceals a non-identity" (1991, 25). And Judith Butler has demonstrated, drawing on the work of Riviere, Wittig, and others, that gender is constructed through performative acts and lacks an essence upon which to hang the mask. Butler and Doane perform similar operations; both show gender and femininity (respectively) to be a role, a masquerade. However, Doane does not theorize the nonidentity she uncovers, whereas Butler seeks to elucidate the mechanics of the production of the " 'outside' to identity" (1993, 194).

In the case of the male, castration anxiety leads to envy of the father's phallic powers, male rivalry, and the compensatory need for virile display. In the male fetishist, this may manifest itself in a kind of macho masquerade, or "homeovestism," or it may appear under the guise of femininity in the effeminate display of the dandy or other figures deeply attracted by the lure of the feminine.[44] On the other side of this paranoid phallic display is dread of the nonphallic woman and a misogynist devaluation of the feminine. Fetishistic homeovestism (exaggerated phallic display to prove one has the phallus), on the one hand, and fetish surrogates for the maternal phallus (the fetish object), on the other, also serve to repair the sadistic aggression launched against the mother and father reintrojected into one's own ego, thus defending the fetishist from his own anxieties of loss.

In his narratives, Strachey explores ways of disavowing the gender division demanded of him by oscillating between pre-oedipal and phallic phantasies of completeness and denial of loss. The male fetishist's effeminate displays (the opposite of macho masquerade or homeovestism) are but a screen for his hidden wish to transgress the injunction of the binary. His is an attempt to evade the effects of the oedipal conflict as melancholic apparatus. The implacable oedipal law, in demanding that he be both like the mother and unlike her (or both like the father and unlike him, respectively), places the child in a paradoxical state of guilt, loss, and melancholia, no matter which of the contradictory commands he (or she) might attempt to obey. Strachey's (and others') gender masquerades and their subversions, based ultimately on mother-father identifications and fear of loss, are further complicated by oedipal jealousies, envy, and interdictions.[45]

John Maynard Keynes incisively captured Strachey's hidden wish to become Essex as he proceeded to write his story and see the latter through Elizabeth's eyes. Through the interplay between projective and introjective identification, Strachey ambivalently wanted both to preserve his aura of melancholic intellectual and to be born anew into this "handsome, charming youth, with his open manner, his boyish spirits, his words and looks of adoration, and his tall figure . . . romantic—passionate, restless, confused" (Strachey [1928] 1968, 5, 178). Essex is also presented as a victim in this universe of appearances, for "the Earl was incapable of dissembling . . . he carries his love and his hatred in the forehead" (119–20). He does not attend to "Apparel, wearings, gestures!" (120).

Strachey's melancholic fascination with the past and all things foreign reveals his struggle to fashion an identity unavailable to him in the midst of the Victorian atmosphere of the time, yet identity remained ultimately a mask or a performance.[46] His tendency to dramatize and his extensive use of dramatic techniques in his writing attests to this.[47] Strachey's correspondence over the period when he was writing *Elizabeth and Essex* shows a precarious state of health that becomes even worse with its progression. This abruptly emerges in the text in passages in which he masochistically lingers over the description of illnesses and afflictions of different sorts. *Elizabeth and Essex* is a masochistic exercise. Strachey wrote it painfully, since he saw many connections between this tragic history and his own. This is probably the cause of its slow process of composition. Michael Holroyd sees most of Strachey's previous work as beneficial and almost therapeutic. *Elizabeth and Essex* is an exception in the sense that he "had been unhappily in love before, yet managed to carry on steadily with his writing because it afforded him relief from his emotional problems. *Elizabeth and Essex* magnified the pain" (1994, 586). What pleasure does Strachey seek to gain from this personal laceration? And what does this say about the textual dynamics implicit in his narrative? What is at stake in the vicious circle of sadistic-masochistic defense mechanisms, and how can one move, if at all, from the paranoid-schizoid to the depressive mode of object relations?

In my reading, even when Elizabeth, in her hysterical and manic disturbances of character, is undeniably the visible effigy of Strachey's figuration of womanliness as a masquerade, Strachey is strategically camouflaged as Essex in a disturbing identification with the successive Others in his personal history. Through this process of alterity and dislocation, Strachey comes to acquire a Janus-faced quality that renders him invulnerable to the law. It is in this terrain of oscillation, which dwells in the partial stage of object love, that Strachey establishes his paranoid-schizoid mode of object relations.

In line with what I have suggested with regard to Klein, in *Elizabeth and Essex* it is this absence of a relationship with the mother as a significant

Other that forecloses the image of the good mother and deprives her daughter (Elizabeth) of a positive image of herself and her own body. In this respect, what can we say of Strachey, inasmuch as he identifies with Elizabeth? The biographers' and critics' perception of Strachey's closeness to and near obsession with his mother could be called into question in fictional form. With the foreclosure of the image of the good mother and what derives from it, Strachey would be a perfect candidate for melancholia. His dissatisfaction with his body and his insecurity about his physical appearance force him to produce an external image of himself, a public image in which he feels more confident, protected and preserved behind the mask. This mask, like the make-believe roles of his characters, is as genuine as anything that may lie behind it. The mask grants Strachey the possibility of having a multiplicity of identities and thus to reject any stable or fixed identity. Strachey's mask-erade elicits the desire to possess by virtue of its very opacity.

In *Elizabeth and Essex*, Strachey presents a new sexual subject produced by Elizabethan England, the effeminate man. Thus, "the flaunting man of fashion, whose codpiece proclaimed an astonishing virility, was he not also, with his flowing hair and his jewelled ears, effeminate?" (9). Whereas the effeminate man showed feminine trends in appearance and extravagant behavior, anxiety and confusion over gender was a sign of the times. From the habitual impersonation of women by young boys on the stage to the sodomite, the fop, or the royal favorite, a whole range of practices was available to be appropriated by the Elizabethans. In Strachey's narrative, Elizabeth's passion for clothes and ornaments causes her to appear in public enveloped in her wealthy costumes, jewels, and wigs. Her excessive attire and Strachey's parodic description of it bring her close to the contemporary aesthetics of drag: "The Queen's costumes were a source of perpetual astonishment. . . . The costume [on that occasion] was completed by a red wig, which fell on to her shoulders and was covered with magnificent pearls, while strings of pearls were twisted round her arms, and her wrists were covered with jewelled bracelets" (156). Let us remember that in the opening pages of *Elizabeth and Essex* Strachey confesses his interest in looking at Elizabeth "below the robes" (11).

With regard to Strachey's own psychic economy, Gabriel Merle has described a variety of neurotic forms that Lytton's character assumed, including psychosomatic problems, development of ghosts, superiority complex, masochistic tendencies, perpetual recriminations, and a plain chronic bad humor" (1980, 182). In the all male atmosphere of his school-ing at Leamington College, the pattern of Strachey's former relations at home within his family change completely. Merle has pointed out that "His brutal change of lifestyle is accompanied by ill-defined, but persistent discomforts, and is expressed in the form of passiveness" (136). Strachey's future love relations will follow the Greek role of the *eron*: "He will always gladly consider himself as older than the others, and the others will always gladly consider him as their superior, their intellectual mentor. Naturally, when one believes himself old and ugly, one looks for younger and more handsome company. Since the greek model has anticipated the role of the *eron*, Lytton Strachey quickly seizes it" (145). Asymmetrical relations of age and class show clearly in the pattern of *Elizabeth and Essex*.

Lytton Goes Camp

I wonder how long it will take the ladies to grasp the obvious fact that the only way out of all their difficulties is universal buggery (on the issue of sufragettes).—Lytton Strachey to Duncan Grant

On the issue of effeminacy in Lytton Strachey, K. R. Iyengar has raised a question that places effeminacy at the center of Strachey's style: "Is it a vein of effeminate timidity that makes it almost impossible for him to use a noun without qualifying it with an adjective?" (1939, 113). In his detailed stylistic approach to Strachey's writings, Gabriel Merle reads Strachey's style as essentially nominal: "It seems to us that there, within this nominal character, lies the essence of Lytton Strachey's style. . . . For Lytton Stra-chey, Biography—and History—are less a succession of processes than a noumenal series. From the Cambridge days, he holds that the 'phenome-nal' is secondary, and that people are more important than facts. That is why it is more important to portrait them than to tell their actions" (1980, 756). In the texture of this nominal style, adjectives are crucial to qualifying substances. But to what extent can we say that Strachey effects a stylistic subversion of the narrative codes used for biography thus far by recourse to a certain gay sensitivity that emerges in camp?

Much has been written about camp and its use by homosexual subcul-tures as a means of subversion. The word *camp* is drawn from the French *camper*, "to pose, to strike an attitude." Here I will only touch on a few definitions that highlight certain aspects of Strachey's method. According to Andrew Ross, "camp is a rediscovery of history's waste. Camp irreverently retrieves not only that which had been excluded from the serious high-cultural 'tradition,' but also the more unsalvageable material that has been picked over and found wanting by purveyors of the 'antique' " (1988, 13–14). Camp also entails undermining our basic assumptions about gender and culture, and, as David Bergman (1993) has noted, it works by drawing attention to the artifice of the gender system through exaggeration, parody, and juxtaposition. Moe Meyer, in turn, has defined camp as the act of being queer in a social context: "I define Camp as the total body of performative practices and strategies used to enact a queer identity, with enactment defined as the production of social visibility" (1994, 5). In his view, camp is manifested in practices and ways of reading and writing "that originate in the 'Camp eye' " (13). He also underscores the parodical element as an instrument through which disenfranchised groups introduce alternate codes into the dominant discourse. Whereas the "original" marks the site of dominance, parody and "Camp, as specifically queer parody, becomes . . . the only process by which the queer is able to enter representation and to produce social visibility" (11).[48] It is important to note that in Meyer's argument camp refuses to derive a fixed identity from its performances, and here precisely lies the challenge that queer sexualities pose to the heterosexist binary.

Elizabeth and Essex allows for a subversive destabilization of normative masculinity by means of camp. Gabriel Merle has remarked that Strachey loved transvestism: "He loved cross-dressing; he had his ears pierced and used to wear ear-rings; he would dream of changing sex; he had a desire for androgyny. And of all this, he was unable to talk" (1980, 182). Strachey would only feel free within his circle of friends. He displays this quasi-transvestism in a conflicting "identity as performance," that of an "effeminate masculinity." We may read effeminacy as a construct that is structured around a phantasmatics of desire and interdiction grounded on a material history, which exceeds the sum of the history of those individual practices that come to articulate it. Susan Isaacs, in her crucial essay on phantasy, highlighted how this materiality interacts with the history of the psyche of each individual: "ordinary bodily characteristics other than illnesses, such as manner and tone of voice in speaking, bodily posture, gait of walking, mode of handshake, facial expression, handwriting and mannerisms generally, also turn out to be determined directly or indirectly by specific phantasies. These are usually highly complex, related both to the internal and external worlds, and bound up with the psychical history of the individual" ([1952] 1983, 100). Strachey's *Elizabeth and Essex* destabilizes the dominant Victorian and bourgeois configurations of gender and class and turns homosexual and upper-class poses into acts of defiance.

Elizabeth and Essex is full of sexual allusions to the late Victorian standards of the time. Thus, a critic in the *Criterion*, the Rev. Charles Smyth, wrote that "In *Elizabeth and Essex* the author shows himself preoccupied with the sexual organs to a degree that seems almost pathological. He positively cannot get away from them" (quoted in Kallich 1961, 18). Smyth deplores the vulgarity of Strachey's sense of humor and complains of the frequency with which he alludes to the sexual organs, which in his view suggests a compulsion neurosis.

In *Elizabeth and Essex*, the Elizabethan milieu and its esprit appear as essentially camp objects. The costumes and props, the setting and atmosphere, all are imbued with an aura of camp. Strachey's impersonations of Elizabeth may aim to achieve a certain degree of self-representation in the open, outside the Bloomsbury milieu, in the larger social sphere. By the end of the narrative, Strachey attributes the execution of Essex to Elizabeth's femininity rather than her royalty, to a psychosexual question rather than a political one. As Gabriel Merle has noted, it is not that Strachey disregards history but rather that he adds up something that for professional historians passes unnoticed: "He [Strachey] adds up what professional historians overlook. Here, national history will be subordinated to individual tragedy. But the former will also be present; it will be the iridescent and blood-colored background against which the history of the two heroes is woven" (1980, 617).

Most of what Strachey said about history can be applied to his idea of biography: "It is obvious that History is not a science: it is obvious that History is not the accumulation of facts, but the relation to them. Only the pedantry of incomplete academic persons could have given birth to such monstruous supposition" (1931, 158). In Strachey's narratives, biography and history are never styled as metanarratives. He rejects the idea of narrating a history that, trying to account for human change, may partake of any totalizing imposition. *Elizabeth and Essex* and most of his other experiments in biography are, in this sense, closer to the anecdotal quality of the fabulistic.

When Strachey completed *Elizabeth and Essex*, Roger Senhouse had not made up his mind as to whether they should continue being lovers.

Strachey sank into a period of melancholia, and phantasies of introjection colored his thoughts: "you [Roger] are somehow with me—as if you could hear me, if I raised my voice—as if I could almost touch you if I could stretch out my hand a little further than usual" (quoted in Holroyd 1994, 617). If *Elizabeth and Essex*, as a text, mitigates a series of losses in the real world through rewriting, it also thematizes within the text how literary language finds itself at a loss, unable to bridge the gap between language and its object. The biographer and the historian engage in a melancholic exercise that both affirms and denies a loss. As Michel de Certeau puts it, "Death is the question of the subject, caught within the impossibility of speaking or writing about it. It is against this life, on this clearing, that the figures of death and the dying will perform their strange dance. They are *ob-scenes*, in as much as it is not me who is represented therein. I deceive myself by placing death in a space or a time where I postulate not to be" (1975, 11). The writing of biography and the writing of history are doomed to fail since the recognition of their respective losses is a utopian project, paranoid-schizoid in its economy and essentially projective in its performance.

11

Melancholia Reborn: Djuna Barnes's Styles of Grief

Unto the woman he said, I will greatly multiply thy sorrow and thy conception; in sorrow thou shalt bring forth children; and thy desire shalt be to thy husband, and he shall rule over thee.—Genesis 3.16

As if, in the case of pain, the body transformed itself into psyche and the psyche into body.—Jean Baptiste Pontalis

If, for Melanie Klein, sexuality is born out of aggression and the subject is shattered into sexuality, for women in Djuna Barnes's *Ryder* sexuality is the clearest possible and embodied manifestation of the workings of the death drive. The first movement of deflection of the death drive fails, and its reintrojection is what determines their troubled status as objects of desire whose agency is curtailed and thwarted by the deceptive status of a law that covers up the domain of the familial and the social, subsuming within itself even its violations, transgressions, and corruption. Because it is in the nature of the law, Julie Ryder's testimony seems to tell us, to dupe us, to make us fall into the trap of delusions, to moralize us in order to compensate for its own immorality. But whose law and whose morality are we talking about? And whose voice is speaking in *Ryder*'s entangled symphony of voices? I want to argue that the waterfall of voices and the pastiche of genres and styles that make up the collage of the novel constitute an alienating and alienated device in which melancholia and paranoia—in one of their many guises—as paraphrenia flourishes. Paranoid defenses are at work to preserve Julie Ryder's fragment of truth and sanity. In an accusatory universe where evidence is set against those who are assigned to bear the burden of victimization, melancholia and paranoia are produced as the very mark of sociality. Paranoia-as-melancholia, I will argue, emerges out of a socially repressive and virtually psychotic scenario in which those who are dispossessed of the good—the good internal object, truth, the phallus, or power/knowledge—are to strategically distance themselves using paranoid, obsessional, and manic defenses. The Ryders' melancholic paranoia, as the novel's own paranoia, is one more instance of the many masks melancholia wears in modernist discourses.

This is neither the time nor the place to make any claims for Barnes's particular sexuality. It is my aim to approach the melancholic nature of her texts in an attempt to grasp the mode melancholia is channeled into in some of her writing and to wonder why this is the case. Why, if at all, is her first novel *Ryder* (1928) a melancholic text, and what is at stake when she gives textual expression to what I have called the constitutive role of melancholia in modernist sexualities? I will try to approach these questions with a reflection on the role of melancholia and paranoia in Barnes's texts, which, as discussed earlier, act as indissociable components of manic depression in psychic organizations that are more prone to it.

I see it as an important and even urgent task to reformulate previous psychoanalytic ideas on paranoia and melancholia and to inquire into their relationship with sexualities outside the heterosexist binary. Inspired by Klein, I will argue for a revision of the role of paranoia as constitutive of all psychosexual development and will counter its marginalized and stigmatized presence within the original Freudian limits of male homosexuality.

In her writings, Barnes inscribes melancholic desire, a desire that by definition is abhorrent to the law but that through the law and by virtue of the law gains the legitimacy of its own abjection. Barnes seeks to counter the unspeakableness and illegibility in culture and history of women's— especifically daughters'—and other outlaw desires, with a complex cluttering of accents, registers, and styles channeled through the distinctive rhythms of modernism.

Implicit in the lesbian melancholic phantasy is the idea of the impossibility of attaining independence and freedom from the constraints of the enforced heterosexual ideology as represented in heterosexual intercourse. The phantasy of incorporation of the penis is frequently literalized in a painful blockage of all creative and emotional possibilities of the lesbian writer.[1] If the penis remains inside, melancholically incorporated, projection is the only possible alternative to psychic illness or death (suicide). But, as we know, projection is forever blocked in the psychic economy of melancholia. It may happen through a violent outburst, expressed in the production of a myriad of deformed and distorted fragments. Here it is projective identification that may be at stake. How does the subject come to project what has been forcibly incorporated in its (phantasy of the) body? How can the subject represent the abyss that mediates between the body in pain (melancholia) and the world? And what is the psychic cost?

Ryder is Djuna Barnes's most important elaboration of how much the subject has to pay for not surrendering to the law. The shifting voices in Ryder seem to be pointing to the impossibility of constructing a subject that is not shattered by the (heterosexuality of the) law, that is not shattered by the enforced demands of a sociosexual code prior to itself and by virtue of whose very ubiquity controls and sanctions.

Violent Excisions

Ryder and Ladies' almanack were both published in 1928. It is astonishing that Ryder, with its focus on patriarchal power, became, albeit briefly, a best-seller.[2] Ladies' almanack, written for a specific female audience and about women's issues, concerns, and interests, was privately printed and circulated among the members of the upper-class Natalie C. Barney's circle on which it draws. The possibility of using Ladies' Almanack as a pretext to provoke a discourse on lesbianism and the erotics of women's bodies marks the book's position outside the economy of the market, both as a position of exclusion and as one of liberation in a clandestine domain, potentially more fruitful by virtue of not being subservient to the law.

It was also in 1928 that Radclyffe Hall's The well of loneliness was banned in England and not published there again until 1959.[3] The Obscene Publications Act was introduced in 1857 in England with the aim of stopping the public circulation of pornography in an attempt to protect audiences from potentially damaging materials. Leigh Gilmore has emphasized how important it is to articulate the significance of obscenity law in the development of modernist notions of authorship and sexuality. She argues that "if we view modernism from the perspective that obscenity is constitutive of rather than corollary to modernism, it is clear that the medicalization of sexuality, the modernization of narrative, and the criminalization of printed material emerged as a constellation of cultural meanings related to identity. . . . Through its engagements with and efforts to control representations of sexuality and identity in both literary and medical writing, obscenity law extended its reach beyond what had already been represented and into which representations could circulate" (1994, 604–5).

In this respect, one of the most important issues at stake in Ryder is the question of the unrepresentability of the barren or sterile female body—in adulthood and childhood—and that of the invert (Dr. O'Connor) and the abject prostitute body as potential threats to the social heterosexual order through nonreproductivity. These other bodies are displaced onto the domains of medicine and the law.[4]

In her foreword to Ryder, Barnes denounces with her superb ironic style the way in which the indiscriminate vogue of censorship had dictated that the novel be expurgated prior to publication. Outraged, Barnes was determined to unveil the forces that would destroy the sense, continuity, and beauty of her work. To avoid speculation, she and her publisher (Liveright) placed asterisks where fragments of text had been removed: "That the public may, in our time, see at least part of the face of creation (which is not allowed to view as a whole) it has been thought the better part of valour, by both author and publisher, to make this departure, showing plainly where the war, so blindly waged on the written word, has left its mark. Hithertofore the public has been offered literature only after it was no longer literature. . . . In the case of Ryder they are permitted to see the havoc of this nicety, and what its effects are on the work of imagination" (vii).

Ryder thus begins its existence as a mutilated text, one that has suffered the violence of the law. Paradoxically, Ryder will also be a novel about the violence that the law inflicts upon many bodies—especially women's and children's bodies but also "deviant" ones (Dr. O'Connor). Barnes's preface is a fiery speech in favor of freedom of expression and against an obscenity law whose linguistic and textual effects are elliptically hidden in diacritical marks. The blatant effects of censorship remain traumatically inscribed in a historical memory impossible to retrieve.[5] And Ryder thus emerges as a corpse, a body that has been aborted upon coming to life. Barnes warns her readers that the text that will reach them is, "so murdered and so discreetly bound in linens that those regarding it have seldom, if ever, been aware, or discovered, that which they took for an original was indeed a reconstruction" (vii). She is herself involved in this process of the mummification of her first novel, willing to render visible the cuts and the scars that censorship has so brutally effected.

In her writing, Djuna Barnes engages in a dialogue with myths of male literary dominance. Her work invites us to read it in light of contemporary debates on gender and sexuality (in the current deliberate destabilizing of sex and gender identifications) and inseparable from critical developments in psychoanalysis. It is in the constant interaction and deconstruction of monolithical categories of masculinity and femininity that Barnes's texts shed light on our present debates, and the categories at work in the present moment can at once enrich and further problematize the already complex Barnesian worldview.

Psychoanalysis, as one of the modernist filiative models of male dominance, was contested on different fronts. The Controversial Discussions were definitive in shaking the foundations of the Freudian edifice, in the realignment of forces, and in the mapping of a terrain where orthodoxy and heresy were separate from the start. In the sphere of the arts, the effects of experimentation, transformation, and change in early modernism provided a ground for challenging former positions in literature, the visual arts, architecture, design, and applied arts and crafts. Artistic innovation, creativity, and insight into the lives and experiences of women and men at the beginning of the century will act as a critique of modernity and a social, political, and aesthetic corrective to it.

In *Ryder*, Barnes explodes the myth of patriarchy by uncovering the ways in which the requirements for sex-appropriate behavior in its formulations of masculinity and femininity foster a modernist culture of gender melancholia. Barnes deliberately seeks to alter our perceptions of the enforced naturalization of gender by narrating a story of a dysfunctional family in which motherhood is enforced as a sociopolitical imperative and fatherhood exists as a function whose only aim is the compulsive reproduction of the law.

Far from being a narrative about the continuation of life, *Ryder* partakes of a culture of the death drive, a culture of modernist melancholia whereby the propagation of the human race manically denies the realities of violence, victimization, and death. Women and children's deaths are erased and hidden from the triumphal and successful history of those who are more apt to survive. This is certainly the case as early as in chapter 2, "Those Twain—Sophia's Parents!" in which we learn of the death of Sophia's mother during her fourteenth childbirth, and in chapter 13, "Midwives' Lament, or the Horrid Outcome of Wendell's First Infidelity," in which Wendell's young lover also dies upon giving birth. Wives and lovers are equals in terms of dying. Nor is the fate of children a felicitous one.

Sophia's first son dies in his sixth month, and Amelia's lullaby is a tragic song upon the death of a child as well as the bedtime story she tells in chapter 36.[6]

Ryder, overlaid as it is by elegiac tension for a longed for and forever lost childhood self and by high familial drama, can undeniably be read as Barnes's own melancholic version of expatriate female modernism. The novel also problematizes the question of women's legibility and the unrepresentable character of their sexuality. Their procreative disclosure points to a deeper opacity that eludes the regime of the gaze. For, as Sophia argues by the end of the novel, "A woman can be civilized beyond civilization and she can be beast beyond beast. A woman is what she loves" (238).

Ryder is a history of bodily expropriation underwritten by the patriarchal parthenogenetic phantasy of magical childbirth. It inscribes a lesson of originary dismemberment, the dismemberment of the mother. Ryder puts forward the megalomaniac idea of massive and indiscriminate reproduction to avoid decay and counter death, to outwit nature with a rationale of ravaging and plundering regardless of the scarcity of its resources. I want to suggest that Barnes's novel acts as a generative phantasy that by way of an expropriation of the female body (specifically the mother's body) reproduces power relations in a context of asymmetrical binaries.

The effects of parturition are evocative of the rift that exists between the legs of the mother and the legs of her daughters, the rift that marks the separation of fiction and theory, of unconscious phantasy and external reality, the rift that simultaneously blurs their boundaries and produces melancholia as an aftereffect. Splitting, ambivalence, and manic denial are predominant psychic strategies in the narrative economy of Ryder.

I also want to suggest that we can read Barnes's fierce rejection of the impositions of patriarchy in Ryder as part of her own subversive avant-garde project to do away with the formalist ideologies of modernism and its multifaceted program of creativity along prescribed licit and illicit forms—high versus popular art. Barnes subverts aesthetic and falsely redemptive paradigms implicit in the ideologies of modernism.

Echoing suffrage activists' and birth control advocates' challenges to gender roles, Ryder mocks biblical, legal, and Freudian representations of female inferiority and dependence as well as the myths of motherhood and penis envy. Through a materialist reformulation of a history built upon women's lack of decision-making capacities, autonomy, and freedom,

Barnes aims to denounce the contemporary social condition of the commodification of women's bodies.

Deformations? Malformations?

Djuna Barnes cancels out the genders by making them obsolete.—Monique Wittig

In her essay "The point of view: Universal or particular?" (1983), Monique Wittig puts forward some important arguments, which relate to her experience as a writer and to Djuna Barnes's texts after Wittig's translation of Spillway into French. It would be interesting to consider to what extent Barnes as a writer and inspiring presence has fuelled some of Wittig's most important thoughts to date, especially when the French philosopher admits that "strategically Barnes is . . . more important than Proust" (67). Wittig's essay opens with some of her well-known aphorisms. There is no "feminine writing"; "Woman" is an imaginary formation, not a concrete reality; and there is only one gender, the feminine, for the masculine is the general.[7] For Wittig, Djuna Barnes's writing "cancels out the genders by making them obsolete" (64). Wittig herself finds it necessary to suppress gender. It is in this state of cancellation or suspension of gender that Barnes will perform, in a tour de force, her exercise of bringing to light new subject positions in the particular historical configuration of modernism.

Wittig's thesis in this essay is that a text by a minority writer is efficient only if it succeeds in making the minority point of view universal. She constantly refers to Proust and Barnes as two of the most relevant contemporary figures in gay and lesbian writing who have succeeded in universalizing their points of view. Wittig argues for the political importance of not limiting Barnes to the lesbian minority, "For it is within literature that the work of Barnes can better act both for her and for us" (1983, 66).

In her reflection on language and form, Wittig tackles two crucial tenets of modernism. The revolution of the word cannot do without formal experimentation in this particular movement. And in Wittig's arguments it is the concern with the sheer materiality of the form that constitutes the writer's task: "For when language takes form, it is lost in the literal meaning. It can only reappear abstractly as language while redoubling itself, while forming a figurative meaning, a figure of speech. This, then, is writer's work—to concern themselves with the letter, the concrete, the visibility of language, that is, material form" (1983, 68). From her materialistic stance, language and form are not so much ideal entities as actualizations; working on their externality at the point where they become visible, meaning is fully realized and explodes in the richness that polysemy brings.[8]

Wittig sees Barnes's texts as constantly shifting and operating through a fracturing of perception: "when the [Barnes's] text is read, [it] produces an effect comparable to what I call an out-of-the-corner-of-the eye perception; the text works through fracturing. Word by word, the text bears the mark of that 'estrangement' which Barnes describes with each of her characters" (1983, 65). This fracturing is for Wittig an aftereffect of the Barnesian text, a disintegrative gesture that makes room for different perspectives. *Estrangement* is the word that most closely approaches Brecht's *Verfremdungseffekt*. In Brechtian theater, the representational scene is more removed from the spectator than is customary, promoting a critical detachment from the spectacle and its ideology. This "distanciation" may be read against the grain, along the lines of the Freudian *uncanny*, and thus it may have a double effect, one of defamiliarization and another of closeness.[9]

In her early fiction, Barnes was much influenced by the decadent aestheticism and morbid sensitivity of symbolism as opposed to naturalism. Instead of focusing on the commonalities of human experience, the symbolist credo advocated a focus on extraordinary sensibilities in an attempt to escape a mundane and vulgar world. The symbolists' use of private symbols to indirectly suggest meanings, their exploitation of the singular and the unusual (from commodities to ideas), their frontal opposition to bourgeois values, and their experiments with technique (non-linearity, breaking narrative progression, and repetition) were designed to produce a new kind of consciousness.

References in Barnes's early work testify to her familiarity with symbolist writers—Gourmont, Hauptmann, Hoffmannsthal, Yeats—and her reading and ample knowledge of Baudelaire.[10] The latter's fascination with the emotions of spleen and melancholia probably find in Walter Benjamin his most attentive and exquisite reader. Benjamin's work on Baudelaire contains his elaborations on the specifically modern, capitalist form of melancholic allegory. In Baudelaire, Benjamin connects melancholia and the commodity structure. In his view, allegory can only be critically represented by means of a confrontation with its source, melancholia. Melancholia, as the most "subjective" moment of Baudelaire's productivity, appears as a mode of intuition that, in the form of *spleen*, is intimately linked to—in a dialectic with—concrete socioeconomic conditions in the early decades of industrial capitalism. For Benjamin, spleen is characterized "as a 'naked horror'; that is, the primitive, infantile fear of being swallowed up by the mass of objects, the fear of flying to pieces, disappearance in the diffraction and multiplication of selfhood. In this way self-alienation, the dispersion of the self through its objects . . . takes the form of an antagonism of the self with itself" (quoted in Pensky 1993, 171). In Benjamin's study of Baudelairean melancholy, in the section he devotes to the commodity as poetic object, he writes that "the commodity will stand as the social reality which underlies the dominion of the death principle in this poetry" (183).

Coming back to the question of form and the concomitant issue of style, in *Ryder* the virtual impossibility of classifying it opens up a space of freedom as far as its public circulation is concerned.[11] It is clear that many of Barnes's readers did not identify Nora and Robin as lesbians in *Nightwood* ([1937] 1961) since they are difficult characters to classify and *Nightwood* is not a realistic novel. Mary Lynn Broe has even called attention to T. S. Eliot's religious appropriation in his preface to *Nightwood*, which is worlds apart from the "morality" of the novel, when he writes: "The test of a book's obscenity is said to be its power of corrupting those who are open to corruption; and, had I a daughter whose passions for mistresses and older girls were beginning to cause scandal and alarm, I should certainly insist that she read *Night Wood*" (quoted in Broe 1991, 7).

We could make a similar case for *Ryder* in terms of the violation of generic and narrative conventions, variation of styles, and even the collagelike quality of mixed media (writing and drawing).[12] Is it possible at all to find the writer behind the text? Barnes elaborates a painful parody of the discourse of autobiography and personal confession—as in the case of Dr. O'Connor in chapter 32.[13] She both discloses and hides. Her modernist masks facilitate her discovery of a voice that both expresses and evades the conscriptions of selfhood and fixed identity.

Mocking Genealogies

Ryder opens with echoes of biblical narratives, a retelling of Genesis as a parable of the procreative power of the almighty God of creation and a word of caution on the abyss that separates the physical body from the spirit and thing from image. There is a chasm between the world of appearances and the world of matter. The narrator chants: "For some is the image and for some the Thing, and for others the Thing that even the Thing knows naught of; and for one only the meaning of That beyond That" (4). There is an almost manic insistence on knowledge, a knowledge whose tyranny operates in a presence or divine absence that requires obedience and consent. The text also insists on an embodiment of identity as a distinctive mark that is written on the body, "that which thou art, that in the end must thou bring as a sign against thy body" (5). *Ryder* begins with the problem of corporeal representation, interrogating the ways in which it is naturalized or acculturated and how it is ultimately imposed by divine law, civil law, or the law of the family.

Genesis contains many passages that delineate genealogical lines, and its focus is on creation and procreation. God's punishment of Adam and Eve in Genesis also provides a legitimate rationale for the sexual division of labor. *Ryder* also begins with a long genealogical line. Barnes narrates the origins of Sophia, the matriarch of the Ryder family, by telling the story of her parents and Sophia's birth. Barnes places us in the fourth generation and devotes a chapter to the great-grandparents in the paternal lineage. Cynthia, Sophia's mother, bore fourteen children and died giving birth to her last son: "Now with her fourteenth, madness had crept upon her, for the bearing of fourteen is no smaller matter" (7). Maternity, in its relation to death and psychic illness, is present in the novel from the start.

Sophia Grieve Ryder is described as an exceptional woman. She was "born robust, leavened at the maternal bosom, and became magnificent" (9). She was intelligent and well read and even managed to hold a salon for women at her home. Sophia used to introduce herself to others casually as "mother," and in the novel, as the matriarch of the *Ryder* clan, she provides for the family, since her son Wendell is out of work (he claims to be an artist-musician, a free thinker, and father of a new race). Sophia passes her maiden name to her son and consequently to the rest of the family. Grieve is a middle name, a painful reminder that oscillates between *grief* and *grave*.[14]

Sophia shows a clear preference for her granddaughter Julie—the daughter of Wendell and Amelia—and tells her stories that she makes up about her youth in an attempt to wipe out the boundaries between the true and the untrue. Throughout the novel, there is a self-conscious attempt to call into question the boundaries between fiction and truth, form and content, phantasy and reality, and projection and introjection. What is narrated in *Ryder* has an underlying melancholic subtext that is concerned with the violent struggle between the life drives and the death drive, between structuring and entropic forces.

It is important to note that Sophia, as a matriarch, is also identified with the law, a law that must be melancholically incorporated before it can be recognized as such. Barnes writes: "She was the law. She gave herself to be devoured, but in the devouring they must acclaim her, saying, 'This is the body of Sophia, and she is greater than we.' Devour her they did, and said, 'This is the body of Sophia, and she is greater than we'; all but Julie who loved her most" (16). Barnes inverts the sexes of the Freudian myth of origin in *Totem and taboo* ([1912–13] 1953), and it is this cannibalistic scenario of the killing and devouring of the primitive mother that provides the ground for narrative.[15] In chapter 5 ("Rape and Repining!"), the splendid parodical discourse on rape, fornication, and the restoration of women's virtue, the narrative voice tells how young girls have sex, ignorant of the consequences: "Yet: Is it not a Woman's quickest way of laying herself open to Legend? For now some say she has whelped Sad Melancholy, and that she do run about in the Night from Hedge to Hedge, and has a Look as if the One who brought her to Great Grief had been Dead a Thousand years" (24). *Ryder* questions the sacrificial logic that grounds language and the social upon the death of the mother, upon what Luce Irigaray calls "originary matricide." In Irigaray's view, the death of the father, inscribed as the founding moment of psychoanalysis, and of civilization in general, masks an originary murder and annihilation of the body of the mother.[16] In *Ryder*, melancholia is the sad, desperate state that lurks behind the fate of women.[17]

Unfatherly Names

A name is a battalion to walk beside you, weak or strong, according to its wording.
—Wendell Ryder

In *Ryder* there is also an obsession with naming and the status of the proper name. As a five year old, Wendell claims a name of his own: "he spoke up for an unfatherly given name, and was handed a history of England to choose from" (17). Finally, it is he who finds his name in a defiant gesture directed against the patronymic.[18] Wendell further declares, "I name myself as I find myself" (164), in his manic delirium in chapter 39, where he splits into many personalities in an attempt to escape Sophia's judgment.[19] In his state of permanent dissatisfaction, Wendell exhibits to the limit the failure to confer singularity that the proper name promises. The sense of Wendell's own unbearable finiteness shows in his malaise over his name—the gap between the time of the subject and the time of language—and fuels his search for immortality in a radical freedom from subjection to the proper name. Wendell manically eschews the vulnerability implicit in the social and linguistic contract in a gesture that subjects him even more strongly to the compulsion to repeat and to the death drive.

In *Ryder*, Amelia, Wendell's wife, is of a melancholic nature.[20] Her mother's advice to her is telling: " 'Never let a man touch you, never show anything, keep your legs in your own life, and when you grow to be a woman, keep that a secret even from yourself.' She shuddered. 'Never, never, have children. And God forgive me!' " (32). We learn that at the age of seven, her violent and abusive father chastised her for something insignificant. And Amelia will pass the same advice on to her daughter Julie: "don't let a man touch you, for their touching never ends, and screaming oneself into a mother is no pleasure at all" (95). Amelia's aversion to having children and passing on her history, in that foreclosed and deadening way, may ironically enable her daughter Julie to gain possession of her sexuality (in all its interconnections with memory and history) by displacing the desire to bear witness from the private to the public sphere, by writing her story. *Ryder*, albeit in a minimalist way, allows Barnes to narrate the origins of the daughter's sexuality, give it a history, or conversely sexualize her history.

Wendell is the youngest of Sophia's three sons and her mother's favorite. He is an eccentric who considers himself an artist and is obsessed with procreation. He holds that "one woman was never enough for a man" (45) and finds in polygamy and adultery the ideal solution. In chapter 13, "Midwives' Lament, or the Horrid Outcome of Wendell's First Infidelity," we learn that Wendell's first affair had a tragic outcome in the death of his lover in childbirth.[21] Wendell lives in his polygamous household with Amelia his wife, Kate-Careless his lover, and their eight children. Sophia also shares the home of this enlarged family.

As Catharine Stimpson has aptly remarked, Djuna Barnes had a "contradictory relationship to language" and anticipates "the post-structuralist anguish about letting loose a word, a sentence" (quoted in Broe 1991, 370–

71).[22] Barnes's body of writing—as much as her own physical body?—is a cryptic and almost intractable one, a body of writing that rejects us even as it entices us with its multiplicity of voices, styles, and forms, with the iconoclasm, ecclecticism, irreverence, and almost obsessive precision. Her deliberate mixture of styles and her violation of generic and even linguistic conventions made her proffer a truth in her particular modernist glossolalia. It is as if Barnes could only possess and be possessed by language. She was too free to be able to accept any further bond or imposition because she was, above all, a language worker. The whole of her oeuvre appears to be raising the question of what makes possible linguistic survival and linguistic death. In this respect, Mary Lynn Broe has noted that Barnes performed a ritual of self-silencing that shows "her refusal to privilege a single 'authentic' voice and her uneasiness with canonical forms" (1991, 8) and suggests that this silencing is a textual response to the father's attempt to violate his daughter and then barter her in ritual exchange. Broe specifically alludes to T. S. Eliot's " 'text-bashing' of the twenty-nine drafts of *The Antiphon*" (8). Eliot's advice led Barnes to suppress and displace parts of Miranda's childhood recollections, especially those that refer to the father's attempts to violate his daughter and then bartering her for a goat.

Barnes's modernist styles place heavy demands on her readers, and her subversiveness comes necessarily to the fore.[23] The trickeries, puns, polysemy, and ambiguity in *Ryder*'s language generate a traffic in meaning that revealingly shows the incommensurability of the effects of narration with narrated events. It is in this gap, this chasm between referentiality and figurality, that we can reflect upon the intersections of the various prisms of meaning in the novel.

Language holds no metaphysical guarantees, and Julie learns that her grandmother Sophia has lied to her. This violation of the pact of truth on which family and kinship rest is also a most intimate violation of the truth that keeps the subject from splitting and disintegration. Barnes's love affair with language also reveals mistrust and misrecognition. Since it is in the nature of language to fabricate fictions and mediate and add complexity to our relationship with reality, Barnes's linguistic virtuosity causes her to flee from the make-believe character of language to seek refuge in other representational apparatuses. Barnes finds freedom in moving from language to drawing. She cannot do without either of them.[24]

The French collection of drawings *L'imagerie populaire* is the source of many images in *Ryder* and *Ladies almanack*. The drawings that accompany *Ryder* were mostly read as illustrations devoid of any further meaning since Barnes took great pains to cover up her personal closeness to their referents. As Frances M. Doughty has noted, in her works Barnes moves ambivalently between revealing and keeping secret. She "encodes her experience, making it unrecognizable to anyone who does not know the original sources for both parts of the image. Because the faces in the published drawings, much reduced from their original size, are so small, because most readers are not trained to look for the telling detail that indicates portrayal of a specific individual, and because fewer readers, if any, know the individuals represented, the drawing is read as a whole simply illustrating the text with which it is associated" (1991, 141).

Whereas language fills in the gaps on the surface of the canvas, painting captures the thick texture of words and signs in its strokes. Barnes's styles subtly and aggressively caress the page. It is in this primary aggression and the scars and marks the pen or the brush leave on the page that the specific quality of her object relations show most vividly. It is through a reflection on her anxieties about creation and in the delicate balance among anxiety, object relations, and superegoic law that we can more fully grasp what is at stake in the particular idiom of Barnes's melancholic modernism.

Illegitimate Laws, Legitimate Acts

Ann [Amelia's sister]: "Have I not, with these very ears, heard him say, time and time again, that one woman was never enough for a man?"

"That," said Amelia, "is a theory which he holds for the race in general, but surely not for persons in particular."—*Ryder*

[Wendell] Was to them all that all wives seek.—*Ryder*

"That," said Amelia, "nicely illustrates the difference between the legitimate and the illegitimate . . . the sole difference between the bastard, per se, and the child of wedlock is, that the wife may leave but the mistress cannot, yet but listen to the nice point of the argument, it is the wife who may enter a house and the mistress who should stay out."—*Ryder*

In *Ryder*, there is an almost manic obsession with the law present in the interest in family genealogies, in the drawing of a clear boundary between the licit and the illicit, in the rights of birth that individuals acquire in the family, and in the civil rights that wives and children gain within a legal union. Barnes launches her strongest critique against the devastating effects that contemporary ideas on heredity had in the lives of the lower classes and the outcast.[25] This obsession with heredity is epitomized in the figure of Kate-Careless, Wendell's official lover. Even when Kate comes to live in the Ryder home in an interesting menage à trois, her origins in her family also suggest that she is a bastard, and thus, as a supreme example of the compulsion to repeat (produce life for the sake of death), she is predisposed to engender bastards herself.[26] We also know that Sophia's eldest son, Gaybert, "lived with a German woman, illicitly" (84).

Wendell lacks coherent motivation. All is nature in him. Male desire, when unruly and abhorrent of the law of the polis, is equivalent to female desire, which is tantamount to saying that male desire can only be represented problematically. Wendell rounds off his stories with stunning naïveté. They all come down to the domestication of sexuality as reproduction, the promise of immortality in unlimited wanton acts of impregnation and fluid mechanics.

In chapter 30, Wendell is accused of violating the law and is charged with not giving his children a formal education at school. In a fiery anarchistic speech, he vehemently maintains that they are better educated at home, and he warns the community, "I may warn you that Ryder as an outlaw is less trouble than citizen Ryder" (131). By the end of the novel, Wendell is obsessed with his violations of the law to the point of paranoia.[27] In a desperate delirium in which he pictures himself as a product of women's manipulations, Wendell appears as an object doomed to be eaten and swallowed by the law: "I have been tempered, cooked, made what I am, by the various heats emanating from the body of woman . . . but I may say that I was never fully roasted, frizzled, and come to a good crisp, until I knew the fair Kate, for there were heats in her like to no woman simmering, and now that I am done to a nice turn, who is to eat me? The authorities of the state and the wiseacres of the nation? For I tell thee, mother, they smell a well-done fowl, my aroma is ripe to the nose of justice, and like a pack of hounds, all slavering at the jaws, with bloody eye and wind in the ears, they snarl down the road of my destiny" (169). Wendell falls prey to the anxiety of being swallowed by the law, of being punished and castrated and no longer able to enjoy sex.

It is also in this chapter that Kate rebels against the tyranny of Wendell and Sophia and against the imposition of motherhood, which she finds disgusting. Kate accuses mother and child of fraud and falsification of reality: "[I will] sing about my house, as I used to, before you and your son came forward with his notions about women loving one another when they were not meant to love one another, or to get their children from the same spigot, or to wail under the same doom. . . . it's disgusting!" (171). It is important to point out that this is the only overt reference to lesbian love in *Ryder*. Kate, free as she was before meeting Wendell and falling into the trap of motherhood, might have lived as many lives as the narrator suggests in chapter 17, where she becomes Kate-Cast-Pot, an independent woman who enjoys her sexuality. This scene has clear sexual overtones, and it places Kate in a different realm, that of fantasy—or fiction within a fiction—untethered from the constraints of reality. She "turned up as a *marchande de poisson* . . . with an odour *tout le temps* of deep-sea matters and changes, digging among the tide-fickle sands, for the bearded Sea-dog. . . . She watched the lustres' iridescent glitter reflected by the aid of a million mirrors from framed Venice . . . and where their glint ceased she, in her imagination, carried it on ad infinitum, so that the fishy mica, and the glory of Venice, in icy precision, worked their way down into the butt of the tail in flawless intervals, ending only where she came to, upon perceiving her own hand grasping the miracle" (91). The specific allusions to feminine sexuality and its pleasures, and to its potential to be carried on ad infinitum, reach total autonomy in autoeroticism and masturbation. Barnes resists subordinating female desire to the law of the father. She knows the price one has to pay for it, which amounts to obliteration, renunciation, and compliance with social expectations. It amounts to mis-recognition of the specificity of female desire in and of itself.

Nevertheless, we cannot locate explicit lesbian love in *Ryder*. Along the lines of melancholia and its symbolics of loss, Carolyn Allen has aptly discussed *Nightwood* and Barnes's legacy in contemporary lesbian writing, noting her interest in reading narratives in which the narrators are obsessed with the loss of a lover, and "That obsession, in turn, creates intricate meditations on women as lovers and constructs an erotics out of the very loss that has occasioned the obsession" (1996, 2). Allen argues that the representation of women's erotics in the context of loss "contribute to personal and political knowledges in particular sociohistorical formations" (3). In the paradigms of experimental novels, this particular erotics occurs in situations of "obsession, loss and inequalities of power" (3).[28]

These novels in the Barnesian tradition inscribe the complexity of emotional and sexual exchanges between women lovers. Allen's approach intends to read novels in the Barnesian tradition "as if they produced theoretical narratives, a few of many such stories inscribing women's erotics" (30). She claims that the "acts and affects" of these novels contribute, albeit in a partial theoretical way, to an understanding of women's erotics as they are enacted beyond the fictional page.[29]

Chapter 17 of *Ryder*, "What Kate Was Not," introduces Kate and her personal history of suffering and misery.[30] The whole chapter is an exercise in phantasy. The unfortunate events reported by the narrative voice lead the reader to conclude that Kate's fate cannot be changed. It turns out to have been easily predictable, since she was "the wench who committed nature on its own scale, preserving the past in the fumes of a voluminous depth, but have a terrible thickness also, herself suffering increase of herself" (89). The final two lines of this chapter are categoric and discard any chance of hope: "Might Kate-Careless not have been this Kate also? Ah never, never, never!" (92). But since desire short-circuits consciousness, it is by virtue of its fleeting intrusion in this phantasy scenario, as well as in Kate's rebellion in chapter 39, that Barnes provides alternative ways to evade patriarchal law.

Projecting Anxiety: Melancholia in Modernist Attire

One of the most important psychic mechanisms at work in *Ryder*'s characters is projective identification. Klein originally defined it as a schizoid mechanism ([1946] 1975) and progressively complemented it with a parallel mechanism, introjective identification. Projective identification appears in *Ryder* in its most pathological form, as a mechanism of defense in the paranoid-schizoid position. And, as noted earlier, it is the death drive that the Kleinians posited as the basis for projective identification.

In chapter 19, "Amelia and Kate Taken to Bed," Julie, through projective identification, identifies with her mother's suffering of Wendell's advances when her brother Timothy attempts to molest her: "he heard . . . the childish treble of Julie, crying, 'Wendell! Wendell!' as she lay on her bed of playful maternity, aged ten, holding to her breast a rag doll thrown from the door to the immediate left by the strong paternal arm of Timothy, who was God and the Father" (95). Julie is a potential mother to be, and Wendell is all fathers, the paradigm of violent sexual potency and brute force. A double process of projective and introjective identification is at work. Even if Julie refuses to be like her mother, she emphatically identifies with her in her suffering.

Chapter 19 is also an exercise in the lessons of the traditional aetiology of melancholia. Amelia is in labor, and Dr. O'Connor is assisting her in the birth of her next son. In the midst of her pain, Amelia longs for a daughter, a sister to Julie. Her discourse is tainted with agonizing pain over her fate and that of all women. She utters a litany charged with distress and lamentation: "It is not enough to be a mother, but memory must bear down also? . . . Yet I shall grieve, for melancholy is mortality remembered" (96–97). When the baby is born, Wendell sees in horror that it is black, and Dr. O'Connor reminds him that "Bile alone is father of its colour" (97).

I want to suggest that in this childbirth scene we are attending to a modernist version of the rebirth of melancholia, black bile in modernist attire.[31] This phantasy of the metaphorical rebirth of melancholia out of the body of a woman has a follow-up in the next chapter, "Amelia Dreams of the Ox of a Black Beauty," where the language of dreams offers a new expressive economy. Amelia's dream parodically operates "to get the black man the attention of the Lord, and a place in his mercies, she having been troubled with the way Wendell had said of her last, 'It's black'. . . . It was also perhaps. . . . an effort to retake Wendell in his own colours" (98). In the narrative of Amelia's dream, Barnes explodes a wide range of reified cultural stereotypes that place women, blacks, and "Others" outside of history by dispossessing them of agency. In a splendid metafictive exercise, Barnes gives us a dreaming Amelia who is watching a woman dreaming on a bed. In this mise en abîme of the scene of dreams and dream discourse, Barnes is operating on a psychoanalytic as well as a narrative level, laying bare the ways in which they both work. Amelia finds in a voyeuristic exercise, "through a prodigious great keyhole" (98), a room, inside a temple, where a woman lies asleep on a bed. Surrounding the bed, the walls are covered with books on the history of mankind, effigies of people, and "pictures . . . of women going nowhere to nothing" (99). The doors to the room open and a great "ox of a Black Beauty" (99) enters. Barnes emphasizes the colossal nature of the shadow the ox casts on the ceiling, which is "mournful and splendid" (99) and its laconic speech, "I am also" (99). The ox requests "a place in your [the woman's] Saviour" (99), and the woman sends it away. But the ox insists, and, kneeling before the crucifix, "A slow downward way a shadow moved on the ceiling, which was his head going inward and downward, and he spoke for her, saying: 'Remember the woman.' And he rose up and went out, down the long steps of the chamber, walking softly and closely, and his shadow went with him, and his feet" (99).

How can we read this shadow of the black ox if not as a sign of melancholia? How can we read the ontological instability of the existential "I am also" if not as an attempt to reach out to others from the depths of the melancholic's afflicted ego? The intertextual movement is clear. The emblems of melancholia as black bile in Burton's *Anatomy of Melancholy* become enmeshed with the Freudian psychoanalytic discourse of the *shadow of the object*. In 1621, Burton referred to the melancholy humor (and melancholy temperament) as black choler or black bile, the cause of melancholia ([1621] 1989–94). Black bile was thus an element in the humoral theory that was understood to be an aspect of normal physiology and a key aspect in the pathology of the disease.[32] Barnes brings to light a melancholia reborn in modernist terms, in the grip of a woman dreaming of another woman's dreams.

Chapter 24, "Julie Becomes What She Had Read," presents an important example of how projective identification works. Barnes narrates the process through which Julie projects and identifies with distressed heroines in children's books. Barnes's epigraph is most telling: "In which Julie is many children, suffering the tortures of the damned, kneeling at the parent knee, in all ages, all times and all bindings, becoming what books make of a child" (106).[33]

As Melanie Klein reminds us, it is in children's books and tales that the infantile imagination nourishes those cruel figures that later come to inhabit the child's inner world. In "The relations between obsessional neurosis and the early stages of the super-ego" ([1932] 1975f), she writes: "It is a known fact that small children feel themselves hemmed in and pursued by phantastic figures. In analysing some quite young children I found that when they were alone, especially at night, they had the feeling of being surrounded by all sorts of persecutors like sorcerers, witches, devils, phantastic figures and animals and that their fears about them had the character of a paranoid anxiety" (156).

Barnes's chapter may function as a parodic illustration of the melodramatic element in children's fiction and simultaneously as a deconstruction of the myth of the ingenuity and naïveté that surrounds infancy. We are introduced to a five-year old girl, Arabella Lynn, the heroine of a story, onto which Julie Ryder projects her emotions and feelings and whose predicament she will later reintroject.[34] Arabella is a playful little girl who, as the narrator voice tells us, "will ask forgiveness for her multitudinous sins" (106). Immersed in the discourse of confession, Arabella, in her solitude, is ready to reveal her wrongdoings and mischievous intentions. It is important to note that Arabella is "in a wide-eyed somnambulic sleep" (107), and the narrator's voice begins to tell of her distress and transformations. In a dreadful nightmare, she is hunted down by "the glistening pack of night, a brightly brindled horde," and accused of something unspecified. Arabella uses splitting as a form of defense.[35] First, she is split into a multitude of figures, "A thousand thousand children now is she, her sins tenfold multiplied" (107). The narrator's voice begins a gloomy discourse about the convenience of her death in the face of what might become of her in the future, given her dubious beginnings. Everything in nature announces her impending death, and the following scene is that of a mourner's procession on its way to her sepulchre.

It is at this time that Julie enters the story as Arabella: "Julie Grieve Ryder, Julie in multitude, follows that little body to the grave. It is Julie now lying on her bed, it is Julie snatched up and flung down into the marketplace, where they are selling Jesus for a price" (109). Whereas earlier Julie had projected onto the story her tremors and fears, reading to some extent what she herself was experiencing, now, in her "voluptuous sixteen," she introjectively identifies with Arabella and the mourners. By the end of the chapter, Julie sees the little mourners as mothers to be, and the vision collapses in a dialogue between the voices of Wendell and Sophia. Barnes writes: "She [Julie] is the total of their running number, and they become mothers and are laden and are large, and the embedded face some this way and some that way. The little girls have little girls' heads, and little girls' hair, and it comes curling, and their feet are children's feet, balancing a child" (109). As Julie's dream resumes, Wendell and Sophia end this chapter in a heated discussion, with Sophia trying to stop her son from striking Julie—whom she phantasizes as the longed for daughter she never had—and Wendell complaining of Julie's "deriding" him. This de-riding undoubtedly condenses much of Barnes's own comment on the sickness of the Ryder family in a portmanteau word that alludes to copulation (ride-her), to the Ryders' name, and to the parodical rendering of incestuous sex in de-ride, which ultimately reads as "mock, make fun of," while in the negative prefix de- suggests the interruption of the act.

In the course of Arabella Lynn's story, she (and Julie) reject the imputation of guilt by the undifferentiated voices in the background. Some crime, some deviation or fault, is attributed, which stands in need of reparation, of restitution. Blaming seeks to put in motion this self-regulatory process. However, in this case the demands of the socioethical apparatus must fail, since the victim fails to acknowledge them as such. A social ethic of victimization collides head on with a subjective oppositional ethics of dissent, even if the price the victim has to pay amounts to her life. Julie Ryder's enraged response to her fate impinges on a crucial question, that of the origins of the law, which in its quasi-infinite specter of versions sets up the foundation of the family and of sexual and class relations.

In chapter 27, Wendell tells Julie and Timothy the story of the beast Thingumbob.[36] Framed as a children's tale and beginning "Once upon a time," Wendell narrates the tragic story of the love that Thingumbob, a supernatural beast—half-lion, half-ram with wings—feels for a strange creature of which he dreams. Her lover is portrayed as "of large limbs and of a beauty outside of the imagination," who was "terrible in her ways, which simply means that her ways were not our ways" (119). Barnes splendidly describes her in her surreal beauty: "Her feet were thinly hoofed, and her hair was many coils, and her face was not yet, and her breasts were ten" (119). She was not "virgin as other women are" and "the underworld had fathered and mothered her" (119). Echoing ancient fertility rituals, this creature is fettered to the earth during the season of harvest and due to her old age and impending death she desires to give children to Thingumbob if he will promise to bury her afterward. The creature's discourse is very eloquent and epitomizes most of the issues Barnes raises in her novel.

> "I shall die beneath you, yet from my body you shall garner ten sons, and they shall be harnessed of terribleness, and you shall bury me quickly, for I am burst asunder at their way within me, for they come marching, and I rejoice and go from this hour no further." And she charged him well, saying: "When you have dragged them forth by their iron locks, smite them with rain-water, and put my name on their tongues, and tell them thenceforth nothing of me, nor picture me to them in any way, saying, 'She was tender-hoofed and her breasts were ten.' For I am, and soon shall be as I am not, and they must know no deception. Nor cut their wings on the right side, nor cut their wings on the left side, nor metal their hoofs, for they are shod of me, at the forge of my heart, and they are." (121)

The story enigmatically ends with Thingumbob, full of sorrow, mourning the death of his lover with a terrible corollary, "for he knows her gift to him was the useless gift of love" (121).

Even when Thingumbob's story is cast as a children's tale, it is obviously written for adults. Barnes's experiment in fantasy turns out to be a children's story that can be read along the lines of the Kleinian concept of unconscious phantasy and situated in the domain of infantile imagination. What lies underneath this phantasy? "What does it mean?" is what Timothy asks his father after listening to the tale. This is certainly a similar question to those formulated by so many of Klein's young analysands. It is similar indeed to the questions little Fritz asks and Klein reports in "The development of a child" ([1921] 1975): "After he had once put the question, 'Where was I before I was born?' it cropped up again in the form 'How is a person made?' and recurred almost daily in this stereotyped fashion. . . . In his more specialized questions ('How can a person move, move his feet, touch something? How does the blood get inside him? How does a person's skin come on him? How does anything grow at all, how can a person work and make things,' etc?), and also in the way he pursues these inquiries. . . . The unconscious curiosity concerning the father's share in the birth of the child (to which as yet he has not given direct expression) may perhaps have been partly responsible for this intensity and profundity" (3, 9).

Timothy formulates the question about origins, which is ultimately a question about sexual difference and how children come into the world. It is important to note that the story occurs in dreams, and as dreams it vanishes with no moral. In Wendell's words, it means "much and little, like all wisdom" (121). In any case, the underlying subtext equates maternity and death. *Ryder* is a novel about the useless gift of love and its reminders, enmeshed as they are in a contemporary culture of the death drive.

Barnes's constant play with phantasy is deployed in the phantasmatic transformations of humans and beasts into one another in multiple variations.[37] In chapter 8, "Pro and Con, or the Sisters Louise," Wendell is pictured as an enormous insect. In this vision, his male attributes are once again brought to the forefront. He is "setting forth from the earth with stupendous great wings, outstripping the cornfields and the mountains, and rising up into the clouds, like an enormous and beloved insect, with strong hands upward and arched feet downward, and thundering male parts hung like a terrible anvil, whereon one beats out the resurrection and the death" (42). Wendell's metamorphosis can be read—as in the case of

Thingumbob—as an instance of monstruous paternity; the absurd, grotesque, and uncanny qualities of its many faces marks the disturbing and familiar aspects of our most feared internal objects.

Bodies in Pain

There is a proper and specific psychic pain, and melancholia shows one of its many faces. As Elaine Scarry has aptly remarked, "Whatever pain achieves, it achieves in part through its unsharability, and it ensures this unsharability through its resistance to language" (1985, 4). Pain cannot be measured concretely or objectively; it cannot be specified. We may only gain an idea of the subjective experience of pain through its outward reflection, as a mark on the body, or through involuntary organic reactions. We can only perceive pain through the Other's description of it. This does not mean, however, that pain does not have a specific vocabulary. Words pertinent to pain have been classified according to whether they fall into the affective or the descriptive category. In medical practice, the intensity of pain is included under affective criteria while the individual characteristics in any episode of pain are descriptive traits. If, as we have just noted, pain resists language, then the latter plays a crucial role in the recollection of pain.

In *Ryder*, language performs a symbolics of pain. Women characters and homosexuals in the novel use language to help them understand their distressed condition in the light of past experiences and what they know about the pain suffered by others.

THE BODY OF THE INVERT

Chapter 32 introduces the brilliant, "Soliloquy of Dr. Matthew O'Connor (Family Physician to the Ryders) on the Way to and from the Confessional of Father Lucas." O'Connor's is a superb dramatic monologue in which the doctor discloses the hidden truth about his personality. O'Connor appears as a cross-dresser, in woman's clothes, "Matthew O'Connor, holding my satin robe about my backsides, tripping up to God like a good woman, and me only seventeen, and taking on something scandalous for the way my sins were with me" (137). The scandalous voice of the body of the invert rises with bitter sarcasm and sexual undertones. In an irreverent farce on the discourse of confession and the authority of the Church, Barnes moves from the priest's words, "Go and live in God and trust to thy better parts" (137) to O'Connor's: "Holy! Holy! Holy! God save the behind, I said, and staggered out into the life and traffic of my days" (138). Barnes mocks the religious discourse of conversion[38] in a series of scenes in which O'Connor appears in the midst of his family of fourteen children mourning the death of his brother Felix. O'Connor, in a speech that borders on ridicule, portrays his family as a respectable one and confesses his sins, repents, and prays for absolution.

Dr. O'Connor engages in a crucial dialogue with Wendell in chapter 45. Vis-à-vis O'Connor, Wendell discloses some of the truth about himself. In his megalomania, he wonders why he is not God (if God is the only thing of which a man can be sure when he is not sure of himself) and, totally confused, asks the doctor about fatherhood, heredity, and religion. Wendell is now obsessed with death and reflects on men's and women's deaths. In his speech, he gives a perfect portrait of a manic suicide in the suicide of man: "A man may commit suicide for any number of the same reasons that a woman commits suicide, but he never lets the effect seal the cause, he reasons it out, he leaves notes, he says it was this, or that, or the other, in an endeavour to place himself on an equal footing with God . . . he goes to his mirror. . . . Troubled—why? Because he cannot kill himself without including his will in that action. . . . If I kill me, my corpse shall be, in my terms, absolute, and by myself, myself made not myself—voilà!" (203). Suicide will ultimately be the genuine expression of Wendell's will to power. The difference with women is that "women know that there is God only, but man knows that there is God and the father" (204). Wendell is obsessed with the law of the father to the point of psychosis. His discourse exhibits splitting, idealization, and manic mechanisms.

To Wendell's question "How would you die, Matthew?" Dr. O'Connor, in his wisdom, answers that he should like to die like a woman. Wendell says that he should die frightened, like a child. But the death of a child is terrible in its ignorance of both God and the father. In an almost Schreberian delirium, Wendell demands justice and charges against the doctor's incredulity: " 'Why,' cried Wendell, exasperated, 'do you, of the Catholic faith, juggle so with words? Justice is a terrible, an irrefutable, and a colossal thing' " (204).

O'Connor possesses an ancient wisdom, which Barnes causes to emanate from the body of the invert. In the novel, O'Connor assists women in childbirth and concedes that he will assist Wendell when he dies. In the figure of O'Connor, the invert reunites within himself a balance between self-preservative instincts and the death drive. His openness to the Kleinian depressive position (whole object love, depressive anxieties) testifies to his specific melancholic stance.

In the 1920s and 1930s, the sexologists' discourse on inversion intersects with emerging discourses on female and male homosexualities. There are two allusions to Oscar Wilde within the novel. The first attributes to Wilde the necessary sensitivity to acknowledge Wendell's physical perfection; the second, more interestingly, alludes to Wilde's trials: "Oscar Wilde was a man of beauty, who looked through a privy-ring at the stars. A man of imagination, a man of parts. A man's man" (166).[39] Wendell also tells of a day when he saw Wilde after the scandal: "The scandal had burst, and though he was the core, the fragrant center of a rousing stench, in a month he was a changed man, not changing, witting within his cell, weeping, writhing, plotting 'De Profundis,' his fingers outside his mouth, shuddering in all his soft female body, direct suffering in his breasts; a bull caught and captured, sentenced, hamstrung, marauded, peered up, peeped upon, regarded and discovered to be a gentle sobbing cow, giving self-suck at the fountain of self, that he might die in his own image, a soft pain chartered she, a girl cast out of heaven, harnessed for a stallion's turn; tremolo to his own swan-song. I turned away and was matchlessly damned" (166).

Wendell uses Wilde's aestheticism to support the argument he makes about his personal beauty. Only a sensitive and perceptive man would be capable of apprehending his many physical virtues. The underlying subtext wittily points to the homosocial bonding that aestheticism, the cult of beauty in its most ample sense, intellectual gifts, a refined education, and a certain upper-middle-class consciousness helped establish for so many gay men, intellectuals and dilettantes alike, who were close to homosexual circles around the turn of the century. Wendell wants to show his virile virtues, his manly attributes, and Barnes parodically does so by recourse to a certain gay sensitivity.[40]

The language of pain proliferates throughout the novel. It is interesting to note that in the period prior to and between the world wars medicine (neurology), psychiatry, and psychology focused research on pain. The trauma of the two world wars brought society and science closer together than ever before and as a result affected the general understanding of pain and its available remedies.

The exaltation of the value of pain as human experience came first under the term *dolorist* in France in the first decades of the twentieth century.[41] The writer and journalist Julien Teppe published two books, *Apologie pour l'anormal, ou Manifeste du dolorisme* in 1935, and *Dictature de la douleur, ou precisions sur le dolorisme* in 1937. Teppe also launched the *Revue Doloriste*, an episodic publication that managed to include such prestigious writers as Gide, Valéry, and Colette, among others. For Teppe, pain is a means of self-discovery and a way to understand basic truth in relation to oneself. He argues: "Pain, of all the psychological states, is the one which takes over the entire being, both the flesh and the spirit, with the greatest urgency and force. It is a disposition which sweeps away, blots out and annihilates all the rest. It does not allow for cheating or compromise. It is there and is enough to eliminate all the rest" (quoted in Rey [1993] 1995, 318). Pain exercises its tyranny over us. In Teppe's view, aggression, hostility, and war all come about because men cannot truly imagine suffering. But *Apologie pour l'anormal* went far beyond its original aim and purported to uncover the merits of pain and to draw up formulas through which to benefit from a practical method of personal enrichment. Teppe, in his campaign in favor of dolorism, proclaimed, "I consider extreme anguish, particularly that of somatic origin, as the perfect incitement for developing pure idealism, created anew in each individual" (318–19). That so many intellectuals should have contributed to the *Revue Doloriste* and debated such issues in the years prior to World War II reveals much about the climate of the times. Attitudes oscillate in a precarious balance between empathic solidarity with those who suffer pain and a dangerously complacent and morbid attitude that anticipates fascism.[42] The socioethical question raised about the value of pain was further complicated with the ideology and teachings of the Christian church, in its advocacy of endurance and its sense of community in Christ's sacrifice.

THE PROSTITUTE BODY, THE LIBERTINE

My dear, stir up the fire for tea, and remember that Hell is not for ladies.—*Ryder*

One may find it disquieting that the most overt appearance of a prostitute in *Ryder* comes at the hand of an adolescent. Chapter 43, "Timothy Strives Greatly with a Whore," is a caustic rendering of a dialogue in which Timothy, knowledgeable in sexual matters, sermonizes a whore "well into her forties" (184) and obsessively inquires whether she has ever repented. The rhythm of this chapter illustrates the crescendo of Timothy's despair when faced with her negative answers. His incessant questions are absurd, and his annoyance is pushed almost to the limit. There is only one moment of repentance the woman can identify, and this is when she was born and found herself thrown out into the world. Timothy engages in a doctrinaire discourse of redemption with the aim of saving her soul, urging her to join him in repentance for their frequent sinning together. The following day, after the whore is gone, almost in an epiphany, he melancholically discovers his many losses: "And in the morning he arose and, lo and behold! he discovered his loss in her, and tore at his hair as he sat on his bed, older and poorer, and he swore a great oath then, as great as he was able" (188). In this illumination, Timothy deplores his inability to distinguish a good from a bad woman, his errors, and his inability to understand women. Anxiety and guilt emerge as almost indistinguishable.

The prostitute body, the feminine commodified body par excellence, brings about confusion and simultaneously reveals a truth so far unknown. In his enraged and desperate speech, Timothy confesses the decline of a dream of omnipotence that resolves itself in impotence and abjection. The availability of the prostitute body does not make it more easily penetrable, more easily apprehensible. In a last obsessional turn, in the compulsion to repeat his numberless questions to his partner forever lost, alone in his solitude, he wonders, "Is the sleep of virgins like the sleep of other women?" (189).

There is another unmanageable and almost intractable female body in *Ryder*, the body of the libertine. It appears in the character of Molly Dance, following the chapter we have just examined, as a further variation on a large gallery of abject bodies. Molly Dance earns her living as a dog fancier who lives with her ten children and no man, "for she got her children where and when it pleased her" (191). Molly totally destabilizes the traditional family, mocks heredity, and even disrupts the prescribed patriarchal relations among mothers and children.[43]

In her encounter with Wendell, he puts her supposed knowledge of the world to test and she finally outwits him. Wendell wants to turn their meeting into a pedagogical scene in an attempt to correct her misapprehensions, clear her confusions, and show her how to distinguish right from wrong. This pedagogical scene dangerously shifts into a seduction scene in which Wendell seduces Molly with unexpectedly terrible consequences for him.

Molly tells a most fabulous parable of the creation of the world, and we are back in the domain of phantasy. Barnes inverts the biblical story of Jonah and the whale. In Molly's version, Jonah, the first man on earth, emerges from the mouth of the whale and the world begins to unfold before his eyes. Upon encountering the first woman, the human race begins. Wendell also inquires about Original Sin. Molly attributes it to man and explains why he and not woman was responsible for pulling the apple from the Tree of Life. Wendell concludes that Molly is mixed up in all things. But Molly has answers for everything: "Molly Dance I am, whichever way you take me, and that's saying more than most. My heart is nearer to my history than yours, that's the bone of contention" (198). As readers may expect, Molly and Wendell have sex, and finally, in a hilarious reversal of roles, Wendell, who wants to give her the certainty of who will be the father of her next son, suffers a terrible narcissistic blow. There is no guarantee of his fatherhood since Molly has recently had sex with other men.

Both the body of the prostitute and that of the libertine undermine traditional notions of family, heredity, and parenthood, simultaneously challenging a religious subtext in which the authority of the church in its discourses of salvation, redemption, and procreation come to be utterly destabilized. These abject bodies explode sexuality and cut it off from reproduction. What does Molly Dance's parable of creation ultimately perform? J. Hillis Miller, placing emphasis on the performative character of parables, has suggested that "Parables do not merely name the 'something' they point to by indirection or merely give the reader knowledge of it. They use words to try to make something happen in relation to the 'other' that resonates in the work. They want to get the reader from here to there. They want to make the reader cross over into the 'something' and dwell there. But the site to which parable would take the reader is something always other than itself, hence that experience of perpetual dissatisfaction" (1990b, ix). I would suggest that this perpetual dissatisfaction invokes melancholia, where the encounter with the "Other" may finally take place, even by detour or by way of indirection.

Molly Dance's phantasies crystallize in a parable that moves from a paranoid-schizoid regime (the paranoid-schizoid position predominates in the interactions among most characters) to one in which the depressive position may find room. As Klein suggests, the encounter with whole objects is characteristic of the depressive position and gives rise to concomitant depressive anxieties.

Molly Dance, by way of a parable, asserts another, nontotalizing knowledge, which discloses some of herself, far from the splitting imposed by the law (into libertine, whore, thief, bad mother). She resists disintegration and appears as whole: "Molly Dance I am, whichever way you take me, and that's saying more than most . . . it's Molly Dance to the end, and that's more than most people can say!" (198–99).

Melancholia Reborn

Yet I shall grieve, for melancholy is mortality remembered.—Amelia

There are four exceptional women in *Ryder* who rebel against the patriarchal imperative and take pleasure in sex: Sophia, Wendell's mother, Molly Dance; the anonymous Haymarket drummer of Wendell's youth (chap. 45); and Lady Terrance Bridesleep, an elderly matron. They are all independent and self-sufficient, and none has followed the path of respectable womanhood. And Dr. O'Connor embodies the formidable figure of the invert. Through all of them, Barnes shows history to be a web of power generated through and maintained by specifically gendered and class, sexual oppression. She painfully negotiates the results of her characters' confrontation with the violence of their history.

Susan Stanford Friedman, in her attempt to examine the ways in which women and men have encoded different concepts of creativity and procreativity in the metaphor of childbirth, argues that women writers have often risked the metaphor's dangerous biologism "in order to challenge fundamental binary oppositions of patriarchal ideology between word and flesh, creativity and procreativity, mind and body" and that women's use of the childbirth metaphor "demonstrates not only a 'marked' discourse distinct from phallogocentric male use of the same metaphor but also a subversive inscription of women's (pro)creativity that has existed for centuries" ([1987] 1989, 74). In what seems to me to be an all too optimistic way of reading the woman's birth metaphor, Friedman notes that "her [a woman's] procreative powers make her specially suited to her creative labors. God the Father is no longer the implicit model of creativity. Instead, the Goddess as Mother provides the paradigm for the (re)production of woman's speech" (80). There is a total absence of nurturing figures in *Ryder*, and the search for empowerment through the mother does not have a place in the novel. *Ryder* exudes a melancholic atmosphere of loneliness, despair, and abandonment. Even in the best possible scenario, Nicholas

Abraham, in a lucid and almost totally Kleinian gloss, has argued that "the mother is the infant's creature. The infant is the mother of all lost and re-created mothers. What is the filial, or matrigenic if you wish, instinct, but a constant repetition of the combat between two melancholies, present and future, between two mothers, one already gained as lost, and the other one whose total loss remains to be gained?" (1978, 346).

In *Ryder*, it is Julie who all by herself must find her way out of hell, and she succeeds in her Barnesian rendering of it. Moreover, Julie suffers from a weak self-image.[44] There is a strong sense that the deprivation of love she feels will last for years to come. In a sense, it is very difficult for her to solve the conflict of the love and uncontrollable hate she feels for her grandmother (as matriarch of the family), and this ambivalence will characterize her relations within the family.[45]

We find in *Ryder* a discourse on the maternal body and also one on the lost adolescent and infantile female body on its way to full-fledged femininity, one that is and can only be guaranteed on the basis of its physical reproduction in flesh and language. Barnes's rebellion against the gender and sexual codes that contemporary culture lays out for women is writ large over a background of misery, distress, melancholy, and family warfare. In *Ryder*, childbirth remains inscribed in the institution of motherhood and of society at large, its meaning being overdetermined by cultural, psychological, ideological, and political factors that contribute to its production and circulation. Barnes also puts to test in the novel the extent to which creative activities—writing and drawing in her case—may be precluded by the exercise of motherhood.[46]

In chapter 46, "Ryder—His Race," Wendell engages in a monologue with a central question, "What is woman?" (206). He speculates with innumerable questions about sexual difference: "Wherein comes that of her which we are not? What destroys our reason in her, when we see it enter her as we would, and come forth as she will? What in her, like a shadow jackal, preys upon the mound of our accomplishment, dragging off that of it we thought most rotten with defeat, to make of it an halter and a noose? For man rides the monster of civilization, but to woman goes the shoe cast of it, in which is the exact record of that journey" (206). Wendell associates women with dark melancholy[47] and, inconclusive as to the true nature of women, he goes to visit Lady Terrance Bridesleep, "a woman of wit" (106) well into her sixties. Lady Terrance had never been a mother, and her ancient wisdom knows of happiness and sorrow, joy and pain. Concerning the pain and suffering of mothers, she argues: "In youth . . . the suffering of the mother is compared to the suffering of Christ; one becomes older, and the suffering is like another's, and one becomes old and the suffering is like everyone's: and one comes to die" (209). Wendell, in one of his most megalomaniac speeches, tells Lady Terrance that she will come to be the "Father of All Things," of a new race, the Ryders: "My children shall come forth, grow, rise, decline and fall in a manner hithertofore unknown to man" (210). By the end of the chapter, they have had sex and Wendell, in his delirium, imagines that he will be father again. Lady Terrance listens to him without turning a hair, she knows Wendell too well to think that his "ambition [is] too heavy for mortal" (211).

At the end of the novel, chapter 48, "Elisha in Love with the Maiden," is devoted to Elisha, the son of Wendell and Kate.[48] In a dream, Elisha thinks about his origins as a bastard and rebels against his father. He wonders about that secret place in his father, "not telling, hiding it forever, hinting the story and hiding the proof" (221). Elisha re-creates in his mind the beginnings of a Familienroman: "Would he have been thus had he gone away like other children? Been brought out of Egypt? But Egypt was the mother wound, the festering that gave off music, and whining, and the power to withstand" (222). In this troubled story of origins, only his mother steps out of the phantasy and appears in the realness of her "experiment-shocked body, heavy of belly, the stiff legs, a distorted shape of death" (222).[49]

In a nightmarish dream, Elisha asks Wendell what a woman is and whether she is good or evil. Wendell has no answers; he only wants to teach his son what a great man is and how he can become one. As to women, they are all evil: "They see too much from the start. . . . They look into their hearts and in their hearts is the whole drama of man" (225–26). This dream places Elisha in an oedipal constellation that distresses him. Uncertain as to his origins, he can only identify a mother who suffers in a very peculiar home. Nevertheless, he is doomed to repeat Wendell's gestures—"playing Beethoven; that had something to do with his father again" (221)—except that he takes revenge in not playing as his father would wish him to do.

Paranoia and Familienroman

Ryder has often been read as autobiography. In the biographical key to the novel, Julie, Amelia and Wendell Ryder's daughter, is taken to represent

Barnes.[50] I want to suggest that we may also read *Ryder* as the inversion of the Freudian notion of the *Familienroman*, one that both partakes of and parodically diverts from the patriarchal myth of origins that Freud places in the neurotic's imaginary. Freud reports that small events in the child's life make him or her feel dissatisfied. This fuels criticism of the child's parents and the thought that in some respects other parents might be preferable. Freud locates the origin of the child's process of estrangement from his or her parents, what he calls *Familienroman der Neurotiker*, in the child's feeling of being slighted: "His sense that his own affection is not being fully reciprocated then finds vent in the idea, often consciously recollected later from early childhood, of being a step-child or an adopted child" ([1909b] 1953, 238). This tendency, fueled by the low opinion the child has of his parents, results in their replacement with others, "who, as a rule, are of a higher social standing" (239). Freud also reminds us that this activity, which persists beyond puberty, starts in children's play and later finds its best expression in daydreaming.

In other words, it is in phantasy that these reversals of role models are effected. Freud, with the accuracy and subtlety of a literature lover, expresses his concern for the issue of technique: "The technique used in developing phantasies like this (which are, of course, conscious at this period) depends upon the ingenuity and the material which the child has at his disposal. There is also the question of whether the phantasies are worked out with greater or less effort to obtain verisimilitude. This stage is reached at a time at which the child is still ignorant of the sexual determinants of procreation" ([1909b] 1953, 239).

At the crossroads of the literary production of phantasy and the phantasy production of literature, Djuna Barnes finds a space in which to effect her personal reversal of roles, her inversion of the Freudian expectations in the romancing of patriarchy. Barnes displaces the neurotic urge to build up a family romance and replaces it with a ruthless narration of facts that are not embellished by the workings of memory. Barnes's experiments in technique are carefully worked out both to undermine and grant verisimilitude to a colossal parodical effort.

The novel's main concerns are those of filiation, of the legitimacy and illegitimacy of any filiation, for Barnes knows all too well that, as Freud puts it, " '*pater semper incertus est*,' while the mother is '*certissima*' " ([1909b] 1953, 239). Freud comes close to saying that family romances are the very stuff of fiction, for "if there are any other particular interests at work they can direct the course to be taken by the family romance; for its many-sidedness and its great range of applicability enable it to meet every sort of requirement" (240).[51] The apparent hostility and ingratitude underneath these stories is not such. The turning away from the child's actual parents is rather a re-turning to the parents in whom he or she believed in the early years of childhood, and "his phantasy is no more than the expression of a regret that those happy days have gone" (241).

Barnes effects a radical inversion of the Familienroman plot by disclosing the legitimacy and illegitimacy of Wendell Ryder's children in a crude hyperrealistic plot. The story becomes entangled with questions of who is legitimate and who is a bastard, and the narrative is contaminated with a discourse on the impurities of the family and the threat it poses to the individual. Barnes, through her analysis of the patriarchal family as a flawed institution, leaves no way open to idealization and regeneration in the claustrophobic domestic space of the family. Nonetheless, with her splendid wit Barnes parodically enacts a minimal scene of Familienroman in chapter 48, where, as we have seen, the Familienroman comes out of the voice of Elisha, bastard son of Kate and Wendell. Not even narrative can grant him a space of stability in his quest for origins and his inquiry into sexual difference.

It is my contention that Barnes in Ryder ventriloquizes voices as a way to convey her innermost thoughts and ideas. By ventriloquize I mean her sustained effort to imitate with a difference, appropriating voices to undermine narrative and even legal authority. For how else can she tell stories about polygamy, rape, child abuse, and infringement of the law?[52] Her rhetorical strategies have the effect of producing resistance to the law. Barnes deploys a vast array of paranoid defenses that, mostly through splitting, allow her characters to find a way out of their predicament.

In a case history, Freud analyzes his analysand Schreber's "feminine wishful phantasy" ([1911] 1953, 47, 48, 55) as "an outburst of homosexual impulse" (12, 45) and as "a passive homosexual wishful phantasy" (47). In other words, it functions as an unconscious mask adopted by Schreber to ward off reprisals from the God-sun-father figure in his delusions. Joan Riviere calls womanliness a "mask" worn "both to hide the possession of masculinity and to avert the reprisals expected if she was found to possess it" (1929, 306). In this respect, we may wonder in what ways Schreber's mission of "redemption," which "must be preceded by his transformation into a woman," and Wendell Ryder's feminine identifications may compare with the masquerade.

In the novel, Wendell, given as he is to innumerable acts of reproduction, has "His children flocking on him every hand" (62). He proclaims: "For this I replenish the world. I have the spirit and the works. And though a child forget a father before a mother, between the lot of them I shall come to memory from time to time" (160). His manic desire to be eternal knows no limit. It is clear that Wendell has a deep feminine identification that shows in his envy and desire to reproduce himself ad infinitum. In a case just opposite to Riviere's theorization, and in which manliness comes to be at stake, Wendell masquerades masculinity in his constant and repetitive virile display, in his flaunting of his procreative potency, in his ars amandi rhetoric: "To Wendell there was no age to a willing woman, the willingness spoke of fecundity" (207). Wendell's anxiety about female fecundity is present precisely in the display of his hyperbolic sexuality.

Multiple narrative voices refer throughout the novel to virginity as "that sweet and lost condition" (21), and there is a morbid curiosity about it.[53] This climaxes in chapter 45, in O'Connor's conversation with Wendell, where the latter identifies with the innocence of a child in a manic attempt to escape death. Passion is reduced to mechanical reproduction and is bound to the compulsion to repeat. The death drive is at work in a narrative that aptly fuses the conservative instincts with its opposite death drives and where the latter finally triumphs.

In the Schreber case, Freud also problematizes the distinction between normalcy and paranoia. He does so by way of a detour in which he places the work of mourning center stage as a primary psychic mechanism: "It is certain that in normal mental life (and not only in periods of mourning) we are constantly detaching our libido in this way from people or from other objects without falling ill. When Faust freed himself from the world by uttering his curses, the result was not a paranoia or any other neurosis but simply a certain general frame of mind" ([1911] 1953, 72). Melancholia and paranoia, in their abnormal quality, share common traits from a similar libidinal economy.

Melanie Klein's definitive work on melancholia and manic-depressive states suggests that melancholia and paranoia may find their way out of the paranoid-schizoid position and into the depressive position if sadistic impulses, paranoid anxieties, and their corresponding defense mechanisms are not too strong. In *Ryder*, splitting, idealization (of Wendell's procreative powers), and denial (of external reality) are predominant. Depressive anxiety cannot find a place in a paranoid economy in which objects are not perceived as whole. The equation of woman with a womb is most telling.

The womb is an artifact for the production of new life, and it is also the artifact through which the inside of the mother's body is projected out into the world. The troubled relationship between inside and outside is constantly at stake.

The last chapter of Ryder presents a moving conversation between Wendell and his mother. Wendell's portrait is one of a desperate man, "his face wet with unusual tears, looking with terror under his eyebrows at his mortal mother" (237). The room they are in smells of corruption due to the impending death of Sophia, and a mortuary atmosphere envelops mother and child. Sophia's wisdom leaves Wendell speechless. She warns him of the problems of "nature" when facing the law—"you are nature, all of you, all of you, and nature is terrible when the law hunts it down" (238)—and cautions him that "A woman is what she loves" (238).

The concern with life and death, with the instinct for self-preservation and the death drive in their intimate fusion, emerges simultaneously with a concern for shape. Implicit in the metamorphoses of the human body from birth to death, there is ultimately a concern with the changing of shapes and the flourishing, decline, and dissolution of forms. Barnes's tribute to her own modernist project crystallizes in a discourse on shapes that carry the mark of death. Sophia tells Wendell that " 'the heart of a man is an insulting shape. That shape,' she continued, 'is an affront, there's something monstrous about it, obscene. It is a shape conceived outside of nature, and that is always terrible' " (238). This monstrous shape is dark and somber in the case of women. Wendell speaks of the "mad obscurity of the female heart" (125) in chapter 29, precisely when he brings back the issue of names, naming and, at this particular point, nicknames. Wendell is trying to "give his version of Amelia's courting" (125), and we come to know that Amelia is the master of nicknames. Barnes gives a hilarious version of how Wendell fell in love with Amelia's exceptional linguistic skills.

By the end of the novel, Amelia's portrait of Wendell also insists on the otherness of his shape: "He has a great sickness that is unknown to other men. . . . He is nature in its other shape. . . . He is a deed that must be committed" (241). Wendell is abhorrent to nature. And, finally, just before the scene of his foretold death, we are told that "everything and its shape became clear in the dark" (242). Barnes enigmatically poses the unsolvable question of the human shape. I take this as evidence of her concern with literary form, which is permanently refashioned out of human creativity.

Wendell is on the verge of committing a melancholic suicide: "I must kill myself . . . I must die and I cannot" (241). Wendell has lost all he had, women and children. "I have unfathered myself" (239), he proclaims in his shameless self-display. And there is something of Wendell that is forever lost in Sophia, entombed in his mother's corpse. Wendell's horror lies in the abrupt discovery of the ultimate truth about life. His terror of mortality is clearly bound up with his excessive sexuality, whose aim was always to produce new subjects for death. Wendell cannot bear the violence of the gaze, and he collapses in an almost paranoid delirium.[54] In deadly combat, he almost drowns but finally rises. And the question remains: "And whom should he disappoint?" (242).

Literally Damned

The painful affection [is] . . . orphan of any representation.—Augustin Jeanneau

Patricia Yaeger has raised an important question that we should try to answer in the context of *Ryder*: "Since we are creatures who delight in reinventing our bodies through elaborate social/epistemological rituals, what does it mean 'to be trapped in a natural function'?" (1992, 265). What does it mean for the women in *Ryder* to be trapped in a natural function? Female reproductive functions are animalistic, a helpless and univocal transfer of the female body in its passage to culture. We may understand that in *Ryder* the symbolic equation literally appears as the death drive compulsively reappears under the guise of reproductive anxiety, in the disruption and destabilization of form that mimics the laboring female body and the irresolution of the work of mourning, emerging in the pervasive cadence of melancholia. Barnes's *Ryder* is fully enmeshed in a culture of the death drive that exhibits aversion to and terror of human mechanical reproduction, a disillusioned culture that foretells the advent of the war.

The work of mourning and the silent workings of the death drive in the state of melancholia parallel the labor of giving birth and extend far beyond. I believe that the discourse of refusal to conceive, the discourse of sterility, is omnipresent in a modernist culture of melancholia.[55] Sterility and the refusal to conceive are only metaphors that do not allude to biological or naturalistic ideas of the body—female or male—but rather want to emphasize the impossibility of finding a sense of direction in existence by reproducing or replicating an individual, be it by way of procreation or by recourse to a work that is designed to remain for the future.[56] During modernism, anxieties about reproduction take on a charged historical specificity.

Djuna Barnes wants to remain "masqué" as a writer, in the intensity of her writing and her art, in her myriad of exploding voices, not in the petty remainders of human fallibility. This is probably why, in a ritual of self-immolation, she burned most of her personal papers before dying. This is probably why she categorically refused mechanical reproduction.[57]

In *Ryder*, the female body appears as torn and fragmented; it returns as a corpse. The female and other abject bodies do not only appear as an image represented but as sites on which cultural tradition has been inscribed. Barnes's technique does not simply retrieve the past from the storehouse of memory; rather, in doing so, she operates through an active process of deciphering cultural inscriptions, which unveils the workings of power and its material effects.

In the whole of Barnes's oeuvre, gender and sexuality are destabilized. Even when there may be a violent attempt to reinscribe the heterosexist binary by enforcing it in the design of the narrative, there is a parallel drive to undermine it. In *Ryder*, Barnes's disruptive narrative contests readerly expectations and explodes in illicit forms such as, poetry, storytelling, fable, dramatic monologue, and a variety of styles. Characters such as Sophia, Julie, Kate, Molly Dance, and Dr. O'Connor strive to flee from the melancholia of gender. Their joint effort subverts the underlying oedipal plot of the narrative. In the collapse of Wendell Ryder, in the impossibility of finding an answer to the oedipal question posed at the end of the novel, "Whom should he disappoint now?" (242), Barnes exonerates us of the teleological imperative dictated by the cruelest superego of the melancholic. In the abrupt breaking of the signifying chain, in the total absence of answers, lies the superb disruptive potential of Barnes's texts.

12

Melancholia, the New Negro, and the Fear
of Modernity: Forms Sublime and Denigrated
in Countee Cullen's Writings

In spite of myself . . . I find that I am actuated by a strong sense of race consciousness. This grows upon me, I find, as I grow older, and although I struggle against it, it colors my writing, I fear, in spite of everything I can do. There may have been many things in my life that have hurt me, and I find that the surest relief from these hurts is in writing.
—Countee Cullen

The white man is convinced that the Negro is a beast; if it is not the length of the penis, then it is the sexual potency that impresses him. Face to face with this man who is "different from himself," he needs to defend himself. In other words, to personify the Other. The Other will become the mainstay of his preoccupations and his desires.
—Frantz Fanon

And if there is any group which is both a problem for itself and a problem for others, and which needs a movement for the solving of both it is the American Negro.—Countee Cullen

In the acclaimed anthology The new Negro ([1925] 1968), Alain Locke attempts to define the emergence of the New Negro as a new figure in the American national landscape, and to reflect upon the larger issue of race consciousness. Locke makes an important statement when he argues that "Subtly the conditions that are molding a New Negro are molding a new American attitude" ([1925] 1968, 8). This means that blacks were defining themselves within the framework of American life and culture and not within a framework created by themselves. And, if in one sense this acknowledges blacks' progressive acquisition of their full rights of citizenship, it also problematizes and to some extent subdues the possibility of a black American nationalism. At the root of the New Negro movement there was what Gerald Early has identified as "a kind of race pride and a sense of group identification that made one a distinct flavor in the American melting pot" (Cullen 1991, 37). Countee Cullen himself, in his "The League of Youth" (1923), also focuses on the "group effect" that increased access to and respect for education is having on the black community. He writes: "it may be that this increased respect for education is selfish in the case of each individual without any concern for the group effect, but that is neither here nor there, the main point to be considered is that it is working a powerful group effect" (167). The almost utopian rhetoric of optimism in his emphasis on altruism and solidarity seeks alternatives to the paranoid-schizoid pattern of relations in the large group in a new reparative morality of depression. Quoting from James Weldon Johnson's prophetic poem "To America," Cullen launches his challenge: "I hope this League will accept my challenge and will answer in the new spirit which seems to be animating youth everywhere—the spirit of what is just and fair and honorable" (168).[1] There is a sense of injustice and dishonor between the elder generations of black and white Americans, and Cullen is calling for a change.

In the last epigraph that opens this section, Cullen by way of an identification with the aggressor introjects the idea that the Negro is "both a problem for itself and for others." In this paranoid-schizoid internalized regime of object relations, the chances of achieving a morality of reparation are drastically curtailed from the start. Cullen exhorts the young to get rid of "passive acquiescence" and move on to "active resistance" in the field of religious belief and, by extension, in all aspects of life. In other words, Cullen, drawing on a strong sense of identification with his disenfranchised group, advocates a politics of active mourning in lieu of one of passive melancholia. Since the black race's many losses are inscribed in its cultural memory there is no need to enumerate them here. In Cullen's feverish discourse, the traces of segregation and discrimination remain encrypted in a short fable of racial hatred and opprobrium, with a colored girl, its protagonist, barred from entering an art school in France "because her presence might be objectionable to certain people who would be along" (1923, 167). Cullen calls for action and harbors some hope for the future, but in his almost utopian dream of group cohesion and in the ideal of interracial brotherhood—since, with astounding naïveté but echoing science (Darwin, Bryan), he reminds us that "we all spring from a common progenitor" (168)—he seems to forget that aggression and retaliation are at the basis of sociality and that large group morality follows paranoid-schizoid lines.

Stephen Frosh has suggested that racism is, among other things, "an expression of a deep and vicious fear of modernity" (1989, 232). In his view, ingrained in the racist psyche is a repudiation of modernity, of multiplicity and heterogeneity: "Racist ideology is the building of a fort, and racist actions, an army to go with it—to defend, frequently through assault, the integrity of the disintegrated self" (233). Frosh's Kleinian reading of the racist ego is in line with my reflections on the phobic character of modernism and the emergence of phobic objects that polarize projections coming from outside.[2] He writes: "The racist ego is one which has to deal with the violence of unfulfilled internal desires in the context of a world which is experienced as threatening rather than containing, as confusing rather than secure. Faced with this, the experience of inner destructiveness is defended against by projection on to external objects, selected for this purpose by their visibility as socially legitimized objects of denigration. The affective content of this projection is envy, regarded by the Kleinians as a pure culture of the death drive—a spoiling hatred which is directed at one and the same time against the admired (for its fantasized cohesion and power) and the despised (because it contains the projected rejects of the self)" (237).[3] In the case of Cullen, his status as a legitimized object of denigration as a black gay man makes him a double target for racism and homophobia. His allegiance to the tradition in poetry also makes him doubly vulnerable to critiques from black and white readers and critics.

In a reading of racism and racial aggression through the post-Kleinian idea of psychotic states, Michael Rustin has argued that "The mechanisms of psychotic thought find in racial categorizations an ideal container. These mechanisms include the paranoid splitting of objects into the loved and hated, the suffusion of thinking processes by intense, unrecognized emotion, confusion between self and object due to the splitting of the self and massive projective identification, and hatred of reality and truth" (1991, 62).[4] Furthermore, in racism projective identification is a crucial mechanism at stake in the attribution of deprecatory and degrading traits to communities and groups of individuals. Manichaean versions of racial difference have a strong paranoid foundation since they do not function to identify differences but rather to channel and align feelings of positive and negative identification.[5] Splitting, idealization, and manic denial are at work in the construction of race as a category of alterity and abjection. Rustin has argued that the most active process at work in the racism of dominant groups "is the projection of negative, repressed, or inaccessible aspects of the individual and social self. Cultures of racial domination, since they are founded on greed, cruelty and the exploitation of weakness, will have many such hateful states of mind to get rid of somewhere" (66).

Much of Cullen's poetry reveals how indebted he felt to the British Romantic tradition and how close he felt to other white poets, but his racial poetry specifically draws inspiration from the rhythms and voices of his African American heritage. Cullen is obsessed with the idea of form and with the issue of the container as mold. His paranoid anxieties about the possibility of closure and fixity, and about any predetermined category that might be imposed on the artist, and by extension the individual, reveal early anxiety situations at play throughout his writing. It is my aim in this chapter to read Cullen's works with recourse to Klein's insights on splitting (of the object and the ego) and the oscillation between the paranoid-schizoid and the depressive mode of object relations. This inquiry will lead to interrogate the specific relationship between the subject's melancholia and the melancholia associated with the race. Can we speak of a sense of collective melancholia in Cullen's writings?

Harlem: The Race Capital

In the 1920s, Harlem became the mecca for Afro-Americans from all over the United States. It constituted the largest black community in the country and attracted many young artists and professionals who were instrumental in the formation of an urban minority culture that flourished in the Harlem Renaissance. In 1925, James Weldon Johnson wrote his essay "Harlem: The culture capital" for Alain Locke's anthology The new Negro ([1925] 1968). Johnson describes Harlem as "the greatest Negro city in the world" (Locke [1925] 1968, 301) and points with racial pride to the atmosphere of harmony between the races, the opportunities for employment, and the absence of crime. The essay ends on this same note of optimism with Johnson's firm belief in the permanence of Harlem as a model of cultural and economic success.[6]

In his preface to The New Negro, Alain Locke described Harlem as the "progressive Negro community of the American metropolis" ([1925] 1968, xvi). He wrote: "In Harlem, Negro life is seizing upon its first chances for group expression and self-determination. It is—or promises at least to be—a race capital. That is why our comparison is taken with those nascent centers of folk expression and self-determination which are playing a creative part in the world today. Without pretense to their political significance, Harlem has the same role to play for the New Negro as Dublin has had for the new Ireland or Prague for the new Czechoslovakia" (7). But, as some critics have remarked, interracial relations resulting from the newly awakened interest in the Negro were not always as "free" as the spirit of the times might suggest. The Harlem nightclubs were a case in point. Drawn by the talent of entertainers like Duke Ellington and other jazz artists, white New Yorkers and visitors toured the Negro cabarets in search of the new. The vogue of the New Negro manifested itself in the affluence of the whites who frequented the district's nightclubs. Paradoxical as it may appear, many of these fancy clubs were exclusively for whites. Eventually, this fad turned against itself when Negro proprietors, eager to attract white audiences, began to exclude their colored customers. The Negro thus became a performer and a spectacle on the stage for mostly white audiences that could afford to pay to be entertained à la mode. As Eric Garber has pointed out, "Harlem and its inhabitants became a symbol of the 'natural' human consciousness, unrestrained and uncontaminated by civilization. A trip to Harlem represented an escape to a primitive, exotic community where the natives were uninhibited, passionate and animalistic" (1983, 9). In the cultural imaginary of the West, the black man becomes for the white man a screen for the projection of his repressed phantasies.

The Harlem Renaissance has also been identified as a swing toward Romanticism that projects a distorted image of the Negro experience. Edward Margolies writes: "No slum dweller, sharecropper, or washroom attendant experiences life more intensely for being exotic, poor, ignorant or Negro. Whatever pleasure he derives from his social activities takes up only a minute proportion of his energies, so absorbed is he with the exigencies of physical survival. Harlem is not—and never was—a happy jungle, and to describe it as such only perpetuates the minstrel stereotype in another form" (1968, 31). But the complexities of the black experience in the bourgeois context of the Harlem Renaissance cannot be limited to a discussion of race and class consciousness or a discussion of the emergence of new aesthetic black forms parallel to those of alternative sexualities. As it has been repeatedly argued, Countee Cullen is one of the representatives of this swing toward Romanticism, or rather toward the British Romantic tradition. At that time, prey to the contradictions, ambivalences, and challenges that the impact of the "new" was causing in the lives of men and women, Cullen wrote: "Just now I can really imagine nothing quite so emblazoned with interest as being a Negro. It is to be à la mode: and who would be the fashion should remember that in a slip shod world to be the vogue is also to be peculiar, and apart" (1927, 272). This figure of the New Negro will constitute itself as the emblem of the Harlem Renaissance. At the same time, Harlem's ghettoization as a bulwark that preserves black heritage and culture is inadvertently oblivious to the inscription of misogyny and homophobia as pure cultures of the death drive in its material practices.

If literary modernism was a heterogeneous movement that radically questioned the nature of modern selves and problematized the means whereby "self" could be expressed, it is understandable that in different modernisms strategies of linguistic mimicry and racial masquerade were widespread among black and white writers alike.[7] The flexibility that the proliferation of styles in modernism offered allowed artists and writers to play self-consciously with issues of identity, sexuality, and community. A model of the self that is autonomous, integral, and continuous, what T. S. Eliot in "Tradition and the individual talent" called "the substantial unity of the soul" ([1919] 1958, 9), was being contested on different fronts. Thus, in African American writing, the notion of the mask as form and the mastery of the minstrel mask, in its questioning personality as indivisible and consistent, constitutes a crucial formative moment in black modernism. In Houston A. Baker's rereading of the minstrel mask for African American modernism, he argues that "The minstrel mask is a governing object in a ritual of *non-sense*. . . . The device is designed to remind white consciousness that black men and women are *mis-speakers* bereft of humanity . . . [and] the *sound* emanating from the mask reverberates through a white American discursive universe as the sound of the Negro" (1987, 21–22). I see in Baker's important argument a doubly subversive maneuver that encompasses both the individual as nonunity by his troping the psychoanalytic split self (the black self would figure here as equally split but with a stronger sense of alienation) by recourse to the mask and also black speech as a double discourse (one that, so to speak, "sounds" in excess of signification) that creeps through the crevices of the high modernist edifice.

We may read Baker's arguments together with Michael North's (1994) incisive account of how modernism mimicked the strategies of dialect and aspired to become a dialect itself. In an unpaginated preface, this critic holds that "dialect became the prototype for the most radical representational strategies of English language modernism" (n.p.). In North's view, African American writing had to fight its way out of the prison of white-created black dialect, and in this sense African American writing and Anglo-American modernism can be discussed in this shared context, which allows us to reflect on their mutual influences in the formation of their singular configurations. For North, "The new voice that American culture acquired in the 1920s, the decade of jazz, stage musicals, talking pictures, and aesthetic modernism, was very largely a black one. In music, on stage, and in film, white artists dubbed a black voice and often wore . . . a black mask. Because this mask, and the voice that issued from it, already embodied white America's quite various feelings about nature and convention, it became an integral part of the cultural and technical innovation of the 1920s" (7–8).

But racial masquerade was "officially" allowable only for whites. As James Weldon Johnson observes, it was deemed "quite seemly for a white person to represent a Negro on the stage, but a violation of some inner code for a Negro to represent a white person" ([1930] 1969, 191). And even if linguistic mimicry could be performed by black and white writers alike the possibility of this double discourse and the effects of its subversive potential were radically different from the start. Social conditions, material practices, histories, audiences, and specific contextual circumstances (from those of transatlantic Anglo-American modernism to those of Harlem or the blacks of the diaspora) determine how to read what is designed as disruptive and in the end may be co-opted by the institutions of modernism, by the apparatuses of production, commodification, and distribution and ultimately by the marketplace. The ideologies of modernism come to perform multiple operations that in a complex dynamics of introjection-projection and aggression-retaliation, and inscribed as they are in the social, cannot escape the psychic as their most contested terrain.

If I am going to be a poet at all, I am going to be a POET and not NEGRO POET. That is what has hindered the development of artists among us. Their one note has been the concern with their race. That is all very well, none of us can get away from it. I cannot at times. You will see it in my verse. The consciousness of this is too poignant at times. I cannot escape it. But what I mean is this: I shall not write of negro subjects for the purpose of propaganda. That is not what a poet is concerned with. Of course, when the emotion rising out of the fact that I am a negro is strong, I express it. But that is another matter.—Countee Cullen

Cullen's open acknowledgment that he is bounded by his race, that his personal freedom is compromised by a priori conditions he has not chosen, causes him to react violently against the simplistic reductionism of the taxonomy, against the convenient classification of his poetry as Negro poetry and of his writings and opinions as collective statements. His fierce individualism is embodied in a distinctive voice that vibrates in its singularity, and also in unison with other voices from his generation, and that shifts from univocality to plurivocality at his wish.

Embedded in the rhetoric of this much quoted statement is the piercing awareness that Cullen cannot escape from the consciousness of his race. He is completely and inescapably inscribed in its cultures, as much as his language is inexorably culturally inflected. If race is here the unwanted container for different parts of the self, we may as well raise the question of how the relationship between container and contained is articulated in Cullen's texts and to what extent the notion of literary form, in its constant refashioning by the writer, may be a more apt container for Cullen's paranoid anxieties.[8]

The year 1903 saw the publication of W. E. B. Du Bois's *The souls of black folk* and the birth of Countee Cullen. In his work, Du Bois gives a vivid portrayal of the black American situation and speaks of the dilemma of "double consciousness," the black man's sense that he is both an American and an Other. Du Bois describes this experience of alienation from white society as the feeling of being "shut out from their world by a vast veil" ([1903] 1990, 8). He comes to know that he was wrong to think that there is simply a true inner world of experience—a soul—that constitutes personhood. As an African American, his identity cannot simply be defined from within; who he is depends on how he is viewed by a racist society, a society that thinks it sees him even as it "veils" him. Du Bois's own experience of racial discrimination is thus at the heart of his theorization about the Negro condition. He writes: "After the Egyptian and Indian, the Greek and Roman, the Teuton and Mongolian, the Negro is a sort of seventh son, born with a veil, and gifted with second-sight in this American world. It is a peculiar sensation, this double-consciousness, this sense of always looking at one's self through the eyes of others, of measuring one's soul by the tape of a world that looks on in amused contempt and pity. One never feels his two-ness—an American, a Negro; two souls, two thoughts, two unreconciled strivings; two warring ideals in one dark body, whose dogged strength alone keeps it from being torn asunder" (8–9). For Du Bois, the history of the American Negro is the history of the struggle to attain self-conscious manhood, to merge his double self into a better and truer self.

Cullen was a precocious talent in the literary and artistic beginnings of the Harlem Renaissance. He was called by his contemporaries the poet laureate of the movement.[9] This does not necessarily mean that assessing his contribution to modernism is an easy task, since his aesthetic paradigm does not openly subscribe to the new ideas about race consciousness and writing of the Harlem Renaissance or to the high modernist poetic credo but rather is situated at the crossroads between the British Romantic tradition and the several idioms of modernism. There was a time when some Harlem writers were closer to their white counterparts in the modernist avant-garde, an avant-garde far from the ideas and postulates put forward by high modernist writers such as Eliot and Pound.[10] Nevertheless, the differences between high modernism and the Harlem Renaissance became increasingly marked as both movements gained momentum with a significant body of writing in their respective sociocultural scenarios. Countee Cullen never felt close to the experimental and avant-garde trend in modernism. An analysis of his poetry reveals how much he felt indebted to the British Romantic tradition (Keats, Shelley) in which he had been trained, but he will achieve a distinctive poetic voice drawing from diverse sources, from his proximity to poets like Edna St. Vincent Millay to his admiration for the French symbolists Baudelaire, Rimbaud, and Verlaine. In his racial poetry, a substantial part of his work, Cullen introduces rhythms, echoes, and voices from his African heritage and comes closer to the poetics of the Harlem Renaissance.

Since a rhetoric of failure has traditionally accompanied the critical evaluation of Cullen's work (especially his latest work), Houston A. Baker, in the only book-length study to date of Cullen's poetry, has raised the question, "What is the task of the Black American author and by what standards is he to be judged?" (1974, 14). Baker finds in Cullen a romantic mode that was not attuned to the more realistic trend of the times: "Cullen's canon reflects all of those characteristics and contain the distinction between a dark romanticism of frustrated love and infidelity and a bright one of harmony with his overall conception of the poet as a man who dwells above mundane realities; for Cullen, the poet is the dream-keeper" (18). The poet is thus removed from the idea of poetry (and art) as social action and from the poet's task of intervening in the political.

Baker identifies Cullen as "the first to achieve monumental success as an author and to substantially express what many of the Renaissance writers felt" (1974, 24). Baker holds that the Harlem Renaissance was simply the artistic expression of the sociopolitical activities of black Americans during the 1920s. Its end was integration into the mainstream, and its means were not very different from those of white creative artists. In Cullen's writings, Baker finds some of the strongest statements on black artistic freedom that emerged from the Renaissance: "His apologies can surely be seen as lamentations that America produced a kind of schizophrenia in the Black artist and made it impossible for him to translate its highest ideals into a unified and consistent body of poetry that would rank with the canons of John Keats and Percy Shelley" (30). Later, in *Modernism and the Harlem Renaissance* (1987), Baker would relate Countee Cullen's and Claude McKay's writings, among others, to their ancestral origins in the minstrel mask: "The trick of McKay and Cullen was . . . the denigration of form—a necessary ('forced,' as it were) adoption of the standard that results in an effective *blackening*" (85).[11] For Baker, minstrel dialect is one of the languages of rebellion against social and linguistic tyranny, against the violence perpetrated on blacks.

Nathan Huggins reports that, "it was Cullen who told Langston Hughes that he wanted to be a poet, not a Negro poet" (1971, 208). Cullen was painfully aware that exclusion on racial grounds benefited some by restricting competition from others and indeed by the idea of superiority embodied in the principles of exclusion. If, on one side in his racial poetry, he struggled to overturn the role of white society in creating conditions for, and legitimizing, racial domination, on the other he aspired to fulfill the criteria of excellence set up by white writers and audiences. Cullen felt that there was very little free space for him to develop his creative potential between traditionalism and the New Negro modernism. We may as well read Cullen's ambivalent movement back and forth from a defiant subject matter in his racial poems to the traditional of love, religion, and death, in their interaction with conventional form, far beyond a strictly literary conflict, insofar as we consider high modernism's prompt identification of African Americans (and Africans) with primitivism and unrestrained impulses. Cullen was simply unable to circumscribe his writing to the rigid either/or alternative between allegiance to the forms of the race and allegiance to tradition in poetry. Cullen's rejection of dialect as inimical to his aesthetic project can be read in line with Michael North's argument that African American poets of the new generation saw "dialect is a 'chain.' In the version created by the white minstrel tradition, it is a constant remainder of the literal unfreedom of slavery and of the political and cultural repression that followed emancipation. Both symbol and actuality, it stands for a most intimate invasion whereby the dominant actually attempts to create the thoughts of the subordinate by providing it speech" (1994, 11).

Cullen's relationship with Africa is at the center of "Heritage," one of his best-known poems. Africa remains the good internal object (mother) forever lost. The non-European elements in his poetry can be read as a romantic escape that strives to challenge the dominance of Anglo-American culture over other, noncosmopolitan modernisms (the West Indies, Africa) and its concomitant forms of violence.

Cullen saw the double obligation of being both a Negro and an American as a construction of his personal and creative freedom. In this sense, we may read the following lines as some sort of response to Du Bois's "double consciousness": "The poet writes out of his experience, whether it be personal or vicarious, and as these experiences differ among other poets so do they differ among Negro poets; for the double obligation of being both a Negro and American is not so unified as we are often led to believe. A survey of the work of Negro poets will show that the individual diversifying ego transcends the synthesizing hue" (1927c, xii). This passage comes from Cullen's own black poetry anthology, *Caroling dusk*, which was published in 1927. In his introduction, which can be read as Cullen's program for what he privileges as the work of Negro poets over generic Negro poetry, his obsession with the form and the issue of the container as mold is omnipresent. He writes: "Negro poetry, it seems to me, in the sense that we speak of Russian, French or Chinese poetry, must emanate from one country other than this, in some language other than our own. Moreover, the attempt to corral the outbursts of the ebony muse into some definite mold to which all poetry by Negroes will conform seems altogether futile and aside from the facts" (1927b, xi). Cullen's blunt rejection of any policing of the borders of these new poetic forms produced by black writers expresses an almost paranoid anxiety over the idea of closure, of fixity, and over any predetermined category that might be imposed on the artist and, by extension, on the individual. The dilemma that Cullen poses is just as crucial and relevant today. He addresses both his audience and future audiences when he wonders whether there is a way for black poets to write free and oblivious of their race.[12] This is a similar concern to the one that, in the sphere of gender, Virginia Woolf was raising in A room of one's own, for "it is fatal for anyone who writes to think of their sex. It is fatal to be a man or woman pure and simple; one must be woman-manly or man-womanly" ([1929] 1957, 156–57).

Is there a way for gay black writers to write and be read as writers tout court? In Cullen's passionate rhetoric, there is also a sense of accuracy and precision and a strong desire to affect critics and readers alike. He argues: "As heretical as it may sound, there is the probability that Negro poets, dependent as they are on the English language, may have more to gain from the rich background of English and American poetry than from any nebulous atavistic yearnings towards an African inheritance. Some of the poets herein represented will eventually find inclusion in any discriminatingly ordered anthology of American verse, and there will be no reason for giving such selections the needless distinction of a separate section marked Negro verse" (1927b, xii). He wants to make an almost impossible point for the achievement of freedom and civilization, which, as Freud was contemporaneously teaching, is always at the cost of repression. In Civilization and its discontents (1930), Freud wrote that "it is impossible to overlook the extent to which civilization is built up upon a renunciation of instinct, how much it presupposes precisely the non-satisfaction (by suppression, repression or some other means?) of powerful instincts" ([1929, 1930] 1953, 97). By the end of this text, Freud hypothesizes that cultural development might lead men and women to master their aggression. The Kleinian account suggests that the issue is not cultural development per se but the way in which the very structure of groups reinforces the most primitive defenses.

For the white American, the New Negro functions as an exotic signifier invested with primitivism, sexual potency, and wild desires, and

Cullen has the brilliant intuition that he should liberate himself from this stereotype. It should thus be important to raise the question of what price is he willing to pay for this. Not to address this question, I believe, is inexcusable in any possible reading of Cullen's oeuvre.

A Sublime Passion for Death

Death cut the strings that gave me life,
And handed me to Sorrow,
The only kind of middle wife
My folks could beg or borrow.
—"Saturday's Child"

Though death should closet me tonight, I swear
Tomorrow's sun would find his cupboard bare.
—"In Spite of Death"

The melancholic dimension of Countee Cullen's poetry has been fore-grounded by several critics, usually in a genealogical sense that links his poems to the tradition of culturally white aesthetic and poetic forms. His proximity to poets like Keats, Shelley, members of the late-nineteenth-century decadent movement, and his American contemporaries, Edna St. Vincent Millay, Alfred E. Housman, and Edwin Arlington Robinson, places Cullen's poetry at a complex intertextual crossroads that initially relates to the forms of "white melancholia" in its literary and artistic codification. Thus, Margaret Perry has emphasized Cullen's "attitude of melancholy youth" (1971, 25); Houston A. Baker reads, mostly in Cullen's *Copper sun*, the "unrequited love, dejection, indifference, *carpe diem* and sighing" (1974, 50) that would have delighted the decadent poets; and Ronald Primeau links Cullen to Keats in his exploration of "the creative dimensions of pain and uncertainty" (1976, 74). Primeau identifies in his poetry an "almost obsessive drive to render poetically the realities of bittersweet human experience" (77). This last ambivalent quality is crucial to my reading of Cullen's poetic and narrative oeuvre. Following Klein, the ambivalences that accompany the splitting of the object into good and bad in the paranoid-schizoid position do not move into a postambivalent state where the splitting decreases in favor of a greater sense of integration. Melancholia, at the border between paranoid-schizoid and depressive modes of object relations, constitutes itself as some sort of psychic barrier that bars the subject from integration. Object loss haunts Cullen's writings from his literary beginnings.

At the end of his college years at New York University (1922–25), Cullen wrote his undergraduate thesis on Edna St. Vincent Millay. His first two books, *Color* (1925) and *Copper sun* (1927) show the important influence of Keats and Millay. In Millay, Cullen had identified "her marked inclination toward form, her superb mastery of word-marriage, her simplicity, which in less capable hands, would degenerate into banality" (Tuttleton 1989, 108).[13] Later he went to Harvard, where he took a course in versification with Robert S. Hillyer, who, in his belief that poetry provides a link between the present and the past, taught the techniques of poetry by assigning exercises in writing the various traditional forms of English verse. The required precision of form and thought was a challenge for the young poet.[14] Cullen's expert manipulation of white poetic forms gained him not only personal recognition but some kind of recognition for the "race." As Houston A. Baker has remarked, "Countee Cullen . . . served a national need in time of 'forced' institution building and national projection. He gained white American recognition for 'Negro poetry' at a moment when there was little encouraging recognition for *anything* Negro" (1987, 86).

In approaching Cullen's love poetry, Alan R. Shucard has stated that "it is patently clear that Cullen's view of love is an uncommonly dismal one, and that in one way or another, as a dark threat to love or as a way out of an already destroyed and destructive love affair, death looms large in that view" (1984, 62). In any case, Shucard neither pursues the reasons for such a view nor examines the implications that Cullen's homosexuality may have had to do with it.

Cullen was attracted to conventional poetic forms that were often at odds with radical literary themes. He was probably drawn to the sonnet, to name but one well-represented instance in the body of his poetry, because of its long tradition, its syllogistic form, and its multiple discursive possibilities. "Yet Do I Marvel," "From the Dark Tower," and "Hunger" are among his best known poems and those that he selected for his personal collection *On these I stand* (1947).

In his approach to poetic form as intimately connected to the body, Amitai F. Avi-Ram's is one of the few attempts to read otherwise what has been called "conventional" poetic form in some gay poetry from the Harlem Renaissance.[15] Avi-Ram understands form as "a *rhetorical* support for the *content* of the poem" (1990, 34), and in his persuasive reading of

Cullen's "For a Poet" (from *Color*) he concludes that its form dramatizes the repression of the voice that "would speak its desire. . . . Yet, ironically, that very dramatization is a way of *naming* the *repression* and thus giving voice to the desire to transcend it" (43).[16]

But what does traditional poetic form signify in the body of Cullen's poetry? If we consider *signify* in the sense that Henry Louis Gates Jr. theorizes, "signifyin(g)" is repetition with a signal difference, a double-voiced utterance (or gesture) that allows the original utterance to be heard along with the speaker's evaluation of that utterance from a different point of view. It frequently holds up to ridicule the first utterance but only through indirect means. Gates cites Roger D. Abrahams at length to explicate the term: "Signifying seems to be a Negro term, in use if not in origin. It can mean any of a number of things; in the case of the toast about the signifying monkey [the African American trickster figure whose origins, Gates argues, can be traced to the Yoruba trickster figure Esu-Elegbara], it certainly refers to the trickster's ability to talk with great innuendo, to carp, cajole, needle, and lie. It can mean in other instances the propensity to talk around a subject, never quite coming to the point." Gates goes on to note that signifyin(g) functions in a way that can be seen to be analogous to "how the unconscious relates to the conscious" (1988, 58).[17] This sense of doubleness understood as repetition via the death drive, and its relation to ambivalence and melancholia, will guide my readings of Cullen.

I want to argue that, as is indeed the case with the issue of form, concerning the content of his poetry Cullen does not simply adhere to the conventional melancholy tone of the Romantics but rather to the new modernist melancholia we have been discussing throughout this book, in which he develops his own specific idiom. A Kleinian approach to Cullen's writings will take insights from Klein and post-Kleinian developments in a consideration of a complex dynamics in which the issue of race plays a central role. What is specific about Cullen's melancholia as it is figured in his poetry, essays, and narratives? To what extent can we say that Cullen's work is traversed by modernist cultures of the death drive that have the issues of race, homosexuality, and a complex oedipal configuration (with the trauma of birth and ultimately the trauma of nonknowledge) as their targets? In my reading of Cullen's oeuvre, melancholia is also inextricably linked to the issue of form and to what has been frequently glossed as his desire to establish a black frame of reference.[18] This desire is assailed by a multiplicity of anxiety situations that are manifest in his work.

Cullen's acute epistemophilic impulse may have to do with the obscure circumstances of his birth. But to what extent is this epistemophilic urge present in his poetry? What can we say of Cullen's sadism/masochism when reading some of his apparently "genteel" verse? Cullen's poems are pervaded with melancholia; there is something forever lost and even denied that emerges in his verse and parallel to this a permanent striving to fill in this void by cannibalistic incorporation. Thus, in his sonnet "To France," he conveys in the closing couplet the insatiable nature of his heart, which only in exile was able to find some nourishment and relief. He writes: "And found across a continent of foam / What was denied my hungry heart at home" (1935, 74).

In *Color* (1925), his first collection of poetry, Cullen gathers some of his best racial poetry together with love poems and epitaphs. A deep feeling of melancholia that is manifested in a morbid passion for death (loss of the self) and a sense of failure and errancy cut across all of his subjects. As paradoxical as it may appear, Cullen uses tradition in a far more liberating way in some of his racial poetry than in his formal elegies.[19] This is certainly the case with poems from different collections such as "The Shroud of Color," "From the Dark Tower," "Heritage," and "The Black Christ."

"Saturday's Child" has been read as an autobiographical poem. It is a poem in which the trauma of birth is central, a prelude of the dismal future that awaits the child protagonist. The last stanza is revealing of the sense of being thrown out into the world that accompanies melancholia: "Death cut the strings that gave me life, / And handed me to Sorrow, / The only kind of middle wife / My folks could beg or borrow" (1925, 18). There is not even a memory of the good internal object, since this child's genealogy is explicitly reduced to "Dame Poverty gave me my name, / And pain godfathered me" (18). The figure of the mother is erased, and only the father's insensitive reaction is captured: " 'Bad time for planting a seed,' / Was all my father had to say, / And, 'One mouth more to feed' " (18). Cullen's only mention of his biological family is limited to a short poem dedicated to his grandmother, in which a feeling of gratitude and recognition prevails,[20] and to the poem "Tribute,"[21] a sonnet dedicated to his mother, on which I will comment further.

In "Saturday's Child," the figure of the mother is thus suspended, and this generates a specific sense of anxiety, effected by traumatic separation. We should remember that the publication of Otto Rank's influential *The trauma of birth* ([1924] 1929) caused Freud's revision of his own theory of anxiety. Rank explained all neuroses on the basis of this initial anxiety, and Freud, who had asserted that birth was "the first great-anxiety state" ([1923] 1953, 58) in a child, later objected to the excessive emphasis placed on the external danger rather than on inner psychic mechanisms ([1925, 1926] 1953). Today many psychoanalysts include birth among the factors making up unconscious phantasies, and in this respect we may read some of Cullen's poems as phantasy responses to this original traumatic scenario, which encompasses not only birth but separation from the mother as the first significant object. In a Kleinian reading, the earliest anxiety is the ego's fear of being annihilated by the death drive. This is best translated as an experience of nonsatisfaction from the breast, which sets in motion the dynamics of deflection-introjection of the death drive and thus aggression and retaliation in a vicious circle that reaches its peak during the course of the paranoid-schizoid position. The importance that Klein places on the danger of annihilation means that the infant's most regressive and psychotic reaction may arise because the fear of separation is equivalent to a fear of annihilation. This scenario is obviously the antechamber of melancholia and object loss, with the loss of the mother as its primary object.

"Suicide Chant" strikes us with its simplicity and rotundity. The poem is pervaded by a feeling of deep suicidal melancholia, and the poetic voice, paralyzed by inaction, engages in a dialectics between being acted upon and being guilty. The voice tries to exonerate itself from guilt, admonitions, and discipline by dissolving into nothingness. There is no good internal object, and the voice strives to disappear by ceasing to exist in a suicidal chant. Words like *chant* and *Sower* (capitalized) echo an ultimate religious meaning that is also lost. Cullen once again obsessively uses the term *seed*, evoking a thwarted coming into being. His anxieties over generation are also patent, but they are rather subdued in this case since the prevailing desire for nonexistence is dominant: "The seed of a weed / Cannot be flowered, / Nor a hero's deed / Spring from a coward" (1925, 87). Cullen's anxieties about generation are patent throughout his work. In his article, "The Negro in art," published one year after *Color*, he writes: "I do believe . . . that the Negro has not yet built up a large enough body of sound healthy race literature to permit him to speculate in abortions and aberrations which other people are all too prone to accept as truly legitimate" (1926, 193). The atmosphere of his poetry is pervaded with metaphors of aborted germination and many allusions to actual life "planted" for death.

"The Shroud of Color" is a poem in which melancholia is associated with race.[22] Cullen is obsessed with closed spaces, boxes, shrouds, and coffers, and images of imprisonment and enforced confinement recur in his poetry. A concomitant sense of claustrophobia contributes to some of the most acute anxiety situations that one can find in his texts. The stifling sense of oppression is experienced through the abjectification that white society imposes upon the Negro: "My color shrouds me in, I am as dirt / Beneath my brother's heel" (1925, 26). The poetic voice longs for death and finally has an apocalpytic vision of the earth and its creatures in which, accompanied by "All sights and sounds and aspects of my race" (33), liberty appears enchained. The poet learns "How being dark, and living through the pain / Of it, is courage more than angels have" (34). Grief and suffering emerge between the interstices of this ruin and devastation. We can read this poem bearing in mind the fact that melancholia has traditionally been associated to the old religious idea of the "fall"—the Luciferian fall, for instance, the fall into an abyssal darkness that goes together with the internal splendor of the dying of the ego in its last moments. This idea of the fall manifests itself psychically in helpless moral pain, in the impotence of unhappiness. The ego strives to get rid of this feeling of incapacity by recourse to the prophetic allure that a catastrophe of universal proportions may offer. It is imperative to add to this archaic mourning—and to the individual version of it—to this moral pain, the redemptive value that accompanies a funereal Freudian rhetoric in his "the shadow of the object falls upon the ego." From here we can read *shadow* as a funereal shadow and even "the shroud of color" as a funereal shadow cast upon the poet. Cullen, oppressed by the burden of color and unable to stand the pressure of living in the world as a black man, expresses his wish to die. There is an ascension toward the heavens and finally a return to life, with the poet's effort to reconcile the split between good and bad into a whole in which ambivalence yields to some recognition of the fusion of the joy as well as the sorrow. Happiness and grief are no longer divorced but fused into a unity: "Right glad I was to stoop to what I once had spurned, / Glad even unto tears; I laughed aloud; I turned / Upon my back, and though the tears for joy would run / My sight was clear; I looked and saw the rising sound" (35). Ultimately, on this return to his former "embodied" state, his spirit finds itself at home: "Lord, I will live persuaded by my own. / I cannot play the recreant to these; / My spirit has come home, that sailed the doubtful seas" (34). This sense of homelessness and errancy has to do with Cullen's profound sense of displacement as a black poet of "deviant" sexuality. His allusion to "spirit" can also be read as a codification of his homosexuality.[23]

In the spring of 1926, Cullen, after the acclaimed publication of *Color*, was invited to speak at the Baltimore City Club at the Hotel Emerson. In a letter to Carl van Vechten, he reported that "on learning that I was a Negro the hotel management would not permit the club to have me there, nor could the club secure another hotel or even a theatre in Baltimore where a Negro poet might read to them. As yet I have not written my second diatribe against Baltimore. Anyhow what good would it do?" (quoted in Perry 1971, 8). The violence of racial interpellation is not only present in Cullen's poetry but also lived and endured in his own personal experience. "Incident," a poem included in *Color*, is reminiscent of the impact that a racial slur had upon the poet in the same city of Baltimore when he was eight years old.[24]

The oxymoronic sense of being alive but dead is present in many of Cullen's poems. In the epitaph "For Myself," he writes: "What's in this grave is worth your tear; / There's more than the eye can see; / Folly and Pride and Love lie here / Buried alive with me" (1925, 72). The discourses of melancholia echo this quality of "living in death" and its concomitant disappearance of affect.

Even when Cullen chose as his poetic ideal the work of the British Romantic poets, Houston A. Baker has identified an even greater proximity to the work of the decadent poets of the fin de siècle, such as Dante Gabriel Rossetti, Charles Swinburne, Ernest Dowson, and Arthur Symons. In Baker's view, "These were the romantics *manqué* who shared the same lyrical impulses but lacked the sweeping vision, the mythicizing potential, and the colossal certainties of their predecessors" (1974, 37). Along the same lines, in his study of French literature Cullen became acquainted with the poetry of Baudelaire. He wrote free translations of several of his poems.[25] Baudelaire's *spleen* reassesses previous philosophical notions about the self in the context of melancholia and propounds the truth of the melancholic subject, immersed in some sort of pensive reverie, as the modern successor of an outdated self as "subject of thought." Inspired by Baudelaire, Cullen wrote "Death to the Poor" (1935, 93), in which, absorbed in the morbid sensitivity and spleen of the French poet, he wrote that death is the only consolation a mortal man may expect as he travels through this sorrowful world.

Some of Cullen's most memorable poetry draws its strength from racial identity. In his racial poetry, Cullen attacks everything that most directly wounded him and his race: racial prejudice. The pattern of aggression-retaliation comes close to Melanie Klein's description of the vicious circle of introjection-projection in "Notes on some schizoid mechanisms" ([1946] 1975).

"Heritage" (1925, 36–41) is one of Cullen's most beautiful poems. It is a long evocation of African landscapes, full of the rhythmic and almost incantatory resonance of tom-toms and of his fascination with ancient gods. The poetic voice's dilemma is that he is neither pagan nor Christian, native African nor inheritor and agent in the transformation of the romantic tradition. Ultimately, the poem raises a similar question to that of "Yet Do I Marvel": Which one among the gods would "make a poet black and bid him sing"? (3). In "Heritage," Cullen reclaims his African roots and poses a crucial question, "What is Africa to me?" The poet is haunted by familiar and ancestral sounds and writes: "Though I cram against my ear / Both my thumbs, and keep them there, / Great drums throbbing through the air" (36–7). Distress and joy are allied, and he conjures up images that connote the sensuality of life in the jungle: "Seek no covert in your fear / Lest a mortal eye should see; / What's your nakedness to me?" (37). The poet exhorts, "Come and dance the Lover's dance!" (39). Out of this experience of recollection and reclaiming his past comes the urge to "fashion dark gods," the gods of black men, and the dilemma between his Christian faith and that of his ancestors is poignantly expressed: "Wishing He I served were black, / Thinking then it would not lack / Precedent of pain to guide it" (40). The poem conveys the ambivalence of being split by two cultures and acknowledges the enormous weight that this remote African past places on him. Finally, Africa is lost forever and what is gained under the guise of civilization generates more distress. The melancholic tone of the last stanza reveals that this good internal object that was lost and remains incorporated still reverberates inside the ego: "All day long and all night through, / One thing only I must do: / Quench my pride and cool my blood, / Lest I perish in the flood. / Lest a hidden ember set / Timber that I thought was wet / Burning like the dryest flax, / Melting like the merest wax, / Lest the grave restore its dead. / Not yet has my heart or head / In the least way realized / They and I are civilized" (40–41).

"Yet Do I Marvel," is a sonnet in which the poetic voice expresses doubts about God's goodness and his benevolent intent in the creation of certain limited beings. The voice oscillates between confidence in God and distrust. "I doubt not God is good, well-meaning, / kind," is the opening line. As the poem advances, it is progressively undermined. For God has created the "little buried mole" to continue blind and "flesh that mirrors

Him to some day die." Cullen illustrates his argument with two cruel predicaments drawn from classical mythology, those of Tantalus and Sisyphus, wherein the death drive appears in full force. Their inexorable fate condemns them to repeat: Tantalus is the man who suffers eternal denial of that which he seeks, and Sisyphus is the man who is forced to toil again and again only to lose his objective each time he thinks he has won it. Cullen's allusion to the mole and the man who must die figures the pathos of all those men and women estranged from God and thrust into a hostile universe. The predicaments of Tantalus and Sisyphus articulate the plight of black artists in America. Cullen raises poignant questions that cannot find resolution, not even in the security provided by the structure of the sonnet. The ninth line of the Petrarchan sonnet, the volta, turns toward resolution, but the apparent progression is undermined by the forceful final couplet from the last stanza: "Inscrutable his ways are, and immune / To catechism by a mind to strewn / With petty cares to slightly understand / What awful brain compels His awful hand. / Yet do I marvel at this curious thing: / To make a poet black, and bid him sing!" (1925, 3).[26] The poem suggests that the black poet is forced to struggle endlessly toward a goal he or she will never be allowed to reach. The death drive is figured from the start in Cullen's literary beginnings. With its quality of deadening repetition, it acquires a specific meaning for the black writer and a specific reading culturally inflected by race. The poem ends with the supreme melancholic irony that reads as inexorable fate. In "Yet Do I Marvel," Cullen inscribes race in the traditional form of the sonnet, modifying it to some extent in an intertextual play among mythology, echoes of William Blake, and religious discourse.[27] In this highly personal elaboration, form and content are to some extent suspended, and we may argue that the symbolic equation, in its very subversion of the symbol and its fracturing of the referential and poetic functions of language, is present in the violation of literary codes (the sonnet) and readers' expectations of a poem dealing with the question of race.

"Harsh World that Lashest Me," (1925, 106–7) is one of Cullen's poems in which the dynamics of aggression, retaliation, and introjection are more clearly inscribed. The poet's body is attacked and violated by a harsh world to which he is unable to respond. He bears the scars of those injuries, and internalizes the pain. The poetic voice rises in resistance, since the poet endures and still lives: "I give my body to be burned. / I mount my cross because I will, / I drink the hemlock which you give / For wine which you withhold—and still, / Because I will not die, I live" (106). The fleeting allusion to God is promptly replaced with a pagan image of the flesh restored from its wounded state, but the possibility of a life un-wounded seems utopian and the poem ends with a line in which "dreams of light [are] eclipsed in shade" (107).

Cullen's recurrent play with death is almost a prelude to his own premature death.[28] Thus, in "Requiescam," the last poem included in *Color*, he writes, "I am for sleeping and forgetting / All that has gone before; / I am for lying still and letting / Who will beat at my door; / I would my life's cold sun were setting / To rise for me no more" (1925, 108). In many of Cullen's poems, death is invested with a protective quality ("The Fall of Hyperion," "Death to the Poor"). It is understood to represent relief from the violence that must be endured in life, in which the loss of love ranks highest: "The loss of love is a terrible thing; / They lie who say that death is worse" ("Variations on a Theme," in 1927a, 25). We may also find a variant of this image of death as closed space in Cullen's metaphor of sleep that is frequently used as a prelude to death and is read as protective, like a shroud. Sleep enshrouds the mind, and the latter is buried deep inside the cloth of sleep.[29] And yet, as Amitai Avi-Ram has suggested in his reading of the epitaph "For a Poet," death and the grave may be read as "sensuous pleasures. . . . The grave is a place of darkness and delight" (1990, 40).

Cullen's second volume of poetry, *Copper sun* (1927), was cryptically dedicated "To the not impossible Her."[30] In this collection, Cullen's love poetry is pervaded by a deep sense of melancholia. Tropes for hunger, thirst, and dispossession of the strength and energy that sustain life char-acterize the dominant mode of a poetic corpus less celebratory than de-pressive, suffused with anxieties of loss, separation, and death. A morbid sensitivity attracted by the lure of the grave finds in its deadening space a place in which to project all those unwanted and split parts of the self. The grave thus figures as an ideal container, as the womb that in its frozen embrace entices the heart with a liberatory promise of escape from the burden of the world.

"From the Dark Tower," is a poem in which anxieties about race render the black man impotent to act; this impotence generates an enraged response that is painfully introjected rather than find its way into the open. Even when the poet asserts his racial dignity, "We were not made eternally to weep," the ability to act is thwarted: "So in the dark we hide the heart that bleeds, / And wait, and tend our agonizing seeds" (1927a, 3). The inner haemorrhage that Freud had identified as constitutive of melancholia is also foregrounded in this poem. "Pity the deep in love," expresses the sorrowful and melancholy condition of those deeply in love who are perilously exposed to an abyss of loss. Cullen writes: "Pity the deep in love / They move as men asleep, / Traveling a narrow way / Precipitous and steep. / Tremulous is the lover's breath / With little moans and sighs; / Heavy are the brimming lids / Upon a lover's eyes" (17). The poet plays with the opposition among phantasy, dreams, and reality. These "brimming lids upon the lover's eyes" simultaneously connote sorrow and affliction and also obscured vision.

"Hunger" is a poem of intense melancholia in which anxieties about introjection are conveyed through metaphors related to nourishment and hunger that cannot be satiated. It is important to note that Cullen refers to "bread" as the bearer of this terrible whiteness that cannot fill his void: "Break me no bread however white it be; / It cannot still fill the emptiness I know; / No wine can cool this desert thirst in me / Though it had lain a thousand years in snow" (1927a, 64). The poetic voice exhibits the inevitability that is figured in its progress to the grave; there is no artifice that can dupe the poet into a false belief in wholeness. Hunger and emptiness trope the supreme melancholia of those who desire to become lost in the grave. The final couplet, by recourse to the metaphors of virginity and marriage, seems to suggest that the emptiness or nonknowledge that result from sexual "inviolability" is useless in a world that is itself empty from the start: "The fool still keeps his dreams inviolate / Till their virginity espouse the grave" (64). In "Love's Way," the lovers appear to be sharing their hunger: "That the beloved hungers, nor drink unless / The cup be shared down to the last sweet dregs" (46).

In "Portrait of a Lover," Cullen attempts to portray the restless lover as trapped in a labyrinth and suffering from this "malady whereby his wits are led" (1927a, 47). The lover's hunger and thirst cannot be satiated. He is assailed by anxieties of cannibalistic incorporation and phantasies of being attacked and poisoned: "Of all men born he deems himself so much accurst, / His plight so piteous, his proper pain so rare, / The very bread he eats so dry, so fierce his thirst, / What shall be liken such a martyr to? Compare / Him to a man with poison raging in his throat, / And far away the one mind with an antidote" (47–48). Love and melancholia can be read interchangeably as "illnesses" that storm the subject in its passage through object relations, specifically through sexuality and aggression. In "Variations on a Theme," Cullen meditates on the loss of love—this is actually the subtitle of the poem—with metaphors of impoverishment, hollowness, and exhaustion. Immersed into the deadening absence of the lover, the two final lines proclaim: "The loss of love is a terrible thing / They lie who say that death is worse" (25).

"The Black Christ" (1929a, 69–110), the poem that gives title to Cullen's third volume, is a contemporary story that leans heavily on the religious symbolism of the death and resurrection of Christ. Cullen deals with another thorny racial subject, this time with the lynching of a Negro boy for a crime he did not commit. The young boy appears to his mother and brother in a vision rising from the dead, like Christ. This poem, full of emotional intensity, shows the firm religious conviction of the mother in contrast to the wavering faith of the younger generation. How can the black protagonist and his brother hold fast to Christianity in the face of the prejudices and violence around them? In any case, the resurrection serves to renew his younger brother's faith in Christ. "The Black Christ" dramatizes black heroism in the face of negrophobia and aggression, and it can be read as a meditation on what it means to be black in a hostile, white world. The violence represented in the poem is an originary violence that can only be figured, read, and decoded as violence against the racial Other.

The only poem that Cullen dedicated to his mother is "Tribute" (1929a, 9). In this sonnet, the specularity coming from the face of the mother rescues the subject from his impure state. The poem opens with an acknowledgment of all the imperfections that plague man and then considers the importance of his race in the aggravation of these qualities. Only by recourse to the mother's beneficial look can the child overcome this abject(ed) state: "So I, least noble of a churlish race, / Least kind of those by nature rough and crude, / Have at the intervention of your face / Spared him with whom was my most bitter feud / One moment, and the next, a deed more grand, / The helpless fly imprisoned in my hand" (9). This protective and beneficial image of the mother (her face, or breast) is what in Cullen's poetry usually remains outside figuration. As I have attempted to demonstrate through my reading of Klein, the foreclosure of the image of the (good) mother is determinant in the production of melancholia.

The dynamics of aggression are also explicitly addressed in the poem "Minutely Hurt," wherein the voice meditates upon the degree of violence that it can tolerate. The heart, depleted of love, is the melancholic target of all these attacks: "Once an atom cracks the heart / All is done and said; / Poison, steel, and fiery dart / May then be buffeted" (1929a, 22).

In *The Medea and some poems* (1935), Cullen writes his version of Euripides' drama in prose and renders its choruses as lyrical poems. In this collection, "Scottsboro, Too, Is Worth Its Song" (96–97) is a protest poem in which Cullen strongly criticizes American poets for ignoring the tragedy of nine Negro boys whose long trial in the South had been so widely discussed and publicized. The poem ends with these lines: "Surely, I said, / Now will the poets sing. / But they have raised no cry. / I wonder why" (97).[31] Their plight was symbolic of the hatred and racial tensions that the Negro cause raised in America during the years of the Depression.

There is also a series of heavily encoded poems in which the ambivalences and conflicts of the poet's love show most clearly. "Spring Reminiscence" (1925, 84) ends with the stanza, "Shall ever your hand lie in my hand, / Pulsing to it, I wonder; / Or have the gods, being jealous gods, / Envied us our thunder?" (84). In this respect, "Tableau" (12) is perhaps one of the most explicitly interracial love poems, in which a black boy and a white boy walk in unison: "Oblivious to look and word / They pass, and see no wonder / That lightning brilliant as a sword / Should blaze the path of thunder" (12). Alden Reimonenq reads this last stanza as a veiled antihomophobic statement: "Under the poetic veil of speaking out against racism, Cullen achieves a larger purpose by also criticizing antihomosexual bigotry" (1993, 150).[32] Throughout the poem, Cullen opposes "The golden splendor of the day" and "The sable pride of night" in flaunting display. By means of projective identification, the reaction of blacks and whites alike show in the same aggravation: "From lowered blind the dark folk stare, / And here the fair folk talk, / Indignant that these two should dare / In unison to walk" (1925, 12). Cullen shows how deeply ingrained in the racist mentality is the mixture of derogation and disguised admiration: what is desired by the threatened ego of the racist is envied and ultimately destroyed.

"Magnets" is an interesting poem of thwarted love in which the poet declares: "But such a strange contrary thing / My heart is, it will never cling / To any bright unblemished thing," and intimately confesses the impossibility of his love: "The loving heart that must deny / The very love it travels by" (1935, 69). With images of magnets that wantonly draw his heart at their will, the poet is dispossessed of agency and passively must follow their course and renounce his love. Melancholia arises out of this loss of love. One of the untitled sonnets in this collection (84) reveals the deadly compulsion to repeat that makes the poet aware that he is just echoing words that have already been used to exhaustion: "What I am saying now was said before, / And countless centuries from now again, / Some poet warped with bitterness and pain, / Will brew like words hoping to salve his sore" (84). The "anguish from that throbbing wound, his brain, / Squeezed out" can be read as his anxiety over having the inside of his body attacked and depleted. In his "Sonnet Dialogue," he sets up a dialogue between himself and his soul, and the latter reveals the ultimate condition of life in its surrender to death, "Because whatever lives is granted breath / But by the grace and sufferance of Death" (86).

In "Medusa," Cullen's allusion to Perseus and his slaying of Medusa reveals how the poet fights a deadly combat with a tradition that gave him birth but dangerously (like a mother?) threatens his existence. In this poem, the link to the mythological tradition also allows him to connect the face of a woman who rejected him with the malign power of Medusa. What blinds the poet in this scenario is the phallic "dart" that poisons after a first mythic moment of wholeness, courage, and absence of fear: "But I was never one to be subdued / By any fear of augth not reason-bred, / And so I mocked the ruddy word, and stood / To meet the gold-envenomed dart instead" (1935, 76).[33] Via Freud, "Das Medusenhaupt" (written in 1922) invokes castration upon the sight of the feminine genitals. Could we say that in Cullen's poem the face of the Medusa coincides with the poet's own face, as Louis Marin ([1977] 1995) has suggested with regard to Caravaggio?[34] What kind of anxieties lie beneath this facade of the evil feminine castratrice? Is Cullen occupying the place of the absent Perseus in his mortal attack on the Gorgon? Marin speculates that "The painter, after all, not only disguises himself as Medusa; he also cross-dresses as a Gorgon, a woman, or at least as the head of a woman. This is a woman of striking beauty" (143). By identifying in the canvas a parodical impulse to disavow the enunciation, Marin reads its plot as erasure, a dissimulation of the subject that enunciates it: it looks as if (*semble* can be translated as "gives the impression that") the event is narrated by itself. Caravaggio's painting shows us this moment of beheading of the "head that narrates," of its generative source, and of the subject of enunciation itself when it looks and cries in pain upon seeing the canvas. It is representation of a cut (*coupure*) as a "cutting blade" (143). Marin reminds us that for Freud the representation of the castrated female among the Greeks has to do with homosexuality as a habitual and extended practice in classical Greece: "Since the Greeks were in the main strongly homosexual, it was inevitable that we should find among them a representation of woman as a being who frightens and repels because she is castrated" (Freud [1922a] 1953, 274). Today it seems outrageous and far-fetched to find in male homosexuality the cause of the representation of women as castrated. But at the same time it raises the question of why Cullen was writing his "Medusa" poem and including it in *The Medea*, one of his most overt homosexual collections.[35] In other words, is this a poem in which Cullen tries to baffle his readers (and critics) by sticking to the misogynistic tradition of the representation of Medusa? Or does he manage, by projecting the reflection of what they want to read, to subvert their expectations by recourse to something rather unexpected? In my reading, the poem is undeniably plagued by anxieties about the female body but also about potency, beauty, logical reason, and a general dispossession of manly attributes. It is a melancholic meditation on the loss of all these manly attributes and qualities inscribed in a sadistic-masochistic dynamics of attack and retaliation. The poet proves his potency, as he makes clear in the last couplet of the sonnet: "Though blind, yet on these arid balls engraved / I know it was a lovely face I braved" (1935, 76). In a Kleinian reading of this poem, the loss of the penis is but an instance of the generalized sense of anxiety that assails the boy and shows in his terror of being attacked in retaliation or enduring the sadistic phantasy of the combined parent figure in copulation. In a self-reflective gesture, Cullen looks at himself in the mirror and perceives the horror of a culture that castrates him as a black gay man.

Cullen's racial poetry is a powerful outcry against the injustices of the white man that lead to humiliating experiences for the black community. We may raise the question of whether there is a symbolics of resistance in Cullen's racial poetry. Or is it rather through the adoption of the master's tools that he endeavors to dismantle the master's house?[36] Through a conscious appropriation of traditional poetic form, Cullen's verse sees the light in print for the first time. I do not mean to suggest that Cullen is a belligerent racial poet. Rather, I aim to show the blind spots that call for a nonsimplistic and complex approach to the reading of his oeuvre today. To perpetuate Cullen's image as a minor conventional poet does not do justice to his importance for current rereadings and revisions of the Harlem Renaissance and its connections to other modernisms and other literatures in English that are written outside the Anglo-American imperial paradigm.

In his training and his painstaking adoption and imitation of poetic forms from the British tradition, Cullen is inadvertently introjecting the paradigm of domination that he consciously rejected in the open. In the case of Cullen, the complex embracing and rejection of racial poetry poses crucial questions for a simple reading of form as mimesis and as divorced from a reading of subject matter as innovative and revolutionary. What seems to be at stake in Cullen is the impossibility of bridging the gap between the paranoid-schizoid and the depressive regime of object relations. Cullen's melancholia and his many ambivalences most commonly find their place in the paranoid-schizoid mode.

In this respect, Cullen's article on miscegenation, published in *The Crisis* (1929b), can be read as his personal response to all those critics and readers who were trying to classify him as a Negro poet regardless of his views. This is another clear instance of fierce rejection of stereotypes wittily narrated by way of an anecdote that places the discussion in another land (France) and thus allows him a greater freedom to parody the assumptions and impositions that threaten his creativity and, by extension, his life. Writing from Paris, Cullen writes of a conversation with Madame Claire Goll, a cultivated woman born of French parents and educated in Germany, who is "sincerely interested in the Negro" (373). On the walls of her home hang African masks and she has the latest German translations of anthologies of Negro literature, since "She speaks English with a prepositional inaccuracy that is at once charming and amusing" (373). Madame Goll and Countee Cullen discuss her latest novel, *Le Nègre Jupiter Enlève Europa*, which Cullen rapidly qualifies as a "story of miscegenation" (373). Since the plot of the story is crucial for my purposes, I will quote Cullen's own summary of it. The story concerns the meeting at the Swedish Embassy in Paris of Alma Valery and Jupiter Djibouti.

> Alma, a lovely blond woman of French and Swedish parentage and of small mental equipment, Jupiter, an African Negro, an executive in the cabinet of the Minister of Foreign Colonies, and in his own land a prince of the blood. They are married and rapidly the story goes forward to what the formula, even in a foreign country, seems to require of such a novel: the husband's embarrassment and the wife's chagrin at the stares and the remarks, as often overt as sotto voce, that attend their presence together at social affairs and in the streets; a growing jealousy on the part of Jupiter and an increasing antipathy on Alma's part, dire portents of an end which even the arrival of a baby does not curtail, the infidelity of Alma and her subsequent murder by Jupiter. (373)

Cullen's critique sees the story as a hackneyed tragic formula of interracial relations. He would rather read stories that present different alternatives, since these circumstances may occur "with any two people, irrespective of their color" (373). He charges Madame Goll with using "outworn shibboleths" like the Negro's desire to be lighter complexioned and his general anxieties about social inequality.[37] Cullen's parodic comments portray Madame Goll as a grotesque character, an extremist in her literary judgment (she believes that "little of artistic merit is now being produced in America except that which is being done by Negroes" (373), and finally the figure of the legislator who indicts Cullen for his love of Keats.

In this apparently innocuous story, Cullen feels himself interpellated by the judges and legislators of the American literary scene. From a foreign land, the land of freedom that he so much admired, he responds in retaliation: "Madame makes me feel that I am recreant, disloyal, a literary heretic, a blind man stumbling along in the light of the new day" (1929b, 373). This is indeed one of Cullen's strongest manifestos on freedom in the arts and the literary imagination. The final lines of the essay are conclusive: "Must we, willy-nilly, be forced into writing nothing but the old atavistic urges, the more savage and none too beautiful aspects of our lives? May we not chant a hymn to the Sun God if we will, create a bit of phantasy in which not a spiritual or a blues appears, write a tract defending Christianity though its practitioners aid us so little in our argument; in short, do, write, create what we will, our only concern being that we do it well and with all the power in us?" (373). What seems to me important in this passage is that, out of his own sense of guilt for being under suspicion of betraying his race, Cullen turns around and responds, confronting his accusers. It is as if in the Althusserian scenario the police would simultaneously indict and abuse this subject ("Hey you, *nigger!*") and Cullen would turn and respond to this imputation of guilt according to the script. But in this turning Cullen responds with a rhetoric of parody and irony that may yet rescue some part of his speech. Cullen needs to acquit himself of guilt, but in the process he cannot escape the burden of its attribution.

It is interesting to note that Cullen passes inadvertently over the issue of rape and does not say a word about the violence implicit in the plot of Madame Goll's novel or about the myth of Jupiter ravishing Europa. He writes: "On the other hand, irrespective of the inroad that black men in various capacities are making into European life, swallowed up as they are among the white population, they are no more to be feared than a handful of sand added to the millions of grains that make the Sahara, no more than a cup of water thrown into the sea" (1929b, 373). What Cullen's overanxious comment explicitly reveals is his concern with the stereotypical ascription of savage sexuality to black men and his interest in deconstructing the myth. In this passage, black men are endowed with more "capacities" than the purely sexual, and instead of being potential rapists and victimizers they are victimized, "swallowed up" by the white population. Oblivious of the woman's sexuality, the rape is only read from the point of view of the black male. Both in the case of the myth and in that of Madame Goll's story, the victim of rape is a white woman. It would probably be too optimistic to think that things would have turned out differently had the victim been a black woman. We might phantasize what Cullen's position vis-à-vis the victim would then be. And we may also wonder if Cullen is silent because white upper class women—like the one portrayed in the novel and Madame Goll herself—had traditionally used lower class black men (and slaves) for sex, with the consequence of "unmanning" or feminizing them. In any case, this passage vividly reveals the conflicts and anxieties over gender that were embedded in the atmosphere of the Harlem Renaissance and Cullen's own conflictual position in his life and writings.[38]

Bal Colonial

The gathering is motley: West Indians from Martinique, French whites with whom they have intermarried or who are their friends, and the usual allotment of tourists. One senses immediately that all the fun is being had on the floor, not at the tables along the walls and along the balcony where congregate with half-amused yet half-intrigued faces the English and American tourists. The Anglo-Saxon, superior species, is in for a deep regretting when he realizes what natural joys he has allowed to decay and grow moth-ridden in his desire to maintain a condescending aloofness.—Countee Cullen

"And do the American whites really dislike the black because of their color?" We would give anything to restore his wavering trust and faith in our land, for we know how the truth will hurt him. "I cannot understand it," he says, "Quelle betise!" What stupidity, indeed. Once more America has lost face in a foreign country.—Countee Cullen

In 1926, Rev. Frederick Cullen, on the occasion of the silver anniversary year of his ministry, was offered a trip to the Holy Land by his congregation. The offer included passage for Carolyn Cullen, his wife, but since she disliked the idea of crossing the Atlantic they thought that Countee could go with his father if the church board approved. The church proved willing, and they began preparing for their trip. The ability to travel was at the time a white prerogative and one of the markers of racial difference. Whereas the white man was free (could afford) to cross the Atlantic and look to Europe, blacks were still forced to occupy the static and reified space of the primitive, fettered to the earth. Cullen's relationship with his adoptive father was very close. After their first trip to Holy Land, Countee came to be his traveling companion and interpreter on his annual vacations.[39] There was also a great familiarity between Frederick Cullen and Countee's friends. Thus, for example, in the summer of 1932 Blanche Ferguson reports that "Customarily Dr. Cullen arrived in Europe for his annual vacation in July or August, and his son usually reserved that time to spend with him. But this July Countee was unable to leave his Sorbonne classes. So his friend Harold Jackman accompanied the older man to Athens, a city Dr. Cullen had long wanted to visit" (1966, 141).

"The Dark Tower" is the title of the column that Cullen wrote for the journal *Opportunity* from 1926 to 1928.[40] In it, Cullen reviewed new books and commented on the literary and artistic scene, writing from Harlem or Paris. The Dark Tower became the name of the literary salon that black heiress A'Lelia Walker founded in 1928 at her home in Harlem. Walker gathered Negro artists (writers, painters, sculptors, and musicians) as well as agents, producers, and publishers; in addition, she tried to attract wealthy men and women to her soirées with the hope that they would become patrons of her friends.[41]

The epigraphs that open this section are from the "Dark Tower" column dated September 1928. In both, he focuses on the face as the first revealing aspect of the race and equates the white provincial faces of English and American tourists at the Bal Colonial in Paris with the face that America shamefully loses abroad on account of racism and discrimination. The striking interracial and cross-cultural mixture of the *bal* is voyeuristically contemplated by the superior white species, which has repressed its "natural joys" almost to the point of extinction and under a facade of "condescending aloofness," seeking its pleasure in the gaze. The faces of black men and women at the bal remain "in the dark," inscrutable, showing only in their agile and flexible movements how these racial Others struggle to maintain their cultural inviolability.

In June 1928, Cullen chose Paris as the place where he would make his home while studying and writing under a Guggenheim grant.[42] Ferguson reports that "To him France meant freedom from the race consciousness he had known at home. No one here seemed to notice the color of his skin"

(1966, 104). Cullen was the greatest francophile in the group of black American writers of the Harlem Renaissance.[43] Between 1930 and 1940, African and West Indian students living in Paris were in close contact with the circle of American Negro writers that Cullen had joined. Claude McKay, Jean Toomer, and Langston Hughes, among others, discussed their work and experiences with other Negroes from the diaspora. In Cullen's sonnet "To France," the country is figured as a generous and bountiful mother to which he would return someday to be nursed and protected from the hardships of the world: "Among a fair, and kindly foreign folk / There might I only breathe my latest days, / With those rich accents falling on my ear / That most have made me feel that freedom's rays / Still have a shrine where they may leap and sear,—/ Though I were palsied there, or halt, or blind, / So I were there, I think I should not mind" (1935, 91).

Terribly excited and prey to the enchantment of Paris, Cullen writes from the French capital his monthly "Dark Tower" column to let his readers know about the Bal Colonial. He describes it as "Probably the most cosmopolitan and democratic dance hall in Paris which may mean in the world. Speaking of it in general terms, one says it is a West Indian dance hall. It is the rendezvous of the Martiniquan Negroes of Paris" (1928, 272). Cullen passionately writes about the music—"a melange or cross between modern jazz and the residue of old West Indian folk pieces" (272)—and the sweet sounds of the French Martiniquan in the voices of men and women who promptly recognize in the Americans "an alien tongue" despite their strenuous efforts to speak French. These Negroes have become Europeanized in dress and manner. This act of cultural cross-dressing reflects back to the white society a distorted mirror image of what they have previously imposed through enforcement in their so-called civilized world. Moreover, in the Martiniquan Bal Colonial there is no need to master language.[44] The confusion of tongues is subsumed under the swift body movements that ignore linguistic boundaries and are built upon rhythmic and tactile sensations in a hybrid symphony. Cullen is fascinated with the dancing, which is sensual and harsh: "The dancing for the most part is harsh and slightly reprehensible, faintly suggestive of the antics of some of the New York night clubs" (272). This atmosphere of mélange, of cultural crossing, holds the promise of transgressive pleasures that can bypass the repressive surveillance of his fatherland.

It was while Cullen was a student at DeWitt Clinton High School in New York that he entered into the most important and enduring relationship of his life with a handsome West Indian boy named Harold Jackman.[45] It is crucial to note that even his relationship with Jackman is marked by substantial differences in culture, background and maybe even skin color. Blanche E. Ferguson describes him as "the light-skinned London-born teacher who was already gaining a reputation for his interest in the Negro theater and his collection of books, playbills, and manuscripts" (1966, 100).[46] Central to my understanding of Cullen's melancholia is this sense of doubleness, which haunts him in his writing, his relationships, and even his psychic economy. In this sense, Michael L. Lomax regards Cullen as "a forced-black man who never adjusted comfortably to his racial identity" (1987, 218). I feel that Lomax's critique ignores the fact that Cullen was a doubly "forced-black man" as a closeted homosexual poet who obviously would never be able to adjust to any identity since his chances to claim one were truncated from the start.

At this point, it is important to be aware that Cullen's many relationships, in both Harlem and Paris, were with men who presented some sort of "double ethnicity." This is certainly the case with Jackman, an American negro of West Indian heritage. Throughout his life, Cullen himself lived the double status of being an orphan and an adopted child, and in the sphere of relationships, even if much of this still remains veiled, he had both male and female lovers.[47] This pattern of doubleness (ethnicity, relationships, family status) bears strong resemblances to his desire to write as a poet eschewing predetermined programs and ascriptions and as a Negro poet embracing the complexities attached to the question of the race. The complexity of Cullen's subject position—an orphan of unknown procedence, adopted and raised in a Methodist parsonage in Harlem and educated (in literature) in the most traditional British style—helps to frame some of the ambivalences and contradictions of his writings. His shifting and contradictory subject positions eschew any fixed mode of object relations, and his texts, from racial to religious, love, and death poems, remain in a perpetual oscillation between the paranoid-schizoid and depressive modes of mastering anxiety.

Cullen's life and writings are marked by a sense of permanent displacement—cultural, racial (African-American heritage), and geographical—and a profound sense of dislocation and displacement due to his condition as an orphan and adopted child.[48] On account of this, he even changes his name, from Countee Porter, to Countee P. Cullen, the name by which he is inscribed in literary history. His original name is dropped in an act of disengagement, deracination, and defamiliarization. Cullen's sense of exile when at home and his longing to go back to Paris, where he was able to find and enjoy his freedom for the first time, lasted throughout his life. As he puts it in his sonnet "To France," "And found across a continent of foam / What was denied my hungry heart at home" (1935, 74).

Perhaps by way of his expatriate life, Cullen came to realize that language and creativity grow through introjection and assimilation and that it is also through loss that one comes to experience language in its radical dispossession and separation from its object.[49] Claude McKay, the Jamaican-born Negro writer who spent most of his life in the United States, explored the sense of alienation that stormed black intellectuals and argued that the loss of a folk tradition and folk wisdom as cultural foundations was one of the main causes of it. In his view, African Americans are uprooted people, doubly uprooted if they are cultured men, educated and policed by the West. The inferiority complex from which most African Americans suffer is still more acute in this intellectual elite, for whom whites represent an ideal that leads them to hide deep within themselves anything that might appear strange to a civilized white.[50]

By the end of his "Dark Tower" column on the Bal Colonial, Cullen indulges in memories of intimacy and discloses part of what he felt in his hotel room with his friend:

> We are back in our hotel . . . it is early morning . . . our room is high with a great circular balcony from which we can see in every direction. Algiers spreading out like a large white fan, its white roofs shining and flashing in the early morning sun, the entire panorama one of bewildering beauty, if one could only forget the dirt and disease which stalks the Arab population. . . . Suddenly there is a knock at the door. We open to one of our boat companions, a young German aviator. In halting English he explains that he would like to indulge in a sun bath on our balcony in the hope that he might tan himself to what he really considers our marvelous complexion. . . . Will we allow him? My companion and I exchange smiles. No similar premium has ever been placed on our color where we came from. . . . Bitters and sweets, aloes and honeysuckle" (1928, 273)

These transient memories of travel and his troping of his inner state with the gleam of the sensuality of the Orient suggest a private world of men behind closed doors. Cullen's vision of Algiers harbors the possibility of fusing black and white and encapsulates a dream of hybridity and miscegenation.[51] The large white fan as sensuous symbol of the feminine may thus become enmeshed with Cullen's and his friend's young black masculine bodies. And, as in some sort of parable, color is restored to this magic prelapsarian moment when it is thought that it could be produced by exposure to the sun. Color is marvelous, then, shining over black bodies. But this is only an alien perception, coming from a foreign land, since the gift of color is not perceived this way at home. The story ends with the irresolution of the dichotomy or rather with the refusal to embrace any dichotomy: "Bitters and sweets, aloes and honeysuckles." Cullen's narrative, interspersed with so many suspension points, ends with a suspension of judgment. In the pure opacity of this figuration of lurid light and suspension points, Cullen's dream of miscegenation and homosexual love remains both encoded and open for all those who may want to read it.

One Way to Heaven: Forms Denigrated?

The word *nigger*, you see, sums up for us who are colored all the bitter years of insult and struggle in America: the slave-beatings of yesterday, the lynchings of today, the Jim Crow cars, the only movie show in town with its sign up FOR WHITE ONLY, the restaurants where you may not eat, the jobs you may not have, the unions you cannot join. The word *nigger* in the mouths of little white boys at school, the word *nigger* in the mouths of foremen on the job, the word *nigger* across the whole face of America! *Nigger! Nigger!* Like the word *Jew* in Hitler's Germany—Langston Hughes

Denigration: stem of Latin denigrare, 1. to blacken, make black or dark. 2. fig. To blacken, sully or stain (character or reputation); to defame (1526).—Oxford English Dictionary

The melancholy of the individual, as the melancholy of the species (of the race) exhibits the imperialism of the pure *culture* of the death drive—Jean Gillibert

The year 1929 is the date that Blanche E. Ferguson, Cullen's biographer, gives for his decline in creativity: "his writing was not progressing to his satisfaction. . . . He was writing now more from force of habit than from inspiration. He was plagued by the fear that he might keep on writing when he no longer had anything significant to say" (1966, 118). A generalized inhibition and depression followed his divorce and the uncertainty about his future career.[52]

The critical reception of *One way to heaven* (1932), Cullen's only novel, was very uneven. Some positive reviews were countered with negative and even hostile judgments following its publication.[53] Critics have said that *One way to heaven* is structurally flawed. Not long ago, Alan R. Shucard suggested that "Cullen, of course, became aware enough of his limitation as a writer of fiction not to attempt a novel ever again." In his critical evaluation of Cullen's career, he even states that "In a sense, then, consideration of *One way to heaven*, a sufficiently interesting exercise in itself, is a digression from an examination of the main business of Cullen's artistic life, the poetry upon which, in the end, he took his stand for posterity" (1984, 72). The main flaw highlighted by critics is the fact that the novel has two plots that are almost independent and that Cullen never quite manages to interrelate and harmonize them. It is mostly a question of structure and narrative design, which were alien to Cullen's long experience in writing poetry.

One way to heaven was published in 1932,[54] following his last book of poetry, *The black Christ and other poems* (1929a). The harsh critique that Cullen received at that time strikes me as particularly negative compared to the acclaim and praise that his poetry had gained. At the very least, it leaves us wondering how the same writer could concentrate such excellent and deficient qualities in his texts. At what level were critics placing their expectations for the first novel of such a precocious and brilliant poet?

In *One way to heaven*, Cullen presents us with a dichotomy that is subject to scrutiny and reflection, and his aim may not have been that of finding a resolution or even giving the structural impression of a coherent whole. As fragmented and discontinuous as the narrative may look to us, we should try to interrogate what it is that Cullen was attempting to convey with this conscious violation of completeness and perfect form. Cullen's readers, and especially his critics, turned out to be incapable of reading *One way to heaven* as other than a minor novel, incapable of assessing its achievements as independent of and apart from his poetry.

The early modernist explosion of narrative and poetic forms had unforeseen disconcerting effects on what was yet to come. During the 1920s and 1930s, the signs of the times seemed to suggest that narrative was less burdened by convention and could move more easily toward the modern. In *One way to heaven*, this possibility of crossing into the new resulted in failure. What does this have to do with Cullen's ideas on form, specifically with poetic as opposed to narrative form (or structure)? And what does this all have to do with the idea of form as the container of experience and in a wider sense with melancholia and its problematization of form?

In *One way to heaven*, Cullen narrates a story of Harlem Negroes from two strata of society. The plot centers mainly around Mattie, whose conversion to religion is fueled by her belief in Sam's conversion. Sam is an embodiment of the trickster, constantly masquerading as a man acting in "good faith."[55] He makes a racket of playing the revivals and in the novel is touched by Mattie's faith in him. He marries her but cannot keep up the pretense of true belief. Their lives are contrasted with those of Mattie's employer, Constancia Brandon, and her circle of Harlem "socialites."

Cullen was familiar to the Negro society represented in his novel by the wealthy Constancia Brandon, but he also knew humble people like Mattie Johnson, the dark-skinned housemaid who is the protagonist of the lower-class plot. Cullen also knew the kind of revival meeting where Mattie and Sam meet, since his father's conversion had taken place at a revival. Cullen's personal experience determined what some critics have identified as the strong element of realism in the novel.[56] He claims in an author's note that "Some of the characters in this book are fictitious." If we take this as an autobiographical statement, Cullen's only narrative could be read in its twofold plot as his personal tribute to Harlem and his race. *One way to heaven* is also a roman à clef in which one can identify some of the best-known figures of the Harlem of the 1920s, including hostess A'Lelia Walker, white novelist and entrepreneur Carl van Vechten, poet Langston Hughes, and black nationalist Marcus Garvey, among others.

Sam Lucas is an openly stereotypical character, but he has a specific idiom of his own. Introduced as an "ill-starred stranger" from the South, Sam is the character through which Cullen is going to play with the issue of Christian belief and make-believe, with the trompe l'oeil character of religion and ultimately with that of human reality as phantasy. Sam's make-believe performance at the revival meeting that opens the narrative will persuade the congregation of his conversion and will even bring Mattie into the new faith. It is important to note how Cullen deftly manipulates this make-believe quality of human action, a self-reflective movement over the make-believe quality of all fiction. Preachers and legislators do not quite grasp why some people are "moved by an action at whose root was the worm of deception" (34). Writers and tricksters see the matter quite differently.

Sam's body is abject from the start. Six years earlier he had lost his left arm on one of his stowaway trips on a freighter. Cullen describes this incident with the uncanny quality granted to those who are "living in death": "with his arm stretched out like an enticement for the sharp rear wheel that had kissed him into unconsciousness. Ever after he had had a feeling of having been buried before his time" (3–4). Cullen's outcast hero has a permanent "hungry, somewhat acidulous look" (4) and sports a scar on one cheek. Sam is indisputably a loser, and even if it will be hard to define him as a melancholic character implicit in his description and in the narrative's general atmosphere there is a sense of losing, of countless losses accumulated through many years in the stories of the dispossessed. Thus, Sam has lost his arm and his dignity from the start. Later Mattie loses her child, who dies shortly after being born, and even language in its repetitive ritualized form loses meaning, as when the congregation's hymns and testimonials "spoke in voices listlessly unintonated, as if they were speaking pieces the import of which was totally lost to them" (4).

Sam is thus limited to gambling and other petty truancies since this is one of the few "occupations" open to a black, uneducated, and mutilated man. Cullen's concern with the economics of sexual exchange cannot possibly pass unnoticed in a reading of the novel. Sam, who used to be a trickster, is now an unemployed man. And what kind of job can an uneducated and mutilated man undertake within a society that looks at the physicality of black men as their only potential in the circuit of economic and sexual exchange?[57]

Mattie works for Constancia Brandon, a wealthy colored lady who exemplifies the gap that Cullen wants to foreground between the lower and the upper classes in the black Harlem of the 1920s. To Sam's incredulity and scorn, Mattie responds that "Black folks know better how to treat black folks every time" (63). By the end of the novel, the differences between Mattie and Sam become more marked, separated as they are between her deep faith and the trap of his past. Mattie's attempt to win Sam back fails (he is having an affair), and she finally loses the child she is expecting.[58] It is important to note that sex is never explicitly addressed in the narrative. Sam and Mattie's sexual relationship is outside figurality; it remains unspeakable. Sex is only insinuated, indirectly alluded to, but sensuality is present in most of Cullen's descriptions of racialized bodies that, by virtue of the signifier race, bear the mark of their entrance into an economy of exchange.

The character of Aunt Mandy is split between her religious faith and her worldly fear, which is "striving to draw her into an opposing channel" (53). There is much that is pagan and occult in her, and she devotes some of her time to reading tea leaves and coffee dregs and to consulting her cards. Constancia Brandon is known as "Harlem's most charming hostess" (97), and her soirees attract writers, artists, and entrepreneurs of all kinds. She embodies the Negro vogue in women, speaks of art and business, and has been psychoanalyzed. Her parties are the only occasions when Negroes and whites interact; this apparent interracial confraternity is a mark of class, since the lower classes only relate with other blacks of the same condition. At some point, a secondary character in the novel comments that "at Constancia's race relations existed in theory only" (157), and this is the crux of the narrative.

Cullen foregrounds the ways in which racial differences are perceived by the black upper and lower classes. Mattie has objected to having whites invited to her wedding at Constancia Brandon's home. She laconically says, "I don't care much for white people" (105), and her employer concludes that she is "prejudiced" (109). The question of passing also briefly arises. The passing of whites for blacks is certainly the case with Carl van Vechten, who often was caricatured in blackface and apparently had passed for black as an undergraduate.[59] This strong desire on the part of some whites to pass for blacks is figured in a hilarious conversation between Constancia and her friend Walter Derwent, in which she tells him, "No, you couldn't pass for colored. Don't be pretentious" (109). This theme of fashionable racial passing from white to black was also reported by Fanon in *Black skin, white masks*, where he includes a series of impersonations in which underneath the facade of some whites' infatuation with black culture there lies a hidden identification: "white 'hot-jazz' orchestras, white blues and spiritual singers, white authors writing novels in which the Negro proclaims his grievances, whites in blackface" ([1952] 1967, 177).[60] During the 1920s, it was not uncommon to find fashionable whites who temporarily passed for blacks.

At Constancia's parties, the habitual concerns of black writers and artists are debated. These include the belief that whites take Negro literature far more seriously than blacks do, race consciousness, new ideas on education, and the recurrent return to Africa theme. Negro music—and at times dance—provides the entertainment for Constancia's soirees, from the blues to the "mongrel music" (203) in which one could trace notes of Africa, Harlem, and the Orient.

One way to heaven is full of debates about literature and art and also about card playing and practices of divination. There is a sense of ancestral magic that the black community identifies in practices that are transmitted through language. Even in church, "They had no hunger for the hard bread of reason, but for the soft, easily digested manna of magic" (14). The priest intones hymns like one possessed,[61] and new converts seem to be exorcizing their past selves. Religious conversion and magic are dangerously equated in the first chapter of the novel, since Sam Lucas, with his performance, is able to gain more converts than the priest himself.[62] Aunt Mandy is indisputably the character who comes closest to magic and occultism. She believes that her niece can win her husband back by recourse to a woman who "can mix a powder strong enough to win any man back" (240).

In the novel, the dichotomy between the lower and upper classes, the primitive and the cultivated, and the African past and an apparently American future is left unresolved. Once again this ambivalent pattern testifies to Cullen's unresolved contradictions and ultimately to his melancholia. We can say that parallel to the axis of class differentiation there runs one of racial differentiation, since in this almost all black context opportunities of class and education make some individuals "more black" than others. Race is also inescapably a construct bounded and inflected by other material, cultural, and sexual factors.[63] What lies below a surface of tolerance and interracial harmony is anxiety and fear of aggression: "we fear what the white world might say about the Negro race" (186–87), says Constancia at one point.

In this narrative, Cullen denounces the dilettantes who come to Harlem for its background, both modern and primitive, with its aura of the avant-garde and its luxuriant exoticism. At the time when race was itself made into a fad, Cullen refrains from an easy ascription to the Negro vogue. But Cullen's critique is never harsh, and even the frivolous figure of Constancia Brandon deserves some recognition because in the end she and her soirees might provide one of the few occasions for free speech: "In my home you are in a veritable temple whose reigning deity is free speech; if I stooped to facetiousness I might even say of unbridled loquacity" (165). In this respect, one of the most hilarious episodes in the narrative takes place at Constancia's salon, when she invites a racist and white supremacist (Professor Calhoun), author of the book *The menace of the Negro to our American civilization*, to lecture on this subject. Constancia parodically pledges "discreet and impartial attention" for a scholar "who has studied us long and ardently, with a microscopic seriousness" (170). Calhoun advocates the return to Africa of all Negroes for reasons far different from those given by characters such as the duchess of Uganda, but Cullen's parodical tour de force makes them appear to be in agreement. The duchess of Uganda argues: "I am in hearty agreement with your ideas on the rehabilitation of Africa by the American Negro. Oh, the green forests of Africa, the amber water of the Nile, the undiscovered oases of the Sahara, what foundations to build upon!" (177).[64]

Some of Cullen's views on language are also implicit in the narrative. The formulaic nature of religious language, worn out through repetition, voids it of all meaning. In Constancia Brandon's speech, language becomes reified in an endless logorrhea. Sam, Mattie, and the lower classes speak in "dialect" and Constancia Brandon and the rest of the upper class characters in perfect American English. Cullen also suggests that mastering the language is a privilege of the upper classes, since Sam's speech is poor and fractured and he, among others, is characterized as a "creature of action and not of speech" (82). Opposite Sam is Constancia Brandon's description as a woman, whose "tongue was her chief attraction. . . . Her schoolmates called her Lady Macbeth, not that she was tragic, but that she never spoke in a monosyllable where she could use a longer word" (92).

Most critics have underscored the structural flaws of Cullen's novel. It is my contention that this collapse has to do with what, following Klein, we have called the symbolic equation. Cullen literalizes experience to the point of hyperreality (physical and psychological descriptions of characters, a wealth of detail in settings), while at the same time he strives to metaphorize, to find a proper symbol for, what he wants to portray as the parodical rendering of the essence of the new in the Harlem Renaissance. The white man's desire for primitive and exotic black bodies is countered by Cullen's narrative of abjection and death. Through the figure of Sam, Cullen throws back the reverse of white desire, a castrating image of black male sexuality.[65]

By the end of the story, Sam, with a make-believe performance similar to the revival meeting experience, and by recourse to a vision, persuades Mattie that he is called to heaven and saves his soul.[66] What is Cullen trying to convey with this self-reflective meditation on the issue of phantasy, narrative, and reality? And what does this have to say about poetry and poetic form? Why is it that the flaws are always attributed to structural failures—in the sense of excessive adherence to traditional form in poetry or divorce of independent plots in narrative? To suggest that Cullen was not sufficiently aware of the new modernist concerns about form or that he was just a renegade of the race is too much of a simplification. What of the psychic dynamics at work in Cullen's texts? I believe that it is by recourse to the psychoanalytic insight into melancholia that we can best understand why these fractures and discontinuities emerge in Cullen's writings, together with almost perfect and coherent poetic constructions. I believe that it is inexcusable to approach all this through a close inspection of the effects that the modernist cultures of the death drive have upon his work.

The critical perception of the decline of Cullen's productivity, his paralysis, may in part be due to the harsh reception of his last books and the kind of expectations that were placed on his writing. Upon his death in 1946, W. E. B. Du Bois wrote an article in which the rhetoric of failure taints his critical evaluation: "It is sheer nonsense to put before Negro writers the ideal of being just writers and not Negroes. . . . The ideal of pure art divorced from actual life is nothing but an ideal of questionable value in any day or time. . . . The opportunity then for literary expression upon which American Negroes have so often turned their backs is their opportunity and not their handicap. That Countee Cullen was born with the Twentieth Century as a black boy to live in Harlem was a priceless experience. . . . Yet, as I have said, Cullen's career was not finished. It did not culminate. It laid [a] fine, beautiful foundation, but the shape of the building never emerged" (quoted in Lomax 1987, 221). Du Bois's negative assessment of Cullen's literary career echoes his militant concern with racial consciousness and his personal engagement with the plight of the black community. In this piece, Du Bois takes Cullen to task because he did not conform to the paradigm of the engaged Negro writer set up by Du Bois himself. But to what extent can we say that Cullen's ambivalence and contradictions were not largely the ferment of this bourgeois movement that we call the Harlem Renaissance? And how can we measure the level of engagement reached by other writers and intellectuals in the same milieu? Isn't it the case that Du Bois's rhetoric in this passage in some ways repeats the concomitant rhetoric of "beginnings"—and thus, not developments or conclusions—that was the target of the harshest critiques launched against the Renaissance?[67]

To conclude, I would like to reflect on the specific relationship between the subject's melancholia and what we may call the melancholia of the race. Is it not the case that in Cullen's writings there emerges a sense of collective melancholia associated with race? When Jean Gillibert argues that "One cannot understand individual 'melancholy' without articulating it with the melancholy of the species (of the Race), with the refusal of this human 'Race' to advance any further into that which determines it, into this barbarity of destruction that rests at the same time both on the deflection of self-destruction (death drive) towards the others, and in the commensalism, the common globality of a primordial 'substance' that can be shared by all in identification" (1979, 182), we should also be ready to raise the question of to what extent "race" encompasses here much more than skin color and is itself implicated in the category of nation (America as a metonymy for the United States and France, versus the colonized, the West Indies, and African and other colonies), species (the human race), and even the gender binary (the male and female race)? And what are the implications that this pure culture of the death drive has for those whose very invisibility dispossesses them of any possible identification? Gillibert's insight does not overlook the fact that the individual's melancholia, as much as the melancholia of the race (or the species), involves this imperialism of the pure culture of the death drive. Countee Cullen's melancholia is the product of this impossible deflection of the death drive toward an Other that results in introjection and internalization inside the ego. His meteoric writing career ends up as that of a loser, at the margins of recent histories of modernism. Is this literary and critical oblivion an effect of his melancholia? To what extent can this psychic malaise cripple a subject's or a writer's life and future? And what, indeed, are the causes that seduce us into this cannibalistic practice of cultural consumption and evacuation?

The unconscious roots of mechanisms of domination and subordination suggest that there is no simple way out of racist beliefs and ideologies. The racist, as Sartre said of the antisemite, "takes his stand from the start on the ground of irrationalism" ([1946] 1948, 26). Cullen himself occupies a precarious space and a role he was never entirely free to occupy or resist. He had enormous difficulty in negotiating his way through the opposing set of black and white expectations that all too early had been placed on him. Whether Cullen speaks from behind Du Bois's "veil" or behind his own poetic persona is not as crucial as recognizing that this doubleness in his discourse has much to do with the problematics of melancholia and its insatiable hunger for introjection. The causes of the melancholic affliction in modernist cultures of the death drive, which sadistically thrive upon racial, sexual, and even class differences, determine the specificity of Cullen's represented and lived melancholia. In his endeavor to express "the heights and depths of emotion which I feel as a Negro," he bordered on the depths of death, loss, and dejection.[68]

Afterword: Modern(ist) Cultures of the Death Drive and the Melancholic Apparatus

In my view the danger arising from the inner working of the death instinct is the first cause of anxiety.—Melanie Klein

To seek reality is both to set out to explore the injury inflicted by it—to turn back on, and to try to penetrate, the state of being *stricken, wounded* by reality—and to attempt, at the same time, to reemerge from the paralysis of this state, to engage reality as an advent, a movement, and as a vital, critical necessity of *moving on*. It is beyond the shock of being stricken, but nonetheless within the wound and from within the woundedness that the event, incomprehensible though it may be, becomes accessible.—Shoshana Felman

The idea of cultures of the death drive developed in the preceding pages moves on ground contested in many urgent, simultaneous debates—in psychoanalysis, gender studies, literature, and the visual arts—and its epistemological and interpretative value derives from its willingness to join them and show their relations. This project has addressed directly the status of melancholia in the object-relations orthodox Freudian debate—showing the dramatic bearing that such melancholia has for the construction of postmodern subjectivity and ethics—and it has approached in the context of Klein's work the recurring problem posed for literary studies by the troubled definitions of *modernism* and *modernity*. We have examined in this light the emergence in the first decades of the twentieth century of a concept of "culture" posed specifically against the Arnoldian tradition, and we have briefly stressed in this examination the status of visuality in literary modernism. This project has also been an attempt to contribute to the current feminist and psychoanalytic reexamination of Klein's work (e.g., in the work of Rose, Mitchell, Butler, Jacobus, and Spivak). It should help us to rethink the status of melancholia following the work of Butler and Kristeva, among others, and it should invigorate and help us to recast the tired debate over the literary "applications" of psychoanalytic models. *Cultures of the death drive* set out to clarify the institutional overinvestment in definitions of the modern and to lay out strategies for articulating the fields of gender, psychoanalysis, subjectivity, and ethics in innovative ways.

The topic of the dialogue at work in these pages can be expressed in two questions. The first involves the question of the relationship between, on the one hand, the novelty of Klein's theorization of the "depressive position" as well as her theorization of that position as an experience of the new (an "experience" of the openness and provisionality of the phantasmatic region of the symbolic). The second concerns the aesthetic valorization of defamiliarization that characterizes literary modernism, both thematically and formally.

In several places, I have argued that the Kleinian depressive position can be read as a theoretical phantasy or as a phantasy of theory, that is, as a phantasy that produces theory as well as phantasmatic settings and scenarios. The depressive position appears as some kind of asymptotic boundary that we constantly strive but always fail to reach. In this Kleinian possibility of another kind of phantasy lies the potential for liberation. The space of the depressive position has no particular shape or site and continually creeps through the subject's behavior and actions, in-forming them, but it is also a space of dissolution. The Kleinian depressive position, I would argue, can be rethought in terms of a theoretical phantasy that unveils the open and provisional nature of a system that avoids fixity and closure. Reparation and integration are only partial outcomes, never fully achieved. The subject is founded on the reproduction of a failure and the repetition of defensive strategies; simultaneously, all this is countered by efforts toward integration and reparation under the stimulus of what is yet to come.

The first question concerning Klein's writing and the Kleinian theorization as modernist per se is posed in a number of different ways in the opening and more general chapters and then again in the consideration of Woolf, Strachey, Barnes, and Cullen. One of its answers comes in the chapter on Woolf's *To the lighthouse*—a novel about which altogether too much has been written, and yet a text explored afresh here by bringing to the question of Woolf's reliance on visuality a dramatic analogue in the work of Magritte. Trompe l'oeil acts, as we have written, "as a frame for the enactment of that flash when something ineluctably occurred," a "something" associated with the unmourned death of the mother. This experience of the persistence of the occurred and its sudden reenacting as failed mourning manifests itself as the compensatory investment of affect in the field of the visual. To the lighthouse expresses in its notorious epistemophilia the fetish value of the eye as a stand-in for the mother one cannot mourn, which is to say that the value of "novelty" in Woolf's text (as that which suddenly strikes the eye, both for Woolf's characters and in the phenomenology of reading as constituted by the work: the "stroke" of the lighthouse for Mrs. Ramsay, the "jar upon the nerves" that Lily describes, as well as the notorious parenthetical instancing of Mrs. Ramsay's death for the reader's eyes) arises as a stand-in for that figure whose loss cannot be mourned or even acknowledged. "Modernist melancholia," as I have named it, can then be understood clinically as the unassimilated or unintrojected anxiety deriving from the asymmetry between the fetish value of what "enacts the flash when something ineluctably occurred" and the ontology of the event that occurs (any event having the "good" dimension of "having occurred," hence of providing consciousness with an instance for reflection and ultimately a ground for self-reflection; and the "bad" dimension of being genuinely new in never having occurred for consciousness, hence of occurring so as to mark consciousness as inescapably retrospective, always what Freud would call nachträglich). As an aesthetic phenomenon, modernist melancholia can be understood, as I have suggested, as the work's memorializing of the "cultural and emotional losses of our pasts," a formulation that joins the work of Abraham (melancholia as the encryptment of the death of the other) to a strong sense of the social or cultural dimension of memory (our pasts).

It is here that we find the second question on which this project turns. What political and social forms of freedom, we ask, can be derived from Klein's theorization of the relationship between melancholia and the depressive position? And to what extent, then, can we return for models of freedom to a modernist aesthetic that dwells on and draws its force from the memorializing of social "loss"? These questions serve strikingly to recast the terms of the arguments about the "politics" of modernism that we have inherited from the Brecht-Lukács-Bloch debates—and in a language grounded on a psychosocial rather than a sociological understanding of the modernist period. Again, this question runs through the many-voiced dialogue in this volume. It is at issue when we discuss different ways of relating Strachey's biography to his writing or Magritte's schematizing of the traumatic event to the sense of history in Woolf or ultimately when we come down to the question of lesbian and gay melancholia in Barnes and Cullen. A tentative answer is given early: the depressive position marks a space of instability and vacillation that is located in our process of construction of ourselves. This space "unveils" the incompleteness and openness of self-construction and sets out the ineluctable insistence of other kinds of phantasy within ourselves—where "other" should be understood as the unassimilable social other. On the basis of a depressive position that faces or comes to terms with this unassimilable social Other, then, and on the basis of the "tension" that marks this encounter, a form of "psychic integration" becomes available as a "precondition of social effectivity." Here the argument rejoins the work of (among others) Rose, Laclau, Butler, Žižek, and critics who paradoxically make such tension into the ground of "social effectivity." Reading with an eye toward modernist melancholia, then, and training oneself to the disciplined aestheticization of this "tension," turns out to provide a model for "social effectivity," for the conversion of the experience of the loss of the ideological field of the social into the experience of the insistence of the social Other for consciousness.

Throughout the preceding pages, the reader may have perceived some tension concerning the "construction of (social) selves." On one hand, I have argued that the unstable space of the depressive position serves to introduce an openness to the social, by means of an awareness of the incompleteness of symbolic phantasies, which must always be supplemented and in-completed by other phantasies that are not properly "ours." This seems to us unassailable and clearly not quite compatible with the image of "psychic integration" presented as the consequence of a full assumption of the depressive position. To the extent that the depressive position is indeed fully assumed, it ceases to be "unstable" in the peculiarly fruitful and open way required (*fully assumed* here meaning something like "arrived at and recognized by means of an analytic working through"). But to say a contrario that it is radically unassimilable, to say that we cannot assume the depressive position at all, is to grant it an ideal status—as the "outside" of "ourselves," something having roughly the status of the Lacanian Real—that does not comfortably fit either the clinical or the analytic scheme Klein outlines. This hesitation is problematically fuzzy in

Klein, and quite unsustainable without careful qualification and working through, when we pass from the domain of analysis to the domain of ethics, as I have very briefly attempted to show in chapter 6. In the domain of ethics, the question assumes a more familiar shape: is the depressive position presented as a regulative ideal of conduct that, being external to "us," commands assent in the form of a duty to a concept that shows itself broader than "our-self"? Or is the depressive position a determining condition of what makes us "ourselves," hence commanding assent in the form of a duty to what will show itself to be most properly our own? The step from modernist melancholia to an ethics of freedom cannot be taken without establishing what it is that is "lost"—where the "mother" is: without, as it were, or within. We should note a couple of things. In the first place, we are in good company here: radical democratic theory in general requires that the status of its representation of ethical ground must remain unresolved, with the use of the notion of "suture" in Laclau and Mouffe being the best-known example. In the second place, Deleuze and Guattari's discussion of Klein in Anti-Oedipus ([1972] 1977) usefully glosses this very problem. Although this distinction between an external, regulative concept and an internal, determining ontology needs a more thorough analysis, one that falls beyond the scope of this volume, we should take it on directly in future work.

I have also echoed Althusser's legacy and explored the role of the Oedipus conflict as a melancholic apparatus. In Althusser's view, whereas the State Apparatus belongs entirely to the public domain, the majority of the Ideological State Apparatuses (ISAs are part of the private domain: "Churches, Parties, Trade Unions, families, some schools, most newspapers, cultural ventures, etc., etc., are private" (1971, 137). The ISAs function by means of "ideology," and "An ideology always exists in a apparatus, and its practice, or practices. This existence is material" (156). And what are the social practices that fuel these modernist cultures of the death drive? If the onset of the Oedipus conflict—the oedipal injunction of sexual difference—coincides with the onset of the Kleinian depressive position, and the latter is described as "a melancholia in statu nascendi" (Klein [1940] 1975, 345), it seems clear that oedipalization runs parallel to melancholization and that the individual's access to gender must go through the experience of some unacknowledged loss.

In Klein's work, we have read a sense of self that involves rebelliousness against the normalizing constraints of conventional gender stereotypes of femininity and masculinity, a sociopsycho material domain in which gender interpellation fails. The foundation of the individual in a primary act of internalization of an object (the breast and/or its substitutes), by definition always already lost, transforms the Kleinian account into a privileged scenario for a reflection on melancholia and the melancholic constitution of the sexual subject. In Klein's theorization, the melancholia of gender comes dramatically to the fore.

Modernism is a discursive field structured by the death drive. I have attempted to show how loss figures in modernist literature and how it might be read in a sustained effort to use the Kleinian theorization for contemporary literary and social analysis. Klein herself was a modernist writer who illuminated some of the key psychic dimensions of modernist literature. Among these dimensions, melancholia becomes especially important since it is the relation to the disavowed past and to what is disowned in desire.

Throughout this volume, I have been pervasively and systematically addressing loss, something that has come to interest many of us during this period, when loss, trauma, and aggression seem to be of great concern. Thus, in current critical discourse Eric Santner has identified the ubiquitous presence of what he calls "the rhetoric of mourning" in recent years and alludes to the overwhelming presence of a "metaphorics of loss and impoverishment" (1990, 7) in postmodern theory. He especifically links these discourses to the collapse of the ideals of modernity and to the current project to open up new ways to live with the complexities and instabilities of new social arrangements. He writes: "These discourses, primarily poststructuralist in inspiration, appear committed to the vigilant and radical critique of what are taken to be the narcissisms and nostalgias central to the project of modernity—namely, Enlightenment faith in progress—and the Western tradition more generally. These discourses propose a kind of perpetual leave-taking from phantasies of plenitude, purity, centrality, totality, unity, and mastery. Such phantasies and their various narrative performances whether cast in the rhetoric of totalization or liberation, are in turn seen as the primary sources of violence in history, the Third Reich being only the most extreme example in a long historical series" (7). In this respect, Shoshana Felman and Dori Laub's work in *Testimony* (1992) figures history through the Holocaust as a trauma to which we must bear witness by deploying the psychoanalytical assumption that an individual history can metaphorically stand in for History. Other psychoanalytical borrowings include a modeling of history as a traumatic event "voided" in its moment of inscription and known only through a retrospective reconstruction produced in a dialogue with a listening Other. And, finally, the problem of knowing one's historical present is figured through the force of a psychic trauma that literally possesses one's subjectivity. Trauma recreates the problem of historicity and our access to it. Crises in accessing the historical truth produced by the specificity of the Holocaust might be generalizable to a more overarching "traumatic" theory of history.

This is not so far from Fredric Jameson's elaboration of the Spinozian-Althusserian understanding of History as an "absent cause" in *The political unconscious:* "History is what hurts, it is what refuses desire and sets inexorable limits to individual as well as collective praxis. . . . History can be apprehended only through its effects, and never directly as some reified force" (1981, 102). This calls for an active "working through" of individual and collective histories in the narrative of modernity in which History dooms us to the shock of events.

Melancholia and trauma have also come together, in a contemporary crisis of unprecedented proportions, in what Linda Singer has called "the age of epidemic": "a rubric under which to link a range of theoretical and political questions that have emerged around sexuality in a variety of registers. It is a discourse prompted by, speaking after, the circulation of AIDS as a social signifier. . . . An epidemic is already a situation that is figured as out of control, hence at least indirectly a recognition of the limits of existing responses, hence a call for new ones. Because the destabilization effect is also represented as a threat, a threat to the very order of things, epidemic conditions tend to reflect a kind of panic logic which seeks immediate and dramatic responses to the situation at hand" (1993, 27–28). The AIDS epidemic has made us aware of the occurrence of death as a social event. When death as a uniquely singular and individual experience loses its private meaning and becomes a social event, both the individual and the community find themselves overwhelmed with irreparable loss. The tidal wave of books about AIDS over the past twenty years, coupled with society's increasing acceptance of the disease as a fact of modern life, has produced a continued cultural rewounding, silent and grieving, compared with the terror and grieving of the early years. The cultural production on and about AIDS (memoirs, documents, grassroots militancy, art) addresses this loss as it chronicles the effort to recognize the integrity of the mortal body—even as that body changes. This living in uncertainty, this state of profound melancholia and radical doubt, parallels, even represents, that engagement with life.

What does a writer do when the world collapses but write? In writing and reading, we search for meaning and perspective and lessons to be shared. Even in its most extreme cases the discourses of melancholia and trauma offer a kind of survivor's guide, not just for those who suffer from some traumatic loss but for anyone who is, after all, only human.

The death drive pedagogy of melancholia reaches for generalization and in some ways resists the lessons of History. What is the appropriate way to write and then read the signs of texts and bodies pushed to their limits by regulatory regimes, by technologies of gender, illness, and death? These states of social abjection always lead us to return to the realm of the literal, sometimes a literal recording or testimony, with no language of its own. Ultimately, when this story of loss requires death, the writing must pass through the self of the witness who remains and holds a stubborn attachment to reference.

The spectacle of this textual and bodily disarray is painful to witness, but it also offers us a horizon against which to launch a project, in the wake of modernism, for future new selves. This is nowhere more apparent than in current accounts of survivors of the Holocaust and in the traumatic AIDS and incest survivors' memoirs. Modernist cultures of the death drive are inseparable from bearing witness to this devastation: not forgotten, but memorialized. For, if the ultimate commandment of History is not to forget, what can be more proper than the will to record?

NOTES

All translations of French texts are mine unless otherwise stated.

Introduction

1   In this book, I write *phantasy* with a *ph*, following common Kleinian usage since the 1920s, when Klein's work began.

2   The International Psychoanalytical Association had been founded in 1910 and Freud had designated Carl Jung as its first president. He was succeeded after World War I by Karl Abraham and later by Ernest Jones.

3   One of Jones's motives for his support of Klein seems to have been his personal interest in keeping her in London to analyze his own children.

4   The discussions, minutes, resolutions, and relevant personal correspondence have been edited by Pearl King and Ricardo Steiner and published as no. 11 in the New Library of Psychoanalysis under the title *The Freud-Klein controversies, 1941–45* (1991). As a result of them, the Society split into three groups, the (Anna) Freudians, the Kleinians, and the Middle Group (Winnicott and others).

5   I am clearly drawing from Louis Althusser's well-known formulation about the notion and function of "apparatuses" in his "Ideology and ideological state apparatuses" (1971). This is amply discussed in several chapters of this book (especially chapter 5), which emphasize the nature of Oedipus as a melancholic apparatus.

6   This well-known quote comes from Lord Alfred Douglas's (Oscar Wilde's lover) poem "Two Loves."

7   This "return to Klein" is present in the recent work of Juliet Mitchell. See, for example, her edition of and introduction to *The selected Melanie Klein* (1986). See also Rose 1993, Doane and Hodges 1992, and Phillips and Stonebridge 1998.

8   See especially Klein's "Love, guilt, and reparation ([1937] 1975) and *The psycho-analysis of children* ([1932] 1975) for accounts of male-female developmental differences.

9   Jacqueline Rose, in her chapter "Negativity in the work of Melanie Klein," has emphasized that much of the critique directed against Klein was centered around the issue of

the death drive: "She was seen as bringing the death drive under the sway of a subject, as making the death drive constitutive of a subject, who is not yet enough of a subject to be mastered or controlled" (1993, 150).

10   The fertilized ovum contains genes derived from each parent and is surrounded by a cell membrane. Later the fetus is covered with its skin. There is a boundary around the embryo, which develops a relationship with its exterior by growing an umbilical cord and a placenta through which nutrients are transmitted. As it grows in size, it moves around in the amniotic fluid, restricted and contained within the uterine walls. Although in a way it seems that at birth it separates from its mother, the real separation is from a part of itself, the placenta.

11   In *Black sun*, Julia Kristeva has argued that "Melancholia . . . ends up in asymbolia, in loss of meaning: if I am no longer capable of translating or metaphorizing, I become silent and I die" ([1987] 1989, 42). Asymbolia is, in her view, an intrinsic element in melancholia: "I shall call *melancholia* the institutional symptomatology of inhibition and asymbolia that becomes established now and then or chronically in a person, alternating more often than not with the so-called manic phase of exaltation" (9).

12   Kristeva has remarked that melancholia "does assert itself in times of crisis; it is spoken of, establishes its archeology, generates its representations and its knowledge" (ibid., 8).

13   In this respect, Luce Irigaray has observed that the male has been constructed as time and the woman as place. Woman, the place from which we emerge, is the name we give to our location in space. Man, understood as action, changes and transforms that space into an evolving entity. She writes: "As a man re-creates woman from outside, from inside-outside, he re-places himself outside, as an actor outside, a creator outside. By actively putting himself outside, he re-sculpts a body for himself. By using a tool? He reconstructs his own body as a result of engendering the body of the other. By using his hand, his penis—which is not merely a tool of pleasure, but a truly useful tool of alliance, incarnation, creation. Woman, insofar as she is a container, is never a closed one. Place is never closed. The boundaries touch against one another while still remaining open" ([1984] 1993, 51).

14   Betsky 1995, 162. Betsky is actually referring to the Bauhaus and the roots of modernism in the Arts and Crafts style and sensibility.

15   In this respect, Mitchell has also argued that Klein's phenomenology dwells within a field of horizontal relationships: "The dominant sociological phenomenologies of the twentieth century in which Klein participated study lateral, horizontal, not vertical relationships" (1986, 29).

16   To my knowledge, Magritte was heterosexual. He was married to Georgette Berger for over forty years (from 1922 until he died in 1967). This does not mean that he unproblematically embraced the gender binary. His canvases show his sexuality in its specific and peculiar forms. I engage these and other questions in chapter 9.

17   With regard to this, Graham Dawson has suggested that the Kleinian elaboration of the depressive position incorporates indispensable notions such as tolerance, openness, and integration. He writes: "Whereas idealization and projective disavowal fix and guard social identity within a sharply polarized boundary between those who are 'like me' and those whose likeness is denied in the name of some irreducible difference, the Kleinian

theory of the depressive position identifies a psychic potential for the movement of these split and defensive modes of composure towards more integrated, open and tolerant modes. The realization of this potential is founded upon the emotional tolerance of once disavowed experiences of pain and loss, and upon recognition of the gendered self as a multiple and contradictory compound of 'masculine' and 'feminine' introjections" (1994, 286–87).

1 Itineraries

1 In a letter dated May 11, 1908, Freud wrote to Abraham: "I was always pleased that Bleuler and Jung so successfully overcame the resistances based on their different personality structure. This makes the change in them all the more painful" (Freud and Abraham 1965, 36).

2 In the last version of "Mourning and melancholia," Abraham is only cited twice. This recognition of indebtedness absent from the original manuscript was added by Freud after Abraham's vindication of his ideas. Freud, in a letter of May 4, 1915, writes: "Your comments on melancholia are very useful to me, and I unhesitatingly incorporated in my paper those parts of them that I could use" (Freud and Abraham 1965, 220).

3 I am thinking specifically of texts such as Freud's *Three essays on the theory of sexuality* ([1905] 1953), "Psycho-analytic notes on an autobiographical account of a case of paranoia (dementia paranoides)" ([1911b] 1953), "On narcissism: an introduction" ([1914] 1953), and "On transformations of instinct as exemplified by anal erotism" ([1917] 1953).

4 On the issue of the melancholic's masochistic self-punishment, in "Notes on the psycho-analytical investigation and treatment of manic-depressive insanity and allied conditions" (1911), Abraham writes: "As a result of the repression of sadism, depression, anxiety, and self-reproach arise. But if such an important source of pleasure from which the active instincts flow is obstructed there is bound to be a reinforcement of the masochistic tendencies. The patient will adopt a passive attitude, and will obtain pleasure from his suffering and from continually thinking about himself. Thus even the deepest melancholic distress contains a hidden source of pleasure" (147).

5 See Ferenczi [1913] 1956, 181–203.

6 See especially Freud's *Three essays on the theory of sexuality* ([1905] 1953) and "Leonardo da Vinci and a memory of his childhood" ([1910] 1953).

7 Being a highly mimetic concept, identification took up different masks and shapes according to context, and it was at times impossible to disentangle it from other forms of internalization. Furthermore, Freud did not differentiate between identification leading to ego development and identifications involved in superego formation. There are different degrees as well as different types of identifications. They usually span a long period of time, but we may also find processes of transitory identification. Identification occurs in various stages of development, and it plays a central role as an intrinsic part of object relationships. For a good account of Freud's manifold and complex views on identification, see Fuss 1995. Incorporation was used rather more specifically by Freud in his *New introductory lectures on psychoanalysis* ([1932, 1933b] 1953) to refer to the aim of the

oral instinct. He had considered it the "prototype" of later processes of identification as early as 1905 in *Three essays on the theory of sexuality*. Abraham was the first analyst to stress that all forms of internalization can be regarded as deriving from oral incorporative impulses ([1924] 1949). Incorporation, in its turn, has also been related in complex ways not only to phantasies of merging with the object (Fenichel [1925] 1953) but to those of destroying the object. This latter and most important relation for our purposes was first mentioned by Freud in the well-known *Little Hans* ([1914, 1918] 1953) case history. It was developed by Melanie Klein in *The psycho-analysis of children* ([1932] 1975e).

8   I am of course alluding to Maria Torok's well-known 1968 essay "The illness of mourning and the fantasy of the exquisite corpse," where she discusses introjection versus incorporation (Abraham and Torok 1994, 107–24).

9   See Abraham's "Introduction de Thalassa" in the French edition of *L'Ecorce et le noyau*: "If our body is language from the origin, it could only have acquired the basic significations by a still more primitive symbolization, achieved during the phylogenesis, through the traumatisms and deprivations that affected the species. The language of organs and functions would then be, in turn, a set of symbols taking us back to a still more archaic language and so on. This considered, it would appear faultlessly logic to view the organism as a hyeroglyphic text, stratified all along the history of the species, that an appropriate research would be able to decipher. This unexpected way of considering of the biological fact opens a whole field of hypotheses, verifiable but radically new. A new science is born: the psychoanalysis of the origins or *bioanalysis*" (Abraham and Torok 1978, 20).

10 In "Mourning and melancholia," Freud writes that "they are far from evincing towards those around them the attitude of humility and submission that alone would befit such worthless people. On the contrary, they make the greatest nuissance of themselves and always seem as though they felt slighted and had been treated with great injustice" ([1915, 1917] 1953, 248).

11 On alimentary orgasm, see Radó 1928.

12 Radó also sees orality as being at the center of mania: "it is a striking fact that in mania the adult with his manifold potentialities of action and reaction reproduces the uninhibited instinctual manifestations which we observe in the euphoria of the satiated suckling. That the quality of the reactions of a period of life in which the super-ego did not as yet exist should be the pattern upon which is modelled the manic state (the basis of which is a temporary withdrawal of the super-ego) is exactly what we should expect" (ibid., 436).

13 The exact quote from the opening passage of "Mourning and melancholia" reads: "Dreams having served us as the prototype in normal life of narcissistic mental disorders, we will try to throw some light on the nature of melancholia by comparing it with the normal affect of mourning" ([1915, 1917] 1953, 243).

14 Freud describes this hole as "an open wound, drawing to itself cathectic energies— which in the transference neuroses we have called 'anti-cathexes'—from all directions, and emptying the ego until it is totally impoverished" (ibid., 253).

15 In this respect, Leo Bersani has suggested that the identification with a lost love object is intrinsically a self-punishment and that the process of decathexis in the relinquishing of

the object implies, in turn, a narcissistic and masochistic action. He writes: "More exactly, in this ambiguously desexualizing process, an object is resexualized (narcissistically and masochistically) by the very move which decathects it. The narcissistic pleasures of these identifications are therefore inseparable from masochistic pleasures, and these perhaps inevitable substitutions of identifications for object-cathexes have to be classified on the dysfunctional side of human development" (1986, 96).

16 As noted, Freud referred to the process whereby the melancholic identified with his lost object of love, setting it up within his ego, as "narcissistic identification" ([1915, 1917] 1953, 249–51). Later, in *Group psychology and the analysis of the ego* ([1921] 1953), Freud abandoned the term *narcissistic identification* and began to use *introjection* instead. There is no clear-cut distinction between *identification* and *introjection* in the Freudian text.

17 In *Group psychology and the analysis of the ego* ([1921] 1953), Freud advances the idea that identification is the basis for community. Donald Meltzer points out that Freud, though rather ambiguous on the subject, actually uses identification in two ways in that book. The first is "introjective identification," in which aggressiveness directed against the father is turned against the self (or that part of the self that identifies with the father). This process is the foundation of civilization, with all the harshness that this implies. The second form is "primary identification," or symbiosis, in which love of another is inseparable from wanting to be like the other (1978, 119–22). Primary identification is based on a tendency to deny the separateness and autonomy of the other. For Meltzer, "the other is simply not recognized as separate" (122). This makes it questionable that identification might be the basis for community at all.

18 In *The ego and the id* ([1923] 1953), Freud places this critical function in the superego, a harsh, cruel, and punishing agency. For Leo Bersani, the excessive severity of the Freudian superego is its true raison d'être. In his view, the postoedipal superego in Freud "legalizes pre-Oedipal aggressiveness, it transforms object-loss into object interdiction, and thereby makes us permanently guilty of those very moves of consciousness by which objects of desire become agents of punishment. . . . [I]t is perhaps really a form of object-relation in which the destruction of the object can be infinitely repeated as a form of masochistic pleasure" (1986, 97–98).

19 Regarding the ego of the melancholic, Bersani has aptly remarked that "What Freud calls the ego is a type of object-relation without the object and strictly speaking, without the relation; the object is appropriated without having been lost. The ego is a collector who transports inert objects from the outside to the inside. Instead of desiring the world, the ego vampirizes it" (1986, 95). W. W. Meissner uses the same trope of vampirism when comparing the eagerness of the infant at the breast and the force of introjection with a scenario of vampire fantasies: "Introjective identification starts with the child's earliest relation to the breast, even in the vampire fantasies of sucking and biting. Introjective identification is thus synonymous with the greed-based oral-sadistic introjection of the mother's breast" (1987, 37).

20 When Klein puts forward her arguments on the relations between obsessional neurosis and early stages of the superego in *The psycho-analysis of children* ([1932] 1975e), she writes about the tendency to heap up possessions observed in many patients. She says that "analyses of adults, too, have shown me that the wish to have ready a sum of money for

any contingency is really a desire to be armed against an attack on the part of the mother they have robbed—a mother who was as often as not in point of fact long since dead—by being able to give her what they have stolen. The fear of being deprived of the contents of their body compels them to be continually accumulating more money so as to have 'reserves' to fall back on" (235).

21 Regarding suicide, Freud argued that "The analysis of melancholia now shows that the ego can kill itself only if, owing to the return of the object cathexis, it can treat itself as an object—if it is able to direct against itself the hostility which relates to an object and which represents the ego's original reaction to objects in the external world" ([1915, 1917] 1953, 252).

22 Jean Gillibert remarks at this point that it is upon this totalizing narcissistic attitude that the fundament of castration rests (1979, 163).

23 Gillibert has noted that omophagic rites give testimony to the blissful quality of orality. Euripides, in *Bacchantes*, shows King Pentheus being devoured by his mother—"Dionysos' maenad." Christian rites repeat in the Eucharist the banquet of eating and drinking the sacrificial body of Christ (1979, 166–67). In a different context but also stressing the crucial quality of orality in development, Wilfred R. Bion has suggested in *Learning from experience* (1962a), that the caretaker engages in a process of "digestion" for the infant, thus enabling it to find meaning, to use it, and to learn from it. Without a caring and receptive atmosphere in early infancy, we would be left with the task of coping with all kinds of strange and incoherent thought fragments. But when the child is able to experience this deeply attuned containing he or she is able to think, dream, feel, and learn.

24 Jacqueline Rose, in her chapter "Negativity in the work of Melanie Klein," writes on the black holes of physics in an illuminating reflection on the role of negativity in psychic structure and the universe of physics, linking all this to the question of knowledge and its origins (1993, 137–90).

25 In *Civilization and its discontents*, Freud's somewhat hopeful vision that men and women may come to master their aggressivity after achieving greater cultural development is striking given the melancholy tone of the book.

26 According to Gillibert, melancholia entails one of the most difficult problems to solve in psychoanalysis, namely, that of the differences and resemblances between the superego and the ego-ideal (1979, 190).

27 In "Mourning and melancholia," Freud makes clear the position of the analyst vis-à-vis the melancholic patient when he writes: "It would be equally fruitless from a scientific and a therapeutic point of view to contradict a patient who brings these accusations against his ego. He must surely be right in some way and be describing something that is as it seems to him to be. Indeed, we must at once confirm some of his statements without reservation" ([1915, 1917] 1953, 41).

2 *Kleinian Metapsychology*

1 After the death of her favorite brother, Emanuel, in 1902, Klein—who was twenty years old—entered a morbid state of mourning. As Phyllis Grosskurth has amply shown, Klein managed to publish her brother's writings in 1906, and her depression became more

marked. In her correspondence around 1907, Grosskurth reveals how Klein was in a state of deep depression during her second pregnancy (her son Hans was born on March 2, 1907). Klein was analyzed by Ferenczi, and in 1916 she began her career as an analyst of children in Budapest. In 1921, she moved to Berlin upon Abraham's invitation. There she had a second analysis with Abraham, which was abruptly broken off by the latter's sudden death in 1925. There are many passages in Grosskurth's biography (1995) in which Klein's depressive character is described (see especially 48–70). Grosskurth remarks that Klein first entered analysis because of acute depression intensified by the death of her mother (72).

2 Robert Hinshelwood has graphically assessed the importance of the death drive in Klein: "The death instinct, clinically silent according to Freud, was noisy in Klein's view. It had very observable clinical derivatives. The primary aggression at the very beginning of life amounted to clinical evidence for the death instinct. The super-ego is manifested as a self-directed aggressive force—or, to put it the other way, the origins of the super-ego are in the first projection of the self-directed aggression into an object which then becomes the danger towards the self" (1994, 140).

3 In her sustained line of social concern, Klein believes that "It is undoubtedly not easy to know to what results the tendencies of a child will lead, whether to the normal, the neurotic, the psychotic, the pervert, or the criminal. But precisely because we do not know we must seek to know. Psycho-analysis gives us the means. And it does more; it can not only ascertain the future development of the child, but it can also change it, and direct it into better channels" (CT, 185).

4 With regard to the mechanisms of introjection and projection, Judith M. Hughes has appropriately remarked that the Kleinian model of the psyche is a corporeal one: "the two mechanisms Klein emphasized [introjection and projection] derived from bodily prototypes—and from Abraham's writing on oral incorporation and anal expulsion. Where Freud believed mind functioned like a machine, Klein saw it working like a digestive tract" (1989, 49–50). W. W. Meissner, in turn, has aptly pointed out that the individual's self-image is shaped out of the interaction of introjective and projective mechanisms: "The interplay of introjective and projective mechanism weaves a pattern of relatedness to the world of objects and provides the fabric out of which the individual fashions his own self-image. Out of this interplay also develops his capacity to relate to and identify with the objects in his environment" (1987, 31).

5 Klein remarks that this process may coincide with Freud's notion of primal repression in Inhibitions, symptoms, and anxiety ([1925, 1926] 1953). In a footnote, she quotes the following passage from this work: "We are not in a position to say whether it may not be the emergence of the super-ego which differentiates primal repression from secondary repression. At any rate we know that the child's earliest outbreaks of anxiety, which are extremely intense, occur before the super-ego has come into being; and it is not at all unlikely that quantitative factors, such as an excessive degree of excitement and the breaking through of the barrier against stimuli, are the immediate cause of primal repression" (94).

6 This figure has come to be called the "combined parent figure" in Kleinian theory. See my discussion of Lewis Aron's ideas on the combined parent figure in chapter 4.

7 Klein explains the negative Oedipus complex at this very early stage as follows: "The

small girl, for instance, while turning from her mother with feelings of hatred and disappointment and directing her oral and genital desires towards her father, is yet bound to her mother by the powerful ties of her oral fixations and of her helplessness in general; and the small boy is drawn to his father by his positive oral attachment, and away from him by feelings of hatred that arise from the early Oedipus situation" (EOC&S, 133).

8 I am referring to Freud's "Screen memories" ([1899] 1953), 303–22, esp. 319–20.

9 Anna Freud's "Beating fantasies and daydreams" ([1922] 1974) replicates Freud's argument in "A child is being beaten" and extends his account by comparing the beating phantasy to conscious daydreams (which serve the purpose of alleviating masturbatory guilt) and with the sublimation of this phantasy in a written story. In Elizabeth Young-Bruehl's reading, Anna Freud, in this public address, transforms "an autistic into a social activity (1988, 157).

10 Klein includes in a footnote the following quotation from *Civilization and its discontents*: "Experience shows, however, that the severity of the super-ego which a child develops in no way corresponds to the severity of the treatment which he has himself met with" and that "the original severity of the ego does not—or does not so much—represent the severity which one has experienced from it (the object), or which one attributes to it; it represents rather one's own aggressiveness towards it" (quoted in EOC&S, 139). Leo Bersani, in his reading of *Civilization and its discontents*, elaborates on these issues and suggests that we are "shattered into sexuality" and that sexuality is essentially masochistic. He writes: "we must sacrifice part of our sexuality and sublimate it into brotherly love in order to control our murderous impulses toward others. But the text [*Civilization*] obliquely yet insistently reformulates this argument in the following way: human love is something like an oceanic aggressiveness which threatens to shatter civilization in the wake of its own shattering narcissistic pleasure. We don't move *from* love *to* aggressiveness in *Civilization and its Discontents*, rather, love is redefined, re-presented, *as* aggressiveness. We have only to see, in concluding this investigation, that civilization itself repeats, rather than opposes, the other two terms and thereby transforms the argument of Freud's work into a triple tautology: Sexuality = aggressiveness = civilization" (1986, 20–21).

11 I will develop the connection of the superego with melancholia in depth in several sections of this book. See especially chapter 5 and 6.

12 From the first attempts to definite melancholia, the concept has shifted and been placed in a sort of middle ground or borderline state between psychosis and neurosis. Melancholia in most cases has been placed in the vicinity of paranoia, schizophrenia, and obsessional neurosis. These ideas will be developed further later in this volume.

13 Ferenczi writes: "Thus arise those intimate connections, which remain throughout life, between the human body and the objective world that we call *symbolic*. On the one hand the child in this stage sees in the world nothing but images of his corporeality, on the other hand he learns to represent by means of his body the whole multifariousness of the outer world" ([1913] 1956, 193–94).

14 General impulses and object relations produce qualitative changes in the superego. Klein's social concerns are explicitly addressed here when she suggests that "If this line of thought is correct, then it would not be a deficiency in the super-ego but a qualitative

difference in it that gives rise to a lack of social feeling in certain individuals, notably in criminals and so-called 'asocial' persons" (ON&ES, 154).

15 According to Klein, the Wolf Man's excessive fear of his father, which is active in his deepest mental layers, had been generated by very strong primary impulses of aggression against him. He could not engage in a struggle with his dangerous, devouring father—as a direct result of oedipal rivalry—and consequently he abandoned his heterosexual position. His passive attitude toward his father was founded on anxiety situations of this order.

16 When Klein wrote these words, she was referring to the Wolf Man's case and similar "analyses of boys on which my present conclusions are based" (ON&ES, 160). Meissner's reading of paranoia with melancholia comes very close to my arguments in this section. He has pointed out that projection is a mechanism that pertains primarily to object relations. The content of projection derives from "introjects," which are in turn derived from object relations, and projection is immediately caught up in the affectual involvement of object relations. It is important to quote Meissner's idea to realize the striking resemblance that projection bears to melancholia and thus the proximity of paranoia and melancholia. He writes: "Jaffe (1968) has pointed to the dualistic and conflictual role of projection in involving the self in a persistent mode of ambivalence in dealing with others. At one pole annihilation of the object is sought, while at the opposite pole internalization and preservation of the object is desired. There is a basic conflict between the impulse to destroy the object to which some threatening subjective impulse has been ascribed, and the wish to protect the object with which the subject has identified, thus investing it with narcissistic cathexis. . . . The paranoid position often seems calculated to preserve both these objects [primary and significant objects] and the object relation. The ambivalence in the relationship is too difficult to tolerate, and the rage against the object cannot be faced. These relations are often the important source of introjects, and the projection to others provides a way of preserving the good aspects of the object relationship. On another level, projection onto such important introjective objects provides a way of preserving the relation, even if on desperate terms" (1987, 33). His description could easily be adscribed to that of melancholia. The proximity of paranoia and melancholia is explicitly addressed in Meissner's account of projection. He goes on to add: "Klein makes projection a necessary process and the point of origin for object relations. The death instinct is postulated as the driving force, and projection as the necessary mechanism for mitigating its internal destructive power. It is the death instinct, through projection, in a sense, that creates objects and the relation to them. The organism then creates powerful, destructive, and persecutory objects" (36).

17 This discussion of female and male homosexualities in the work of Klein will be further elaborated later. See especially chapter 3 and chapter 4.

18 In her analysis of her patient Erna, narrated in "An obsessional neurosis in a six-year old girl" ([1932] 1975, 35–57) Klein draws attention to the patient's excessive fear of her mother and the presence of strong homosexual tendencies from early childhood alternating with paranoid phantasies of persecution. Following analysis of her early, strong, sadistic phantasies, Erna's homosexual fixation upon her mother lessened and her heterosexual impulses grew stronger.

19 See "The Effects of Early Anxiety Situations on the Sexual Development of the Girl" and "The Effects of Early Anxiety Situations on the Sexual Development of the Boy" in chapter 3.

20 In 1896, Kraepelin was the first psychiatrist to speak of involutional depression (or melancholia) as a diagnostic entity. In the fifth edition of Kraepelin's manual *Psychiatrie: Ein Lehrbuch für Studierende und Aertze* (1896), he introduces new ideas on melancholia and depression. The types of depression appearing in the young subject are related to early dementia, generalized paralysis, or periodic psychosis (manifested as mania and periodic depressions). Only the types of melancholia appearing during the "involutional" years offer sufficient similarity to warrant being grouped under one category, which Kraepelin classifies as "melancholia" and which defines as all pathological manifestations of sadness or anxiety, appearing at an advanced age. Melancholia has specific characteristics, and to a depressive mood diminished intellectual capacity, irritability, and possibly considerable anxiety are added. In subsequent editions of his manual, Kraepelin opposes the symptomatology of melancholia to that of the new "manic-depressive illness." The latter is characterized by inhibition, unlike the former, in which inhibition is replaced with anxiety.

21 Klein gives the following examples to illustrate the reappearance of these anxiety situations: "If a normal person is put under a severe internal or external strain, of if he falls ill or fails in some other way, we may observe in him the full and direct operation of his deepest anxiety-situations. Since, then, every healthy person may succumb to a neurotic illness, it follows that he can never have entirely given up his old anxiety-situations" (EASDE, 193).

3 Femininities

1 Although this is probably Freud's most overlooked case study, there are some significant exceptions to this silent rule. See Irigaray ([1974] 1985), Merck 1986, Hamer 1990, Roof 1991a, De Lauretis 1994a, Fuss 1995, and Jacobus 1995.

2 Kaja Silverman rigorously distinguishes the look and the gaze in Lacanian terms in *Male subjectivity at the margins* (1992). She writes: "*Four Fundamental Concepts* stresses not only the otherness of the gaze, but its distinctness from what Lacan calls the 'eye,' or what I have been calling the 'look'. . . . Although the gaze might be said to be 'the presence of other as such,' it is by no means coterminous with any individual viewer, or group of viewers. It issues 'from all sides,' whereas the 'eye' sees 'only from one point.' Moreover, the gaze's relationship to the eye is sufficiently antinomic that Lacan can describe it as 'triumph[ing] over the look' " (129–30).

3 On aphanisis, see Lacan 1978, 216–29. Lacan speaks of aphanisis as the fading of the neurotic subject in his or her phantasy as the object cause comes to the fore. It is the Lacanian object (a) that comes to center stage and takes the leading role in phantasy, overshadowing the subject.

4 Jones developed this concept in his well-known essay "The early development of female sexuality" (1927), in which he described the fear of destruction of the capacity to obtain libidinal gratification. In the case of the girl, this constitutes an early and dominating anxiety situation.

5 Helene Deutsch developed these ideas in her *Psychoanalyse der weiblichen Sexualfunktionen* ([1925] 1944).

6 At this point, Klein stresses in a footnote the importance of Abraham's ([1924] 1949) ideas and illustrates this with the example of her patient Erna, as narrated in her "An obsessional neurosis in a six-year-old girl," chapter 3 of *The psycho-analysis of children*.

7 I am of course ironically referring to Charles Bernheimer's rather disturbing but correct allusion explored in his essay "Penile reference in phallic theory" as well as in other essays included in the excellent special issue on the phallus published in *differences* (1992, 116–32).

8 In the Kleinian account of the Oedipus complex, both girls and boys turn away from the primary object, the mother—or, most primitively, the breast. The early oral characteristics of the breast, and phantasies—sadistic and paranoid—determine that both girls and boys will turn away from the mother and toward the father, adopting a position of femininity. From a different angle, but along not too dissimilar lines, Kaja Silverman argues that female melancholia is "a psychic condition which is somehow endemic to the female version of the positive Oedipus complex" (1988, 152).

9 For Lacan, desire has no object; there is no object that can assuage it. The only object involved in desire is the object that causes desire, in Lacanian parlance, the object (a). See Lacan 1966.

10 Kaja Silverman (1988) writes about the "voice-over" in film as that which always escapes the viewer's gaze. She defines the notion of an "acoustic mirror" as "the function which the female voice is called upon to perform for the male subject. Within the traditional familial paradigm, the maternal voice introduces the child to its mirror reflection." Nevertheless, she argues that "whereas the mother's voice initially functions as the acoustic mirror in which the child discovers its identity and voice, it later functions as the acoustic mirror in which the male subject hears all the repudiated elements of his infantile babble" (80–81). In Lacanian terms, both the Other's desire—manifested in the voice and in the gaze, both of which are unspecularizable—can be read as instances of object (a). They cannot have mirror images, and they are almost impossible to symbolize. Resisting imaginarization and symbolization, they belong to the Real.

11 It is understandable that at this point there is some confusion in Klein's writing between sexual and love relationships, which holds throughout the text. She seems to be referring only to sexual relationships in this passage.

12 This is summarized by Klein in a footnote on page 212 of *The psycho-analysis of children*. In her book, *Like subject, love objects* (1995), Jessica Benjamin has underscored the fundamental agreement of Klein's and Horney's views on issues such as penis envy. She writes: "Perhaps, Horney theorized, penis-envy becomes salient only when the little girl backs off from father love, fears competing with mother, and chooses instead to identify with father. Thus penis-envy would not be the trigger of the Oedipus complex, as Freud thought, but indeed the result of a misfired Oedipal situation, a 'flight from womanhood.' The perception of her own organs as damaged or inadequate might occur, Horney and Klein agreed, because the little girl fears injury a retribution for her envious wish to supplant mother by stealing her father penis or injure her by stealing her babies. Klein's sense of the multiple meanings of penis-envy remains clinically interesting and

fresh, and Horney's work in particular deserves to be rescued from the disparagement it received from the psychoanalytical establishment" (117–18).

13 With regard to the issue of prescribed (or compulsory) heterosexuality, Jacqueline Rose has most accurately argued that "if heterosexuality is preestablished for the subject, it is so only as part of an unmanageable set of phantasies which are in fact incapable, in the theory, of ensuring heterosexuality itself" (1993, 167).

14 Later, in her 1948 essay "On the theory of anxiety and guilt" Klein will modify her position on superego formation, including its negative as well as its helpful aspects. This latter idea finds expression in her positing a superego based on traces and features coming from both parents. She argues: "Thus the super-ego is built up from the devouring breast (mother) to which is added the devouring penis (father). These cruel and dangerous internal figures become the representatives of the death instinct. Simultaneously the other aspect of the early super-ego is formed first by the internalized good breast (to which is added the good penis of the father), which is felt as a feeding and helpful internal object, and as the representative of the life instinct" ([1948] 1975, 30).

15 It would be interesting to trace the vicissitudes of the parenthetical aside Klein includes in the original German version of *The psycho-analysis of children* (*Die Psychoanalyse des Kindes*, 1932), which Alix Strachey relegates to a footnote in the parallel 1932 English version ([1932] 1949, 321–22). Klein writes: "Nur wenn das vom Vater in der Phantasie gezeugte oder erwartete Kind ein 'gutes' und 'schönes' Kind bedeutet, wenn also das Körperinnere der Frau in ihrer Phantasie eine Stätte vorstellt, in der Harmonie un Schönheit herrscht (eine Phantasie, die übrigens auch mit der des Mannes korrespondiert) nur dann kann sie sich dem väterlichen Uber-Ich und dessen Repräsentanten in der Außenwelt sexuell und psychisch voll und ganz hingeben" (1932, 247). Obviously, Klein is assessing here the common traits girls and boys share in their psychosexual development by imagining a beautiful and potentially fruitful space that corresponds to the demands of the paternal superego and reality. But it seems quite clear that the elided parenthesis is restricted to the issue of the good internal object, which populates a beneficial inner space for both sexes. The question of the "surrendering" (*voll und ganz hingeben*) to the paternal superego will definitely take at least two (in the conscription of the binary) totally different paths. In *The psycho-analysis of children* ([1932] 1949), the parenthetical information appears in a footnote that reads "This phantasy is also present in the boy" (321).

16 See sections on the Oedipus complex in both sexes in this chapter and in chapter 4.

17 For Klein, this synthesis goes hand in hand with "a greater synthesis between the various aspects of the analyst" (*ELI*, 47).

18 Klein does not add anything beyond her former work in *The psycho-analysis of children* and "The Oedipus complex in the light of early anxieties" ([1945] 1975). She very briefly mentions the leading anxieties in both sexes. For an analysis of this, see also chapter 5.

19 Fairbairn and Winnicott are the only ones who get redeemed, and that is because their work "is largely devoid of any mention of homosexuality, and does not contain a specific theory of sexuality in the way that Kleinian theory, for example, does" (O'Connor and Ryan 1993, 14).

20 The main critiques directed against the Kleinian elaboration over the years can be sum-

marized as follows: excessive emphasis on internal phantasies at the expense of external reality, lack of clarity concerning the relationship between phantasy and the establishment of psychic structure, and reification of internal objects, which become real entities with a seemingly independent existence. As far as phantasy is concerned, in *The thread of life* (1984), Richard Wollheim defends Klein against the charge of "misplaced internality"—that is, of attributing internality to what phantasies are made of rather than the phantasies themselves. In Wollheim's view, this criticism fails to understand Klein's purpose; rather than confusing phantasies with their objects, she attempts some sort of classification of phantasies in terms of their relationships with objects (26–27). Klein strives to differentiate between phantasies about external objects and those that become internal through the process of incorporation. Wollheim emphasizes that unconscious phantasies in Kleinian theory are a product of our experiences of external objects as mediated by conflicts of ambivalence and the corresponding defense mechanisms against these conflicts.

21 In both the special issue devoted to the publication of King and Steiner's volume on the Controversial Discussions by the *International Journal of Psychoanalysis* and in other recent essays, Roy Schafer has emphasized Klein's attempts to abandon gender stereotypes. He writes: "I read her foundational work as a compromise between, on the one hand, retaining Freud's flawed, overgeneralized propositions concerning gender and, on the other, subordinating them to the dynamic variables that did somewhat shift the emphasis away from Freud's steady focus on gendered sexuality" (1994a, 21).

22 From a different angle, and within a feminist project, Teresa Brennan has emphasized the importance of envy of the "creativeness embodied in the mother and mother's breast" (1993, 93). In her view, envy focuses on creativity understood as the possession of certain attributes rather than as a force in itself. She remarks that envy, from the Latin verb *videre*, in its etymology ties the concept to visualization: what matters is the appearance of the thing. For Brennan, if we say that what is envied is the mother's possession of the breast, we are already moving within the terms of envy, which are those of possessions and appearances. From here, Brennan argues that the fantasy of controlling the breast can survive at the imaginary level through hallucination. She writes that "by this account, the fantasy of controlling the breast and the act of hallucination are one and the same, which means that the amazing visual power of hallucination is tied to a desire for omnipotence from the outset" (98). Brennan also acknowledges the blow that the reality of dependence from the mother poses to narcissism: "When realities are seen in terms of their opposites, the fact of nurturance and the means to grow becomes a threat to narcissism; it establishes the reality of dependence. From this perspective, the envy of the mother's breast is the resentment of that dependence, and the reason why nurturance, or love, or protection, or assistance, are interpreted as assertions of superiority and power" (96). In Brennan's account, envy would thus be very close to mania. This will fit into the last stage of her suggested pattern of a three-stage historical process in the West in which, "containment is breaking down in an hallucinatory culture" (114). This will tentatively lead us to a decrease in melancholia tout court and an increase in complex narcissistic pathologies.

23 Klein addresses these issues in her discussions of the Oedipus complex in "Early stages

of the Oedipus conflict" ([1928] 1975), "The effects of early anxiety-situations on the sexual development of the girl" ([1932] 1975d), and "The Oedipus complex in the light of early anxieties" ([1945] 1975).

4 Masculinities

1 This section, entitled "The effect of E.A.S. on the sexual development of the boy," is one of the central papers included in Klein's *The psycho-analysis of children* ([1932] 1949, 240–78).

2 On the development of the girl, see chapter 3. In order to fully understand to what extent the analogies between the development of both sexes hold, Klein refers her readers to chapters 8 and 9, "Early stages of the Oedipus conflict and of super-ego formation" (EOC&S) and "The relations between obsessional neurosis and the early stages of the super-ego" (ON&ES), respectively.

3 For a splendid and illuminating essay on the Leonardo narrative, see Bersani 1986, 339–88; and Silverman 1992, 339–88.

4 Klein suggests that these are the main causes of impotence in later life. The boy's fear of being castrated by his conjoint "bad" parents and his fear of having his penis shut up inside his mother's body are also at the root of various forms of claustrophobia: "It seems certain that claustrophobia goes back to the fear of being shut up inside the mother's dangerous body" (EASB, 242, n. 2).

5 See Aron 1995.

6 Klein's combined parent figure is the earliest and most primitive version of the primal scene. It consists of the child's phantasy that the parent's sexual organs are locked together permanently in violent sexual intercourse. As a consequence of the child's attacks on to the mother's body—which also imply a struggle with the father's penis, which is imagined to be inside the mother—he fears retaliation by the "united parents" (IASWA, 213).

7 Aron underscores that the primal scene should not be interpreted as the child's literal viewing of sexual intercourse between the parents. From his perspective, the nature and quality of the primal scene phantasies, reflect, in symbolized form, the child's perceptions, understandings, and experience of the parental relationship and interactions.

8 Wilfred R. Bion contributed a most innovative elaboration of the Kleinian combined parent figure in his work, which "led him to describe learning and knowing as activities that entail bringing things together in the mind: bringing together preconceptions (anticipations) with things as they actually are; bringing one idea together with another; putting two and two together, and so on. He likened such activities to the parent's coming together in their sexuality. Bion considered that things linked together in the mind may create reactions similar to parents linking together sexually. The experience of things coming together in the mind is a version of the combined parent figure, located internally (or internalized). . . . We could, then, expect the tensions and aggression normally associated with the Oedipus complex to appear in the intellectual arena, as a thought disorder based in disturbance caused by the coupling of ideas—a mental intercourse" (Hinshelwood 1994, 180).

9 Aron also acknowledges and values the importance of the paranoid-schizoid position,

which in his view contributes the capacity for multiplicity, difference, and discontinuity. The depressive position basically contributes the capacity for integration and identity (see Aron 1995, esp. 219).

10   Bersani comes close to these arguments when he writes: "The post-Oedipal superego is the climax of a fantasy which fixes the passionate, and passionately shifting, object-relations of our childhood in the linear narrative of the Oedipus story. To put this in another way, we could say that the *oedipus complex represses the unintelligibility of Oedipal relations*" (1986, 101).

11   Aron also devotes attention to the analytical situation in his section "Fusion, splitting, and integration of gender in relation to the analyst" (1995).

12   The title of this section appears between quotation marks in the original.

13   See especially her remarks in footnotes on pages 242, 245–46, and 249.

14   Klein remarks that the boy's identification with his "bad" father is in part based on his identification of himself with his anxiety object (EASB, 249).

15   Klein refers her readers to Chadwick's 1925 essay "Über die Wurzel der Wissbegierde."

16   Paranoia may act as an obstacle to the maintenance of heterosexuality. Nevertheless, Klein's persuasive argument in this essay proves that paranoid traits are pervasive in, and to some extent constitutive of, infantile sexuality as a whole.

17   As noted earlier, epistemophilia provides a motive force for the performance of the sexual act. Klein illustrates the role of epistemophilia in early homosexual relations as follows: "The homosexual act is designed to realize his early childhood desire of having an opportunity of seeing in what respect his father's penis differs from his own and to find out how it behaves in copulating with his mother" (EASB, 263).

18   Whereas there are several instances of male and female homosexual phantasies and behaviors in early infancy, the case of Mr. B. is the only one devoted to the analysis of homosexuality in an adult.

19   At this point, Klein remarks that the patient's power of dissimulation goes along with his paranoid characteristics, which were very strong.

20   With regard to this issue, Klein most graphically writes: "The standards imposed by his super-ego upon his sexual activities were very high. In copulation he had to make good every single thing he had destroyed inside his mother. His work of restoration began, for the reason we have seen, with the penis, and there, too, it ended. It was as though a person wanted to put up a particularly fine house but was filled with doubts as to whether he had well and truly laid the foundations. He would keep on trying to make those foundations more solid and would never be able to leave off working at them" (EASB, 271–72).

21   Klein, in a surprisingly concise fashion, writes that "he had had great admiration and love [for Leslie] . . . partly, no doubt, on account of the early satisfaction of his oral cravings which he had received from him through the sexual act" (ibid., 268). The lack of detail obviously has to do with the rigid attitude of censorship and prudery that enveloped the issue of children's sexuality in that period.

22   Klein writes that her patient's greatest ambition was to become worthy of Leslie's friendship and to follow in his footsteps. In fact, he chose the same profession as his brother (ibid., 268).

23   Feminist readings of Dora have emphasized how fellatio was foregrounded by Freud,

while cunnilingus in the couple Dora and Frau K was never even considered. See Bernheimer and Kahane 1985 and Roof 1991b.

24 Klein explains that this perception of her patient's penis as ugly stems from his having taken on anal qualities as a consequence of his repression of anal matters (see EASB, 270).

25 All relationships reported by Klein in this case are incestuous. She even adds the following in a footnote: "On one occasion he had an affair with a third type of person who corresponded to his father. It happened against his will, but he could not avoid it and aroused great anxiety in him" (EASB, 271).

26 It is clear that the good mother-imago is also lost in heterosexuality, but apparently its retrieval is not blocked, as seems to be the case in homosexuality.

27 It seems that there is nothing worse than to be a "good mother" today. They tend to be intrusive in their omnipotence, potential seducers or inhibiting influences in infantile sexuality, and less than zero in all other activities. Following Winnicott and current rereadings of his work, "good enough" versions are preferred. See Winnicott 1965, 1971, 1986.

5 Kleinian Melancholia

1 Klein points out that from the beginning of psychic development there is a constant correlation of real objects with those installed within the ego (M-DS, 266).

2 Later Klein again uses the obstetric metaphor to refer to melancholia and the failure of introjection: "If the infant at this period of life [between four and five months] fails to establish its loved object within—if the introjection of the 'good' object miscarries—then the situation of the 'loss of the loved object' arises already in the same sense as it is found in the adult melancholic" (ibid., 287).

3 Later in the essay Klein collapses introjection, incorporation, and internalization when she writes that "the process of internalization, which sets in the earliest stage of infancy, is instrumental for the development of the psychotic positions" (ibid., 284). The fundamentals of the critique of Klein by Abraham and Torok are based on a consideration of "introjection" as radically different from "incorporation," drawing from Ferenczi's introduction of the term in his essays, "Introjection and transference" ([1909] 1956) and "On the definition of introjection" ([1912] 1955), among others. This has also been a major area for criticism of the work of the Kleinian school. My views on Abraham and Torok's ideas can be found in chapter 1.

4 With regard to the question of the bad object, Jacqueline Rose has remarked: "The lost object is not, therefore, only the hallucinated object of satisfaction, it is also and simultaneously, an object which, because of this failure of negative hallucination, is required—is actively sought after in order to be bad" (1993, 151).

5 Klein points out that young children's difficulties in taking food have a paranoid root. As the child (or adult) identifies more fully with a good object, libidinal urges increase; the individual develops a greedy love and the desire to devour this object. Thus, the mechanism of introjection is reinforced.

6 The advantages that Klein and her group find in holding this highly controversial view

are summarized as follows, "As we study the relations of the early infantile ego to its internalized objects and to the id, and come to understand the gradual changes these relations undergo, we obtain a deeper insight into the specific anxiety-situations through which the ego passes and the specific defence mechanisms which it develops as it becomes more highly organized. Viewing them from this standpoint in our experience, we find that we arrive at a more complete understanding of the earliest phases of psychic development, of the structure of the super-ego and of the genesis of psychotic diseases" (M-DS, 267).

7 Klein writes of the id's hate of the ego. In her view, it "accounts even more for its [the ego's] feelings of unworthiness and despair. I have often found that these reproaches [of the depressive] and the hatred against bad objects are secondarily increased as a defence against the hatred of the id, which is even more unbearable" (ibid., 270).

8 See Althusser 1971, 121–73.

9 Klein is using the terms *depressive* and *melancholic* interchangeably here. She has not yet introduced her theory of the depressive position.

10 Klein closely associates perfection with beauty. What is perfect—in the sense of whole— is also beautiful: "It is a 'perfect' object which is in pieces; thus the effort to undo the state of disintegration to which it has been reduced presupposes the necessity to make it beautiful and perfect" (M-DS, 270).

11 Klein had argued in *The psychoanalysis of children* that the absence of a good mother-imago was the cause of homosexuality and disturbances in the development of heterosexuality. Implicit here is the suggestion that virtually any position can be sublimated by recourse to the trompe l'oeil device and ultimately by splitting (dissociation of the real object from its image) and disavowal (of the negative aspects of the object).

12 Klein refers to several inhibitions and anxieties that manifest themselves differently in the paranoiac and the depressive. These include inhibitions and anxieties about food and hypochondriacal symptoms. Anxiety about absorbing dangerous substances destructive to one's interior is typically paranoiac, while anxiety about destroying external good objects by biting and chewing, or of endangering the internal good object by introducing bad substances from outside into it, is depressive. In hypochondria, the pains that result from the attacks of internal persecuting objects against the ego are paranoiac, while the identification of the ego with the sufferings of its good objects is depressive (M-DS, 272–73).

13 Klein holds a different position from that of Helene Deutsch, who states that this denial is connected with the phallic phase and the castration complex and in girls it is a denial of the lack of the penis. According to Klein, the mechanism of denial originates at a very early phase when the yet undeveloped ego endeavors to defend itself from its most profound anxiety, namely, its dread of internalized persecutors and the id (ibid., 277). She refers to Deutsch's "Psychologie der manisch-depressiven Zustände insbesondere der chronischen Hypomanie" (1933).

14 The underlying phantasy in mania allows the maniac to prevent dangerous coitus between the parents he or she has internalized and their death within. Klein acknowledges that this "reparation" is almost always of a "quite unpracticable and unrealizable nature" (M-DS, 278).

15 See the section devoted to Radó in chapter 1.

16 Klein stresses that ambivalence is "partly a safeguard against one's own hate and against the hated and terrifying objects" (M-DS, 288).

17 Here I am borrowing Eric Santner's felicitous expression "stranded objects," which also provides the title of his book *Stranded objects: Mourning, memory, and film in postwar Germany* (1990).

18 In her later work, Klein sticks to her idea that the process of unification depends on more realistic splitting of the object. See especially her "Some theoretical conclusions regarding the emotional life of the infant" ([1952] 1975c) for a detailed discussion of the splitting that is a characteristic of the depressive position.

19 Klein quotes from "Mourning and melancholia" to illustrate her point: "Why, then, after [mourning] has run its course, is there no hint in this case of the economic condition for a phase of triumph? I find it impossible to answer this objection straight away" (Freud [1915, 1917] 1953, 255).

20 In "Absence of grief," Helene Deutsch describes situations in which there is a complete absence of the manifestations of mourning. She puts forward the hypothesis that the ego of the child, unsufficiently developed to bear the strain of the work of mourning, utilizes some mechanisms of "narcissistic self-protection to circumvent the process" (1937, 13). She is in agreement with Klein's views on the persistence of the ongoing necessity to mourn in the psychic apparatus.

21 See, for example, "An obsessional neurosis in a six-year-old girl," chapter 3 of *The psycho-analysis of children* (Klein 35–57).

6 The Death Drive and Aggression

1 See Freud ([1915] 1953, 122–24).

2 See Freud ([1915] 1953). At any rate, the Freudian concept of drive (Trieb) is opposed to the biological notion of instinct—as in self-preservative instincts versus erotic or libidinal drives. This stems from the absence of a predetermined or given object. In *Three essays on the theory of sexuality* ([1905] 1953), Freud writes, "It has been brought to our notice that we have been in the habit of regarding the connection between the sexual instinct and the sexual object as more intimate that it in fact is. Experience of the cases that are considered abnormal has shown us that in them the sexual instinct and the sexual object are merely soldered together—a fact which we have been in danger of overlooking in consequence of the uniformity of the normal picture, where the object appears to form part and parcel of the instinct. We are thus warned to loosen the bond that exists in our thought between instinct and object. It seems probable that the sexual instinct is in the first instance dependent of its object; nor is its origin likely to be due to its object's attractions" (147–48). The major characteristics of the drives are: they are derived from and supported by instincts, they have no pregiven objects, and they are dominated by an erotogenic zone (182–83). Later, with his description of perversions, which can be defined in terms of both object and goal, as Laplanche puts it, "the text is an eloquent argument in favour of the view that drives and forms of behaviour are plastic, mobile and interchangeable. About all, it foregrounds their *Vertretungsfähigkeit*, or vicariousness, the

ability of one drive to take the place of another, and the possibility of a perverse drive taking the place of a non-perverse drive, or vice versa" ([1987] 1989, 30).

3 In a footnote, Klein explains that when the essay was published she was using *paranoid position* synonymously with W. R. D. Fairbairn's *schizoid position* and decided to use the combined name. Nevertheless, Klein makes clear her differences with Fairbairn's approach, which she characterizes as taken "from the angle of ego-development in relation to objects, while mine was predominantly from the angle of anxieties and their vicissitudes" (SM, 3).

4 W. W. Meissner (1987) has pointed out that "internalising and externalizing processes may be differentiating rather than defensive processes, and thus directed to the formation and establishment of boundaries between the inner and the outer worlds, between self and object. They would then be the fundamental processes through which internality and externality are constituted" (30).

5 Klein once again remarks in a footnote on the insufficiency of language to express those primitive phantasies that arise in the infant previous to the acquisition language: "I am using the expression 'to project into another person' because this seems to me the only way of conveying the unconscious processes I am trying to describe" (SM, 8).

6 Joseph Sandler has approached the complexity of the notion of projective identification by distinguishing three stages. The first stage corresponds to Klein's formulation in SM, and Sandler remarks that "M. Klein can be taken to refer here to shifts and displacements within the child's representational world. *Identification* with parts of an object can be regarded as 'taking into' the self-representation aspects of an object representation. Projection is then a displacement in the opposite direction" (1987a, 16). In this context, splitting involves a division of parts of the self-representation or the object representation and projection in the process of identification of the object with split parts of the self. The "real" object is not regarded as being affected, Sander writes, because "the parts of the self put into the object are put into the fantasy object, the 'internal' object, not the external object" (17). The second stage corresponds to the notion of countertransference as theorized from a Kleinian perspective by Paula Heimann (1950). According to Sandler, Heimann and others made a significant extension of projective identification by bringing it into conjunction with the analyst's identification with the self or object representation in the patient's unconscious phantasies and with the effect of this on the countertransference. The countertransference reaction could then be a possible source of information for the analyst about what was occurring in the patient. The third stage was theorized especially by Bion in the late 1950s and found expression in his concept of the "container" (see Bion 1962a, 1963). Projective identification is now described as if the externalization of parts of the self or of the internal object occurs directly into the external object. Bion describes a concrete "putting into the object," as when he writes, "An evacuation of the bad breast takes place through a realistic projective identification. The mother, with her capacity for reverie, transforms the unpleasant sensations linked to the 'bad breast' and provides relief for the infant who then reintrojects the mitigated and modified emotional experience, i.e., reintrojects . . . a non-sensual aspect of the mother's love" (quoted in Sandler 1987, 19). In Sandler's view, Bion's formulations can be related to Winnicott's "holding" function of the "good enough mother"

(see Winnicott 1958). From a different angle, Otto F. Kernberg has suggested a developmental line from primitive projective identification to projection, which he sees as proceeding "from projective identification, which is based on an ego structure centered on splitting (primitive dissociation) as its essential defense, to projection, which is based on an ego structure centered on repression as a basic defense" (1987, 94).

7   In this appendix, Klein acknowledges Freud's contributions to the study of schizophrenia and paranoia, together with Abraham's important insights—especially in his "The psycho-sexual differences between hysteria and dementia praecox" (1908), which opened up the possibility of understanding and studying psychoses.

8   In one of her footnotes, Klein notes that in *Civilization and its discontents* Freud adopted her hypothesis (put forward in her 1928 "Early stages of the Oedipus complex" and 1930 "The importance of symbol-formation in the development of the ego") that the severity of the superego to some extent results from the child's own aggression, which is projected onto this psychic instance (A&G, 26).

9   Klein refers to the well-known Freudian attempt to distinguish between both of them: "Real danger is a danger that is known, and realistic anxiety is anxiety about a known danger of this sort, Neurotic anxiety is anxiety about an unknown danger. Neurotic danger is thus a danger that has still to be discovered. Analysis has shown that it is an instinctual danger" (Freud [1925, 1926] 1953, 165).

10 Klein explains that during latency "the child deals with his strict super-ego by projecting it on to his environment—in other words, externalizing it—and trying to come to terms with those in authority. However, although in the older child and in the adult these anxieties are modified, changed in form, warded off by stronger defences, and therefore are also less accessible to analysis than in the young child, when we penetrate to deeper layers of the unconscious, we find that dangerous and persecutory figures still co-exist with idealized ones" (DMF, 242). As it is clear from this passage, Klein problematizes the achievement of any stable position, since anxiety always poses a threat.

11 Klein has been accused from some fronts, especially Lacanian and other "discursive" postmodern positions, of a disregard for the issue of language. I would argue that she does not aim to give a prelinguistic version of the process of becoming subject; rather, acknowledging the precarious position of mothers and infants in the turbulence of Europe between the wars, her focus is in the complex syntax of unconscious phantasy that comes before language acquisition in the infant. Surely, the field of culture is always there. Klein showed in several occasions her concern with language, with the inadequacies and the impossibilities one has to face when trying to translate unconscious phantasy into words. Her play technique and child analysis provided her with an exceptional vantage point from which to become aware of and reflect on these issues. For a detailed account of the Kleinian group's position on this, see chapter 7, especially my discussion of Mary Jacobus's (1990) reading of Klein's "The importance of symbol formation in the development of the ego" ([1930] 1975) with Lacan and Kristeva.

12 Klein advances, more clearly than even before, her contention about the precarious stability of the ego: "Full and permanent integration is never possible for some polarity between the life and death instincts always persists and remains the deepest source of

conflict. Since full integration is never achieved, complete integration and acceptance of one's own emotions, phantasies and anxieties is not possible and this continues as an important factor in loneliness" (SL, 302).

13 Klein's interest centers on what she calls "the psychological aspect in bi-sexuality" (ibid., 306).

14 Freud also left unfinished his insightful "Splitting of the ego in the process of defence" ([1938] 1940b). Freud's later work, especially his "Splitting of the ego" ([1938] 1940b] 1953) and *An outline of psycho-analysis* ([1938] 1940a), has aroused an unprecedented amount of critical writing and interdisciplinary debate in recent times. I am referring to work in the areas of perversion—fetishism in particular—and psychosis. In analytic circles, much has been said on the challenge that Freud's later work poses to some of his earlier positions. The structural theory of the psyche and the question of narcissism are two salient instances of it.

15 The editors of Klein's works point out that she had not submitted "On the sense of loneliness" for publication before her death. Apparently, the present version has undergone some slight editorial changes. They argue that this may be due to the fact that she did not consider it yet ready for the press, because, as her editors say, "it seems in places incomplete, and its thought is not altogether resolved" (Klein 1975a, 336).

16 Butler explains that the term *foreclosure*—borrowed from Lacanian theory—is different from Freud's *Verwerfung*: "Distinguished from repression, understood as an action by an already formed subject, foreclosure is an act of negation that found and forms the subject itself" (1990a, 171).

17 Butler provocatively argues, following from her argument, that "In this sense, the 'truest' lesbian melancholic is the strictly straight woman, and the 'truest' gay male melancholic is the strictly straight man" (ibid., 177).

18 Butler herself seems to be close to this argument when at the end of "Melancholy gender-refused identification" (1995), she writes: "Indeed, we are all made the more fragile under the pressure of such rules [imposed by a logic of repudiation], and all the more mobile when ambivalence and loss are given a dramatic language in which to do their acting out" (180).

19 This is the second of the introductory essays—the first one was written by Naomi Schor— to the excellent *Engaging with Irigaray*, edited by Carolyn Burke, Naomi Schor and Margaret Whitford (1994, 15–33).

20 Whitford makes reference to Richard Boothby's Lacanian interpretation of the death drive in his *Death and desire: Psychoanalytic theory in Lacan's return to Freud* (1991). I am drawing what follows from Whitford's account of his ideas. For Boothby, each of Lacan's registers—Symbolic, Imaginary, and Real—seems to claim the death drive for its own. Whitford writes: "Imaginary identity involves exclusion and also violence. Its integrity and form are threatened by pressure from the unrepresented, to which it reacts with anxiety and aggression. On the other side the symbolic functions as a disruptive and disintegrative factor. Boothby calls this a sublimation of the death drive. The symbolic can negate or transform the imaginary, break up imaginary formations. The stablity of the imaginary allows life to continue, but it impedes creation or transformation. In so far as it breaks up fixed forms, the death drive as symbolic may be creative. However, this

may also be experienced by the imaginary as symbolic violence. The death drive may be purely destructive, but it may also be creative" (1994a, 391).

21 For her discussion of Irigaray's image of nuptials, see Whitford 1994a, 392–93.

22 See especially Klein [1946] 1975 and [1957] 1975.

7 The Setting (Up) of Phantasy

1 In this essay, Isaacs clarifies why the Kleinians write *phantasy* with *ph*: "The English translators of Freud adopted a special spelling of the word 'phantasy,' with the *ph*, in order to differentiate the psychoanalytical significance of the term, i.e., predominantly or entirely unconscious phantasies, from the popular word 'fantasy,' meaning conscious day-dreams, fictions and so on" ([1952] 1983, 81).

2 The exact quote is found on page 104 of the 1933 edition of the *New introductory lectures*. This passage was heavily altered in the new translation for the standard edition: "We picture it as being open at its end to somatic influences, and as there taking up into itself instinctual needs which find their psychical expression in it" ([1932, 1933b] 1953, 73).

3 Here I am borrowing Teresa de Lauretis's notion of "structuring" as defined in her "Habit changes": "By *sexual structuring* I want to designate the constructedness of sex, as well as of the sexual subject, its being a process, an accumulation of effects that do not rest on an originary materiality of the body, that do not modify or attach to an essence, matter or form—whether corporeal or existential—prior to the process itself. In other words, neither the body nor the subject is prior to the process of sexuation; both come into being in that continuous and life-long process in which the subject is, as it were, permanently under construction" (1994b, 301–2).

4 Isaacs refers specifically to language acquisition and to the interval that mediates between comprehension and use of words ([1952] 1983, 74).

5 See Freud's "Formulations on the two principles of mental functioning" ([1911a] 1953, 215).

6 Isaacs quotes the following fragment from Freud's essay: "The objects presenting themselves, in so far as they are sources of pleasure, are absorbed by the ego into itself, 'introjected' (according to an expression coined by Ferenczi): while on the other hand, the ego thrusts forth upon the external world whatever within itself gives rise to pain (*v.infra*: the mechanism of projection)" (Freud [1915] 1953, 136).

7 See Ferenczi [1913] 1956.

8 Jacobus quotes from Lacan's graphic critique: "She slams the symbolism on him with complete brutality, does Melanie Klein, on little Dick! Straight away she starts off hitting him large scale interpretations. She hits him a brutal verbalization of the Oedipal myth, almost as revolting for us as for any reader—'You are the little train, you want to fuck your mother' " (Jacobus [1930] 1975, 166).

9 Kristeva's "Freud and love: Treatment and its discontents" appeared originally in a shorter version as "L'abjet d'Amour" (1982). It later became chapter 1 of *Tales of love* ([1987] 1989).

10 In this respect, Jacqueline Rose, referring to the mechanism of scotomization and to Isaacs's ([1952] 1983) reporting of the phantasy, "It is all right if it comes out of my anus

as flatus or faeces, but it mustn't come out of my mouth as words," has written, "For if the body can become a mechanism of disavowal for language, then the body is already being inscribed in a linguistic process, is being called up as a metaphor even as it is metaphor that the subject exists" (1993, 158). From here it follows that for Rose the Kleinian view is not outside of language, even when language is not at the center of her elaboration.

11 Jacobus refers to the following passage in Klein's analysis of Dick: "The early operations of the reactions originating on the genital level was a result of premature ego-development, but further ego-development was only inhibited by it. This early identification with the object could not as yet be brought into relation with reality. For instance, once when Dick saw some pencil shavings on my lap he said 'Poor Mrs Klein.' But on a similar occasion he said in just the same way, 'Poor curtain' " (Klein [1930] 1975, 227).

12 By "critical response" I mean engagement on the part of critics or scholars outside the strict psychoanalytical domain.

13 Here Isaacs directly addresses one of the most important objections to the Kleinian group raised during the Controversial Discussions, namely, that of the differences between phantasy and mechanism—that is to say, between incorporation and introjection—and the definition of *drive*. She elaborates on Freud's "Negation," defines *imago*, and offers innumerable examples of how to distinguish between an internal object and a bodily concrete one.

14 Klein first develops her concept of the symbolic equation in "The importance of symbol-formation in the development of the ego" ([1930] 1975).

15 See Hinshelwood 1989, 452–55.

16 Born in Poland, Segal was trained as a doctor in Great Britain and then as a psychoanalyst, becoming an important member of the Kleinian group. She pioneered the psychoanalysis of schizophrenics in the 1940s. She also devoted much effort to the investigation of symbol formation and aesthetics.

17 In "A psychoanalytical approach to aesthetics" (1952), Segal had already remarked: "With the establishment of the depressive position the object becomes more personal and unique and the ego more integrated, and an awareness of an integrated, internal world is gradually achieved. Only when this happens does the attack on the object lead to real despair at the destruction of an existing complex and organized internal world, and with it, to the wish to recover such a complete world again" (198).

18 See Klein's definition of *position* in "A contribution to the psychogenesis of manic-depressive states" ([1935] 1975, 276).

19 Roland Barthes published his well-known essay "The death of the author," in 1968, while Michel Foucault questioned artistic authority in the pages of "Qu'est-ce qu'un auteur?" (1969).

20 Bersani points out that "identification . . . works as an extension of regions of pleasure" (1990, 16–17) and quotes the following from Klein to support his view: "Objects and activities, not in themselves sources of pleasure, become so through this identification, a sexual pleasure being displaced onto them" (EA, 85).

21 Bersani (1990, 21) argues that Freud's views in "Leonardo da Vinci" are very much like those in Klein's "Early analysis."

22 The complete quotation of the passage I am referring to in Bersani's essay reads: "In Freud, and particularly in Klein, the kind of spectral repetitions on which art in Proust seems to depend are presented as a goal of normative development" (1990, 22).

23 See Klein [1929] 1975, [1930] 1975, [1932] 1975c, [1932] 1975d, her central essays on manic-depressive states ([1935] 1975, [1940] 1975), and [1937] 1975.

24 In Jacqueline Rose's view, the Kleinian concept of reparation cannot be detached from the issue of knowledge and "as psychic process, reparation requires a suspension of absolute knowledge if it is not to turn into pure omnipotent defence" (1993, 111). In this refusal of mastery, I believe Rose accurately captures the Kleinian reparative impulse in its fundamental form.

25 Bion, Meltzer, Tustin, and others have focused their research on what happens to symbolization in psychotic and autistic states.

8 Modernist Cultures of the Death Drive

1 Merton (1968) elaborates on social anomie and the strategies available for the subject's response to it. Among them, *rebellion* means the total rejection of the goal-oriented content of socially sanctioned behavior and its substitution for private means and ends. Retreatism, in Merton's view, is another strategy in which the "supreme value of the success-goal has not yet been renounced" although its attainment seems impossible and the capacity for instrumental action is thus repressed. Lepenies focuses on Merton's notion of retreatism and thus comes close to the latter description of anomic social exclusion. For Merton, among all those who are marginalized from society and have no access to any plan of instrumental action whatsoever, are "psychotics, outcasts, vagrants, vagabonds, tramps, chronic drunkards, and drug addicts" (1968, 207).

2 In literary history, the modernist period usually extends from 1890 to 1939. The 1920s were the age of "high modernism." In the visual arts, modernism coincides with the rise of avant-garde artistic groups whose main concerns were artistic innovation and questions of perception. In art criticism, formalist modernism is associated with the Bloomsbury aesthetic of Roger Fry and Clive Bell.

3 During the first years of her short marriage and motherhood, Klein moved constantly due to her husband's work as a chemical engineer. She was first analyzed by Ferenczi in Budapest and then moved to Berlin to undergo a second analysis with Abraham, which abruptly ended with his sudden death. In 1927, she moved to England, where she remained until her death in 1960.

4 I am borrowing this idea from Michael Levenson's *A genealogy of modernism* (1984), in which he maintains that the founding of *The Criterion* takes precedence over the publication of Eliot's *The waste land* and Joyce's *Ulysses* in the institutionalization of modernism.

5 Some critics have recently taken up the question of modernism's relationship with imperialism, but there is still a long way to go. See especially Jameson 1990 and Lane 1995.

6 Russian socialists considered art to be an ineffective instrument of revolution. Fascists saw it as superfluous and representative of capitalist decadence.

7 In the context of feminist rereadings of modernist texts, Rita Felski (1989) has warned us

of the risks of embracing any discourse as subversive or radical in a straightforward manner: "Feminist theories of 'textual politics' grounded in a modernist aesthetics—for example, the celebration of the writings of Virginia Woolf as radically subversive of patriarchal ideology—are thus open to criticism on the grounds that they continue to draw upon static oppositions between realism and modernism without taking into account the changing social meanings of textual forms. The assumptions that the political value of a text can be read off from its aesthetic value as defined by a modernist paradigm, and that a text that employs experimental techniques is therefore more radical in its effects than one which relies on established structures and conventional language is too simple. Such an opposition takes for granted an equivalence between automatized language and dominant ideology and between experimentalism and oppositionality, an equation which is abstract and ultimately formalist in its failure to theorize the contingent functions of textual forms in relation to socially differentiated publics at particular historical moments" (161).

8   Rita Felski (1994) has cautioned against the dangers of considering some modernisms to be representative of the wide range of experiences (of disenfranchised groups) that often remain hidden and erased in modernity: "Such writings [as those of Woolf or Stein] offer us elegant and ironic explorations of the fragility of linguistic and sexual norms, embodying the view that human nature is 'elusive, indeterminate, multiple, often implausible, infinitely various and essentially irreducible' (McFarlane 400). They thereby invoke a particular consciousness of modernity prevalent among the cosmopolitan, bohemian, white, middle- and upper-class female artists of the period, a consciousness shaped by the impact of Freudianism and feminism, of linguistic philosophies and artistic manifestos. However, they tell us much less about those aspects of modernity that shaped the lives of other kinds of women: the modernity of department stores and factories, of popular romances and women's magazines, of mass political movements and bureaucratic constructions of femininity. Such concerns are not of course completely absent from modernism, but they are mediated and refracted through an aesthetic lens of irony, defamiliarization and montage specific to an artistic and intellectual—if not necessarily political—elite of the period" (196).

9   In its extreme version, this objectivism leads to a futurist and ultimately fascist aesthetics. The paintings and novels of Wyndham Lewis, in which human bodies and activities acquire machinelike qualities, are a good example of this.

10 Rosalind Krauss (1985, 151–72) points out that originality is a constant in vanguardist discourse. In her argument, originality is bound to a notion of repetition, and they operate as a sort of binary code. For Krauss, both the avant-garde and modernism depend on repression of the second term of the binary code.

11 The concept of nowness is Harry Levin's and was introduced in his classic "What was modernism?" (1960).

12 I will address Klein's theory of phobias and her differences from Freud subsequently.

13 Sinfield understands the term queer as belonging to "that historical phase [Wilde's epoch]—not contradicting, thereby, its recent revival among activists—and 'gay' for post-Stonewall kinds of consciousness" (1994, 3).

14 Among the most remarkable examples, we can include Nisbet's The insanity of genius

[1900] 1973, Max Nordau's *Degeneration* ([1892] 1993), and Cesare Lombroso's *The man of Genius* ([1863] 1913).

15 Hitchens's novel circulated in homosexual circles close to Wilde and Lord Alfred Douglas. He decided to withdraw his novel by the time Wilde was in court, as he was much concerned with its possible influence on Wilde's ruin.

16 In this respect, Alan Sinfield quotes a telling passage from Havelock Ellis's *Sexual inversion* (1936): "the celebrity of Oscar Wilde and the universal publicity given to the facts of the case by the newspapers may have brought conviction of their perversion to many inverts who were before only vaguely conscious of their abnormality" (Sinfield 1994, 125–26).

17 Teresa de Lauretis has given us one of the most original and persuasive readings of Hall's mannish lesbian in relation to her idea of the lesbian fetish in *The practice of love: Lesbian sexuality and perverse desire* (1994a).

18 According to the summary of Judge Biron's ruling that was published in the *Times* (November 17, 1928), Hall's novel appears to be the motive that provoked the British authorities into legal action by bringing an unacceptable sexual doctrine into the open in an *earnest* tone: "He agreed that the book had some literary merit, though defaced with certain deplorable lapses of taste. The mere fact that the book was well written could be no answer to these proceedings; otherwise the preposterous position would arise that, because it was well written, every obscene book would be free from proceedings. The mere fact that the book dealt with unnatural offences between women would not in itself make it an obscene libel. It might even have a strong moral influence. But in the present case there was not one word which suggested that anyone with the horrible tendencies described was in the least degree blameworthy. All the characters were presented as attractive people and put forward with admiration. What was even more serious was that certain acts were described in the most alluring terms." Sir Robert Wallace, chief magistrate, in his concluding speech at court, alluded to the authorities' use of certain laws of literary interpretation in reaching their verdict: "The character of the book cannot be gathered from the reading of isolated passages. They give an indication as to the general tendency, but the book must be taken as a whole. The view of the Court is that this book is a very subtle work. It is one which is insinuating and probably more dangerous because of that fact. . . . Put in a word, the view of this Court is that this is a disgusting book when properly read" (quoted in Parkes 1996, 145, 151).

19 Feminist theorists engaged in studies of the British suffrage movement have focused their attention on the visual representation of the female body. Lisa Tickner (1988) has traced the "spectacle of woman" in suffrage artistry, and Jane Marcus (1989) has located a feminist fetishism in suffrage iconography. The suffragettes made themselves "spectacular" in order to attract public attention to their cause.

20 Dora Marsden, a member of the British Women's Social and Political Union and an activist and writer, figures among the first women who embraced anarchist ideas in a complex mixture of individualism and spiritual philosophy. She was one of the editors of the *Freewoman* and the *New Freewoman*. In 1909, the British government authorized the "treatment" of the force feeding for hunger-striking suffragettes. The episodes surrounding Marsden's repeated arrests, hunger strikes, and forcible feedings are well known. Djuna Barnes's "How it feels to be forcibly fed" (1914) is her personal account of

the experience of being forcibly fed. It was part of a series of sketches and journalistic pieces she wrote to support herself in New York. Barnes, even when she was skeptical about suffragism—as about almost everything else—launched her satire against male impositions on women's bodies. She reports that she had "a vision of a hundred women in grim prison hospitals, bound and shrouded on tables just like this, held in the rough grip of callous warders while white-robed doctors thrust rubber tubing into the delicate interstices of their nostrils and forced into their helpless bodies the crude fuel to sustain the life they longed to sacrifice" (1989, 178).

21 During the latter decades of the nineteenth century, in both the United States and Great Britain, there was a clear increase in public attention paid to issues of childbearing and family limitation. Throughout this period, when the terms contraception and birth control were first used, the birth rate declined steadily and childbirth practices changed. Recent studies suggest that from the mid–nineteenth century through the 1920s the nature and functions of motherhood were being radically redefined. Historical trends reveal that by the end of the nineteenth century the birth rate dropped sharply due to a variety of factors, including the increased industrialization and urbanization that complicated the existence of large families. Another historical trend in childbearing is a high maternal mortality rate, which persisted in Great Britain and America even after infant mortality began to decline. This resulted in an increased perception of motherhood as a social and political problem, with important repercussions in the social fabric in the early decades of the twentieth century. See Lewis 1990 and McLaren 1990.

22 Carl van Vechten was a white writer, music critic, and photographer who acted as a patron of the arts in Harlem and helped many talented black and white artists to become established. He was deeply attracted to black arts and culture and is well known for his photographs of black intellectuals and artists.

23 Art Berman has grounded the connection between the artist and his or her public in modernism in terms of a formal relation: "The formal properties of art relate to the essence of art just as the formal properties of the material world relate to its immaterial essence. The exterior formal properties of art, which the body perceives through the senses (color, sound, shape, texture), are the physical medium through which the inner forms of consciousness of the artist are linked to the inner forms of consciousness of the observer. The validity of the connection is demonstrated in proportion to the intensity of the aesthetic experience" (1994, 275).

24 In psychological representation, formalist criticism seeks meaning in the artwork in a correspondence between the experience conveyed by it and a psychic structure whose reality the artwork both stimulates and reveals.

25 Hayden White illuminatingly describes the dissolution of the ontological distinction between realistic and fictional discourses in recent theories of discourse in favor of a view of their aspects in common. In these semiological approaches, narrative "is revealed to be a particularly effective system of discursive meaning production by which individuals can be taught to live a distinctively 'imaginary relation to their real conditions of existence,' that is to say, an unreal but meaningful relation to the social formations in which they are indentured to live out their lives and realize their destinies as social subjects" (1987, x).

26 The container-contained relationship is at the core of Wilfred R. Bion's post-Kleinian

theorization. Bion argued that the human personality is made up of these two components, whose mating occurs at every stage of development and determines mental growth. In his view, psychological symbols are containers for bodily sensations. Sensations accumulate in the mind, which, through reflection, makes some sense of them (i.e., gives them a meaning) and can then use them for thinking. See Bion 1963.

27 Meltzer's concept of the aesthetic may be understood to refer to the pleasure obtained from the recognition of order, from the containment of experience in symbolic form. See Meltzer and Williams 1988.

28 As Art Berman has argued, "Literature is an intermediary between objects and the conditions of their existence for us. Art remains situated between the realm of ordinarily experienced reality and some other realm, a (higher) reality of another kind, an idea inherited from idealism; in this regard, modernism reinvigorates while it also reconfigures romanticism. . . . Modernist art reveals not a metaphysical geography, but an aesthetic state" (1994, 36).

29 Fowlkes observes in her essay that the loneliest and the most destructive grief of all is the grief following a loss that is not merely socially and morally undervalued but actually devalued. She identifies what she calls "stigmatized loss"—an illegitimate social loss—in contemporary American society as most openly expressed in homophobia and by extension in its association with AIDS: "When stigma persists to this extent, family members themselves sit in judgment of their own loss as morally illegitimate, thereby blocking the avenue for expression and enactment of their grief" (1991, 546). Most importantly, "The homosexual, then, stands to be condemned equally for loving and for grieving the loss of love" (549).

30 I am thinking especially of the work of analysts such as Wilfred R. Bion, Herbert Rosenfeld, and Donald Meltzer and the contributions of younger analysts from the Tavistock Clinic.

31 The entire quotation from A room of one's own reads: "the shadow shaped something like the letter 'I' which falls across the page of Mr. A's writing" ([1929] 1957, 103).

9 Framing the Fetish

1 In her diary, Virginia Woolf re-creates a scene in which Vanessa brings into the room a small canvas painted by Cézanne and given to Maynard Keynes, with Roger Fry's comments on the perfect roundness and greenness Cézanne had splendidly captured. Woolf writes: "The apples positively got redder and rounder and greener" (1977–84, 1:40). The discovery of Cézanne was for Fry a true revelation.

2 Mary Ann Caws has documented the importance that the art of Cézanne and Matisse had for Vanessa Bell: "The flat surfaces of Cézanne and Gauguin, their particular palette of colors, their portraits and their still lifes, the ways Matisse had of treating sunlight and windows and especially studio interiors, all of this is clearly traced in her work" (1990, 108–9) Caws speaks of the influence of Cézanne on Vanessa's still lives and portraits and of Matisse on her interiors (see especially 109–14).

3 Fry wrote of Cézanne something that is too close to Lily's aesthetics and technique: "there is always something still lurking behind the expression, something he would

grasp if he could. In short, he is not perfect, and of many modern works one might predicate perfection" (1927, 2).

4 As is well known, Woolf divides her narrative into three sections: "The Window," "Time Passes" and "The Lighthouse."

5 Elliott and Wallace write that her amateur status "is represented almost entirely by the *absence* of references to, for example, the apparatus of professional associations, exhibitions and connoisseurship" (1994, 75).

6 Marie-Claude Lambotte has considered the question of the empty frame as part of a larger problem that has to do with the specularity of the image and the pathologies associated with it: "The melancholic subject cannot afford to let the trick of his defensive behavior show in front of the others, for fear of sinking within this emptiness which seems not to have an edge or a frame . . . despite the absence of an imaginary frame within which its singular originary image is formed, a symbolic frame is elaborated whose specificity has been granted by a certain kind of discourse. And from this stems the dissociation between image and word that we have already mentioned" (1993, 253–55).

7 In the context of object relations theory (she explicitly mentions Melanie Klein and D. W. Winnicott), Lambotte relates this problem to the failure in early object relations and "holding." She argues that there are "pathologic deviations that can appear if certain qualities necessary for the framework of life of the infant, for that which D. W. Winnicott calls 'holding,' are not put together . . . [so] the melancholic subject seems . . . to miss the frame which would have allowed him to recognize his image; it is precisely the search for it which would have been missing in this primary stage of development, up to a point such that the feelings of love and hate, conceived at the same time and differentiated on the ingestion and expulsion model, would not succeed in creating a universe of values" (ibid., 273).

8 In his *Project for a scientific psychology* ([1887–1902, 1950] 1953), Freud writes of an inner bleeding (*innere Verblutung*) and goes on to say that it reaches several instincts and functions and thus determines a generalized inhibition (*Hemmung*) accompanied by the pains of a wound. Following a true pumping effect, sexual excitation in melancholia leaks as if through a hole (*Loch*) placed in the psyche, whereas in the case of mania, close to the economic model of neurasthenia, the hole would be placed in the somatic. For a discussion of this trope in the context of melancholia, see Lambotte 1984, 45.

9 Magritte's obsession with representing canvases and reality juxtaposed is well known. *The Human Condition* (*La Condition Humaine*) of 1933 shows an easel set up before a window in such a way that the scene on the canvas overlaps the image on outside, which is visible through the window. David Sylvester has noted that "It was in 1924 the René Magritte painted his first picture. It represented a window seen from an interior. In front of the window, a hand seems to be trying to grasp a flying bird" (1992, 62–63).

10 See Spitz's discussion of the visual in Magritte in her section "Optical appetites," (1994, esp. 19–21).

11 There are two versions of this picture, which was originally called *Motherhood*. Both were painted between 1936 and 1937, and it is not certain which came first. See Whitfield 1992.

12 Magritte attached great importance to the titles of his paintings, which were typically chosen after the picture had been completed (see Hammacher 1973, 25–30). Spitz has remarked that "In their seeming irrelevance, [Magritte's titles] not only fail to give us clear interpretive directions and thus work to subvert convention but also create in their viewers a heightened sense of cognitive dissonance" (1994, 45).

13 The most explicit reference to death by water is a work painted at the end of 1926, *The Musings of a Solitary Walker*. The setting presents a river with a footbridge across it. In the foreground there appears a naked figure floating in the air, which evokes a mythic image of the dead. The back view of a solitary bowler-hatted man walking away into the landscape is also one in the series of this recurrent image in Magritte's work, which is sometimes identified with him.

14 David Sylvester reports these events as follows: "She shared a room with her youngest child, who, finding himself alone in the middle of the night, woke up the rest of the family. They searched in vain all over the house; then, noticing footprints on the door-step and on the pavement, followed them as far as the bridge over the Sambre, the local river" (1992, 12). Her body was found seventeen days later, drowned in the river.

15 Mary M. Gedo associates Magritte's predilection for scenes in which darkness and light coexist in a single space with a screen memory that she relates to his childhood plays. She reports that as a young boy "His favourite occupation [during his summers] involved exploring a disused cemetery in the company of a special little girl. One day, as they emerged from an underground vault, the children came upon an artist from the capital who was serenely working at his easel among the broken stone columns and piles of dead leaves. From that moment, painting seemed a magical occupation for Magritte, and the course of his future was determined" (1994, 182).

16 *Simulacrum* can be defined as "a copy without an original." Recent approaches to the simulacrum have underscored the concept of mass reproduction and reproducibility that characterizes the postmodern electronic media culture. See Baudrillard [1981] 1994.

17 A careful reflection on the operations and effects of trompe l'oeil may lead us to consider the Freudian notion of *Vorstellungsrepräsentanz* in a new way. Laplanche and Pontalis ([1967] 1973) translate this concept as "representative-representation."

18 See Abel 1989 for a detailed reading of James's and Cam's relationships with their parents, especially their father. Abel argues that "Both children construct stories that hinge on a renunciation of (the memory of) their mother" (46).

19 See Pierre Bourdieu's "La domination masculine," especially the section "L'illusio et la genèse sociale de la libido dominandi" (1990b, 21–31).

20 It is crucial to note how, in the context of his discussion of *To the lighthouse*, Bourdieu's notion of "habitus" evokes something very close to what I am calling trompe l'oeil or simulacrum. He writes: "The habitus, a second nature that never presents such an appearance of nature and of instinct as in those cases, such as this one, where the socially instituted libido is carried out as a particular form of desire, of libido, in the most common sense of the term" (ibid., 25). Here Bourdieu alludes to Mrs. Ramsay and the fate of women who participate "par procuration," at a distance, as spectators, in the games designed by the libido dominandi. His idea of illusio, also sends us back to the question of trompe l'oeil. He argues that domination is built upon symbolic violence or *méconnaissance* (30).

21 In the novel, Lily also finds herself in solitude, for "she liked to be alone; she liked to be herself; she was not made for that" (50). Woolf is obviously writing about Lily's rejection of the assumption of patriarchally imposed women's roles such as those of wife or mother.

22 In this respect, Woolf writes that her beauty "was apparent. She had been admired. She had been loved. She had entered rooms where mourners sat. Tears had flown in her presence. Men, and women too, letting go the multiplicity of things, had allowed themselves with her the relief of simplicity" (ibid., 41).

23 As I have mentioned, in *The psycho-analysis of children* ([1932] 1975e), Klein wrote that "It would seem that for the unconscious nothing is more distant and more unfathomable than the inside of the mother's body and, still more, the inside of one's own body" (266 n. 2).

24 See my discussion of the girl's achievement of heterosexuality in chapter 3.

25 In this respect, Rachel Bowlby has pointed out that "The middle section, 'Time Passes,' makes Mrs. Ramsay's death parenthetical, literally, to a general lack of differentiation from which individual human agency is absent, except for the ambivalent questioning of 'sea airs' (T, 195), or the half-acknowledged place of the narrator" (1988, 75). Parenthetical or elliptical strategies are recurrent in the style of Woolf. Jane Marcus, in her important discussion of *A room of one's own*, speaks of a "poetics of interruption" in Woolf's texts. Woolf "transform[s] interruption, the condition of the woman writer's oppression . . . into a deliberate strategy as a sign of woman's writing. The narrator of *A Room* continually interrupts herself. In following the interrupted text the reader reproduces the female experience of being interrupted and joins Woolf in making interrupted discourse a positive female form. The tyranny of the interrupter is forgotten as the woman writer interrupts herself" (1987, 187).

26 Woolf writes: "That dream of sharing, completing, of finding in solitude on the beach an answer, was then but a reflection in a mirror, and the mirror itself was but the surface glassiness which forms in quiescence when the nobler powers sleep beneath? Impatient, desparing yet loth to go (for beauty offers her lures, has her consolations), to pace the beach was impossible; contemplation was unendurable; the mirror was broken" (*To the lighthouse*, 134).

27 "The Lighthouse" abounds in rhetorical questions. This profusion of unanswerable or "empty" questions points to the larger representational crisis of language in modernist literature and philosophy. Lily, in her mind, poses questions such as: "What does one send (to the Lighthouse)? What does one do? Why is one sitting here, after all?" (146).

28 One of the most memorable episodes of "writing on the wall" is H. D.'s account of her trance in the section of the same title included in her *Tribute to Freud*. H. D. went through a disturbing hallucinatory experience during her stay in Corfu with her friend Bryher and began to see signs on the wall of her hotel room with strange forms and supposedly encrypted meanings. H. D. feared that the visions of writing she saw were the workings of an artist's mind "got out of hand, gone too far, a 'dangerous symptom' " (1974, 51).

29 For a new reading of the combined parent figure, one free of the heterosexist imperative, see chapter 4.

30 It is interesting to note that Lily "attacks" problems in painting and that Woolf chooses this verb, and no other, to describe Lily's position vis-à-vis her creation: "She had not

obviously taken leave of her senses. No one had seen her step off her strip of board into the waters of annihilation. . . . Lily squeezed her tubes again. She attacked that problem of the hedge" (181).

31 Woolf writes: "For in the rough and tumble of daily life, with all those children about, all those visitors, one had constantly a sense of repetition—of one thing falling where another had fallen, and so setting up an echo which chimed in the air and made it full of vibrations" (199).

32 In a persuasive reading of the fetish inspired by the Kleinian combined parent figure, Angela Moorjani has argued that "Fetishism will exist as long as people are culturally required to channel into univocal gender manifestations, one of two, driving them to fetishize what they fantasize as lost" (1994, 37). This is in line with my critique of binarisms in my readings of Klein throughout this book.

33 Foucault defines *heterotopia* as follows: "there is a worse kind of disorder than that of the *incongruous*, the linking together of things that are inappropriate; I mean the disorder in which a large number of possible orders glitter separately, in the lawless and uncharted dimension of the *heteroclite*. . . . *Heterotopias* are disturbing, probably because they secretly undermine language, because they make it impossible to name this *and* that, because they shatter or tangle common names, because they destroy syntax in advance, and not only the syntax with which we construct sentences but also that less apparent syntax which causes words and things (next to but also opposite one another) to 'hang together' " ([1966] 1970, 48).

34 Foucault specifies that this version can be found in *Aube à l'antipode*, a book with illustrations by Magritte. As is the case with many of the subjects of Magritte's paintings, *Ceci n'est pas une Pipe* has many variants, which range from 1929 almost until the end of his life.

35 For Foucault, whereas the small pipe is inside "a stable prison," the larger one lacks coordinates and "Its enormous proportions render uncertain its location" ([1968] 1983, 17).

36 In his view, this problematic relationship "symbolizes" the exteriority of written and figurative elements so obvious in Magritte's work. See "Burrowing Words," ([1968] 1983, 36–42).

37 Foucault explicitly refers to the paintings *L'Alphabet des Révélations* (1929) and *Personnage Marchant vers l'Horizon* (1928–29) in their contrasting perspectives.

38 Foucault refers explicitly to Magritte's *Les Grâces Naturelles* (1967) and raises the question: "Is it the plant whose leaves take flight and become birds, or the birds that drown and slowly botanize themselves, sinking into the ground with a final quiver of greenery?" ([1968] 1983, 49–50).

39 Karen Smythe has used the term *fiction-elegy* (which she defines as "an elegy in fictional form") to read some of Woolf's narratives. She argues that "Woolf's experimental attempt to find a vehicle for the verbal expression of grief using methods of psychonarration paradoxically involves a quest for convention, for form" (1992, 65). In her view, Woolf uses the novel form in the exploration and alternation of elegiac conventions, and she sees this fiction-elegy as "a formal framing device" (70). I am not sure what Smythe understands as convention and form (literary convention and form, I believe). It is my

contention that Woolf's exploration of form has to do with a deeper (more inward) level of complexity connected with melancholia in its problematization of boundaries and its particular spatialization, in its blurring of inside and out, introjection and projection. Her exploration of form can be seen not only as literary but as artistic and psychic in the most ample sense. My reading of the denouement of *To the lighthouse* also differs from Smythe's more optimistic interpretation—"The vision [Lily's] evokes the resurrecting think-act that retrieves Mrs. Ramsay via the transformation of memory into permanence, into art" (74)—and from her idea that Woolf's poetics both renders private and public grief and "offers a sense of consolation in aesthetic and historical continuity" (75–76). In my discussion of phantasy and reparation in this book, I argue that art cannot repair, redeem, or offer consolation for human despair.

40 Susan Isaacs has pointed out that the quality of some images makes the subject believe that the object is incorporated: "Such images, however, draw their power to affect the mind by being 'in it,' i.e., their influence upon feelings, behaviour, character and personality upon the mind as a whole, *from their repressed unconscious somatic associates* in the unconscious world of desire and emotions, which *form the link with the id*; and which do mean, in unconscious phantasy, that the objects to which they refer are believed to be inside the body, to be incorporated" ([1952] 1983, 105–6).

41 See especially chapter 5 and specifically the section "Oedipal Melancholia."

42 Klein reports that Richard, in his drawings, named a destroyer that stood for himself *Vampire*, which is evocative of the oral-sadistic character that Klein sees in his reactions and behavior.

43 I am including the full text of Keats's sonnet to facilitate the follow-up of Klein's reading: "Much have I travell'd in the realms of gold, / And many godly states and kingdoms seen; / Round many western islands have I been / Which bards in fealty to Apollo hold. / Oft of one wide expanse had I been told / That deep-brow'd Homer ruled at his demesne: / Yet did I never breathe its pure serene / Till I heard Chapman speak out loud and bold: / Then I felt like some watcher of the skies / When a new planet swims into his ken; / Or like stout Cortez, when with eagle eyes / He stared at the Pacific—and all his men / Look'd at each other with a wild surmise— / Silent, upon a peak in Darien" (1990, 32).

44 For Walter Benjamin, the allegorical mode of representation of baroque *Trauerspiel* testifies to this melancholic dimension of all signification. He writes: "For the baroque sound is and remains something purely sensuous; meaning has its home in written language. And the spoken word is only afflicted by meaning, so to speak, as if by an inescapable disease; it breaks off in the middle of the process of resounding, and the damming up of the feeling, which was ready to pour forth, provokes mourning, and will continue to be encountered as the reason for mournfulness" ([1928] 1977, 209).

45 Mr. Ramsay looks patronizingly at his wife and the book in her hands. Apparently, he can only appraise her beauty and is ignorant and unconcerned about the rest. He "wanted the thing she always found it so difficult to give him: wanted her to tell him that she loved him" (*To the lighthouse*, 123).

46 It is important to note that this essay was published only one year after Klein's crucial "Early stages of the Oedipus conflict" ([1928] 1975) and before "A Contribution to the

psychogenesis of manic-depressive states" ([1935] 1975). At this point, she holds that there exist pregenital stages of the Oedipus conflict and that guilt is present in the latter from the start. The Oedipus conflict starts when sadism is at its height. As I have previously remarked, later, in OCEA ([1945] 1975), Klein maintains that the Oedipus conflict coincides with the onset of the depressive position, basically when persecutory anxiety decreases and hate is not dominant.

47 Jean Walton has challenged "psychoanalysis's unacknowledged racial whiteness" (1995, 777) and its obliviousness to race as a crucial fact in the construction of subjectivity. Among other texts, she reads Klein's "Infantile anxiety-situations reflected in a work of art and the creative impulse" ([1929] 1975) and focuses on Ruth Kjär's first painting of a naked Negress as one of the instances in which the reparative impulse of the daughter is channeled into the production of "a racialized figure that, once gain, goes unremarked by the analyst" (1995, 791). Walton sees this as an important dismissal of a racialized figuration in the phantasy life of a female subject. Her comments on the differences between the terms naked and nude in the domain of art history are also central to her discussion of Kjär's, and by extension other women's, entry into the male domain of high art by "stealing" the phallus. She writes: "A nude, then, is a depiction of a (female) body whose whiteness is not in any way suspect, since it is assumed that to be white is not to be specifically 'raced.' To paint an unclothed black woman is, it would seem, by definition to paint a 'naked,' sexualized woman" (797).

48 Interestingly, Klein refers to the conclusions we may draw from Kjär's story in her direct allusion to her paintings as "instructive": "it is instructive to consider what sort of pictures Ruth Kjär has painted since her first attempt" (IASWA, 217). In this pedagogical scene, Klein aims to teach us how her theory of early anxiety situations, in her divergent views from Freud's doctrine, can provide a more balanced account of girls' and the boys' different psychosexual evolutions, one that does not reduce everything to the law of castration. In any case, at this moment in her career, Klein has not completely established her main differences from and disagreements with Freud.

49 In Magritte's letter to Michel Foucault dated June 4, 1966, he writes about those paintings he calls "Perspective:" "I believe it should be pointed out that the paintings named Perspectives have a connotation distinct from the two ordinary meanings of the word. This word and others have a precise meaning in a context, but the context—you show it better than anyone else in Les Mots et les Choses—can say nothing, is confused, save the mind that imagines an imaginary world" (quoted in Foucault [1968] 1983, 58).

50 They specifically refer to Bell's portrait of Mary Hutchinson (1915), "where the brush work of the face blends into a flesh-toned background which is bordered on the left and right edges by an abstract pattern of stripes that gestures to Vanessa Bell's own abstract paintings from the period" (1994, 61). In their view, the dissolving images of women in Bell's work should be explored and interrogated in the wider context of images of women in the suffrage campaigns and of the position of women in the Bloomsbury Group.

51 Sublimation is not the focus of my discussion, but it plays an important part in Heimann's. She briefly defines it as "a form of discharge of the instinctual drive to creation (procreation)" (1942, 8). She remarks that gratification on the part of the ego is an essential element in sublimation: "the conscious gratification, bound up with the experi-

ence of expansion and development of the ego, seems to me an important indication that a sublimatory activity is successful" (8). I have extensively discussed sublimation in chapter 7.

52 Heimann writes that her patient was unable to eat "because [the devils] would poison her with their excrement and thus turn the food into poison. Owing to these persecutions she was in agony, especially when painting" (ibid., 10).

53 Heimann alludes to her patient's design as if it actually were a shape, a form: "Gradually the design became more and more established, and she developed a firm faith in its existence, and was no longer dependent on getting constant visible proofs of it. The working of her design could be applied more and more to her painting, and her pictures became more and more manifestations of the design" (ibid., 10–11). We may read this form container as a frame, as a boundary that delimits experience, which, as it turns out, progressively becomes "established," materialized, and solidified.

54 It is important to note that a good number of the analysts who participated in the Controversial Discussions were lay analysts; in fact, many of them were in the humanities. Some were (or had been) teachers (Ella Sharpe), expert translators (the Stracheys, Joan Riviere), or educators (Susan Isaacs), which means that the relationship between psychoanalysis and other disciplines in the humanities was alive and flourishing.

55 These phantasies of bad internal objects figured as demons seem to be a recurrent element in Heimann's analysand, in Lily Briscoe, and even in Magritte. Mary M. Gedo has remarked that the extreme panic and disorganization with which Magritte reacted to his mother's death shows in the repetition of rituals—mostly religious, such as genuflections, signs of the cross, and the like—"to fend off internal experiences that the boy concretized as 'demons,' demonic presences that may have involved actual hallucinations as well as disturbing, frightening thoughts" (1994, 182).

56 Woolf narrates this episode as follows: "[These forces] had much ado to control her impulse to fling herself (thank Heaven she had always resisted so far) at Mrs. Ramsay's knee and say to her—but what could one say to her? 'I'm in love with you?' No, that was not true, 'I'm in love with this all' " (To the lighthouse, 19).

57 In his respect, Mary M. Gedo has pointed out that "Magritte always insisted that his images were not symbols, but rather poetic mysteries—mysteries that he evidently intended his public to contemplate, but not to penetrate" (1994, 180).

58 I am including a full quotation of Heimann's passage: "if she had no other function in life but that of restoring her childhood objects, she would not attain the full range of a boundless territory in which to develop herself" (1942, 13).

59 In Heimann's view, guilt and anxiety interfere with the work of sublimation "because they lead to the employment of various mechanisms for magical control of the internal persecutors. This control, however, in its turn keeps the ego under control and interferes with the independent ego-expanding activities which are implied in successful sublimation" (ibid., 15).

60 In Elliot and Wallace's view, both To the lighthouse and Between the acts "enact the difficulty of holding in suspension, much less reconciling, the competing claims of professionalism and artistry, the public life and the private life, the polemical and the visionary" (1994, 76).

1   If, as I am suggesting, we think of biography as always already autobiographical, it would be helpful to consider Paul de Man's idea of autobiography as a conflicted generic category. De Man argues that autobiography "lends itself poorly" to generic classification because each instance seems an exception to the norm. He also claims that, although autobiography seems to depend on the actual and verifiable, in fact the "distinction between fiction and autobiography is not an either/or polarity but . . . undecidable" (1979, 921). He suggests that, while we assume that life produces the autobiography, we can as easily maintain "that the autobiographical project may itself produce and determine the life" (920). It is precisely in this sense that I believe we can reflect upon and further problematize Strachey's notion of biography.

2   See especially sections "Modernist Form(ation)s," "The Concreteness of the Form," and "An Aesthetics of Phantasy?" in this book.

3   Here, I am using writerly in the sense that Roland Barthes gave to the term in S/Z ([1970] 1974) when he was exploring texts that violate the conventions of realism and thus force the reader to produce different meanings from those that are "authorized." He wrote: "The writerly text is a perpetual present, upon which no consequent language (which would inevitably make it past) can be superimposed; the writerly text is ourselves writing, before the infinite play of the world (the world as function) is traversed, intersected, stopped, plasticized by some singular system (Ideology, Genus, Criticism) which reduces the plurality of entrances, the opening of networks, the infinity of languages" (5).

4   Constance Garnett was David "Bunny" Garnett's mother.

5   An attempt to discuss the debates about the status of facts and evidence among historians would be too pretentious given my critical position. In any case, I can see some similarities between the controversies about the status of the facts in history and psychoanalysis today. In this respect, analyst Roy Schafer has argued that he and others "have been asserting that, for the most part, the idea of evidence has been misunderstood in psychoanalysis. The traditional claims of proof and evidence do not stand up well to close inspection, and that is why, in my opinion, controversy cannot be settled by appeals to 'the facts' as they are called and research can never be reduced to mere fact-finding" (1994b, 362). Schafer goes on to say that even the use of therapeutic results for evidence does not help, for analysts are often unable to agree on the presence, extent, depth, and basis of alleged change for better or worse. In his words, "This state of affairs may be attributed to the fact that each therapeutic position uses somewhat different modes of conceptualisation and rules of evidence" (362).

6   Strachey "The Italian Renaissance," Spectator 101 (Nov. 21, 1908), quoted in Sanders 1957, 188.

7   It is interesting to note that when Charles R. Sanders echoes the impressions of Strachey's readers with regard to his innovations in biography, points out that "They have agreed too that Strachey possessed a rare gift for breathing life into his subjects" (1957, 198).

8   Strachey writes: "But, after all, posterity is privileged. Let us draw nearer; we shall do no wrong now to that Majesty, if we look below the robes" ([1928] 1948, 11).

9   In 1908, Strachey published a study on Racine in the *New Quarterly*.

10   In "A sidelight on Frederick the Great" *New Statesman* (Jan. 27, 1917), 397, quoted in Sanders 1957, 195. Strachey writes of Boswell's *The life of Johnson* that it showed "Boswellian artistry . . . that power of selection and evocation which clothes its objects with something of the palpable reality of life" (1917, 397). In the English biographical tradition, Strachey deeply admired Boswell and Johnson.

11   This was written in Woolf's diary on October 9, 1927, and is quoted in Sackville-West in, "V.W. & Orlando," *The Listener* (27 January 1955).

12   Here, in her essay "The new biography," Woolf is referring to Harold Nicholson's *Some people*. Nicholson's work becomes, for Woolf, an example of how to solve the problem of transmitting personality through a biography.

13   Strachey began his love affair with Roger Senhouse around 1926, when they set off on a trip to Rome. Senhouse was an intelligent and cultivated young man (in his early twenties when Lytton was almost fifty) who read eagerly and had translated Colette into English. Theirs was loving, playful, and highly literary friendship (Strachey wrote many poems and limericks for him). Strachey's fairly frequent melancholic and depressive episodes were an issue of concern for Senhouse, who gradually distanced himself from him. On and off, they would meet and spend a short time together. By 1931, their relationship had almost totally faded away. See Holroyd 1994, esp. 566–88, 660–68.

14   Holroyd is proposing an idea that involves psychoanalytic notions such as projective and introjective identification and defense mechanisms such as splitting, idealization, and manic denial. He writes: "In his affair with Duncan Grant he had tried to force a reality out of his day-dreams by assuming, almost literally, the form and personality of the man he loved. With Henry Lamb, he had resorted to sexual infantilism only in moments of crisis or reconciliation, so that fantasy and actuality had run alongside in a makeshift partnership that eventually broke apart. With Ralph Partridge he had attempted to alter the object of his love so that they might become closer in everyday life" (ibid., 581).

15   Holroyd reports that when it was first published in 1928 the book sold more than forty thousand copies within six months. In the United States, Harcourt Brace rapidly sold out its first edition of thirty thousand copies and many more were shipped to meet the increasing demand. See ibid., 616.

16   Harrison 1928. As an expert in the field, Harrison's reception of this narrative was not altogether negative, even when he objected to Strachey's "suppressions" and "manipulations" of the facts. See G. B. Harrison, "Elizabeth and Her Court," *Spectator* 141, Nov. 24, 1928.

17   There are several ways of understanding animism in both primitive cultures (as some sort of superstitious form of religion) and later societies. In this case, I am not referring to any notion of objects and bodies being inhabited by souls but rather to a wider consideration that may ascribe life endowed with meaning (or the absence of meaning) to all natural objects and nature and, by extension, culture as a whole. If cultures are living organisms, they are susceptible to being read and reread. History intervenes in this cognitive, hermeneutic, and (re)constructive process of endlessly reading and reorganizing materials.

18   I am borrowing the term *emplot* from Hayden White's discussion of "emplotment" in

Metahistory. He defines it as: "Providing the 'meaning' of a story by identifying the kind of story that has been told is called explanation by emplotment. If, in the course of narrating this story, the historian provides us with the plot structure of a Tragedy, he has explained it in one way; if he has structured it as a Comedy, he has 'explained' it in another way. Emplotment is the way by which a sequence of event fashioned into a story is gradually revealed to be a story of a particular kind" (1973, 7).

19 Sanders writes: "The primary purpose [of *Elizabeth and Essex*] is not to be that of inform-ing and explaining through the use of historic data; rather, it is to be that of one of the greatest forms of literary art—tragedy—in order to arouse the intellect, vitalize and intensify the imagination, and stir the emotions deeply" (1957, 239). The rhetoric of the text shows that Strachey is constantly striving to develop a style appropriate to a tragic history. Strachey's dramatic techniques make his readers approach the text as if they were members of an audience, presenting them with the spectacle of a cast of characters performing onstage. He shifts from narration to soliloquy to stream of consciousness. In "The Art of Biography," Woolf also remarked that Strachey's biographies are the product of a frustrated dramatist ([1942] 1967, 223).

20 See Kallich 1961.

21 In an oedipal reading of Strachey's identifications in *Elizabeth and Essex*, John Ferns has suggested that "Strachey felt that his manhood had been denied and thwarted by a female presence that he could not get beyond . . . [and he] was unable to struggle free of the oedipal web. If one sees *Elizabeth and Essex* in the Freudian terms that Strachey himself used in writing the book, one might ultimately identify Elizabeth with Strachey's mother and Strachey himself with Essex" (1988, 101). In Ferns's view, "*Elizabeth and Essex* is as much a romantic biography as a 'tragic history,' a romantic biography with a personal meaning for Strachey" (100).

22 Klein had been lecturing in London since the summer of 1925 thanks to the initiative of Alix and James Strachey. Karl Abraham's premature death in December 1925 brought Alix's and Melanie Klein's analyses to an abrupt end. Both women met in Berlin at that time. As Judith M. Hughes has reported, "Alix's account of Klein's talk in Berlin had aroused James's interest. In London, he wrote, 'the little ones' [children] were stirring 'people's feelings' to such an extent that discussion of them occupied successive meet-ings. To that discussion James thought an abstract of the talk would make a fine addi-tion. He proved correct: when he read the document Alix provided, Klein received universal acclaim, with Jones turning out to be 'an absolutely heart-and-soul whole-hogging pro-Melanie' " (1989, 12).

23 See especially chapter 8 in this book and my comments on the figure of Wilde in chapter 11.

24 *Elizabeth and Essex* has been repeatedly compared to Shakespeare's *Anthony and Cleopatra*. See McCarthy 1933, Iyengar 1939, and Holroyd 1994.

25 In *Elizabeth and Essex*, there is also an obsession with the mutilation of the ears that relates to castration anxiety: "And the curious society which loved such fantasies and delica-cies—how readily would it turn and rend a random victim with hideous cruelty! A change of fortune—a spy's word—and those same ears might be sliced off, to the laughter of the crowd, in the pillory; or, if ambition or religion made a darker embroilment, a more ghastly mutilation" ([1928] 1948, 9–10).

26 As is well known, Foucault makes the point that the cruelty of the punishment could easily result in a dangerous reversal of public opinion toward the criminal: "It was as if the punishment . . . [were] to make the executioner resemble a criminal, judges murderers, to reverse roles at the last moment, to make the tortured criminal an object of pity or admiration" ([1975] 1995, 9).

27 Sanders has pointed out that "Violence and blood are no more out of place here in the vivid accounts of uprisings, wars, and gory executions than in the sensational means which the Elizabethan stage used to produce its effects of terror" (1957, 242).

28 In line with other critics, Sanders recognizes Strachey's successful treatments of Manning, Gordon, Queen Victoria, Queen Elizabeth, Cecil, and Bacon. Among his failures, he mentions Dr. Arnold and "some of the other portraits which have been objected to" (ibid., 210).

29 Strachey writes of Essex's changing moods and disposition, noting that "suddenly health would ebb away from him, and the pale boy would lie for hours in his chamber, obscurely melancholy, with a Virgil in his hand" ([1928] 1948, 4). After his victory over the Spanish army in Cadiz, he is seized by a profound melancholia. He desires to be "Away from the glory and the struggle—to be back at home, a boy again at Chartley—to escape irrevocably into the prolonged innocence of solitude and insignificance and dreams! With a play upon his own name—half smiling, half melancholy—he wrote some lines" (105).

30 As Sanders reports, "Lopez had once made the queen and others laugh at him. Harrison questioned such suppressions and manipulations as 'privileges denied to the pedestrian scholar' " (1957, 204).

31 We may raise the question of whether being afflicted with melancholia was possible at all for women during the Renaissance. In this respect, the argument of Juliana Schiesari's work on the "gendering of melancholia" attempts to show how male "lack" is predicated upon female loss. Schiesari sets herself up to examine "feminism, psychoanalysis, and the symbolics of loss in Renaissance literature" and argues that we are, at the present moment, at the end of an epistemic formation, a great age of melancholia that began in the Renaissance. She draws a parallel between this beginning and ending of melancholia and the formation and decline of the "subject." In tracing this movement, she identifies Freud's "Mourning and melancholia" as a text that foregrounds, through the figure of Hamlet, how the "blessed lack or holy course" (1992, 7) of melancholy bestows on men a "keener eye for the truth" (Freud [1915, 1917] 1953, 246). She notes that "it is significant that melancholia—at least this form of it—became an elite 'illness' which afflicted men precisely as the sign of their exceptionality, as the inscription of genius within them" (1992, 7). She argues that for male creativity melancholia thus converts "the feeling of disempowerment into a privileged artifact" (13). In her conclusions, she makes clear the hierarchical nature of "loss" as a category and the legitimation of male loss through female dispossession of it.

32 See my brief discussion of Klein's ideas on the horror of spending money and melancholia in chapter 1.

33 Elizabeth is a Hamletian figure in Strachey's narrative. We could probably say about her what Stephen Reid has said about Shakespeare's best-known dramatic hero: "we have in

Hamlet's story a real loss (the death of his father) which ought to have led to mourning, together with the intolerable injunction to avenge that death, as well as the unrecognized loss which lies at the heart of melancholia" (1974, 380). In Elizabeth's case, we are obviously facing the premature and violent death of her mother. All other circumstances are very similar to those just mentioned.

34 In his narrative, Strachey underlines the fact that Essex, "Elizabeth's first cousin twice removed," possessed "high birth, great traditions, Court influence, even poverty—for the making of a fine career" ([1928] 1948, 3). Later Elizabeth would give him a monopoly over wine, "the right to farm the customs on the sweet wines imported into the country" (36).

35 Strachey portrays Elizabeth's vicarious pleasure in subjugation: "Her servants, struggling with each other for influence, remained her servants still" ([1928] 1948, 47).

36 Strachey condenses this atmosphere of struggles over power and prerogatives with the statement "Below the surface of caracoling courtiers and high policies, there was cruelty, corruption and gnashing of teeth" (ibid., 64).

37 Bacon is described as a learned man, interested in literature and philosophical speculation, with an extremely "sensitive nature" (ibid., 61). In a state of anxiety, he could attack, "in a style suggestive of a female cat" (63).

38 In the militaristic tone present in the discourse of Elizabeth, Essex, and the courtiers, there is usually an element of sadism followed by a state of mania. Before Essex launches the final offensive against Spain, Strachey says: "He urged an exactly contrary policy—a vigorous offensive—a great military effort, which would bring Spain to her knees" (ibid., 165). Mania goes hand in hand with the defeat of its objects.

39 In the second chapter of Elizabeth and Essex, Strachey gives us a portrait of Elizabeth's "neurotic condition," which is of "an hysterical origin" (ibid., 19). At this point, Strachey attributes hysteria to his hero in a masterful operation of masquerade: "Hysterical and distracted, he was still hesitating, when letters were brought to him from England" (207).

40 See chapters 4 and 5.

41 Strachey's portrait of Bacon is splendidly completed now, with more details added to his sagacious character. He was "Inspired with the ingenious grandeur of the serpent" and believed that "Private friendship and private benefits were one thing; the public duty of taking the part required of him by the state in bringing to justice a dangerous criminal was another" ([1928] 1948, 245, 243).

42 In his detailed study of Strachey's personality, Gabriel Merle finds no trace of guilt in him. Strachey was an atheist throughout his life, and he maintained a critical attitude toward the Church of England and all institutionalized religion (1980, 179–83).

43 It was particularly during modernism when the primacy of the visual was challenged as a guarantor of gender and racial knowledge. Sexual and racial styles proliferated, and strategies of passing gained currency. Passing problematizes the notion of identity insofar as identity is predicated upon the (false) promise of the visible as that which grants access to epistemological inquiry and ultimately to some truth about the individual. Modernism's wealth of instances in literature of sexual and racial passing presents characters who pass as an Other, gays who pass as straight, and blacks who pass as

whites in a wide variety of modes. The visible has never easily or simply been a guarantor of truth. As Judith Butler puts it, "Can sexuality even remain sexuality once it submits to a criterion of transparency and disclosure, or does it perhaps cease it to be sexuality when the semblance of full explicitness is achieved?" (1991, 15).

44 The term *homeovestism* was coined by the Canadian psychoanalyst George Zavitzianos, on the model of *transvestism*, to refer to the perverse "dressing up in the clothes of the same-sex person" (quoted in Kaplan 1991, 249).

45 In an interesting essay, Kim Michasiw approaches gay male masquerade and camp and develops an interesting argument with what he understands as the "ironized identifications of camp" (1994, 150) and gay male masquerade as a "mode of appropriating and articulating the gap between masculinity understood in heterosexist terms—as being bounded by heterosexual object-choice—and masculinity understood differently" (150). As far as the question of identification is concerned, Michasiw concludes that "Both camp and masquerade are structured around a conscious parody overlying an unconscious identification. The objects of unconscious identification, however, differ radically. Camp's identification, as we have seen, is with the signs of the symbolic father at his most hystericized; masquerade's identification is with the father's ego-ideal" (168).

46 Strachey began his career writing articles and his *Landmarks in French literature* ([1912] 1945), a survey commissioned by the Home University Library.

47 In this respect, Jack Babuscio has argued that this theatrical element in gay experience derives in part from the social exigency placed on gays to pass as straight (see Bergman 1993, 26).

48 Meyer follows Judith Butler's idea of gender performativity. For Butler, "Performativity . . . is always a reiteration of a norm or set of norms, and to the extent that it acquires an act-like status in the present, it conceals or dissimulates the conventions of which it is a repetition" (1993, 12). She has argued that the parodic repetition of the original "reveals the original to be nothing other than a parody of the *idea* of the natural and the original" (1990a, 31).

11 *Melancholia Reborn*

1 I do not mean to imply in any essentialist way that this melancholic phantasy of violent incorporation of the penis is exclusive to lesbians. A similar phantasmatic structuring may be found in other women, especially heterosexual women—more so than in bisexuals—when they face creativity and emotional independence. This is in line with my reflections on the specificity of the girl's Oedipus conflict in Klein, the proximity of melancholia and paranoia, and my understanding of the melancholia of gender. See especially chapters 3 and 5 in this book.

2 Mary Lynn Broe, among other contributors to *Silence and power* (1991), has emphasized that *Ryder*, despite being censored, was a best-seller in the United States (6).

3 In the United States, publishers Covici-Friede defended their right to publish the novel, which they finally accomplished in 1929.

4 From the trials of *The well of loneliness*, it is clear that the body of the "invert" acquired legal meaning, and thus illegal status, under the repressive obscenity law.

5   The publisher's note to the last edition of *Ryder* to date (1990) states that the only text available is expurgated since the original manuscript was destroyed during World War II. Barnes declined to restore the censored passages for a 1979 St. Martin's reprint. Some of the original illustrations were also censored, but they survived and were included in the 1990 edition.

6   It is important to remark how Barnes, in a covert manner and in the form of a lullaby, tells the story of a filicide, the drowning of a child by its mother. Since there is no further comment about this incident, Barnes seems to be asking her readers what motives could force a woman to kill her child. The anxieties linked to motherhood and the enormous pressure that society has traditionally placed on mothers are obviously factors to be considered in melancholia and related pathologies and in women's depression in its most general sense.

7   The reasons for Wittig's aphorisms are also well known. In her view, " 'Feminine writing' is the naturalizing metaphor of the brutal political fact of the domination of women, and as such it enlarges the apparatus under which 'femininity' presents itself: that is Difference, Specificity, Female Body/Nature . . . 'feminine writing' amounts to saying that women do not belong to history, and that writing is not a material production" (1983, 63).

8   In this respect, Wittig's own words put it clearly: "This work on the level of the words and of the letter reactivates words in their arrangement, and in turn confers on meaning its full meaning: in practice this work brings out in most cases—rather than one meaning—polysemy" (ibid., 68).

9   See Brecht 1964.

10 Cheryl Plumb has explored this dimension in the fiction, plays and journalism of Barnes's literary beginnings (1986, esp. 7–13).

11 In this respect, Leigh Gilmore refers to similar questions in the case of *Nightwood*. Gilmore makes the point that T. S. Eliot's presentation of the text in catachrestical terms (as a "poetic novel") prevented the distinctions upon which obscenity law depends from being attached to *Nightwood*. She writes: "Whereas Barnes' 'deviance' was strictly a matter of literary style, Radclyffe Hall was perceived not as the lesbian in the text and the lesbian writing the text" (1994, 623); see also 617–24.

12 If we stick to Fredric Jameson's definition of *genre* in *The political unconscious* (1981, 106)— "Genres are essentially literary institutions or social contracts between a writer and a specific public, whose function is to specify the proper use of a particular cultural artifact"—Barnes's deliberate blending and confusion of genres, in her effort to eschew classification, baffles readers' expectations and society at large.

13 It has been noted that Barnes wrote *Ryder* along the lines of the literary tradition of great parody in the West, one that begins with Aristophanes and continues with Rabelais, Fielding, Sterne, and Joyce. In this respect, Sheryl Stevenson places *Ryder* in the Rabelaisian carnivalesque tradition in a reading of the novel that elaborates on Bakhtin's ideas in *Rabelais and his world*. See Stevenson 1991 and Marcus 1991.

14 A choir of her sisters' voices, the first words that accompany Cynthia Ryder in the novel, gloomily alludes to graves and good times gone just before Amelia's wedding to Jonathan Buxton Ryder: " 'I lament o'er graves of hopes and pleasures gone' (she then but sixteen!)" (6). Amelia's maiden name, de Grier, is also evocative of grief.

15 It would be interesting to trace this cannibalistic element associated with feminine characters who are devoured and who devour in the whole of Barnes's oeuvre and in relation to its melancholic subtext. In this respect, Bertha Harris writes: "When D. Barnes wrote Nightwood she was creating, in the silent, devouring magic of her lesbian, Robin Vote, a sleepless swimmer in the depths of all our imaginations; and her new name is Jaws—and her ancient name Beauty" (1977, 8). Carolyn Allen in Following Djuna (1996), explains Harris's passage as follows: "Harris's reference to 'Jaws' (she is referring especially to the film of that title) places Robin in what Harris delineates in her essay as the tradition of the lesbian as monster, by which she has in mind not only an outsider to various cultures of domination, but also 'a creature of tooth and claw, of passion and purpose: unassimilable, awesome, dangerous, different: distinguished' " (quoted in Allen 1996, 115). Allen writes of Robin's "devouring music" (13), which involves her with others and finally captures her lovers.

16 See especially Irigaray 1991. Aeschylus' Oresteia and Sophocles' Oedipus Rex are two canonical instances of this operation of concealment.

17 I will endeavor to prove the validity of the argument put forward in the first chapter of this book, namely, that women, feminine masochists, and female and male homosexuals are most prone to melancholia. In Ryder, women (mothers and daughters) and "inverts" exhibit a devastating form of melancholia.

18 There is virtually no trace of Wendell's father in the novel. We know that Wendell was first called John, and in chapter 2 there is a fleeting allusion to this man: "Truth impels me to say that Sophia had indeed a son, but it was three days bastard, got of John Peel, the tutor, before he mended the matter" (8). We also know that Sophia had many lovers and finally married Alex, a "handsome Swede" (13), a figure also shrouded in mystery.

19 In chapter 39, "Wendell Discusses Himself with His Mother," Barnes describes Wendell's mania in full force: "I sport a changing countenance. I am all things to all men, and all women's woman. At one moment I am a young and tender girl, with close-held legs, and light bones becoming used to the still, sweet pain that is a girl's flesh, metaphorically speaking, of course. At other times, this face, is not a dowager's? Sometimes I am whore in ruffle petticoat, playing madly at a pack of rufians, and getting thrippence for my pains; a smartly boxed ear, or, a bottom-tingling clap a-hind. Yet, again I am a man-with-a-trowel, digging at the edge of my life for the tangible substance of re-creation; and once I was a bird who flew down my own throat, twanging at the heart chord, to get the pitch of my own mate-call. And once I was a deer stalking myself" (164).

20 As Barnes describes her early in the novel: "Now Amelia gave way to her nature, which was sentimental and longing, and took up violin and singing at the Conservatory of Music" (32).

21 Barnes brilliantly narrates this episode in a poetic vein as a limerick: "And died so . . . / Who died as women die, unequally / Impaled upon a death that crawls within; / For men die otherwise, of man unsheathed / But women on a sword they scabbard to. / And so this girl, untimely to the point, / Pricked herself upon her son and passed / Like any Roman bleeding on the blade—" (77).

22 In the afterword to the collection of essays edited by Mary Lynn Broe, Silence and power: A

reevaluation of Djuna Barnes, Stimpson refers to the self-immolation of Barnes's letters as a "symbol of her contradictory relationship to language" (Stimpson 1991, 370). Even when the motives for their burning remain an enigma, Stimpson presumes that Barnes's much cherished sense of privacy together with her desire not to be studied and thus "possessed"—in Stimpson's words—and her anger and frustration with this world might be plausible reasons for her decision to make them disappear.

23 Her radical political views have not received as much critical attention. Jane Marcus's remarkable feminist discussion of *Nightwood* and her argument that the novel makes a modernism of marginality are two of the few exceptions (1991).

24 Frances M. Doughty has noted that "Barnes does not seem to have used visual art as a primary means of expression but as a means of illustrating something preexisting, whether a concept, as in her antiwar work; a text, as in her illustrations to her fiction; or a person, as in the portrait sketches accompanying her interviews." Nevertheless, she observes that in 1913 alone, and in six months, "Barnes produced thirty-eight articles accompanied by eighty-eight drawings, as well as more than twenty drawings apparently not associated with any text" (1991, 138).

25 The Darwinian and Lamarckian models of heredity were competing models debated in the natural sciences at the end of the nineteenth century. Whereas classical Darwinian theory was based on the principle of natural selection, for Lamarck acquired traits were inheritable. Later neo-Lamarckism held that the environment acts directly on organic structures, resulting in adaptation.

26 Barnes writes with supreme wit about Kate's condition: "At times it seemed that the two [Kate's parents] were not united in lawful wedlock. / Does it seem to follow that Kate-Careless was a bastard? It would seem to follow, and yet who can tell how craftily a child makes legitimate prey upon her condition?" (83).

27 This is especially evident in chapter 39, "Wendell Discusses Himself with His Mother," where Wendell shows his frailty and dependence on Sophia and other women in an almost psychotic discourse.

28 In her book *Following Djuna: Women's lovers and the erotics of loss* (1996), Allen focuses on what she calls the Djuna Barnes tradition (as opposed to the Radclyffe Hall tradition) and studies lesbian romance, tracing its progress from Bertha Harris to Jeanette Winterson and Rebecca Brown. By "tradition" she refers to the ways in which "some of Barnes's themes and textual obsessions, preference for lyrical prose, and experimental forms are 'handed down,' and continue in such contemporary writers as Bertha Harris. The term also marks how these writers have acknowledged Barnes's work and/or how critical commentators have compared them to Barnes" (14). She places her use of the term tradition close to what Elaine Marks has called "lesbian intertextuality" (1979).

29 In her book, Allen opts for the broader term *erotics between women*—though she acknowledges that she uses it interchangeably with *lesbian erotics*—for several reasons: "to avoid reifications of 'lesbian' and to enable recognition of the historical specificity of 'lesbian' as a descriptive term. Most important, 'erotics between women' underlines my argument's focus on relational, dyadic interchanges rather than on individual 'identity' issues. I intend 'erotics between women' to signal the complicated sexual and emotional dynamics of desire between women, however they name themselves" (1996, 3). She

defines *erotics* as being opposed to *poetics* and *politics*: "If 'poetics' signifies the formal aesthetics of texts being read and 'politics' their contextual networks of power, 'erotics' points to the working out readerly desire in the production of a genealogy, a tradition, a paradigm. At the same time 'erotics' intersects both with 'poetics' and with 'politics' by signifying the reader's performances of textual scripts charged with the relation of power to desire" (15).

30 Wendell patronizingly describes Kate's low-class origins and his own instrumental role in her salvation: "Kate, a girl brought up in penury, beached from the gutters, has been vouchsafed an offering from the shades" (159).

31 Throughout the novel, there is ample evidence that not only childbirth but also pregnancy are melancholic states, the work of mourning definitely gone astray. See chapter 5, "Rape and Repining!": "A Girl hath come to mourning in Spring again . . . when Unripe Woman falls to Ripening!" (23). In chapter 8, Mazie, a twenty-year-old mother, appears as a "mourner" (41).

32 Hippocrates, in his *On the nature of man* (fifth century B.C.) was the first to bring together the four humors—blood, yellow bile, phlegm, and black bile—in his account of the body and psyche. In his classic *Melancholia and depression*, Stanley Jackson explains at length Burton's definition of melancholia. Burton "essentially accepted the definition subscribed to by the majority: '*a kind of dotage without a fever, having for his ordinary companions fear and sadness, without any apparent occasion.*' Dotage, following Du Laurens, mean that '*some of the principal faculty of the mind, as imagination, or reason, is corrupted, as all melancholy persons have*'; our closest equivalent would be *delusional.* He took note of the tendency to consider the mental disturbance as less pervasive than in madness (mania) and commented that '*Fear* and *Sorrow* make it different from *madness* [mania].' And '*without any apparent occasion*' or '*without a cause*' is lastly inserted, to specify it all from all ordinary of *Fear* and *Sorrow*. . . . He went on in some detail to indicate that such sufferers were frequently discontent, restless, and tired of life; and often they were suspicious and jealous, given to solitariness" (1986, 332–38; emphasis in original). In many cases, they were also troubled by a particular, circumscribed fear or delusion, and Burton elaborated a list of such possible fears and delusions, perhaps the most extensive and certainly the most colorful of such accounts (327–32). But regarding these fears and delusions he added: "Yet for all this . . . *in all other things they are wise, staid, discreet, and do nothing unbeseeming their dignity, person or place*" (96; emphasis in original).

33 This chapter has been read and decoded as the central piece of evidence for Djuna Barnes's molestation by her father. Both *Ryder* and her play *The Antiphon*, which is written in an autobiographical vein, are read as narrative testimonies of her experience as incest survivor. See especially DeSalvo 1991 and Dalton 1993.

34 Carolyn Allen stresses the importance on the figure of the "little girl" as narrator in some of the stories published prior to *Nightwood*. She specifically traces the little girl in "Cassation"—originally entitled "A little girl tells a story to a lady" (1925)—"The grand malade" (1925), and "Dusie" (1927), all of them in Barnes (1996), a figure that is missing in *Nightwood*. In *Ryder*, the little girl reappears in the figures of Arabella and Julie. Even when they are not, properly, narrators of their own stories, paradoxically *Ryder* comes to be "their" narrative.

35 Barnes in a most telling way translates Arabella's wish: " 'Oh, empty out thy stars, and let the sky, in unpeopled multitude, take up my case!' Throughout that long night she tosses on her bed. A thousand thousand children now is she" (107).

36 Anne B. Dalton has suggested that the narration of the events of the fishing excursion of Wendell, Timothy, and Julie in chapter 27 uses "charged metaphorical description of Julie 'playing' with Wendell's 'flute' and of Wendell and Julie's brother Timothy playing with crabs to portray Julie's molestation" (1993, 178).

37 See Scott 1993.

38 In her essay, "What's a nice lesbian like you doing in the Church of Torquemada? Radclyffe Hall and other Catholic converts" (1990), Joanne Glasgow asks why, paradoxical as it may appear—since, as Glasgow remarks, "lesbianism did not exist as a Catholic reality" (242)—a significant number of lesbians chose Roman Catholicism as their professed faith in the first decades of the twentieth century. In chapter 12 of *Ryder*, "Amelia Hears from her Sister in re Hisodalgus, That Fine Horse," Ann, Amelia's sister—who amalgamates traditional values with lack of instruction—speaks of the current decline of morality in society and of the precarious state of religion: "And speaking of women, dear sister, was there ever a woman made a good convert? Tell me your mind on this, for I would know your opinion. Mine is most terribly set on it that they are but poor at anything but that which they laid hands on in the cradle. And no matter how they do turn from their natures, it is with perfect intuition of where that nature is left, and with a backward looking. Not so is it with a man, for his nature is never of a certainty with him, because of his notions of chemistry and such logic, and when he leaves it, it is with a conviction (born of this philosophy) that he is stalking it. No such muddle can be in a woman, and I'll tell you the why of my conclusion: My last lady, whereto I'll go no more a-dusting and sweeping, turned from Catholic to Protestant overnight, for that she had bedded with dissension in the shape of a pair of heathen breeches, and I heard of the matter as she sat upon the commode. Now, imagine a new-blown Protestant sitting upon a sempiternal pot managing aught from her converted bottoms that would give pleasure or relief to those parts that had been Catholic all the days of her life!" (73).

39 Barnes narrates this brief episode as follows: "Had not Oscar Wilde himself, with his then not-to-be-denied right hand, lifted his, Wendell's auburn forelock, murmuring, 'Beautiful, beautiful, beautiful!' " (18).

40 I take up this issue at length in chapter 10, where I discuss Lytton Strachey's writings.

41 Roselyne Rey (1995) remarks that the term *dolorist* first appeared in France in 1919 in a review about a book by Georges Duhamel, *La Possession du Monde*, published in the newspaper *Le Temps*, though in this instance the term had definite pejorative connotations.

42 Jane Marcus (1991) has noted *Nightwood's* relation to the trial concerning *The well of loneliness* and the rise of nazism.

43 Barnes amusingly narrates the peculiarities of this alternative family as follows: "Molly had borne six sons and four daughters. Every one of the six was a liar, thief, drunkard and pickpocket. A merry household it made of an evening, as they whittled away the legs of the tables and chairs, boasting of this and of that, with many stolen watches as a basis. . . . Molly would say, as she was their mother, so their watches were also hers, but Molly was only fooling. For, as she said, she had been an honest woman all the days of

her life, and had a wholesome picture of the likeness of the Lord, of damnation and hell-fire" (192).

44　In the conversation between Laura Twelvetree and Wendell in chapter 37, Julie does not appear as a beautiful and attractive young woman. Laura says, " 'You have a little daughter . . . and she has no breasts. I've often noted Julie—where,' she said, rummaging in her scented case, 'are those jujubes I brought for her?' " (158).

45　Julie finds out that her grandmother has betrayed her with her lies and is unable to forgive her: "[A]nd I [Sophia] went further where was Julie in the deep of the garden, and I said, 'I love you,' and I could not kiss her, as I had kissed the others, because she was thinking something outside the family. Therefore I leaned my head upon her little breast, and she said, 'You have betrayed me,' and she held me with her arm, and because she doubts me, and because there is trouble in the house, I shall remember her always, and she will walk to my grave, and will doubt me long" (169).

46　Discussions of the incompatibility of motherhood and authorship abound in literature. Two of the most telling examples are Virginia Woolf's A room of one's own ([1929] 1957) and Adrienne Rich's Of Woman born: Motherhood as experience and institution (1976).

47　As in chapter 19, here Wendell connects the traditional humoral theory of melancholia to women. He says: "Has not some dove cooed lost its perch, to give her the voice in which she says, 'Lovest thou mee?' / Aye, what brisket, shoulder, leg, rump, brought her to her knees crying, 'I am thine, O Lord!' What snaring turned her on the lathe to gentleness? What cloven hoof tramped out her vintage of dark melancholy, to bring her down with mortal lowing?" (206).

48　The chapter alludes to "Death and the Maiden," a song composed by Schubert in 1817 after a poem by Claudius from which comes the title. In 1824, Schubert composed a quartet with the same title, and later this subject was treated by artists such as the German painter Egon Schiele (Girl Clutching the Figure of Death, 1915) and playwright Ariel Dorfman. In 1994, Roman Polanski directed a movie by the same name based on Dorfman's play.

49　The narration at this point can be read along the lines of the traditional 'pater semper incertus est, mater certissima': "And who can doubt the word of the mother when she is shameless in her nakedness before you, to show you how a body goes down into death?" (223).

50　Barnes wittily uncovers for her readers a complicitous path they may follow on their way to her personal history. It is important to note that Barnes even gives us the name, à la Ryder, of the place where she was born: Cornwall-on-Hudson comes to be Storm-King-on-Hudson (84), where the Ryders have their family house.

51　Freud exemplifies two common variants of the family romance to demonstrate the versatility of such narratives: "An interesting variant of the family romance may then appear, in which the hero and author returns to legitimacy himself while his brothers and sisters are eliminated by being bastardized . . . the young phantasy-builder can get rid of his forbidden degree of kinship with one of his sisters if he finds himself sexually attracted by her" ([1909] 1953, 240).

52　In the context of the novel, leaving aside biographical questions, child abuse is well documented in the Ryder children's deprivation of education and in Wendell's obsession with sex, which shows in his intrusive narration of stories that have to do with sex and procreation to his children.

53 In chapter 15, Kate's virginity is an enigma: "It was queried, was she a virgin?" (83).

54 Barnes splendidly narrates this scene of horror of the gaze. It is set in the fields, where all creatures look at Wendell: "And everything and its shape became clear in the dark, by tens and tens they ranged, and lifted their lids and looked at him; in the air and in the trees and on the earth and from under the earth, and regarded him long, and he forbore to hide his face. They seemed close ranged, and now they seemed far ranged, and they moved now near, now far, as a wave comes and goes, and they lifted their lids and regarded him, and spoke not in their many tongues, and they went far way, and there was a little rest, and they came close, and there was none" (242).

55 Eliot's *The waste land* was considered to be an emblem of this modernist discourse of sterility. But it also emerges in a multitude of works written by both men and women. I am thinking of Joyce, Woolf, Barnes, Mallarmé, Camus, Sartre, García Lorca, and Mann.

56 In a postmodern vein, Donna Haraway exemplifies a similar antireproductive impulse in her "Manifesto for cyborgs" (1985). Elsewhere she writes: "I would suggest that cyborgs have more to do with regeneration and are suspicious of the reproductive matrix and of most birthing. . . . We require regeneration, not rebirth, and the possibilities for our reconstitution include the utopian dream of the hope for a monstruous world without gender" (1991, 181).

57 Here I am referring both to Barnes's voluntary choice not to be a mother—we know she had an abortion in 1932—and to her blunt refusal to have her work massively published and distributed, which would have made it more vulnerable to censorship. This second Benjaminian sense of "mechanical reproduction" (see Benjamin 1968a) shows in her private publication of *Ladies almanack* and its restricted circulation among her friends and members of Natalie C. Barney's circle.

12 *Melancholia, the New Negro, and the Fear of Modernity*

1 Weldon Johnson's poem reads as follows: "How would you have us? As we are? / Or sinking 'neath the load we bear? / Our eyes fixed forward on a star? / Or gazing empty at despair? / Rising or falling? Men or things? / With dragging pace or footsteps fleet? / Strong willing sinews in your wings? / Or tightening chains about your feet?" (quoted in Cullen 1923, 168, originally published in Johnson's *Fifty years and other poems* [1917]).

2 See Chapter 8. In *Black skin, white masks*, Frantz Fanon writes about white men's phantasies in which black men function as "phobogenic objects" ([1952] 1967, 151).

3 In his essay, "Psychoanalysis and racism" (1989), Frosh discusses the precariousness of the sense of ego integrity of the racist and the terror derived from the encounter with the black Other: "the *visibility* of difference undermines the abstract sense of homogeneity which so shakily supports the ego. Into this is poured the sexual distress of the white; supported by the economic and political pay-offs of oppression, racism becomes a fortress for the fragments of the self" (241).

4 Rustin's ideas rest on the Kleinian and post-Kleinian elaborations on psychotic states of mind, which imply that "psychotic attributes of mind are universal, original and latent

components of human mentality; never wholly banished from the self; liable to become more salient in conditions of fear and anxiety than in more benign settings; and of course more central and pathogenic in some individuals than in others, sometimes for individual reasons in an individual's psychic history" (1991, 62). See also Bion 1961, 1967; and Steiner 1993.

5 From a post-Kleinian perspective, sociologist Michael Rustin shares this view when he writes: "Racism can thus be seen to involve states of projective identification, in which hated self-attributes of members of the group gripped by prejudice are phantasied to exist in members of the stigmatized race" (1991, 68).

6 Johnson closes his essay with the following lines: "I believe that the Negro's advantages and opportunities are greater in Harlem than in any other place in the country, and that Harlem will become the intellectual and the financial center for Negroes of the United States, and will exert a vital influence upon all Negro peoples" (Locke [1925] 1968, 311).

7 We have previously engaged the issue of masquerade. For an important and influential elaboration, see especially Homi K. Bhabha's "Of mimicry and man: The ambivalence of colonial discourse" and "Sly civility," in The location of culture (Bhabha 1994, 85–92, 93–101).

8 If we were to take a psychobiographical approach, we may as well suggest that the problematics of container-contained in Cullen have to do with his anxieties about his origin and separation from his original family and his biological mother. As his close friend Arna Bontemps wrote, Cullen "was in many ways an old-fashioned poet. He never ventured very far from the Methodist parsonage in which he grew up in New York. A foster child, drawn into this shelter at an early age, he continued to cherish it gratefully" (quoted in Baker 1974, 24).

9 In this respect, Gerald Early, in his introduction to My soul's high song (1991) has argued that it was Cullen's initial success with his 1923 poem "The Ballad of the Brown Girl" and the winning of the Empire Federation of Women's Clubs first prize for his poem "I Have a Rendezvous with Life" that marked the beginning of the Harlem Renaissance (rather than the publication of Jean Toomer's Cane in September 1923). He writes that "if anyone was being groomed, being intellectually and culturally conditioned and bred, first by whites and then by blacks, to be a major black crossover literary figure, it was this thin, shy black boy. America has always loved precocious children and Cullen's was the race's first honest-to-goodness child literary star" (19). In Early's view, this precociousness may have to do with his mature anxieties and the decline of his literary production.

10 I am specifically thinking of writers such as H. D., Marianne Moore, Gertrude Stein, and William Carlos Williams. To explore the connections between white modernism and the Harlem Renaissance, see North 1994, especially chapters 6 and 7.

11 For Baker it is "the mastery of the minstrel mask by blacks that constitutes a primary move in Afro-American discursive modernism" (1987, 17).

12 Critics contended that Cullen's points about race in the preface to Caroling dusk were mostly theoretical, since Cullen himself had admitted that there were certain experiences, such as racial injustices, peculiar to Negro life. See Ferguson 1966, 92–97.

13 Cullen's undergraduate thesis has been reproduced and studied by James W. Tuttleton, in his essay "Countee Cullen at 'The Heights' " (1989). I am quoting from this material.

14 Hillyer's emphasis on perfect form has been reported by Blanche Ferguson (Cullen's biographer). She writes: "According to Hillyer, Countee Cullen was the first American poet to publish a poem in rime royal the difficult seven-line stanza made famous by Chaucer and Masefield" (1966, 58). Ferguson refers to a poem by Cullen, "To Lovers of Earth, Fair Warning" (1927c, 51–52), which was used as an example of poetic form in one of Hillyer's books.

15 Avi-Ram argues that, "The form of the poem . . . must have something to do with the body, since it is to the body that rhythm and sound effects make their most immediate appeal" (1990, 32). This critic reads some of Claude McKay's and Countee Cullen's poems with a hidden gay content, led by his idea that the "conventionality" of the form does not necessarily signal political conservatism; in some instances—as in the cases he selects for his reading—the form undermines the very dichotomy of form and content and causes us to confront "the form of the poem as well as the body of a human being" (43).

16 In his reading, Avi-Ram focuses on the metaphor of the "box" and reads it as "closet," arguing that "a poet's voice, is both hidden and protected by a box in Cullen's poetic corpus" and that in relation to black and gay experience the poem's form, "as a protective box or shroud . . . allows the themes only faintly (but the more poignantly) to be heard through it, [and] draws together these two experiences of social repression" (ibid., 42–43).

17 Indeed, Gates goes so far as to argue that "signifyin(g), in Lacan's sense, is the Other of discourse" (1988, 50).

18 This is an idea that Lloyd W. Brown, among others, has identified mostly in Cullen's racial poetry. See his "The expatriate consciousness in black American literature" (1972).

19 In this respect, Ronald Primeau has argued that in Cullen's racial poetry, his "adoption of Keats is more pervasive and liberating than in the obviously allusive and formal elegies" (1976, 78).

20 See "For My Grandmother," in *Color* (1925, 46).

21 Gerald Early has suggested that "Tribute" was written for Carolyn (Mitchell) Cullen, the poet's foster mother, in 1929 while Cullen was in Paris. He reads line 8, "To one the victor loved a world away," as follows: "The phrase 'a world away' not only implies that Cullen is writing this poem abroad, far from his mother, but also that he and his mother are, not surprisingly, different, of separate worlds, if you will" (Cullen 1991, 11).

22 "The Shroud of Color" has often been compared to Edna St. Vincent Millay's "Renascence." The influence of Millay on Cullen's early poetry has been highlighted by Harvey C. Webster (1947), Margaret Perry (1971), and James W. Tuttleton (1989) among others.

23 I am borrowing this idea from Alden Reimonenq (1993), who suggests that "spirit" and its derivatives can be read as encoding Cullen's homosexuality.

24 The central "incident" from which the poem draws its title is narrated in the second stanza: "Now I was eight and very small, / And he was no whit bigger, / And so I smiled, but he poked out / His tongue, and called me, 'Nigger'" (1925, 15).

25 Cullen also wrote two sonnets on cats since he shared Baudelaire's interest in these independent and mysterious creatures. "The Cat" and "Cats" are included in *The Medea and some poems* (1935, 94–95).

26 Cullen's "Yet Do I Marvel," exhibits the form of the Petrarchan sonnet. Its rhyme scheme is: the first two quatrains abab, cdcd, and a sestet, ee ff gg. The poem is divided into the octave, wherein the problem is stated, and the sestet, in which some sort of resolution is attempted. The ninth line, or volta, marks the movement toward resolution.

27 Some critics have noted Blake's influence on Cullen's poetry. John C. Shields (1992) and Ronald E. Sheasby (1995) trace the presence of Blake in Cullen's "Yet Do I Marvel" and "Heritage," respectively.

28 Cullen died in 1946 of uremic poisoning at the age of forty-four.

29 See, for instance, "Sleep" (Cullen 1935, 75).

30 Blanche Ferguson has remarked that the critical reception of Cullen's second volume of poetry, "while generally favorable, did not measure up to that burst of acclaim that had greeted his first book, *Color*. But Countee was encouraged to read among the reviews a statement in *The Nation* that said in part, 'Best of all he can forget that he is of the colored race and be just 'poet' most of the time' " (1966, 91–92).

31 As Gerald Early reports, this poems refers to the trial of nine black boys ranging in age from thirteen to nineteen in Scottsboro, Alabama, between 1931 and 1933. The children were accused of raping two white prostitutes and were sentenced to death. Finally, after several legal appeals and much public outcry, the convictions were overturned. In the end, the children spent four years in prison (Cullen 1991, 258).

32 For Reimonenq, in his letters and some of his poetry Cullen's relationships exhibit an oxymoronic rhetoric of "closeted openness" (1993, 152).

33 Should the reader wish to find a misogynist trend in Cullen's poetry, he or she can find it in Cullen's translations of Baudelaire. For instance, in "The Cat" he writes: "I see revived in thee, feline cast, / A woman with thine eyes, satanic beast / Profound and cold as scythes to mow me down" (1935, 94).

34 Marin's discourse is within a Lacanian framework, but it provides an important insight into the reading of Cullen's "Medusa."

35 I use *overt* cautiously, within a context of closeted homosexuality. Alden Reimonenq (1993) identifies in *The Medea* a group of poems "gay in theme, imagery, and argument" (158). He explicitly refers to: "Sonnet Dialogue," "These Are No Wind-Blown Rumours," "Interlude," "Any Human to Another," "Bilitis Sings" and "I Would I Could, as Other Poets Have."

36 This is obviously a reference to Audre Lorde's "The Master's tools will never dismantle the Master's house" (1984, 110–13).

37 Cullen pokes fun at Goll's naive descriptions of Jupiter as obsessed with cleanliness. He also has special gifts—like an acute olfactory sense—and is obsessed with his salvation and the existence of "black angels" in the heaven of Christianity. At bottom, all his anxieties reflect a desire to become "more like the whites" (1929b, 373).

38 In this respect, Alden Reimonenq reads Cullen's poetry as essentially androcentric. Cullen's "is an androcentric poetry replete with overt confessional self-analysis—a feature most evident in *Copper Sun* (1927) and *The Medea and Some Poems* (1935)" (1993, 148).

39 See Ferguson's comments in her biography of Cullen (1966, esp. 130).

40 *Opportunity* was the journal of the African Urban League. The league was concerned with problems confronting Negroes in urban areas—housing, employment, education, and race relations—especially after the rural exodus from the South to northern cities after

World War I. Charles S. Johnson, the editor of *Opportunity*, hired Cullen as an assistant editor. Johnson wanted to make the magazine's pages available for the manuscripts of talented young Negroes and prepare the way for acceptance of their works by more prominent publications. With Cullen's background as a poet and a graduate of Harvard, it was felt that he could provide advice and suggestions as to which manuscripts should be published in the journal.

41 Walker was heiress to the fortune of her mother, Madam C. J. Walker, who became rich by inventing a method for straightening hair. See Ferguson 1966, 83.

42 When Cullen was able to extend his grant for a second year, he continued to write in Paris.

43 For an account of Cullen's activities and his life in Paris, especially during 1928–30, see Fabre ([1985] 1991).

44 In Fanon's chapter "The Negro and language," in *Black skin, white masks*, he emphasizes the importance of mastering the colonizer's language so as to be able to pass as white: "to speak a language is to take on a world, a culture. The Antilles Negro who wants to be white will be the whiter as he gains greater mastery of the cultural tool that language is" ([1952] 1967, 38).

45 Very few critics have broken the silence concerning Cullen's homosexuality (or bisexuality). Among them, see Lewis (1981), Wagner [1963] 1973, Rampersad 1986, Avi-Ram 1990, and Reimonenq 1993. More recently, Marjorie Garber (1995), in the context of her assessment of bisexuality in the Harlem Renaissance and modernism, has underscored Cullen's bisexuality. Cullen's biographer, Blanche E. Ferguson, mentions in passing that Jackman was one of the friends with whom Countee enjoyed discussing literature, for Harold had made himself an authority on the Negro in the arts. In addition, he was an excellent bridge partner.

46 Gerald Early reports that Cullen and Jackman met at DeWitt Clinton High School in New York City and that he was from the West Indies (Cullen 1991, 19). Blanche E. Ferguson, in her biography of Cullen, says that Jackman was born in London (1966, 100). I have not been able to locate his exact place of birth. One of the few physical descriptions we have of Cullen is also given by Ferguson. In 1934, when he began his career as a teacher of French at Frederick Douglass Junior High School 139 in New York, "his boyish expression made him appear younger. He never wore a hat and his hair was the color and texture Negroes sometimes called 'meriney,' a crinky reddish tan. His skin was somewhat darker. His eyes could best be described as 'earnest,' though a closer look revealed a mischievous twinkle in their brown depths. He was not very tall, and his figure was somewhat plump from the gourmet dishes he had learned to love in France" (144).

47 One of the aspects that has baffled his biographer and many critics for years is precisely the place and circumstances of Cullen's birth. Apparently, he told different versions of his birth and upbringing to different people. There are at least three versions. One, given by him for his anthology *Caroling dusk*, specifies New York and Reverend Cullen's parsonage. A second, which appeared in an article at the time of his death, gives Baltimore as the place of birth of Countee LeRoy Porter and claims that he was brought up in New York by his mother after his father's death. It was said that he was adopted by the Cullens in 1918 after his mother's death. The third version gives Louisville, Kentucky, as his birthplace (this is the story that his widow, Ida M. Cullen deems accurate). Gerald Early

provides a variation on the second version, describing Cullen's upbringing by a Mrs. Porter, his grandmother, who brought him to New York at the age of nine. Early adds still another account, which holds that Cullen's biological mother reappeared in his life in the 1920s, by which time he was famous. He is said to have helped her financially for the rest of her life and to have attended her funeral in Kentucky in 1940. See Cullen 1991, 9–10.

48 Cullen's deep sense of displacement can be found in such poems as "Atlantic City Waiter" (1925, 10), "Brown Boy to Brown Girl" (5), "Pagan Prayer" (20–21), and "Heritage" (36–41).

49 Here I am referring to Paula Heimann's concept of assimilation as introduced in her 1942 essay "A contribution to the problem of sublimation and its relation to processes of internalization" (1942). See my discussion in chapter 9.

50 See McKay 1929.

51 When Freud writes about inversion, which is "widespread among savage and primitive races" ([1905] 1953, 139), and considers the influence that climate, race, and geographical factors have on its appearance, he has in mind Richard Burton's theory of the "Sotadic zone," from his *The book of one thousand nights and a night*, where he argues that "There exists what I shall call a 'Sotadic Zone,' bounded westwards by the northern shores of the Mediterranean (N.Lat.43°) and by the Southern (N.Lat.30°). Thus the depth would be 780 to 800 miles including meridional France, the Iberian Peninsula, Italy and Greece, with the coast-regions of Africa from Morocco to Egypt" (1885, 10:206). In Burton's account, Algiers was one of the most dangerous of all zones after the conquest because of its potential for spreading the "vice" of homosexuality to French soldiers and, by extension, to civilian society (216).

52 As is well known, Cullen married Yolande Du Bois, the daughter of W. E. B. Du Bois. The relationship lasted only a few months, and in two years they were divorced. Their marriage was an important social event in Harlem. As Ferguson has reported, Dr. Du Bois "stressed that this was no ordinary wedding. He saw it as a pageant symbolic of the beauty and power of a new breed of American negro" (1966, 100).

53 There are different critical opinions concerning the reception of Cullen's novel. Blanche Ferguson writes that, "in general, Countee's novel went well" (1966, 140), whereas Alan Shucard argues that it "suffers the consequences of having two plots that touch each other only tangentially and are never adequately reconciled by incident or tone" (1984, 72).

54 In 1935, the Hedgerow Theater, a repertory company based in Moylan, Pennsylvania, expressed an interest in producing a dramatic version of *One way to heaven*. Cullen arranged the story as a play in ten scenes, and, as Blanche Ferguson reports, "The opening production was so successful that the company decided to include the play in its repertory" (1966, 156).

55 In the novel, Cullen even uses the word *masquerade* to describe Sam's activities. Thus, when he describes Sam and Mattie's first encounter outside a church, he writes: "He had seen this same light shining on the preacher's face, but on hers it glowed with a strength that he felt might burn sheer through his masquerade and reveal him for the arrant trickster he was" (42–43).

56 In this respect, Ferguson has argued that Cullen's experience at the Methodist par-

sonage enabled him to "make these [religious] scenes in his story strikingly realistic" (1966, 139).

57 Furthermore, in the novel Sam appears as a "good-looking" man (109), and at his wedding party some women say of him, "How romantic! How perfectly like a lover!" (127). But he is also a rebel. This is most clearly shown at his wedding at Constancia's home, when he recognizes that the people that surround him "were not of his world . . . they were society" and proudly reacts: "He eyed them insolently, not bending his head when they bowed to him, raging inwardly as he saw them gaze in astonishment at his lonely arm" (119).

58 In the novel, Mattie also is torn between her newly embraced faith and her belief in alternative supernatural practices to obtain what she desires. Cullen's obsession with boxes and shrouds is also conveyed in relation to their multiple uncanny powers. Thus, for instance, Mattie keeps Sam's razor and cards (his tools for performing at revival meetings) "in a little golden box" (46). In a different context, Cullen describes Mattie as follows: "Shame and misery encircled her like a shroud, pressed in upon her and disturbed her waking hours, kept her suffocated and dream-ridden at night" (227).

59 Michael North reports that van Vechten (and also Waldo Frank's, author of the racial melodrama *Holiday*) passed while traveling in the South with Jean Toomer (1994, 8). North speaks of a "pattern of rebellion through racial ventriloquism" (9) in white modernist writing.

60 Similar reverse situations are repeated at the wedding party of Mattie and Sam. On the matter of blacks who may pass as whites: " 'My dear,' said Constancia, with a trace of hurt in her voice, 'do you think I would betray you? He's [Stanley Bickford, a musician and one of her guests] *colored*' " (122).

61 See the episode narrated in chapter 1 in which Reverend Johnson relieves his anxiety about new conversions with a song.

62 Cullen explicitly refers to magic throughout the first chapter of the novel: "Here was magic which not even the preacher had been able to deal out of them [congregation] . . . a sinner's heart all displayed on the altar of the Lord. The very devil had been laid low before them" (23).

63 Constancia makes this clear when she confesses that "It isn't being colored that annoys me. I could go white if I wanted to, but I am too much of a hedonist; I enjoy life too much, and enjoyment isn't across the line. Money is there, and privilege, and the sort of power which comes with numbers" (187).

64 The reader can compare Cullen's sarcasm upon forcing the coincidence between the duchess of Uganda's idealized speech and Professor Calhoun's fierce racist and white supremacist discourse: "It is the duty of white America to look to itself, to protects its sons and daughters from the insidious and growing infiltration of black blood into the arteries of this glorious Republic. There can be no quarter between the white man and a race which can truthfully be stigmatized as indolent, untrustworthy, unintelligent, un- clean, immoral, and cursed of heaven. Their only salvation and ours lies in a congressio- nal enactment returning them to Africa, the land of their fathers" (175).

65 When Constancia learns from Mattie that she is going to marry a man who has lost an arm, she is horrified and asks, "will you manage with a husband lacking an appendage?"

(103). Ironically here, and more seriously at other times, Cullen refers to this "lack" throughout the novel.

66 In this fake conversion, Sam feigns hearing some music and seeing the lights in his room brighter than ever before (278–79).

67 As Gerald Early has pointed out, "Perhaps the biggest criticism that can be made against the Renaissance was that it seemed to be nothing more than a series of beginnings. . . . It seemed a movement that was always getting started but never going anywhere" (Cullen 1991, 33). Early lists a series of these "beginnings," such as the publication of Claude McKay's *Harlem shadows* (1922), Johnson's anthology *The book of American Negro poetry* (1922), Jessie Fausset's novel, *There is confusion* (1924), Countee Cullen's *Color* (1925), Langston Hughes's *The weary blues* (1926), and Alain Locke's anthology *The new Negro* ([1925] 1968).

68 Cullen wrote these words in the *Chicago Bee*, December 24, 1927 (quoted in Turner 1971).

BIBLIOGRAPHY

Abel, Elizabeth. 1989. *Virginia Woolf and the fictions of psychoanalysis*. Chicago: University of Chicago Press.

Abercrombie, Nicholas, Stephen Hill, and Bryan S. Turner. 1986. *Sovereign individuals of capitalism*. London: Allen and Unwin.

Abraham, Karl. [1907] 1955. On the significance of sexual trauma in childhood for the symptomatology of dementia praecox. In *Clinical papers and essays on psychoanalysis*. Ed. Hilda Abraham. New York: Basic Books. 13–20.

——. [1908] 1949. The psycho-sexual differences between hysteria and dementia praecox. In Abraham [1927] 1949, 64–79.

——. [1911] 1949. Notes on the psychoanalytical investigation and treatment of manic-depressive insanity and allied conditions. In Abraham [1927] 1949, 137–56.

——. [1920] 1922. Manifestations of the female castration complex. *International Journal of Psycho-Analysis* 3: 1–29.

——. [1924] 1949. A short study of the development of the libido viewed in the light of mental disorders. In Abraham [1927] 1949, 418–501.

——. [1927] 1949. *Selected papers of Karl Abraham, M.D.* Trans. Douglas Bryan and Alix Strachey. London: Hogarth.

Abraham, Nicolas, and Maria Torok. 1967. *Melanie Klein: Essais de psychanalyse, 1921–1945.* Trans. into French by Marguerite Derrida. Paris: Payot. Also in Abraham and Torok 1978, 184–99.

——. 1978. *L'Ecorce et le noyau*. 2d ed. Paris: Flammarion.

——. 1994. *The shell and the kernel: Renewals of psychoanalysis*. Trans. Nicholas T. Rand. Vol. 1. Chicago: University of Chicago Press.

Alford, C. Fred. 1989. *Melanie Klein and critical social theory: An account of politics, art, and reason based on her psychoanalytic theory*. New Haven: Yale University Press.

Allen, Carolyn. 1996. *Following Djuna: Women lovers and the erotics of loss*. Bloomington: Indiana University Press.

Althusser, Louis. 1969. Freud and Lacan. Trans. Ben Bewster. *New Left Review* 55 (May–June): 49–65.

——. 1971. Ideology and ideological state apparatuses. In *Lenin and philosophy and other essays*. Trans. Ben Brewster. London: New Left. 121–73.

——. 1993. Freud et Lacan. In *Ecrits sur la psychanalyse: Freud et Lacan*. Paris: Stock. 22–46.

Anderson, Perry. [1984] 1988. Modernity and revolution. In *Marxism and the interpretation of culture*. Ed. Cary Nelson and Lawrence Grossberg. Urbana: University of Illinois Press. 317–33. Reprinted from *New Left Review* 144 (March–April 1984): 96–113.

Aron, Lewis. 1995. The internalized primal scene. *Psychoanalytic Dialogues* 5 (2): 195–237.

Auerbach, Erich. 1953. The brown stocking. In *Mimesis: The representation of reality in Western literature*. Princeton: Princeton University Press. 525–53.

Avi-Ram, Amitai F. 1990. The unreadable black body: "Conventional" poetic form in the Harlem Renaissance. *Genders* 7:32–46.

Babuscio, Jack. 1993. Camp and the gay sensibility. In Bergman 1993, 19–38.

Baker, Houston A. 1974. *A many-colored coat of dreams: The poetry of Countee Cullen*. Detroit: Broadside.

——. 1987. *Modernism and the Harlem Renaissance*. Chicago: University of Chicago Press.

Baliteau, Catherine. 1990. Karl Abraham, un disciple entre savoir et penser. *Psychanalyse à l'Université* 15 (58): 35–63.

Barbier, André. 1991. Réflexions sur la place de la douleur dans la théorie psychanalytique. *Revue Française de Psychanalyse* 55 (4): 801–17.

——. 1992. Empire, action, origine. *Revue Française de Psychanalyse* 56 (5): 1499–1505.

Barnes, Djuna. [1914] 1989. How it feels to be forcibly fed. In *New York*. Ed. Alyce Barry. Los Angeles: Sun and Moon. 174–79.

——. [1928] 1990. *Ryder*. Lisle, IL: Dalkey Archive.

——. 1928. *Ladies almanack: Showing their signs and their tides, their moons and their changes, the seasons as it is with them, their eclipses and equinoxes, as well as a full record of diurnal and nocturnal distempers*. Paris: Printed for the author.

——. [1937] 1961. *Nightwood*. New York: New Directions.

——. 1989. *New York*. Ed. Alyce Barry. Los Angeles: Sun and Moon.

——. 1996. *Collected stories*. Ed. Philip Herring. Los Angeles: Sun and Moon.

Barthes, Roland. [1968] 1977. The death of the author. In *Image, music, text*. Ed. Stephen Heath. New York: Hill and Wang. 142–48.

——. [1970] 1974. *S/Z*. Trans. Richard Miller. New York: Hill and Wang. Original edition *S/Z* (Paris: Editions du Seuil).

Baudrillard, Jean. [1981] 1994. *Simulacra and simulation*. Trans. Sheila Faria Glaser. Ann Arbor: University of Michigan Press. Original edition *Simulacres et simulation* (Paris: Galilée).

Benhabib, Seyla, Judith Butler, Drucilla Cornell, and Nancy Fraser. 1995. *Feminist contentions: A philosophical exchange*. New York: Routledge.

Benjamin, Jessica. 1995. *Like subjects, love objects: Essays on recognition and sexual difference*. New Haven: Yale University Press.

Benjamin, Walter. [1928] 1977. *The origin of German tragic drama*. Trans. John Osborne. London: NLB. Original edition *Ursprung des deutschen Trauerspiels* (Berlin: E. Rowohlt).

——. 1968a. *Illuminations*. Trans. Harry Zohn. Ed. Hannah Arendt. New York: Harcourt, Brace and World.

——. 1968b. The work of art in the age of mechanical reproduction. In Benjamin 1968a, 217–51.

Benstock, Shari. 1986. *Women of the Left Bank: Paris, 1900–1940*. Austin: University of Texas Press.

——. 1990. Expatriate sapphic modernism. In Jay and Glasgow 1990, 183–203.

Bergman, David, ed. 1993. *Camp grounds: Style and homosexuality*. Amherst: University of Massachusetts Press.

Berman, Art. 1994. *Preface to modernism*. Urbana: University of Illinois Press.

Bernauer, James William, and David M. Rasmussen. 1988. *The final Foucault*. Cambridge: MIT Press.

Bernheimer, Charles. 1992. Penile reference in phallic theory. *differences: A Journal of Feminist Cultural Studies* 4 (1, The Phallus Issue): 116–32.

Bernheimer, Charles, and Claire Kahane. 1985. *In Dora's case: Freud, hysteria, feminism*. New York: Columbia University Press.

Bersani, Leo. 1986. *The Freudian body: Psychoanalysis and art*. New York: Columbia University Press.

——. 1990. *The culture of redemption*. Cambridge: Harvard University Press.

Betsky, Aaron. 1995. *Building sex: Men, women, architecture, and the construction of sexuality*. New York: William Morrow.

Bhabha, Homi K. 1994. *The location of culture*. London: Routledge.

Bilu, Yoram. 1987. Dybbuk possession and mechanisms of internalization and externalization: A case study. In Sandler 1987b, 163–78.

Bion, Wilfred Rupert. 1961. *Experiences in groups and other papers*. New York: Basic Books.

——. 1962a. *Learning from experience*. London: William Heinemann.

——. 1962b. A theory of thinking. *International Journal of Psycho-Analysis* 43:306–10.

——. 1963. *Elements of psycho-analysis*. New York: Basic Books.

——. 1967. *Second thoughts: Selected papers on psycho-analysis*. London: Heinemann Medical.

——. 1970. *Attention and interpretation: A scientific approach to insight in psycho-analysis and groups*. New York: Basic Books.

——. 1977. *Seven servants: Four works*. New York: Aronson.

Boehm, Felix. 1920. Beiträge zur Psychologie der Homosexualität, pt. I: Homosexualität und Polygamie. *Internationale Zeitschrift für Psychoanalyse* 6:298–319.

——. 1926. Beiträge zur Psychologie der Homosexualität, pt. III: Homosexualität und Ödipuskomplex. *Internationale Zeitschrift für Psychoanalyse* 12:66–79.

Bonnet, Marc. 1995. Prototypes identificatoires dans le travail de Mélancolie. *Topique: Revue Freudienne* 25 (56): 107–52.

Booth, Alison. 1992. *Greatness engendered: George Eliot and Virginia Woolf*. Ithaca, NY: Cornell University Press.

Boothby, Richard. 1991. *Death and desire: Psychoanalytic theory in Lacan's return to Freud*. New York: Routledge.

Borch-Jacobsen, Mikkel. [1982] 1988. *The Freudian subject*. Trans. Catherine Porter. Stanford: Stanford University Press. Original edition *Le sujet freudien* (Paris: Flammarion).

Bourdieu, Pierre. [1980] 1990a. *The logic of practice*. Trans. Richard Nice. Stanford: Stanford University Press. Original edition *Le sens pratique* (Paris: Editions de Minuit).

——. 1990b. La domination masculine. *Actes de la Recherche en Sciences Sociales* 84 (2): 2–31.

Bowlby, Rachel. 1988. *Virginia Woolf: Feminist destinations.* New York: Blackwell.

Brecht, Bertolt. 1964. *Brecht on theatre: the development of an aesthetic.* Ed. and trans. John Willett. New York: Hill and Wang.

Breen, Dana, ed. 1993. *The Gender conundrum: Contemporary psychoanalytic perspectives on femininity and masculinity.* London: Routledge.

Brennan, Teresa. 1993. *History after Lacan.* London: Routledge.

Breton, André. 1972. *Manifestoes of surrealism.* Trans. Richard Seaver and Helen R. Lane. Ann Arbor: University of Michigan Press.

Britton, Ronald. 1995. Reality and unreality in phantasy and fiction. In Person et al. 1995, 82–106.

Broe, Mary Lynn. 1989. My art belongs to daddy: Incest as exile—the textual economics of Hayford Hall. In Broe and Ingram 1989, 41–86.

——, ed. 1991. *Silence and power: A reevaluation of Djuna Barnes.* Carbondale: Southern Illinois University Press.

Broe, Mary Lynn, and Angela J. C. Ingram, eds. 1989. *Women's writing in exile.* Chapel Hill: University of North Carolina Press.

Bronfen, Elisabeth. 1992. *Over her dead body: Death, femininity, and the aesthetic.* New York: Routledge.

Bronz, Stephen H. 1964. *Roots of Negro racial consciousness: The 1920s, three Harlem Renaissance authors.* New York: Libra.

Brown, Dennis. 1989. *The modernist self in twentieth-century English literature: A study of self-fragmentation.* Basingstoke: Macmillan.

Brown, Lloyd W. 1972. The expatriate consciousness in black American literature. *Studies in Black Literature* 3 (2): 9–12.

Buci-Glucksmann, Christine. 1986. Catastrophic utopia: The feminine as allegory of the modern. *Representations* 14:220–29.

Bürger, Peter. 1984. *Theory of the avant-garde.* Trans. Michael Shaw. Minneapolis: University of Minnesota Press.

Burgin, Victor, James Donald, and Cora Kaplan. 1986. *Formations of fantasy.* London: Methuen.

Burke, Carolyn, Naomi Schor, and Margaret Whitford, eds. 1994. *Engaging with Irigaray: Feminist philosophy and modern European thought.* New York: Columbia University Press.

Burton, Richard Francis. 1885. *A plain and literal translation of the Arabian nights' entertainments now entituled* The Book of the Thousand Nights and a Night. 10 vols. N.p.: Burton Club.

Burton, Robert. [1621] 1989–94. *The anatomy of melancholy.* Ed. Thomas C. Faulkner, Nicolas K. Kiessling, and Rhonda L. Blair. 3 vols. Oxford: Clarendon.

Butler, Judith. 1990a. *Gender trouble: Feminism and the subversion of identity.* New York: Routledge.

——. 1990b. Performative acts and gender constitution: An essay in phenomenology and feminist theory. In *Performing feminisms: Feminist critical theory and theatre.* Ed. Sue-Ellen Case. Baltimore: Johns Hopkins University Press. 270–82.

——. 1990c. The pleasures of repetition. In *Pleasure beyond the pleasure principle.* Ed. Robert A. Glick and Stanley Bone. New Haven: Yale University Press. 259–75.

——. 1991. Imitation and gender insubordination. In Fuss 1991, 3–31. Reprinted in *The Lesbian and Gay Studies Reader,* ed. Henry Abelove, Michele Aina Barale, and David M. Halperin (New York: Routledge, 1993), 307–20.

——. 1993. *Bodies that matter: On the discursive limits of "sex."* New York: Routledge.

——. 1995. Melancholy gender-refused identification. *Psychoanalytic Dialogues* 5 (2): 165–80.

Butler, Judith, and Joan Wallach Scott, eds. 1992. *Feminists theorize the political.* New York: Routledge.

Caws, Mary Ann. 1990. *Women of Bloomsbury: Virginia, Vanessa, and Carrington.* New York: Routledge.

Chadwick, Mary. 1925. Über die Wurzel der Wissbegierde. *Internationale Zeitschrift für Psycho-analyse* 11:54–68. Abstract in *Int. J. Psycho-Anal.* 6.

Chambers, Ross. 1993. *The writing of melancholy: Modes of opposition in early French modernism.* Trans. Mary Seidman Trouille. Chicago: University of Chicago Press.

Chasseguet-Smirgel, Janine. [1975] 1985. *The ego ideal: A psychoanalytic essay on the malady of the ideal.* Trans. Paul Barrows. New York: Norton. Original edition *L'idéal du moi: Essai psychanalytique sur la "maladie d'idéalité"* (Paris: Tchou).

——. 1984. *Creativity and perversion.* London: Free Association Books.

——. 1995. "Creative writers and day-dreaming": A commentary. In Person et al. 1995, 107–21.

Chodorow, Nancy. 1994. *Femininities, masculinities, sexualities: Freud and beyond.* Lexington: University Press of Kentucky.

Cooper, Virginia S. 1995. Virginia Woolf, 1882–1941: A Kleinian perspective. *Melanie Klein and Object Relations* 13 (1): 91–111.

Court, Raymond, ed. 1988. *L'Effet trompe-l'oeil dans l'art et la psychanalyse.* Paris: Dunod.

Cullen, Countee. 1923. The League of Youth. *The Crisis* 26 (August): 167–68.

——. 1925. *Color.* New York: Harper and Brothers.

——. 1926. The Negro in art: How shall he be portrayed? *The Crisis.* 32:193–94.

——. 1927a. *Copper sun.* New York: Harper and Brothers.

——. 1927b. The Dark Tower. *Opportunity* 5 (9): 272–73.

——. 1928. The Dark Tower. *Opportunity* 6 (9): 272–73.

——. 1929a. *The black Christ and other poems.* London: Putnam.

——. 1929b. Countee Cullen on miscegenation. *The Crisis* 36 (11): 373.

——. 1932. *One way to heaven.* New York: Harper and Brothers.

——. 1935. *The Medea and some poems.* New York: Harper and Brothers.

——. 1947. *On these I stand: An anthology of the best poems of Countee Cullen.* New York: Harper and Brothers.

——. 1991. *My soul's high song: The collected writings of Countee Cullen, voice of the Harlem Renaissance.* Ed. Gerald Lyn Early. New York: Doubleday.

——, ed. 1927c. *Caroling dusk: An anthology of verse by Negro poets.* New York and London: Harper and Brothers.

Dalton, Anne B. 1993. Escaping from Eden: Djuna Barnes' revision of psychoanalytic theory and her treatment of father-daughter incest in *Ryder. Women's Studies* 22 (2): 163–79.

Daniel, Walter C. 1971. Countee Cullen as a literary critic. *College Language Association Journal* 14:281–90.

Dawson, Graham. 1994. *Soldier heroes: British adventure, empire, and the imagining of masculinities.* London: Routledge.

De Beauvoir, Simone. 1952. *The second sex.* New York: Knopf.

De Certeau, Michel. 1975. Écrire l'innomable. *Traverses* 1:9–15.

——. 1986. *Heterologies: Discourse on the other.* Trans. Brian Massumi. Minneapolis: University of Minnesota Press.

De Jongh, James. 1990. *Vicious modernism: Black Harlem and the literary imagination.* Cambridge and New York: Cambridge University Press.

DeKoven, Marianne. 1991. *Rich and strange: Gender, history, modernism.* Princeton: Princeton University Press.

De Lauretis, Teresa. 1994a. *The Practice of love: Lesbian sexuality and perverse desire.* Bloomington: Indiana University Press.

——. 1994b. Habit changes. *differences: A Journal of Feminist Cultural Studies* 6 (2–3, More Gender Trouble: Feminism Meets Queer Theory): 296–313.

De Man, Paul. 1979. Autobiography as de-facement. *Modern Language Notes* 94:919–30.

De Saussure, Raymond. 1929. Les fixations homosexuelles chez les femmes névrosés. *Revue Française de Psychanalyse* 3:50–91.

Deleuze, Gilles. [1964] 1972. *Proust and signs.* Trans. Richard Howard. New York: Braziller.

Deleuze, Gilles, and Felix Guattari. [1972] 1977. *Anti-Oedipus: Capitalism and schizophrenia.* Trans. Robert Hurley, Mark Seem, and Helen R. Lane. New York: Viking.

Derrida, Jacques. [1967] 1978. Freud and the scene of writing. In *Writing and difference.* Trans. Alan Bass. Chicago: University of Chicago Press. 196–231. Original edition *L'Écriture et la difference* (Paris: Seuil). First published in English in *Yale French Studies* 48 (1972): 74–117.

DeSalvo, Louise A. 1989. *Virginia Woolf: The impact of childhood sexual abuse on her life and work.* Boston: Beacon.

——. 1991. To make her mutton at sixteen: Rape, incest, and child abuse in *The Antiphon.* In Broe 1991, 300–315.

Deutsch, Helene. [1925] 1944. *The psychology of women: A psychoanalytic interpretation.* New York: Grune and Stratton. Original edition *Psychoanalyse der weiblichen Sexualfunktionen* (Leipzig: Internationaler Psychoanalytischer Verlag).

——. 1933. Psychologie der manisch-depressiven Zuständen insbesondere der chronischen Hypomanie. *Internationale Zeitschrift für Psychoanalyse* 19:358–71.

——. 1937. Absence of grief. *Psychoanalytic Quarterly* 6:12–22.

differences: A Journal of Feminist Cultural Studies. 1992. 4 (1, The Phallus Issue).

Diprose, Rosalyn, and Robyn Ferrell, eds. 1991. *Cartographies: Poststructuralism and the mapping of bodies and spaces.* North Sydney, NSW, Australia: Allen and Unwin.

Doane, Janice L., and Devon L. Hodges. 1992. *From Klein to Kristeva: Psychoanalytic feminism and the search for the "good enough" mother.* Ann Arbor: University of Michigan Press.

Doane, Mary Ann. 1991. *Femmes fatales: Feminism, film theory, psychoanalysis.* New York: Routledge.

Domenici, Thomas, Ronnie C. Lesser, and Adrienne Harris, eds. 1995. *Disorienting sexuality: Psychoanalytic reappraisals of sexual identities.* New York: Routledge.

Doughty, Frances M. 1991. Djuna Barnes as illustrator of her life and work. In Broe 1991, 137–55.

Doyle, Laura. 1994. "These Emotions of the Body": Intercorporeal narrative in *To the Lighthouse. Twentieth Century Literature* 40 (1): 42–71.

Du Bois, W. E. B. [1903] 1990. *The souls of black folk.* New York: Vintage.

Duparc, François. 1989. Les objets infinis du mélancolique. *Revue Française de Psychanalyse* 53 (1): 481–86.

Eliot, T. S. [1919] 1958. Tradition and the individual talent. In *Selected essays*. 3d ed. London: Faber and Faber. 3–11. First published in *Egoist* 6 (4): 909–910; 6 (5): 72–73. Reprinted in Eliot 1920, 47–50.

———. 1920. *The sacred wood: Essays on poetry and criticism*. London: Methuen.

———. 1922. *The waste land*. New York: Boni and Liveright.

Elliott, Bridget, and Jo-Ann Wallace. 1994. *Women artists and writers: Modernist (im)positionings*. London: Routledge.

Ellis, Havelock. 1936. *Sexual inversion*. New York: Random House.

Emanuel, James A., and Theodore L. Gross, eds. 1968. *Dark symphony: Negro literature in America*. New York: Free Press.

Epstein, William H. 1987. Recognizing the life-course: Strachey's *Eminent Victorians*. In *Recognizing biography*. Philadelphia: University of Pennsylvania Press. 138–71.

Eysteinsson, Astradur. 1990. *The concept of modernism*. Ithaca: Cornell University Press.

Fabre, Michel. [1985] 1991. Countee Cullen: "The Greatest Francophile." In *From Harlem to Paris: Black American writers in France, 1840–1980*. Urbana: University of Illinois Press. 76–91. Original edition *La rive noire: De Harlem a la Seine* (Paris: Lieu commun).

Fanon, Frantz. [1952] 1967. *Black skin, white masks*. Trans. Charles Lam Markmann. New York: Grove. Original edition *Peau noire, masques blancs* (Paris: Seuil).

Fauset, Jessie Redmon. 1925. *There is confusion*. New York: Boni and Liveright.

Felman, Shoshana, and Dori Laub. 1992. *Testimony: Crises of witnessing in literature, psychoanalysis, and history*. New York: Routledge.

Felski, Rita. 1989. *Beyond feminist aesthetics: Feminist literature and social change*. Cambridge: Harvard University Press.

———. 1994. Modernism and modernity: Engendering literary history. In Rado 1994, 191–208.

Fenichel, Otto. [1925] 1953. Introjection and the castration complex. In *The collected papers of Otto Fenichel*. First series. Ed. Hanna Fenichel and David Rapaport. New York: Norton. 39–70.

Ferenczi, Sándor. [1909] 1956. Introjection and transference. In *Sex in psychoanalysis*. Trans. Ernest Jones. New York: Dover. 30–79.

———. [1912] 1955. On the definition of introjection. In *Final contributions to the problems and methods of psycho-analysis*. Ed. Michael Balint. Trans. Eric Mosbacher et al. New York: Basic Books. 316–18.

———. [1913] 1956. Stages in the development of the sense of reality. In *Sex in psychoanalysis*. Trans. Ernest Jones. New York: Dover. 181–203.

———. [1922] 1955. Freud's "Group psychology and the analysis of the ego": Its contribution to the psychology of the individual. In *Final contributions to the problems and methods of psycho-analysis*. Ed. Michael Balint. Trans. Eric Mosbacher et al. New York: Basic Books. 371–76.

———. [1926] 1952. Psycho-analysis of sexual habits. In *Further contributions to the theory and technique of psycho-analysis*. Comp. John Rickman. Trans. Jane Isabel Sutie et al. New York: Basic Books. 259–97.

———. [1933] 1955. Confusion of tongues between adult and child: The languages of tenderness and of passion. In *Final contributions to the problems and methods of psycho-analysis*. Ed. Michael Balint. Trans. Eric Mosbacher et al. New York: Basic Books. 156–67.

Ferguson, Blanche E. 1966. *Countee Cullen and the Negro renaissance*. New York: Dodd, Mead.

Ferns, John. 1988. *Lytton Strachey*. Boston: Twayne.

Fink, Bruce. 1995. *The Lacanian subject: Between language and jouissance*. Princeton: Princeton University Press.

Fordham, Michael, and Roger Hobdell. 1995. *Freud, Jung, Klein, the fenceless field: Essays on psychoanalysis and analytical psychology*. London: Routledge.

Foucault, Michel. [1966] 1970. *The order of things: An archaeology of the human sciences*. London: Tavistock. Original edition *Les mots et les choses* (Paris: Gallimard).

———. [1968] 1983. *This is not a pipe*. Ed. and Trans. James Harkness. Berkeley: University of California Press.

———. 1969. Qu'est-ce qu'un auteur? *Bulletin de la Société Française de Philosophie* 63 (July–September): 73–104.

———. [1975] 1995. *Discipline and punish: The birth of the prison*. Trans. Alan Sheridan. 2d ed. New York: Vintage. Original edition *Surveiller et punir* (Paris: Gallimard).

Fowlkes, Martha R. 1991. The morality of loss: The social construction of mourning and melancholia. *Contemporary Psychoanalysis* 27 (3): 529–51.

Frank, Joseph. [1963] 1968. Spatial form in modern literature. In *The widening gyre: Crisis and mastery in modern literature*. Bloomington: Indiana University Press. 3–62.

Frankiel, Rita V. 1994. *Essential papers on object loss*. New York: New York University Press.

Freud, Anna. [1913] 1956. Stages in the development of the sense of reality. In *Sex in psycho-analysis*. Trans. Ernest Jones. New York: Dover. 181–203.

———. [1922] 1974. Beating fantasies and daydreams. In *Introduction to psychoanalysis: Lectures for child analysts and teachers, 1922–1935, early writings*. New York: International Universities Press. 137–57.

———. [1953] 1968. About losing and being lost. In *Indications for child analysis and other papers, 1945–1956*. New York: International Universities Press. 302–16.

Freud, Sigmund. 1953. *The standard edition of the complete psychological works of Sigmund Freud*. 24 vols. London: Hogarth. (Hereafter S.E.)

[1887–1902, 1950] 1953. Project for a scientific psychology. S.E. 1:283.

[1895?] 1953. Draft G. S.E. 1:200–206.

[1899] 1953. Screen memories. S.E. 3:301.

[1900] 1953. The interpretation of dreams. S.E., vols. 4 and 5.

[1901, 1905] 1953. Fragment of an analysis of a case of hysteria. S.E. 7:3.

[1905] 1953. Three essays on the theory of sexuality. S.E. 7:125.

[1907, 1908] 1953. Creative writers and day-dreaming. S.E. 9:143.

[1909a] 1953. Analysis of a phobia in a five-year-old boy. S.E. 10:3.

[1909b] 1953. Family romance. S.E. 9:235.

[1910] 1953. Leonardo da Vinci and a memory of his childhood. S.E. 11:59.

[1911a] 1953. Formulations on the two principles of mental functioning. S.E. 12:215.

[1911b] 1953. Psycho-analytic notes on an autobiographical account of a case of paranoia (dementia paranoides). S.E. 12:3.

[1912–13] 1953. Totem and taboo. S.E. 13:ix.

[1914, 1918] 1953. From the history of an infantile neurosis. S.E. 17:3.

[1914] 1953. On narcissism: An introduction. S.E. 14:69.

[1915] 1953. Instincts and their vicissitudes. S.E. 14:111.

[1915, 1917] 1953. Mourning and melancholia. S.E. 14:239.

[1916] 1953. Some character-types met with in psycho-analytic work. S.E. 14:311.

[1917] 1953. On transformations of instinct as exemplified in anal erotism. S.E. 17:127.

[1919] 1953. "A child is being beaten": A contribution to the study of the origin of sexual perversions. S.E. 17:177.

[1920a] 1953. Beyond the pleasure principle. S.E. 18:3.

[1920b] 1953. The psychogenesis of a case of homosexuality in a woman. S.E. 18:147.

[1921] 1953. Group psychology and the analysis of the ego. S.E. 18:67.

[1922a] 1953. Medusa's head. S.E. 18:273–74.

[1922b] 1953. Some neurotic mechanisms in jealousy, paranoia, and homosexuality. S.E. 18:223.

[1923] 1953. The ego and the id. S.E., 19:3.

[1924] 1953. The economic problem of masochism. S.E. 19:157.

[1925, 1926] 1953. Inhibitions, symptoms, and anxiety. S.E. 20:77.

[1925a] 1953. Negation. S.E. 19:235.

[1925b] 1953. Some psychical consequences of the anatomical distinction between sexes. S.E. 19:243.

[1927] 1953. Fetishism. S.E. 21:149.

[1929, 1930] 1953. Civilization and its discontents. S.E. 21:59.

[1931] 1953. Female sexuality. S.E. 21:223.

[1932, 1933a] 1953. Femininity. S.E. 22:112–35.

[1932, 1933b] 1953. New introductory lectures on psycho-analysis. S.E. 22:3.

[1938, 1940a] 1953. An outline of psycho-analysis. S.E. 23:141.

[1938, 1940b] 1953. Splitting of the ego in the process of defence. S.E. 23:273.

Freud, Sigmund, and Karl Abraham. 1965. *A psycho-analytic dialogue: The letters of Sigmund Freud and Karl Abraham, 1907–1926.* Ed. Hilda C. Abraham and Ernst L. Freud. Trans. Bernard Marsh and Hilda C. Abraham. London: Hogarth.

Freud, Sigmund, and Sándor Ferenczi. 1993. *The correspondence of Sigmund Freud and Sándor Ferenczi.* Ed. Eva Brabant, Ernst Falzeder, and Patrizia Giampieri-Deutsch. Vol. 1. Cambridge: Harvard University Press.

Friedman, Susan Stanford. [1987] 1989. Creativity and the childbirth metaphor: Gender difference in literary discourse. In *Speaking of gender.* Ed. Elaine Showalter. New York: Routledge. 73–100.

Frosh, Stephen. 1989. Psychoanalysis and racism. In Richards, 1989, 229–44.

———. 1994. *Sexual difference: Masculinity and psychoanalysis.* London: Routledge.

Fry, Roger Eliot. [1920] 1924. *Vision and design.* New York: Brentano's.

———. 1927. *Cézanne: A study of his development.* New York: Macmillan.

———. [1933] 1969. The double nature of painting. *Apollo* 89 (May): 362–71. Originally delivered as a lecture in Brussels in the fall of 1933. The published version is an abridged translation by Pamela Diamand.

Fuchs, S. H. 1937. On introjection. *International Journal of Psycho-analysis* 18:269–93.

Fuss, Diana. 1995. *Identification papers.* New York: Routledge.

———, ed. 1991. *Inside/out: Lesbian theories, gay theories.* New York: Routledge.

Gamman, Lorraine, and Merja Makinen. 1995. *Female fetishism.* New York: New York University Press.

Garber, Eric. 1983. T'ain't nobody's bizness: Homosexuality in 1920s Harlem. In *Black men/ white men: A Gay anthology*. Ed. Michael J. Smith. San Francisco: Gay Sunshine Press. 7–16.

Garber, Lawrence. 1976. Techniques of characterization in Strachey's *Elizabeth & Essex*. *Dalhousie Review* 56:405–28.

Garber, Marjorie B. 1992. *Vested interests: Cross-dressing and cultural anxiety*. New York: Routledge.

———. 1995. *Vice versa: Bisexuality and the eroticism of everyday life*. New York: Simon and Schuster.

Gates, Henry Louis. 1988. *The signifying monkey: A theory of Afro-American literary criticism*. New York: Oxford University Press.

Gedo, Mary Mathews. 1994. *Looking at art from the inside out: The psychoiconographic approach to modern art*. Cambridge: Cambridge University Press.

Gillibert, Jean. 1979. *L'image réconciliée: L'homme de constitution*. Paris: Payot.

Gilman, Sander L. 1993. *The case of Sigmund Freud: Medicine and identity at the fin de siècle*. Baltimore: Johns Hopkins University Press.

Gilmore, Leigh. 1994. Obscenity, modernity, identity: Legalizing *The Well of Loneliness* and *Nightwood*. *Journal of the History of Sexuality* 4 (4): 603–24.

Glasgow, Joanna. 1990. What's a nice lesbian like you doing in the church of Torquemada? Radclyffe Hall and other Catholic converts. In Jay and Glasgow 1990, 241–54.

Glover, Edward. 1933. The relation of perversion formation to the development of reality sense. *International Journal of Psycho-Analysis* 14:486–504.

Glover, James. 1927. Notes on an unusual form of perversion. *International Journal of Psycho-Analysis* 8:10–24.

Good, Michael I. 1995. Karl Abraham, Sigmund Freud, and the fate of the seduction theory. *Journal of the American Psychoanalytic Association* 43 (4): 1137–67.

Goodwin, Sarah McKim Webster, and Elisabeth Bronfen. 1993. *Death and representation*. Baltimore: Johns Hopkins University Press.

Greenacre, Phyllis. 1953. Certain relationships between fetishism and faulty development of the body image. *Psychoanalytic Study of the Child* 8:79–98.

———. 1968. Perversions: General considerations regarding their genetic and dynamic background. *Psychoanalytic Study of the Child* 23:47–62.

Grosskurth, Phyllis. 1995. *Melanie Klein: Her world and her work*. New York: Aronson.

Grosz, Elizabeth A. 1994. *Volatile bodies: Toward a corporeal feminism*. Bloomington: Indiana University Press.

———. 1995. *Space, time, and perversion: Essays on the politics of bodies*. New York: Routledge.

H. D. [Hilda Doolittle]. 1974. *Tribute to Freud*. Boston: Godine.

Hall, Radclyffe. 1928. *The well of loneliness*. London: Cape.

Halperin, John. 1980. Eminent Victorians and history. *Virginia Quarterly Review* 56:433–54.

Hamer, Diane. 1990. Significant others: Lesbianism and psychoanalytic theory. *Feminist Review* 34 (Perverse Politics: Lesbian Issues): 134–51.

Hammacher, Abraham Marie. 1973. *René Magritte*. New York: Abrams.

Handley, William R. 1994. The housemaid and the kitchen table: Incorporating the frame in *To the Lighthouse*. *Twentieth Century Literature* 40 (1): 15–41.

Haraway, Donna. 1985. Manifesto for cyborgs. *Socialist Review* 15:65–105.

———. 1991. *Simians, cyborgs, and women: The reinvention of nature*. New York: Routledge.

Harris, Andrea L. 1994. The third sex: Figures of inversion in Djuna Barnes' *Nightwood*. In

Eroticism and containment: Notes from the flood plain. Ed. Carol Siegel and Ann Kibbey. New York: New York University Press. 233–59.

Harris, Bertha. 1977. What we mean to say: Notes toward defining the nature of lesbian literature. *Heresies* 3 (fall): 5–8.

Hayman, Anne. 1994. Some remarks about the "Controversial Discussions." *International Journal of Psycho-Analysis* 75 (2): 343–58.

Heimann, Paula. 1942. A contribution to the problem of sublimation and its relation to processes of internalization. *International Journal of Psycho-Analysis* 23:8–17.

——. 1950. On counter-transference. *International Journal of Psycho-Analysis* 31:81–4.

Hichens, Robert Smythe. [1894] 1929. *The green carnation.* Chicago: Argus.

Hinshelwood, R. D. 1989. *A dictionary of Kleinian thought.* London: Free Association Books.

——. 1994. *Clinical Klein: From theory to practice.* New York: Basic Books.

Holroyd, Michael. 1987. Bloomsbury and the Fabians. In *Virginia Woolf and Bloomsbury: A centenary celebration.* Ed. Jane Marcus. Bloomington: Indiana University Press. 39–51.

——. 1994. *Lytton Strachey.* London: Chatto and Windus.

——, ed. 1971. *Lytton Strachey by himself: A self-portrait.* London: Heinemann.

Horkheimer, Max. 1972. *Critical theory: Selected essays.* Trans. Matthew J. O'Connell et al. New York: Herder and Herder.

Horney, Karen. 1924. On the genesis of the castration complex in women. *International Journal of Psycho-Analysis* 5:50–65.

Huggins, Nathan Irvin. 1971. *Harlem Renaissance.* New York: Oxford University Press.

Hughes, Judith M. 1989. *Reshaping the psychoanalytic domain: The work of Melanie Klein, W. R. D. Fairbairn, and D. W. Winnicott.* Berkeley: University of California Press.

Hughes, Langston. 1926. *The weary blues.* New York: Knopf.

——. [1940] 1963. *The big sea: An autobiography.* New York: Hill and Wang.

Hutch, Richard. 1988. Strategic irony and Lytton Strachey's contribution to biography. *Biography* 11 (1): 1–15.

Hutchinson, George. 1995. *The Harlem Renaissance in black and white.* Cambridge: Harvard University Press.

Huyssen, Andreas. 1986. *After the great divide: Modernism, mass culture, postmodernism.* Bloomington: Indiana University Press.

Irigaray, Luce. [1974] 1985. *Speculum of the other woman.* Trans. Gillian C. Gill. Ithaca: Cornell University Press. Original edition *Speculum de l'autre femme* (Paris: Editions de Minuit).

——. [1980] 1991. *Marine lover of Friedrich Nietzsche.* Trans. Gillian C. Gill. New York: Columbia University Press.

——. [1982] 1992. *Elemental passions.* Trans. Joanne Collie and Judith Still. New York: Routledge.

——. [1984] 1993. *An ethics of sexual difference.* Trans. Carolyn Burke and Gillian C. Gill. Ithaca: Cornell University Press. Original edition *Ethique de la différence sexuelle* (Paris: Editions de Minuit).

——. 1985. *This sex which is not one.* Trans. Catherine Porter and Carolyn Burke. Ithaca: Cornell University Press.

——. [1987] 1991. The bodily encounter with the mother. In *The Irigaray Reader.* Ed. Margaret Whitford. Trans. David Macey. Cambridge: Blackwell. 34–46. Original edition *Sexes et parentes* (Paris: Editions de minuit).

——. 1989. *Le temps de la différence: pour une revolution pacifique*. Paris: Librairie Generale Française.

——. 1992. *J'aime à toi: esquise d'une felicité dans l'histoire*. Paris: B. Grasset.

Isaacs, Susan. [1952] 1983. The nature and function of phantasy. In Riviere [1952] 1983, 67–121.

Iyengar, K. R. Srinivasa. 1939. *Lytton Strachey: A critical study*. London: Chatto and Windus.

Jaccard, Roland. 1971. *Mélanie Klein et la pulsion de mort*. Lausanne: Editions l'Age d'Homme.

Jackson, Stanley W. 1986. *Melancholia and depression: From Hippocratic times to modern times*. New Haven: Yale University Press.

Jacobus, Mary. 1990. "Tea Daddy": Poor Mrs. Klein and the pencil shavings. *Women: A Cultural Review* 1 (2): 160–79.

——. 1995. *First things: The maternal imaginary in literature, art, and psychoanalysis*. New York: Routledge.

Jaffe, Daniel S. 1968. The mechanism of projection: Its dual role in object relations. *International Journal of Psycho-Analysis* 49 (4): 662–77.

Jameson, Fredric. 1981. *The political unconscious: Narrative as a socially symbolic act*. London: Methuen.

——. 1990. Modernism and imperialism. In *Nationalism, colonialism, and literature*. Fredric Jameson, Terry Eagleton, and Edward W. Said. Minneapolis: University of Minnesota Press. 43–66.

Jay, Karla, and Joanne Glasgow, eds. 1990. *Lesbian texts and contexts: Radical revisions*. New York: New York University Press.

Jeanneau, Augustin. 1977. A partir de la douleur psychique. *Revue Française de Psychanalyse* 41 (1–2): 253–56.

Johnson, James Weldon. 1917. *Fifty years and other poems*. Boston: Cornhill.

——. 1922. *The book of American Negro poetry*. New York: Harcourt, Brace.

——. [1930] 1969. *Black Manhattan*. New York: Atheneum.

Jones, Ernest. 1926. Obituary of Karl Abraham. *International Journal of Psycho-analysis* 7:155–81. Reprinted as an introductory memoir in Abraham [1927] 1949, 9–41.

——. 1927. The early development of female sexuality. *International Journal of Psycho-Analysis* 8:459–72.

——. 1953–57. *The life and work of Sigmund Freud*. 3 vols. New York: Basic Books.

Jouffroy, Alain. 1966. *Aube à l'antipode: Carnets de bord tenus sous forme de notes analogiques expeditives*. Illustrations by René Magritte. Paris: Editions du soleil.

Kallich, Martin. 1961. *The psychological milieu of Lytton Strachey*. New York: Bookman.

Kaplan, Louise J. 1991. *Female perversions: The temptations of Emma Bovary*. New York: Doubleday.

——. 1994. Female castration anxiety. *American Imago* 51 (4): 471–89.

Kavaler-Adler, Susan. 1993. *The compulsion to create: A psychoanalytic study of women artists*. New York: Routledge.

Keats, John. 1990. *John Keats: A critical edition of the major works*. Ed. Elizabeth Cook. Oxford: Oxford University Press.

Kernberg, Otto F. 1985. *Internal world and external reality: Object relations theory applied*. New York: Aronson.

——. 1987. Projection and projective identification: Developmental and clinical aspects. In Sandler 1987b, 93–115.

Kesteloot, Lilyan. 1974. Negritude and its American sources. *Boston University Journal* 22 (2): 54–67.

Kiely, Robert, and John Hildebidle. 1983. *Modernism reconsidered*. Cambridge: Harvard University Press.

King, Pearl, and Riccardo Steiner, eds. 1991. *The Freud-Klein controversies, 1941–45*. London: Tavistock.

Klein, Melanie. 1932. *Die Psychoanalyse des Kindes*. Wien: Internationaler Psychoanalytischer Verlag.

——. [1932] 1949. *The psycho-analysis of children*. Trans. Alix Strachey. 3d ed. London: Hogarth. Original edition *Die Psychoanalyse des Kindes* (Vienna: Internationaler Psychoanalytischer Verlag).

——. [1961] 1975. *Narrative of a child psycho-analysis*. Vol. 4 of *The writings of Melanie Klein*. Ed. Roger Money-Kyrle, Betty Joseph, Edna O'Shaughnessy, and Hanna Segal. New York: Free Press.

——. 1975a. *Envy and gratitude and other works, 1946–1963*. Vol. 3 of *The writings of Melanie Klein*. Ed. Roger Money-Kyrle, Betty Joseph, Edna O'Shaughnessy, and Hanna Segal. New York: Free Press.

——. 1975b. *Love, guilt, and reparation and other works*. Vol. 1 of *The writings of Melanie Klein*. Ed. Roger Money-Kyrle, Betty Joseph, Edna O'Shaughnessy, and Hanna Segal. New York: Free Press.

[1921] 1975. The development of a child. In *Love, guilt, and reparation and other works*, 1–53.

[1923] 1975a. Early analysis. In *Love, guilt, and reparation and other works*, 77–105.

[1923] 1975b. The role of the school in the libidinal development of the child. In *Love, guilt, and reparation and other works*, 59–76.

[1927] 1975a. Criminal tendencies in normal children. In *Love, guilt, and reparation and other works*, 170–85.

[1927] 1975b. Personification in the play of children. In *Love, guilt, and reparation and other works*, 199–209.

[1928] 1975. Early stages of the Oedipus conflict. In *Love, guilt, and reparation and other works*, 186–98.

[1929] 1975. Infantile anxiety situations reflected in a work of art and in the creative impulse. In *Love, guilt, and reparation and other works*, 210–18.

[1930] 1975. The importance of symbol-formation in the development of the ego. In *Love, guilt, and reparation and other works*, 219–32.

[1932] 1975a. Appendix: The scope and limits of child analysis. In *The psycho-analysis of children*, 279–82.

[1932] 1975b. Early stages of the Oedipus conflict and of super-ego formation. In *The psycho-analysis of children*, 123–48.

[1932] 1975c. The effects of early anxiety-situations on the sexual development of the boy. In *The psycho-analysis of children*, 240–78.

[1932] 1975d. The effects of early anxiety-situations on the sexual development of the girl. In *The psycho-analysis of children*, 194–239.

[1932] 1975e. *The psycho-analysis of children*. Vol. 2 of *The writings of Melanie Klein*. Ed. Roger

Money-Kyrle, Betty Joseph, Edna O'Shaughnessy, and Hanna Segal. New York: Free Press.

[1932] 1975f. The relations between obsessional neurosis and the early stages of the super-ego. In The psycho-analysis of children, 149–75.

[1932] 1975g. The significance of early anxiety-situations in the development of the ego. In The psycho-analysis of children, 176–93.

[1933] 1975. The early development of conscience in the child. In Love, guilt, and reparation and other works, 248–57.

[1934] 1975. On criminality. In Love, guilt, and reparation and other works, 258–61.

[1935] 1975. A contribution to the psychogenesis of manic-depressive states. In Love, guilt, and reparation and other works, 262–89.

[1936] 1975. Weaning. In Love, guilt, and reparation and other works, 290–305.

[1937] 1975. Love, guilt, and reparation. In Love, guilt, and reparation and other works, 306–43.

[1940] 1975. Mourning and its relation to manic-depressive states. In Love, guilt, and reparation and other works, 344–69.

[1945] 1975. The Oedipus complex in the light of early anxieties. In Love, guilt, and reparation and other works, 370–419.

[1946] 1975. Notes on some schizoid mechanisms. In Envy and gratitude and other works, 1946–1963, 1–24.

[1948] 1975. On the theory of anxiety and guilt. In Envy and gratitude and other works, 1946–1963, 25–42.

[1950] 1975. On the criteria for the termination of a psycho-analysis. In Envy and gratitude and other works, 1946–1963, 43–47.

[1952] 1975a. On observing the behaviour of young infants. In Envy and gratitude and other works, 1946–1963, 94–121.

[1952] 1975b. The origins of transference. In Envy and gratitude and other works, 1946–1963, 48–56.

[1952] 1975c. Some theoretical conclusions regarding the emotional life of the infant. In Envy and gratitude and other works, 1946–1963, 61–93.

[1955] 1975a. On identification. In Envy and gratitude and other works, 1946–1963, 141–75.

[1955] 1975b. The psycho-analytic play technique: Its history and significance. In Envy and gratitude and other works, 1946–1963, 122–40.

[1957] 1975. Envy and gratitude. In Envy and gratitude and other works, 1946–1963, 176–235.

[1958] 1975. On the development of mental functioning. In Envy and gratitude and other works, 1946–1963, 236–46.

[1959] 1975. Our adult world and its roots in infancy. In Envy and gratitude and other works, 1946–1963, 247–63.

[1963] 1975. On the sense of loneliness. In Envy and gratitude and other works, 1946–1963, 300–313.

Klein, Melanie, Paula Heimann, and R. E. Money-Kyrle, eds. 1955. New directions in psycho-analysis: The significance of infant conflict in the pattern of adult behaviour. London: Tavistock.

Klein, Melanie, and Joan Riviere. [1937] 1962. Love, hate, and reparation. London: Hogarth.

Kraepelin, Emil. 1896. *Psychiatrie: Ein Lehrbuck für Studierende und Aerzte.* 5th ed. Leipzig: Johann Ambrosius Barth.

Krauss, Rosalind E. 1985. The originality of the avant-garde. In *The originality of the avant-garde and other modernist myths.* Cambridge: MIT Press. 151–72. A previous version appeared in *October* 18 (fall 1981): 47–66.

Kristeva, Julia. 1982. L'abjet d'amour. *Tel Quel* 91:17–32.

———. [1983] 1987. *Tales of love.* Trans. Leon S. Roudiez. New York: Columbia University Press. Original edition *Histoires d'amour* (Paris: Denoel).

———. [1987] 1989. *Black sun: Depression and melancholia.* Trans. Leon S. Roudiez. New York: Columbia University Press. Original edition *Soleil noir* (Paris: Gallimard).

Lacan, Jacques. 1966. *Écrits.* Paris: Editions du Seuil.

———. [1973] 1988. *The seminar of Jacques Lacan.* Ed. Jacques-Alain Miller. 3 vols. New York: Norton. Original edition *Le Seminaire de Jacques Lacan* (Paris: Seuil).

———. [1973] 1978. *The four fundamental concepts of psycho-analysis.* Ed. Jacques-Alain Miller. Trans. Alan Sheridan. New York: Norton. Original edition *Les quatre concepts fondamentaux de la psychoanalyse* (Paris: Seuil).

Lambotte, Marie-Claude. 1984. *Esthétique de la mélancolie.* Paris: Aubier.

———. 1993. *Le discours mélancolique: De la phénoménologie à la métapsychologie.* Paris: Anthropos.

Lampl–de Groot, Jeanne. [1947] 1965. On the development of ego and superego. In Lampl–de Groot 1965a, 126–37.

———. [1962] 1965. Ego ideal and superego. In Lampl–de Groot 1965a, 317–50.

———. 1965a. *The development of the mind: Psychoanalytic papers on clinical and theoretical problems.* New York: International Universities Press.

———. 1965b. The origin and development of guilt feelings. In Lampl–de Groot 1965a, 114–25.

———. 1965c. Superego, ego ideal, and masochistic fantasies. In Lampl–de Groot 1965a, 351–63.

Lane, Christopher. 1995. *The ruling passion: British colonial allegory and the paradox of homosexual desire.* Durham: Duke University Press.

Laplanche, Jean. [1987] 1989. *New foundations for psychoanalysis.* Trans. David Macey. Oxford: Blackwell. Original edition *Nouveaux fondements pour la psychanalyse la seduction originaire* (Paris: Presses Universitaires de France).

Laplanche, Jean, and Jean Baptiste Pontalis. [1964] 1986. Fantasy and the origins of sexuality. In Burgin et al. 1986, 5–34. Original English translation published in 1968 in *International Journal of Psycho-analysis* 49 (1): 1–18.

———. [1967] 1973. *The language of psychoanalysis.* London: Hogarth. Original edition *Vocabulaire de la psychanalyse* (Paris: Presses Universitaires de France).

Laqueur, Thomas. 1986. Female orgasm, generation, and the politics of reproductive biology. *Representations* 14:1–82.

Lee, Hugh, ed. 1992. *A Cézanne in the hedge and other memories of Charleston and Bloomsbury.* Chicago: University of Chicago Press.

Lepenies, Wolf. [1969] 1992. *Melancholy and society.* Trans. Jeremy Gaines and Doris Jones. Cambridge: Harvard University Press. Original edition *Melancholie und Gesellschaft* (Frankfurt: Suhrkamp).

Levenson, Michael H. 1984. *A genealogy of modernism: A study of English literary doctrine, 1908–1922.* Cambridge: Cambridge University Press.

—. 1991. *Modernism and the fate of individuality: Character and novelistic form from Conrad to Woolf.*
Cambridge: Cambridge University Press.

Levin, Harry. 1960. What was modernism? *Massachusetts Review* 1:609–30.

Lewis, David L. 1981. *When Harlem was in vogue.* New York: Knopf.

Lewis, Jane. 1990. Motherhood issues in the late nineteenth and twentieth centuries. In
Delivering motherhood: Maternal ideologies and practices in the nineteenth and twentieth centuries.
Ed. Katherine Arnup, Arnée Levesque, and Ruth Roach Pierson. London: Routledge. 1–
19.

Lezra, Jacques, ed. 1995. *Depositions: Althusser, Balibar, Macherey, and the labor of reading.* Yale
French Studies, no. 88. New Haven: Yale University Press.

Locke, Alain LeRoy, ed. [1925] 1968. *The new Negro: An interpretation.* New York: Arno.

Lomax, Michael L. 1987. Countee Cullen: A key to the puzzle. In *The Harlem Renaissance re-
examined.* Ed. Victor A. Kramer. New York: AMS. 213–22.

Lombroso, Cesare. [1863] 1913. *The man of genius.* London: W. Scott. Original edition *L'uomo di
genio* (Turin: Fratelli Bocca).

London, Bette Lynn. 1990. *The appropriated voice: Narrative authority in Conrad, Forster, and Woolf.*
Ann Arbor: University of Michigan Press.

Lorand, Sándor, and Michael Balint, eds. 1956. *Perversions, psychodynamics, and therapy.* New
York: Random House.

Lorde, Audre. 1984. *Sister/outsider: Essays and speeches.* Trumansburg, NY: Crossing Press.

Lupton, Mary Jane. 1993. *Menstruation and psychoanalysis.* Urbana: University of Illinois Press.

MacCannell, Juliet Flower, and Laura Zakarin. 1994. *Thinking bodies.* Stanford: Stanford University Press.

Macherey, Pierre. [1990] 1995. *The object of literature.* Trans. D. Macey. Cambridge: Cambridge
University Press. Original edition *À quoi pense la litterature?* (Paris: Presses Universitaires
de France).

Marcus, Jane. 1987. *Virginia Woolf and the languages of patriarchy.* Bloomington: Indiana University Press.

—. 1989. The asylums of Anthaeus: Women, war, and madness—is there a feminist fetishism? In *The new historicism.* Ed. H. Aram Veeser. New York: Routledge. 132–51.

—. 1990. Sapphistory: The Woolf and the Well. In Jay and Glasgow 1990, 164–79.

—. 1991. Laughing at Leviticus: *Nightwood* as woman's circus epic. In Broe 1991, 221–50.

Marks, Elaine. 1979. Lesbian intertextuality. In Stambolian and Marks 1979, 353–77.

Margolies, Edward. 1968. *Native sons: A critical study of twentieth-century Negro American authors.*
Philadelphia: Lippincott.

Marin, Louis. [1977] 1995. *To destroy painting.* Trans. Mette Hjort. Chicago: University of
Chicago Press. Original edition *Détruire la peinture* (Paris: Galilée).

Masters, William H., and Virginia E. Johnson. 1966. *Human sexual response.* Boston: Little,
Brown.

Maurois, André. 1942. *I remember, I remember.* Trans. Denver Lindley and Jane Hastings Hickok
Lindley. New York: Harper.

McCarthy, Desmond. 1933. Lytton Strachey: The art of biography. *Sunday Times,* 5 November.

McKay, Claude. 1922. *Harlem shadows.* Harcourt, Brace.

—. 1929. *Banjo, a story without a plot.* New York and London: Harper.

McLaren, Angus. 1990. *A history of contraception: From antiquity to the present day.* Oxford: Blackwell.

Meissner, William W. 1987. Projection and projective identification. In Sandler 1987b, 27–49.

Meltzer, Donald. 1966. The relation of anal masturbation to projective identification. *International Journal of Psycho-Analysis* 47:335–42.

———. 1968. Terror, persecution, and dread: A dissection of paranoid anxieties. *International Journal of Psycho-Analysis* 49 (2–3): 396–401. Reprinted in Spillius 1988a, 1:230–38.

———. 1978. *The Kleinian development.* Perthshire: Clunie.

Meltzer, Donald, and Meg Harris Williams. 1988. *The apprehension of beauty: The role of aesthetic conflict in development, violence, and art.* Old Ballechin, Strath Tay: Clunie.

Merck, Mandy. 1986. The train of thought in Freud's "Case of homosexuality in a woman." *m/f* 11–12:35–46.

Merle, Gabriel. 1980. *Lytton Strachey, 1880–1932: Biographie et critique d'un critique et biographe.* Ph.D. diss. University Lille III, Lille (France).

Merton, Robert King. 1968. *Social theory and social structure.* 2d. ed. New York: Free Press.

Meyer, Moe, ed. 1994. *The Politics and poetics of camp.* London: Routledge.

Michasiw, Kim. 1994. Camp, masculinity, masquerade. *differences: A Journal of Feminist Cultural Studies* 6 (2–3, More Gender Trouble: Feminism Meets Queer Theory): 146–73.

Miller, C. Ruth. 1988. *Virginia Woolf: The frames of art and life.* New York: St. Martin's.

Miller, J. Hillis. [1983] 1990a. Mr. Carmichael and Lily Briscoe: The rhythm of creativity in *To the Lighthouse.* In Miller 1990b, 151–70. First published in Kiely and Hildebidle 1983, 167–89.

———. 1990b. *Tropes, parables, performatives: Essays on twentieth-century literature.* New York: Harvester Wheatsheaf.

Mitchell, Juliet, ed. 1986. *The selected Melanie Klein.* Harmondsworth: Penguin Books.

Money-Kyrle, Roger. 1944. Toward a common aim: A psychoanalytical contribution to Ethics. *British Journal of Medical Psychology* 20 (2): 105–17.

Moorjani, Angela. 1994. Fetishism, gender masquerade, and the mother-father fantasy. In Smith and Mahfouz 1994, 22–41.

Moraga, Chérrie. 1986. *Giving up the ghost: Teatro in two acts.* Los Angeles: West End.

Moses, Rafael. 1987. Projection, identification, and projective identification: Their relation to political process. In Sandler 1987b, 133–50.

Nisbet, John Ferguson. [1900] 1973. *The insanity of genius and the general inequality of human faculty physiologically considered.* Rpt. of 4th ed. Folcroft, PA: Folcroft Library Editions. Original edition published in 1891.

Nordau, Max Simon. [1892] 1993. *Degeneration.* Lincoln: University of Nebraska Press. Original edition *Entartung* (Berlin: C. Duncker).

North, Michael. 1994. *The dialect of modernism: Race, language, and twentieth-century literature.* New York: Oxford University Press.

O'Connor, Noreen. 1990. Is Melanie Klein the one who knows who you really are? *Women: A Cultural Review* 1 (2): 180–88.

O'Connor, Noreen, and Joanna Ryan. 1993. *Wild desires and mistaken identities: Lesbianism and psychoanalysis.* New York: Columbia University Press.

Oldham, John M., and Stanley Bone, eds. 1994. *Paranoia: New psychoanalytic perspectives.* Madison, CT: International Universities Press.

Parkes, Adam. 1996. *Modernism and the theater of censorship.* New York: Oxford University Press.

Parkin, Alan. 1976. Melancholia: A reconsideration. *Journal of the American Psychoanalytic Association* 24 (1): 123–39.

Pedder, Jonathan R. 1982. Failure to mourn and melancholia. *British Journal of Psychiatry* 141:329–37.

Pensky, Max. 1993. *Melancholy dialectics: Walter Benjamin and the play of mourning.* Amherst: University of Massachusetts Press.

Perlow, Meir. 1995. *Understanding mental objects.* London and New York: Routledge.

Perry, Margaret. 1971. *A bio-bibliography of Countee P. Cullen, 1903–1946.* Westport, CT: Greenwood.

Person, Ethel Spector, Peter Fonagy, and Servulo A. Figueira, eds. 1995. *On Freud's "Creative writers and day-dreaming."* New Haven: Yale University Press.

Phillips, John, and Lyndsey Stonebridge, eds. 1998. *Reading Melanie Klein.* New York: Routledge.

Plumb, Cheryl J. 1986. *Fancy's craft: Art and identity in the early works of Djuna Barnes.* Selinsgrove, PA: Susquehanna University Press.

Ponsot, Marie. 1991. A reader's Ryder. In Broe 1991, 94–112.

Pontalis, Jean Baptiste. [1977] 1981. *Frontiers in psychoanalysis: Between the dream and psychic pain.* Trans. Catherine Cullen and Philip Cullen. New York: International Universities Press. Original edition *Entre le rêve et la douleur* (Paris: Gallimard).

Pound, Ezra. [1934] 1968. *Literary essays of Ezra Pound.* Ed. T. S. Eliot. Norfolk, CT: New Directions.

Primeau, Ronald. 1976. Countee Cullen and Keats' "Value of soul making." *Papers on Language and Literature* 12:73–86.

Proust, Marcel. [1914–19] 1981. *Remembrance of things past.* Trans. C. K. Scott Moncrieff and Terence Kilmartin. 3 vols. New York: Random House.

Quinodoz, Jean-Michel. 1989. Female homosexual patients in psychoanalysis. *International Journal of Psycho-Analysis* 70 (1): 55–63.

——. 1993. *The taming of solitude: Separation anxiety in psychoanalysis.* London: Routledge.

Radden, Jennifer. 1987. Melancholy and melancholia. In *Pathologies of the modern self: Postmodern studies on narcissism, schizophrenia, and depression.* Ed. David Michael Levin. New York: New York University Press. 231–50.

Rado, Lisa, ed. 1994. *Rereading modernism: New directions in feminist criticism.* New York: Garland.

Radó, Sándor. 1928. The problem of melancholia. *International Journal of Psycho-Analysis* 9:420–38.

——. 1933. Fear of castration in women. *Psychoanalytic Quarterly* 2:425–75.

Rampersad, Arnold. 1986. *The life of Langston Hughes.* 2 vols. New York: Oxford University Press.

Rank, Otto. [1924] 1929. *The trauma of birth.* London: K. Paul, Trench, Trubner. Original edition *Das Trauma der Geburt und seine Bedeutung für die Psychoanalyse* (Leipzig: Internationaler Psychoanalytischer Verlag).

Rapaport, Herman. 1994. *Between the sign and the gaze.* Ithaca: Cornell University Press.

Reid, Stephen A. 1974. Hamlet's melancholia. *American Imago* 31 (4): 378–400.

Reimonenq, Alden. 1993. Countee Cullen's Uranian "Soul Windows." In *Critical essays: Gay and lesbian writers of color.* Ed. Emmanuel S. Nelson. New York: Haworth. 143–65.

Rey, Roselyne. [1993] 1995. *The history of pain.* Trans. Louise Elliott Wallace, J. A. Cadden, and S. W. Cadden. Cambridge: Harvard University Press. Original edition *Histoire de la douleur* (Paris: La Découverte).

Rich, Adrienne. 1976. *Of woman born: Motherhood as experience and institution.* New York: Norton.

Richards, Barry, ed. 1989. *Crises of the self: Further essays on psychoanalysis and politics.* London: Free Association Books.

Riviere, Joan. 1929. Womanliness as a masquerade. *International Journal of Psycho-Analysis* 10:303–13.

——, ed. [1952] 1983. *Developments in psychoanalysis.* New York: DaCapo.

Roazen, Paul, and Bluma Swerdloff. 1995. *Heresy: Sándor Radó and the psychoanalytic movement.* Northvale, NJ: Aronson.

Roof, Judith. 1991a. Freud reads lesbians: The male homosexual imperative. In Roof 1991b, 174–215.

——. 1991b. *A lure of knowledge: Lesbian sexuality and theory.* New York: Columbia University Press.

Rose, Jacqueline. 1986. *Sexuality in the field of vision.* London: Verso.

——. 1993. *Why war? Psychoanalysis, politics, and the return to Melanie Klein.* Oxford: Blackwell.

Rosenberg, Benno. 1986. Le travail de mélancolie ou la fonction élaborative de l'identification ou le role du masochisme dans la resolution de l'accès mélancolique. *Revue Française de Psychanalyse* 50 (6): 1523–43.

Rosenfeld, Herbert A. 1949. Remarks on the relation of male homosexuality to paranoia, paranoid anxiety, and narcissism. *International Journal of Psycho-Analysis* 30:36–47.

——. [1952] 1988. Notes on the psychoanalysis of the superego conflict in an acute schizophrenic patient. In Spillius 1988a, 14–51. First published in *International Journal of Psycho-analysis* 33:111–31.

——. 1988. Contribution to the psychopathology of psychotic states: The importance of projective identification in the ego structure and the object relations of the psychotic patient. In Spillius 1988a, 117–37.

Ross, Andrew. 1988. Uses of camp. *Yale Journal of Criticism* 2 (2): 1–24. Reprinted in Bergman, 1993, 54–77.

Roy, David. 1973. Lytton Strachey and the masochistic basis of homosexuality. *Psychoanalytic Review* 59 (4): 579–84.

Rustin, Michael. 1991. *The good society and the inner world: Psychoanalysis, politics, and culture.* London: Verso.

Saladin, Linda. 1993. *Fetishism and fatal women: Gender, power, and reflexive discourse.* New York: Lang.

Sanders, Charles Richard. 1957. *Lytton Strachey, his mind and art.* New Haven: Yale University Press.

Sandler, Joseph. 1987a. The concept of projective identification. In Sandler 1987b, 13–26.

——, ed. 1987b. *Projection, identification, projective identification.* Madison, CT: International Universities Press.

Sandler, Joseph, and Meir Perlow. 1987. Internalization and externalization. In Sandler 1987b, 1–11.

Sanger, Margaret. [1920] 1969. *Woman and the new race.* Elmsford, NY: Maxwell. Original edition New York: Brentano.

——. [1922] 1970. *The new motherhood*. Elmsford, NY: Maxwell. Original edition London: J. Cape.

——. [1928] 1956. *Motherhood in bondage*. Elmsford, NY: Maxwell. Original edition New York: Brentano.

Santner, Eric L. 1990. *Stranded objects: Mourning, memory, and film in postwar Germany*. Ithaca: Cornell University Press.

Sartre, Jean Paul. [1946] 1948. *Anti-Semite and Jew*. Trans. George Joseph Becker. New York: Schocken. Original edition *Réflexions sur la question juive* (Paris: Morihien).

Sass, Louis Arnorsson. 1992. *Madness and modernism: Insanity in the light of modern art, literature, and thought*. New York: Basic Books.

Sayers, Janet. 1991. *Mothers of psychoanalysis: Helene Deutsch, Karen Horney, Anna Freud, Melanie Klein*. New York: Norton.

Scarry, Elaine. 1985. *The body in pain: The making and unmaking of the world*. New York: Oxford University Press.

Schafer, Roy. 1994a. On gendered discourse and discourse on gender. In Smith and Mahfouz 1994, 1–21.

——. 1994b. One perspective on the Freud-Klein controversies, 1941–45. *International Journal of Psycho-Analysis* 75 (2): 359–65.

Schenck, Celeste. 1989. Exiled by genre: Modernism, canonicity, and the politics of exclusion. In Broe and Ingram, 1989, 211–50.

Schiesari, Juliana. 1992. *The gendering of melancholia: Feminism, psychoanalysis, and the symbolics of loss in Renaissance literature*. Ithaca: Cornell University Press.

Schor, Naomi. 1995. *Bad objects: Essays popular and unpopular*. Durham: Duke University Press.

Schor, Naomi, and Elizabeth Weed, eds. 1994. *The essential difference*. Bloomington: Indiana University Press.

Scott, Ann. 1990. Melanie Klein and the questions of feminism. *Women: A Cultural Review* 1 (2): 127–34.

Scott, Bonnie Kime. 1993. Barnes being "beast familiar": Representation on the margins of modernism. *Review of Contemporary Fiction* 13 (3): 41–52.

——. 1995. *Refiguring modernism: The Women of 1928*. Bloomington: Indiana University Press.

Sedgwick, Eve Kosofsky. 1990. *Epistemology of the closet*. Berkeley: University of California Press.

——. 1993. *Tendencies*. Durham: Duke University Press.

Segal, Hanna. 1952. A psychoanalytical approach to aesthetics. *International Journal of Psycho-Analysis* 33:196–207. Reprinted in Klein et al. 1955, 384–405; and Frankiel 1994, 486–507.

——. 1957. Notes on symbol formation. *International Journal of Psycho-Analysis* 38:391–97.

——. 1964. *Introduction to the work of Melanie Klein*. London: Heinemann.

——. 1980. *Melanie Klein*. New York: Viking.

——. 1990. Hanna Segal interviewed by Jacqueline Rose. *Women: A Cultural Review* 1 (2): 198–214.

——. 1994. Phantasy and reality. *International Journal of Psycho-Analysis* 75 (2): 395–401.

Sheasby, Ronald E. 1995. Dual reality: Echoes of Blake's tiger in Cullen's heritage. *College Language Association Journal* 39 (2): 219–27.

Shields, John C. 1992. Countee Cullen. In *Critical survey of poetry: English language series*. Ed. Frank Northen Magill. 2d ed. Pasadena: Salem. 783–91.

Showalter, Elaine. 1990. "Mrs. Klein": The mother, the daughter, the thief and their critics. *Women: A Cultural Review* 1 (2): 144–48.

Shucard, Alan. 1984. *Countee Cullen*. Boston: Twayne.

Silverman, Kaja. 1988. *The acoustic mirror: The female voice in psychoanalysis and cinema*. Bloomington: Indiana University Press.

———. 1992. *Male subjectivity at the margins*. New York: Routledge.

———. 1996. *The threshold of the visible world*. New York: Routledge.

Sinfield, Alan. 1994. *The Wilde century: Effeminacy, Oscar Wilde, and the queer moment*. New York: Columbia University Press.

Singer, Linda. 1993. *Erotic welfare: sexual theory and politics in the age of epidemic*. Ed. and introd. Judith Butler and Maureen MacGrogan. New York: Routledge.

Smith, Gary. 1984. The Black protest sonnet. *American Poetry* 2 (1): 2–12.

Smith, George. 1994. Woolf, Cézanne, and the Nachträglichkeit of feminist modernism. In Rado 1994, 67–95.

Smith, Joseph H., and Afaf M. Mahfouz, eds. 1994. *Psychoanalysis, feminism, and the future of gender*. Baltimore: Johns Hopkins University Press.

Smythe, Karen. 1992. Virginia Woolf's elegiac enterprise. *Novel* 26 (1): 64–79.

Sohn, Leslie. 1985. Narcissistic organization, projective identification, and the formation of the identificate. *International Journal of Psycho-Analysis* 66 (2): 201–13.

Sontag, Susan. [1966] 1969. *Against interpretation and other essays*. New York: Dell. Original edition New York: Farrar, Straus and Giroux.

———. 1980. *Under the sign of Saturn*. New York: Farrar, Straus and Giroux.

Spencer, Charles. 1981. *Erté*. 2d ed. New York: Potter.

Sperling, Melitta. 1963. Fetishism in children. *Psychoanalytic Quarterly* 32:374–92.

Spillius, Elizabeth Bott, ed. 1988a. *Melanie Klein today: Developments in theory and practice*. Vol. 1: Mainly theory. London: Routledge.

———, ed. 1988b. *Melanie Klein today: Developments in theory and practice*. Vol. 2: Mainly practice. London: Routledge.

Spitz, Ellen Handler. 1994. *Museums of the mind: Magritte's labyrinth and other essays in the arts*. New Haven: Yale University Press.

Spivak, Gayatri Chakravorty. 1987. Unmaking and making in *To the Lighthouse*. In *In other worlds: Essays in cultural politics*. New York: Methuen. 30–45.

———. 1992. French feminism revisited: Ethics and politics. In Butler and Scott 1992, 54–85.

———. 1994. Examples to fit the title. *American Imago* 51 (2, Psychoanalysis in the left field): 161–96.

Spurr, Barry. 1990. Camp Mandarin: The prose style of Lytton Strachey. *English Literature in Transition, 1880–1920* 33 (1): 31–45.

Stambolian, George, and Elaine Marks, eds. 1979. *Homosexualities and French literature: Cultural contexts, critical texts*. Ithaca: Cornell University Press.

Stanton, Domna C., ed. 1992. *Discourses of sexuality: From Aristotle to AIDS*. Ann Arbor: University of Michigan Press.

Steiner, John. 1982. *Psychic retreats: Pathological organizations in psychotic, neurotic, and borderline patients*. London: Routledge.

Stevenson, Sheryl. 1991. Writing the grotesque body: Djuna Barnes' carnival parody. In Broe 1991, 81–93.

——. 1993. *Ryder* as contraception: Barnes v. the reproduction of mothering. *Review of Contemporary Fiction* 13 (3): 97–106.

Stewart, Susan. 1993. *On longing: Narratives of the miniature, the gigantic, the souvenir, the collection.* Durham: Duke University Press.

Stimpson, Catherine. 1982. Zero degree deviancy: The lesbian novel in English. In *Writing and sexual difference.* Ed. Elizabeth Abel. Chicago: University of Chicago Press. 243–60.

——. 1991. Afterword. In Broe 1991, 370–73.

Stokes, Adrian Durham. 1963. *Painting and the inner world.* London: Tavistock.

Strachey, Lytton [1912] 1945. *Landmarks in French literature.* London: Oxford University Press. Original edition London: Williams and Norgate.

——. 1918. *Eminent Victorians.* London: Chatto and Windus.

——. 1922. *Books and characters: French and English.* New York: Harcourt, Brace.

——. [1928] 1948. *Elizabeth and Essex: A tragic history.* London: Chatto and Windus.

——. 1931. *Portraits in miniature and other essays.* London: Chatto and Windus.

——. 1969. *Ermyntrude and Esmeralda: An entertainment.* London: Blond.

Sylvester, David. 1992. *Magritte: The silence of the world.* Houston: Menil Foundation.

Teppe, Julien. 1935. *Apologie pour l'anormal, ou manifeste du dolorisme.* Paris: La Caravelle.

——. 1937. *Dictature de la douleur ou precisions sur le dolorisme.* Paris: La Caravelle.

Tickner, Lisa. 1988. *The spectacle of women: Imagery of the suffrage campaign, 1907–14.* Chicago: University of Chicago Press.

Turner, Darwin T. 1971. *In a minor chord: Three Afro-American writers and their search for identity.* Carbondale: Southern Illinois University Press.

Tustin, Frances. 1972. *Autism and childhood psychoses.* London: Hogarth.

——. 1987. *Autistic barriers in neurotic patients.* New Haven: Yale University Press.

——. 1992. *Autistic states in children.* 2nd ed. London: Tavistock.

Tuttleton, James W. 1989. Countee Cullen at "The Heights." In *The Harlem Renaissance: Revaluations.* Ed. Amritjit Singh, William S. Shiver, and Stanley Brodwin. New York: Garland. 101–37.

Waddell, Margot. 1990. Gender identity: Fifty years on from Freud. *Women: A Cultural Review* 1 (2): 149–59.

Wagner, Jean. [1963] 1973. *Black poets of the United States. From Paul Laurence Dunbar to Langston Hughes.* Trans. Kenneth Douglas. Urbana: University of Illinois Press. Original edition *Les poetes negres des Etats-Unis: Le sentiment racial et religieux dans la poesie de P. L. Dunbar a L. Hughes, 1890–1940* (Paris: Librairie Istra).

Walton, Jean. 1995. Re-placing race in (white) psychoanalytic discourse: Founding narratives of feminism. *Critical Inquiry* 21 (4): 775–804.

Watson, John B. [1924] 1925. *Behaviorism.* New York: Norton.

Webster, Harvey C. 1947. A difficult career. *Poetry* 70 (4): 224–25.

Weininger, Otto. 1908. *Sex and character.* London: Heinemann.

——. 1992. *Melanie Klein: From theory to reality.* London: Karnac.

White, Hayden. 1973. *Metahistory: The historical imagination in nineteenth-century Europe.* Baltimore: Johns Hopkins University Press.

——. 1987. *The content of the form: Narrative discourse and historical representation.* Baltimore: Johns Hopkins University Press.

Whitfield, Sarah. 1992. *Magritte.* London: South Bank Centre.

Whitford, Margaret. 1994a. Irigaray, utopia, and the death drive. In Burke et al. 1994, 379–400.

——. 1994b. Reading Irigaray in the nineties. In Burke et al. 1994, 15–33.

Whyte-Earnshaw, Christina E. 1994. Toward the articulation of a Kleinian social theory. *Melanie Klein and Object Relations* 12 (1): 59–82.

Wilde, Oscar. [1890] 1981. *The picture of Dorian Gray.* Ed. Isobel Murray. Oxford: Oxford University Press.

——. 1958. *Teleny, or the reverse of the medal.* Paris: Olympia.

Williams, Linda Ruth. 1995. *Critical desire: Psychoanalysis and the literary subject.* London: Arnold.

Williams, Raymond. 1980. The Bloomsbury fraction. In *Problems in materialism and culture: Selected essays.* London: Verso. 148–69.

——. 1989. *The politics of modernism: Against the new conformists.* Ed. Tony Pinkney. London: Verso.

Wilson, Stephen. 1995. *The cradle of violence: Essays on psychiatry, psychoanalysis, and literature.* London: Jessica Kingsley.

Winnicott, Donald W. 1958. *Collected papers: Through paediatrics to psycho-analysis.* London: Tavistock.

——. 1965. The development of the capacity for concern. In *The maturational processes and the facilitating environment: Studies in the theory of emotional development.* Madison, CT: International Universities Press. 73–82.

——. 1971. The mirror-role of mother and family. In *Playing and reality.* New York: Basic Books. 111–18.

——. 1986. The mother's contribution to society. In *Home is where we start from: Essays by a psychoanalyst.* Ed. Clare Winnicott, Ray Shepherd, and Madeleine Davis. New York: Norton. 123–27.

Wittig, Monique. 1983. The point of view: Universal or particular? *Feminist Issues* 3 (2): 63–69.

Wollheim, Richard. 1984. *The thread of life.* Cambridge: Harvard University Press.

Women: A Cultural Review. 1990. 1 (2, Positioning Klein).

Woolf, Virginia. 1924. *Mr. Bennett and Mrs. Brown.* London: Leonard and Virginia Woolf.

——. [1927] 1958. The new biography. In *Granite and Rainbow.* New York: Harvest. 149–55.

——. [1927] 1981. *To the Lighthouse.* New York: Harcourt Brace Jovanovich.

——. 1928. *Orlando: A Biography.* London: Leonard and Virginia Woolf at the Hogarth Press.

——. [1929] 1957. *A room of one's own.* New York: Harcourt, Brace, Jovanovich.

——. [1942] 1967. The art of biography. In *Collected Essays.* Ed. Leonard Woolf. London: Hogarth. 221–28.

——. 1975. *The letters of Virginia Woolf.* 6 vols. Ed. Nigel Nicolson and Joanne Trautmann Banks. New York: Harcourt Brace Jovanovich.

——. 1977–84. *The diary of Virginia Woolf.* 5 vols. Ed. Anne Olivier Bell. New York: Harcourt Brace Jovanovich.

——. 1985. *Moments of being.* Ed. Jeanne Schulkind. 2d ed. London: Hogarth.

Wright, Elizabeth, ed. 1992. *Feminism and psychoanalysis: A critical dictionary.* Oxford: Blackwell.

Yaeger, Patricia. 1992. The poetics of birth. In Stanton 1992, 262–96.

Young-Bruehl, Elisabeth. 1988. *Anna Freud: A biography.* New York: Summit.

——. 1994. What theories women want. *American Imago* 51 (4): 373–96.

——. 1996. *The anatomy of prejudices.* Cambridge: Harvard University Press.

Zavitzianos, Georges. 1977. The object in fetishism, homeovestism, and transvestism. *International Journal of Psycho-Analysis* 58 (4): 487–95.

Zwerdling, Alex. 1986. *Virginia Woolf and the real world.* Berkeley: University of California Press.

Art: as institution, 204; Kleinian ideas about, 254; and loss, 179; Magritte's ideas about, 15; and market value, 200, 202; and reparation, 179, 185, 262, 271; Woolf's ideas about, 15

Assimilation, 264, 270

Autobiography, 274; of De Man, Paul, 430 n.1. See also Biography

Avi-Ram, Amitai F., 356, 364

Baker, Houston A.: on Cullen, 351–52, 355–56, 361. See also Mask, minstrel

Barnes, Djuna, 14, 16; and abjection, 307; avant-garde project of, 311; cannibalistic elements in work of, 316, 320; childbirth scenes in work of, 323, 334; and depression, 217; and glossolalia, 318; and *Ladies' Almanack*, 308, 318; and lesbian writing, 312; *The little review*, 208; and the market, 308; and mechanical reproduction, 341; and melancholia, 307, 321; *Nightwood*, 211, 314, 321; and obscenity law, 314 (*see also* Obscenity law); and phantasy of penis incorporation, 307; political views of, 318; projective identification of, 308; and Proust, 312; and sexuality and aggression, 306; styles, 319; and symbolics of loss, 321; symbolism in work of, 313; and Thelma Wood, 217. See also *Ryder* (Barnes)

Barney, Natalie C., 210, 308

Barthes, Roland, 430 n.3

Baudelaire, Charles, 12, 361; and spleen, 314, 361

Behaviorism, 198

Bell, Clive, 219; and pacifism, 210

Bell, Vanessa: influences of, 219; and pacifism, 210; portrait painting by, 263

Benjamin, Walter: and the camera, 11; and melancholia in Baudelaire, 313; and woman as allegory, 12

Benstock, Shari, 204

Bergman, David, 303

Berman, Art, 421 n.23

Bersani, Leo, 398 n.15, 399 nn.18, 19; on *Civilization and its discontents* (Freud), 52; on Klein, 48, 185–88

Biography: as autobiography, 274; as camp, 302; and cannibalism, 277; and epistemophilia, 283; form, 274; as history and fiction, 275, 304; and introjective identification, 280; as melancholic exercise, 15, 274, 304; and projection, 274; in Woolf, 273, 278. See also Autobiography; Strachey, Lytton

Bion, Wilfred Rupert, 9, 54; on analyst vs. patient, 249; *Attention and interpretation*, 249–50; on combined parent figure, 244

Birth control, 208–9

Bloomsbury group, 14, 209, 282–83, 304; and pacifism, 210

Body, abject: in *Ryder* (Barnes), 16

Boehm, Felix, 100, 104

Bourdieu, Pierre: on *To the lighthouse* (Woolf), 237, 424 nn.19, 20

Bowlby, Rachel, 225, 237

Breast, 86; good, 139; mother's, mourning, 129; persecuting, 140; and relation, 133; return to, 136

Brecht, Bertolt, 313

Breton, André, 233

Briscoe, Lily: as amateur, 220; bereavement of, 223, 238, 245, 248, 249; as melancholic, 221, 242; as product of Victorian England, 269. See also *To the lighthouse*

British Psychoanalytical Society, 2, 89, 118

Britton, Ronald, 214

Broe, Mary Lynn, 314, 318

Bürger, Peter, 204

Burton, Robert, 324

Butler, Judith, 151–54, 299; and drag performance, 153; on gendering of the ego, 151; and gender melancholy, 152; and gender performativity, 153; and melancholic identification, 151

Camp, 206, 302; in *Elizabeth and Essex* (Strachey), 303

Cullen, Countee (cont.)

Shroud of Color," 358, 359; "Sleep," 364; "Sonnet Dialogue," 368; "Spring Reminiscence," 367; "Suicide Chant," 359; "Tableau," 367; On These I Stand, 356; "Tribute," 358, 366; "Variations on a Theme," 364, 366; "Yet Do I Marvel," 356, 362–63. See also One way to heaven (Cullen)

Culture(s) of the death drive, 16, 194, 266, 345; in Countee Cullen, 357, 384, 385; in Ryder (Barnes), 310

Dada, 198

Dawson, Graham, 158

Daydreams (Freud), 181

Death drive, 137–58; and anxiety, 5; and construction of sexualities, 189; creativeness and, 179; criticisms, 7; deflection of, 139; and envy, 86; Freudian theory of, 137; and guilt, 141; modernist cultures of, 2, 13, 391, 393; patriarchal, 155; in Ryder (Barnes), 16; and superego, 67

Death drive, cultures of the. See Culture(s) of the death drive

De Certeau, Michel, 305

De Chirico, Giorgio, 233

Defences: manic, 127; obsessional, 127

Deflection: and destructive drives, 68

DeKoven, Marianne, 207

De Lauretis, Teresa, 249

Delirium: and object loss, 49. See also Hallucination

Denial, 140; in Mania, 125; of reality, 125, 127. See also Scotomization

Depressive position (Klein), 6, 123–34, 387; and ability to mourn, 130; creativeness and, 178; and damage to internal object, 160; failure of reparation and, 129; failure to mourn and, 132; and guilt toward object, 123; and inner good objects, 129–30; as melancholia in statu nascendi, 3; and Oedipus complex, 3; onset of, 134; and paranoid-schizoid position, 5; phantasies

in, 161; reactivation of, 130; remorse, 124; and tolerance, 19

De Saussure, Raymond, 73

Desire: of the mother's body, 173; and phantasy, 168–69

Deutsch, Helene, 75–76

Displacement of fear, 59, 63

Doane, Mary Ann, 298

Dolorist, 331

Doughty, Frances M., 319

Drag: in Butler, 153

Drive(s): definition (Kleinian), 166; homeostatic character of, 138; life, 58; partial, 168; phantasy and, 166; and self-preservation, 138; sexual, 138. See also Death drive

Du Bois, W. E. B.: on Countee Cullen, 384, 385; and double consciousness, 350

Early, Gerald, 344

Effeminate masculinity, 16, 206, 274, 283, 299, 303; dandy as, 206; dissoluteness, 206; in Elizabeth and Essex (Strachey), 16, 299, 301

Ego, 69; immature, 59; in modernism, 198

Ego (Klein): early, 139; fragility of, 150

Ego-ideal: Chasseguet-Smirgel on, 183; Freud on, 182

Elegy: and fiction-elegy, 426 n.39; in To the lighthouse (Woolf), 252

Eliot, T. S., 197, 201, 348; and The Antiphon (Barnes), 318; preface to Nightwood (Barnes), 314

Elizabeth and Essex (Strachey), 16, 273–305; aggression and retaliation in, 289; Bacon, Francis in, 291, 294–95, 296; as bestseller, 279; and body politic, 297; camp in, 303; drag in, aesthetics of, 301; effeminate man and, 16, 299, 301; Elizabeth's melancholia in, 289–90; Essex's melancholia in, 288; Freudian arguments about, 282, 294; Freud's reaction to, 282; good mother image in, 296, 301; and historical representation, 275; homosociality

Freud, Sigmund (*cont.*)

repeat, 60; exile of, 196; on feminine masochism, 79; and Ferenczi, 23, 34; and Fliess, 24; Fort-Da game analysis by, 68; and identification, 33–35, 397 n.7; and introjection, 32–34; Klein's influence on, 48; and melancholia (*see* Melancholia [Freud]); mourning of, 50, 215; and narcissism, 30, 137; on pleasure principle, 51; on reality principle, 51; re-readings of, 5; Richard III study by, 174; and satisfaction by hallucination, 165; screen memories of, 60, 227 (*see also* Screen memories); on sexual aetiology of anxiety, 27; and shadow of the object, 324; and the superego, 35; on the uncanny, 313. Works: "Analysis of a phobia in a five-year-old boy," 134; *Beyond the pleasure principle*, 60, 68, 77, 79, 137; "Certain neurotic mechanisms in jealousy, paranoia and homosexuality," 105; "A child is being beaten," 60; *Civilization and its discontents*, 35, 48, 52, 61, 142–43, 354; "Creative writers and daydreaming," 181; Draft G, 44; "The economic problem of masochism," 79; *The ego and the id*, 47, 83, 122, 132, 151, 152, 169, 171, 187, 358; *Familienroman der Neurotiker*, 337; "Female sexuality," 85; "Fetishism," 236; *Fragment of an analysis of a case of hysteria*, 110; *Group psychology and the analysis of the ego*, 34, 47, 66; "From the history of an infantile neurosis," 182; *Inhibitions, symptoms and anxiety*, 58, 65, 66, 74, 143, 359; "Instincts and their vicissitudes," 60, 138, 165; *The interpretation of dreams*, 44, 181; *Leonardo da Vinci and a memory of his childhood*, 94; "Mourning and melancholia," 24–26, 34, 36, 43–50, 51, 70, 128, 151, 274–75; "On narcissism: an introduction," 33, 45–46, 137, 182; "Negation," 166; *New introductory lectures on psychoanalysis*, 94, 162; "Notes upon a case of obsessional neurosis" (The Rat Man), 25; *Project for a scientific psychology*,

48; "Psychoanalytic notes on an autobiographical account of a case of paranoia (dementia paranoides)," 338; "The psychogenesis of a case of homosexuality in a woman," 72; "Screen memories," 60; "Some character-types met with in psycho-analytic work," 174; "Some psychological consequences of the anatomical distinction between the sexes," 82; *Three essays on the theory of sexuality*, 96, 227, 232; *Totem and taboo*, 51, 316

Freud, Sigmund, cases of: Dora, 110, 115; Little Hans, 65; Schreber, 66, 115, 141; Wolf Man, 65–66, 115

Friedman, Susan Stanford, 334

Frosh, Stephen, 345

Fry, Roger: and Cézanne, 2, 218; design in, 219; form in, 219; vision in, 219

Garber, Eric, 347

Gates Jr., Henry Louis, 357

Gaze, 238, 245, 259, 268

Gedo, Mary M., 223, 225

Gender: binary, 1–2; modernism and, 1–2

Gillibert, Jean, 384, 400 nn.22, 23, 26; on melancholia, 48, 50–52

Gilmore, Leigh, 308

Glover, Edward, 3

Good mother: foreclosure of the image of, 249, 261

Greenacre, Phyllis, 234

Guilt: death drive and, 141; early sense of, 145; envy and, 146; in Freud, 142; in Kleinian thinking, 159–60; and restoration, 178; toward object, 123

Hall, Radclyffe, 274, 308. *See also* Obscenity trials

Hallucination, 15, 165, 265. *See also* To the lighthouse (Woolf): hallucination

Harkness, James, 233

Harlem: ghettoization of, 348; homophobia in, 348; interracial relations in, 347, 370;

as mecca for Afro-Americans, 346; and the New Negro, 348

Harlem Renaissance, 14, 210, 346–49; and anxieties over gender, 16, 372; and fear of modernity, 345; and group identification, 344; and race, 350; and uprootedness of African Americans, 376; and white modernism, 351

Harrison, G. B., 288

Hatred: in Klein, 129, 134. See also Aggression

Heimann, Paula: and analysis of a painter, 15, 264–71; and assimilation, 37; "A contribution to the problem of sublimation and its relation to processes of internalization," 37, 254, 264–71; "the design," 265; as early Kleinian, 2, 9, 283; and internalization and sublimation, 38; and rhetoric of freedom, 270

Heterosexual position, 136; boy's attainment of, 100

Heterosexual tendencies: and Oedipus conflict, 50

Heterotopia, 250

Hinshelwood, Robert, 160; and the death drive, 401 n.2

Hitchens, Robert, 206

Holroyd, Michael, 278–79, 282, 298, 300

Homeostatic principle of drives, 138

Homeovestism, 299

Homosexual(ity): depressive position of, 108; and displacement and disavowal, 103; love, 135; and melancholia, 175; modern, 205; position, 136; relations in early childhood, 103; restitutive, in boy, 99; sexologists and 205; tendencies, and Oedipus conflict, 59. See also Mr. B's case (Klein)

Homosocial(ity): bonding, in *Ryder* (Barnes), 330; ties, 135

Horney, Karen, 81

Hughes, Judith M., 196

Hughes, Langston, 374, 379

Humoral theory, 324

Huyssen, Andreas, 204

Id, 69, 122

Identification: in Ferenczi, 34; in Freud, 33–34

Identity-as-performance: in Strachey, 303

Imagism, 11, 202

Imago: good mother, 15; Kleinian theory, 167

Imagos, object: in Klein, 64

Impressionism, 198, 212

Inhibition: in creative work, 264; and melancholia, 193

Instincts. See Drive(s)

Integration, 147; impossibility of achieving, 150

International Journal of Psycho-analysis, 197

International Psychoanalytic Association, 197

Introjection: in Ferenczi (see Ferenczi, Sándor: introjection); in Klein, 57; of lost object of love, 145; vs. phantasy of incorporation, 166; projection and, 63. See also Projection

Inversion, 206; as abnormality, 207

Irigaray, Luce, 154–58, 396 n.13; and originary matricide, 155, 316; and patriarchal death drive, 155

Isaacs, Susan: case stories, 171–76; compulsive confession, 37; as early Kleinian, 2, 9, 283; on Freud's study of Richard III, 174; on "The nature and function of phantasy," 10, 162–69, 171–76, 234; on phantasy, 37, 303; on repression of the body, 246

Jacobus, Mary, 169–71

Jameson, Fredric, 392; on genre, 436 n.12

Jealousy: in the boy's development, 105

Johnson, James Weldon: on Harlem, 346, 349; "To America," 344

Jones, Ernest, 2, 197; and aphanisis, 73, 74; and female homosexuality, 73, 81; and Freud's biography, 23, 137; and invitation to Melanie Klein, 196

Jung, Carl, 23

Kallich, Martin, 282
Keats, John, 258
Keynes, John Maynard, 299
Kjär, Ruth, 259–62, 268–69
Klein, Melanie: and Abraham, Karl, 55, 58, 61, 86, 119; Abraham and Torok's critique of, 36–37; and adaptation to reality, 63; and aesthetic texts, 215; and aggression and defence, 194; and ambivalence, 127; and antiessentialism, 3; on anxiety and the death drive, 5; on aphanisis, 74; children, on benefits of analysis, 56; on the death drive, 56, 59, 137, 138, 156; and deconstructive potential, 3; on early anxiety situations, 56, 58; on early oral stage of development, 58; on early stages of superego formation, 61; on external objects, 59; on feminine masochism, 79; feminist return to, 5, 387; and form, 214; Freud, on differences with, 4, 7, 57; Glover's opposition to, 3; and hatred, 129; on the id, 122; and the imaginary penis, 136; on the immature ego, 59; on incorporated object as superego, 59; and independence of thought, 197; on interiority and exteriority, 11; on internal objects, 139; on introjection, projection and self-image, 57–58; on introjection of the good object, 120; Jacobus's critique of, 170; Keats, reading of, 258; and location in psychoanalytic movement, 196–97; London, move to, 2, 196, 283; on mania, 118–19; on masochism, 70; on masquerade, 15; on masturbation phantasies, 67; on melancholia (see Melancholia [Klein]); as monstrous mother, 36; on mother-child relation, 7; on mourning, 54, 128, 215; on mourning as melancholia, 56; and Mr. B (see Mr. B's case [Klein]); and "the new," 6; on object as perceived from birth, 53; on object imagos, 64; on object loss, 5; on object relations, 62; Oedipus complex, changing ideas on, 253; on Oedipus conflict (see Oedipus conflict [Klein]); on oral sadism,

58; on origin of bad conscience, 122; on overfeminization of psychoanalysis, 6; and paranoia, 119; on phantasy (see Phantasy); on phobias, 204; on play technique, 163; and positions, 5, 123–34, 194; on primal scene of male homosexuality, 108; on primitive ego, 120; on psychosexual development, 2; on psychosis, 57, 119; on reality testing, 59; on regression, 66; on relational view of the subject, 195; on reparative phantasies, 258; Richard, analysis of, 15, 254–57; Rita, analysis of, 133, 254; sadism, 58; on scotomization, 119; on sculpture, 258; on social function of psychoanalysis, 57; on space, 11–13; on splitting, 127, 255; on sublimation, 123, 185; on the superego, 35, 58, 60; superego, late ideas on, 148–51; as the theorist of melancholia, 4, 8–9; translation issues, 406 n.15; on vicious circle, 129, 141; on world of infant, 7. Works: "A contribution to the psychogenesis of manic-depressive states," 118–28, 128, 143; "Criminal tendencies in normal children," 57; "On the criteria for the termination of a psychoanalysis," 89; "On the development of mental functioning," 146–47; "Early analysis," 168, 185; "Early stages of the Oedipus conflict," 74, 90, 142, 219; "Early stages of the Oedipus conflict and of super-ego formation," 57–63; "The effects of early anxiety-situations on the sexual development of the boy," 94–95, 98–117; "The effects of early anxiety-situations on the sexual development of the girl," 74–86; Envy and gratitude, 86–87, 92–93, 141, 145; "On functioning, 146–47; "The importance of symbol-formation in the development of the ego," 62, 168, 169–70, 186; "Infantile anxiety-situations reflected in a work of art and in the creative impulse," 96, 259; "Love, guilt and reparation," 92–93, 257; "Mourning and its relation to manic-depressive states," 3,

Medusa, 368

Meissner, W. W., 401 n.4, 403 n.16

Melancholia: Abraham's ideas on (see Abraham, Karl: melancholia); and absence of frame, 221; and acedia, 194; affective and cognitive states in 194; black hole in, 51; classic theorization about, 193; and container/contained, 214; concept of, 4–5; delusions of grandeur in, 27; and dispossession of spaces, 195; Djuna Barnes' rewriting of, 17; as empty frame, 221; as epochal sign, 215; and fall in self-esteem, 39; feminine, 82; as flight from reality, 39; Fowlkes' ideas on, 216; inferiority in, 27; as illness of love, 5; individuals prone to, 195; involutional, 69; and manic-depression, 69; melancholic depression and, 25; modernist, 13, 17; and modernist sexualities, 1–2; and narcissism, 26, 195; Oedipus conflict and, 145; orality in, 26; and phantasy, 5, 11, 195; and political dimension in modernism, 201; as social rebellion, 194. See also Melancholia (Freud); Melancholia (Klein)

Melancholia (Freud), 4, 24–28, 30–38, 43–53; affect in, 44; and alterity of lost object, 27; and ambivalence, 47; and cannibalistic ingestion, 52; concept of, 193–95; and denial of alterity, 43; and disavowal of object loss, 52; and disavowal of reality, 45; ego-ideal in, 46; ego in, 43, 53; and failure in symbolization, 44; identification, 34, 46, 151; and inhibition, 44; as libidinal illness, 51; and loss of self-esteem, 45; and lost object, 45, 50, 52; and mania, 52; as mental revolt, 48; normal vs. pathological affect in, 43; nostalgia of, 53; and psychic impoverishment, 45; and psychic pain, 44; and psychic vs. external realities, 44; and punishment, 44; and self-alienation, 47; and shadow of the object, 46; and space, 44; splitting of the ego in, 46; and the superego, 46, 47. See also Freud, Sigmund

Melancholia (Klein), 3; blockage of projection, 63; and changes of mood, 65; concept of, 195; and denial of external reality, 62; and feeling of not belonging, 150; and feminine masochists, 70; vs. Freudian melancholia, 9; homosexuality and, 9, 65; and internal objects, 4, 131; loss of loved object and, 119; as main tenet in her theory, 196; as a mode of object relations, 9, 70, 195; paranoia and, 9, 66, 121; post-Kleinian developments on, 217; and preservation of good objects, 122; and The psycho-analysis of children, 9; and psychotic states, 62; of the race, 384; and reality, 195; as rebellion, 39; in the Renaissance, 15; reproaches in, 26; and retreat into interiority, 194; and right to grieve, 216; and sexualities, 307; and the social, 5–7, 194, 215; and space, 213; and suicide, 66, 124; and the superego, 121; and voice in conscience, 122

Melancholic. See Melancholia

Melancholic apparatus, 3, 85, 145; Oedipus complex as, 254

Meltzer, Donald, 9, 214

Merle, Gabriel, 286, 297, 301–4

Merton, Robert, 194

Meyer, Moe, 303

Michaelis, Karin: on Ruth Kjär, 259–60, 268

Miller, J. Hillis, 333

Mimesis, 198, 212

Mimicry: linguistic, 17, 348, 349

Miscegenation: Cullen on, 370

Mitchell, Juliet, 6, 12

Modernism: academicism and, 200; aesthetic experience of, 200; aesthetic form of, 211; and alternative sexualities, 207; and anxieties, 205, 207, 342; avant-garde in, 201; bohemian, 210; canonicity politics of, 204; and capitalism, 198, 199–200; and challenge to family values, 217; concept of, 1, 386; and content, 211; as cosmopolitan and diasporic movement, 195–96; and crisis of genre, 213; and dialect, 348; early, 198; ego in, 198; ethical ideal of, 199; and exclusionary practices, 204; and exiles, 196; and formalism, 199; freedoms in, 199, 200; and gender, 1–2; high, 198; and historical impasse, 204; ideologies, 349; impersonality of art and, 199; inside/outside dilemma and, 11; and institutionalization, 197; and linguistic self-consciousness, 203; literary, and self, 17; metropolitan centers of, 195; narrative form of, 213; negativistic worldview of, 203; and the new, 197; new forms of representation in, 11–12; nowness of, 204; object in, 203; objective detachment in, 212; originality of, 202; peripheral, 195; phobia and, 204; and politics, 200; and progress, 198; and psychoanalysis, 1, 4, 196–97; and reliance on psychology, 198; and Romanticism, 199; and salons, 196; and self-referentiality, 212; and sexual styles, 206–7; and social revolution, 200; and space(s), 12, 196, 215; and stream of consciousness, 11; technology and, 200; truth and, 211–12; utilitarian credo of, 199; visual, 212; and war, 10

Modernisms, 190, 198; noncosmopolitan, 353

Modernist texts: collage and montage, 213; denial of temporality in, 211; hybridization of, 213; poetic image of, 211

Modernity, 198, 386; alienation in, 200; deterministic worldview of, 202; empiricist principles of, 199; imperialistic policies of, 200; and social malaise, 200

Money-Kyrle, Roger, 159–60

Morality, 159, 160. See also Ethics

Mourning: ability, 131; creativity and, 179; failure to experience, 132; of internal lost objects, 195; in Klein, 53, 56, 128–29, 130, 215; and manic-depressive states, 128, 215; as melancholia, 56; mother's breast, 129; and reality testing, 128

Mr. B's case (Klein), 106–17; and creativity, 113; and fear of bad imagos, 111; and feeling of emptiness, 114; and *fellatio*, 109; and feminine position, 113; and good mother-imago, 115; homosexuality and melancholia in, 112; hypochondria in, 107; idealization of the penis in, 107; identification with mother in, 114; impossibility of mourning in, 112; losses in, 112; mother's aversion to sex in, 110; obsessional symptoms in, 107; phantasy of "good" and "bad" penis in, 109; restitutive tendencies in, 111; seduction by his brother in, 109; superego in, 110–16

Narcissism: in Freud, 30, 137; and melancholia, 26; states, 182

Narration, historical, 274

Narrative: as non-neutral discursive form, 212

Naturalism, 198; literary, 212

Negrophobia, 366

New Freewoman, 208

New Negro: as exotic signifier, 354; in Harlem, 16, 348. See also Harlem Renaissance

Nonheterosexual love, 267; brotherly, 175

Normality: in Money-Kyrle, 159

North, Michael, 349, 353

Nostalgia: in Freudian melancholia, 53

Nowness: in modernism, 204

Objectivism, 202

Object loss. See Loss, object

Object relations, 62, 70; and Lacanian theory, 169; melancholia as a mode of, 9, 70, 195

Object(s): aesthetic, 15; breast, 86; camp, 16; as commodity fetish, 203; external, 69, 176; frustrating, 165; good, 120, 122, 129; good, and loneliness, 149; internal, 4, 69, 139, 160, 176; in Kleinian theory, 4; lost, 4, 12, 15, 165, 194 (see also Loss, object); in modernism, 203; as "objective" thing, 203; part, 76, 177; partial, 120; as physical thing, 203; pleasure, 168; preservation of, 61; as subjective phenomenon, 203; whole, 120; world, 203

conquest of mother's body, 98; depressive position of, 161; devil, 264, 266, 269; *fellatio*, 77; "good" and "bad" penis, 76, 109; incorporation of the penis, 74, 134, 307; incorporative oral desire, 77; and language, 171; lesbian melancholic, 307; masturbation, 60, 67; and melancholia, 5, 11, 195; mother-imago, 80; mother with penis, 135; and omnipotence, 96, 98, 125, 178; oral, 134; penis, 78, 134; and reality, 69; restitution, 99; and the somatic, 181; and *trompe l'oeil*, 123; unconscious (Klein), 1, 3, 9, 18, 214; woman with a penis, 99. *See also* Phantasy (Isaacs); Phantasy (Laplanche and Pontalis)

Phantasy (Isaacs), 162–76; body, 164; compulsive confession, 37; and drive, 166; early, 166; function of, in psychic life, 10; incorporation, 166; and perversion, 172; structuring function of, 163; thinking, 167; unconscious, 162. *See also* Phantasy

Phantasy (Laplanche and Pontalis), 181; desire and, 168–69; originary, 168; structural character of, 168. *See also* Phantasy

Phobias (Klein), 63, 65

Play technique (Klein), 163

Pleasure, 168

Politics: and feminist movement, 207; and melancholy, 201; repressive policies and, 202; socialist movement and, 207

Pontalis, Jean-Baptiste. *See* Phantasy (Laplanche and Pontalis)

Positions (Klein): and flexibility, 2. *See also* Depressive position (Klein); Heterosexual position; Mania; Paranoid-schizoid position

Post-Kleinian thinking: and ethics, 158–61

Pound, Ezra, 11, 197, 201; *The Criterion*, 197; on imagism, 202–3; and poetic image, 211

Primal scene: internalized, 96; of male homosexuality (Klein), 108

Primeau, Ronald, 355

Projection: and distrubances, 62; in Klein, 58, 61. *See also* Introjection

Projective identification, 87, 136; as communication form, 160; "concrete identificate" and, 177; and empathy, 160; ethics and, 160; for Jacobus, 169–70; and loss of capacity to love, 140; as mechanism of defence, 160; and split-off parts of ego, 140; stages of, 413 n.6; and symbolic equation, 176

Proust, Marcel, 179, 185, 312

Psychoanalysis: and exile, 196; feminism and, 6; and images, 12; and institutionalization, 197; and migrant movement, 196; and modernism, 1, 4, 196–97; and rise of nazism, 196; and space, 11–12

Psychosexual stages: in boys, 94; in girls, 75; and homosexual tendencies in development, 91; and latency period, 69

Psychosis, 193; in Klein, 119, 127, 131; and symbolic equation, 177

Queer: in cultural history, 205; visibility, 206

Race: as container, 350; face in, 373; in Harlem Renaissance, 351

Racine, Jean, 278

Racism: and denigration of blacks, 345; idealization in, 345; manic denial of, 345; and melancholia of the race, 384; racist ego and, 345

Radó, Sándor: and alimentary orgasm, 40; and bad object, 41; differences with Klein, 40; on double introjection, 39, 41, 43; on femininity and depressive position, 41; and flight from reality, 39; on guilt, 40; and ideas on melancholia, 39–43; on mania, 41; on obsessional neurosis, 42; and rebellion, 39; "The problem of melancholia," 39, 126; on synthetic function of child, 41

Rank, Otto, 358

Redemption: art and, 185

Reimonenq, Alden, 367

Reparation, 132, 185

Representation: in psychoanalysis, 232

Esther Sánchez-Pardo is an Associate Professor of English at
Complutense University in Madrid. She is coauthor of
Ophelia's Legacy: Schizotexts in Twentieth Century Women's Literature
(2000) and has coedited *Women, Identities and Poetry* (1999) and
Feeling the Worlds (2001).

Library of Congress Cataloging-in-Publication Data
Sánchez-Pardo, Esther
Cultures of the death drive : Melanie Klein and modernist
melancholia / Esther Sanchez-Pardo
p. cm. — (Post-contemporary interventions)
Includes bibliographical references and index.
ISBN 0-8223-3009-1 (cloth : alk. paper)
ISBN 0-8223-3045-8 (pbk. : alk. paper)
1. Death instinct. 2. Psychoanalysis. 3. Klein, Melanie.
I. Title. II. Series.
BF175.5.D4 S26 2003   150.19′5′092—dc21   2002010948